The Palgrave Lacan Series

Jacques Lacan is one of the most important and influential thinkers of the 20th century. The reach of this influence continues to grow as we settle into the 21st century, the resonance of Lacan's thought arguably only beginning now to be properly felt, both in terms of its application to clinical matters and in its application to a range of human activities and interests. The Palgrave Lacan Series is a book series for the best new writing in the Lacanian field, giving voice to the leading writers of a new generation of Lacanian thought. The series will comprise original monographs and thematic, multi-authored collections. The books in the series will explore aspects of Lacan's theory from new perspectives and with original insights. There will be books focused on particular areas of or issues in clinical work. There will be books focused on applying Lacanian theory to areas and issues beyond the clinic, to matters of society, politics, the arts and culture. Each book, whatever its particular concern, will work to expand our understanding of Lacan's theory and its value in the 21st century.

Ernesto Espindola

The Paternal Imago in Ruins

Messianic Leadership and Constitutional Instability in Ecuador

palgrave
macmillan

Ernesto Espindola
Department of History and Political Science
Johnson County Community College
Overland Park, KS, USA

ISSN 2946-4196 ISSN 2946-420X (electronic)
The Palgrave Lacan Series
ISBN 978-3-032-07506-2 ISBN 978-3-032-07507-9 (eBook)
https://doi.org/10.1007/978-3-032-07507-9

Cover credit : ilbusca

This Palgrave Macmillan imprint is published by the registered company Springer Nature Switzerland AG.
The registered company address is: Gewerbestrasse 11, 6330 Cham, Switzerland

To my parents

Introduction[1]

This book advances the dialogue between Lacanian psychoanalysis and political theory. As *Family Complexes* (Lacan, 1938), *The Sublime Object of Ideology* (Žižek, 1990), and *Lacan & the Political* (Stavrakakis, 1999) show us, the ontology of lack allows us to account for the failure and peril of utopian politics. And this, I argue, is one of the main contributions made by Lacanian psychoanalysis to political theory.

Freud's (1939) understanding of monotheism, heroism, and caudillismo (as presented in *Moses and Monotheism*) also permits us to explain the question of political fantasy. Freud has contributed to the history of political thought by offering an intergenerational account of how societal guilt—for the original parricide—*returns* and buttresses the inverted fantasy of the religious and political Messiah (discussed below). *Moses and Monotheism's* theoretical and practical values have been praised by Lacan: 'Nothing seems to me to be more firmly articulated in any case and more in conformity with all Freud's previous thought than this work' (1959–60/1997, p. 172).

This investigation analyses classic ideas put forward by Ovid, Rousseau, Freud, Lacan, and Lagache. In doing so, it contributes to the Essex School of Discourse Analysis, whose political theorists (Laclau, Mouffe,

[1] Certain sections of this book (i.e., those related to the 2015 constitutional reform in Ecuador) were previously published in the *Journal of Psychosocial Studies* (Espindola, 2023). My deepest thanks to this journal for granting me the permission to reproduce these parts herein. My article (Espindola, 2023) does not include the original text in the footnotes. The translations of quotations and paraphrasing are my own.

Stavrakakis, Glynos, Norval, Howarth, among others) have drawn on Lacanian psychoanalysis to better understand the persistence of controversial phenomena in politics, such as populism, utopian politics, and the transgressive dimension of ideology (its 'grip'). In particular, this endeavour discusses Laclau's (2005) interpretation of Freudian theory regarding the centrality of the leader in *the political*. While Laclau is interested in the ontology of populism, this book delves into the narcissistic and authoritarian logic that appears to underpin, in part, the leader–followership dynamic in postcolonial contexts. Lacan's (1938) concept of a diminished *paternal imago*, his (1953–1954/1991) problematization of the distinction between the ideal-ego and the ego-ideal, and Lagache's (1961) notion of *heroic identification* seek to fill, in part, the gap left by Laclau (2005) on the question of postcolonial identification with the 'populist' leader, that is, the 'primus inter pares' (the first among equals). Albeit Ecuador serves as my case study, the following theoretical reflections could be of utility in other postcolonial contexts.

Drawing on Freud (1939), Lacanian psychoanalysis, and political theory (i.e., the contractarian theory), this book contributes to our understanding of the intertwined dynamics of narcissism, authoritarianism, and messianism in postcolonial contexts. Freud (1939) conjectures that the guilt for the killing of the father of the primal horde *returns* through the inverted *fantasy* of Messiahs, capable of delivering redemption and the promised land. Courtesy of Freud's conjecture, alongside Lacanian insights, my overall argument reads as follows. Ecuador's long-lasting history of political instability has fostered a culture prone to supporting *messianic* leaders, that is, lawgivers whose personages have been invested with the hope and aspiration of perpetual stability, epitomized by the setting up of Constituent Assemblies (CAs) themselves. More precisely, the affective pull of 'messianic leadership' in the constitutional politics of Ecuador, influenced by a diminished *paternal imago* resulting from colonialism, has set the scene for a constant process of *heroic identification* with authoritarian leaders, who have led constitutional replacements in this postcolonial country (analysed below).

Ecuador has sanctioned 20 constitutions since independence (1830).[2] This presidential country has supplanted its *social contract* every decade, a

[2] Namely, in 1830, 1835, 1843, 1845, 1851, 1852, 1861, 1869, 1878, 1883, 1897, 1906, 1928-1929, 1938, 1944-1945, 1946-1947, 1966-1967, 1978, 1998, and 2008. Cf. http://archivobiblioteca.asambleanacional.gob.ec/constituciones-anteriores.

dramatic average some would argue. Ecuador's constitutional history reflects this country's long run of political instability since independence. Constituent Assemblies (CAs), convened by non-democratic and democratic leaders alike, have been mobilized 19 times to rewrite its constitution. ***How can we best characterize and account for Ecuador's constitutional volatility***? Existing literature on constitutional instability focuses on philosophical, legal, economic, regionalist, and institutionalist explanations. While important, these accounts do not sufficiently elucidate the way Ecuador's political elites are affectively invested in such constitutional 'abolition-replacement events'. Based on historical archives and Lacanian psychoanalysis, in this book I conduct a discourse analysis of their 'ideological grip', focusing on the 1869 and 2007–2008 CAs, as well as the 2015 reform that abolished presidential term limits, processes influenced by Presidents García Moreno, Alfaro, and Correa, three key 'lawgivers' in Ecuador's history. This historical, theoretical, empirical, and qualitative endeavour offers a novel understanding of 'constitutional instability' in general and that of Ecuador in particular.

Throughout its postcolonial history, an important number of Ecuador's constitutional replacements have stemmed from putsches or revolutions. As the jurisconsult Manuel E. Flor put it against the backdrop of the 1945 convention, 'the constitutions have emanated from revolutions. One revolution, one constitution. Ecuador's constitutional regime has lived by the edge of the sword' (as cited in Ayala Mora, 2014, p. 16, own translation). The historical replacement of the constitution was often supported by regional elites whose conflicting interests spurred them to rebel against the charter in force. Despite this frequent abolition, it was commonplace for the victorious 'caudillo' (a personalist and authoritarian leader) to convene a CA to legitimize the abandonment of the previous constitution. With a few exceptions (e.g., the secularization of the state), many constitutional reforms were implemented and then erased by successive charters, such as term limits for elected authorities, the creation of a senate, and the provision of more power to either the executive or the legislative branch as a counterbalancing measure (Ayala Mora, 2008; Ayala Mora, 2014; Espinosa, 2010; Ibarra, 2010; Negretto, 2013; Salvador Lara, 2005).

In distinguishing Ecuador from politically stable countries in Latin America such as Costa Rica, Negretto emphasizes that 'Ecuador ... has had highly unstable political regimes almost since its independence' (2008, p. 11). Indeed, if we add up all the periods in which the democratic regime was in force in Ecuador between 1830 and 2012 (i.e., 154 years), the average life of each one of its 20 constitutions is an ephemeral 7.7 years. This constitutional volatility finds an echo in the large number of different administrations that Ecuador has had since 1830, whether constitutional presidents, acting officials, or individual or collective dictatorships. On average, from 1830 to 2020, each head of the executive (democratic or not) has remained in office for 1.6 years (Ayala Mora, 2014, p. 15, the updated recalculation for the executive branch is mine). Ayala Mora, a prestigious historian, offers an insightful and somehow pessimistic diagnosis regarding Ecuador's constitutional tradition:

Given these realities, one would think that we Ecuadorians … have developed a solid constitutional doctrine, and that we have accumulated a great doctrinal heritage throughout the successive assemblies. But this has not been the case. Generally, each constitution has been conceived of as a way of founding the country from a tabula rasa. In fact, not even this was possible, nor did great changes occur between one constitution and the following one. Every time we have returned to page one. (ibid., own translation)

The kernel motivating this book concerns the enigma of Ecuador's *constitutional instability*. By *constitution* here I mean 'the set of the most important rules and common understandings in any given country that regulate the relations among that country's governing institutions and also the relations between that country's governing institutions and the people of that country' (King, 2011, p. 3). In this book I utilize, interchangeably, the terms constitution, charter, higher law, social contract, and fundamental law. By constitutional *instability* I mean the frequent replacement of the constitution in force with a new one. This definition of constitutional instability, borrowed from Negretto (2008), differs from less radical institutional alterations, such as constitutional amendments (the US constitution has 27 amendments) or new judicial interpretations of the operative constitution.

Constitutional instability is not endemic to Ecuador; it occurs in many Latin American countries. If we consider this region's presidential democracies, Venezuela is the country with the highest number of different constitutions (26) since independence, while Ecuador occupies the second place in the Latin American 'constitutional instability league' (20), Bolivia comes third in this list with 16 constitutions, followed by El Salvador (15), Honduras (14), Peru (13), Nicaragua, and Costa Rica (12), just to mention a few examples. Moreover, these constitutional replacements in this region have occurred in both democratic and non-democratic contexts

(Negretto, 2008, p. 12). In 2025, the president of Ecuador Daniel Noboa proposed a new CA to replace Ecuador's 20th constitution.

Although Central and South America adopted the US presidential system, there is a key difference between the constitutional tradition in Hispanic and North America. The 1787 US Charter pertains to the *preservative* family of constitutions whose purpose is to limit and preserve the constituted power. Differently, the Latin American constitutional tradition can be regarded as *aspirational*, a conception that enhances political will. Rousseau, Sieyès, Marx, and Schmitt are part of this tradition. Despite their theoretical differences, the distinctive feature of aspirational constitutionalism, also present in India and South Africa, is its resemblance to a *political promise* of progress. This distinction, of course, serves analytical purposes. In practice, not all aspirational constitutions derive from the French tradition. Moreover, preservative *legal* discourses and *political* promises can coexist in the same constitutional document. As for Latin America, 'it is usually thought that the society's destiny depends on the goodness of the constitutions' (García Villegas, 2012, pp. 90–93, own translation).

Ecuador has had 20 CAs, but only a small number stand out as worthy of closer analysis. Two cases—the 1869 and 2007–2008 CAs—promise to offer us special insight into the character of Ecuador's history of political instability, specifically in relation to the issue of messianic leadership and, relatedly, regarding the indigenous question.

Previous research on the significance of the tithe's survival in Ecuador and the centrality attributed to President García Moreno (1861–1865, 1869–1875) partially justifies my case selection. The tithe was a tribute to God administered by the Catholic Church since the Spanish conquest, and it formally levied 10% of the individuals' production. Historiography regards García Moreno as a key leader in nineteenth-century Ecuador; he began the building of the modern state. However, his Catholic effort to modernize/centralize the political power and combat anarchy was contradictory. The tithe had detrimental effects in socio-economic terms, not to mention its anachronistic character. The Catholic García Moreno did not replace this tribute. The Republic, the Church, and the landowners (the tithe's collectors) benefitted from this colonial and Catholic tribute. The mistreatment of the indigenous population, key taxpayers in postcolonial Ecuador, was commonplace. The constant disputes around the tithe created political instability at the local level. This colonial tribute survived until 1889 (Espindola, 2016). *Garcianismo* (1861–1875), a period in which Gabriel García Moreno played a key role in Ecuadorian politics, has provoked controversy amongst scholars (ibid., p. 96). García Moreno, who was highly idealized by the 1869 CA, was the intellectual author of the 1869 constitution. Back then, his leadership was regarded as indispensable to combat political instability. The 1869 constitution, the eighth since independence in 1830, endeavoured to institutionalize the Catholic nation, including the native population. The 1869 debates on the 'miserable race' (i.e., the indigenous peoples) showed the fragmented character of Ecuador's *social contract* since independence.

The 1869 CA was established after a putsch prompted by García Moreno, while the 2007–2008 CA was approved via referendum. García Moreno was not a popular leader (Espinosa, 2010, p. 530). President Rafael Correa (2007–2017) is known for his popularity and charisma. Why are the 1869 and 2007–2008 CAs worthy of comparison? There is a similarity/connection between these CAs, which suggests a link between 'messianic' leadership and constitutional instability in Ecuador.

The two CAs in question were prompted by two 'strong' leaders from across the ideological spectrum: the Catholic and conservative García Moreno, and the Catholic and left-wing Rafael Correa. (The latter was inspired by President Eloy Alfaro, another 'lawgiver' whose deeds inspired both the 1906 liberal constitution and the 2008 left-wing charter.) García Moreno and Correa served as presidents for a total of ten years, an atypical period of stability. Both leaders influenced their comrades during the conventions that wrote the 1869 and 2008 constitutions, and both constitutions strengthened the executive branch. The 1869 charter extended term limits for authorities, stipulating a six-year presidential mandate. The consecutive re-election allowance was permitted, as a result of which García Moreno was re-elected for a third period (Ayala Mora, 2008, pp. 35–36; Salvador Lara, 2005, p. 392). Similarly, the 2008 charter instituted the consecutive re-election concession for one time only for the president (Article 144 of the 2008 charter), which abolished a constitutional prohibition in this regard (Article 164 of the 1998 constitution). In 2014 President Correa proposed a constitutional amendment to abolish presidential term limits. While the longing for García Moreno becomes clear in the 1869 CA, the idealization of Rafael Correa needs to be interpreted in two phases: in the 2007–2008 CA and during the 2014–2015 reform in favour of the constitutional amendment just mentioned. From a psychoanalytic perspective on messianism, this thesis sheds new light on the discourse praising 'strong' leaders. And this offers a novel understanding of

Ecuador's long-lasting history of constitutional instability. Moreover, the 2008 constitution stipulates for the first time the 'pluri-national' nature of the Ecuadorian state (Article 1 of the constitution). This recognition implies that *the peoples* and *nationalities* that inhabited Ecuador before the Spanish and Inca conquests are part of the *social contract*. The 2007–2008 CA was composed of indigenous deputies, who indicated that racism survives in this postcolonial country.

Ecuadorian historiography has focused on the backdrop against which Ecuador's 20 constitutions have been sanctioned but little attention has been paid to specific constitutional assemblies. This book, therefore, can be said to contribute to this literature by dint of providing an in-depth discourse analysis of the debates associated with the 1869 and 2007–2008 conventions, and the 2015 abolition of presidential term limits.

I advance my argument as follows. In Chap. 1 I propose a psychoanalytic (Freudian and Lacanian) framework for the analysis of Ecuador's constitutional processes. Chapter 2 offers the research strategy for the subsequent discourse analysis. This methodological chapter is located within a broader discussion about the feasibility and desirability of using psychoanalysis beyond the clinical setting. Chapter 3 analyses the debates of the 1869 CA. Chapter 4 addresses the 2007–2008 CA, as well as the parliamentary reform process resulting in the abolition of presidential term limits in Ecuador, in the hope of realizing a third mandate of President Correa. Throughout the text I discuss pertinent competing explanations accounting for constitutional instability. Chapter 5 draws together some of the findings of the empirical chapters, not only to consolidate in comparative fashion their psychoanalytic insights but also to better ascertain how the psychic factors isolated in this way relates to other explanatory elements. In doing so, I seek to put different disciplines and explanatory hypotheses into dialogue with each other in a way that averts psychoanalytic reductionism. In other words, while I suggest that an appeal to Lacanian psychoanalysis enhances our understanding of the non-rational elements of political processes, by no means do I want to suggest that a focus on the psychic dimension alone can deliver a full account of Ecuador's constitutional instability.

References

Ayala, E. (2008). *Manual de historia del Ecuador II. Época Republicana*. Corporación Editora Nacional.

Ayala, E. (2014). Rasgos históricos de la evolución constitucional del Ecuador. In A. Mora (Ed.), *Historia constitucional: estudios comparativos*. Corporación Editora Nacional

Espindola, E. (2016). *La construcción del Estado ecuatoriano y de su ciudadanía tributaria a la luz del diezmo*. E-book Retrieved January 24, 2023, from https://www.flacso.edu.ec/node/111?id=4283

Espinosa, C. (2010). *Historia del Ecuador en contexto regional y global*. Lexus.

Freud, S. (1939/2015b). *Moisés y la religión monoteísta*. Amorrortu Editores.

García Villegas, M. (2012). Constitucionalismo aspiracional: Derecho, Democracia Y Cambio social En América Latina. *Revista Análisis Político, 75*, 89–110.

Ibarra, H. (2010). *Visión histórico-política de la Constitución del 2008*. Centro Andino de Acción Popular.

King, A. (2011). *The British constitution*. Oxford Scholarship Online.

Lacan, J. (1938). Family complexes in the formation of the individual. Encyclopédie française (A. de Monzie, Editor), Vol. 8, translated by Cormac Gallagher.

Laclau, E. (2005/2007). *On populist reason*. Verso.

Lagache, D. (1961). El psicoanálisis y la estructura de la personalidad. Asociación Psicoanalítica del Uruguay – Revista Uruguaya de Psicoanálisis

Negretto, G. L. (2008). The durability of constitutions in changing environments: explaining constitutional replacements in Latin America. Kellogg Institute, working paper 350, pp. 1–34. Retrieved February 7, 2020, from https://kellogg.nd.edu/documents/1658

Negretto, G. L. (2013). *Making constitutions. Presidents, parties, and institutional choice in Latin America*. Cambridge University Press.

Salvador Lara, J. (2005). *Breve historia contemporánea del Ecuador*. Fondo de Cultura Económica.

Stavrakakis, Y. (1999). *Lacan & the political*. Routledge.

Žižek, S. (1990). Eastern Europe's Republics of Gilead. *New Left Review* (I/183, September-October).

Acknowledgements

A special thanks to Derek Hook, Jason Glynos, and David Howarth. This book is indebted to their insightful comments.

This work has also benefitted from the contributions made by John Bartle, Sandy Macmillen (University of Essex), Guillaume Fontaine (Facultad Latinoamericana de Ciencias Sociales, Ecuador), Enrique Ayala Mora (Universidad Andina Simón Bolívar, Ecuador), and Pete Gentry. To all these people, my thanks. I would like to acknowledge the support of Ecuador's National Assembly's Archives.

Competing Interests The author has no competing interests to declare that are relevant to the content of this manuscript.

Contents

CHAPTER 1

Building an Argument: The Psychology of Constitutional Instability

The application of psychoanalytic ideas to socio-political issues is not new—Freud himself wrote about societal themes. Among other endeavours, Lacan's contribution to Freud's discoveries has been fruitfully operationalized by the Essex School of Discourse Analysis. Slavoj Žižek is arguably the first scholar who has systematically applied Lacanian theory to the study of ideology (cf. *The Sublime Object of Ideology*, 1989). As Stavrakakis (2007/Stavrakakis, 2010) notes, the list of political theorists who draw on Lacanian theory has considerably grown since the 1990s.

In this chapter I argue that a Lacanian approach to Ecuador's *social contract* offers a productive perspective from which to explore its enigmatic instability. Freud, Lacan, the Essex School of Discourse Analysis, and other scholars have theorized about the founding moment of the law ('the social contract'), its *repetitive* transgression, and the role played by *identification* in politics. Their theories can be applied to shed light on my research question, thereby also offering a way to complement other explanations accounting for constitutional instability. As we will see, there are some important psychoanalytic concepts that I will develop that are of different relevance within the realm of ideology.

This chapter proceeds as follows. Firstly, I introduce the reader to a debate on the origins of the state, with particular reference to the French version of the modern contractarian theory, the cradle of the constitutional moment in nineteenth century in Latin America. I then present

E. Espindola, *The Paternal Imago in Ruins*, The Palgrave Lacan Series, https://doi.org/10.1007/978-3-032-07507-9_1

Freud's theory on the founding moment of the law from which the first 'social contract' emerged, followed by key criticisms of Freud's account. Afterwards, I build and discuss the psychoanalytically informed notions of *heroic identification* and *messianic leadership*. This is followed by a discussion of Freud's myth on the founding moment of the law in view of Lacanian psychoanalysis; here I operationalize the Lacanian categories of (amongst others) *enjoyment* and *fantasy* in ways aiming to guide the discourse analysis of the 1869 and 2007–2008 constituent assemblies (CAs), as well as of the 2014–2015 constitutional reform.

A Brief Comment on the Contractarian Theory in Latin America

Bobbio et al. (2005, *contractualismo*) note that the history of Western political thought has produced three main theories on the origins of the state: the organicist, the contractarian, and that based on conflict. Each of these theories has its own nuances depending on both the historical period analysed (ancient, medieval, modern) and the scholar in question. In modern times the organicist discourse is expressed by authors such as Hegel and Burke, while the contractarian theory finds popular exponents in Hobbes, Locke, and Rousseau. Amongst others, Marx and Freud represent the current based on conflict. While the former author bases his theory on the classist dialectic, the latter draws on the Oedipus complex.

In mainstream academia, it is commonly accepted that while Locke's *Second Treatise on Civil Government* partly inspired the American Revolution, Rousseau's *Social Contract* partially influenced Latin American independence. More precisely, the revolutionary constitutionalism of France influenced the presidential system in Latin America. As Zolo puts it (Zolo, 2007, section 3.4), for this revolutionary tradition the popular-national sovereignty was exclusively embodied in Parliament. Thus, this power prevailed over the other branches of the state. Article 3 (Ch.5, Title 3) of the 1791 Constitution in France established that the judicial power could not interfere with the legislation nor prevent the implementation of laws. In line with Rousseau's maxim that popular sovereignty was unalienable, Emmanuel Sieyès coined the distinction between *constituent power* and *constituted powers*. As a *pre-legal power*, constituent power was deemed to be the *collective legislator* in charge of establishing the values and rules upon which a political community ought to be built. Differing from the limited attributions of constituted powers, constituent power was conceived of as one with unlimited authority. Indeed, Article 28 of the 1793 *Declaration of Rights* explicitly indicated that the people were always authorized to reconsider, amend, and replace their constitution, and that no generation was obligated to follow the laws sanctioned by past generations. The outcome of this doctrine was twofold: (1) Parliament was prone to act as both constituted and constituent powers, constantly re-evaluating the constitution; (2) a constitutional inclination 'towards rejecting both constitutional rigidity and judicial control over the constitutional legitimacy of ordinary laws' came into existence (p. 15).

Rousseau's influential exaltation of the ancient *demos* had to be operationalized in Latin America in times when the words *revolution* and *independence* were highly valued. For this French tradition (Rousseau was a Swiss citizen who lived in Paris), the legislative branch became the fundamental pillar for this revolutionary tradition; hence, no judge could weigh up the decisions of the 'general will'. Furthermore, Sieyès' distinction between the almighty *constituent power* and the limited constituted powers paved the way for accepting that the people's representatives could draft a new constitution as many times as they saw fit. In short, this tradition has endowed Latin American systems with the key notion of *constituent power*, an element partly informing this region's legal feasibility to replace its constitutions.

Despite its usefulness, this philosophical and legalistic approach to constitutional instability, arguably the most popular in political science and legal studies, has a limitation. Many of the Ecuadorian CAs were organized by non-democratic 'caudillos' to legitimize their putsches, after which these leaders convened the people's representatives to sanction a new constitution. In this hybrid context (putsch—CA), Sieyès' notion of *constituent power* becomes problematic, as the latter alludes to the prevalence of Parliament over the executive, a maxim stemming from Rousseau's *Social Contract.* A second limitation, however, concerns the status accorded to the indigenous peoples. For this French School, everyone's equality before the law informs its founding premise. But this postulate was problematic in the Americas because it did not take into account the native population inhabiting these territories. As Clavero summarizes it, from Argentina to Canada modern states were established 'by a population of European origin faced with native populations that, initially, were a majority but who were destined to become foreigners in their own lands' (Clavero, 2007, p. 443).

In this book I reach out to psychoanalysis, for it provides insightful ideas for the analysis of the origin of the *social contract* in general and its characteristic instability in postcolonial Ecuador in particular.[1]

The Freudian Contribution to the Contractarian Theory

Drawing on anthropological studies, in the fourth essay of *Totem and Taboo,* Freud implicitly questions the idea of a civilized consensus as the founding base of the *social contract.* He partly sides with Darwin's (1871) hypothesis: there was a prehistoric time when the women of the horde were reserved for the primeval father. Thus, his sons were expelled from the horde once they reached adulthood. From this point, Freud adds the following conjecture. To occupy the place of the father, 1 day the expelled and jealous brothers united and killed their genitor. (This league of primal brothers was governed by an ambivalent feeling also found in children and neurotic adults in present times, i.e., the hate-love sentiment informing the *paternal complex.*) Once the murder in question was materialized, the sentiments of love and guilt towards the dead father prevailed. These primitive brothers realized that their father's fatal destiny could also befall any of them at any time. Consequently, and despite their initial desire, they decided to prohibit incest, a pact that brought about two byproducts: exogamy and totemism. 'Social institutions, ethical limitations and religion' resulted from this foundational parricide, an act that marked the passage from the Darwinian *paternal horde* to the *clan of brothers* ruled by totemism (Freud, 2015a, pp. 203–206, 208–209, own translation).

For the members of the tribe, 'the totemic animal … was most of the time deemed as their ancestral father' (Wundt, as cited in Freud, 2015a, p. 160). Freud underscores that the worshipped totem was both loved and feared as much as the primal father. It is in this ambivalent context (love/hate—father/totem) that one can understand why the tribal members were banned from killing and eating their sacred animal. Indeed, a profound sense of guilt was the foundation of the totemic religion, a religion seeking to redeem the sons for their primal parricide by obeying the

[1] It is beyond the scope of this book to evaluate the strengths and weaknesses of the organicist theory. Aristotle's *Politics* and Hegel's *The Philosophy of Law* provide key insights in Ancient and Modern times. *The Manifesto of the Communist Party* illustrates, in a pedagogical way, Marx and Engel's notion of the origin and role of the state.

totemic father. 'All the successive religions prove to be essays solving the same problem ... all of these are reactions ... facing the same great episode with which culture was initiated' (Freud, p. 207). Despite the guilty nature of the totemic religion, every now and then the tribe allowed its members to enjoy the 'cruel' assassination and ingestion of its godly animal. 'Whereas the individual is banned from executing this action, it becomes legitimate if everyone participates ... no one is allowed to abstain from both the murder and the banquet' (Freud, pp. 201–202). As time passed, the rancour towards the primal father diminished, while the longing for him increased. His formerly unlimited power was idealized and respected. Of note here is that this immemorial parricide produces a long-lasting psychical sequel for the following generations (Freud, pp. 211, 222–224).

The Critics of Freud's Thesis on the Origin of Organized Power

Political philosophy highlights the importance of consensus as the base upon which politically organized power emerges. For instance, Bobbio et al. note that after the killing of the father of the primal horde, his sons still had to make a *pact* for the new community (*contractualismo*, Bobbio et al., 2005). There is a more general critique of those theories based on conflict:

> The limitation of all these theories consists in the fact that they do not allow any realist alternative, except the nostalgia of a lost golden age or the utopian perspective of an absolute emancipation. In the present there is only force, power, repression, and each state as such is always a dictatorship. By the way, the contractarian thought does not deny the existence of force, though it is to be seen as operating in different forms in the state of nature and in the social state. (Bobbio et al., 2005, p. 358, own translation)

As for the Freudian theory on the origin of society, modern anthropology cannot corroborate a type of early human organization governed by one single male such as the father of the primal horde. Although his 'fantasy story' is 'a compelling one', Freud builds his theory with 'inaccurate data' (Thurschwell, 2000, p. 102).

The Marxist-Feminist stance has also criticized psychoanalysis. The excessive emphasis on the *Oedipus complex* and the *nuclear family triangle* mistakenly universalizes to the status of the human condition a rather historically conditioned structure, that of the patriarchal family (in Žižek, 2008, p. 51).

Despite these necessary critiques, the appearance of the psychoanalytic *myth* of the primal parricide under the *contractarian* theory section of the *Dictionary of Politics* (Bobbio et al.) brings to the fore the politico-philosophical relevance of *Totem and Taboo*. At this point, though, it suffices to note that Freud's conjecture addresses two intertwined psychosocial dynamics present in my research puzzle: the ambivalent idealization of the authority figure and the enjoyment procured by the transgression of the social pact (Ecuador's constitution). Thus, Freud's conjecture begs further problematization.

From the Father of the Primal Horde to Moses and Other Substitutive Figures

As mentioned, *Moses and Monotheism* (Freud, 2015b) constitutes a fundamental piece of writing for Lacan, for it systematizes Freud's early and late work. Freud's thesis on the psychic factor underpinning the longing for a Messiah sheds light on the constitutional processes analysed here, a point to which I now turn.

Certain ideas mentioned above (e.g., the killing of the father of the primal horde, the *paternal complex*) were later refined by Freud in *Moses and Monotheism*. For him (2015b, pp. 133, 135, 144–149, 158, 167, 182), the compulsive nature of monotheism, expressed by the idea that only one all-powerful God exists, derives from an early psychic dynamic found in contemporary and prehistoric times. The compulsive nature of monotheistic phenomena relates to Freud's phylogenetic thesis on *archaic heredity*. Besides the subject's own experiences, his/her psychic life is constituted (from birth) by *predispositions*, *contents*, and *mnemic traces* of what previous generations went through. The assumption that *archaic heredity* exists shortens the gap between the psychology of the subject and that of its people, as 'human beings have always known … that, previously, they possessed a primordial father whom they killed' (p. 147, own translation). This memory became part of the *archaic heredity* because it was sufficiently relevant, and it occurred several times throughout millennia. Also, it was reignited (though in a deformed way) through the repetition of the same events: the assassinations of Moses and then Christ. The development of religions is predicated on the killing of the primal father (*the primordial image of God*) as well as that of his reincarnations. Destiny put the Jewish people in a situation in which they repeated the prehistoric parricide on the father figure of Moses. 'The clarity of thought, the force of will, the strength in action, are constitutive of the father's image, but, above all, autonomy and independence' (p. 158). These traits, attributed to *the great man* (e.g., Moses), make people admire, trust, and fear him. In group psychology, the great man plays the role of the super-ego.

This conceptual synthesis allows Freud to put forward the case study of *Moses and Monotheism*. This links the death of the father of the primal horde to the emergence of Christianity in a way conducive to this book on Ecuador's frequent 'lawgivers'. Freud (2015b, pp. 45, 98–100, 123, 129–130, 134) agrees with the old hypothesis according to which Moses was an Egyptian. Freud conjectures that Moses was sympathetic to Aton's monotheistic religion. Around 1350 BCE, this religion was abolished in Egypt. Moses chose a group of foreigners (the Jewish people) whom he led (the *Exodus*) and whom he provided with both laws and Aton's religion. But one day, argues Selling (1922) and Freud, the Jewish people rebelled against Moses, killed him, and abolished Aton's religion. 'It is an attractive conjecture', argues Freud, that after a period of time the guilt for the killing in question began manifesting in the *fantasy* of a Messiah. Freud posits that this fantasy was underpinned by repentance for the killing. According to this fantasmatic narrative, the Messiah's return would bring 'redemption' and the 'promised universal empire'. The assassination of a Son of God/Father would redeem humanity for its *original sin*, which instituted the law. In a nutshell:

> If Moses was this first Messiah, Christ is his substitute and his successor ... [I]n Christ's resurrection there is certain historic-experiential truth, since it was ... the resurrected Moses and before him ... *the returned primordial father of the primal horde who was glorified and situated as the son instead of the father.* (Freud, 2015b, p. 134, own translation, emphasis added).

Freud (2015b, p. 131) conjectures that this Messiah may personify the 'principal rebel and caudillo' (amongst the primal brothers) who assassinated the father on his own. Freud offers another interpretation: this redeemer represents the *unfulfilled fantasy* that each of these brothers had, that is, their desire to kill the father on their own to become the predominant figure and a *substitute for the father identification that was being renounced* after the parricide. Either way (Freud leaves this question open), the meaning of the redeemer/hero sheds light on the psychic phenomenon of heroes: '[H]ere is the origin of the representation of the hero, the hero that always revolts against the father and kills him in any of his figures. Also, here is the real foundation of the "tragic guilt" of the hero in the drama, if not hard to locate' (ibid., own translation).

Freud's myth on the 'origin' of the *social contract* and his subsequent understanding of *messianism* allow us to discuss frequent constitutional replacements in Ecuador from a novel perspective. 'Caudillos' in Ecuador have inspired political movements whose support in CAs has legitimized the new constitution. To what extent does these movements' support of their leaders resonate with the league of brothers' *unfulfilled fantasy* to occupy a privileged place within the community? In this process, the dethronement of the previous constitution appears to be the means to conquer the promised land. The idealization of this land blends with that of their promoters/leaders: 'Idealization is a process that concerns the *object*; by it that object, without any alteration in its nature, is aggrandized and exalted in the subject's mind' (Freud, 1914, p. 94). This process relates in part to a formula on the libidinal constitution of a group dependent on a leader presented above. In this process, 'a number of individuals ... have put one and the same object [the leader] in the place of their ego ideal and have consequently identified themselves with one another in their ego' (Freud, 1959, p. 48). I say in part because, as I shall argue in the empirical chapters, the postcolonial conditions in Ecuador have set the scene for a recurrent type of identification within the Ecuadorian community (that of *heroic identification*) which complexifies Freud's initial formula on group formation.

In this thesis I analyse three idealized leaders located across Ecuador's ideological spectrum: the Catholic and conservative García Moreno, the liberal Eloy Alfaro, and the Catholic and socialist Rafael Correa. In one way or another, these persons have inspired the 1869, 1906, and 2008 constitutions, as well as the 2015 constitutional amendment that allowed indefinite presidential re-elections in Ecuador.

A Lacanian Reading of Freud's Myth and its Relevance for the Study of Ideology

Freud's (2015a) conjecture on the killing of the father of the primal horde finds a compelling case study in *Moses and Monotheism* (1939) which, among other aspects, discusses the notion of *archaic heredity*. According to this thesis, since the dawn of history human beings have known—and passed on to future generations—a thorny legacy; namely, that once upon a time, our ancestors committed on several occasions a series of parricides against our primal fathers, our *original sin*.

The above phylogenetic conjecture on *archaic heredity* is problematized by Lacan in a useful way for the analysis of the transgressive grip of ideology. As he puts it, Freud's 'myth' is predicated on the *Oedipus complex*. In Book IV, Lacan interprets the 'tyrannical' Freudian myth in terms of *The-Name-of-the-Father*. This *myth* relates to the Oedipus complex, which is intertwined with the castration complex. Thanks to *castration*, which is executed by the *symbolic father*, the infant is introduced to the realm of law (Lacan, 2016, pp. 229, 365–369). In Book VII, Lacan (1997, pp. 67, 176–177) highlights that Freud's breakthrough is predicated on the notion that incest is the subject's constituent desire, which has been repressed. Lacan further problematizes Freud's myth—which, according to Lacan, was created by Freud himself. There is an ambivalent compromise underpinning the original pact amongst the league of brothers, an ambivalence characteristic of the relations between son and father. In addition, and against all odds, we should recall that the removal of the 'obstacle' (the killing of the father of the primal horde) did not open the way to incestuous enjoyment (the prehistoric pact established exogamy). However, and this is important, the prohibition of incest did not extinguish its desire. Freud's myth shows us that the law and the desire to transgress it are co-constitutive for psychoanalysis. Maybe this is what Lacan means in part when he posits that '[e]very act of *jouissance* gives rise to something that is inscribed in the Book of debts of the Law' (p. 176). The intertwined logic between the law and the enjoyment procured by the fantasy of its transgression, presented by Lacan in the *Ethics of Psychoanalysis*, becomes useful as a tool for the analysis of the transgressive dimension of ideology found in Ecuador's history of constitutional instability.

Lacan emphasizes that Freud's contribution consisted in highlighting that the subject–object relation is a troubled one. It initiates in childhood and accompanies the subject throughout his/her life. This relation entails the subject's quest for the *lost object*, the *first object*, that is, the mother. As a result of this, there will be a continual disharmonious disunion between the object found and the object sought (Lacan, 2016, pp. 27–28, 55). This is neatly summarized in Book VII: 'The world of our experience … assumes that it is this object, das Ding [the Mother], as the absolute Other of the subject, that one is supposed to find again. […] One doesn't find it, but only its pleasurable associations' (Lacan, 1997, p. 52).

The disharmony between the object sought and the one found relates to the logic of desire which, as presented in Book V, is composed of (amongst others) the letter *a*, a sign that abbreviates *autre*, that is *other* in French. This lower-case *a*, which differs from *Autre*/Other, denotes the fellow man/woman whose *image* captivates us (discussed below). It is around a particular relationship with this image that our narcissistic identification—and thus our ego—is formed, and this identification goes through various phases (Lacan, 1999, pp. 311, 319, 324).

As noted in Book III, the first experience of the subject with its primary object is characterized by the rivalry of jealousy, for this primordial object constitutes the object of the other's desire. A primeval otherness is already part of the subject's first experience (Lacan, 2000, p. 39). 'This rivalrous and competitive ground for the foundation of the object is precisely what is overcome in speech insofar as this involves a third party. Speech is always a pact … [T]his is yours, this is mine, this is this, that is that' (Lacan, pp. 39–40). The notion of a pact helps us to distinguish *the other* from *the Other* unknown to us, which Lacan conceives of in terms of a *unifying entity somewhere*. When the Other speaks it does so beyond the reality of the other who is talking at length. In fact, this Other is a *symbolic* entity recognized by subjects, thanks to which subjects make themselves recognized, such as the case of the following dynamic: You are my *slave* —You are my *master*. Both slave and master are alluding not only to one another but, more importantly, to a symbolic entity which they recognize as that which provides the coordinates 'master' and 'slave' (pp. 36, 50–51, 56). By contrast, 'in delusional speech the Other is truly excluded, there is no truth behind' (p. 53).

As for the above discussion on the subjects' constant quest for the *lost object*, it must be noted that this search is doomed to failure, and the latter has crucial consequences in politics:

> The affective dimensions of speech ... are rooted in a compulsion in subjectivity to recover the primordial lost object. ... The public world is replete with debates, disagreements and arguments that express, for example, anxieties, threats and dangers, resentment and paranoia ... and the idealisation of events and figures—a vast range of emotions, feelings and affective states that attach to and are conveyed, momentarily, via controversies that characterise our shared loss. (Martin, 2019, p. 21)

This primordial loss institutes an ontology of *lack* with key political consequences. As Stavrakakis (1999) puts it, the symbolic 'imposition' of *The-Name-of-the-Father* constitutes a signifier prohibiting the imaginary and incestuous relation with the mother. Given this necessary 'imposition', Stavrakakis (pp. 13, 31, 35) highlights that for Lacanian theory the subject's identity is, from this imposition onwards, split. The latter has lasting consequences because the subject will constantly desire to overcome his/her split and be alienated in the level of representation. In other words, 'what we have is only attempts to construct a stable identity, either on the imaginary or the symbolic level, through the image or the signifier' (p. 29). In Lacanian theory there are no identities as such but only failed processes of identifications, that is, 'a play between identification and its failure, a deeply political play' (ibid.). By indicating the distinction between imaginary and symbolic identifications, as well as the unstable character of this psychic process, Lacan refines Freud's conception of identification (Stavrakakis, 1999, p. 30). And these nuances have a crucial consequence for the political arena, as 'instead of identity politics we should speak of identification politics' (ibid.).

On the Puzzle of Postcolonial Lawgivers in Ecuador

The political theorist Ernesto Laclau draws partial inspiration on Freud's *Group Psychology and the Analysis of the Ego* when justifying the centrality of the leader in populism (2005/2007, ch. 3). In fact, Freud's famous formula on group formation is cited by Laclau: 'A primary group of this kind is a number of individuals who have put one and the same object [the leader] in their place of their ego ideal and have consequently identified themselves with one another in their ego'. Notwithstanding, Laclau takes note of Freud's nuanced examination of the leader–followership dynamic, which problematizes his own 'formula' on group formation:

> In many individuals the separation between the ego and the ego ideal is not very far advanced; the two still coincide readily; the ego has often preserved its earlier narcissistic self-complacency. The selection of the leader is very much facilitated by this circumstance. He need often only possess the typical qualities of the individuals concerned in a particularly clearly marked and pure form, and need only give an impression of greater force and more freedom of libido; and in that case the need for a strong chief will often meet him half-way and invest him with a predominance to which he would otherwise perhaps have had no claim. (Freud, in Laclau, 2007, pp. 58–59).

To justify the *populist reason*, Laclau interprets Freud's (1921) nuanced observation as follows. Identification is not based exclusively on a shared loved for the leader (as Freud's 'formula' suggests at first sight), but also on personal traits shared by followers and their chosen leaders. Hence, a degree of identification with the leader becomes plausible. If the leader assumes the leading position due to his noticeable traits—which are shared by his followers—he can no longer be regarded as the despotic, narcissistic leader; instead, he becomes a primus inter pares (first among equals). This means that the leader's identity is cut into two: he is the father and the brother of those whom he leads and, as such, is accountable to a more democratic community (Laclau, 2007, pp. 59–60). For Laclau, the Freudian breakthrough opens up new avenues of research for thinking about a plurality of socio-political alternatives (e.g., populism). In his own words:

> If that distance [between the ego and the ego ideal] increases (why?—this is a question we will have to ask ourselves), we will find the central situation described by Freud: identification between the peers as members of the group and transference of the role of ego ideal to the leader. [...] *If, on the contrary, the distance between ego and the ego ideal is narrower ... the leader will be the object-choice of the members of the group, but he will also be part of the group, participating in the general process of mutual identification.* In that case there would be a partial immanentization of the ground of the communitarian order. (Laclau, 2007, p. 62, emphasis added)

So far two elements stand out: firstly, in *Group Psychology* Freud is dealing with different degrees of *narcissism* as a factor that influences the type of leaders we select. Secondly, Laclau's question mark ('Why' does the distance between the ego and the ego-ideal increase?) hints at the enigma of a plurality of socio-political formations, such as populism. This book is interested in a particular socio-political formation, namely that which underpins the unstable dynamic of the constitutional politics of postcolonial Ecuador. In what follows, I seek to unpack the *psychic* element accounting in part for this country's long-lasting history of constitutional replacements led by often authoritarian leaders.

Narcissism, Identification, the Ideal-Ego, and the Ego-Ideal

The question of narcissism finds its origin in Ovid's *Narcissus and Echo* (circa 8 CE). Tiresias (the seer) predicted that Narcissus would live long enough '[i]f he ne' er know himself'. But his fatal destiny, which came sooner than expected, unfolded when he fell in love with his own image, the latter reflected on the surface of a pool. Ovid brings to our attention the potentially dangerous nature of an extreme form of self-love and pride. Full of pride and self-love, Narcissus had rejected the love of Echo and other women, as well as the overall company of men. Narcissus embodies the idea of a person who is not fit for any type of bonding in society which, ultimately, led to his death. The story tells us that one of the scorned youths asked heaven to punish Narcissus: 'So may he himself love, and not gain the things he loves!' (Ovid, 1977, p. 153). Nemesis heard this prayer and actioned the punishment. The vengeance inflicted on Narcissus consisted in realizing, in a rather painful way, how unsubstantial his infatuation was:

> Unwittingly he desires himself. [...] What he sees he knows not; but that which he sees he burns for, and the same delusion mocks and allures his eyes. O fondly foolish boy, why vainly seek to clasp a fleeting image? What you seek is nowhere; but turn yourself away, and the object of your love will be no more. [...] 'I am charmed, and I see; but what I see and what charms me I cannot find'—so serious is the lover's delusion. (Ovid, p. 155)

How does something as private as narcissism influence politics? Freud contends that there is a *primary* and infantile *narcissism* (self-love) in all of us which never goes away completely (Freud, 1914, pp. 88, 93–94). '[W]e form the idea of there being an original libidinal cathexis of the ego, from which some is later given off to objects, but which fundamentally persists' (p. 75). Freud also points out an antithesis present in this condition: whenever the ego-libido prevails, the object-libido weakens and vice versa (p. 76). Ovid's Narcissus illustrates an extreme case where the ego-libido is highly at work in detriment to object-libido relations with his outside world. For Freud, 'normal' adults have successfully repressed their early megalomania (ego-libido) in light of cultural and ethical mandates learned from civilization. But this repression does not amount to total erasure; in fact, subjects transform their early narcissism into an *ideal* which they establish to measure their ego (pp. 93–94).

> The subject's narcissism makes its appearance displaced on to this new *ideal ego*, which, like the infantile ego, finds itself possessed of every perfection that is of value. [...] He is not willing to forgo the narcissistic perfection of his childhood; ... he seeks to recover it in the new form of an *ego ideal*. What he projects before him as his ideal is the substitute for the lost narcissism of his childhood in which he was his own ideal (p. 94). [...] In addition to its individual side, this [ego] ideal has a social side; it is also the common ideal of a family, a class or a nation. (p. 101, emphasis added)

Apparently, Freud uses ideal-ego and ego-ideal interchangeably. But there is no synonymy in Freud's (1914) text. In Book I, Lacan (1991) contends that, for Freud, the ideal-ego and the ego-ideal denote diverse functions: '[o]ne [the ideal ego] is on the plain of the imaginary, and the other [the ego ideal] is on the plane of the symbolic—since the demand of the Ichideal [ego ideal] takes up its place within the totality of demands of the law' (p. 134). By way of illustration, argues Lacan, the seeming command of the mirror image experienced by the child speaks to an ideal mastery, the ideal-ego. Lacan and Leclaire (Lacan, 1991) (amongst others) problematize Freud's foundational text on narcissism (Freud, 1914) in a conducive way. In summarizing one of Freud's key points, Leclaire emphasizes that the evolution of the ego consists in a separation from primary narcissism that produces a strong attempt to win back that primary state. This separation is caused by the displacement of libido on to an *ego-ideal* introduced from the outside and whose fulfilment pleases the subject. Leclaire goes further and hypothesizes that the subject's libido could be displaced on to *two ideal* destinations: 'an image of the ego ... or something which is quite properly an ideal, and which comes closer to the idea', a distinction with which Lacan agrees (Leclaire in Lacan, 1991, pp. 135–136; Lacan, p. 148).

Apart from the case of love, I would like to explore the idea that under certain political circumstances the libido is displaced on to an ideal image of the ego. Is there a link between narcissism and Ecuador's enigmatic constitutional instability led by often authoritarian figures with whom Ecuadorians have identified? To what extent has Laclau's justification of the centrality of the leader in populism (as first among equals) left unattended the psychology of authoritarian leadership in postcolonial Latin America, a region known for its recurrent 'populism'?

The Super-ego and Heroic Identification

In *Psychoanalysis and the Structure of the Personality* (1961, section VII), Lagache addresses the structure of the super-ego in a clarifying way. He reminds us that in *The Ego and the Id* Freud (1923) conceives the super-ego as a sum or system of privileged identifications stemming from the decline of the Oedipus complex. But this has led post-Freudians to wonder about the pre-oedipal ancestors of the super-ego and the post-oedipal reconfigurations. However, this genetic interest in the super-ego has often left unattended its structural elements. In *On Narcissism*, comments Lagache, Freud understands the origin of the ego-ideal as the union of primary narcissism and the identifications with parents, their substitutes, and the collective ideals. Hence, moral consciousness, self-observance, and censorship are the ego-ideal's functions. In *The Ego and the Id*, continues Lagache, Freud introduces the notion of the super-ego, while preserving the ego-ideal and the ideal-ego. In *The New Introductory Lectures*, Freud (1933) preserves the terminological 'confusion', although one precision is made, namely that the ego-ideal is a *function* of the superego. From a structural perspective, the ego-ideal speaks to how the individual must behave in order for the ego-subject—identified with the parental authority—to authorize the ego-object.

When discussing the different types of personality, Lagache highlights those instances in which subjects do not develop/identify with a super-ego—ego-ideal; instead, they identify with their ideal-ego. And this, as I shall soon argue, has consequences in politics.

> In those cases, the figures of moral authority are objectivized but not "recognized", they are devaluated, despised, considered as enemies or rivals. The identification with the ego ideal is out of the question: the conformists are criticized, ridiculed. The personal ideal is a narcissist ideal of omnipotence which only admits identifications with exceptional and prestigious celebrities. [...] In this regard, I have previously described the concept of "heroic identification" ... [...] These subjects are by no means incapable of

> imagining the others' viewpoint, but with no adherence to it. [O]ne of their typical reflections is 'I know I have a bad character'... [...] Their "chosen circle" is composed of persons for whom these subjects, who are identified with their ideal ego, constitute an object of tolerance, admiration, and imitation. (Lagache, 1961, p. 36, own translation)

There are other cases in which one can note how the ego-ideal and ideal-ego of the analysands rapidly fluctuate back and forth. Here, the analysands' ideal-ego uncovers through the passionate admiration of strong historical and contemporary personae due to their independence, pride, and authority. But as the cure progresses, their ego-ideal emerges and becomes irreducible to their ideal-ego (Lagache, 1961, p. 37).

The formation of the ideal-ego stems from a primary process of identification. Lagache cites Nuremberg for whom the ideal-ego, which pertains to a pre-oedipal phase, stems from the union between the Ego and the Id. But Lagache is not satisfied with this, for Nuremberg's account ignores an early intersubjective dynamic. Lagache notes that pre-oedipal and parasitic relation between the mother and the child creates a primary identification, that of the child with the omnipotent mother. After this period, the subject starts to experience a *primary conflict* with the mother (her *NO*), which takes place from the age of 12 to 18 months. At this point the infant has an alternative: either she/he goes back to the parasitic relationship with the mother, or she/he identifies with the 'aggressor'. In a nutshell, the infants' ideal-ego is a narcissistic ideal of omnipotence that results from their identification with a figure of omnipotence: their mother. The subsequent emergence of the *primary conflict* foreshadows the alternative to either go back to the parasitic relation with the mother or to identify with the 'ego ideal or the superego' (Lagache, 1961, pp. 37–38).

Lagache's (1961) pre-oedipal findings contribute to Freud's (1921) account of identification. Back then, Freud conceived this conflicting process as the infant's first manifestation of emotional affection. As he puts it, just before or during the *Oedipus complex*, little infants idealize their father and thus want to be like him when they grow up. However, during this process of identification (or soon after) the child starts to manifest an *object-cathexis* towards his/her mother. For a while, these two sentiments coexist without tension. Nevertheless, at some point the necessary unification of the psyche generates a collision of these emotions, a convergence whereby a normal *Oedipus complex* arises. 'Identification, in fact, is ambivalent from the very first; it can turn into an expression of tenderness as easily as into a wish for someone's removal' (Freud, 1921/Freud, 1959, p. 37).[2]

While Freud (1921) emphasizes the role of the father in the process of identification, Lagache (1961) pays special attention to the process of identification with the mother during the pre-oedipal dynamic. It is intriguing to note Lagache's nuanced contribution, namely, that there are adults who identify with their ego-ideal, while others with their ideal-ego. Moreover, there are cases in which there is a back-and-forth fluctuation between the ideal-ego and the ego-ideal in adults (only when the *psycho-analytic experience* advances can this oscillation stop in favour of the ego-ideal). Under certain limits, this persistent fluctuation cannot be considered pathological (Lagache, 1961, pp. 38–39).

In this light, a few political reflections are in order. A psychoanalytic understanding of *Narcissus and Echo* (Ovid, 8 CE) allowed Freud (1914, 1921) to refine his notion of the leader–followership dynamic, with particular emphasis on the idea that many followers have not renounced their early narcissism as much as others have. More precisely, as Laclau (2005) observes, Freud (1921) brings to our attention how the selection of leaders is influenced, at least partially, by the degree of differentiation between the followers' egos and their ego-ideals. Lacan and Leclaire (1953–1954) refine the imaginary and symbolic nature of the ideal-ego and the ego-ideal (respectively) put forward by Freud in his foundational text (Freud, 1914). And their distinctive nature speaks to the different avenues that subjects can transit in trying to recover their early narcissism. To clarify post-Freudian 'confusion', in 1961 Lagache reminds us that Freud's typology *Ego-Id-Superego* encompasses the ego-ideal, the latter a function of the super-ego (I further problematize the super-ego in the methodological chapter when addressing Hook's contribution (2017, 2018a, 2018b)). In addition, Lagache makes a contribution by linking the ideal-ego/ego-ideal distinction to the notion of *heroic identification*. In doing so, he distinguishes those individuals who identify with their ideal-ego (i.e., a narcissistic ideal of omnipotence) from those who identify with their ego-ideal (i.e., the authoritative commands from their parents, their substitutes, and collective ideals). In short, the French School of

[2] In his essay on *Femininity*, Freud indicates that both little girls and boys manifest the *object-cathexis towards the mother*. Notwithstanding, there are differences as to how women and men enter, transit, and exit the *Oedipus complex*. Cf. *New Introductory Lectures on Psycho-Analysis*.

Psychoanalysis fleshes out Freud's (1921) observation as to how the degree of distance between the followers' ego and ego-ideal influences their preferred leader.

I agree with Laclau (2005) in positing that leaders who share traits with their followers can be understood as primus inter pares (first among equals) within the populist logic. Thanks to these shared features, leaders serve as the element that helps the unification of heterogeneous and unmet social demands. And this makes the populist logic possible. Admittedly, Laclau was occupied with the task of making sense of Freud's (1921) text when justifying the centrality of the leader in populism. In doing so, he was responding to those rushed critiques against the so-called manipulative character of 'populist' leaders.

But my contribution sidesteps the controversial and overly discussed topic of populism. Freud's (1921) comment on the degree of differentiation between the ego and the ego-ideal, a topic further refined by Lacan, Leclaire, and Lagache, paves the way for thinking about two types of political leadership (notwithstanding other alternatives): (1) one that builds a collective endeavour (e.g., a nation) through shared and prevalent ego-ideals; (2) another that builds the nation through shared and prevalent images of ideal-egos. Two questions ensue: (1) under what circumstances are followers and leaders inclined to develop a majoritarian identification with the nation's ego-ideals or, differently, with certain ideal-egos personified in 'strong' leaders? (2) Can the colonial trauma shed partial light on this bifurcation? If so, how would this split account in part for Ecuador's constitutional instability?

The Trauma of Colonialism and the Diminished Paternal Imago in Ecuador

As of today, 20 constitutions have been sanctioned, most of which under the auspices of authoritarian leaders known as 'caudillos'.[3] What is intriguing about the Ecuadorian case (and maybe other cases of which I am not aware) is the 'father' imagery present in its CAs, at least in those analysed here. By this I mean a blend of those fatherly qualities described by Freud and the type of narrative found in the CAs in view of the idealization of García Moreno, Alfaro, and Correa. This can often resonate with Freud's

[3] I borrow this idea from historian Enrique Ayala Mora, with whom I shared my reflections.

description of the *father's image*, namely '[t]he clarity of thought, the force of will, the strength in action, are constitutive of the father image, but, above all, autonomy and independence' (Freud, 2015b, p. 158). However, a nuance must be noted. The father's image in postcolonial Ecuador resonates with that of an authoritarian father whose authority relies more on force than speech, as the archives will show in subsequent chapters. (Even in the present day, it is common to hear that politicians are effective in so far as they have the 'necessary' macho skills to dominate their political adversaries.)

Although Lacan's (1938) *Family Complexes* can be problematic as it speaks to its early theory, some of its elements are helpful when making sense of political identification in Ecuador in the nineteenth and twentieth centuries, a clearly patriarchal epoch. Lacan (1938) posits that while the ego-ideal exerts a conscious influence on the subject, the super-ego has an unconscious sway on it. And this is so considering how subjects exit the Oedipus complex (under normal circumstances). Within the simple form of oedipal conflict for the male child, which was the typical case explained by Freud during his early writings, 'the parent of the same sex appears to the child both as an agent of sexual prohibition and as an example of its transgression' (Lacan, 1938, pp. 36, 38). This dynamic leads subjects to repress their incestual desires and to sublimate the parental image, a twofold process that establishes two subsequent agencies in the subject: one that represses (the super-ego) and one that sublimates (the ego-ideal) (Lacan, 1938, p. 37).

Lacan (1938) acknowledges that the Oedipus complex must be understood in light of its narcissistic antecedents (cf. our discussion with Lagache above). However, Lacan also highlights that this complex must be comprehended considering the *sociological relativity* that surrounds it. Take the case of a paternalistic family. Here, argues Lacan, what provides the most enduring psychic effect of suppression and sublimation is the imago of the father. More precisely, the suppression of the *Oedipus complex* leads to a twofold and sublimated psychic experience beyond self-interest, namely that of the emergence of an unconscious super-ego and a conscious ego-ideal. But how does this complex sublimate reality? The resolution of this drama initiates through the process of identification. 'It is in fact because of an identification of the subject with an imago of the parent of the same sex that the super-ego and ego-ideal can be seen to have traits that correspond to particular characteristics of this imago' (Lacan, 1938, pp. 44, 46, 49). Albeit later Lacan established a clear prevalence of the symbolic register over the imaginary one (I address this in the next chapter), the question of the decline of the paternal imago as discussed by Lacan in 1938 is of help in this book. In Lacan's own words:

> [T]he forms of neurosis dominating the end of the last century revealed that they were intimately linked with the conditions of the family. [...] Our experience leads us to designate its principal determinant [that of the 'great neurosis of our time'] in the personality of the father which is always lacking in some way or another, whether he be absent or humiliated, divided or sham. It is this lack which, as explained by our theory of the Oedipus complex, exhausts institutional energy and vitiates the dialectic of sublimation. (Lacan, 1938, pp. 55–56)

The decline of the paternal imago, which manifests itself in humiliated and divided personalities, degrades the dialectic of sublimation from which the ego-ideal emerges. An imago is an unconscious model figure (in this case that of the father) which orientates the subject's mode of perceiving others. More precisely, an imago is an 'acquired imaginary set rather than an image ..., a stereotype through which ... the subject views the other person. Feelings and behaviour ... are just as likely to be the concrete expressions of the imago as are mental images' (Laplanche & Pontalis, 1973, p. 211). As I shall suggest below, there might be a partial connection between the humiliating logic of racism in postcolonial Ecuador, the subsequent declination of its *paternal imago* (the figure of authority back then), and its long-lasting history of constitutional replacements led by authoritarian figures.

But how can we apply Lacan's clinical and sociological reflections to nineteenth-century Ecuador? A universal novel might be of help here. In *The Failure of the Parental Metaphor: A Lacanian Reading of James Joyce's "Eveline"*, Sharoni (2016) interprets Eveline's tragic incapacity to love someone. Despite the daily nightmare that Eveline endures with her violent father at home, she does not escape with her beloved Frank to Buenos Aires when the opportunity presents itself. To make sense of this classic contradiction, Sharoni draws on Lacan's understanding of the link between the mother's desire and the paternal metaphor/function to account for the (un)successful overcoming of the oedipal drama in childhood. For Lacan, the subject's sexual desire can come to fruition thanks to the instantiation of the Name-of-the-Father which, according to Sharoni, did not take place in the case of Eveline. Although Sharoni correctly indicates that the instantiation of the Name-of-the-Father is not necessarily prompted by the biological father, he can embody this symbolic function:

> [Q]ua symbolic father, every father ought to have certain authority in the child's eyes to lay down this law of society. The father is, after all, the one whose "no" prevents the child from remaining the mother's object in order to become a subject. [...] This function does not necessitate any specific individual, let alone an actual father. [...] The point I will make nonetheless is that in "Eveline", a father is depicted who does not take the role of "father" ... as an authority with the power to lay down the law by means of speech... There is, I argue, only the semblance of a patriarchal authority, fabricated by the violence. In the gap between the father's illusion of potency and the reality of haplessness, we can see the failure of the implementation of the paternal metaphor. (Sharoni, 2016, p. 41)

Due to this failed instantiation of the Name-of-the-Father, Eveline's desire remained attached to her mother's desire. And this, ultimately, prevented Eveline from travelling with her beloved Frank to Argentina. Sharoni's interpretation of Eveline's incapacity to love Frank speaks to how a particular biography accounts for someone's difficulty to embrace love, a problem often treated in the clinical setting. Notwithstanding the impossibility of utilizing the psychoanalytic technique outside the clinic, let alone the ethical implication of such a ludicrous endeavour, a Lacanian interpretation of Eveline's drama and Lacan's notion of the decline of the paternal imago under certain societal circumstances open the door for further political analysis.

Ecuador has had a history of racism initiated in colonial times. This type of violence has been perpetrated against most of its inhabitants, that is, the non-white population (the indigenous, mestizo—mixed race—and African Americans). I would like to speculate on the partial link between this racism (and its other side, i.e., the national shame stemming from a mixed race), a diminished paternal imago, and frequent constitutional replacements led by authoritarian leaders. Although this history of racist exploitation has been perpetrated against women and men alike, the realm of politics in Ecuador, a patriarchal and postcolonial country, has been dominated by men (this is slowly changing in the twenty-first century). Should this conjecture prove in part eloquent (I let the reader judge this), could we suggest, then, that a systematic diminishing of the paternal imago in nineteenth-century Ecuador accounts, at least in part, for its long-lasting history of constitutional instability? If so, how? Is the violent/humiliating logic of the (post) colonial authority linked to a particular type of political identification? Why would this be of relevance?

By identification here I mean the '[p]sychological process whereby the subject assimilates an aspect, property or attribute of the other and is transformed, wholly or partially, after the model the other provides. It is by means of a series of identifications that the personality is constituted and specified' (Laplanche & Pontalis, 1973, p. 205). This definition, to be refined in the methodological chapter in which *symbolic identification* is presented, is useful for three reasons. Firstly, it allows us to account for the transformational character of the subject once it assimilates the properties of its admired 'model'. Secondly, this definition speaks to an ongoing process which starts in the pre-oedipal phase (as discussed above) and continues throughout life. Thirdly, this ongoing collection of identifications does not result in a consistent relational system. In addition to certain demands of the super-ego conflict with one another, some societal ideals—with which the subject identifies—are not in accord with one another (ibid., p. 208). The cultural ideas stemming from a postcolonial society constitute fertile ground for exploring this lack of harmony within the ego-ideals of a postcolonial nation.

Concluding Remarks

According to Freud, the killing of the father of the primal horde instated the first social contract amongst the league of brothers; the law, ethics, and religion derived from this pact. This conflict-based hypothesis is one amongst other theories on the origin of the state. The contractarian discourse (the predominant perspective in the liberal and contemporary constitutional doctrine) and Marxism are popular alternatives in academia.

But Freud's thesis has been questioned. Contemporary anthropology cannot corroborate that a primal father such as that described by Freud existed in prehistoric times. Moreover, feminism and Marxism have contested the universal and ahistorical nature of the *Oedipus complex*, its 'patriarchal' character, and its determinism in accounting for socio-political phenomena. These critiques are important, but these should not lead us to simply jettison Freud's conjecture, as it sheds light on the psychic factor underpinning my research puzzle.

Freud's hypothesis on the origin of law and its subsequent and frequent transgression—which arguably resonates with the totemic banquet—later refined in *Moses and Monotheism*, is productive insofar as it is regarded as a *myth*. It allows us to explain, in part, how the question of 'messianic' leadership/caudillismo relates to Ecuador's constitutional instability. As I shall argue below, the idealization of key authoritarian lawgivers (García Moreno, Alfaro, and Correa) speaks to the 'return' of the *fantasy* of the messiah. This trans-ideological experience in Ecuador, I will suggest, has played out in a context-dependent manner. That is, in terms of a heroic and narcissistic identification with authoritarian figures, the flip side of a diminished paternal imago shaped in part by the racist structure of colonialism. But this should not mislead us to believe that imaginary identification takes precedence over symbolic identification, not even in postcolonial Ecuador. In the following methodological chapter, I tackle this and other concerns, while setting the scene for the subsequent discourse analysis.

References

Bobbio, N., Matteucci, N., & Pasquino, G. (2005). *Diccionario de política*. Siglo Veintiuno Editores.

Clavero, B. (2007). The rule of law and the legal treatment of native americans. In P. Costa & D. Zolo (Eds.), *Law and philosophy library* (Vol. 80). Springer.

Freud, S. (1914) *On Narcissism*. The Standard Edition of the Complete Psychological Works of Sigmund Freud, Volume XIV (1914-1916): On the History of the Psycho-Analytic Movement, Papers on Metapsychology and Other Works, pp. 67-102. Retrieved February 28, 2023, from https://www.sas.upenn.edu/~cavitch/pdf-library/Freud_SE_On_Narcissism_complete.pdf

Freud, S. (1921/1959). *Group psychology and the analysis of the ego*. The Hogarth Press and The Institute of Psycho-Analysis.

Freud, S. (2015a). *Tótem y tabú*. Amorrortu Editores.

Freud, S. (1939/2015b). *Moisés y la religión monoteísta*. Amorrortu Editores.

Hook, D. (2017). What is "enjoyment as a political factor"? *Political Psychology, 38*(4), 605–620.

Hook, D. (2018a). Racism and jouissance: Evaluating the "racism as (the theft of) enjoyment" hypothesis. *Psychoanalysis, Culture & Society, 23*, 244–266.

Hook, D. (2018b). *Six moments in Lacan. Communication and identification in psychology and psychoanalysis*. Routledge.

Lacan, J. (1938). Family complexes in the formation of the individual. Paris: Encyclopédie française (A. de Monzie, Editor), Vol. 8, translated by Cormac Gallagher.

Lacan, J. (1991). *Freud's Papers on Technique 1953-1954. Book I.* Norton.
Lacan, J. (1997). *The ethics of psychoanalysis 1959-1960. Book VII.* Norton.
Lacan, J. (1999). *Las formaciones del inconsciente 1957-1958. Libro 5.* Paidós.
Lacan, J. (2000). *The Psychoses 1955–1956. Book III.* Norton.
Lacan, J. (2016). *La Relación de objeto. seminario 4.* Paidós.
Laclau, E. (2005/2007). *On populist reason.* Verso.
Lagache, D. (1961). *El psicoanálisis y la estructura de la personalidad.* Asociación Psicoanalítica del Uruguay – Revista Uruguaya de Psicoanálisis.
Laplanche, J., & Pontalis, J.-B. (1973). *The Language of Psycho-analysis.* Norton.
Martin, J. (2019). *Psycho-politics of speech. Uncivil discourse and the excess of desire.* Transcript.
Ovid. (1977). *Metamorphoses, Book III (Narcissus and Echo).* Harvard University Press. translation by Frank Justus Miller.
Sharoni, J. (2016). The failure of the parental metaphor: A Lacanian reading of James Joyce's "Eveline". *Journal of Modern Literature, 39*(4), 33–48.
Stavrakakis, Y. (1999). *Lacan & the political.* Routledge.
Stavrakakis, Y. (2010). *La izquierda lacaniana. Psicoanálisis, teoría, política.* Fondo de Cultura Económica.
Thurschwell, P. (2000). *Sigmund Freud.* Routledge Critical Thinkers.
Žižek, S. (1990). Eastern Europe's Republics of Gilead. *New Left Review* (I/183, September-October).
Žižek, S. (2008). *The sublime object of ideology.* Verso.
Zolo, D. (2007). The rule of law: A critical reappraisal. In P. Costa & D. Zolo (Eds.), *The rule of Law. History, theory and criticism* (Vol. 80). Springer.

CHAPTER 2

The Research Strategy

On the Case Study and Comparative Methodologies

The case study methodology provides the following advantages (amongst others): an in-depth analysis of the phenomenon under investigation, a better understanding of the crucial periods of history, and a way to provide a voice to those historically excluded. This methodology requires an adequate definition of the unit of analysis (Sjoberg et al., 1991, pp. 31, 51, 54, 65). This book's main units of analysis are Ecuador's *founding discourses*, and their analyses allow us to relate the question of messianic leadership to the long-lasting problem of 'constitutional instability' in this postcolonial country.

There are overt similarities between the conservative García Moreno, the liberal Alfaro, and the socialist Correa. These presidents promoted the 1869, 1906, and 2007–2008 conventions, as well as the 2015 constitutional amendment that allowed indefinite presidential re-elections in Ecuador. Moreover, these leaders served as presidents for a rather long period (10–11 years), an exception to Ecuador's long-lasting history of political instability in the executive branch. Relatedly, their idealization by their followers follows a rather similar pattern, despite ideological differences. Notwithstanding their resemblances, I expect that some scholars (especially historians) may seek to contest my case selection. For instance, Espinosa (2010) has argued that the charismatic Rafael Correa shares similarities with the charismatic José María Velasco Ibarra, the five-time

E. Espindola, *The Paternal Imago in Ruins*, The Palgrave Lacan Series, https://doi.org/10.1007/978-3-032-07507-9_2

president in twentieth-century Ecuador. Nevertheless, in this book I am interested in highlighting, from a psychoanalytic perspective, the *messianic* role played by García Moreno, Alfaro, and Correa in key constitutional replacements and reforms in three centuries.

The decision of mixing the case study and comparative methodologies stems from my *problem-driven research strategy*, that is, a strategy underpinned by certain ontological premises that have guided the *construction* of what I deem to be a *problematic* phenomenon: Ecuador's constitutional volatility understood as the frequent abolition of the constitutional order led by 'caudillos', a process followed by Constituent Assemblies (CAs) seeking to rewrite this postcolonial country's history from *tabula rasa*. In this research, the comparative methodology serves the purpose of highlighting the meaning of certain similarities underlying Ecuador's long-lasting desire to abolish/replace its higher law (for this research strategy, see Glynos & Howarth, 2007, pp. 167, 201, 206).

It is worth revisiting this question: does instability explain 'messianism' or vice versa? While the affective pull of 'messianic leadership' in the constitutional politics of Ecuador can develop because of the need for political stability, this messianism can also be triggered by a psychic mechanism fleshed out in the previous chapter. That is, the ambivalent and heroic identification with authoritarian leaders, the flip side of a diminished paternal imago in postcolonial Ecuador. In this national context, Ecuador's long-lasting history of political instability has reproduced a culture prone to supporting *messianic* leaders, that is, lawgivers whose personae have blended with the aspiration of perpetual stability epitomized by the setting up of CAs themselves. My explanatory hypothesis thus conforms to a retroductive mode of reasoning, in which 'the posited hypothesis accounts for a problematized phenomenon by rendering it intelligible' (Hanson, as cited by Glynos & Howarth, 2007, p. 39). To render my psychoanalytically informed hypothesis intelligible, which comprises an extra-clinical approach to constitutional instability in Ecuador, my arguments are conjectural, speculative. By speculation here I mean a rigorous conjecture whose aim is not to 'prove' something *à la* positivism but to persuade the reader of its partial validity/usefulness in explaining the puzzle of constitutional instability in this country.

A Lacanian Approach to the Grip of Ideology

Ecuador's constitutionalist tradition has been self-transgressive since independence. By this I mean that the constant abolition of the constitution in force by the elites has sabotaged their own hope for stability. The 1869 and 2007–2008 CAs speak to this hope for stability. To discuss this nation's self-transgressive constitutional tradition, I now propose a methodology to capture *enjoyment* (and related concepts) in the subsequent discourse analysis.

Glynos (2008) addresses how the concept of *enjoyment* can productively converse with the difficulties underlying our pursuit of freedom. He begins by highlighting the common phenomenon of self-transgression as illustrated by an academic goal. Although the latter requires a proper and self-disciplined management of time, it is many times transgressed by procrastination. The pleasure brought about by the transgression of our own goals (co-constitutive for psychoanalysis) is an ontological mode of our subjectivity informed by *enjoyment* (pp. 679, 685–687). Self-transgressive enjoyment can manifest in 'those situations in which a subject appears both to affirm an ideal and, at the same time, systematically to transgress it' (Glynos, 2008, p. 679). Of course, there are other plausible explanations for the issue of self-transgression, such as competing ideals or the 'false consciousness' account (ibid.). Glynos conceives the self-transgressive nature of *enjoyment* as the logic that informs, in part, the grip of ideology. This grip, according to a common critique of ideology, works in detriment to our freedom (p. 685).

A community remains together because its inhabitants identify with one another via ideals such as 'fraternity' and 'equality'. Psychoanalysis, however, identifies a complementary but countervailing logic to this process of community identification. Counterintuitively, the union of a community also relies on its people's identification with the *enjoyment* procured by a shared transgression of those ideals (Glynos, 2021, pp. 7–8). I would like to suggest, therefore, that Ecuador's self-transgressive constitutional tradition follows this logic.

As Hook (2017) puts it, libidinal *enjoyment* (in its various manifestations) influences the realm of the political. The psychoanalytic (Lacanian) nature of *enjoyment* does not equate to pleasure; in fact, it is blended with pain. *Enjoyment*, which is linked to the *death drive*, is a kind of *stimulation* that subjects experience once the affective dimension reaches the beyond-the-pleasure-principle threshold. How can we identify this particular logic of *enjoyment* in psychosocial phenomena such as ideology? To find the grip of a particular ideology, it becomes useful to map the prevalent modes of *enjoyment* contravening its professed goals, that is, the inconsistencies between the *presentable symbolic formations* of ideology and its *disavowed libidinal components*. The *libidinal* ingredient of ideology should not mislead us to assert that *enjoyment* is an 'ordinary' emotion (e.g., anger, joy), or an 'extra-discursive' element related to the *real* without symbolic mediation. *Jouissance* is linked to the symbolic order, as this is the field in which social limitations are instituted and disobeyed. '*Jouissance* can be thought of as *subliminal* in the sense that we are not fully conscious of—or willing to admit to—the thrills ... we get in pursuing those activities that trigger libidinal intensity' (p. 608), activities that are excessive, transgressive par excellence. But *enjoyment* does not work on its own; *fantasy* structures the frame whereby subjects experience *stolen enjoyment* at the individual and collective level. '[I]nsofar as groups share fantasies about themselves (attributions regarding what is most precious about themselves, about what is their greatest threat of "castration"), then they have shared modes of *jouissance*' (Hook, 2018b, pp. 606–614).

The application of *enjoyment* as a tool for socio-political analysis of postcolonial Ecuador requires the discussion of interconnected concepts (Hook, 2017, 2018a), such as the notions of *castration*, the *lost object*, *fantasy* (presented above), and the super-ego. The transgressive dimension of *enjoyment* and its association with the law and the super-ego might appear contradictory, for the implementation of the law produces a type of reward or 'jouissance payment' (and this furtive payment buttresses the symbolic law). In virtue of the super-ego, which also generates *jouissance*, societal ego-ideals are adopted and devotedly implemented. Among other practices, denouncing lawbreakers, passing out punishments, and allocating severe sentences produce 'jouissance payment' in subjects (Hook, 2018a, pp. 259–260). In addition, the linkage between the super-ego and *enjoyment* allows us to appreciate a practice that is often overlooked by accounts that emphasize the common aspects of racism, such as ignorance, baseless hate, and intolerance. While racism can certainly come from all of these roots, it 'is also a type of indignation; an impetus to blame and punish, involving a sense of laws, societal (if racist) norms, and ideals that been violated' (Hook, 2018a, p. 261).

In sum, *enjoyment*, the super-ego, and the law are intertwined—a brief illustration is in order. The 1869 constitution established the Catholic faith as a legal requisite for those citizens seeking to hold a public post.

This, I would like to suggest, required state vigilance, a monitoring underpinned in part by the *enjoyment* procured by 'the righteous indignation of constantly denouncing' (Hook, 2018a, p. 260) non-Catholic infiltrators. In this case, the super-ego could have connected the *law* with *enjoyment*, thus guaranteeing that the ego-ideals of the Catholic nation were successfully enacted and accepted as enthusiastic investments (ibid.). Amongst other aspects, 'the superego produces enjoyment ... by means of the exhilarating intensities (of hate, anger, punishments, etc.) that accompany the enactment of symbolic law' (Hook, 2017, p. 618).

The Capturing of Symbolic and Imaginary Identification: On the Coming of the Messiah

Hook's (2018b) problematization of imaginary and symbolic identification in politics, a process in which the symbolic register takes precedence, offers further insights and methodological tools for this book. The following section operationalizes an aspect addressed in the previous chapter, that is, Lacan's problematization of the ideal-ego and the ego-ideal.

Hook (2018b, ch. 4) draws on Lacanian psychoanalysis to complement Freud's understanding of the libidinal economy underpinning group formation. In doing so, Hook reminds us that identification is, for the most part, an unconscious and unfinished process whereby images and signifiers mould the personality of the subject. Take, for instance, the case of symbolic identification in post-apartheid South Africa, where Nelson Mandela became the symbolic father of this new social contract. In this context, social and symbolic ideals fostered the emergence of a leader who represented a moment in which a foundational law inscribed a given sociocultural order.

> [W]hen a set of social and symbolic ideals are powerfully animated, then a leader is never far away. [...] [W]hen a social contract is put in place, when a foundational gesture confers (social, historical, subjective) identity, then a symbolic father is likewise never distant. We have a nice instance here of a Lacanian amendment to Freudian theory: it is not simply the case that charismatic leaders embody social and symbolic ideals; a surge of such ideals also engenders leaders and—by extension—symbolic fathers. [...] *Apropos* any symbolic identification (or any collective or mass bond) we can ask: '*Who's your daddy?*' (Hook, 2018b, p. 121)

Hook 'amends' Freud's 'love of the leader' argument by changing the focus of analysis: it is not the charismatic personality of the leader as such what is most important but rather *the symbolic place* this leader occupies. More precisely, the desired features attributed to the leader are mediated by the Other, which means that traits such as integrity, intelligence, leadership are always underpinned by historically informed symbolic coordinates. Hook stresses that Freud's understanding of the ego-ideal resonates with Lacan's notion of the Name-of-the-Father. 'The symbolic place of the leader corresponds to what Freud calls the "ego–ideal", that is, the collection of the cherished and respected societal ideals which mean more than the ego itself' (Hook, 2018b, p. 125).

Freud's theory on mass identification relies on two emotional attachments: (1) to one's fellow group members and (2) to the leader. In fact, it is thanks to the presence of a leader (or to a series of ego-ideal values with which followers identify) that intragroup tensions can be significantly neutralized. What is important here is that Freud's theory, when complemented by Lacan's insights, allows us to appreciate two modes of identifications operating in group psychology: a hierarchical (symbolic) and a horizontal (imaginary) one. The hierarchical dimension entails symbolic identifications not with other peers but with values (signifiers) located outside the subject, that is, ego-ideals linked to the totality of the socio-cultural network *as embodied in the big Other* (Hook, 2018b, pp. 126–127). Differently, the horizontal mode of identification—that between fellow group members—consists in ideal-ego identifications between *like others,* that is, with those

> who represent my own possible mirror image (alter egos, we might say). [...] On the one hand we have an *imaginary* type of identification ... which unfolds along the lines of likeable images that have a self-valorizing, affirming quality. These are the grandiose or idealized, indeed, narcissistically gratifying, images of ourselves—or our group—that we hold dear; our preferred self-images. This imaginary dimension prioritizes visual markers, the dimension of the image and the factor of resemblance. It comprises the field of mirror-images through which the inter-subjective dialectic of *seeing others as one's self* and *one's self as others* play out. (Hook, 2018b, p. 127)

Hook's unpacking of Lacanian theory in light of Freud's notion of mass identification is illustrated by the shared behaviours of soccer fans in the 2010 South African World Cup. The imaginary dimension of identification became evident in the fans' ritual of painting their faces and dressing in the colours of their national teams. While the latter is important to generate an identity, the adoption of mirror images is not enough if one is to fully (and thus symbolically) identify with their team/nation. A symbolic identification will necessitate the adoption of signifiers from the field of the Other (Hook, 2018b, pp. 127–128). Apropos, Lacan argues that symbolic identification takes precedence, for it

> [is the] support [of specular, immediate identification]. [Symbolic identification] supports the perspective chosen by the subject in the field of the Other, from which specular identification may be seen ...The point of the ego-ideal is that from which the subject will see himself ... *as others see him* ... [A] specular image ... is situated in the field ... centered on the ideal point ... placed in the Other, from which the Other sees me. (Lacan, 1981, p. 268, as cited in Hook, 2018b, p. 129)

As we shall see below, the ***historical continuity*** of the Ecuadorian community, certain ***symbolic debts*** (e.g., the need to compensate for the historic mistreatment of the Indigenous Peoples), and ***unfulfilled promises*** (e.g., national progress) are part of the symbolic dimension of identification found in Ecuador's foundational moments. Worthy of note here is that symbolic identification provides the foundational basis from which a particular set of given images ensue. Hence, the ideal-ego is always dependent on the intervening element of the ego-ideal, the latter situated in the terrain of the Other (Hook, 2018b, pp. 129–130).

The foregoing discussion is of use in thinking about Ecuador's historic constitutional instability, a process driven by authoritarian leaders from across the ideological spectrum. The idea that symbolic identification takes precedence and influences how imaginary identification plays out will be discussed in the context of a postcolonial country whose national ego-ideals have been influenced by European colonization. And this might shed partial light on the recurrent type of heroic identification that Ecuadorians have had with authoritarian leaders: García Moreno, Alfaro, and Correa. Saving their differences, these personae have promised a new social contract inspired by European ideals: Catholic conservatism, radical liberalism, and Catholic socialism, respectively. Albeit counterintuitive, the prioritization of symbolic over imaginary identification is logic, for 'unless there was some delimitation and prioritization of what particular imaginary features are most lovable, how would [we] even know what images, and as importantly, *what faces of those images*, to love?' (Hook, 2018b, p. 131).

In a similar fashion to that of South Africa, in Ecuador there is a shame that accompanies the mixed-race identity (*mestizaje*), on account of the pejorative connotations associated with it. Apparently, the Freudian framework of intra-communal ties between members of the ingroup does not offer a suitable loupe for thinking about how shame operates within the group. But if we visualized ourselves as perceived from the location of the symbolic ideals—which may exist beyond the internal identifications within the national boundaries—shame is a plausible option within a national and postcolonial dynamic (Hook, 2018b, p. 131).

Methodological Notes on the Capturing of Fantasy in Politics

The way that *fantasy* operates in politics requires clarification. *Castration* instates the ontological *lack* with which subjects live throughout their life, that is, *a lack of full enjoyment*. As important as the latter, castration allows them to access the symbolic order of language (Lacan, as cited in Stavrakakis, 1999, pp. 41–42). Stavrakakis (1999) underscores that the lack in the subject and the *lack in the Other* are two sides of the same coin. The failed attempts to identify with something do not exclusively derive from the lack in the subject but also 'as a result of the lack within the structure, the structure of the social Other'. This is Lacan's novel understanding of the classic bipolarity subjective/objective. In virtue of this structural lack of the social Other, the symbolic register cannot provide a stable identity to subjects, whose resulting frustration leads them to restore the 'quasi-imaginary *objet petit a,* the field of fantasy' (pp. 40–41, 45). As Stavrakakis puts it, fantasy entails the 'promise to attain the mythical jouissance'. While fantasy is not there to 'fill up' the lack in the Other (impossible per se), it seeks to 'achieve a "forgetting of origins" of reality … It attempts to do so by offering us the object as metaphor of our lacking fullness' (pp. 45, 47).[1] And this 'lacking fullness' has a link to utopian

[1] 'In "Direction of the Treatment" (1958) Lacan restates that what is at stake in metaphor is the substitution of one term for another, while in metonymy we have the combination of one term with another' (as cited in Stavrakakis, 1999, p. 57).

discourses. Utopia derives from the Greek 'u' and 'tópos', that is, the 'non-existent place' (Arlotti, 2003, p. 417). The interplay between the *metonymic logic of desire* and the *metaphor of our lacking fullness* accounts, at least in part, for the ongoing glue of substitute utopian *fantasies* in politics. Take the case of Ecuador's constitutional instability since independence. In this process, the recurrent promise of a new constitution (the *object petit a*) speaks to this never-ending desire animating the quest for a fantasized (and always lacking) fullness, such as that of a fully developed, independent, and emancipated nation. The gap in Ecuador between what was sought (the fullness in question) and what is found (a lacking reality) incentivizes an ongoing disruption/crisis at the constitutional level. 'Desire ... is animated by the quest for a lacking/impossible fullness, around the promise of encountering *jouissance* and *jouissance* always has "the connotation of fullness"' (Stavrakakis and Forrester, as cited in Stavrakakis, p. 45). *Apropos*, Žižek provides a useful systematization of how *castration*, the *lost object*, and *fantasy* relate to one another:

> The 'impossible' relationship of the subject to this object the loss of which constitutes the subject is marked by the Lacanian formula of fantasy: $\$\Diamond a$. Fantasy is then to be conceived as an imaginary scenario the function of which is to provide a kind of positive support filling out the subject's constitutive void. And the same goes, mutatis mutandis, for social fantasy: it is a necessary counterpart to the concept of antagonism, a scenario filling out the voids of the social structure, masking its constitutive antagonism by the fullness of enjoyment (racist enjoyment, for example). (Žižek, 2005, pp. 242–243)

How can we identify shared fantasmatic narratives—sustained by *the fullness of enjoyment*—amongst liberals, conservatives, socialists, etc.? Glynos and Howarth's beatific and horrific dimensions of fantasy offer a productive operationalization, which allows us to identify political narratives seeking to 'fill up' the subjects' lacking identity. The beatific dimension manifests itself through speeches promising a full harmony-to-come, provided that the named or implied enemy (i.e., the 'stealer' of 'our' *enjoyment*) is defeated. Its horrific dimension can be identified through narratives foreseeing an apocalyptic future if the 'obstacle' is not defeated (Glynos & Howarth, 2007, pp. 146–147, 149).

Racism in Ecuador: On the Explanatory and Methodological Power of Jouissance

This book focuses on the relation between messianic leadership and constitutional instability in a postcolonial and racist country: Ecuador. Thus, Chap. 3 and 4 also discuss the indigenous question in light of the 1869 and 2007–2008 debates. The role that the native population ought to play in the new *Social Contract* created insightful controversies amongst the parliamentarians. Whereas the 1869 convention erased the ways that the indigenous peoples organized their communities prior to the nation state, the 2008 constitution recognized their demand for a pluri-national state. Also, the 2007–2008 convention criticized the fact that racism was still present in twenty-first-century Ecuador. Psychoanalysis offers insightful theoretical and methodological tools for thinking about and capturing the grip of racism in postcolonial contexts.

Since independence, the indigenous, black, and mestizo populations in Ecuador have been treated as racially inferior by Europeans and their 'white' descendants (most white-looking people in Ecuador have some type of racial mixture). Unfortunately, the premise of this 'racial inferiority' has structural consequences, as *Black Skin, White Masks* shows. In this book, Fanon (2017/1967, ch. 4) criticizes Mannoni's assumption according to which certain colonized peoples (e.g., the Malagasy) were the possessors of a primordial *dependency complex* prior to the arrival of the colonizers. Supposedly, this *complex* made colonialism viable. Fanon argues that it is the domination of a colonial society as a whole that creates and perpetuates an inferiority complex: 'If he [his black patient] is overwhelmed to such a degree by the wish to be white, it is because he lives in a society that makes his inferiority complex possible … in a society that proclaims the superiority of one race' (p. 81). Saving contextual differences between Madagascar, Martinique, and Ecuador, the 1869 debates in Ecuador show the tension between this so-called inferiority complex in the colonized, the societal logic of colonialism, and the liberal and Catholic humanitarian efforts in favour of Ecuador's 'miserable class'. The 2007–2008 convention evidences that the indigenous peoples continued to be treated as racially inferior.

Above it was mentioned that *fantasy* (in its horrific and beatific dimensions) builds the frame through which the subject experiences *enjoyment*. It was also indicated that this experience can take the imaginary form of something that has been 'stolen', which relates to the retroactive effect of *castration*: 'What we conceal by imputing to the Other the theft of enjoyment is the traumatic fact that *we never possessed what was allegedly stolen from us*: the lack ("castration") is original; enjoyment constitutes itself as "stolen"' (Žižek, 1990, p. 54). Lacanian psychoanalysis has theorized the link between *enjoyment* and racism to shed light on the phenomenon of exclusionary nationalism:

> The national Cause is ultimately nothing but the way subjects of a given ethnic community organize their enjoyment through national myths. What is therefore at stake in ethnic tensions is always the possession of the national Thing. We always impute to the 'other' an excessive enjoyment; *s/he wants to steal our enjoyment (by ruining our way of life) and/or has access to some secret, perverse enjoyment*. (Žižek, 1990, pp. 53–54, emphasis added)

Hook (2018a, pp. 246, 252) problematizes the explanatory power of the theft of enjoyment thesis when accounting for racism, a thesis gradually conceived by Lacan, Miller, and Žižek. Amongst other criticisms, this hypothesis can be regarded as a depoliticized narrative in view of its apparent psychological reductionism. Moreover, its all-encompassing logic, summarized in the 'theft' formula, can be applied to a myriad of other phenomena besides racism. But from a formalist perspective, which is loyal to Lacan's grammar, what at first sight appears to be a deficiency can be regarded as an analytical advantage, namely this formula's capacity to explain various phenomena.

Hook (2018a, pp. 254–258) notes that *jouissance* allows us to grasp the different modes of *enjoyment* informing racism. For instance, the passionate and *embodied* 'thrill of hate', such as that of a hate speech, is a conscious transgression of what is politically correct on account of the libidinal compensation that this trespass brings about. Another mode of enjoyment can be identified in light of a 'libidinal treasure', that is, when subjects deem something to be rightly 'theirs' and at continual risk of being stolen by 'them'. This 'property', a *fantasy object*, can take any form, such as the idea that the local language will eventually disappear given the influx of immigrants. Moreover, there is a mode of *enjoying* in which others are perceived to have a harmful 'surplus vitality'. In this dynamic, the *object a*, that is, the object cause of desire for the subject, is 'placed' in the Other. This '*object a* is the subject's own lack as it is positivized, materialized in an external attribute or object *possessed by the other*' (Hook, p. 258). But in lieu of just equating racism to *projection*, a nuanced and Lacanian approach to this phenomenon is needed, for the subject's 'structural incapacity is transformed into the certainty that some troubling substance of enjoyment has been illicitly procured by the other', as a result of which jealousy emerges (ibid.). The *theft of enjoyment* thesis and the modes whereby *jouissance* can be experienced will be of methodological assistance for the discourse analysis of the indigenous question in Ecuador.

On Rhetorical Political Analysis

My research strategy also benefits from rhetorical analysis, which allows us to identify and analyse the complexities and nuances of key fantasies found in the empirical chapters, namely those of the Messiah (1869, 1906, 2015), the Catholic Nation (1869), and the Pluri-National State (2007–2008).

Finlayson develops Rhetorical Political Analysis (RPA) to better understand the activity of persuading in politics. For RPA one has to set out clearly the context and the 'act' of the rhetorical argument; that is, one must first make explicit the setting in which the political rhetoric is analysed, since it is only against this backdrop that the character and significance of the rhetorical act can be appreciated. One must then come to terms with the fact that the form and content of a given argument are not always so clear and must therefore be unpacked as part of the RPA. A number of concepts serve to facilitate this process of unpacking, such as 'points of argument', 'genres', 'commonplaces', and 'appeals'. According to Roman rhetorical theory, there are *four points of argument*: 1) arguments of conjecture relating to what is 'factual'; 2) arguments of definition that name something one way or the other; 3) arguments of quality (moral assertions); 4) arguments of place that establish whether something is still relevant. All these points are contestable. Finlayson also draws on Aristotle's typology based on three genres of rhetoric: (1) an epideictic or ceremonial element that approves or disapproves something or someone; (2) a forensic component dealing with what is just or unjust; (3) a deliberative element in charge of either advocating or dissuading a course of action (Finlayson, 2007, pp. 552–556).

Argumentative *commonplaces* are crucial in structuring a rhetorical strategy, and they relate to a set of appeals (Finlayson, 2007, p. 557). Commonplaces, which are elements usually taken for granted, are mobilized in various ways to make one's case more persuasive through certain appeals, such as *ethos*, *pathos*, and *logos*. In the case of ethos, it is the type of authority evoked by the argument that confers validity to it: 'the people' in left and right populist speeches, and the authority of 'science' in the liberal narrative. As for pathos, certain ideologies spark specific emotions (e.g., love, hate) while others do not, or, if they do so, these emotions manifest themselves in different forms and/or degrees of intensity depending on the topics. When invoking logos, political actors try to 'demonstrate' the 'quasi-logical' tie between their premises and conclusions. The art of persuasion thus forms an important part of any ideological analysis (Finlayson, 2013, pp. 206–208).

On the Productive Dialogue between Rhetoric and Psychoanalysis

> In exploring the linkages between the psychic and the rhetorical, we might develop greater insight into the ways that—'beneath' overt appeals to emotion or to knowledge—political arguments continue to animate our desires and recruit our support. (Martin, 2016, p. 158)

As Martin (2014, Ch. 7) rightly puts it, emotion cannot be dissociated from reason, and this has been corroborated by neuroscience and psychoanalysis. From distinct epistemologies, both disciplines account for the intertwined logic of *affect*, emotion, and reason. 'Rather than distortions of reason, emotions are better conceived as conduits of affect that prompt feelings and shape cognition' (p. 108). Emotions are a constitutive part of any process of deliberation. But this, for some, can become problematic; hence formal procedures are required for a proper democratic deliberation. Many theorists of deliberative democracy mistrust emotions (and thus rhetoric), as they can lead to deception. For them, '[e]fforts to change the preferences of others ... must appeal solely to reason ... which is deemed entirely separate from ethos and pathos' (p. 111). This attempt is unrealistic, some would argue. From a psychoanalytic perspective as discussed above, ethos, logos, and pathos are often intertwined and allow us to enquire into the psychosocial outcome triggered by a *rhetorical strategy*. This 'denotes the purposeful assemblage of arguments for a particular occasion and setting in light of its anticipated effects and by means of available techniques' (Rowland, 2002, as cited in Martin, 2014, p. 94). An illustration is in order. The 1869 invocation of God and the 'lessons of history' referred to ethos and logos to legitimize the leadership of President García Moreno. These appeals, I would like to suggest, could have detonated the affective dimension, such as that of fantasy. 'Practices of mourning or fantasizing are fabricated ways of channelling feelings, calling up deep memories and reactivating traumatic experiences' (Martin, 2014, p. 119). This type of practice, which can rely on the link between *enjoyment* and fantasy, is *socially constructed* (Žižek, 2008, as cited in ibid.).

In this book I mainly analyse the link between the fantasy of the Messiah and the question of constitutional instability in postcolonial Ecuador. The examination of other fantasmatic narratives (the Catholic Nation and the Pluri-National State) is supplementary. In this endeavour, rhetorical analysis helps me to identify the multifaceted rationale with which this type of social fantasy is produced via speech. To preclude dispersion, this empirical endeavour will rely on the following scheme.

Martin (2014, pp. 57, 77–78, 99–101) proposes a method for rhetorical analysis focused on the *rhetorical context*, the *rhetorical arguments*, and the *rhetorical effects*, three moments informing the political strategy of a speech. The *rhetorical context* comprises the historical conditions forming the backdrop to a *speech occasion*, namely, 'the historical time and place of the intervention, the exigence(s) to which it is a response … and any broader circumstances the intervention also seeks to shape' (p. 100). Parliamentary speeches and press conferences (amongst others) are types of discourses linked to particular kinds of audiences. While the dyad *generic occasion*–respective audience establishes limits to someone's freedom of speech, it also provides chances for conveying a message in a legitimate way. The *rhetorical argument* denotes the moment in which a discourse seeks to shape a given situation in one way or another. Rhetorical techniques are deployed to persuade audience(s), such as, amongst others, the appeal to logos, ethos, and pathos; the usage of rhetorical questions (raised and answered by the speaker); and recourse to metaphors to define the premise for an argument. Let us recall that fantasy endeavours to 'achieve a "forgetting of origins" of reality … It attempts to do so by offering us the object as metaphor of our lacking fullness' (Stavrakakis, 1999, p. 47).[2] Speakers also draw on metaphors to induce an *analogical reasoning* in the audience, in the style of something 'being like' that which the speakers mean. The *rhetorical effects* allude to whether a 'a rhetorical strategy has contributed to defining the parameters of choice and conflict, compelling others to accept its terms of reference to the situation and positioning themselves accordingly' (p. 101).

[2] Ibid.

Finally, Can we Use Psychoanalysis in the Social Sciences?

As Hook (2008, pp. 398–399) puts it, an attempt to generalize the psychoanalytic technique beyond the clinical setting is problematic. Epistemic and ethical concerns derive from 'expert' interpretations of research participants in qualitative endeavours, such as the understanding of the 'real' meaning of what was said by the Ecuadorian parliamentarians. However, there are legitimate ways whereby psychoanalysis can complement psychosocial studies. Freud himself shows this in *Group Psychology and the Analysis of the Ego*, where he focuses on the libidinal economy of this phenomenon: 'Libidinal economy is a fundamental vector of group identification: the push-pull cohesion of its ego-ideal and ideal-ego dynamics is precisely what for Freud proved constitutive of social bonds' (Hook, 2008, p. 399). Relatedly, in the empirical chapters I discuss these symbolic and imaginary identifications (Hook, 2008) and their link to Ecuador's constitutional instability. This is analysed during the nation-building process put forward in CAs prompted by idealized leaders. I will focus on privileged *fantasmatic objects-cause of desire* (Hook, 2008, p. 400), namely the constitution (the one to be written), the Catholic Nation (1869), the Pluri-National State (2007–2008), and the 1869, 1906, and 2015 Messiahs. These *fantasmatic objects,* 'which contain ... something "in them more than themselves"' (ibid.), support the discourse whose master signifier is the *Ecuadorian nation.* This signifier 'remain[s] somehow open, but [it] anchor[s] meaning ... and organize[s] the ideological field' (ibid.) of different political elites.

Cavalletto (2007, pp. 33, 36–37) foregrounds that *Civilization and Its Discontents* puts forward key mental processes integrated into the social. The following are pertinent to this research strategy: 1) *The Narcissism of Minor Differences*; 2) the *Cultural Superego*; 3) and *Communal Neuroses.* As regards the *Narcissism of Minor Differences*, it must be noted that the social is continually at risk of disunion due to the *death instinct*, as this underpins the subject's aggressive nature. Eros counterbalances this risk via libidinal ties that keep the social as one. A key mechanism for this libidinal union is the process of *identification* (discussed above), namely the transformation of the subject's identity based on the resemblance shared with another person. This type of fellowship identification almost inexorably exaggerates the characteristics of the group, making them its collective ideal.

> By means of these idealized common traits, the members of the group are then enabled to love their fellow members narcissistically and, at the same time, to deflect their own innate aggressivity outward toward others who do not share these common traits, a double-edged social dynamic that Freud titles "the narcissism of minor differences". Combining solidarity and intolerance, "the narcissism of minor differences" is Freud's formula for the understanding of the politics of social identity, postulated as the inherent connection of in-group narcissism and out-group aggression. (Cavalletto, 2007, p. 37)

The narcissism of minor differences will be illustrated in the empirical chapters, where the 'us–them' dynamic between opposing parties is evident. I now address the cultural super-ego, arguably a redundant concept (after all, the subject's super-ego is, by definition, linked to cultural mandates). The cultural super-ego represents the ideals and prohibitions of a given society. Like the process leading to the emergence of the subject's super-ego, which involves love, rivalry, guilt, and *identification*, a community also develops a super-ego. This is characterized by the influence left by extraordinary and heroic leaders in a way that resembles the subject's super-ego. The *impression left behind* by these persons, whose fate has often been tragic, grips society: it reveals certain reputed possibilities of the community with a magnified pureness and power.

> [A]t the same time it [*the impression left behind*] implicates this society in the hero's downfall, tying it to the hero not only through love but guilt. Bound thus to the hero … the community comes to identify … with this "impression left behind" … Through the narratives of its heroes, civilizations propagate the values that bespeak of a cultural conscience, of the ideals and prohibitions that inform society's ethical and religious beliefs, its art and its collective narratives of self-understanding. (Cavalletto, 2007, p. 38)

In Chap. 4 I draw on the notion of the cultural super-ego to offer a meaningful understanding of the discourse that praised Eloy Alfaro, one of Ecuador's founding fathers. I now turn to the notion of *communal neuroses*. Drawing on Freud, Cavalletto summarizes a neurotic disorder as the deformation and upsetting of the subject's psychic life caused by the return of what was repressed in a particular way. Unlike individual neurosis, which is distinctive to each person's biography, *communal neuroses* speak to trans-individual neuroses stemming from a society's particular development. More precisely, this type of communal or social neurosis derives from 'trans-individual stresses and immaturities that have occurred as part of that society's history' (Cavalletto, 2007, pp. 38–39). Freud speaks of religion as the social counterpart of obsessional neurosis. In the next chapters I focus on the religious aspect of messianic leadership to address the 'neurotic' (repetitive-ritualistic) character of Ecuador's constitutional tradition.

On a final note, Glynos (2021) warns us against *psychoanalytic imperialism*, that is, an academic endeavour that tends to *exaggerate* the explanatory power of psychoanalysis. For instance, the concept of *enjoyment* could become as imperialistic as 'class' has in certain economistic approaches to political and ideological analysis. To prevent this, Glynos suggests a theoretical challenge, that is, a dialogue between non-psychoanalytically informed accounts of a given phenomenon and a psychoanalytic approach to this same phenomenon. The conceptualization and articulation of these relationships constitute the kernel of this challenge (pp. 12–13). Drawing on this suggestion, in Chap. 5 I discuss my argument in view of competing hypotheses on constitutional instability. This comparative exercise creates a bridge whereby institutionalist, economic, historic, and psychic accounts of constitutional instability can enter into dialogue, in the hope of improving our understanding of this complex phenomenon in presidential Ecuador.

Concluding Remarks

The methodological strategy put forward in this chapter mixes the case study and comparative methodologies given by problem-driven approach to research, which accounts for the enigma of constitutional instability in Ecuador.

Psychoanalytically informed scholars have been discussed in this chapter to link the theoretical elements presented in Chap. 1 to appropriate methodological tools, such as the imaginary and symbolic axes of identification, the non-rational 'grip' of ideology, and rhetorical analysis. This methodological bridge will allow us to shed light, via discourse analysis, on Ecuador's transgressive, authoritarian, and heroic constitutional tradition.

My research strategy focuses on the psychosocial (as opposed to personal) dynamic of the movements that have supported Ecuador's lawgivers in different constitutional processes. That said, my endeavour is and must remain conjectural, with a caution of psychoanalytic *imperialism*/reductionism.

References

Arlotti, R. (2003). *Vocabulario técnico y científico de la política*. Dunken.

Cavalletto, G. (2007). *Crossing the psycho-social divide. Freud, Weber, Adorno and Elias*. Ashgate.

Espinosa, C. (2010). *Historia del Ecuador en contexto regional y global*. Lexus.

Finlayson, A. (2007). From Beliefs to Arguments: Interpretive Methodology and Rhetorical Political Analysis. *British Journal of Politics & International, 9*, 545–563.

Finlayson, A. (2013). Ideology and Political Rhetoric. In *The oxford handbook of political ideologies*. Oxford University Press.

Glynos, J. (2008). Self-transgressive enjoyment as a freedom fetter. *Political Studies, 56*, 679–704.

Glynos, J. (2021). Critical fantasy studies. *Journal of Language and Politics, 20*(1), 95–111.

Glynos, J., & Howarth, D. (2007). *Logics of critical explanation in social and political theory*. Routledge.

Hook, D. (2008). Articulating psychoanalysis and psychosocial studies: Limitations and possibilities. *Psychoanalysis, Culture & Society, 13*, 397–405.

Hook, D. (2017). What is "enjoyment as a political factor"? *Political Psychology, 38*(4), 605–620.

Hook, D. (2018a). Racism and jouissance: Evaluating the "racism as (the theft of) enjoyment" hypothesis. *Psychoanalysis, Culture & Society, 23*, 244–266.

Hook, D. (2018b). *Six moments in Lacan. Communication and identification in psychology and psychoanalysis*. Routledge.

Lacan, J. (1981). *The four fundamental concepts of psychoanalysis (Book XI)*. London.

Martin, J. (2014). *Politics and rhetoric: A critical introduction*. Routledge. Available at: University of Essex (E-book).

Martin, J. (2016). Capturing desire: Rhetorical strategies and the affectivity of discourse. *The British Journal of Politics and International Relations, 18*(1), 143–160.

Sjoberg, G., Williams, N., Vaughan, T., & Sjoberg, A. (1991). The case study approach in social research: Basic methodological issues. In J. Feagin, A. Orum, & G. Sjoberg (Eds.), *A case for the case study*. The University of North Carolina Press.

Stavrakakis, Y. (1999). *Lacan & the political.* Routledge.
Žižek, S. (1990). Eastern Europe's Republics of Gilead. *New Left Review* (I/183, September-October).
Žižek, S. (2005). Beyond Discourse Analysis. In *Interrogating the real.* Bloomsbury Publishing Plc.
Žižek, S. (2008). *The sublime object of ideology.* Verso.

CHAPTER 3

On the Religious Spirit of the 1869 Constituent Assembly

In this chapter I proceed as follows. First, I present the rhetorical context informing the need of the 1869 Constituent Assembly (CA). Afterwards, I deploy a psychoanalytically informed discourse analysis of my primary sources. The corpus analysed consists of the officially transcribed debates provided by Ecuador's National Assembly (NA). The paraphrasing and quotations that follow are based on my own translations, but the original text is provided in the footnotes. The page numbers of the handwritten transcripts are sometimes confusing (e.g., the folio number at the upper right corner is partly or totally missing). Thus, the sheet numbers referenced below correspond with those of the PDF documents provided by Ecuador's NA. To facilitate the process of navigating these primary sources, below I always refer to the year, month, and day of a given debate. A letter after the date (e.g., 1869–06-01a) indicates those days in which ordinary and extraordinary sessions occurred: during the day (1) or during the evening (2).

The Rhetorical Context

Since ancient times, the Ecuadorian Pacific has been the *locus* of much maritime commerce. After independence in the first half of the nineteenth century, the commercial interests in this country made liberalism a popular doctrine on its coast. Differently, the presence of large estates and the

E. Espindola, *The Paternal Imago in Ruins*, The Palgrave Lacan Series, https://doi.org/10.1007/978-3-032-07507-9_3

Church in the Ecuadorian highlands made this region more prone to Catholic conservatism. As Espinosa (2010) puts it, during the nineteenth century the animosity between conservatives and liberals characterized Latin American politics. In Ecuador the first president (Juan José Flores) and his followers adhered to a conservative agenda supported by the popular sectors in the highlands. The second president (Vicente Rocafuerte) and his successors aligned with the liberal programme, backed by the popular sectors on the coast. Despite the existence of these two ideologies, political parties as such only emerged towards the end of the nineteenth century. During this period conservative and liberal leaders relied on a fractionalized army to conduct putsches. The political life of this 'republic' excluded all those who were not part of the elites, such as women, black, indigenous, illiterates, and those whose property did not reach a defined threshold. 'Although the successive constitutions of the new republic proclaimed the principle of popular sovereignty, in practice the vast majority were totally excluded from the electoral processes, and all the more so from the decision-making process' (Espinosa, pp. 484, 488, own translation).

In line with Martin's (2014) methodology, Ecuador's 1869 constituent discourse cannot be fully grasped without realizing the contextual 'necessity' of this *speech occasion*, that is, an overall state of national disunion and anarchy. In what follows, I analyse the *rhetorical context*, the key *rhetorical argument*(s), and the *rhetorical effects* of this assembly. In capturing the appeals to pathos, logos, ethos, forensic, epideictic, and deliberative arguments, I will better frame and analyse those aspects related to certain fantasies discussed in the 1869 convention. Among others are the Catholic nation and García Moreno's messianic leadership.

The 1869 CA began its discussions on 16 May and ended on 30 August. The rhetorical audience during the 1869 CA was composed of males only. These property owners represented the upper classes, the latter a part of the target audience. Back then the Members of the Assembly (hereinafter MAs) spoke on behalf of both the citizens and those who were not entitled to the citizenship.

Since the transcriptions lack each day's agenda, it is hard to tell whether the samples used are quantitatively representative of the totality of the 1869 debates transcribed in 689 folios. Having read the totality of this transcription, I can confidently state that the following were key elements discussed by this convention: the Catholic religion, armed rebellions, García Moreno's leadership, and the indigenous question. Previous constitutions recognized Catholicism as the only permitted religion, but the 1869 charter established for the first time the requisite of the Catholic faith for the exercise of political rights. The topics of rebellions and the idealization of García Moreno also appear in newspapers of the epoch: the March 1869 armed uprising in *Boletín Oficial*; the idealization of García Moreno outside parliament in *El Joven Conservador* (the conservative elites outside parliament were part of the rhetorical audience of this convention); and García Moreno's messages to the 1869 convention in *La Estrella de Mayo*. The 1869 constitution was proposed by García Moreno, a fervent Catholic. As for the indigenous question, the 1869 attempt to evangelize 'barbarians' offers an entry point for thinking about racism in postcolonial Ecuador. I now turn to the contextualization of these themes to better understand the rhetorical strategies deployed by the 1869 deputies.

Political Instability, Strong Leaderships, and the Catholic Church

The transgression of the constitutional order in Ecuador dates to the beginning of the republic and continued throughout the nineteenth century. As Espinosa puts it, General Juan José Flores (the first president) inherited the 'dictatorial' style of Bolívar. Flores, the predominant political figure from 1830 to 1845, disobeyed presidential term limits and governed for three terms. Between 1845 and 1860 the political power was held by liberal politicians under the leadership of 'caudillo' General José María Urbina. He conducted a putsch in 1851, followed by a CA that appointed him president. During the period 1859–1875, the pendulum swung in favour of Conservatives led by the 'Catholic caudillo' Gabriel García Moreno. During his first presidential mandate, he disobeyed the 1861 constitution when nominating the provincial governors, in lieu of allowing the popular elections of these authorities. The dictatorship of the liberal Ignacio de Veintemilla (1876–1884) and the putsch conducted by liberal Eloy Alfaro in 1895 (2010, pp. 473, 505, 508, 515, 541–542) closed a century characterized by authoritarian leaders, whose leadership went beyond the constitution, after which a new one was crafted.

Above I conjectured that Ecuador's long-lasting history of postcolonial violence has diminished the paternal imago of this patriarchal society, an outcome that has influenced its constitutional politics. In particular, I posited that the racist violence exerted on males in the public sphere was then passed onto the household environment. And this, as I suggested, could have shaped in part Ecuadorians' propensity to identify with strong and often authoritarian figures in politics. The cases of Flores, Urbina, García Moreno, de Veintemilla, and Alfaro (above) seem to illustrate my conjecture. I come back to this.

García Moreno was not a popular leader. His 'rational and scientific' Catholic agenda and his policy on compulsory work for public works clashed with the Catholic traditions and economic interests of the popular sectors in the highlands (Espinosa, 2010, p. 530). Even so, it is the idealization of García Moreno by the conservative elites and the fact that he proposed a draft of the new constitution that are at stake in the analysis of this 'lawgiver'.

During the nineteenth century the gravest Ecuadorian civil war occurred from 1859 to 1861. This conflict was triggered by the Peruvian declaration of war in 1859 against its neighbour. Peru justified the invasion alleging that Ecuador gave certain Peruvian territories to England in exchange for debt renegotiation. The international war revealed long-lasting regional disputes within Ecuador. While the Peruvian army took control of Ecuador's principal port, the rest of its territory was 'governed' by militias and then by four autonomous governments in Quito, the coast, Cuenca, and Loja. The last three regions had traditionally advocated for federalism in opposition to the centralism of Quito, the latter governed by García Moreno during the civil war. The intensity of this internal struggle led to official talks about either dismembering Ecuador to append it to both Peru and Colombia, or to transform it into a French protectorate (a failed diplomatic attempt led by García Moreno). With the military assistance of 'legendary' general Flores, at that time living in exile in Lima, García Moreno managed to reconstruct national unity (Espinosa, 2010, pp. 511–513).

Once the civil war came to an end, Quito hosted a new CA presided by Flores, who validated García Moreno as the new president. The 1861 constitution (the seventh in Ecuador's history) introduced significant changes to the democratic regime: the direct suffrage, the abolition of property requisites for citizens, and a decentralized institution that allowed the popular election of local authorities. Nonetheless, during his first presidency García Moreno disobeyed the fundamental law by directly appointing governors, by amputating both citizens' rights and municipal prerogatives, and through the execution of political competitors. This was despite the fact that the 1861 charter had maintained the tradition of banning the death penalty for political reasons (Ayala, 2008, p. 34). From a more favourable stance towards García Moreno's legacy, one historian highlights key accomplishments courtesy of this leader. As 'the standard bearer of the conservative doctrine, [García Moreno] was one of the great builders of Ecuador'. He managed to defeat militarism, build roads on a large scale, introduce the train to Ecuador, provide education for the indigenous, and foster the Ecuadorian 'culture' and 'technique'. But his attempt to materially and spiritually unite the nation resulted in an 'excessive' allowance in favour of the church's role in politics (Salvador Lara, 2005, p. 385, own translation).

García Moreno's attempt to expand the church's power was predictable, as this institution's dominance rested on both material and ideational bases. Throughout the nineteenth century, the church was the main landlord in Ecuador and benefitted from this status as a letting agency. This religious institution legitimated the landowner class system in the highlands (Ayala, 2011, pp. 193–194), and it exerted considerable influence on the political elites when they drafted new constitutions:

> The [official] discussion ... about whether the constitutions [were] to be issued in the name of God or in the name of the people always ended favouring the former, for it was God the Creator of the universe and thus the source of the laws. The [public] authority, the representative of this divinity, was in charge of executing them. (ibid., p. 193, own translation)

In January 1869, García Moreno overthrew President Xavier Espinosa, alleging his incapacity to prevent an imminent revolution. As a self-proclaimed 'supreme chief', García Moreno convened the eighth CA since independence. The opposition named the 1869 constitution the 'Black Charter', as it extended term limits for authorities, provided extraordinary prerogatives to the executive, and established that only Catholics could become citizens of the republic. 'The constitution was also approved by an overwhelming plebiscite, and ... García Moreno governed again from 1869 to 1875', the year a political machete assassinated him (Salvador Lara, 2005, p. 392).

From 1861 to 1875 García Moreno, the persona who has received the most attention throughout Ecuador's history, managed to consolidate the *oligarchic state*. This was possible due to his ability to promote the difficult coexistence of two economic models: *latifundismo*[1] in the highlands (Quito is located here) and a project seeking to modernize and stimulate commerce, the latter favouring the economic interests of the Establishment on the coast (Guayaquil city is situated here) (Ayala, 2008, pp. 32, 36).

In sum, the *rhetorical context*/historical conditions informing the 'necessity' of the 1869 CA were the following: (1) a highly politically unstable country whose constitution had been transgressed by several authoritarian executives since independence; (2) a war with Peru (1859–1861) followed by self-proclaimed governments; (3) a metastasis of the rivalries between the national elites; (4) the almost complete disappearance of Ecuador as an autonomous state; (5) a constitution (1861) that aimed to come to terms with those long-standing rivalries to provide a (precarious) national unity; (6) internal rebellions; (7) a church whose ideational and economic power was intertwined with the landowner class, the latter the 'representative' of the people. García Moreno's armed insurrection against his comrade President Espinosa was the immediate precursor to the 1869 CA. In this convention García Moreno proposed a Catholic charter to unite the country in political, economic, and religious terms.

The 1869 Convention and its Arguments

In this section I present the 1869 convention. I then analyse some of its arguments accounting for the *messianic* nature of constitutional instability in postcolonial Ecuador. By way of summary, the 1869 CA was predominantly composed by deputies representing the highlands. Nonetheless, by 1869 the coastal elites had become influential in national politics. Although García Moreno managed to come to a national equilibrium, the fear of anarchy was still present in 1869. Below I flesh out and discuss how the chaos stemming from armed rebellions set the scene for the horrific dimension of fantasy in 1869, which foresaw an apocalyptic outcome if the enemy was not eliminated. The longing for a strong leader revealed the beatific dimension of fantasy, which promised a full-harmony-to-come led by a *Messiah* who prompted a new constitution. This intertwined dynamic

[1] *Latifundium*, from the Spanish latifundio, denotes '[a] large landed estate or ranch in ancient Rome or more recently in Spain or Latin America, typically worked by peasants or slaves'. Cf. https://www.lexico.com/definition/latifundium

was underpinned, I would like to suggest, by a process of *heroic identification* with certain postcolonial signifiers and images which have shaped Ecuador's constitutional tradition.

From 1861, the representation of the legislative branch was determined in proportion to the provincial population (Ayala, 2011, p. 34). The 1869 constitution contains a list of the MAs who participated in this convention. Out of 28 Mas, 20 represented the highlands (Constitución de, 1869), which shows the demographic relevance of the Andean region in nineteenth-century Ecuador.

As for its *modus operandi*, the 1869 CA established technical commissions in charge of addressing and issuing reports on (amongst others) citizens' petitions, and economic, military, and ecclesiastical affairs. In general, the MAs had to debate three times a given matter before the constitutional articles, laws, and decrees could be sanctioned. At the beginning of each debate, the secretary indicated which deputies were present, after which the previous session's debate minutes were read and approved. The secretary paraphrased what MAs said, and on a few occasions used quotation marks to indicate the parliamentarians' words. When the new constitution was discussed, the point of reference was the text proposed by García Moreno.

Officially, the main goal of the 1869 convention was to discuss and elaborate the new fundamental law to *constitute* the republic. However, from May to August 1869 the convention had to carry on with its daily business. Thus, at all times and in the same sessions, the people's representatives addressed both constitutional and non-constitutional affairs. The CA received and discussed the citizens' petitions to undertake economic enterprises, personal requests, taxation-related issues, the civil code's reform, reprieves, the provision of resources for public services (water, schools, warships), the building of a monument, official appointments, the restitution of political rights, charitable funds, disciplinary action against those attempting to commit suicide, cockfighting, amongst other non-constitutional topics (Carvajal, 1869). In line with King's (2011) definition of a constitution, fewer themes discussed in this convention were constitutional, for example, the requisite of the Catholic faith for citizens, the political organization of the state at the subnational level, the debates on the electoral law, the necessity of a national law on public instruction, and whether the trials of the republic should follow the written or verbal format (Carvajal, 1869). I can confidently say that the majority (approximately 60–70%) of the 1869 CA did not address 'the set of the most important rules and common understandings' (King, 2011, p. 3) of the Ecuadorian republic. I come back to this, as this 'deficit' hints at the strong attachment to a *constituent* practice transgressive of the formerly valid constitution.

On the Constant Rebellion against the Constitution and the 1869 Lawgiver

In 1869 it was vox populi that putsches and revolutions were commonplace and thus part of Ecuador's political culture. While the 1869 convention condemned these types of actions, it legitimated García Moreno's non-democratic rise to power in that year. The 1869 deputies were García Moreno's comrades (Ayala, 2008, p. 35). Besides armed rebellions, which constitute a clear revolt against the constitution in force, the disobedience of the Ecuadorian charter was also a common practice amongst presidents. As one 1869 deputy put it, '[t]he presidents before the 1861 charter swore an oath to respect and sustain seven Constitutions and obey the laws, and they scandalously ran over them without even remembering their oath' (Noboa, 1869, p. 3).[2]

The fear of anarchy and the longing for García Moreno's unlimited leadership set the scene for the horrific and beatific dimensions of fantasy in 1869. Whereas the former foresaw an apocalyptic future if the 'enemy' was not defeated, the latter promised a full-harmony-to-come. It is in this twofold context that the following discourse analysis needs to be understood, an analytical endeavour guided by my retroductive argument, that is, a thesis whose 'criterion of validity depends on whether the posited hypothesis accounts for a problematized phenomenon by rendering it intelligible' (Hanson, as cited by Glynos & Howarth, 2007, p. 39). My conjecture in this chapter reads as follows. Ecuador's postcolonial history of violence prompted the support of a *messianic* leader in 1869, a Catholic lawgiver whose persona blended with the 1869 aspiration of stability. The violence in question was twofold: armed rebellions and structural racism. Given that nineteenth-century Ecuador was a patriarchal society in which the notion of authority blended with that of the father figure, I cannot

[2] 'Los Presidentes anteriores á la Constitución de 1861 juraron respetar i sostener siete constituciones, i obedecer las leyes, i las atropellaron escandalosamente sin recordar siquiera sus juramentos'.

help but ask: to what extent (if any) can political violence and structural racism account for the type of *heroic identification* characteristic of the constitutional politics of postcolonial Ecuador?

On the Justification of the 1869 Putsch and the Proposed Constitution

Once the 1869 CA's president (Carvajal MA) and vice-president (Lazo MA) were elected, García Moreno began his inaugural speech: 'In the name of God I declare the National Convention established: long live the Republic' (García Moreno, 1869, p. 2).[3] García Moreno emphasized the critical situation the country was facing: (1) the commercial prohibitions established by Spain in response to Ecuador's relations with certain allies; (2) the 1868 earthquake; (3) the conspiracy organized by those who had ruled in 1859–1860 in the midst of the civil war. García Moreno criticized the previous government for its inability to stop the agitators. He also condemned the *demagogic press* as it had *insulted religion*, while rallying dangerous *revolutionary passions* leading to anarchy. Backed by 'the people' and the armed forces, García Moreno had 'provisionally accepted' to take control of power, 'which I now give back to you [to the MAs]' after four months of temporary presidency (pp. 2–4).

For García Moreno, the dishonour to which the official religion was subjected, as well as the fear of anarchy, legitimized the overthrowing of President Espinosa. The appeal to a particular authority (ethos) and the approval or disapproval of something or someone (an *epideictic* strategy) are two powerful rhetorical strategies. García Moreno's appeal to the legitimacy of his deeds drew on two sources of ethos: God-Catholicism and the people. The former had been insulted and the latter benefitted from the avoidance of anarchy. Four months after the putsch, Moreno's self-sacrificing feat was corroborated by his eagerness to give back power to those who owned it: the sovereign's representatives. García Moreno approved the earlier transgression of the constitutional order for the sake of both the reputation of God/Catholicism and the survival of democracy.

During García Moreno's inaugural speech, which coincided with the convention's first day, he suggested a draft of the new constitution before the actual debate had even begun. He argued that, given conflicting

[3] 'En el nombre de Dios declaro instalada la Convención Nacional: Viva la República'.

interests and passions stemming from various territories, parties, and 'races', Ecuador was a 'divided' nation whose 'only bond' was the Catholic faith. In this context, García Moreno told the convention that his proposed constitution had two objectives:

> [F]irst, to harmonize our political institutions with our religious faith; second, to invest public authority with sufficient strength in order to resist the attacks of anarchy. ... [R]eason and experience have proven that a weak government is insufficient in our turbulent Republics ... Since I cannot accept the presidency given the solemn oath I took on 17 January, neither can I be accused of egoism nor of ambitious plans in asking you to strengthen the authority [the executive branch] that I will not exercise. (García Moreno, 1869, p. 6)[4]

Patriotism and selflessness sought to enhance the speaker's authority (ethos). The sought communion between Catholicism and political institutions might have appealed to the audience's emotions (pathos), for it wanted to remedy the fractured republic via the universal harmony provided by the Catholic faith. The conclusion that a strong executive was needed to fight off anarchy derived from the premises of reason and experience (logos). García Moreno's strategic reminder (his promise not to serve as president during the convention) becomes eloquent.

Making the Catholic Nation

Above we saw that the objectives of García Moreno's proposed constitution were to provide the executive branch with enough power to combat political violence against the established order, as well as to harmonize the state with Catholicism. In this section I analyse the inconsistencies stemming from the official attempt to make the Catholic nation a reality by focusing on the 1869 discourse on Article 10.1 of the constitution and the 1869 debate on the indigenous question.

[4] '[E]l primero, poner en armonía nuestras instituciones políticas con nuestra creencia religiosa; i el segundo investir a la autoridad pública de la fuerza suficiente para resistir à los embates de la anarquía. (...) [L]a razón y la experiencia han puesto fuera de duda que un Gobierno débil es insuficiente en nuestras agitadas Repúblicas ... No pudiendo aceptar el Poder por el solemne juramento que hice el diezisiete de enero, no puedo ser acusado de egoismo ni de designios ambiciosos cuando os pido que robustezcais la autoridad que yo no voy á ejercer'.

Catholicism was constitutionally recognized as Ecuador's official religion in the CAs of 1830, 1835, 1843, 1845, 1851, 1852, and 1861. The 1869 constitution inscribed this principle in Article 9: 'The Religion of the Republic is Apostolic and Roman Catholicism, excluding any other' (Martínez, 1869, p. 10).[5] What distinguished the 1869 charter from previous constitutions was the people's requirement to practise Catholicism to exercise their political rights (Martínez, 1869, p. 4). The watershed in question revolved around three articles of the proposed constitution:

Article 6.1	This aimed to grant Ecuadorian citizenship to 'distinguished' individuals from other countries who were not necessarily Catholics
Article 9	This established that Catholicism was the only faith officially permitted in Ecuador
Article 10.1	This stipulated that only *practising* Catholics could exercise their political rights (to elect or be elected for public posts)

During the 21 May session, Article 10.1 of the proposed constitution was debated. Uquillas MA opposed this clause because of its 'anti-social' character, the practical difficulty of enforcing it, and its threat to the citizens' civil rights. (The secretary of the treasury intervened before the MAs to answer all those enquiries questioning the Catholic component of the proposed constitution.) Martínez MA also spoke of the practical difficulty of 'checking' on others' faith, let alone how unacceptable it would be if the Catholic faith were serving party interests. Salazar MA also criticized the inconsistency between Article 10.1 and Article 6.1, as the latter proposed to grant citizenship to eligible 'foreigners' who had provided 'great services' for the country (pp. 1–3). In view of the criticism of the exclusionary and Catholic clause in question, the counterargument of the secretary of the treasury was cutting:

> It [is] necessary to raise a wall of division between the followers of the true God and those of Satan ... Failing to declare the truths about this religion on account of the fear of being persecuted by a victorious party is a vile and disgraceful fear ... By no means can fear authorise an apostasy. (the treasury secretary, pp. 3–4)[6]

[5] 'La Religión de la República es la católica, apostólica, romana, con exclusión de cualquier otra'.

[6] 'El H. Señor Ministro dijo: que éra necesario levantar un muro de división entre los adoradores del verdadero Dios i los de Satanas... (...) Dejar de declarar las verdades de esta religión por el temor de la persecución de un partido triunfante, es un temor vil é ignomioso. (...) ...el miedo no puede autorizar de ninguna manera, para dar lugar à una apostasía'.

Underpinned by an appeal to pathos ('Satan'), the minister resorts to a puzzle solution strategy, that is, a problem whose solution is provided by the speaker. Apostasy requires a clear distinction between those who follow the orthodoxy and those who do not (believers and Satan's followers). The proposed article (10.1) aimed to solve the problem of apostasy, though it created an inconsistency. Through this clause the MAs were transgressing the universal precept of the republic, a commonwealth hosting and naturalizing non-Catholic inhabitants whose deeds were regarded as beneficial to Ecuador.

During this session (21 May), García Moreno spoke in full support of Article 10.1. Amongst other things, he argued that its exclusionary character complemented Article 9 of the proposed constitution, that is, the decision to regard Catholicism as the only faith permitted in Ecuador. For him, Article 10.1 provided practicality to the theory condensed in Article 9. The former provided the legal means to prevent public authorities (e.g., presidents, magistrates, teachers) from acting on behalf of non-Catholic beliefs. If this failed, the infiltration of non-Catholic sentiments 'in the heart of the Ecuadorian society' would create chaos and 'immorality'. After a 'long debate', Article 10.1 passed to the third discussion (García Moreno, 1869, pp. 5, 10).

On 28 May García Moreno's and his followers' words had a clear rhetorical effect: Article 10.1 was approved. This debate speaks to—and expands—the horrific dimension of fantasy discussed above (armed rebellions): the official discourse added the fear of a probable propagation of non-Catholic beliefs within Ecuadorian society. The latter was preventable with Article 10.1 of the new constitution. The discussion around this article showed competing accounts of the horrific dimension of fantasy:

> All in all, Mr President, why do we want to increase the already numerous causes of division amongst Ecuadorians? ... We cannot deny that there are some who, albeit having been baptized, do not practise the Catholic religion. Excluding them from political rights would exasperate their mood, and this would introduce a new germ of discord. (Martínez, 1869, p. 4)[7]

[7] 'En fin Señor Presidente ≤por qué queremos aumentar las causas ya numerosas de división entre los ecuatorianos?... No podemos negar que hai algunos que aunque hayan sido bautisados no profesan la religión católica, i excluirlos de los derechos políticos, es agriar sus ánimos è introducir un nuevo jérmen de discordia'.

Despite nuances, at all times the MAs invoked the same Catholic God. Nonetheless, this national community seemed to be fractured by 'true' and 'false' believers. The risk of allowing 'pretenders' to serve as magistrates demanded a constitutional censor, that is, the citizens' requirement to practise Catholicism to exercise their political rights. This was despite the contradiction that this censor brought about in terms of granting Ecuadorian citizenship to certain illustrious foreigners.

From a Freudian perspective, Article 10.1 of the proposed constitution (later sanctioned) can be regarded as the 'institutional manifestation' of the super-ego of the official discourse, thanks to which the ego-ideals of the Catholic nation were sustained.[8] Lacanian psychoanalysis complements our understanding of the super-ego in terms of a 'cold judge or censor', for it shows how *jouissance* can also work in favour of the conservation of the law. In Chap. 1 I highlighted the transgressive nature of *enjoyment*. Notwithstanding, the interconnection between enjoyment, the law, and the superego has been problematized by Lacanian theory. Albeit *seemingly* contradictory, the imposition of the law also brings out a kind of compensation (a 'jouissance payment'), a covert reward that buttresses the symbolic law. Thanks to the superego, which causes jouissance, societal ego-ideals are enthusiastically adopted and put into effect. Among other acts, blaming lawbreakers, distributing punishments, and allocating tremendous sentences produce *jouissance payment* in subjects (Hook, 2018a, pp. 259–260). It is safe to argue that prohibiting the service of non-Catholic citizens in public posts in nineteenth-century Ecuador required the persecution and espionage of fellow citizens. In this context, I would like to suggest that Article 10.1, the institutional super-ego of the Catholic nation, could have relied in part on the *enjoyment* procured by the punishment of the lawbreakers, namely those who betrayed the Catholic dogma. In other words, this *jouissance payment* could have strengthened, at least partially, the enthusiastic adherence to the symbolic law, at least during the lifespan of the 1869 constitution. I now turn to the indigenous question, which sets the scene for the analysis of racism in postcolonial Ecuador.

[8] '[T]he super-ego's role in relation to the ego may be compared to that of a judge or a censor. Freud sees conscience, self-observation and the formation of ideals as functions of the super-ego' (Laplanche & Pontalis, 1973, p. 435).

On the Evangelization of 'Barbarians'

The 1869 CA knew that Ecuador was ethnically and culturally diverse. Villavicencio (1856) provides a useful estimate of Ecuador's ethnic composition for the period under study. In 1856, out of a total of 1,108,042 inhabitants,

(A) 601,219 individuals were 'whites descended from Europeans';
(B) 462,400 were 'Indians descended from the conquerors';
(C) 7831 were 'blacks without mixture';
(D) 36,592 were a 'mixture of blacks with whites and Indians'.

Despite the lack of precision of this report, its categorization of races is helpful. In 1856, the 'purely' white race (A) represented 54% of the population, while the remaining races (B+C+D) amounted to 45% of this total. This would rise to 54% if the 200,000 'savages from the East' (the jungle) were included in the study in question (own calculation). The decision to exclude these natives stemmed from the fact that a non-rigorous calculating method was used in the jungle (Villavicencio, as cited in Paz y Miño, 1936, pp. 9–11). In short, mid-nineteenth-century Ecuador was ethnically split into two relatively equal parts: one composed of 'whites descended from Europeans' and the other made of both non-whites (Indians and blacks) and the mestizo population.

The Catholic convention foregrounded that 'barbarism' was still a reality in Ecuador. This is illustrated by the 3 June session on the special jurisdiction of certain Ecuadorian territories, namely that of the Galapagos Islands, Esmeraldas (a coastal province inhabited by a significant population of black people), and the East (the jungle region inhabited by various ethnic groups since immemorial times):

> *[T]here are vast places in a state of barbarism to the east of the mountain chain, places where the population would increase and exit from barbarism through the predication of the Gospel by the missions to be established* (Ordónez MA, p. 3, emphasis added). In agreement with these reasons, H. Martínez modified his motion as follows: 'Art. 86. The Ecuadorian populations of the East, the Esmeralda province, and all the places whose isolation and distance … do not allow them to be part of a canton or province … will be ruled by special regulations until the growth of their population *or the*

> *progress of their civilization allow them to govern themselves as the others*'. The voting proceeded and this motion was approved. (the secretary, Martínez, 1869, pp. 3–4, emphasis added)[9]

As Hook eloquently puts it, accounts of racism often highlight its identifying features, such as ignorance and intolerance. While racism can in indeed entail all of these features, a Lacanian understanding of the link between the super-ego, the law, and *enjoyment* (discussed above) allows us to capture the subtle grip of racism. Racism 'is also a type of indignation; an impetus to blame and punish, involving a sense of laws, societal (if racist) norms, and ideals that have been violated' (Hook, 2018a, p. 261). Admittedly, the above excerpt is neither blaming nor punishing 'barbarians' for the violation of certain laws. However, and in light of Hook's observation, I would like to suggest that in nineteenth-century Ecuador the societal ideals linked to the notion of civilization were, in part, racist. The idea and notion of 'barbarism' presented and approved by the 1869 convention linked European civilization to the readiness for self-government, ignoring that the peoples 'to the East of the mountain' (the jungle) had had their own government before the Spanish conquest. As for the 'barbarians' from Esmeraldas, note that this coastal province has hosted an important number of African Ecuadorians since colonial times. As the above speech indicates, special rules had to be implemented in distant, sparsely, isolated, and 'barbarous' territories (the jungle and Esmeralda) until the growth of the population or 'the progress of their civilization' would enable them to govern themselves. I suggest that the proposal to 'cure' the problem of 'barbarism', a cure that would help to sustain the ego-ideals of a 'civilized' society, overshadowed the partly racist component of this motion.

[9] 'el H. Ordoñez… [:] existiendo bastos lugares en estado de barbarie en la banda oriental de la cordillera, lugares en que se aumentaría la población i saldría esta de la barbarie mediante la predicación del evangelio por las misiones que iban à establecerse. De acuerdo con estas razones el H. Martínez modificó su moción en estos términos.—"Art. 86. Las poblaciones ecuatorianas de la banda Oriental, la provincia de Esmeraldas i todos los lugares que por su aislamiento i distancia… no pueden hacer parte de algún cantón ò provincia…serán regidos por disposiciones especiales hasta que el aumento de su población ò los progresos de su civilización les permita gobernarse como los demas".—i puesta à votación se aprobó'.

Let us apply other Lacanian concepts to the analysis of the above excerpt. The appeal to Catholicism (ethos) justified the continuation of a colonial practice, that is, the taming of 'barbarians' *through the predication of the Gospel*. This was needed to build the Catholic Nation, the 1869 *object petit a*, and this points us in the direction of how *jouissance* can shape the manifestation of racism. The above speech hints at how the *national Thing* could have been experienced by the convention, that is, in terms of a *full enjoyment* under the threat of a potential *theft* of what was most precious to it: its language (Spanish) and its Catholic ceremonies. If barbarism was removed via evangelization, the fantasy of the nation's unity/full identity could be sustained. I suggest that it was the *libidinal treasure* of the Catholic nation that underpinned, at least in part, the 1869 attempt to build a fully fixed Catholic Nation, the beatific dimension of fantasy.

The indigenous question in Ecuador is expanded in the next chapter, where I address the 2007–2008 indigenous demand for a pluri-national state. Suffice to note here that García Moreno's (1869) religious project required further evangelization. This process, which began with the Spanish conquest, erased the cultural and political forms whereby the native population organized itself prior to the Incan and European conquests.

In sum, Article 10.1 of the 1869 constitution and the evangelization of non-Catholics sought to tackle the first challenge/goal of García Moreno's (1869) Catholic charter, that is, the harmonization of Catholicism with the nation-state. I now address his other goal.

On Anarchy and the Repressive Prerogatives for the President

The other objective of García Moreno's constitution was to fortify the executive branch to repress anarchy. As a major historian puts it, 'a great part of García Moreno's proposal [of the new constitution] was adopted. A quasi-monarchical, confessional, and exclusionary system was adopted' (Ayala, 2008, p. 35, own translation). The citizens' rights were 'restricted' and the death penalty for political reasons was re-established. The president (whose mandate consisted of 6 years) could be consecutively re-elected (ibid.). García Moreno's constitution was influenced by his religious faith and the fear of anarchy.

García Moreno was not the only one who advocated in favour of a strong executive in view of Ecuador's turbulent history. A week after the inaugural session, certain MAs also supported the idea of a strong(er) head of state:

> Lectured by the frequency of our political revolts, I am convinced that the Executive power must be strengthened through enough prerogatives to uphold public order, though in a way that these are not detrimental to the Nation. Once the state of siege is declared, the prerogatives given [to the Executive] concern the military operations and must be limited to the *theatre in which these aberrations take place*, as there is no reason to extend these prerogatives to the province or provinces where there is peace. (Martínez, 1869, p. 3, emphasis added)[10]

Martínez's argument built its premise on the experience provided by the lessons of history ('Lectured by ...'), a clear appeal to *ethos*. Apparently, his strategy sought to induce an ***analogical reasoning*** in the audience by regarding revolutions as ***aberrations***, implying the 'perverted' nature of rebellions. Martínez advocated for enough—though limited—military power granted to the executive to extinguish internal armed conflicts. Salazar MA added:

> This prerogative regarding the Executive and the state of siege would allow ***the trial of civilians under the military law ... To remedy great misfortunes, measures of the same magnitude are indispensable.*** If this clause were removed, the Executive's extraordinary prerogative would disappear ... the most effective way to prevent and repress revolutions. (Salazar MA, ibid., pp. 3–4)[11]

[10] 'Aleccionado por la frecuencia de nuestras revueltas políticas, me hallo convencido de que se debe robustecer el Poder Ejecutivo con facultades suficientes para sostener el orden público; pero de manera que ellas no puedan ser perjudiciales à la Nación. Las facultades que se conceden al declararse el estado de sitio se refieren à las operaciones militares, i deben limitarse a los lugares que sean teatro de estas aberraciones, pues no hay razón para extenderlas à la provincia ò provincias que se hallen en paz'.

[11] 'Esta facultad del Poder Ejecutivo y el estado de sitio consistía en que sean juzgados los paisanos conforme à las ordenanzas militares, ..., que para remediar grandes males eran indispensables medidas de igual magnitud, i que si se quitara esta circunstancia, desaparecería la facultad extraordinaria del Poder Ejecutivo, el estado de sitio i el medio más eficaz para precaver y contener las revoluciones'.

The excerpts on what needed to be written at the constitutional level to prevent frequent armed rebellions spoke to the horrific dimension of fantasy. This conjured an apocalyptic prospect. In supporting the expansion of the executive's prerogative in military terms, the 1869 speakers and their audience preferred order over individual liberty. The latter is understandable considering that, from 1859 to 1861, Ecuador almost disappeared as an autonomous state. Further arguments were given in favour of treating civilian 'agitators' under the military law:

> Honourable Alcázar added new reasons in support of this [constitutional] article by demonstrating the slowness of the trial procedures under the common law, and the necessity of a prompt punishment for the cases of political disruptions. (the secretary, ibid., p. 4)[12]

A few days later, the *rhetorical effect* of the speeches on 24 May was felt: part of the constitutional article (63.7) in charge of preventing the subversion of the constitutional order was approved. 'Be stipulated the military trial … [with] military punishments for those who directly or indirectly promote or favour the internal commotion or the external invasion' (Alcázar et al., 1869, pp. 1–2).[13] (Although a minor change was made to this article in a subsequent session, its kernel remained unchanged.) I would like to conjecture that the enactment of the law on the military punishment for rebels might have been facilitated, in part, by the interaction between jouissance, the law, and the superego (discussed above). To begin with, the sustainment of the *ego-ideal* of the Catholic (and thus united) nation relied on the convention's *superego*. In instructing *jouissance*, this superego (amongst Catholic deputies) helped to perpetuate the affective attachment to the symbolic law. It did so by offering the bonus of a *jouissance payment* procured by the promise to enact a harsh ('military') punishment to those seeking, directly or indirectly, to transgress the law.

Let us examine one last intervention signalling the revolutionary culture denounced by the Catholic convention:

[12] 'El H. Alcazar añadió nuevas razones en apoyo del artículo demostrando la lentitud de los trámites de enjuiciamiento por las leyes comunes, i la necesidad de un castigo pronto en los casos de trastornos políticos'.

[13] 'Disponer se juzguen militarmente…i con las penas de las ordenanzas militares "à los que directa o indirectamente promuevan ò favorezcan la conmocion [sic] interior ò la invación [sic] exterior"'.

> In the Hispanic American republics, he said, there is a ferment or tendency towards political disturbances. Unfortunately, we have some men who can be called *revolutionary speculators* as they aim to make a fortune from revolutions. It is indispensable to restrain them *via the fear of punishment*. (minister of the treasury, 1869-06-01b, p. 3, emphasis added)[14]

As the minister emphasized, anarchy was a constant in Hispanic America. His stance, clearly against the revolutionary method, appealed to an epideictic (disapproving) and deliberative argument prompting a given action: *revolutionary speculators* needed to be contained by the fear of institutionalized punishment. The notion of 'revolutionary speculators' adds a nuance to the horrific dimension of fantasy so far discussed, for the signifier 'speculator' alluded to two types of rebels: the truly revolutionary ones (e.g., those who fought the war of independence) and those rebelling for the sake of personal benefits. The latter had to be dissuaded through fear, which was being institutionally designed by the 1869 convention. I cannot help but note the recurring recourse to the rhetorical figure of 'punishment' during the 1869 convention, for it hints at the theoretical usefulness of the interconnection between jouissance, the law, and the super-ego discussed above, especially when thinking about the mechanisms by which subjects enthusiastically adhere to the symbolic law.

What else can Lacanian theory say about the political violence characteristic of Ecuador? As discussed above, for Lacanian psychoanalysis there is a clear distinction between the *paternal function* and the biological father. Notwithstanding, as Sharoni (2016) puts it, *qua* symbolic father a biological father can embody the law. The analysis of Joyce's *Eveline* led her to conclude that Eveline's father failed to embody the law, as his 'authority' did not stem from speech, but from the force manufactured by patriarchal violence. And this prevented Eveline from disentangling herself from her mother's desire. If biological fathers can embody this symbolic function, I now ask: was it likely for most fathers in postcolonial Ecuador to embody this function? Albeit speculative, this question provides us with a potential path of investigation, as it might bridge the chasm between patriarchal violence and heroic identification in Ecuador.

[14] 'Existe, dijo, en las repúblicas Hispano-americanas un fermento o una tendencia á los trastornos políticos, tenemos por desgracia ciertos hombres, á quienes puede llamarse especuladores revolucionarios pr. [sic] el propósito de hacer fortuna en las revoluciones, i es indispensable contenerlos por el temor del castigo'.

The Longing for García Moreno, the 1869 Lawgiver

On the inaugural day of the convention García Moreno resigned the temporary presidency. The promoter of the 1869 constitution supported his resignation on the oath he took, that is, on the promise not to extend his temporary presidency during the 1869 convention. At first, his resignation, which showed patriotism and a lack of egoism, was not welcomed by the convention, but compensatory measures made up for this loss (discussed below).

In view of García Moreno's resignation, the CA's first task was to overcome the lack of a leader. Another temporary president had to be immediately elected, while the new constitution was being discussed and shaped. Noboa, Sáenz, and Eguiguren MAs proposed a decree whereby García Moreno's resignation was not accepted, on the grounds that his departure would result in a state without a head. As these MAs put it, García Moreno had to remain as temporary president until another head of state was constitutionally elected. The CA voted in favour of this decree; García Moreno was immediately informed. Despite this new resolution, he insisted on resigning the temporary presidency. At the end of that day the MAs finally accepted García Moreno's resignation, while praising him for his services to the country (García Moreno, 1869, pp. 7–8, 16). Why was García Moreno's resignation so hard to accept by the 1869 convention? As Aragundi MA put it,

> Sirs, by no means should we accept the resignation proposed by Mr G. Moreno, as the oath upon which it stands is invalid. Had he sworn for a better good, his promise would be valid; but, quite the contrary, *if this oath were kept, only evils would emerge in this homeland, hence we must firmly reject it* [Moreno's decision]. (Aragundi, 1869, p. 9, emphasis added)[15]

The above *evils* imply in part the constant anarchy in nineteenth-century Ecuador, the basis on which the horrific dimension of fantasy was elaborated by the 1869 convention. Not only was García Moreno praised by the official convention, but he was also supported by his followers outside parliament. Was he, then, a popular leader backed by 'the people'? As

[15] 'No debemos, S.S., aceptar de ningun [sic] modo la renuncia propuesta por el Sor. G. Moreno, por que el juramento en que se apoya es nulo. Si él hubiera jurado por un mejor bien, su promesa sería válida; pero muy al contrario, de llevar a cabo su juramento solo nacerían males para la patria, i asi debemos negarle con firmeza'.

already indicated, historiography regards García Moreno as an unpopular leader, but some of García Moreno's followers, that is, the readers of the newspaper *El Joven Conservador* (The Young Conservative), could have argued otherwise. In the context of the coming presidential election, which followed the approval of the 1869 constitution, this newspaper praised García Moreno while criticizing liberals. It argued that the liberal ambition for power, which stemmed from its 'caudillos', created 'sects' with different 'masters' (candidates) *à la* Protestantism. By contrast, conservatism proposed a unified candidate on the following grounds:

> The conservative party has put the distinguished Mr García Moreno forward [as presidential candidate] because that is what two thirds of the Republic want, in virtue of the knowledge they have about this illustrious Caudillo ... Indeed, Ecuador owes to Mr García Moreno its moral, intellectual, and material advancement. There has been no one else who, as president, would have given more beautiful brushstrokes in the painting of *progress* for the country's good than García Moreno. (*El Joven Conservador*, 1869-01-08, emphasis added)[16]

In the theoretical chapter we discussed Lacan's notion of the Other (Book III) as a symbolic and unifying entity perceived by non-psychotic subjects, an entity through which individuals make themselves recognized (e.g., slave–master). The voice of the Other surpasses the existence of the 'little other' who is conversing extensively. Relatedly, in the methodological chapter we distinguished and operationalized imaginary and symbolic identification, a twofold process whereby group members identify with images and signifiers. The message voiced by the conservative party in 1869 highlights the value of progress in its moral, intellectual, and material components. Arguably, *historical progress* served as the master signifier shaping the process of symbolic and imaginary identification in 1869. Imaginary identification played out between 'little others', that is, between the members of the conservative party and their leader, whose idealized persona was elevated. What is not so evident in the above excerpt is the process of symbolic and triangulated identification with a third party. The

[16] 'El Partido conservador ha presentado al esclarecido Sor. García Moreno, porque así lo quieren las dos terceras partes de la República, en virtud del conocimiento que tienen de este ilustre Caudillo ... Con efecto, al Sor. García Moreno se le debe el adelantamiento moral, intelectual i material del Ecuador, sin que haya habido otro, que en calidad de Presidente, hubiese dado pinceladas tan hermosas en el cuadro del progreso para el bien del país'.

1869 conservative faction was acquiring signifiers from 'little others' (conservative comrades) as well as from the Other, that is, *historical progress*. Symbolic identification 'involves the assumption of signifiers from a second party (a 'little other') that puts the identifying subject into the position of *being desired by a third* (the Other)' (Hook, 2018b, p. 133). In this light, the conservative party in general and García Moreno in particular became the 'tools' of the *Other's will*, namely *historical progress*.[17] Notwithstanding the prevalence of symbolic identification and its triangular nature, note that the conservative party appeared to prioritize the persona of García Moreno over its doctrine: 'Ecuador owes to Mr García Moreno its moral, intellectual, and material advancement. There has been no one else '. And this begs further problematization.

As discussed in Chap. 1, Laclau (2005) highlights one of Freud's discoveries, that is, the predisposition of more *narcissistic* followers to choose certain leaders over others. Freud's discovery was later refined by Lacan (1991), who problematized the distinction between the ideal-ego and the ego-ideal on account of the imaginary and symbolic registers. Lagache (1961) added value to this collective endeavour by offering the notion of *heroic identification*. If the subject's primary identification with the omnipotent Mother was not successfully traversed, he/she would be later predisposed to identifying with omnipotent figures in politics. How does Lacan's (1938) early concept of a diminished paternal imago fit into this collective endeavour, which seeks to refine Freud's notion of narcissism in the leader–followership dynamic? At this point, I would like to suggest one conjecture. The structural violence that results from racism might account in part for certain 'vitiated' societal ego-ideals, such as the cause of *national progress* predicated on political violence/retaliation. Here the idealization of authoritarian personalities from across the ideological spectrum becomes a constant and a value per se. In other words, the omnipotent logic of the ideal-ego which is placed in the figure of the admired leader, underpins a political logic based on caprices and thus force. I come back to this in the next chapter where I address the case of Alfaro.

[17] Here I am also indebted to Žižek's (Žižek, 1990, p. 36) operationalization of this triangulation in light of the purges of the Communist Party under the leadership of Stalin. For that case, the party 'adopted the position of the big Other's will', that is, the Progress of Humanity.

As mentioned, García Moreno proposed a draft of the new constitution whose kernel, according to historian Ayala (2008), was adopted by the 1869 convention. This CA and the conservative elites outside parliament praised García Moreno, their *only* presidential candidate. To add extra credence to my argument regarding the idealization of García Moreno, his active participation before and after the 1869 CA cannot go unnoticed. Not only did García Moreno propose the draft of the new constitution, but he also recommended the 1869 MAs to approve certain executive decrees that he had sanctioned before the convention. In addition, the CA appointed him as general of the national army. The fact that a newspaper of the epoch publicized García Moreno's recommendation shows his influence on the conservative elites inside and outside the CA:

> Deputies: ... V. In the four months in which I have exercised the temporary presidency, I have always been guided by the Republic's well-being. ... VI. The decrees issued by the temporary Presidency, which will be presented to you all by the respective Ministries, comprise all the substantial acts relative to the Republic's interior Administration. *I recommend their examination and approval,* with particular reference to the Finance Ministry ... Also, I recommend the reform and extension of public education ... As it has been the case for the temporary government, it ought to be of special consideration and gratitude to you all everything relative to the Army. (García Moreno, 1869, as cited in La Estrella de Mayo, 1869, emphasis added)[18]

The very next day after García Moreno's resignation, the longing for his leadership continued. Seven deputies (García Moreno, 1869, pp. 1–4) proposed a motion to appoint him as general of the national army. The president of the assembly reminded his peers that the convention was established to sanction the new constitution, after which secondary laws could be sanctioned. He argued that given this priority and the 'urgent necessity' to appoint García Moreno as general for the sake of national order, the proposal to discuss this appointment on three occasions ought

[18] 'Señores Diputados: [...] V. En los cuatro meses que he ejercido la Presidencia interina, he llevado siempre por norte el bien de la República. [...] VI. Los decretos expedidos por la Presidencia interina, que os será presentados por los respectivos Ministerios, contienen todo lo sustancial de los actos relativos a la Administración interior de la República. —Os recomiendo su examen y aprobación, principalmente en lo concerniente a la hacienda nacional...[...] Os recomiendo igualmente la reforma y extensión de la instrucción pública... [...] Objeto de especial consideración y gratitud debe ser para vosotros, como lo ha sido para el Gobierno interino, todo lo relativo al ejército'.

to be dismissed. It was agreed that one single debate was sufficient to appoint García Moreno as general of the army. In supporting this designation, Pablo Bustamante MA contended that this would anyway 'sanction the general will of Ecuadorians, who knew that Providence had brought up ... Moreno ... with the greatest military skill' (p. 2).[19] Here the *forensic* element of rhetoric, that is, the *just* decision to appoint Moreno as general, as well as the deliberative component advocating for a specific *action*, was supported by the appeal to a twofold *ethos*: *the general will* and the Providence. In a country heavily influenced by both Rousseauian and Catholic discourses, Bustamante's rhetorical effect was clear. Two weeks later the appointment in question was formally accepted by García Moreno, and the convention acknowledged his acceptance on 2 June (García Moreno, 1869, p. 1).

On 29 July the new constitution was read, and García Moreno was appointed President of the Republic for the period 1869–1875. A few days later he accepted this appointment as follows: 'If the Honourable National Convention considers that my separation will produce appreciable misfortunes to this country, I will accept the Power' (García Moreno, 1869, p. 4).[20] He was to swear to the new constitution on 10 August.

Concluding Remarks

I began this chapter by presenting a rhetorical context informing the 1869 convention. The turbulent decades that preceded this CA (particularly the 1859–1861 war) moulded the military tone of the 1869 convention, in charge of writing a Catholic and repressive constitution.

To account for constitutional instability in Ecuador, in this chapter I have addressed the psychoanalytically informed question of messianic leadership. By way of summary, the 1869 CA built the horrific dimension of fantasy based on Ecuador's frequent armed rebellions since independence. The transgressive nature of Ecuador's constitutional politics—characterized by caudillos who disobeyed the fundamental law—paved the way for the emergence of the beatific dimension of fantasy: the messianic

[19] 'Al aprobarse el proyecto no se haría otra cosa que sancionar la voluntad general de los ecuatorianos, quienes conocían que la Providencia había criado al Sor. G. García Moreno adornado de las más relevantes dotes militares'.

[20] 'Si, pues, en el ilustrado concepto de la H. Convención Nacional mi separación ha de producir males considerables al país, aceptaré el Poder'.

leader. The yearning for García Moreno 'fulfilled' the desire for an everlasting protection/stability entwined with the 1869 constitution, a Catholic charter.

The non-acceptance of García Moreno's resignation, his idealization by the conservative elites outside and inside the convention, his designation as both the army's general and then the new President of the Republic spoke to a key issue discussed in the theory chapter. That is, the psychoanalytic interpretation of the fantasy of the coming of the Messiah. In *Moses and Monotheism*, Freud suggests that the guilt for the killing of the father of the primal horde *returns* through the fantasy of a Messiah as a Son of God/Father. The latter is personified in substitutive figures (Moses, Christ, etc.) in charge of delivering both redemption and the promised land. This promise, according to the Ecuadorian *conservative party*, was being delivered by García Moreno: 'Ecuador owes to Mr García Moreno its moral, intellectual, and material advancement. There has been no one else who, as president, would have given more beautiful brushstrokes in the painting of progress for the country's good than García Moreno'. This idealization illustrates the libidinal constitution of the conservative party in 1869. From a Freudian perspective, it could be argued that in this process the Catholic leader was put in the place of the conservatives' ego-ideal, as a result of which they identified with one another in their ego. However, the case of García Moreno resonates more with the notion of narcissistic identification discussed in this book; that is, a process of identification in which the leader and his followers share some traits. Here, the leader is not put in the place of his followers' ego-ideal, but rather in the place of their ideal-ego. This narcissistic identification sets the scene for thinking about what appears to be a constant in Ecuador's history, namely the link between heroic identification, a diminished paternal imago, and its flipside: authoritarianism across the ideological spectrum. These intertwined conjectures become clearer in the next chapter, where I analyse the further idealization of 'substitutes' messiahs: Alfaro and Correa.

References

Alcázar, N. N., Martínez, N. N., & Salazar, J. (1869). *Sesión del 24 de mayo.* Archivo de la Asamblea Nacional del Ecuador, 24 May.

Aragundi, M. A. (1869). *Acta de instalación.* Archivo de la Asamblea Nacional del Ecuador, 16 May.

Ayala, E. (2008). *Manual de historia del Ecuador II. Época Republicana*. Corporación Editora Nacional.
Ayala, E. (2011). *Ecuador del siglo XIX. Estado Nacional, Ejército, Iglesia y Municipio*. Universidad Andina Simón Bolívar – Corporación Editorial Nacional.
Carvajal, M. A. (1869). *Acta de instalación*. Archivo de la Asamblea Nacional del Ecuador, 28 May, 21 July.
Constitución de. (1869). https://www.cancilleria.gob.ec/wp-content/uploads/2013/06/constitucion_1869.pdf
Espinosa, C. (2010). *Historia del Ecuador en contexto regional y global*. Lexus.
García Moreno, G. (1869). *Acta de instalación*. Archivo de la Asamblea Nacional del Ecuador, 16, 21 May, 9 August.
Glynos, J., & Howarth, D. (2007). *Logics of critical explanation in social and political theory*. Routledge.
Hook, D. (2018a). Racism and jouissance: Evaluating the "racism as (the theft of) enjoyment" hypothesis. *Psychoanalysis, Culture & Society, 23*, 244–266.
Hook, D. (2018b). *Six moments in Lacan. Communication and identification in psychology and psychoanalysis*. Routledge.
King, A. (2011). *The British Constitution*. Oxford Scholarship Online. oxford.universitypressscholarship.com
La Estrella de Mayo (1869). Convencion De 1869, 24 May. Quito: Biblioteca Aurelio Espinosa Pólit.
Lacan, J. (1938). Family complexes in the formation of the individual. Paris: Encyclopédie française (A. de Monzie, Editor), Vol. 8, translated by Cormac Gallagher.
Lacan, J. (1991). *Freud's Papers on Technique 1953-1954. Book I*. Norton.
Laclau, E. (2005/2007). *On populist reason*. Verso.
Lagache, D. (1961). *El psicoanálisis y la estructura de la personalidad*. Asociación Psicoanalítica del Uruguay – Revista Uruguaya de Psicoanálisis.
Laplanche, J., & Pontalis, J.-B. (1973). *The Language of Psycho-analysis*. Norton.
Martin, J. (2014). *Politics and rhetoric: A critical introduction*. Routledge. Available at: University of Essex (E-book).
Martínez, M. A. (1869). *Sesión del 19 de Mayo*. Archivo de la Asamblea Nacional del Ecuador, 19, 21, 28 May, 3 June.
Noboa, N. N. (1869). *Sesión del 31 de Mayo*. Archivo de la Asamblea Nacional del Ecuador, 31 May.
Salvador Lara, J. (2005). *Breve historia contemporánea del Ecuador*. Fondo de Cultura Económica.

Sharoni, J. (2016). The failure of the parental metaphor: A Lacanian reading of James Joyce's "Eveline". *Journal of Modern Literature, 39*(4), 33–48.

Uquillas, M. A. (1869). *Sesión del 21 de Mayo.* Archivo de la Asamblea Nacional del Ecuador, 21 May.

Žižek, S. (1990). Eastern Europe's Republics of Gilead. *New Left Review* (I/183, September-October).

CHAPTER 4

The 2007–2008 Constituent Convention and the 2015 Constitutional Amendment

In this chapter I proceed as follows. Firstly, I present the rhetorical context shaping the 'necessity' of both the 2007–2008 Constituent Assembly (CA) and the 2015 constitutional reform (this section is longer than that presented in the previous chapter). Afterwards, I conduct a discourse analysis of the officially transcribed debates (2007–2008; 2014–2015) provided by Ecuador's National Assembly (NA). The 2007–2008 CA addressed many non-constitutional topics, that is, themes that do not speak to ***the most important rules and common understandings*** of the state, for example, the import of food and its price limits, drug trafficking, Colombia's bombing of *Fuerzas Armadas Revolucionarias de Colombia* (FARC) on Ecuadorian soil in 2008, amongst others (National Assembly, 2007–2008). The convention's order of the day facilitated the mapping, organization, and selection of those debates relating to the question of leadership. This has been mainly expressed during the 2008 debates on Alfaro's legacy and the presidential re-election allowance. The 2014–2015 discourse that led to indefinite presidential re-elections is also presented in this chapter, on account of its link to my research puzzle. The chapter includes an analysis of the indigenous' demand for a pluri-national state, a demand widely discussed by the 2007–2008 CA. As Betty Amores MA contended, this demand 'has been one of the most debated topics' by this convention. International thinkers such as de Sousa Santos participated in the workshops dedicated to discussing this theme (2008, p. 69). The 1869

E. Espindola, *The Paternal Imago in Ruins*, The Palgrave Lacan Series, https://doi.org/10.1007/978-3-032-07507-9_4

CA led by the Catholic García Moreno sought to include the indigenous peoples in the *Social Contract* via further evangelization. The 2007–2008 CA led by the Catholic Rafael Correa welcomed the constitutional recognition of the pluri-national nature of the Ecuadorian state.

The Rhetorical Context

The *rhetorical context* denotes the historical conditions that form the backdrop to a *speech occasion*, that is, 'the historical time and place of the intervention, the exigence(s) to which it is a response … and any broader circumstances the intervention also seeks to shape' (Martin, 2014, p. 100). The rhetorical context informing Ecuador's latest CA was characterized by (1) the locus of Ecuador's convention ('Alfaro's City'), on account of its symbolic importance; (2) the ethnic and gender-based composition of the Assembly; (3) its participatory character and subsequent challenges; (4) Ecuador's political instability during the last decades of the twentieth century; (5) the role played by the indigenous movement since the 1980s. All these contextual phenomena will help us better understand the anti-neoliberal rhetoric informing the convention that replaced the 1998 constitution.

Ecuador's latest CA was in session from 29 November 2007 until 25 July 2008. The 2008 constitution was crafted in Montecristi, the coastal city where general Eloy Alfaro was born. Alfaro was the leader of Ecuador's Liberal Revolution (1895) and the Citizens' Revolution's main historical reference. Once Alfaro overthrew President Lizardo García in 1905, he convened a CA. Key liberal reforms were enshrined in the 1906 constitution, namely the separation of the state from the church and the secular character of education (Espinosa, 2010, pp. 563–564). Alfaro's legacy is discussed in the context of a parliamentary session (28 January 2008) dedicated to him.

According to the 2001 census valid at the time of the 2007–2008 convention, the ethnic composition in Ecuador was as follows: out of 12,156,608 inhabitants, 77.42% were mestizo, 10.46% white, 6.83% indigenous, 2.23% black, amongst others (as cited in Ayala Mora, 2008, p. 129).

The 2007–2008 CA was composed of formerly excluded groups—45 out of the 130 MAs were women (Misión de Observación Electoral de la Unión Europea (MOE UE), 2007, p. 47). In line with the maxim of gender equality, ten women and ten men were elected as presidents and vice-presidents of the 2007–2008 *constituent tables* (subcommittees—explained below) (The Carter Center, 2008, p. 10). The indigenous movement participated in this CA with 4 out of 130 parliamentary seats via its political party, Pachakutik (Cordero, 2018, p. 4). Since the 1990s, the political actions of the indigenous had influenced the public agenda (ibid.—discussed below). In this CA there were indigenous MAs who did not belong to Pachakutik, such as Mónica Chuji (Alianza País). Ecuador's census operates through self-identification, and people are asked which ethnic group they identify with. It is hard to tell the 'real' percentage of indigenous MAs in this convention. Even so and unlike previous CAs, in the 2007–2008 CA the indigenous MAs (representing both Pachakutik and other organizations) directly participated in the writing of Ecuador's *social contract*, a point worthy of emphasis.

The 2007–2008 CA was opened to public involvement. Amongst others, the constituent tables/subcommittees, the citizens' fora, a postbox, and an email welcomed the people's proposals. The CA created the *Social Participation Unit* in charge of 'collecting, organising, channelling, and systematizing the thousands of proposals that arrived at Alfaro City' (The Carter Center, 2008, p. 11). Citizens' observatories were established to check that their demands were considered during the drafting and sanctioning of constitutional articles. Afterwards, these were shared with the citizenry in view of the upcoming referendum that was going to approve the constitution (*Social Participation Unit*, as cited in ibid., p. 12).

Which exigencies and broader circumstances underpinned the *rhetorical necessity* to replace the 1998 constitution with the 2008 charter? To what extent did these circumstances shape the rhetoric of a convention fostered by Rafael Correa, an outsider with a PhD in Developmental Economics, strong Catholic beliefs, and an anti-neoliberal discourse?

The following processes allow us to understand how the Washington Consensus became popular in Ecuador in the 1980s and 1990s and became unpopular from 1999: first, the failed attempt to industrialize Ecuador (1972–1979), a military endeavour leveraged by the oil *boom*; second, a neoliberal programme (1982–2006) followed by severe political instability (1997–2005). (I present these opening points in the first subsection); lastly, the indigenous movement's shift (1930–2007) from being a *classist* and Catholic organization to a confederation demanding both the transformation of the nation-state and the end of neoliberalism. As we shall see in the analytical section, the longing for the return of a state as the planner of development and the critique of neoliberalism merged into the need for a strong and democratic president. This will become clear during the 2008 discourse analysis in favour of presidential re-elections put forward by Alianza País and prohibited by the 1998 'neoliberal' constitution. The demand for a pluri-national state was also critical of neoliberalism, as well as of racism in Ecuador (discussed below). The yearning for a stronger and democratic leadership/state, the hope for economic and political stability, and the indigenous demand for a pluri-national state coincided on one point: their critique of neoliberalism, the arch enemy of this predominantly left-wing CA.

The Oil Boom, the Army and Its Failed Process of Industrialization, the Neoliberal Catastrophe, and Democratic Instability in Ecuador (1972–2005)

In contrast to the right-wing and highly repressive military dictatorships in the 1970s in Argentina, Brazil, and Chile, the Ecuadorian dictator Rodríguez Lara (1972–1976) led a relatively non-repressive and 'centre-left' government. This regime implemented redistributive policies, such as agrarian reforms and subsidies (Espinosa, 2010, pp. 649–650).

The 1972–1979 military regime in Ecuador did not have a monolithic approach to policy-making. From 1972 to 1976 the 'revolutionary' and 'nationalist' faction focused on agrarian, fiscal, and administrative reforms for the benefit of the poor. From 1976 to 1979 a less radical and less nationalistic faction seized power and stopped the agrarian reform, while crafting a new constitution for the return of democracy in 1979 (Ayala, 2008, pp. 112–113).

Although the exploration and exploitation of oil in Ecuador began in the first half of the twentieth century, it was only in the 1960s that significant fields of oil were found. In 1968 Texaco and Gulf found the Shushufindi field, 'one of the richest [fields] in South America at that time. ... Ecuador had entered the oil prosperity, which was consolidated once the oil prices in the global market began their rise in 1973' (Espinosa, 2010, pp. 645–646). This enabled the armed forces to finance certain reforms inspired by the *Cepalist* thought, reforms that were compatible with those of previous governments. But unlike Rodríguez Lara, his predecessors did not rely on the oil revenue to finance the modernization of Ecuador. General Lara and the 1976–1979 military triumvirate used part of this income for industrialization. Public soft loans, tax exemptions, and protectionist measures were implemented. Industrial production quadrupled from 1970 to 1976, but its share in the gross domestic product was comparatively small (less than 20%). The bulk of the industries were either elementary (e.g., cigarettes) or imported components for assembling (Espinosa, pp. 648–649, 655). 'The industrialisation dream never materialised' (ibid., pp. 655–656); however, this dream was reignited by Rafael Correa.

Although 'the oil revenue evened out in 1975' (ibid., p. 657), the military continued to finance its developmentalist policy. The bureaucracy, public investment, and subsidies were financed by both the oil revenue and loans from international private banks. In the 1970s the national debt corresponded to US$ 324 million; by 1979 it had risen to US$ 4500 million. The citizens and the civilian governments that followed the dictatorship had to deal with the repayment of this 'onerous' obligation. The 'hard adjustments' and the economic deadlocks of the 1980s were the immediate outcome of both the corruption and the 'modernizing messianism' of the military, not to mention the environmental damage resulting from the oil *boom* (Espinosa, 2010, pp. 657, 659).

The 1980s was a difficult decade for the whole of Latin America. Once Mexico *defaulted* in 1982, flows of capital halted, and this led to the external debt crisis in this region. The 1982–1999 period in Ecuador was characterized by (1) the endeavour to constrain the fiscal deficit (1982–1991); (2) the execution of the reforms stemming from the Washington Consensus (1992–1995); (3) and the international and national financial crisis (1996–1999), an event that put an end to Ecuador's monetary sovereignty. The following policies and events were critical within the 1982–1999 period: (1) the economic resources formerly channelled to investment and public spending were prioritized for the repayment of the external debt; (2) the IMF conditioned its assistance in favour of the interests of its external creditors, while equating development to economic growth. Two conflicts with Peru in 1981 and 1995, two climatic disasters attributed to El Niño in 1982–1983 and 1997–1999, and the 1987 earthquake further complicated Ecuador's 'fragile productive structure' (Oleas, 2018, pp. 40–41).

By the end of 1998, the international financial crisis (originating in Russia) had reduced the export of Ecuadorian goods and the influx of foreign capital. In a few months the price of the oil barrel decreased from US$ 20 to 7 (the Ecuadorian government was in a financial crisis). The 1994 law on the financial system had created one of the key conditions leading, from December 1998 to mid-1999, to the collapse of 18 out of

38 banks. This law reduced the legal banking reserve, that is, the amount of money that banks must not lend in the event that savers decide to withdraw it. This law authorized *linked loans*, that is, the making of loans to firms associated with the banks. The evaluation of whether potential debtors were capable of repaying their loans did not follow a technical criterion, hence 'there was a high risk for these debts to become uncollectible' (Espinosa, 2010, p. 702). From 1994 the liberated interest rates and the non-regulated influx of international capital created a financial bubble. This burst in 1998 when the government levied a 1% tax on the flow of international capital, which provoked a widespread flight of capital. When the banks began collapsing, the government responded with a bailout. Even so, people rushed to withdraw their savings, as a result of which the government froze bank deposits. This measure increased poverty and created massive unrest. Ecuador *defaulted* in September 1999 and adopted the US dollar as its official currency (9 January 2000). Mahuad's presidential campaign was financed by a famous banker, 'which induced public opinion to think that throughout the financial crisis Mahuad had acted to protect the banks' interests'. On 21 January 2000, a coalition of the indigenous and the military compelled the president to resign (Espinosa, 2010, pp. 696–698, 702).

Although the 1999 financial crisis resulted from 'complex' causes, it is undeniable that the 1994 law on the financial system and the 1998 worldwide financial hysteria contributed to it. The agenda implemented in the 1980s and 1990s was heavily criticized by the World Social Forum, ex-civil servants of the World Bank (e.g., Joseph Stiglitz), and the 2006 electoral candidate Rafael Correa. Between 2000 and 2007 Ecuador's representative democracy reached the peak of its crisis (Espinosa, 2010, pp. 741–742, 744).

Between 1996 and 2007 several individuals presided over the Ecuadorian nation (one of which lasted in office for 2 days): Abdalá Bucaram (1996–1997), Fabián Alarcón (1997), Rosalía Arteaga (1997), Fabián Alarcón (1997–1998), Jamil Mahuad (1998–2000), Colonel Lucio Gutiérrez (2000), General Carlos Mendoza (2000), Gustavo Noboa (2000–2002), Lucio Gutiérrez (2002–2005), and Alfredo Palacio (2005–2007) (Political Database of the Americas Georgetown University, 2009). Rafael Correa (2007–2017) is the president who has presided over Ecuador for the longest *uninterrupted* period since independence (El Universo, 2017).

The day before Correa took office, he commemorated Latin American integration and the region's 'turn' towards *twenty-first-Century Socialism* before the indigenous population of Zumbahua, a rural community in the highlands. The Bolivian and Venezuelan presidents Evo Morales and Hugo Chávez were part of this non-official but symbolic celebration where Correa conveyed a message of change. Informed by antagonism, President Correa's discourse was constantly communicated via nomadic cabinets throughout the country, as well as through his Saturday TV broadcast. (The ministers and the president used to travel to small and large cities throughout Ecuador to discuss how the central government could contribute to local development.) This created an inclusionary feeling for those historically ignored by the central government. Unlike the traditional elite, Correa 'distinguished himself' by making decisions in accordance with his electoral promises. 'His ability to alternate the well-aimed insult, technical explanations, and the invocation of collective dreams has allowed him to satisfy the complex expectations that the citizenry has of its leaders' (Espinosa, 2010, pp. 763, 765, own translation).

Correa's antagonistic rhetoric has affinities with that of the most influential Ecuadorian politician of the last century, the many-time president José María Velasco Ibarra (1934–1935, 1944–1947, 1952–1956, 1960–1961, 1968–1972) (Political Database of the Americas Georgetown University, 2009). However, Correa has been 'much more' strategic in 'neutralizing' his adversaries. Unlike Velasco Ibarra, who was 'always defeated by his enemies', Correa re-established the democratic edifice to legitimize his programme, while relying on his own political movement. Velasco Ibarra depended on unstable alliances that left him isolated, and his authority was lost as soon as he proclaimed himself dictator. As for these leaders' affinities, that is, their antagonism and readiness to disregard legality on behalf of the people, 'these are a product of ... the Ecuadorian political culture that expects politicians to both personally berate their adversaries and to overlook the formal rules to prove their power' (Espinosa, 2010, pp. 765–766, own translation).

The psychosocial meaning of Correa's uninterrupted leadership in such an unstable country, as well as that of Ecuador's political culture—which expects politicians to berate their adversaries—is addressed below. Here it suffices to stress that Correa's discourse has criticized Ecuador's party-based democracy and the neoliberal agenda, while partly sympathizing with the Indigenous Cause, another highly debated topic in the 2007–2008 CA.

On the Indigenous Cause: The Agrarian Reform (1964) and Its Anti-Neoliberal and Anti-Racist Demand for a Pluri-National State (2008)

In what follows, a selective genealogy of the Ecuadorian indigenous movement is presented. I highlight its shift from being a *classist* and Catholic organization to a confederation demanding the establishment of a plurinational state, later recognized by the 2008 constitution.

Until the 1960s, the indigenous in Ecuador were regarded as peasants. Their demands, channelled through the left and trade unions, were treated as part of the Agrarian Question (Zúñiga, 2004, p. 195). At the beginning of the 1960s economic inequality was severe and was criticized; 1% of the haciendas hogged 56% of the cultivated land, while the long-lasting institution of *huasipungo* continued, as it were the counterpart to a feudal relation in Europe. 'Here [huasipungo] the landowner granted the indigenous labourer a plot of land in exchange for his/her work on the main fields of the hacienda' (Espinosa, 2010, p. 491). The labourer could use this land for cultivation, but it belonged to the hacendado. In 1954, 20,000 families lived under the huasipungo regime. In 1964, the military junta (1963–1966) implemented an agrarian reform, guided by the US *Alliance for Progress.* Amongst other measures, the Law on the Agrarian Reform and Colonisation abolished huasipungo. The state granted lands to about 80% of former huasipungeros, expropriated unproductive lands, and established an 800-hectare limit for landowners in the highlands. Although the reform was limited in its scope, it 'helped dismantle a system of social domination and racial subjection incompatible with a democratic society' (Espinosa, 2010, p. 645). In 1970, Velasco Ibarra aimed to broaden this reform, and this continued during the military government of Rodríguez Lara (1973–1976). But the military triumvirate (1976–1979) discontinued the distribution of nonproductive lands, as this measure had fostered a battle between landowners and peasants (Espinosa, 2010, pp. 643–645, 652, 654).

According to Cordero (2018, pp. 122–125), the history of the indigenous movement dates back to the First Conference of Indigenous Leaders in 1936, the precursor to the National Federation of Indians founded in 1944. In the 1930–1970 period, the indigenous' demands for land and better living conditions in rural areas were intertwined with the communist and socialist programmes, as well as that of the Catholic Church. Despite this bottom-up struggle carried out by the indigenous and peasants in favour of land redistribution, their know-how was ignored during the 1964 and 1973 agrarian reforms. The military conducted these reformations neglected by both political parties and modernizing landowners (Cosse, as cited in Cordero, 2018, p. 125). From 1979 to 2013, continues Cordero, the Ecuadorian Confederation of Indigenous Nationalities (CONAIE) played a key role in the evolution of the indigenous movement. From its foundation in 1986, CONAIE has grouped together all the indigenous associations across the Ecuadorian regions. The demands stemming from the indigenous organizations of the Amazonian region have converged with those of the highlands. The Amazonian demand for *territory* now underpins CONAIE's political programme of *self-government*. CONAIE's political movement (Pachakutik) has allowed the electoral participation of a confederation composed of heterogeneous indigenous cultures.

CONAIE influenced the 1998 and 2008 CAs. Throughout the 1990s, the indigenous movement succeeded in articulating various social demands, and the indigenous' mobilization reached its peak in the 1998 convention. The 1998 charter recognized (for the first time) the collective rights of the indigenous peoples, as well as the pluri-cultural and pluri-ethnic nature of the Ecuadorian state. CONAIE also played a part in the socio-political process leading to the 2007–2008 convention, where the indigenous movement repudiated Ecuador's corrupted and unstable democracy. CONAIE also criticized the inefficient and elitist character of the Ecuadorian state. This created the conditions that led to the 1999 financial crisis and the dollarization of the economy in 2000. The resulting socio-economic unrest forced a large number of Ecuadorians to emigrate (Cordero, 2018, p. 3). In 2007–2008 CONAIE brought to the convention's attention 'the demand for a Pluri-National State constructed by the indigenous movement since the 1990s, which brought to the fore the demands for an inclusive society and State' (ibid.).

The constitutional recognition (2008) of the pluri-national nature of the Ecuadorian state was an achievement. Nonetheless, it was followed by setbacks for CONAIE. This comes as no surprise if we consider Pachakutik's participation in the crafting of Ecuador's latest constitution. The 2007–2008 convention was composed of 130 deputies out of which 80 belonged to the incumbent's movement (Alianza País), while only 4 represented Pachakutik. Even so, CONAIE's active involvement in national politics since the 1990s had created a political capital that could not go unnoticed in this convention. This was acknowledged and supported by

Alberto Acosta, the first president of this assembly and Correa's former comrade. Once the constitution was approved, President Correa implemented a top-down process of decentralization that clashed with the autonomist demands of the indigenous peoples (Cordero, pp. 4, 122, 144).

The Rhetorical Context of the 2015 Reform that Abolished Presidential Term Limits

The 1998 constitution prohibited presidential re-elections in Ecuador. During the 2007–2008 CA, the opposition contended that the proposal for the presidential re-election allowance put forward by Alianza País aimed at allowing the future re-election of President Correa. The 2008 constitution instated the presidential re-election concession 'for one time only', consecutive or not. In 2014, Alianza País proposed a constitutional amendment to abolish presidential term limits *tout court*, in the hope of Correa's third presidential mandate. As I will argue, the 2008–2015 question of presidential re-elections in Ecuador, which accounts in part for its constitutional volatility, relates to the issue of messianic leadership analysed here.

Ecuador's constitutional instability resonates with the volatility of the executive branch. Between 1830 and 2014 there was a total of 114 governments, whether constitutional presidents, acting officials, or individual or collective dictatorships (Ayala, 2014, p. 15). Although the democratic regime prevailed during the 1978–2000 period, gridlocks between the legislative and executive branches were commonplace, which created ungovernability (Espinosa, 2010, p. 711–712). In addition, in the 1980s and 1990s the political parties lost their legitimacy, as they failed to collect the people's demands and translate them into fruitful policies (Echeverría, 2006, as cited in Espinosa, p. 713). In this crisis of representativeness, the new social movements proposed demands beyond the traditional left-right rhetoric, while 'populist' or 'managerial anti-politics' appeared. Anti-politics 'can be defined as the rejection of the political class and the preference for outsiders' (Espinosa, pp. 715, 719, own translation). The ideology of the charismatic Rafael Correa fused the following elements: the discourse of the outsider, an 'innovative populism', and a leftist agenda in favour of both a participatory democracy and social equity. 'Not only did he promise to dethrone the traditional politicians, but also to re-establish democracy and to bury neoliberalism to foster a nationalist policy on oil derived in more social and economic inclusion' (Espinosa, p. 760, own translation).

The presidency of Dr. Correa is an exception to Ecuador's long-lasting history of political instability. He served as president for a whole decade (2007–2017), that is, the longest uninterrupted presidency since 1830. His left-wing movement (Alianza País) also constituted the majoritarian force in the legislature from 2009 to 2017, that is, immediately after the 2007–2008 CA. How can we explicate Alianza País' atypical popularity/ stability in this highly unstable presidential system? Correa has been a critic of neoliberalism and was part of the group of presidents that led Latin America's turn to the left in the twenty-first century (i.e., Hugo Chávez, Néstor Kirchner, Michelle Bachelet, Evo Morales, amongst others). The literature on the turn to the left has mainly explained this shift in terms of a disapproval of the economic reform implemented in this region under the guidelines of the Washington Consensus (Arditi, 2009; French, 2009; MacDonald and Ruckert, 2009, as cited in Basabe, 2017, p. 317). Arguably, Alianza País' atypical stability derives from its anti-neoliberal and thus popular discourse, considering that the 1999 financial crisis, which was devastating for the population, was partly influenced by the 1994 neoliberal reform on the banking system and the 1998 international fear (Espinosa, 2010, p. 742).

However, Basabe-Serrano (2017) posits that the turn to the left hypothesis, which focuses on the ideological dimension, is problematic for the Ecuadorian case. If compared to other Latin American countries such as Argentina and Bolivia, the implementation of the neoliberal programme in Ecuador was weak. Besides, the left has not been a popular force in the Ecuadorian legislature since the return of democracy. On average, between 1979 and 2007 only 10.75% of parliamentary seats were obtained by the left. Surprisingly, Alianza País won 47.58% of the congressional seats for the 2009–2013 mandate and 76.33% of these seats for the 2013–2017 period. Basabe conjectures that this continued support of the Citizens' Revolution was motivated, 'at least in part', by an atypical prosperity, namely the unseen prices of oil, which coincided with President Correa's consecutive governments. (Ecuador's economy is highly dependent on this fossil fuel.) The price of oil skyrocketed in 2008 (99 US$ per barrel), and it remained very high for some years (e.g., 98 US$ per barrel in 2013). But this price began a dramatic decrease in 2015, a year in which a barrel was worth 49 US$. Ecuador's prosperity (2007–2014) might have played a key role in Correa's decision to run for presidency for the third time, for which reason Alianza País proposed a constitutional amendment to allow indefinite re-elections in 2014 (pp. 315–319, 321–328, 330; Fontaine, 2002, as cited in Basabe-Serrano, 2017, p. 325; Lora y Panizza, 2002, as cited in Basabe-Serrano, 2017, pp. 318–319).

The above criticism of the turn to the left hypothesis for the Ecuadorian case exhorts us to reflect on the explanatory power of ideology in this politically unstable and economically dependent country. As I shall argue below, a Lacanian approach to the grip of ideology allows us to explicate, at least in part, the unexpected abolition of presidential term limits prompted by the Citizens' Revolution.

The 2007–2008 Constituent Assembly and its Arguments

The disenchantment provoked by the failed attempt to industrialize Ecuador, the socio-economic austerity stemming from the neoliberal agenda, the Indigenous Cause, and political instability were all elements upon which Dr. Correa built his 2006 political campaign. This charismatic outsider promised a new deal with the replacement of the 1998 constitution.

This second part of the chapter begins by describing the composition and modus operandi of Ecuador's latest CA. I then forge the argument according to which the idealization of Eloy Alfaro set the 'psychic scene' for the 2007–2008 CA. More precisely, his idealization, I suggest, triggers in part the CA's longing for its 'founding father'. In other words, it is the meaning of the *fantasy* of the Messiah that is at stake in the mourning of Alfaro (to be discussed below). The reference to Alfaro's sensibility towards the indigenous question begins to hint at the link between the indigenous demand for a non-racist and pluri-national state and the land promised by the 2007–2008 CA. The problematization of the 'theft of enjoyment' thesis underpins the analysis of the indigenous demand. Afterwards, I come back to the question of messianic leadership. There I conduct a discourse analysis of the 2008 debate on presidential re-election and the 2014–2015 reform that abolished presidential term limits in Ecuador, in the hope of Correa's third presidential re-election. In drawing on the argument on the *return* of guilt for the killing of the father of the primal horde, the appearance of *substitute* 'fathers' (García Moreno, Alfaro, and Correa) in the 1869, 2008, and 2014–2015 debates allows us to grasp the psychic factor informing, in part, Ecuador's history of frequent 'lawgivers' or, put differently, its history of 'constitutional instability'.

The Assembly's Composition and Modus Operandi

On 15 January 2007, Rafael Correa took office. The very next day he decreed the future referendum to convene a national CA with full authority (The Carter Center, 2008, p. 63). The April referendum asked the people if they would agree to craft a new constitution. The people replied favourably, with a vote of more than 80% supporting the creation of a CA. On 30 September, 130 MAs were elected for the convention (2007, p. 6), out of which 24 represented the nation, 100 the provinces, and 6 the migrants (2 for Latin America, 2 for the US and Canada, and 2 for Europe). As mentioned earlier, Alianza País (Correa's movement) had 80 MAs for this convention, out of which 7 were part of an alliance. During the assembly's first day Correa was confirmed as president, while the former Congress was suspended. Since the CA approved its resolutions via absolute majority (this was agreed by the people in the April referendum), Alianza País had an ample leverage throughout this process. Partido Sociedad Patriótica (PSP) and Partido Renovador Institucional Acción Nacional (PRIAN) were the second and third largest political forces in this CA with 18 and 8 MAs respectively. The remaining forces had five, three, two, and one MAs in the convention. Out of a total of 20 parties and movements present in this assembly, 13 forces (in alliance or not) represented their constituents with 1 MA only. Despite the dispersed composition of the convention, in the April plebiscite 81.72% of Ecuadorians voted in favour of crafting a new constitution (The Carter Center, 2008, pp. 5–7, 63). Alianza País had the democratic monopoly on the convention because it held 61% of the voting power.

The CA's regulation, adopted with 86 out of 130 votes, stipulated that up to two debates were allowed for the plenary to approve the constitutional articles. The 2007–2008 convention was structured via 'Constituent Tables', that is, subcommittees in which the MAs conducted their work before the plenary discussion. Each subcommittee had 13 MAs, 8 of whom belonged to Alianza País, on account of its popularity. There were ten subcommittees in charge of deliberating on the following: (1) Fundamental Rights and Constitutional Guaranties; (2) Organization, Social and Civic Participation, and Systems of Representation; (3) Structure and Institutions of the State; (4) Territorial Code and

Competency Allocation; (5) Natural Resources and Biodiversity; (6) Labour, Production, and Social Inclusion; (7) Development's Regime; (8) Justice and Battle against Corruption; (9) Sovereignty, International Relations, and Latin American Integration; and (10) Legislation and Audits. The MAs could visit other subcommittees to offer their opinion; nonetheless, their vote was restricted to their assigned subcommittees where an absolute majority was required to propose constitutional articles to the plenary session. Either collectively or individually, the population was allowed to put forward its suggestions before the convention. Besides crafting the constitution, the convention was in charge of both carrying out audits of the *constituted powers* and legislating under the following three circumstances: first, when the proposal stemmed from the citizens, so long as the bill was backed by a required minimum (0.1%) of the electoral register; second, when the bill was proposed by the MAs with at least 5% of the convention's support; third, when the bill was presented by the president, the latter also the case for the 1869 assembly (2007, pp. 11–12, 22–24; The Carter Center, 2008, pp. 7, 10; Misión de Observación Electoral de la Unión Europea, 2007, p. 80; Villacís & Carrillo, 2012, p. 11).

The Idealization of Eloy Alfaro, the 1906 and 2008 Lawgiver

Ecuadorian historiography constantly underscores that Ecuador's constitutions have been mainly prompted by 'caudillos'. As McLean and McMillan (McLean & Alistair, 2003, p. 68) remind us, *caudillismo* emerged because of the socio-political disturbances that followed Latin American independence. 'Caudillos … filled the power vacuum and became guarantors of order and stability. Their rule style was personalist'. Ecuador's latest convention referred to various leaders and independence heroes, such as Simón Bolívar. Alfaro was the one who received most of the 2007–2008 praising. From a psychoanalytic perspective, in what follows I examine how the 2008 emotional attachment to 'caudillo' Eloy Alfaro (the 1906 'lawgiver') speaks to the partial nature of Ecuador's historic constitutional instability.

As historian Salvador Lara contends, only two 'authentic' revolutions have occurred throughout Ecuador's history: the war of independence and the liberal revolution led by Alfaro, who presided over the nation on two occasions (1895–1901 and 1906–1911). Amongst other reforms, his revolution brought about the separation of the church from the state, secular education in public schools, the 'definite consolidation' of citizens' civil rights, gender equality within the formal work force, and a sensibility towards the indigenous question. Two factions emerged from this revolution: *alfarismo* and *placismo,* the latter led by President Leonidas Plaza (1901–1905), Alfaro's former general. In 1911, these liberal wings went to war with each other, and Alfaro was taken prisoner. On 28 January 1912, a 'mob' assassinated, dragged, and burnt Alfaro and his comrades (2005, pp. 422–423, 429, 431–432), a murder provoked in the last instance by *placismo* (Jaramillo Alvarado, as cited in Salvador Lara, p. 432).

Although the convention began its sessions in November 2007, it was from 2008 onwards that the assembly approved the articles of the new constitution, with the people's participation. During the 4 January session Fernando Cordero MA suggested the assembly to organize the citizens' fora to be conducted in January and February. It is in this preparatory context that we need to frame the 28 January session, dedicated to commemorating the life and work of General Alfaro. Public authorities were invited to the 28 January event. This session sought to inspire the spirit of the future constitution. A note on my case selection is in order. I choose two speeches and one resolution for the subsequent analysis, namely the discourse of the president of the convention (Alberto Acosta MA); the speech given by Martha Roldós MA; and the resolution that consecrated Alfaro's home town as national heritage. Acosta's speech fulfils the representativeness criterion, as he was the most voted for MA for the 2007–2008 CA (Roldós, 2008, p. 27). Roldós' speech illustrates the several progressive reforms led by Alfaro. Moreover, Acosta's and Roldós' discourses share a key characteristic related to my research puzzle, that is, they treat the 1906 and 2008 constitutions, García Moreno, and Alfaro as privileged '(*object petit a*) objects, which contain ... something in "them more than themselves," and hence take on a disproportionate libidinal status by virtue of the degree of investment of a given community' (Hook, 2008, p. 400), the Ecuadorian community. The *unanimous* resolution praising Alfaro's home town as national heritage shows the relevance of this 'founding father' in Ecuador's history, at least in the context of Ecuador's latest CA. Choosing the analysis of the longing for Alfaro over that of other historic leaders (e.g., Bolívar) is appropriate.

As mentioned, only the war of independence and Alfaro's revolution can be regarded as 'authentic' revolutions in Ecuador's history. This can be better understood in view of the scope of Alfaro's deeds. In 2008,

Martha Roldós MA (RED) drew on *pathos* and rhetorical questions to address Alfaro's legacy:

> Why do we remember you … on the anniversary of your terrible death? *Why do those who seek to write a new future for the country remember you in this Alfaro's City in Montecristi?* … What do you still have to say to us? … Since a child and thanks to my father, *I was clear on the difference between those who fight for their people's rights and those, such as García Moreno, who want power for tyranny and despotism.* … Not only did you lead the most important revolution that Ecuador has known, but you were also a great builder of our identity as a national State. The public and secular education was an indispensable social achievement for building and gestating the citizenry … We must also thank you for our incorporation, that of women to the political life … In addition, you made yours the cause of the indigenous peoples and nationalities in Ecuador … The indigenous have continued with their centenarian fight and they too accompany us today in politics and in this Assembly. … Thanks to your revolution, an environment—which opened us to new ideas of all signs—was created. … *Here you are today in this mud pot with your divided ashes, but your heart is one, your heart that belongs to the whole of Ecuador, your heart that still beats while Ecuador exists.* (Roldós, 2008, pp. 25–26, 28–30, emphasis added)[1]

Martha Roldós provides a helpful description of key progressive policies led by Alfaro's revolution in favour of various social sectors. These ranged from public education to gender and ethnic equality and thus show the societal relevance of Alfaro. By criticizing García Moreno, this description

[1] 'Por qué te recordamos … en el aniversario de tu terrible muerte? Por qué te recordamos en esta Ciudad Alfaro de Montecristi, quienes buscamos escribir un nuevo futuro para el país? […] Qué tienes que decirnos todavía? […] Desde niña y gracias a mi padre tuve muy clara la diferencia entre quien lucha por los derechos de su pueblo y quien como García Moreno quiere el poder para la tiranía y el despotismo. […] No solo lideraste la más importante revolución que haya conocido el Ecuador, sino que fuiste un gran constructor de nuestra identidad como Estado nacional. […] La educación pública laica fue una conquista indispensable para construir y gestar ciudadanía … También debemos agradecerte nuestra incorporación, la de las mujeres a la vida política …[…] También hiciste tuya la causa de los pueblos y nacionalidades indígenas en el Ecuador …, los indígenas han continuado con su lucha centenaria y nos acompañan también hoy en la política y en esta Asamblea. […] Gracias a tu revolución se creo un clima para abrirnos a nuevas ideas de todo signo. […] Aquí estas hoy en tu vasija de barro, con tus cenizas divididas, pero tu corazón uno solo, tu corazón que es de todo el Ecuador, tu corazón que aun late mientras exista el Ecuador'. (Martha Roldós MA, ibid., pp. 25–26, 28–30) Martha Rina Roldós Bucaram/MovimientoRED/Guayas

also incorporates the importance of caudillos—across the ideological spectrum—in Ecuador's history of constitutional replacements.

From a classic and Freudian approach to group formation, Roldós' account allows us to grasp the libidinal constitution of a group dependent on a leader. In this process, a group of people have put one and the same object (Alfaro) in place of their ego-ideal and have thus identified with one another in their ego. From a Lacanian and Lagachian perspectives, which problematize the distinction between the ideal-ego and ego-ideal suggested by Freud since 1914, the above speech hints at the usefulness of *heroic identification* in thinking about the 'personalistic' character of the 2008 convention: *Why do those who seek to write a new future for the country remember you in this Alfaro's City in Montecristi?* See also: *Thanks to your revolution, an environment—which opened us to new ideas of all signs—was created.* These enunciations allow me to suggest a different interpretation of Freud's formula. The above process of group formation, which speaks to the will of *Alfaristas* (Alfaro's followers), I argue that Alfaro is put in the place of the followers' ideal-ego, the latter reminiscent of an early feeling of imaginary omnipotence. The omnipresent persona of Alfaro in Ciudad Alfaro adds credence to my argument.[2] In a similar way to García Moreno in 1869, the 2008 session on *Alfarism* speaks to how Alfaro is praised by most of the Assembly, the latter point corroborated by the unanimous decision to declare Alfaro city a historical heritage of the nation (discussed below). This type of speech allows us to appreciate how the new constitution (2008) and Alfaro served as fantasmatic objects-cause of desire in this convention, considering that *Alfaro City* was built for the writing of the 2008 constitution. The apparent presence of *heroic identification* in 2008 speaks to the key role played by the imaginary realm in this Ecuadorian convention. Notwithstanding, symbolic identification was also present. Note that Roldós' comment speaks to a triangular and symbolic identification which takes precedence: 'What do you [Alfaro] still have to say to us [before the eyes of History]?' While talking to her peers or *little others* in the convention, Roldós' speech also converses with a more radical alterity, that of History, that of the Other.

Alfaro (the 1906 lawgiver) and the 2008 charter were interconnected thanks to the power of persuasion. A *deliberative* strategy in rhetoric seeks to foster a particular course of action. Resorting to this technique, President Acosta (MA) exhorted the convention to draw inspiration from

[2] See: https://ciudadalfaro.gob.ec/#.

Alfaro's *transformative legacy* when writing the new charter. Alfaro's struggle to reconstruct the country, enshrined in the 1906 constitution, needed to be *recovered* in the twenty-first century. This legacy would allow the elaboration of a *participatory* and *deeply liberating* constitution in political, social, cultural, and environmental terms. It was also said that 'maybe' thanks to the 1906 charter, which separated the church from the state, Ecuador had not experienced cruel civil wars motivated by religion. But the 12th constitution (that of 1906) since independence was not able to guarantee the permanence of the benefits earned nor the opportunities proposed, because its opponents were not completely defeated, while a faction of liberalism 'betrayed' the revolution (Acosta, 2008, pp. 4–6). Let us focus on these and other ideas expressed by the president of the convention:

> On this occasion, namely, 96 years since the assassination of general Eloy Alfaro, *his memory* develops renewed force. ... [I] believe that the opportunity opened to the Ecuadorian people by this Constituent Assembly should be transformed into an exercise of historical recovery of his transformative legacy. This would be the greatest and best tribute to the 'Old Fighter' and his work. *Also, this would be an atonement for an assassination left in absolute impunity.* And for this nothing better than to prepare the way for a participatory constitution, but above all, a constitution profoundly liberating in political, social, cultural, and environmental terms. The duty of rethinking and transforming the country, which is our duty now, was crystallised a little more than 100 years ago in the 1906 constitution during the 'Liberal Revolution'. (Alberto Acosta MA, ibid., pp. 3–4, emphasis added)[3]

For Acosta MA, the 1906 constitution condensed Alfaro's revolution. The new constitution (2008) ought to draw inspiration from the same

[3]'En estas ocasión a los 96 años del asesinato del general Eloy Alfaro, cobra renovada fuerza su memoria. [...] [C]reo que la oportunidad que se abre al pueblo ecuatoriano con nuestra Asamblea Constituyente, debe transformarse en un ejercicio de rescate histórico, de su herencia transformadora. Ese sería el mayor y mejor homenaje al "Viejo Luchador" y a su obra. Sería, además, un acto de desagravio a un asesinato que quedó en la más absoluta impunidad, y para ello, nada mejor que dar paso a una Constitución participativa, pero sobre todo, profundamente liberador en lo político, profundamente liberador en lo social, profundamente liberador en lo cultural, profundamente liberador en lo ambiental. [...] Es [sic] tarea de repensar y transformar el país, que es ahora nuestra tarea, se cristalizó hace poco más de 100 años, durante la "Revolución Liberal", con la Constitución de 1906.' (Acosta Alberto MA, 2008-01-28, pp. 3–4)

leader. More importantly, the president of the convention suggested that, in embracing Alfaro's 'transformative legacy', the Constituent Assembly could contribute to atone for his assassination. This required, amongst other elements, a 'participatory constitution', namely a process in which both the people and their representatives configure the new constitution. The enunciation 'his memory [that of Alfaro]' and the idea of a necessary national 'atonement' for Alfaro's assassination help us to locate the Other in this speech. Here, again, the Other is History, that is, as Lacan neatly puts it, *the unifying entity* that preserves Alfaro's memory and waits for the nation's redemption. Borrowing in part Žižek (1990) grammar, it could be argued that the 2008 convention (composed of little others) became the Other's tool for the redemption of Ecuadorians' *original sin*. While Roldós' speech highlights the imaginary dimension of identification (which, as shown, does not exclude symbolic identification), Acosta's words stress the symbolic component of identification, the latter composed of societal values and ideals. Take, for instance, this fragment: *The duty of rethinking and transforming the country, which is our duty now, was crystallised a little more than 100 years ago in the 1906 constitution during the 'Liberal Revolution'*. From a logical perspective in line with Hook (2018b) operationalization, it is the *liberal ideal* what makes the image of the liberal *Old Fighter* lovable and not vice versa.

The prevalence of symbolic over imaginary identification does not contradict my intuition, that is, that the history of frequent constitutional replacements—led by authoritarian leaders—speaks to a predominant process of *heroic identification* in Ecuador. On the contrary, the said prevalence has a direct link to my puzzle. Why do three different ideologies (conservatism, liberalism, and socialism) result in similar personalistic/imaginary instantiations (García Moreno, Alfaro, and Correa) in the constitutional politics of Ecuador? When discussing the psychic effect of colonialism in Chap. 1, I argued that violence in the public sphere—on account of racist laws and social codes—might have metastasized within the Ecuadorian family and thus society. Arguably, this might have resulted in a diminished paternal imago, whose flip side has been a process of national identification with authoritarian/despotic figures. What is important here is that this predominant type of identification with authoritarian leaders became part of the societal ego-ideals of postcolonial Ecuador. In this suggested light, seeking 'strong leaders'—whose power went beyond the limits of the constitution and the rights of their adversaries—became a societal value per se. The political culture in Ecuador, which embraces leaders who berate their adversaries and transgress the law (as suggested by historian Espinosa, 2010), appears to reproduce the colonial logic in extenso, namely the prevalence of force over speech in the public sphere (Sharoni, 2016).

Roldós' and Acosta's speeches led to a substantive rhetorical effect in this predominantly left-wing convention. At the end of the 28 January session (transcribed in 40 pages), which was fully dedicated to Alfaro's legacy, the 2007–2008 CA approved a resolution in tribute to Alfaro's home town (Montecristi). This resolution was unanimously supported by 118 MAs (out of a total of 130) present during the voting (NA, ibid., p. 39). It read as follows:

> The Plenary of the Constituent Assembly. Considering: ... That the hero and promoter of the liberal and radical revolution José Eloy Alfaro Delgado was born in this city on June 25, 1842 ... That Montecristi is currently home to the National Constituent Assembly, which sessions in the civic complex Alfaro's City; and, That part of the ashes of general Eloy Alfaro Delgado are in the mausoleum located within the civic complex Alfaro's City ... Exercising its powers ... approves the following Agreement: To declare the city of Montecristi and its areas of influence a Natural, Cultural and Historic Heritage of the Nation. (NA, ibid., pp. 32, 35–36)[4]

The above resolution can be said to entail an amendment to Ecuador's original social contract. When enquiring into the founding moment of the law, the notion of a pact is useful for the contractarian and psychoanalytic theories. The above Agreement on Alfaro's city fosters dialogue between said theories considering the Lacanian premise that symbolic identification takes precedence over imaginary identification. Unlike the other, as Lacan puts it, the Other can be understood as a symbolic pact among neurotic subjects. Albeit unknown to us, this pact unites us and speaks beyond the materiality of us, and this makes possible triangular and thus effective recognition. See, for instance, the unanimous resolution above: the

[4] 'El Pleno de la Asamblea Constituyente. Considerando: [...] Que. el 25 de junio de 1842 nació en esta ciudad el héroe y artífice de la revolución liberal radical José Eloy Alfaro Delgado ...; Que. Montecristi es actualmente sede de la Asamblea Nacional Constituyente, la cual actúa en el complejo cívico Ciudad Alfaro; y, Que. parte de las cenizas del general Eloy Alfaro Delgado se encuentran en el mausoleo que está situado dentro del complejo cívico Ciudad Alfaro ... En ejercicio de sus atribuciones y facultades ..., aprueba lo siguiente, Acuerdo: Declarar a la ciudad de Montecristi y sus áreas de influencia Patrimonio Natural, Cultural e Histórico de la Nación'. (NA, ibid., pp. 32, 35–6)

peoples' representatives agree, *before the eyes of History*, the resolution in question. This triangular recognition would not be possible in psychoses, for this pact is excluded (Lacan, 1991, pp. 36, 50–51, 53, 56).

The foregoing discussion on the social contract hints (once again) at the usefulness of Freud's myth as put forward in *Totem and Taboo* and later refined in *Moses and Monotheism*. Note that Acosta's and Roldós' speeches as well as the unanimous resolution have a mourning tone, which begs another question: how can the Ecuadorian people in the twenty-first century be 'implicated' in the 1912 magnicide of Alfaro?

From a societal perspective as presented by Cavalletto (2007), the 'cultural superego' denotes the societal ideals and prohibitions of a given community. This super-ego manifests in society in an ambivalent way resonant with early dynamics in subjects. This means that the ambivalence once felt towards the beloved father is displaced towards the hero(es), whose idealization and frequent tragedy unites society in a particular way:

> [T]*he impression left behind* by these heroes implicates this society in the hero's downfall, tying it to the hero not only through love but guilt. Bound thus to the hero … the community comes to identify … with this "impression left behind" … Through the narratives of its heroes, civilizations propagate the values that bespeak of a cultural conscience, of the ideals and prohibitions that inform society's ethical and religious beliefs, its art and its collective narratives of self-understanding. (Cavalletto, 2007, p. 38)

For psychoanalysis, society's ethical beliefs depend in part on a conflicting human condition. At the cultural level, the super-ego mandates universal love, which can be summarized in the maxim *you shall love your neighbor*. But this precept is unachievable and unreasonable, on account of the subject's natural propensity towards aggressiveness (Freud, 1930, p. 111 as cited in Billiet, 2023).[5] In the *Ethics of Psychoanalysis*, Lacan contributes to Freud's idea that individuals are inclined to cruelty as opposed to benevolence, for not only my neighbour but I too desire what is destructive. The mutual aggressivity against one another speaks to an evil that dwells within each person. Lacan's own words are worth citing in extenso:

[5] https://nlscongress2023.amp-nls.org/blogposts/lievebillieten (accessed on 03/10/2025).

> [E]very time that Freud stops short in horror at the consequences of the commandment to love one's neighbor, we see evoked the presence of that fundamental evil which dwells within this neighbor. *But if that is the case, then it also dwells within me. And what is more of a neighbor to me than this heart within which is that of my jouissance and which I don't dare go near?* For as soon as I go near it, as *Civilization and Its Discontents* makes clear, there rises up the unfathomable aggressivity from which I flee, that I turn against me. (Lacan, 1997, p. 186, my emphasis)

In a nutshell, the subject's contradictory *enjoyment* is transgressive of the promises of civilization, such as that that commands subjects to love their neighbour. In this light, further problematization of the parliamentary session that commemorated Alfaro is in order. Ecuador's ego-ideal in 2008 was informed by an idealization of certain reforms implemented by Alfaro (e.g., public education) as well as a thorny task, that is, the atonement for the killing of that same hero, a murder perpetrated by his own people, the convention's ancestors. What does the mourning of Alfaro tell us about the character of constitutional instability in Ecuador?

In *Moses and Monotheism*, Freud foregrounds that the conjecture put forth in *Totem and Taboo* is a 'condensation' of an incident (that of the killing of the father of the primal horde) that occurred countless times throughout millennia. Thus, it 'affected all the primordial men, hence all our ancestors' (Freud, 2015, pp. 123–125). The killing in question, now part of humanity's *archaic heredity*, had a clear consequence for future generations. The guilt for the original parricide, which passed from one generation to the next, has triggered the fantasy of redemption delivered by inverted Messiahs. Freud analyses two cases: Moses and Christ, the Sons of God/Father.

Under certain circumstances, some psychosocial phenomena in everyday life stem, at least in part, from the *return of the repressed*. That is, the '[p]rocess whereby what has been repressed—though never abolished by repression—tends to reappear, and succeeds in doing so in a distorted fashion ' (Laplanche & Pontalis, 1973, p. 398). In this light, let us reinterpret Freud's mythological *archaic heredity* in light of Lacan's idea that there is a wicked substance (*enjoyment*) that dwells within subjects. As mentioned, as soon as they go near their *enjoyment*, this triggers an aggressivity from which they try to flee. The mourning characteristic of the session dedicated to the memory of Alfaro hinted, I would like to suggest, at a twofold process. On the one hand, there was overall jubilation. On the other, there was societal guilt for the cruel assassination—by his own people—of Ecuador's national hero, a tragedy resonant with that of the father of the primal horde, Moses, Christ, and, arguably, subsequent substitutive figures. The coexistence of joy and guilt in Ecuador's convention speaks to a psychosocial substance (*enjoyment*) underpinning the social fabric of communities. *A propos*, as Hook (2018b) puts it, the lesson we can learn from *Totem and Taboo* is that communities are also bound by a sense of a shared loss and guilt, which leads me to a necessary detour. Hook analyses the case of post-apartheid South Africa during the 2010 World Cup. In thinking about the psychoanalytic meaning of the national pride and sense of 'inter-racial' unity that characterized the mood of South Africans during this event, it is worth asking: was the ego-ideal of inter-racial unity masking (*repressing*)—in part at least—the traumatic division created by the apartheid regime? 'What comes into view then is the possibility of an alliance of repressed losses which, paradoxically, comes to the fore precisely in shared moments of jubilant national togetherness' (pp. 122–123). The Ecuadorian and South African cases seem to validate a Lacanian interpretation of Freud's myth when thinking about processes of identification in postcolonial societies. Admittedly, this myth, which problematizes the complexity and nuances of this troubling bodily substance called *jouissance* (a non-rational and effective glue sustaining communities), does not create a distinction between colonial and non-colonial communities. We, however, can problematize this myth from a nuanced and context-dependent approach, such as the one provided here.

In *Moses and Monotheism*, we also find the 'return' of a failed quest for the *lost object* (a constant in the life of neurotic subjects) through the fantasy of a fullness-to-come, the latter embodied in the image of a promised land, a clear roundabout some would argue.[6] Needless to say, the mother figure is a key element in the psychosocial dynamic analysed so far. For instance, at the end of the 28 January session on Alfaro's legacy the convention's president told the secretary 'that it would be convenient to distribute ... a facsimile of the 1906 constitution which I want everyone to keep as a memory of this historic day' (Acosta MA, p. 31). At first sight a trifle, this symbolic gesture speaks in part to Martin's (2019) thesis, which

[6] '[The step taken by Freud at the level of the pleasure principle is to show us that there is no Sovereign Good—that the Sovereign Good, which is das Ding, which is the mother, is also the object of incest, is a forbidden good, and that there is no other good. Such is the foundation of the moral law as turned on its head by Freud'. (Lacan, 1991, p. 70)

suggests that '[t]he affective dimensions of speech ... are rooted in a compulsion in subjectivity to recover the primordial lost object' (2019, p. 21). Freud's key discovery, according to Lacan (2000), consisted in realizing that the object we find is always different from what we had *desired*; thus, our search never stops. Despite the fact that the 1906 constitution was understood to be 'precious' and in theory 'ready' for its re-establishment (updates/amendments would have been required), a new charter was again longed for in 2007–2008. The yearning for a new constitution appears to be an important political instantiation (among a myriad of other possibilities) of the failed quest for the *lost object* in Ecuadorian politics. The notion of the *lost object* also relates to another aspect beyond messianic leadership, namely the nation *qua* the first Other under the threat of 'others', those 'racially different'. This issue is linked to the fragmented character—and maybe also volatile nature—of Ecuador's *social contract*. I address this in the next section.

As for the fantasy of the father figure embodied in the Messiah, this can be grasped in view of Ecuador's CAs. While García Moreno 'fulfilled' this fantasy in 1869, Alfaro served this purpose in 2007–2008. Alfaro, the bearer of the promised land consecrated in the 1906 constitution, is the *great man* whose assassination is atoned by the 2007–2008 CA. At first sight, the resonance between the religious characters of Moses or Christ and Alfaro seems unfit, for his liberal revolution was antagonistic to the Catholic Church. After all, Freud's (1939) thesis creates a link between *Totem and Taboo* and the emergence of monotheism in view of his case study, that of the 'Egyptian' Moses. But what appears to be a weakness underpinning my suggestion might be a strength. It is the understanding of a Messiah as both the redeemer of the *original sin* (the early desire to eliminate one of the parents) and the bringer of the promised land that seems to be productive in shedding light on Ecuador's frequent constitutional replacements prompted by idealized and strong father figures or 'caudillos'. In the nineteenth century, for instance, several CAs in Ecuador 'served to legitimise a putsch' (Espinosa, 2010, p. 558). The legitimization of putsches via CAs, which ultimately legitimized new 'lawgivers', suggests that Ecuador's constitutional politics has resembled a religious phenomenon, at least in the nineteenth century. By this I mean the compulsive practice in which there is one 'great' caudillo (democratic or not) whose perceived omnipotence—with which Ecuadorians have identified—blends with that of the new charter that promises a new land. I come back to this.

The Demand for a Non-racist and Pluri-National State

The demand for a pluri-national state led by the indigenous movement in Ecuador since the 1990s was a key topic discussed by the 2007–2008 CA. The 2008 constitutional recognition of this demand was a watershed in the constitutional politics of postcolonial Ecuador, a country where informal racism survives.

More than a century passed before the 1869 erasure of the indigenous' identity was amended. Article 1 of the 1998 charter recognized the 'pluri-cultural and multi-ethnic' nature of the state. This charter recognized certain collective rights that the indigenous and Afro-Ecuadorians were entitled to. Both points were acknowledged by the 2008 majority report during the first debate on the *Character and Constitutive Elements of the State*. In this session Carlos Pilamunga MA highlighted that, thanks to the 1990 indigenous' uprising, collective rights were enshrined in the 1998 constitution (Pilamunga, 2007, pp. 6–7, 35).

On 27 December 2007, the assembly discussed the work plan of the subcommittee on *Territorial Code and Competency Allocation*. Grefa MA began his speech by highlighting a crucial and recent event, namely the United Nations' official recognition (that of 13 September 2007) of the rights of the indigenous peoples. The 1998 constitution had already incorporated some of the indigenous' demands. '[I]n light of the current constitution ... the territorial divisions of both the indigenous and Afro-Ecuadorians are considered, but the colleagues of the table [subcommittee] have not contemplated them within the levels of the state' (Grefa MA, ibid., p. 10).[7] He continued that these divisions needed to be further discussed in the 2007–2008 CA, a point supported by Mónica Chuji, another indigenous MA (ibid., pp. 10, 16).

Grefa's intervention drew on both the UN's 2007 resolution on the rights of the indigenous peoples and the 1998 constitution to set the basis for his argument. He appealed to a purportedly logical connection between the premise and the conclusion (*logos*): since the international and national doctrines recognized the indigenous rights and their territorial divisions, the 2007–2008 convention could not work in detriment to this progression of rights. His rhetorical strategy/petition obtained non-indigenous support in the CA:

[7] 'Así mismo, en la Constitución actual, nosotros contamos, están consideradas las circunscripciones territoriales indígenas y afroecuatorianas ..., pero los compañeros de la Mesa no lo han considerado dentro de los niveles de gobierno'.

> Amongst others, the constitutional recognition [1998] of their territorial divisions is an achievement of both the Indigenous Movement and Afro-Ecuadorians. Ten years have passed, and this right has not been legislated for its materialization. This is a problem attributable to the legislature. I deem it important to support the petition made by the workmate César Grefa, so these territorial divisions are considered in Subcommittee four … as this request constitutes their accomplished right. (Burbano, 2007, p. 17)[8]

The constitutional recognition in question was an achievement of CONAIE's and Pachakutik's historical struggle. Both organizations earned their rightful place in the 1998 and 2007–2008 CAs. The demand for a pluri-national state was put forward in the 2007–2008 CA by Pachakutik. For the indigenous movement, this demand asked for the constitutional recognition of crucial aspects. As an MA representing Pachakutik put it, the CA had to 'recognize all its [Ecuadorian] sons'. Accepting the pluri-national nature of the Ecuadorian state implied the recognition of the nationalities' various forms of traditions, as well as their governing institutions in their local territories. However, this demand did not imply the secession of all the 'peoples' and 'nationalities' (Afro-Ecuadorians are mentioned) from Ecuador, which was to remain a unitary though diverse state. Considering its importance, the pluri-national character of Ecuador ought to be enshrined in Article 1 of the constitution (Sarango, 2008, pp. 21–24). Supportive of this demand, Rosana Alvarado MA stated that the panic of pluri-nationalism had created the spectres of separatism and those of two states within the same territory, a distortion of the indigenous' request (ibid., p. 42).

Sarango MA (Pachakutik) and Alvarado MA (Alianza País) were clear: the demand for a pluri-national state did not entail separatism nor the creation of another state within the existing one. Nonetheless, as an indigenous deputy put it, the presence of indigenous parliamentarians in this CA caused fear. The following long quote addresses this dread, while

[8] 'En la Constitución vigente, uno de los logros que consiguió de parte del Movimiento Indígena y de los pueblos afroecuatorianos, fue precisamente conseguir la vigencia de las circunscripciones territoriales, que durante estos diez años no se haya podido legislar, para que efectivamente este derecho pueda ser utilizado, ha sido un problema de la Legislatura. Pero considero importante en virtud de la solicitud del compañero César Grefa, apoyarla y que estas circunscripciones territoriales sean consideradas en la Mesa número cuatro …, ya que es un derecho alcanzado'.

highlighting the ethnic and organizational diversity of Ecuador, a country invaded by the Incan and Spanish empires in modern times.

> It is necessary to remember all this historic process. *In the 19 previous constitutions no one spoke about what is being spoken today. For many, some words and terms are causing fear, maybe because they think that we, the Ecuadorians and peoples who lived before the colony and before the republic, appear now and speak with our own voice.* ... We also say that today the peoples appear and recognize their identity, their self-esteem. The Afro-Ecuadorian peoples and the Montubios peoples are proudly demanding to be recognized by the constitution. We too refer to the indigenous peoples and nationalities in Ecuador. Here we are: 22 peoples. For example, Quechuas, but Guaranga Quechua, myself, Quechua for the Amazon, Cayambis or Otavaleños Quechuas. *We all speak Quechua in the Andean region. Although different peoples, having this language [Quechua] allow us to say that we are also a nationality of ancestral roots, of original peoples. Not a nationality to establish another State within the Ecuadorian Republic* ... [T]he Montubio people cannot say that it is a nationality of ancestral roots because it does not have its own language; it speaks Spanish ... *We also say that both the Montubio and the Indigenous peoples have our own culture and organizational forms.* (Carlos Pilamunga, 2007, pp. 96–97, emphasis added)[9]

To begin with, I would like to note Ecuador's ethnic composition in view of its various 'nationalities'. The reference to the Cayambis people and the Quechua language evidences the cultural diversity of a country invaded by the Incan empire. The Spanish invasion complexified the

[9] 'Es necesario recordar todo este proceso histórico, las diecinueve Constituciones anteriores donde no se habla ... lo que hoy se está hablando algunas palabras, algunos términos, para muchos, causando temor, miedo porque, a lo mejor, piensan que los ecuatorianos y los pueblos que vivíamos antes de la Colonia y antes de la República, hoy aparece y habla con su propia voz. [...] Decimos también que hoy en la actualidad, aparecen también ya los pueblos reconociendo su identidad, su autoestima, ahí están los pueblos afroecuatorianos ..., ahí están los pueblos montubios que, con orgullo, están reclamando que se escriba en la nueva Constitución y consten. Hablamos también de los pueblos y nacionalidades indígenas en el Ecuador. Veintidós pueblos aquí estamos, por ejemplo, kichwas, pero kichwa guaranga, el que habla, kichwa de la Amazonía, kichwa de los cayambis o kichwa de los otavaleños, todos hablamos el kichwa en la región Andina y, por tener la lengua, aunque somos diferentes pueblos, decimos que también somos nacionalidad, de raíces ancestrales, de pueblos originarios. No nacionalidad para fundar dentro de la República del Ecuador otro Estado ... [E]l pueblo montubio no puede decir que es nacionalidad de raíces ancestrales, porque no tiene su propio idioma, habla el español ... Decimos también, que tanto el pueblo montubio o el pueblo indígena tenemos cultura, tenemos nuestras formas organizativas propias'.

ethnic composition of Ecuador. Moreover, the distinction between a people and a nationality is based on whether a (non-)European language is spoken. The case of Montubios (a people but not a nationality because they speak Spanish) illustrates this. Nonetheless, both Montubios and indigenous peoples have various 'organizational forms'. According to Pilamunga MA, *nationalities* can be defined as those 'human groups whose existence is millenary and, as such, before the Spanish conquest'. These nationalities have their own languages, cultures, and laws (Pilamunga, 2007, p. 36).

The above speech also hints at the exclusionary nature of Ecuador's *Social Contract* throughout its history. Moreover, this discourse speaks to the 2007–2008 watershed. Unlike the case of the 19 previous constitutions, in 2007–2008 the indigenous peoples were an important part of the *constituent power*. But this inclusion did not come without a price: *For many, some words and terms are causing fear, maybe because they think that we, the Ecuadorians and peoples who lived before the colony and before the republic, appear now and speak with our own voice.* Why would the presence of indigenous MAs cause fear amongst certain non-indigenous people?

I venture one possible answer to this question. The demand for a pluri-national state was seeking to alter a 'civilized' notion of the nation instated after independence and influenced by the *Social Contract*. This political philosophy has accompanied Ecuador throughout its constitutional history, and it is predicated on the subordination of all minorities to the *general will*. The indigenous' demand for a pluri-national pact/state aimed at recognizing cultural/ethnic minorities at the constitutional level. This, of course, questioned Rousseau's monolithic social contract.

Another interpretation is in order: *for many, some words and terms are causing fear, maybe because they think that we, the Ecuadorians and peoples who lived before the colony and before the republic, appear now and speak with our own voice.* If this fear was prompted in part by racism, we might find it helpful to discuss how the logic of *jouissance* clarifies this supposition. Following Žižek's (1990) early reasoning, we can argue that subjects experience this bodily 'substance' called enjoyment in terms of a theft, which speaks to the retroactive effect of the imposition of the Name-of-the-Father. In other words, although the incestuous desire and ambivalent feeling related to this early 'theft' were *repressed*, they can *return* by means of a *projection* onto others. This account of racism, valid in its own right, begs further problematization. As Hook (2018a, pp. 255–256, 259–261) argues, to properly address *enjoyment* as an explanatory tool for racism, it needs to be understood as connected to the law, the ego-ideal, the super-ego, and *fantasy*, amongst other categories. I suggest that the non-indigenous 'fear' denounced by Pilamunga MA relates in part to the dread of those ethnically different. And this can be understood as a fear of losing what is most precious for a particular community, for instance, the national unity condensed in the *general will* thesis. Ecuador's ego-ideal (i.e., its national unity) speaks to the *libidinal treasure* (i.e., the fantasy of the *nation-state*) supposedly at risk in view of the cultural others, that is, those who favour the *pluri-national state*. Thus, the 'nation' needs to be maintained at all costs to preclude the, as it were, *extinction of being* of 'us'. Following this rationale further, it can be said that keeping the nation-state (a particular configuration of the law since independence) in place has provided a 'libidinal reward' to those safeguarding a particular ordering of the Ecuadorian republic. As mentioned above, this reward derives from the commands of a censor, that of the super-ego. The relation between the super-ego and *jouissance* may clarify an element of racism that is often omitted, that is, that '[r]acism also pivots on a series of ideological values which, crucially, involve a potent "moral" dimension' (Hook, 2018a, p. 261). In this line of thought, the apparently racist critique of the pluri-national thesis could be 'justified' by the moral precept of national unity.

As for the non-indigenous support of the indigenous demand, which was a majoritarian support during the 2007–2008 CA, this can be understood, at least in part, as the need for national atonement. I suggest this in the context of Ecuador's national remorse for the systematic mistreatment of the indigenous peoples since colonial times. In fact, in the previous subsection we saw how the national mourning of Alfaro was linked to his sensibility towards the indigenous question. Here we can observe how the psychic dimension, in general, and its guilty component, in particular, link the question of messianic leadership to that of postcolonialism. The national regret for the inhumane mistreatment of the indigenous peoples in Ecuador, whose cause was hoisted by Alfaro, could have merged with the remorse for Alfaro's killing. Be that as it may, many non-indigenous MAs welcomed the proposal of a pluri-national state. From an enthusiastic point of view, it can be argued that racism in Ecuador, a product of colonialism, can begin its process of extinction through cultural exchanges prompted by Article 1 of the 2008 constitution. As the president of the 2007–2008 CA put it,

> Through the recognition of the pluri-nationality we re-engage in a State that, while being one in its sovereignty and territoriality, recognizes and incorporates the distinct original and ancestral nations that are part of Ecuador. We reaffirm, then, that this coexistence, without colonial power relations, supposes a permanent process of interculturality. (Alberto Acosta MA, 2008, p. 20)[10]

Appealing to a *forensic* strategy, Acosta highlighted the *fairness* of the CA's decision in recognizing the pluri-national nature of the Ecuadorian state. He also resorted to a *deliberative* strategy; he exhorted his fellow citizens to embrace the challenge of interculturality by means of which the former nation-state could be decolonized. This decolonization relates in part to the 2008 constitutional recognition of the indigenous' forms of organization. The first collective right granted by the 1998 constitution to the indigenous peoples read: the *indigenous peoples* have the right 'To maintain, develop, and strengthen their identity and traditions at the spiritual, cultural, linguistic, social, political and economic level' (Article 84.1). The first collective right bestowed on the indigenous peoples by the 2008 constitution provided a key nuance to this right: 'To maintain, develop, and freely strengthen their identity, sense of belonging, ancestral traditions, *and forms of social organization*' (Article 57.1, emphasis added).

As mentioned, at some points the indigenous question in 2007–2008 was linked to Alfaro's leadership. As Roldós, 2008) foregrounded above, Alfaro was sympathetic to the demands of the native population: *[Y]ou [Alfaro] made yours the cause of the indigenous peoples and nationalities in Ecuador … The indigenous have continued with their centenarian fight and they too accompany us today in politics and in this Assembly.* The speaker drew on the authority of Alfaro, that is, an appeal to ethos. By highlighting his legacy in Ecuador's historic struggle for ethnic equality, Roldós' *rhetorical strategy* linked Alfaro's leadership to the indigenous' demand in 2007–2008. Alvarado's, Roldós', and Acosta's discursive strategies (all of them inspired by *Alfarism*) contributed to guaranteeing enough voting support to consecrate the pluri-national nature of Ecuador in the 2008 constitution. Let us recall that Pachakutik, the promoter of the

[10] 'A través del reconocimiento de la plurinacionalidad nos reencontramos en un Estado, que siendo único en su soberanía y territorialidad, reconoce e incorpora las distintas naciones originarias y ancestrales que forman parte del Ecuador. Reafirmamos, entonces, que esa convivencia, sin relaciones coloniales de poder, supone un permanente proceso de interculturalidad'.

indigenous' demand under discussion, only obtained 4 parliamentary seats out of a total of 130.

I would like to suggest that the atonement for the historical mistreatment of the indigenous peoples influenced, at least in part, the massive non-indigenous support for the demand for a pluri-national state in Ecuador's latest CA. This conjectural argument resonates—and is indebted—with Muldoon's (2017) paper: *A Reconciliation Most Desirable: Shame, Narcissism, Justice and Apology*. Here he draws on psychoanalysis to assess how narcissism can be said to influence the process of reconciliation in postcolonial contexts. The *Federal Parliamentary Apology to the 'Stolen Generations'* in Australia sought to atone for the twentieth-century policy of forced removal of children of mixed descent from their aboriginal parents, a policy implemented for the 'sake' of these Australian infants. This apology, per se valid from a political philosophy perspective, sheds light on the power of narcissism in reconciliatory politics. Freud's (1914) paper on *Narcissism* puts forward the idea that the ego-ideal (the nation is one of its social byproducts) emerges as the substitutive repository of our early feeling of perfection. Drawing on this maxim, Muldoon argues that what motivated the national apology in Australia stemmed, in part, from a necessity to repair the self-image of perfection. In other words, the apology in Australia speaks to the ego's narcissistic desire to recuperate its ego-ideal at the individual and social/national levels (Muldoon, pp. 214, 216, 217, 220, 222–223).

Muldoon's (2017) contribution adds an interesting layer to the analysis of the motivations underpinning the non-indigenous support of the indigenous demand for a pluri-national state. The 2008 charter renounced to a previous understanding of the *Social Contract* predicated on the monolithic 'general will'. From 2008, the Ecuadorian contract is no longer a homogeneous pact with uniform rules. As one of the MAs put it,

> The pluri-national state is another form of social contract with the various peoples of our country. It is another form of national solidarity. The declaration of the pluri-national state constitutes a recognition of the nationalities that exist in our country, and who have their own cultural model, their own social institutions, their own legal systems. (Martínez, 2008, p. 84)[11]

[11] 'El Estado plurinacional es otra forma de contrato social con los pueblos diversos de nuestro país, es otra forma de solidaridad nacional. La declaratoria del Estado plurinacional, es un reconocimiento a las nacionalidades que existen en nuestro país y que tienen su propio modelo cultural, sus propias instituciones sociales, sus propios sistemas legales'.

This speech, voiced in twenty-first century Ecuador, would have been unthinkable in the nineteenth and part of the twentieth centuries. Two historic taxes are illustrative of this. The persistence of the 'Indian' tax until the 1850s revealed the systematic mistreatment of the indigenous population after the Republic was founded. The anachronistic survival of the tithe until 1889 also showed the mistreatment in question, the latter orchestrated by the state, the Church, and the landlords in the highlands. A discourse analysis of the reform that led to the abolition of the tithe highlighted how the *Progressive* party favoured the elimination of this colonial tribute due to the human suffering caused by it (Espindola, 2016). The history of Ecuador's official attempt to compensate for the historic and racist exploitation of the indigenous peoples was not an invention of the 2008 constituent assembly. Nonetheless, this CA recognized something that was ignored since independence. That is, the indeed plurinational character of the Ecuadorian state, Ecuador's new though conflicting national ego-ideal.

Back to the Question of Messianic Leadership: The 2008 Debate on Presidential Re-elections and the 2015 Amendment that Abolished Presidential Term Limits

This section begins by providing an overview of President Correa's influence on the 2007–2008 CA. Of note here is the internal quarrel that at some point emerged between comrades President Correa and Acosta MA, the president of this CA. Correa's influence on Ecuador's 2007–2008 convention serves as an introduction to the subsequent sections: the 2008 debate on presidential re-elections, and the 2015 reform that abolished presidential term limits in Ecuador, in the hope of Correa's third presidential mandate.

On 24 June the CA accepted the resignation of its president, Alberto Acosta MA. Acosta's early retirement sent a clear message to the convention: President Correa had exerted an influential power on the last stage of the CA. As stated, Acosta was the most voted for candidate for the 2007–2008 CA. Considering his democratic legitimacy, as well as his 'human quality and professional capacity', the CA had appointed him as its president on 29 November 2007 (2008, p. 27). Despite his legitimacy, Acosta's leadership turned out to be undesirable for some of his comrades. His resignation speaks for itself:

> This disposition and personal position, which does not sacrifice the debate over the urgency of the deadline, is not shared ... by the majority of the leadership of Acuerdo País, movement to which I belong and to which I reaffirm my registration. In withdrawing their support de facto, from there, from the political bureau to which I belong, *they asked me to give way to another leadership that speeds up the approval of the texts in order to comply with the due date, July 26.* (Acosta MA, ibid., pp. 24–25, emphasis added)[12]

Acosta's disagreement with the political bureau of Alianza País should be read in dialogue with President Correa's opinion:

> I would like to begin by quoting ... President Correa's assertion yesterday ... In an unequivocal reference to both the Constituent Assembly and Alberto Acosta, he [Correa] states: 'the first step for achieving change is to put aside false democracies; *they want us to believe that everyone can debate interminably*; there is an attempt to enshrine in the constitution the agendas of those party groups that lost the elections.' And here comes what is the most critical of President Correa's statement: 'if that is democracy, I am not a democrat'. ... I reject that the decisions come from outside the Assembly. I reject the rudeness against both the Assembly and Alberto Acosta. (León Roldós MA and Correa, as cited by Roldós, 2008, pp. 23–24, emphasis added)[13]

Roldós' (RED) criticism of Correa's influence on the *constituent power* was further supported by Vicente Taiano MA (PRIAN), who argued that Correa 'was giving instructions to the Constituent Assembly' (ibid., pp. 24–25). Moreover, and on behalf of *Unidad Plurinacional Pachakutik*, Luis Guamangate showed his support to Acosta. Guamangate expressed

[12] 'Esta disposición y posición personal, de no sacrificar el debate por la premura del plazo, no es compartida ... por la mayoría de la cúpula de Acuerdo País, movimiento al cual pertenezco y al que reafirmo mi adscripción. Desde allí, desde el buró político al que pertenezco, al retirarme de facto su apoyo, me solicitaron dar paso a otra dirección que apresure la aprobación de los textos para cumplir con la fecha tope del veintiséis de julio'.

[13] 'Quiero iniciar mi intervención citando ... la intervención del Presidente Correa, el día de ayer... Refiriéndose en forma imposible de equivocarse, a la Asamblea Constituyente y a Alberto Acosta, señala, "el primer paso para lograr el cambio es dejar a un lado las falsas democracias, nos quieren hacer creer que todo el mundo puede debatir interminablemente, se intenta introducir en la Constitución las agendas de los grupos partidistas que perdieron las elecciones," y aquí viene lo más grave de la intervención del Presidente Correa, "si eso es democracia, yo no soy demócrata." [...] Las decisiones vienen de afuera acá a la Asamblea, yo rechazo aquello, rechazo las groserías contra la Asamblea y contra Alberto Acosta'.

his concern for how the dispute between Acuerdo País' leadership and Acosta was detrimental to democracy (Acosta, 2008, pp. 28–29). But there were those who disagreed with the idea that President Correa was exerting an illegitimate influence on the Convention. As Jorge Escala MA (MPD) put it,

> We do not share the opinion of the hacks and those loudspeakers of the oligarchy who say that Correa has taken over the Constituent Assembly, and that this Assembly is dependent on the executive power. (Escala, 2008, p. 26)[14]

The resignation of comrade Acosta to the presidency of the CA illustrates the significant influence that President Correa exerted on the 2007–2008 assembly. As for the idealization of Correa, on whom his followers' ego-ideal was placed (while identifying with one another in their ego), it further speaks to a key issue discussed here: the role played by the 'lawgiver' in Ecuador's CAs. However, as I shall argue below, a closer look at the idealization of Correa (as much as that of García Moreno and Alfaro) appears to derive, in great part, from the logic of the ideal-ego. This identification/idealization will become clearer when analysing the hope of Correa's third presidential mandate. But to better understand this hope, linked to the reform that abolished presidential term limits in Ecuador in 2015, first we need to examine the 2008 official discourse on the presidential re-election allowance. Since the 1998 constitution prohibited presidential re-elections tout court, Alianza País' 2008 support of this allowance ('for one time only') showed, according to some, its ambition for power.

The Citizens' Revolution's Unexpected Shift from a Liberal to a Non-liberal Stance on Presidential re-Elections

This section addresses the relation between leadership and constitutional volatility in view of Alianza País' 2008 and 2014–2015 stances on presidential re-elections. I proceed as follows. Firstly, I frame the rhetorical strategies underpinning the discussion on the presidential re-election

[14] 'No compartimos la opinión de los plumíferos y de aquellos parlantes de la oligarquía que dicen que Correa, se ha tomado la Asamblea Constituyente, y que esta Asamblea es dependiente del poder Ejecutivo'.

allowance. This concession, which permitted the re-election 'for one time only', was proposed by Alianza País and was later enshrined in the 2008 charter. Secondly, I analyse Alianza País' unexpected support of unlimited presidential re-elections, which led to the 2015 constitutional amendment that abolished presidential term limits, hence contradicting Alianza País' previous stance on re-elections. Alianza País' shift from its liberal stance on re-elections to the thesis on the possible indispensability of a particular leader (2015) further accounts for the unstable/messianic character of Ecuador's constitutional regime.

The 2008 Ecuadorian Debate on Presidential re-Elections

As mentioned earlier, the gridlocks between the executive and legislative branches can explain, in part, the frequent constitutional reforms in presidential Latin America. Amongst other topics, this 'endemic tension' between these branches of the state was discussed by Ecuador's latest CA on 8 and 13 May 2008. In these sessions, the MAs addressed this tension amidst a broader debate on the proposed characteristics, structure, and rules for the executive branch.

Betty Amores MA (Alianza País) began her intervention by highlighting the 'known' conflict between the executive and legislative branches in Ecuador. She did not criticize the presidential system for its purported inherent instability compared to parliamentary democracies. Instead, she noted that the conflict in question had a different cause, namely, 'the increasing looting of the powers and institutional competencies [pertaining to these branches of the state] by groups that represent and have represented private interests' (Amores, 2008, p. 49). On a different front, the increasingly 'chronic' and widespread discrediting of institutions has led, during the last decade and a half, to a 'spiral of procedures or "anti-institutional putsches"'. Purportedly, these procedures sought to put an end to obstacles and emergencies; however, they further languished the democratic edifice. In this context, the majority report comprised the proposed constitutional changes for the executive branch, so the Ecuadorian democracy could rebound its legitimacy and thus work in support of national development (ibid., pp. 49–50). The presidential re-election allowance was one of the proposed reforms. In 2008, the official discourse drew on the lessons of an unstable political history (an appeal to ethos and the premise of an argument) to propose the presidential re-election allowance as part of the solution (logos).

The majority report elaborated by Subcommittee 3—in charge of the structure and institutions of the state—justified the presidential re-election concession as follows: 'On presidential re-elections *for one time only*. The re-election finds its basis on the necessity to strengthen and broaden democracy by bestowing the people with the power to recognise and ratify their trust on those who govern and deserve it' (ibid., p. 32, own translation, emphasis added). Here we see how the appeal to the people as the agent capable of strengthening democracy bestowed legitimacy (ethos) to the official claim in favour of presidential re-elections. Moreover, this report noted that, while other democratic authorities could be re-elected, the president of the republic could not, which was unacceptable because the source of legitimacy was the same: the people's will via their vote (ibid).

According to the opposition, which had slightly different views on re-elections, the presidential re-election concession '[was] being forged for the current President of the republic [Rafael Correa] ... the constitution is being made for the current government' (Leonardo Viteri MA/PSC, ibid., p. 55). In different ways, this assertion was insinuated by Pablo Paredes MA/MCIFY (ibid., p. 111) and further highlighted by Vicente Taiano MA (PRIAN) a few days later (Taiano, 2007, p. 54).

Since the 1998 constitution did not allow presidential re-elections, the opposition regarded the 2008 proposal for this concession as a clear indication of Alianza País' ambition for power. The opposition denounced Alianza País' supposed interest in the eventual re-election of its leader: Rafael Correa. This added an emotional tone (pathos) to its rhetorical strategy and thus sparked the 'us–them' rivalry typical of politics. And this points us in the direction of Freud's *Narcissism of Minor Differences* discussed above, namely the psychic mechanism whereby the in-group narcissism and out-group aggression manifest. By way of a reminder, for Freud the social is always under the threat of the *death instinct*. Thus, *Eros* counterbalances this destructive tendency through (amongst others) the process of identification. But this fellowship identification embellishes the traits of the group to which the narcissistic subject belongs; these exaggerated traits become the group's collective ideal.

> By means of these idealized common traits, the members of the group are then enabled to love their fellow members narcissistically and, at the same time, to deflect their own innate aggressivity outward toward others who do not share these common traits, a double-edged social dynamic that Freud titles "the narcissism of minor differences". (Cavalletto, 2007, p. 37)

In the context of this in-group–out-group dynamic in Ecuador's latest CA, Virgilio Hernández MA (Alianza País) rejected the opposition's contention according to which Correa was exerting influence on the CA. Relying on the fact that the CA was composed of 130 MAs, Hernández drew on a puzzle solution rhetorical strategy, a technique in which the speaker presents the problem as well as the solution:

> On several occasions it has been ironically said that there is here the Member of the Assembly number 131 [Rafael Correa], and that this MA is the one who makes the decisions. I want to say it in a very clear way. There is a President of the Republic who is part of a political project, and this political project has the right to decide and deliberate in order to propose serious institutions for the country. (Hernández, 2008, p. 59)[15]

If approved, Alianza País' proposal (i.e., the authorities' possibility to be re-elected for one time only) was going to change the political dynamic at the subnational level. As Eduardo Zambrano MA (Alianza País) reminded the plenary, according to the 1998 constitution the president of the republic could not be re-elected, while other authorities (e.g., mayors) were allowed to run for office indefinitely (Zambrano, 2008, p. 66). In short, the 'spirit' of the official proposal aimed at unifying the re-election allowance for one time only for all the democratic authorities at both the national and subnational levels (Félix Alcívar MA/Alianza País, ibid., p. 76). Implicitly, the official discourse appealed to logos, that is, to a 'logical tie' between the premise and the conclusion: if democratic authorities are elected by the people, the re-election institution ought to be uniform in all cases. The following speech, which incorporated the means to tackle the problem of the ambition of power, illustrated the Citizens' Revolution's reasoning in 2008:

> I totally agree with the concern of having a President of the Republic who perpetuates in power. That is why we say that he/she can be re-elected one time only. But we also have the concern of having subnational authorities who have in fact converted their municipalities into small principalities. So,

[15] 'Aquí varias veces se ha ironizado en el sentido de que aquí hay un Asambleísta ciento treinta y uno y que ese Asambleísta es el que toma las decisiones. Yo quiero decirlo en forma muy clara, aquí hay un Presidente de la República, que es parte de un proyecto político y ese proyecto político tiene el derecho de poder decidir y de poder deliberar, para proponer instituciones serias al país'.

> I believe that we are working on … the same rules for all elected authorities. (Amanda Arboleda MA/Alianza País, ibid., pp. 82–83)[16]

The Citizens' Revolution's 2008 proposal on re-elections, whose spirit was neatly expressed by the above speech, was enshrined in the 2008 charter. From that year until 2015, Article 114 of the 2008 constitution stipulated the re-election allowance—consecutive or not—for one time only for all elected authorities. Article 144 extended this stipulation to the president of the republic, while adding other elements pertaining to the head of the executive. But in 2015 these articles (amongst others) were amended by the same revolution that supported them in 2008, a shift worthy of analysis.

The 2015 Abolition of Presidential Term Limits

The spirit underpinning the *Citizens' Revolution* was undermined on 24 May 2014. During the State of the Nation speech, President Correa petitioned the legislative branch to abolish presidential term limits. Correa foregrounded that this request emanated from his movement, and it entailed a dilemma for him (Alianza País was hoping for Correa's third presidential mandate—discussed below). The official discourse justified the abolitionist reform on account of the 'gestation' of the 'Conservative Restoration' in Ecuador and Latin America, that is, the electoral victory of right-wing candidates supported by non-democratically elected actors (e.g., the media) in a purportedly invalid way. Some might argue that this justification stemmed from paranoid reasoning, a common phenomenon in politics. In fact, it has been suggested that '[p]aranoia is a "style" that … can be adopted by people pursuing a wide range of political goals, but it does not mean that they as individuals have paranoid personalities' (Hofstadter, as cited in Richards, 2018, p. 21). Whether or not paranoid, President Correa's request was approved by the legislature, as a result of which Article 144 of the constitution was amended, amongst other amendments to the charter.

[16] 'Estoy totalmente de acuerdo con la preocupación de que haya un Presidente de la República que se perennice en el poder, por eso hablamos de que solo sea reelegido por una sola vez. Pero nosotros también tenemos la preocupación de que haya autoridades seccionales, que realmente han convertido sus municipios en pequeños principados. Entonces, yo creo que estamos trabajando sobre principios de las mismas reglas, para todos los funcionarios de elección popular'.

How can we account for Alianza País' sudden decision to abolish presidential term limits, considering it had ratified these limits as early as 2008? Correa's stable presidency (2007–2017), the longest uninterrupted presidency in Ecuador since independence, can be partly understood as a result of his renowned charisma, which led his movement to support the abolition of presidential term limits. Charisma derives from the Greek *charismoi*, which means to please and free gift, the latter with a theological meaning (Arlotti, 2003, p. 64, own translation). Weber defines charisma as the 'extraordinary quality ... of a personality in virtue of which he/she is regarded as the possessor of supernatural strength' (1922/2005, p. 193, own translation). According to Breslauer (2019, p. 128), Weber regarded charisma as revolutionary in nature and an inexorably momentary event to be supplanted by bureaucracy. President Correa's charisma can account for his followers' indefinite support in Alianza País. Of note here is that his natural charm could have coexisted with other types of charisma, such as that obtained via Correa's achievements and/or the charisma stemming from the prestige of the presidential office (Peters, 2010).

The classic notion of charisma can account for Alianza País' sudden shift from a liberal to a non-liberal stance on presidential re-elections. Nonetheless, this perspective falls short in identifying and analysing the ideological process whereby leaders and followers transgress their officially affirmed stance. By this I mean the Citizens' Revolution's sudden shift from its founding position on presidential re-elections—enshrined in the constitutional limit of one-re-election only—to the thesis on the possible indispensability of a particular leader. By way of contribution, in what follows I analyse the shift in question from a Lacanian understanding of messianism as put forward in *Moses and Monotheism*.

The Longing for Rafael Correa's Indefinite Leadership

Before we address the longing for Correa's indefinite re-election, a summary of the 2014 and 2015 parliamentary arguments for and against the abolition of presidential term limits is in order. The following were the main assertions implied or called upon by the MAs opposing the abolitionist reform: the liberal maxim of the rotation of democratic power, and the necessity to ask the citizens—via referendum—whether they wanted indefinite re-elections in Ecuador on account of their 'altering' the 'nature' of the polity. Conversely, the representatives of Alianza País supported the reform on the basis of the citizens' 'democratic rights' to run for candidacies and to elect their authorities without institutional restrictions. For the official stance, this meant 'broadening' the citizens' democratic right to participate in politics. It was also argued that, as long as the people so decided, the indefinite re-election of someone guaranteeing the stability of an 'excellent' project was a democratic and legitimate practice (Primer debate de la Solicitud de Enmienda Constitucional (PD), 2014; Continuación del primer debate de la solicitud de enmienda constitucional, 2014; Segundo Debate de la Solicitud de enmiendas Constitucionales, 2015.

A Discourse Analysis of the Abolitionist Reform

After independence and until 1979, the Members of the Ecuadorian Congress were allowed to run for office indefinitely. The 1979 (1978) constitution established the non-consecutive re-election allowance for parliamentarians, and the 2008 charter authorized only one re-election (consecutive or not) for all elected authorities (PD, 2014, pp. 19, 21). In fact, in November 2007 President Correa shared his movement's stance on re-elections with *La Tercera*, a media outlet from Chile. The leader of the *Citizens' Revolution* was categorical:

> Our stance is that only one re-election can be allowed, from the President to the town councillor. (President Correa, as cited in *El Universo*, 2007)

The above *only one re-election* maxim was enshrined in Article 114 of the 2008 charter prompted by the Citizens' Revolution. When asked in January 2014 whether he was considering altering the constitution to run for a third consecutive presidential term in 2016, President Correa replied:

> It would be very harmful if one person became so indispensable that the constitution had to be changed in order to affect the rules of the game. There are capable people [to take the lead]. (as cited in *La Nación*, 2014)

Correa's statement adds extra credence to the previous analyses of the cases of García Moreno and Alfaro, for it shows how symbolic identification takes precedence over imaginary identification. Lacan (2000, ch. III) suggestion to conceive the Other in terms of a pact—which links and makes neurotic/normal subjects recognizable in the eyes of a third party—is of help here. Where can we find this pact in Correa's above statement?

Arguably and partly, in the 'rules of the game' agreed in 2008 by his majoritarian movement in Ecuador's Constituent Assembly. In that year, the presidential re-election allowance (for one time only) served as the ideal (amongst others) upon which the *Citizens' Revolution* presented its *symbolic formation*, which was inscribed in the Constitution, a pact in the History of Ecuador. The transgression of this pact entailed the surrender of this ideal to the thesis on the indispensability of one revolutionary subject, as Correa himself lamented: *It would be very harmful if one person became so indispensable that the constitution had to be changed in order to affect the rules of the game.* Here we appreciate the power exerted by this Other on the little and revolutionary other Correa, the primus inter pares amongst the revolutionary subjects to use Laclau's populist jargon. I would like to add extra credence to my argument. As Patricio Donoso MA reminded the plenary, in May 2013 President Correa had also stated:

> I reject the re-election. It would be our gravest failure not to have one person to take the baton after having prepared young people for ten years, and it is not that I am going to take it. (as cited in Continuación del primer debate de la solicitud de enmienda constitucional, 2014, p. 20)

But the above avant-garde spirit underlying the *Citizens' Revolution*, which originally hinted at the stability of the 2008 constitution, was undermined on 24 May 2014. In a radically different way, during his State of the Nation speech President Correa addressed (amongst other aspects) the issue of indefinite presidential re-elections as follows:

> Ecuador continues its struggle between the Citizens' Revolution and the Conservative Restoration, which is gestating in the country and in the whole of Latin America. We must keep adjusting our institutions to the new reality, and we must prevent the return of the elites' control. In its fourth Convention on May 1 ... Alianza PAIS resolved to ask our bloc of parliamentarians to amend the constitution regarding the presidential re-election provision. ... *My stance—sincere, authentic, as people know me—was always contrary to it, or at the most informed by analysis and respite. After careful consideration and realizing that sometimes only the lesser evil can be chosen, since, I insist, I believe in the stability of institutions, I have decided to support these initiatives.* Thus, I request our bloc of parliamentarians ... to amend the Constitution of the Republic to allow indefinite re-elections for all elected authorities ... With all liberty the Ecuadorian people will elect the continuity or rotation of their leaders. ... *I hope that some day this type of*

> *institutional change will no longer be necessary.* (President Correa, Presidencia República del Ecuador, INFORME A LA NACIÓN, 2014, pp. 11–13, emphasis added)

Alianza País' unexpected shift in favour of indefinite presidential re-elections was justified at its grassroots national convention, as articulated by President Correa, and later by his bloc of parliamentarians. President Correa drew on a metaphor (the 'Conservative Restoration') to set the premise of his argument. For the Citizens' Revolution, the adjustment of the Ecuadorian democracy to a context characterized by this 'Restoration' was necessary to prevent the return of the 'elites' control'. This was a real possibility due to presidential term limits. I argue that this institution was the indirect obstacle around which the official discourse elaborated the beatific dimension of fantasy. This type of fantasmatic narrative promises a full harmony-to-come, provided that the *stealer* of 'our' *enjoyment* is removed, a removal—through the abolition of presidential term limits—that would keep alive the Citizens' Revolution. This narrative as well as Alianza País' democratic decision on 1 May prompted President Correa to request indefinite re-elections not only for presidents but for all elected authorities.

It is important to note how this official discourse was accompanied by vacillation: *After careful consideration and realizing that sometimes only the lesser evil can be chosen, since, I insist, I believe in the stability of institutions. … I hope that some day this type of institutional change will no longer be necessary.* Some might argue that this hesitant fragment evidenced Alianza País' ambition for unlimited power, which contradicted its 'own' constitution. Another interpretation of Alianza País' shift is worth exploring. I propose that the wavering in question may speak, at least in part, to the grip of ideology, the latter predicated on the transgressive notion of *enjoyment*. Maybe this is what Hook means when he suggests the following *analytical imperative* for the 'deployment' of *jouissance* as a tool for psychosocial studies:

> The making of laws produces the very conditions of possibility for enjoyment. … When it comes to grasping the hold of an ideology upon subjects, look not simply to *the meanings they produce* but *to how they enjoy*. We should expect, furthermore, that their predominant modes of enjoyment often contradict many of their avowed moral or political beliefs. It is crucial then to

prioritize points of contradiction between ideology in its *presentable symbolic formations* and its disavowed *libidinal components.* (2017, pp. 609–610)

The ideological contradiction between the Citizens' Revolution's *symbolic formation* and its disavowed libidinal element can be captured by juxtaposing excerpts expressing these opposing views. As presented earlier, Alianza País' 2007 stance on re-elections read as follows: *Our stance is that only one re-election can be allowed, from the President to the town councillor.* This was corroborated in 2013 when Correa claimed that: *It would be our gravest failure not to have one [another] person to take the baton after having prepared young people for ten years, and it is not that I am going to take it.* But Alianza País' original stance on re-elections radically changed in 2014. As its bloc of parliamentarians put it when justifying the abolitionist reform before the Constitutional Court,

> Leaderships are neither decreed nor established by fate or destiny. They are a series of aspects condensed in one person who has been capable of representing values, expectations, wishes, and collective aspirations. In a given moment of a country or a region, [these leaderships] are essential for consolidating processes. (as cited in Segundo Debate de la Solicitud de enmiendas Constitucionales, 2015, p. 29)

In a less formal fashion, one of the above parliamentarians stated in the plenary:

> [W]e, the 100 parliamentarians of PAIS, hope that President [Correa] makes this decision [of running for president for a third consecutive term] ... in the year 2016 ... [T]here are personal motives that he needs to analyse. But let us hope that the President continues to be in command of the country because that will be beneficial for the homeland. (Nicolás Issa MA, Continuación del primer debate de la solicitud de enmienda constitucional, 2014, p. 213)

It is safe to argue that the person *capable of representing values, expectations, wishes, and collective aspirations* was Rafael Correa, at least for the parliamentarians of Alianza País in 2014. From the point of view of a classic approach to charisma, the Citizens' Revolution's sudden shift in favour of a non-liberal democracy speaks to the extraordinary attributes of those leaders regarded as essential for the continuation of a given political process. Therefore, according to this rationale, these persons deserve to be re-elected indefinitely. From a 'rushed' understanding of *Group Psychology*, the quotations in question permit us to understand how 'a number of individuals … have put one and the same object [Correa] in the place of their ego-ideal and have consequently identified themselves with one another in their ego' (Freud, 1921/1959, p. 48). But this formula needs to be revamped under certain circumstances, as Freud himself (1921) notes and Laclau (2005) reminds us when drawing on Freud (1921). Alianza País' socialist idealization of Correa before the Constitutional Court and parliament (above) resembles the cases of conservative García Moreno and liberal Alfaro. Instead of emphasizing the ideas and values that these leaders represented, their idealization hinted at a predominant process of *heroic identification*. In it, the narcissistic image of omnipotence and perfection blended with that of the leader, which allows us to modify Freud's formula as follows: 'a number of individuals … have put one and the same object [García Moreno, Alfaro, and Correa] in the place of their ideal-ego and have consequently identified themselves with one another in their ego'. This history of 'omnipotent' and authoritarian messiahs across the ideological spectrum adds reliance to part of my argument; namely, that colonial violence in Ecuador led to a diminished paternal imago, whose flip side (amongst others) manifests in its *heroic* constitutional politics.

In line with Glynos and Howarth (2007), the above idealization of Correa—which complements Correa's State of the Nation Speech—allows us to grasp a shared fantasy, namely that of an irreplaceable leader for the consolidation of the Ecuadorian Citizens' Revolution, a deliverable promise as long as the obstacle of presidential term limits is abolished. Alianza País' transgression of its ideal (i.e., that no leader is indispensable within the Ecuadorian Citizens' Revolution) bolstered the identification amongst its partisans inside the NA. Alianza País' transgression of its original stance on presidential re-elections strengthened its unity, a non-rational phenomenon highlighted by Glynos (2021).

Above I foregrounded that libidinal enjoyment needs to be understood in relation to other concepts, such as the *death drive* and the law. I would like to add another element to this analysis, that of the super-ego. This sheds light on a controversial punishment that followed the abolitionist reform under discussion. Within the realm of ideology, the super-ego can produce a twofold process. Once the subject identifies with the symbolic law, the super-ego commands him/her to *enjoy* the punishment of those lawbreakers. And here we appreciate the *obscene gratification* underpinning in part the grip of ideology (Hook, 2017, pp. 17–18). Maybe the latter psychosocial mechanism played its part in the punishment received by Fernando Bustamante MA, a former member of Alianza País. Unlike the block of parliamentarians cited above, Bustamante abstained from voting in favour of the constitutional amendment that abolished presidential term limits. The response was immediate. The Ethics Committee of Alianza País sanctioned Bustamante MA for his abstention, after which he was asked to resign the presidency of the parliamentary committee on International Relations (El Universo, 2016). Here we can appreciate how the official super-ego became the ambassador of the new law on indefinite presidential re-elections and thus punished the lawbreaker. Whether or not the official super-ego and *enjoyment* played their part in this punishment, I cannot help but suggest a link between Hook's (2017) theoretical contribution and this empirical conjecture.

The abolitionist reform supported by the parliamentarians of Alianza País, which entailed the transgression of its original stance on re-elections, was seen as a blunt quest for unlimited power by the opposition, and this created social unrest. By November 2015, amidst social protests for and against indefinite re-elections, the official stance had affirmed that the eventual constitutional amendment would include a clause preventing Rafael Correa from running for the presidency in 2016, while allowing him to do so from 2020 onwards (elDiario.es, 2015). The clause in question, the Second and Temporary Provision of the constitutional amendment, was actually sanctioned by the legislature in December 2015 (ESN, 2015).

The above provision can be understood as the government's means to alleviate the political tension caused by this rather controversial reform. In fact, this provision allowed the official stance in parliament to claim a lack of interest in President Correa's third and consecutive presidential mandate. However, and this is important, his eventual and *indefinite* participation as a presidential candidate could resume from 2020. In other words, according to the official discourse President Correa was not the reform's raison d'être, although his return in 2021 ('God willing') was desired. It was purported that this reformation did not alter the principle of the rotation of democratic power, for the ultimate decision relied on the sovereign's will (cf. Segundo Debate de la Solicitud de enmiendas Constitucionales, 2015, pp. 136–137, 245).

With 109 parliamentarians (out of 137) present during the voting, the constitutional amendment allowing indefinite presidential re-elections was approved with 100 favourable votes, 8 negatives, and 1 abstention (Segundo Debate de la Solicitud de enmiendas Constitucionales, 2015, p. 294).

In sum, the fantasy of an unstoppable revolution led by a charismatic leader outweighed the adequate *symbolic formation* of the Ecuadorian Citizens' Revolution. In this process both the followers (i.e., Alianza País' grassroots movement and its parliamentarians) and their leader transgressed the spirit with which the Citizens' Revolution emerged in 2006. This transgressive shift speaks to one way (among many others) through which the logic of *enjoyment* operates in ideology.

Concluding Remarks

A failed attempt to industrialize Ecuador, an unpopular neoliberal agenda, unstable governments, and the strength of the indigenous' movement since the 1990s informed the rhetorical context against which the outsider Rafael Correa promised a new beginning. With the people's massive approval, the 2007–2008 CA sanctioned Ecuador's 20th constitution, which is currently valid.

This chapter on the relation between messianic leadership and constitutional instability contributes to Chap. 3. There I argued that Ecuador's postcolonial history of violence motivated the support of the 1869 messiah. In part, it was Ecuador's long-lasting history of political violence the phantom against which the substitutive messiahs Alfaro and Correa gained sway on the 2007–2008 CA and 2015 constitutional reform. The 2008 inspiring discourse on Alfaro's leadership, the mourning of his assassination, and the 2014–2015 yearning for Correa's indefinite leadership are suggestive of my psychoanalytically informed interpretation of 'constitutional instability' in Ecuador.

The abolition/replacement/alteration of the constitution in force (1869, 1906, 1998, 2008/2015) can be interpreted, in part, as a result of a similar 'psychic' fascination across the ideological spectrum in Ecuador. As argued throughout this chapter, this trans-ideological fixation is predicated on the psychosocial mechanisms of (among others) *heroic identification* and transgressive *enjoyment*. As for the *theft of enjoyment* thesis, this has allowed us to capture the racist element that, seemingly, buttressed in part the fear of the pluri-national state proposed by the indigenous peoples in twenty-first-century Ecuador.

Alfaro's and Correa's influence on the 1906 constitution, the 2007–2008 CA, and the 2014–2015 abolitionist reform speak to the psychosocial factor underpinning constitutional volatility in Ecuador. The recurrent longing for 'omnipotent' personae, whose programmes have vowed to establish the promised land, hints at one of the potential byproducts of colonialism, that is, a diminished paternal imago and its political flipside: patriarchal authoritarianism.

References

Acosta, A. (2008). *Asamblea constituyente.* Archivo de la Asamblea Nacional del Ecuador, 28 January, 24 June.

Amores, B. (2008). *Asamblea constituyente.* Archivo de la Asamblea Nacional del Ecuador, 8 May, 9 June.

Arlotti, R. (2003). *Vocabulario técnico y científico de la política.* Dunken.

Ayala, E. (2008). *Manual de historia del Ecuador II. Época Republicana.* Corporación Editora Nacional.

Ayala, E. (2014). Rasgos históricos de la evolución constitucional del Ecuador. In M. E. Ayala (Ed.), *Historia constitucional: estudios comparativos.* Quito.

Basabe-Serrano, S. (2017). El fin de la hegemonía de Rafael Correa y los espejismos del giro a la izquierda en Ecuador: un análisis desde la perspectiva del electorado. In C. Arqueros & A. Iriarte (Eds.), *Chile y América Latina. Crisis de las izquierdas del siglo XXI* (pp. 313–334). Instituto Res Publica.

Billiet, L. (2023). The cultural superego or the demand for universality. Retrieved March 10, 2023, from https://nlscongress2023.amp-nls.org/blogposts/lievebillieten

Breslauer, S. D. (2019). Negative charisma, leadership, and Martin Buber's myth of Zion. *Jewish Culture and History, 20*(2), 123–139.

Burbano, F. (2007). *Asamblea constituyente.* Archivo de la Asamblea Nacional del Ecuador, 27 December.

Cavalletto, G. (2007). *Crossing the psycho-social divide. Freud, Weber, Adorno and Elias.* Ashgate.

Cordero, S. (2018). *La plurinacionalidad desde abajo. Autogobierno indígena en Bolivia y Ecuador.* FLACSO, Ecuador – Programa de las Naciones Unidas para el Desarrollo.

Correa, R. (2007). Es absurda la reelección indefinida. El Universo, 10 November. Retrieved February 28, 2023, from https://www.eluniverso.com/2007/11/10/0001/8/F275D24BD604403AA42BF797883984AD.html

Correa, R. (2014). INFORME A LA NACIÓN.

El Universo. (2016). *Fernando Bustamante es el tercer asambleísta en dejar Alianza PAIS.* Retrieved February 9, 2023, from https://www.eluniverso.com/noticias/2016/01/28/nota/5373631/fernando-bustamante-es-tercer-asambleista-dejar-alianza-pais/

El Universo. (2017). *Rafael Correa, entre los cinco presidentes con más tiempo en el poder*. Retrieved February 24, 2023, from https://www.eluniverso.com/noticias/2017/05/22/nota/6195727/rafael-correa-cinco-presidentes-mas-tiempo-poder/

elDiario.es. (2015). Protestas en Ecuador contra enmiendas a Constitución y reelección indefinida. *elDiario.es*, 25 November. Retrieved February 28, 2023, from https://www.eldiario.es/politica/Protestas-Ecuador-Constitucion-reeleccion-indefinida_0_456005501.html

Enmienda S/N (Enmiendas a la Constitución de la República del Ecuador) (2015). *Cancillería del Ecuador*. Retrieved from https://www.cancilleria.gob.ec/wp-content/uploads/2016/01/enmiendas-a-la-constitucion-de-la-republica-del-ecuador.pdf

Escala, J. (2008). *Asamblea constituyente*. Archivo de la Asamblea Nacional del Ecuador, 25 June.

Espindola, E. (2016). *La construcción del Estado ecuatoriano y de su ciudadanía tributaria a la luz del diezmo*. E-book Retrieved January 24, 2023, from https://www.flacso.edu.ec/node/111?id=4283

Espinosa, C. (2010). *Historia del Ecuador en contexto regional y global*. Lexus.

Freud, S. (1914) *On Narcissism*. The Standard Edition of the Complete Psychological Works of Sigmund Freud, Volume XIV (1914-1916): On the History of the Psycho-Analytic Movement, Papers on Metapsychology and Other Works, pp. 67-102. Retrieved February 28, 2023, from https://www.sas.upenn.edu/~cavitch/pdf-library/Freud_SE_On_Narcissism_complete.pdf

Freud, S. (2015). *Moisés y la religión monoteísta*. Amorrortu Editores.

Georgetown University. (2009). Republic of Ecuador. Chronology of Presidents. *Political Database of the Americas*. Retrieved February 28, 2023, from https://pdba.georgetown.edu/Executive/Ecuador/pres.html

Glynos, J. (2021). Critical fantasy studies. *Journal of Language and Politics, 20*(1), 95–111.

Glynos, J., & Howarth, D. (2007). *Logics of critical explanation in social and political theory*. Routledge.

Hernández, V. (2008). *Asamblea constituyente*. Archivo de la Asamblea Nacional del Ecuador, 13 May.

Hook, D. (2008). Articulating psychoanalysis and psychosocial studies: Limitations and possibilities. *Psychoanalysis, Culture & Society, 13*, 397–405.

Hook, D. (2017). What is "enjoyment as a political factor"? *Political Psychology, 38*(4), 605–620.

Hook, D. (2018a). Racism and jouissance: Evaluating the "racism as (the theft of) enjoyment" hypothesis. *Psychoanalysis, Culture & Society, 23*, 244–266.

Hook, D. (2018b). *Six moments in Lacan. Communication and identification in psychology and psychoanalysis.* Routledge.
Issa, N. (2014). *Continuación del primer debate de la solicitud de enmienda constitucional.* Archivo de la Asamblea Nacional del Ecuador, 2 December.
La Nación. (2014). Correa descartó reformar la Constitución para buscar reelección. Retrieved February 28, 2023, from https://www.lanacion.com.co/correa-descarto-reformar-la-constitucion-para-buscar-reeleccion/
Lacan, J. (1991). *Freud's Papers on Technique 1953-1954. Book I.* Norton.
Lacan, J. (1997). *The ethics of psychoanalysis 1959-1960. Book VII.* Norton.
Lacan, J. (2000). *The Psychoses 1955–1956. Book III.* Norton.
Laplanche, J., & Pontalis, J.-B. (1973). *The Language of Psycho-analysis.* Norton.
Martin, J. (2014). *Politics and rhetoric: A critical introduction.* Routledge. Available at: University of Essex (E-book).
Martin, J. (2019). *Psycho-politics of speech. Uncivil discourse and the excess of desire.* Transcript.
Martínez, M. (2008). *Asamblea constituyente.* Archivo de la Asamblea Nacional del Ecuador, 9 June.
McLean, I., & Alistair, M. M. (2003). *Oxford concise dictionary of politics.* Oxford University Press.
Misión de Observación Electoral de la Unión Europea. (2007). *Informe Final.* https://aceproject.org/ero-en/regions/americas/EC/ecuador-final-report-constituent-assembly-eu-2007-1/view
Muldoon, P. (2017). A reconciliation most desirable: Shame, narcissism, justice and apology. *International Political Science Review, 38*(2), 213–226.
National Assembly. (1869). *Sesión ordinaria del 2 de Junio.* Archivo de la Asamblea Nacional del Ecuador, 2 June.
Oleas, J. (2018). *Ecuador 1972-1999: del boom del petróleo a la pérdida del signo monetario (o los costos del cambio de régimen de desarrollo).* Editorial IAEN.
Peters, R. (2010). The riddle of charisma. *Society, 47*, 516–520.
Pilamunga, C. (2007, 2008). *Asamblea constituyente.* Archivo de la Asamblea Nacional del Ecuador, 11 December 2007; 5 March, 7 June 2008.
Primer debate de la Solicitud de Enmienda Constitucional. (2014). Archivo de la Asamblea Nacional del Ecuador, 1 December.
Richards, B. (2018). Exploring malignancies: Narcissism and paranoia today. *Psychoanalysis, Culture & Society, 23*, 15–27.
Roldós, M. (2008). *Asamblea constituyente.* Archivo de la Asamblea Nacional del Ecuador, 28 January, 25 June.
Sarango, J. (2008). *Asamblea constituyente.* Archivo de la Asamblea Nacional del Ecuador, 9 June.
Segundo Debate de la Solicitud de enmiendas Constitucionales. (2015) Archivo de la Asamblea Nacional del Ecuador, 3 December.

Sharoni, J. (2016). The failure of the parental metaphor: A Lacanian reading of James Joyce's "Eveline". *Journal of Modern Literature, 39*(4), 33–48.

Taiano, V. (2007, 2008). *Asamblea constituyente*. Archivo de la Asamblea Nacional del Ecuador, 13 December 2007; 13 May, 25 June 2008.

The Carter Center (2008). *Informe sobre la Asamblea Constituyente de la República del Ecuador*. Retrieved February 28, 2023, from https://www.cartercenter.org/resources/pdfs/peace/americas/informe_final_ac_-_centro_carter_distribuido.pdf

Villacís, B., & Carrillo, D. (2012). *País atrevido: la nueva cara sociodemográfica del Ecuador*. INEC and Analitika. https://www.ecuadorencifras.gob.ec/wp-content/descargas/Libros/Economia/Nuevacarademograficadeecuador.pdf

Weber, M. (2005/1992). *Economía y sociedad. Esbozo de sociología comprensiva*. Fondo de Cultura Económica.

Zambrano, E. (2008). *Asamblea constituyente*. Archivo de la Asamblea Nacional del Ecuador, 13 May.

Žižek, S. (1990). Eastern Europe's Republics of Gilead. *New Left Review* (I/183, September-October).

Zúñiga, N. (2004). Un estudio de caso: Los derechos de los pueblos indígenas en Ecuador. In F. Mariño & D. Oliva (Eds.), *Avances en la protección de los derechos de los pueblos indígenas*. Dykinson.

CHAPTER 5

A Comparative Reflection on Constitutional Instability in Ecuador

The research puzzle driving this book concerns the enigma of Ecuador's dramatic constitutional instability, illustrated by 20 constitutions since 1830. Competing explanations speak of philosophical, legal, institutionalist, economic, and context-dependent regional variables accounting for this type of instability. As I have argued throughout this book, the psychic processes of identification, idealization, guilt, and the transgressive dimension of ideology shape, in part, the ritualistic and repetitive character of constitutional replacements in Ecuador. Theoretical resources drawn from psychoanalysis and the Essex School of Discourse Analysis have helped grasp these psychosocial factors in the empirical cases. While indebted to Freud's *Moses and Monotheism*, my approach also draws on the Lacanian notions of (amongst others) *enjoyment* and *fantasy*, which are rearticulated in this chapter in light of Cavalletto's (2007) contribution. Rhetorical political analysis has served as a useful tool in previous chapters. It was 'deployed' as a method for an in-depth discourse analysis of the 1869 and 2007–2008 Constituent Assemblies (CAs), allowing us to better identify, characterize, and highlight how the psychic factor appears and operates in these discourses. Overall, I argue that Ecuador's postcolonial history of political violence has fostered a political culture prone to supporting *messianic* leaders, that is, lawgivers whose personages have been invested with the hope and aspiration of perpetual stability, epitomized by the setting up of CAs themselves. Presidents García Moreno, Eloy Alfaro, and Rafael

E. Espindola, *The Paternal Imago in Ruins*, The Palgrave Lacan Series, https://doi.org/10.1007/978-3-032-07507-9_5

Correa have illustrated my case studies. In this final chapter my main objective is to better contextualize how political messianism, as discussed in this book, operates in relation to other variables that seek to explain Ecuador's constitutional instability.

This chapter is structured as follows. Firstly, I reflect comparatively on the hybrid and conflictive nature of the Rousseau-inspired presidential system in Latin America, after which I show how the psychic factor can be said to complement this French understanding of democracy. I focus, in particular, on how the psychoanalytic notion of 'messianic leadership' fills the gap found in Sieyès' democratic theory when applied to Ecuador, a country where strong caudillos/messiahs (democratic and non-democratic) have convened CAs. I then address the relationship between economic and psychic factors influencing the 'urgent need for' a Messiah in an underdeveloped nation, after which I highlight the contribution that a rational choice approach—and related perspectives—can make to our understanding of Ecuador's constitutional instability. I show how psychoanalysis adds value by acknowledging the non-rational aspect that informs constitutional volatility.

Rousseau and the Constituent Power in Ecuador: The 1869 and 2007–2008 Conventions

In this section I argue that the hybrid, conflictive, and volatile nature of Ecuador's constitutional tradition, which is underpinned by Rousseau's doctrine and the US presidential model, can be better understood in light of a psychoanalytic approach to messianism. This understanding of messianism cuts across the Left/Right and Democratic/Non-Democratic distinctions. In this light, in what follows I foster dialogue between political philosophy, Ecuadorian historiography, and psychoanalysis.

In this work I have borrowed King's (2011) definition of a constitution, the latter inspired by two values: neutrality and universal applicability. He defines a constitution as 'the set of the most important rules and common understandings in any given country that regulate the relations among that country's governing institutions and also the relations between that country's governing institutions and the people of that country' (p. 3). This definition avoids moral and political judgements, such as those suggesting that a given constitution is 'good' or 'bad'. Almost every nation has a constitution as defined above, apart from, perhaps, 'failed states'. Codified and non-codified charters (e.g., the British) fit the same definition of a constitution. King's definition can capture what is constitutional in one country in two dramatically different contexts, such as the constitution of Nazi Germany and that of today's Germany (pp. 3–4). This 'neutral' definition of constitutions, which 'are never ... written down in their entirety' (King, 2011, p. 5), allows us to navigate through cultural differences. It also distinguishes what is (and what is not) constitutional in a non-codified and codified charter. For instance, Ecuador's 1869 and 2007–2008 CAs discussed non-constitutional and highly *aspirational* themes (García Villegas, 2012) in 'the hope of a new beginning' (Negretto, 2008). Some of these themes were later enshrined in its codified constitutions.

The 1789 Revolution and Rousseau's *contractarian* edifice influenced the independence and framing of the new constitutions in Hispanic America. But this founding moment in the former Spanish colonies had already been impacted by another architecture: the presidential system built in the US in 1787. The new constitutions in Latin America resulted in a hybrid comprising a strong executive, the doctrine of the separation of powers, and a legislature 'representing' the *general will.*

Sieyès' operationalization of Rousseau's doctrine has exercised some influence in presidential Ecuador. The *constituent power* (i.e., the *collective* capacity to legislate on any matter) has been bestowed on the people's deputies. This has allowed the legislature to legally change the constitution as many times as it has seen fit. Since presidents are also elected by the people in this country, these leaders too have prompted constitutional replacements 'in favour of' the people's well-being. There is a philosophical and legal basis for frequent constitutional replacements in presidential Ecuador, but this country's hybrid constitutional edifice, inspired by the precept of the 'general will', creates short-circuits, as the 1869 and 2007–2008 CAs show.

The 2007 referendum asked the following question: *Do you approve the call and installation of a Constituent Assembly with full authority in line with the attached electoral statute to transform the constitutional frame of the State and to elaborate a new Constitution?*[1]

[1] '¿Aprueba que se convoque e instale una Asamblea Constituyente con plenos poderes de conformidad con el estatuto electoral que se adjunta para que transforme el marco constitucional del Estado y elabore una nueva Constitución?' Retrieved from: https://www.notimerica.com/politica/noticia-ecuador-tribunal-electoral-aprueba-propuesta-correa-convoca-consulta-popular-15-abril-20070302185318.html.

The way this referendum was framed illustrates the operationalization of Rousseau's legacy in Ecuador's contemporary democracy because the bearer of sovereignty is the people, and it follows that its representatives—convened in a constituent assembly—should have 'full authority' within state affairs. While the 2007–2008 CA was in session, Subcommittee 10 legislated and performed audits of the state. This situation, which favoured the majoritarian movement in the convention (Alianza País), created controversies in the opposition. The third force in the assembly (PRIAN) claimed that the CA's power to legislate had not been authorized by the sovereign in the April plebiscite (Taiano, 2007, p. 20). Leonardo Viteri MA also disapproved the legislative function of the convention, though he did not rely on the people's will to support his argument (ibid, pp. 23–24).

Taiano's (2007) complaint is similar to that voiced in 1869, the proposition that the *constituent power* delegated by the people to their representatives did not automatically entitle them to legislate. This prerogative is inherent to a *constituted power*, e.g., Congress. Despite contextual differences, this type of complaint invites us to reflect on the practical difficulty of the Rousseauian nature of presidential Ecuador. In view of the above referendum question, it could be argued that while the sovereign agreed to delegate its 'full authority' to its representatives to write a new *pact*, it did not delegate its legislative power. From a similar perspective, the opposition in the 2007–2008 convention contended that the plebiscite's statute only bestowed the *constituent* prerogative—to write a constitution—on the assembly (The Carter Center, 2008, p. 23). There are at least two plausible counterarguments to this. As Lenin Hurtado MA put it, the notion of 'full authority' inscribed in the above referendum entailed the convention's ability to legislate (Hurtado, 2007, p. 26). Also, it could be that during the eight-month period in which the convention deliberated, the republic could not stop its daily business, such as legislating. These grey zones bring to the fore the criticism of the short-circuits characteristic of presidential systems imbued with Rousseau's legacy.

Rousseau's influence on Ecuador's latest CA is indisputable. The 2007–2008 CA could modify this country's legal system (this was explicitly stipulated in the Assembly's Regulation). But this philosophical *ethos* required some historical amendments. Unlike 1869, the Rousseauian legacy in 2007 embraced politico-cultural minorities. If an MA's first language was not Spanish, he/she was entitled to address the plenary in their native tongue. Up to five minutes were granted for the translation of their speech into Spanish. The CA's documentation was made available to the public in both Spanish and Quechua. This non-European language was also spoken in Bolivia, Colombia, and Peru, as Carlos Pilamunga MA stressed in a speech that began in Quechua (Pilamunga, 2007, pp. 18–19, 28, 32, 34). By including Quechua as part of the CA's official languages, the character of this convention 'lost' the cultural homogeneity praised by Rousseau in its *Social Contract*.

Despite these disputes about whether a constituent assembly can legislate, as well as the nuances between the exclusionary logic of the 1869 CA and the inclusionary one of the 2007–2008 CA, both conventions drew on Rousseau. His doctrine, as it has been operationalized for contemporary times, allows the people's representatives to replace the constitution as many times as they see fit. In fact, on average, Ecuador has replaced its codified constitution every 10 years.

Ecuadorian History and the Psychic Factor

It is hard to believe that every 10 years 'the set of the most important rules and common understandings' of the Ecuadorian republic was changed. As the 1869 and 2007–2008 CAs have shown, the majority of topics discussed by these assemblies were non-constitutional articles. Various themes were addressed by these conventions, ranging from the citizens' petitions to national laws (these CAs served as the legislature during the period in which they were in session). But there is a clear difference between these two processes. Rousseau's maxim that the legislature prevails over the executive applies to the 2007–2008 CA. It was thanks to the people's vote that the CA became the ultimate authority in presidential Ecuador while the convention was in session. By contrast, the 1869 CA was preceded by a putsch conducted by former president García Moreno, whose proposed constitution was sanctioned by an assembly composed of his supporters. This difference speaks to the limited applicability of Rousseau's maxim in understanding the non-democratic character of some CAs in Ecuador. Constitutional instability in this country cannot be simply equated to the 'general will' enacted by the people's representatives in the almighty legislature, a regular legislature, or a CA.

The role played by the leader in the frequent processes of replacements in Ecuador appears to be a key explanatory factor. The legitimation of García Moreno's putsch by the 1869 CA was not an isolated event in the nineteenth century. Once García Moreno was assassinated, Antonio Borrero was elected president, later overthrown by Ignacio Veintimilla.

'Besides approving the new constitution [that of 1878], the convention elected Veintimilla as president for four years. *As on other occasions, the scheme of Constitutional Conventions served to legitimize a putsch*' (Espinosa, 2010, pp. 554–555, 558, emphasis added, own translation). Just like former *caudillos* (e.g., Flores, García Moreno), Veintimilla relied on force to perpetuate his presidency for another 4 years, which caused a civil war between competing caudillos (Alfaro was one of them). After the 1883 civil war came to an end, there were constitutional governments from 1883 to 1895, when Alfaro overthrew the democratic government, and he convened a CA in 1896. Alfaro, the leader of the liberal revolution, conducted another putsch in 1905, this time against a liberal government, and convened another CA in 1906. The 1906 constitution 'consecrated the changes introduced by Alfaro since the beginning of the Alfarist revolution: the separation between the State and the Church and secular education' (Espinosa, 2010, pp. 559–564, own translation).

A psychoanalytic approach to messianic leadership amongst the Ecuadorian elites contributes to our understanding of constitutional replacements in presidential Ecuador. In this country the substitution of the previous charter by a new one has been preceded by either putsches or democratic processes. As the 1869 and 2007–2008 CAs have shown, these conventions relied on Rousseauian terminology, corroborating the influence that Rousseau's doctrine has had in Ecuador since independence. Democratic and non-democratic constitutional replacements have been inspired by strong and authoritarian leaders or caudillos. The non-democratic (García Moreno, 1869) and democratic (2007–2008) cases analysed here serve as a partial illustration. I say partial because I cannot generalize the findings of this book based on 2 out of a total of 20 CAs in Ecuador's history. Nonetheless, there is a common denominator in my case selection, that is, the idealization of the 'lawgivers' García Moreno, Alfaro, and Correa in the 1869, 2007–2008, and 2014–2015 processes. These figures were regarded as capable of bringing a long-lasting stability for the Ecuadorian nation. Alfaro's leadership, which entailed the non-democratic rise to power in 1895 and 1905, was admired by a highly democratic convention in 2007–2008. How can we account for this contradiction?

Freud's *Moses and Monotheism* allows us to grasp the psychosocial meaning of the messiahs, the lawgivers, regardless of their ideological affiliation and (un)democratic beliefs. In line with Freud's myth and from the followers' perspective, these extraordinary personae 'return' as the Son of the Father once killed by the *league of brothers*. This inverted father figure offers redemption and the promised land. From a non-mythical point of view, this 'return' speaks to the guilty element underpinning the aftereffect of 'castration', namely the guilt that subjects feel for having desired the 'removal' of their admired authority figure in childhood.

The idea of a promised and perfect/utopic land was found in the 1869 and 2007–2008 CAs. This utopic scenario, according to a Lacanian approach to ideology, relates to a 'forgetting of origins' (i.e., *castration*) that *fantasy* provides for subjects. The fantasy of a promised land blends with the image of the Messiahs. And here we see how Freud's thesis on messianism combines productively with the Lacanian notion of *castration-fantasy* and its function in utopian politics, that is, the 'filling up' of the subjects' ontological lack, that of their mythical *jouissance* (Stavrakakis, 1999). Utopian messianism is related with the psychic processes of *idealization* and *identification*. From a classic understanding of group formation, García Moreno, Alfaro, and Correa were the persons on whom their followers' ego-ideals were deposited, while they identified with one another in their *ego*. From a Lacanian and Lagachian perspectives, which shed light on Ecuador's constitutional instability, the idealization of these three leaders hints at a nuanced phenomenon. As argued in the previous chapters, these lawgivers appear to be the recipients on whom most of their followers have deposited their ideal-egos, while identifying one another in their ego.

Above I have tried to create a meaningful bridge between three disciplines: political philosophy (i.e., Rousseau's legacy in Ecuador), Ecuadorian historiography (i.e., the narrative according to which CAs in Ecuador have been prompted by democratic and non-democratic caudillos), and Freudian-Lacanian literature (the role played by these leaders in a CA from the followers' perspective). The role that messianism plays in the constitutional politics of Ecuador needs further problematization.

A Psycho-Economic Approach to Constitutional Instability in Ecuador

This section hints at the partial link between an economic understanding of constitutional instability and the psychoanalytic factor discussed here, complemented by a reflection on the question of charismatic leadership in light of Correa's presidency. Drawing on the contributions of Rueschemeyer et al. (1992), Cavalletto (2007), and Hirschorn (1990), below I suggest that political 'Messiahs' might be more likely to emerge in developing countries than in developed nations.

Ecuadorian historians referenced throughout this book (e.g., Ayala Mora, Espinosa, Salvador Lara) have identified a common pattern in Ecuador's history of constitutional replacements. During the second half of the nineteenth and most of the twentieth centuries, Ecuador hosted frequent armed disputes between regional elites whose economic interests—based on commodities—were linked to the international market. This evidenced Ecuador's underdeveloped industry and the presence of a weak state.

In 1992, Rueschemeyer et al. put forward an argument on *Capitalist Development & Democracy*, which is of help in this discussion. In light of this mainstream hypothesis, some would argue that the underdevelopment of capitalism in Ecuador has influenced its democratic instability and, subsequently, its constitutional volatility. During the second half of the nineteenth century, there was an accelerated expansion of industrial capitalism in the *advanced capitalist countries*. This economic growth translated to a greater empowerment of the working class through its representatives, trade unions, and socialist parties. Even more, in countries such as Belgium and the Netherlands the working class participated in rushing confessional parties towards a more democratic stance. In addition, the demands created by World War I (e.g., labour assistance for both production and war) only consolidated this reconfiguration of the balance of class power in favour of the interests of the working class, especially in belligerent nations. By contrast, in contemporary Latin America and the Caribbean the landed class was more powerful than the working class. Consequently, the process of democratization was less propitious than that in the core countries. In accounting for the rise and stabilization of democracy in Latin America, Rueschemeyer et al. analyse, amongst others, the *consolidation of state power, export expansion, industrialization, and agents of political articulation, class forces,* and *import substitution industrialization*. Worthy of notice is that 'of the four cases [Brazil, Colombia, Paraguay, Ecuador] with labor intensive agriculture, Ecuador and Paraguay experienced very late and limited industrialization and thus very weak pressures for democratization' (Rueschemeyer et al., 1992, pp. 8, 91, 97, Ch. 5, 324).

Rueschemeyer et al. emphasize that a democracy has a chance to prosper as long as contestation has been institutionalized, for which the consolidation of state power constitutes a prerequisite. Ultimately, the latter means that the monopoly of the state's coercive authority has become undisputed nationwide (Rueschemeyer et al., 1992, pp. 159, 163). During the nineteenth century and most of the twentieth, Ecuador failed to institutionalize its political contestation. As mentioned, 'the [Ecuadorian] constitutions have emanated from revolutions. One revolution, one constitution. Ecuador's constitutional regime has lived by the edge of the sword' (Manuel E. Flor, as cited in Ayala, 2014, p. 16). The weakness of the Ecuadorian state throughout the nineteenth and most of the twentieth centuries paved the way for non-institutionalized disputes between elites who frequently 'legitimized' their power via CAs. The working and middle classes did not participate in this armed 'negotiation' due, in part, to Ecuador's economic underdevelopment (the frail contradictions of capitalism have not empowered these classes). The regular constitutional replacements in Ecuador have not meant a further step towards the consolidation of its democracy. Instead, this volatile practice could be seen as a symptom of this country's weak capitalism, the latter favouring the interests of the landed upper class, which has mainly prompted an unstable constitutional regime.

In sum, the lack of material preconditions for a stable democracy has made constitutional replacements a possible and frequent practice in Ecuador. This country's lack of industry has precluded the emergence of strong working and middle classes capable of strengthening the nation's democracy through strong parties and trade unions. The upper classes have ruled the democratic game, changing the constitution for the sake of minority interests. This has resulted in frequent constitutional replacements, a symptom of Ecuador's underdeveloped (capitalist) economy. Argentina's greater industrial development compared to Ecuador (especially between 1850 and 1950), and the fact that the 1853 Argentinian constitution lasted for 100 years, supports the thesis on *Capitalist Development & Democracy*. Ecuadorian caudillos and the elites supporting them have been key actors in the constitutional politics of Ecuador. In fact, on several occasions the constant abolition and replacement of the constitution in force served to legitimize putsches in nineteenth-century Ecuador (Espinosa, 2010, p. 558). The elites' agendas have created political instability, and this has led to a change of the constitutional architecture in favour of their political, economic, and social interests. Albeit sound, this mainstream hypothesis does not quite account for my research puzzle, that is, the underlying meaning of the followers' historic and frequent support of constitutional replacements, irrespective of whether this practice has altered *the most important rules and common understandings* of Ecuador.

The psychic factor put forth in this book may tangentially complement our understanding of the relationship between underdevelopment in Ecuador and its constitutional instability. Despite the distance between 1869, 2007–2008, and 2015, there are key common characteristics in all these constitutional processes. First, Ecuador has been dependent on the unstable price of commodities, from cocoa in the nineteenth century to banana and oil in the twentieth and twenty-first centuries. The socio-economic status of the vast majority of the population has been precarious since independence, making it possible for the 'need' for a Messiah to become an 'urgent matter' in this underdeveloped country. This can be inferred from the 1869, 2007–2008, and 2014–2015 discussions on the 'indispensability/uniqueness' of a particular leader, as the following fragments from quotations (cited above) remind us:

> Sirs, by no means should we accept the resignation proposed by Mr. G. Moreno… [I]f [his] oath [to resign] were kept, only evils would emerge in this homeland, hence we must firmly reject it [Moreno's oath not to extend his non-democratic and temporary presidency during the 1869 CA]. (Aragundi, 1869)

> What do you [Alfaro] still have to say to us? … Since a child and thanks to my father, I was clear on the difference between those who fight for their people's rights and those, such as García Moreno, who want power for tyranny and despotism. … Not only did you lead the most important revolution that Ecuador has known, but you were also a great builder of our identity as a national State. (Roldós, 2008)

> [W]e, the 100 parliamentarians of PAIS, hope that President [Correa] makes this decision [of running for president for a third consecutive term] … in the year 2016 … [L]et us hope that the President continues to be in command of the country because that will be beneficial for the homeland. (Issa, 2014)

For the sake of analysis, let us assume that the content and the style of these individual speeches are representative of three movements (I argue that this is not at ludicrous assumption): Garcianismo, Alfarismo, and Correismo. Despite ideological differences between conservative García Moreno, liberal Alfaro, and socialist Correa, these collectives share one common denominator, that of *heroic identification*. In this process, the identification with strong figures resonates more with those characteristics of the ideal-ego than those of the ego-ideal. While the ideal-ego is reminiscent of an early experience of narcissistic and imaginary omnipotence, the ego-ideal entails symbolic agreements (recognized by the Other) that make interindividual coexistence less conflicting. The transgression of the constitutional order by these nonetheless idealized lawgivers has been located in a broader debate on the psychic aftereffect of colonialism. Above I suggested that this heroic identification has a context-dependent characteristic, namely the reproduction of a diminished paternal imago through the recurrent emergence of an inverted process, that of national identification with authoritarian leaders.

Above I conjectured that the lack of economic development influences the longing for a strong Messiah. And this fosters dialogue between psychoanalysis and economics about the role of 'caudillos' in the constitutional politics of developing countries. In *Crossing the Psycho-Social Divide*, Cavalletto (2007, pp. 4, 10–13) addresses the relationship between the social and the psychic, one found in scholars such as Weber and Freud. He notes that *The Future of an Illusion* (1927) and *Civilization and Its Discontents* (1929) are Freud's 'great books on civilization', although their approach to the relationship between the psychic world and the social varies. *The Future of an Illusion* discusses the relationship between the *paternal complex* (i.e., the ambivalence once felt towards the father) and its transference to the monotheistic experience, where the idea of the Messiah fulfils a wish for protection. This thesis is later refined by Freud in *Moses and Monotheism* (1939). As Cavalletto notes, in the first part of *The Future of an Illusion*, Freud links the social to the psychic, while focusing on the latter: '[T]he text tends to conceptualize this world in terms of the impact it has upon the psyche' (Cavalletto, 2007, pp. 11–12). In other words, there is a shift from social economy to psychic economy. Freud notes that throughout history there has been an inconsistency between the social production of every civilization and how wealth has been distributed: '[C]ivilization is something which was imposed on a resisting majority by a minority which understood how to obtain possession of the means to power and coercion' (Freud, as cited in Cavalletto, 2007, p. 12).

For Freud, modern civilization guarantees the education and leisure whereby the social elite can benefit from the products of progress. Most people are deprived of these assets (Cavalletto, p. 13). This socio-economic inequality has a political consequence for Freud: social revolt. But the sociological aspect of Freud's text, which is indeed preoccupied with the unequal distribution of wealth, is the first layer of his argument. What drives subjects to dissatisfaction and potential insurrection against civilization? As Cavalletto argues, this class-based analysis of social inequity in Freud is later understood in terms of psychic inequity: the *surplus of privation* of the *underprivileged classes* speaks to their instinctual privation whose external signal is material privation.

> [A]nd when he [Freud] then adds that "the satisfaction" of civilized privileged classes "depends upon the suppression" of the unprivileged classes, we begin to understand that the words "satisfaction" and "suppression" refer as much or more to instinctual suppression and satisfaction than to their material or social variants. ... [E]strangement is grounded upon the extraction and transfer of instinctual energies and pleasures from the underprivileged to the privileged classes. Thus, social concepts become psychic concepts, as an inequitable distribution of instinctual gratifications. *Freud's thought here presumes a translational correspondence between inner and outer, although the mechanisms by which this occurs are never spelled out.* (Cavalletto, 2007, p. 13, emphasis added)

These *never-spelled-out mechanisms* can be, in part, elucidated here. Let us consider Hirschorn's (1990) contribution and my suggestion that developing countries might be more prone to experience the emergence of messianic leaders than developed nations. It cannot be overstated that 'castration' has an important repercussion in the 'us–them' rivalry typical of politics. For instance, as Hirschorn (1990) puts it, there is a challenge that people face whenever they unconsciously revisit the infantile feeling towards the parent whom they regarded as their protector and rival. As we grow, this ambivalent feeling becomes our super-ego, which punishes the ego for having felt hostility towards the beloved parent.

> [In this context], people frequently cannot contain this ambivalent relationship to their superego. They cannot simultaneously be punished and guided by this introjected authority figure. Under conditions of stress they tend to split their unconscious experience of this fantasized authority figure, projecting the hatred part onto other people and retaining the good, idealized part for themselves. In this way they feel less bad and guilty. ... *A group that feels at risk may erect and support a charismatic leader in whom they invest all their hopes* ... To protect their now idealized leader from their own hatred for authority, they must project their hatred onto others. (p. 203, emphasis added)

Freud's idea on the instinctual privation felt by the majority and Hirschorn's comment on why charismatic leaders emerge allow us to conjecture about the compensatory mechanism underpinning Ecuador's constitutional instability. It is safe to argue that in a developing nation there is a real sense of 'risk' for those that lack the material means for subsistence. In this socio-economic adversity, which leads to a psychic trigger, people are likely to deposit their hope in one person deemed to be extraordinary, a trait 'thanks to which material problems can be solved'. This has been the case in the 1869, 2007–2008, and 2015 constitutional processes previously analysed. In one way or another, during these reforms the idealization of and the identification with the leader have played their part. These processes have occurred despite differential traits amongst these leaders (according to the bibliography consulted, only Correa can be understood to be charismatic).

According to *The Future of an Illusion*, *identification* in adulthood is in part triggered by the ambivalent feeling that the person once felt towards her beloved parent in childhood. The idealization of the subject's father accompanies him/her in adulthood and is later transferred to the figure of the Messiah (charismatic or not), such as García Moreno. This figure represents the fantasy of the redeemer (of the original parricide) and that of the person promising the new land (cf. *Moses and Monotheism*). As part of the same psychosocial mechanism, the hatred once felt towards him (the father) is *projected* on to the antagonistic 'other' (Hirschorn, 1990). *Messianism* (as presented in *Moses and Monotheism*) and the *theft of enjoyment* thesis can productively converge in different topics, such as constitutional instability in Ecuador and racism. Although both conjectures can be said to have an origin in oedipal dynamics, the *theft of enjoyment* hypothesis differs from the phylogenetic thesis on *archaic heredity* on which *messianism* relies. While Freud's thesis emphasizes the intergenerational guilt underpinning the fantasy of the Messiah, the theft of enjoyment hypothesis highlights the fantasy of the transgression of the law. In other words, the type of fantasy put forward by Freud seems to prioritize the father figure, while the *theft of enjoyment* conjecture appears to highlight the mother figure. Be that as it may, Lacan's emphasis on the importance of the first Other (the Mother) in the life of the lacking subject resonates, in part, with Lagache's (1961) contribution. That is, the long-lasting role that the Mother plays in those common cases where the subjects' pre-oedipal identification with Her is not successfully traversed.

Micro-Economic, Institutional, and Historic Approaches to Constitutional Instability in Ecuador

From a Lacanian perspective, in this section I venture the suggestion that the aftereffect of *castration* manifests itself in Ecuador's long-lasting history of CAs. This conjecture adds value to mainstream accounts focused on the subject's rational calculus in general and in relation to Ecuador's constitutional instability in particular.

Why is an institution such as the social pact important in politics? The rational choice theory and affiliated approaches answer this question by stressing their concern about the unpredictable outcomes to be expected in 'open' interactions between parties and individuals. Plainly put, for these perspectives, institutions are needed to constrain our behaviour. By doing so, they foster stability and resolve cooperation, coordination, and agency problems. In other words, political equilibria (i.e., stable outcomes) can be produced through reasonably stable institutions (Shepsle, 1979, 1986, 1989, as cited in Colomer, 2001, pp. 235–236). Despite theoretical differences, there seems to be a consensus regarding the paramount role of institutions. For instance, 'rational choice practitioners and historic institutionalists were largely in agreement on one essential definition and premise: that institutions constitute the "humanly devised constraints that shape human interaction" (North 1990)' (Sanders, 2009, p. 3).

But will institutions remain stable? If so, why? According to the theory of equilibrium institutions, organizations are likely to remain stable for the following reason: institutional development generates increasing returns, in the sense that the benefits of relying on existing institutions outweigh the costs of replacing them (North and Thomas, 1973; North, 1990a, Pierson, 2004, as cited in Colomer, 2001, p. 236).

The guilt stemming from the aftereffect of the mythical parricide is encapsulated in Freud's totemic banquet, a repetitive, destabilizing, and transgressive practice in which the community puts into action what was prohibited and repressed, that is, the desires underpinning the social contract.

According to rational choice theory, and related perspectives, including equilibrium theories, institutions are designed to restrain our behaviour via sanctions/costs/rewards. These theories are buttressed by the neoclassic assumption that individuals try to maximize their utility. Rewards and sanctions are established under the presupposition that individuals will abide by these incentives. The cost of deviation from the established pattern of conduct, according to this neo-classic approach, implies that institutions are stable, and this provides a degree of predictability in different institutional edifices at the local, national, and international levels.

A constitution is a national edifice that seeks to provide stability and continuity to 'the set of the most important rules and common understandings' of any given country. Mainstream scholars assume that, for the most part, institutions will remain stable, on account of the costs stemming from deviation from the path established by an institutional arrangement.

From these related theories, how can we account for Ecuador's historic constitutional instability, a phenomenon already addressed by the 1869 convention? It could be argued that rational choice theory and similar perspectives do not properly account for Ecuador's instability by pointing out how convening a constituent convention every 10 years (on average) has been costly, inefficient, and ineffective. The writing of a new constitution every decade does not provide political and legal stability required for long-term investment in favour of national development, to mention one among many examples of the economic and political costs of constitutional volatility. But from the point of view of elites' interests, it could be contended that the *path dependence* established since independence (i.e., frequent constitutional replacements) is beneficial.[2] After all, the sanctioning of a new constitution legitimizes the rules of the game needed to advance the elites' political, social, and economic interests, which can converge in elitist alliances. And this can happen even if *the set of the most important rules and common understandings* of the republic remains pretty much the same after the abolition of the constitution in force. Ecuador's constitutional instability can be criticized or justified by its losers and winners alike.

A psychoanalytic approach to constitutional instability in Ecuador allows us to address a phenomenon overlooked by the above accounts premised on a rational benefit cost calculus. It is by pointing to the non-rational and ritualistic element underpinning Ecuador's constitutional volatility that psychoanalysis can be said to add value. The 1869, 2008,

[2] 'Path dependence has to mean, if it is to mean anything, that once a country or region has started down a track, the costs of reversal are very high. There will be other choice points, but the entrenchment of certain institutional arrangements obstructs an easy reversal of the initial choice' (Levi, as cited in Pierson, 2004, p. 20).

and 2014–2015 highly emotional debates on the 'indispensable' leaderships of García Moreno, Alfaro, and Correa illustrate this. The longing for a leader whose knowledge and deeds are purportedly irreplaceable for the nation's prosperity suggests, at first sight, that the constitutions proposed or supported by them are to last for a long time. In other words, if the leaders or 'designers of the constitution' are so extraordinary, so should 'their' constitutions be. But Ecuador's history tells us otherwise. The frequent 'replacement' of the 'Messiah' and the corresponding Ecuadorian constitution makes more sense if approached via psychoanalysis. The hypothesis on the 'need for redemption' (cf. *Moses and Monotheism*), which is predicated on the guilt stemming from the *ambivalent* identification with the father figure in childhood, invites us to hypothesize that the constitutional replacements in Ecuador are influenced in part by this dynamic. For instance, as the case of Alfaro allows us to conjecture, the *identification* with the father figure whose death has to be atoned for—Alfaro's—epitomizes this ambivalence. As *Totem and Taboo* indicates, the two repressed wishes underpinning the original pact (or castration to put it in Lacanian terms) are incest and the murder of the father. The return of these deformed wishes, as psychoanalytic theory assumes, influences our political behaviour. In this context, the new constitution can be understood as this 'fullness-to-come' which, of course, is one among many other instantiations of the failed quest for the lost object. The mourning of Alfaro—accompanied by national guilt—speaks to those heroes whose fate has been tragic, such as that of the father of the primal horde or that of King Laius, who was also killed by his own son, Oedipus Rex.

Needless to say, there are other political processes (beyond constituent assemblies in Ecuador) where the father figure appears to predominate. As Žižek (2008, pp. 64–65) highlights, it is guilt for the killing of Caesar—the biological person—that drives repetition to anoint subsequent Caesars. The title 'Caesar' keeps alive the memory of and the attempt to atone for the killing of Caesar, the 'great man' to use Freud's words. This illustrates the usefulness of Freud's thesis on *Moses and Monotheism* (as cited by Žižek, ibid.) beyond Hispanic America.

Freud's case study has been applied to the Ecuadorian case, with particular reference to Eloy Alfaro. In this work I have not included the mourning of García Moreno (Chap. 3), as this does not appear in the 1869 official transcription provided by Ecuador's NA. García Moreno was similarly killed by his own people with a machete, six years after his constitution was sanctioned. The mourning of both García Moreno and Alfaro may have had a similar psychic logic since these persons shared key traits in the eyes of their followers. They mourned the death of a father figure whose authoritarianism was admired; their murder was lamented and atoned by the right-wing and left-wing Catholic republic.

Despite ideological differences, García Moreno and Alfaro were authoritarian leaders in nineteenth and twentieth-century Ecuador. As Ecuadorian historiography highlights, both leaders led putsches, transgressed constitutional provisions, and violently repressed (or even killed) political opponents. Scholars also regard Correa as a contemporary case of authoritarianism. But their authoritarianism was not problematic for their supporters in 1869, 2008, and 2015. *Apropos*, I now circle back to Sharoni's (2016) problematization of Eveline's weak though violent father, as well as Lacan's (1938) notion of a diminished paternal imago and its impact on social neurosis. An imago is an 'unconscious prototypical figure which orientates the subject's way of apprehending others; it is built up on the basis of the first real and phantasied relationships within the family environment' (Laplanche & Pontalis, 1973, p. 211). But this imago is more than just an unconscious image; it is an ***acquired imaginary set*** through which stereotypical mental images, feelings, and behaviour mould the way subjects view others (ibid.).

In this light, how can we make sense of Ecuador's long-lasting history of constitutional instability? Colonialism in Ecuador has distorted the notion of the law. Take the case of racism. Racist humiliation and force were the rule in this country's public sphere, as the case of the tithe shows. Until 1889, the Ecuadorian central government would organize auction blocks to sell the right to collect the tithe to white landowners. These public auctions were facilitated by the Catholic Church, the agent in charge of the demographic statistics at the local level. Under the umbrella of the law of the Republic, the landowners' greed and racism would exploit the indigenous peoples in the highlands by charging them more than 10% of their production. To achieve this theft, these *hacendados* would recourse to humiliating practices to extort illegitimate amounts of money beyond the percentage stipulated in the law. The government and the Church knew about theses racists and illegal inconsistences (Espindola, 2016). In addition to this humiliation suffered by the indigenous peoples, mestizos (those descending from European and indigenous lineages) have too undergone racist mistreatment due to their non-white skin. The mestizo population in Ecuador accounts for 77.5% of its inhabitants.[3] Despite its majoritarian nature, this population illustrates a case of in-group racism. In view of informal codes inherited from colonialism, the *microphysics of power* (to use Foucauldian jargon) is displayed on a daily basis along the following lines: the whiter someone is as a mestizo, the 'better' he/she is. In this day-to-day social interaction and categorization, in which European physical features are regarded as 'superior', it is not surprising to hear racist comments amongst family members, friends, and strangers. 'Longo' and 'indio', for instance, are two terms used as insults against those whose phenotype is 'Indian' or 'not so European'. At this point I am reminded of one of Fanon's assertions in *Black Skin, White Masks*; namely, that it is colonialism (and not the so-called natural inferiority of the colonized) the structure that creates an inferiority complex in colonies. Arguably, the flip side of this inferiority complex in Ecuador manifests in a sense of superiority that disavows the mestizo identity of the nation, a case of 'social splitting' some would argue.

In this light, I would like to suggest that racism has affected the Ecuadorian paternal imago, that is, the behaviour and image of the Ecuadorian father. As Sharoni (2016) reminds us, a father can (or cannot) embody the first instantiation of the law in the private sphere. If systematized violence in the public sphere was exerted on the father in Ecuador, a negative byproduct might have ensued, namely, the reproduction of violence in the household. Assuming this was the case, how has this general state of patriarchal violence influenced, in part, Ecuador's predisposition to *identify* with authoritarian figures in politics? The Lacanian maxim that *we need to go back to Freud* is of help here. In *Group Psychology*, Freud stresses that identification, the first manifestation of emotional attachment, makes subjects want to be like their fathers when they grow up. However, '[i]dentification, in fact, is ambivalent from the very first; it can turn into an expression of tenderness as easily as into a wish for someone's removal' (Freud, 1959, p. 37). This maxim needs contextualization. The new constitution in Ecuador has promised a fullness-to-come, that is, the beatific dimension of fantasy (Glynos & Howarth, 2007). But this promise has depended on the abolition of the previous constitution, and this has required the removal of the substitute father figure implanted in the anterior charter. At this point I cannot help but ask: has heroic

[3] Cf. https://www.cia.gov/the-world-factbook/countries/ecuador/factsheets/ (accessed on 04/12/2025).

identification with the flip side of a diminished paternal imago (authoritarianism) in postcolonial Ecuador influenced the nature of its constitutional tradition? If so, to what extent? I leave these as open-ended questions.

In *Moses and Monotheism*, Freud describes Moses as this severe (and maybe authoritarian) Egyptian caudillo. This makes sense in light of the tyrannical nature of the mythical father of the primal horde. However, Freud's religious and political myth begs context-dependent operationalizations. He himself analyses two different reincarnations of the dead and tyrannical Father: the severe Moses and the more democratic Christ. And this, I argue, opens the possibility of adding nuances to how this myth plays out in different contexts and epochs, such as the suggested case of a diminished paternal imago in the constitutional politics of postcolonial Ecuador.

Besides the explicit sway that Presidents García Moreno and Correa exerted on the 1869 and 2007–2008 CAs, the invocation of previous caudillos/heroes was a common practice in the archives analysed. For instance, while Urbina was critically invoked by the 1869 CA, Alfaro was praised by the 2007–2008 convention. But the mourning tone that characterized the 2008 parliamentary session seeking to atone for Alfaro's 'terrible' death was indeed worthy of attention. This session brought together different parties and organizations beyond Alianza País. This 'blurring' of the Left-Right distinction in 2008 resonates with the mythical totemic banquet, a ritual in which the whole of a community re-experiences pleasure and guilt for the killing of its founding Father.

Concluding Remarks

In this final chapter, I have visited key competing understandings of constitutional instability, integrating these into my account of the Ecuadorian case. In doing so, I have sought to establish a dialogue between these non-psychoanalytic explanations and my psychoanalytically informed argument on Ecuador's history of constitutional instability.

The nature of the alternative hypotheses discussed in this chapter is multifaceted. It entails philosophical, legal, institutionalist, and economic rationales. In different degrees, my comparative reflection has prompted the invocation of psychoanalysis as a complementary approach in explaining constitutional instability in Ecuador. For example, the philosophical and legal feasibility of frequent constitutional replacements in

Ecuador—predicated on Rousseau's and Sieyès's democratic doctrine—is complemented by my argument, namely, that the *fantasy* of the Messiah occurs across the ideological spectrum. The need for *redemption* for the killing of the father of the primal horde and the desire for the promised land are aspects beyond political affiliations. The putsches conducted by the conservative García Moreno and the liberal Alfaro to sanction the 1869 and 1906 constitutions, as well as the democratic character of the 2008 charter, are illustrative of the trans-ideological and trans-democratic dimensions of the phenomenon under analysis.

It is noteworthy that, although General Alfaro rose to power via non-democratic means, a highly democratic and participatory convention (that of 2007–2008) praised him. Relatedly, the messianic discourse found in a constituent assembly—the foundational moment of the Ecuadorian republic—is similar in two highly different contexts: that of 1869 and 2007–2008. It could be argued, then, that Rousseau's influence on Ecuador's democracy is in tension with its hybrid messianism. Alternatively, it could be contended that the Rousseauian nature of presidential Ecuador fits its messianism. After all, in the *Social Contract* Rousseau highlights the importance of the *legislator*, a person whose extraordinary knowledge serves as the basis for the laws to be written and then voted for by the sovereign (*the populus*). Irrespective of the fact that Rousseau prioritizes the legislative over the executive, the idea that there is one person whose wisdom is pivotal in the law-making process resonates with the idea of the Messiah/lawgiver, that is, this extraordinary leader who 'ought' to exert influence on the writing of the fundamental law. However, Freud's myth can and should be contextualized. I have sought this through the operationalization of the ideal-ego and the notion of a diminished paternal imago in a postcolonial context. This operationalization has allowed me to suggest a partial link between the psychosocial condition of patriarchal and postcolonial Ecuador and its recurrent constitutional replacements, processes led by authoritarian leaders from across the ideological spectrum (García Moreno, Eloy Alfaro, and Rafael Correa).

References

Aragundi, J. M. (1869). *Acta de instalación*. Archivo de la Asamblea Nacional del Ecuador, 16 May.

Ayala, E. (2014). Rasgos históricos de la evolución constitucional del Ecuador. In M. E. Ayala (Ed.), *Historia constitucional: estudios comparativos*. Quito.

Cavalletto, G. (2007). *Crossing the psycho-social divide. Freud, Weber, Adorno and Elias*. Ashgate.

Colomer, J. (2001). Disequilibrium Institutions and Pluralist Democracy. *Journal of Theoretical Politics, 13*(3), 235–247.

Espindola, E. (2016). *La construcción del Estado ecuatoriano y de su ciudadanía tributaria a la luz del diezmo*. E-book Retrieved January 24, 2023, from https://www.flacso.edu.ec/node/111?id=4283

Espinosa, C. (2010). *Historia del Ecuador en contexto regional y global*. Lexus.

Freud, S. (1959). *Group Psychology and The Analysis of The Ego*. The Hogarth Press and The Institute of Psycho-Analysis.

García Moreno, G. (1869). *Acta de instalación*. Archivo de la Asamblea Nacional del Ecuador, 16, 21 May, 9 August.

García Villegas, M. (2012). Constitucionalismo aspiracional: Derecho, Democracia Y Cambio social En América Latina. *Revista Análisis Político, 75*, 89–110.

Glynos, J., & Howarth, D. (2007). *Logics of critical explanation in social and political theory*. Routledge.

Hirschorn, L. (1990). Work and reparation. In *The workplace within: Psychodynamics of organisational life*. MIT Press.

Hurtado, L. (2007). *Asamblea constituyente*. Archivo de la Asamblea Nacional del Ecuador, 13 December.

Issa, N. (2014). *Continuación del primer debate de la solicitud de enmienda constitucional*. Archivo de la Asamblea Nacional del Ecuador, 2 December.

King, A. (2011). *The British Constitution*. Oxford Scholarship Online. oxford.universitypressscholarship.com

Lacan, J. (1938). Family complexes in the formation of the individual. Paris: Encyclopédie française (A. de Monzie, Editor), Vol. 8, translated by Cormac Gallagher.

Lagache, D. (1961). *El psicoanálisis y la estructura de la personalidad*. Asociación Psicoanalítica del Uruguay – Revista Uruguaya de Psicoanálisis.

Laplanche, J., & Pontalis, J.-B. (1973). *The Language of Psycho-analysis*. Norton.

Negretto, G. L. (2008) The durability of constitutions in changing environments: explaining constitutional replacements in Latin America. Kellogg Institute, working paper 350 (pp. 1–34). Retrieved February 7, 2020, from https://kellogg.nd.edu/documents/1658

Pierson, P. (2004). *Politics in time. History, institutions, and social analysis*. Princeton University Press.

Pilamunga, C. (2007, 2008). *Asamblea constituyente*. Archivo de la Asamblea Nacional del Ecuador, 11 December 2007; 5 March, 7 June 2008.

Roldós, M. (2008). *Asamblea constituyente*. Archivo de la Asamblea Nacional del Ecuador, 28 January, 25 June.

Rueschemeyer, D., Huber Stephens, E., & Stephens, J. (1992). *Capitalist development and democracy*. University of Chicago Press.

Sanders, E. (2009). Historical Institutionalism. In S. Binder, R. Rhodes, & B. Rockman (Eds.), *The oxford handbook of political institutions*. Oxford University Press. E-Book retrieved from the University of Essex Library. https://doi.org/10.1093/oxfordhb/9780199548460.003.0003

Sharoni, J. (2016). The failure of the parental metaphor: A Lacanian reading of James Joyce's "Eveline". *Journal of Modern Literature, 39*(4), 33–48.

Stavrakakis, Y. (1999). *Lacan & the political*. Routledge.

Taiano, V. (2007, 2008). *Asamblea constituyente*. Archivo de la Asamblea Nacional del Ecuador, 13 December 2007; 13 May, 25 June 2008.

The Carter Center (2008). *Informe sobre la Asamblea Constituyente de la República del Ecuador*. Retrieved February 28, 2023, from https://www.cartercenter.org/resources/pdfs/peace/americas/informe_final_ac_-_centro_carter_distribuido.pdf

Žižek, S. (1990). Eastern Europe's Republics of Gilead. *New Left Review* (I/183, September-October).

Žižek, S. (2008). *The sublime object of ideology*. Verso.

Final Comments

The strong colonial state in Ecuador (Ayala, 2011) disappeared after independence. The lack of capitalist development aggravated the weakness of the central state (Rueschemeyer et al., 1992) that followed the failed attempt to instate *Gran Colombia* (1822–1830). From 1830, the power vacuum in Ecuador was filled by *caudillos* (McLean & Alistair, 2003). In this national context of political and economic adversities, a strict adherence to the constitution in force was unlikely. As the 1869 CA put it, 'Presidents before the 1861 charter swore an oath to respect and sustain seven Constitutions and obey the laws, and they scandalously ran over them without even remembering their oath' (Noboa MA, as referenced by the secretary, Noboa, 1869, p. 3).

This book has been guided by the following overarching question: *how can we best characterize and account for Ecuador'sconstitutional volatility*? To answer this, I have focused on the psychoanalytic factor accounting in part for this instability. In light of available archives stored in Ecuador's National Assembly (NA), as well as a contextualized and problematized interpretation of *Moses and Monotheism*, I have put forward the following overarching argument. Ecuador's history of postcolonial political violence has fostered a culture prone to supporting *messianic*leaders, that is, lawgivers whose personages have been invested with the hope and aspiration of perpetual stability, epitomized by the setting up of Constituent Assemblies (CAs) themselves. The messianic leaders analysed here (García

E. Espindola, *The Paternal Imago in Ruins*, The Palgrave Lacan Series, https://doi.org/10.1007/978-3-032-07507-9

Moreno, Eloy Alfaro, and Rafael Correa) are known for their authoritarianism and popularity amongst their followers, who have identified with them in a *heroic* way. This heroic identification, as I have conjectured above, can be understood as the flip side of a diminished paternal imago in patriarchal Ecuador, on account of the colonial violence perpetrated against its authority figure, a violence likely reproduced in the private sphere. In sum, a Lacanian understanding of *messianism* (and related concepts such as *enjoyment, castration, fantasy, the super-ego, identification, the ideal-ego, a diminished paternal imago*) has allowed me to grasp that which appears to underpin, in part, the affectively invested and ritualistic dimension of constitutional instability in Ecuador.

This book has studied the Ecuadorian context, leaving unattended necessary comparisons within the region, all the more so considering that 'constitutional instability' is not endemic to Ecuador alone but to all Hispanic America. Although my hypothesis cannot be generalized to the whole of Latin America, further research may open up the possibility of exploring this potential and its limits. And this might be so considering the well-known prevalence of 'strong leaders/caudillos' (charismatic or not) in the politics of this politically unstable region. CAs play an important role in Hispanic America as one can infer from Negretto's (2008) study. Since psychoanalytically informed endeavours tend to call for an in-depth discourse analysis, an initial two-country comparison might appear a promising way forward for a future book. Such a comparative study would have to consider the clear contextual differences between sub-regions within postcolonial South America. For instance, that between the Andean area and the Rio de la Plata, regions with different ethnic and economic histories. In this comparative context, and from a psychoanalytic perspective, one could imagine asking: what 'psychic nuance' makes Argentina—where a genocide occurred at the end of the nineteenth century—a more stable country in terms of constitutional replacements than Ecuador, where the state did not implement a genocide? Relatedly, how do colonial variants affect differently the operationalization of Freud's myth?

My appeal to psychoanalytically informed categories in this book has sought to contribute to our understanding of a highly discussed topic in political science: 'constitutional instability'. However, the psychoanalytic factor discussed here is not restricted to shedding light on cases of instability; it can very plausibly be used to shed light on cases of constitutional stability too, such as that of the 1787 US constitution. In other words, we can readily imagine the analytical category of *messianism* being applied to the American case, often linked to its *founding fathers*. The key point, of course, in establishing these different uses of the psychoanalytic factor lies in the difference in context. Whether political instability or stability underpins the research puzzle is a context-dependent matter. In this investigation I have unpacked certain elements of psychoanalytic theory to better understand the unstable and cyclical rewriting of the Ecuadorian constitution. In this same line of thought, the ritualistic aspect underlying the constitutional politics of Ecuador might very well operate in CAs elsewhere, as well as in other political processes. However, this comparative observation raises a broader explanatory issue that may invite future research regarding how to negotiate the relationship between psychoanalytic categories in different contexts, not least because rituals are present in most (if not all) political phenomena?

On a final note, I would like to pose a few open-ended questions regarding the 'so what?' query of this book. This is a work whose main purpose is to offer a novel understanding of Ecuador's long-lasting history of 'constitutional instability'. But the author is also interested in the practical impact that this volatility has had in Ecuador's development. After all, setting up CAs every decade since independence has not solved the basic needs of the population, despite the promises made by the people's representatives in these assemblies. Can this book, then—or a fraction of it—be of any relevance for the political elites in Ecuador? Maybe the psychoanalytic factor emphasized in this work, which relates to the 'instability' of a postcolonial country, can be 'treated' in reconciliation conventions where a particular society seeks cultural transformations. But first, Ecuadorians would need to ask: what is exactly that which needs to be 'treated' in postcolonial Ecuador which seems to be underpinning the *frequent* need for 'strong' (authoritarian) messiahs across the ideological spectrum?

References

Acosta, A. (2008). *Asamblea constituyente.* Archivo de la Asamblea Nacional del Ecuador, 28 January, 24 June.

Aguirre, G. (2007). *Asamblea constituyente.* Archivo de la Asamblea Nacional del Ecuador, 27 December.

Alcázar, N. N., Martínez, N. N., & Salazar, J. (1869). *Sesión del 24 de mayo.* Archivo de la Asamblea Nacional del Ecuador, 24 May.

Alcívar, F. (2008). *Asamblea constituyente.* Archivo de la Asamblea Nacional del Ecuador, 13 May.

Alvarado, R. (2008). Asamblea Constituyente. Archivo de la Asamblea Nacional del Ecuador, 9 June.

Amores, B. (2008). *Asamblea constituyente.* Archivo de la Asamblea Nacional del Ecuador, 8 May, 9 June.

Aragundi, J. M. (1869). *Acta de instalación.* Archivo de la Asamblea Nacional del Ecuador, 16 May.

Arboleda, A. (2008). *Asamblea constituyente.* Archivo de la Asamblea Nacional del Ecuador, 13 May.

Arlotti, R. (2003). *Vocabulario técnico y científico de la política.* Dunken.

Asamblea Constituyente. (2007). *Asamblea constituyente.* Archivo de la Asamblea Nacional del Ecuador, 11, 27 December.

Asamblea Nacional. República del Ecuador. (2023) Constituciones de la República del Ecuador de 1998 a 1830. Retrieved February 28, 2023, from http://archivobiblioteca.asambleanacional.gob.ec/constituciones-anteriores

Ayala, E. (2008). *Manual de historia del Ecuador II. Época Republicana.* Corporación Editora Nacional.

E. Espindola, *The Paternal Imago in Ruins*, The Palgrave Lacan Series, https://doi.org/10.1007/978-3-032-07507-9

Ayala, E. (2011). *Ecuador del siglo XIX. Estado Nacional, Ejército, Iglesia y Municipio*. Universidad Andina Simón Bolívar – Corporación Editorial Nacional.

Ayala, E. (2014). Rasgos históricos de la evolución constitucional del Ecuador. In M. E. Ayala (Ed.), *Historia constitucional: estudios comparativos*. Quito.

Basabe-Serrano, S. (2017). El fin de la hegemonía de Rafael Correa y los espejismos del giro a la izquierda en Ecuador: un análisis desde la perspectiva del electorado. In C. Arqueros & A. Iriarte (Eds.), *Chile y América Latina. Crisis de las izquierdas del siglo XXI* (pp. 313–334). Instituto Res Publica.

Billiet, L. (2023). The cultural superego or the demand for universality. Retrieved March 10, 2023, from https://nlscongress2023.amp-nls.org/blogposts/lievebillieten

Bobbio, N., Matteucci, N., & Pasquino, G. (2005). *Diccionario de política*. Siglo Veintiuno Editores.

Bohórquez, X. (2008). *Asamblea constituyente*. Archivo de la Asamblea Nacional del Ecuador, 4 January.

Breslauer, S. D. (2019). Negative charisma, leadership, and Martin Buber's myth of Zion. *Jewish Culture and History, 20*(2), 123–139.

Burbano, F. (2007). *Asamblea constituyente*. Archivo de la Asamblea Nacional del Ecuador,27 December.

Bustamante, P. (1869) *Sesión del 17 de Mayo*. Archivo de la Asamblea Nacional del Ecuador, 17 May.

Bynander, F., & Hart, P. (2006). When Power Changes Hands: The Political Psychology of Leadership Succession in Democracies. *Political Psychology, 27*(5), 707–730.

Carey, J. (2003). The Reelection Debate in Latin America. *Latin American Politics and Society, 45*(1), 119–133.

Carvajal, M. A. (1869). *Acta de instalación*. Archivo de la Asamblea Nacional del Ecuador, 28 May, 21 July.

Cavalletto, G. (2007). *Crossing the psycho-social divide. Freud, Weber, Adorno and Elias*. Ashgate.

Chacón, S. (2008). Asamblea Constituyente. Archivo de la Asamblea Nacional del Ecuador, 15 July

Chuji, M. (2007). *Asamblea constituyente*. Archivo de la Asamblea Nacional del Ecuador, 27 December.

Clavero, B. (2007). The rule of law and the legal treatment of native americans. In P. Costa & D. Zolo (Eds.), *Law and philosophy library* (Vol. 80). Springer.

Colomer, J. (2001). Disequilibrium Institutions and Pluralist Democracy. *Journal of Theoretical Politics, 13*(3), 235–247.

Comité Especializado. (2014). *Primer debate de la Solicitud de Enmienda Constitucional* Archivo de la Asamblea Nacional del Ecuador, 1 December.

Constitución de. (1869). https://www.cancilleria.gob.ec/wp-content/uploads/2013/06/constitucion_1869.pdf

Constitución de. (1998). http://archivobiblioteca.asambleanacional.gob.ec/constitucion-1998

Constitución política del Ecuador. (2008). https://www.cancilleria.gob.ec/wp-content/uploads/2013/06/constitucion_2008.pdf

Continuación del primer debate de la solicitud de enmienda constitucional. (2014). Archivo de la Asamblea Nacional del Ecuador, 2 December.

Cordero, F. (2008). *Asamblea constituyente*. Archivo de la Asamblea Nacional del Ecuador, 4 January.

Cordero, S. (2018). *La plurinacionalidad desde abajo. Autogobierno indígena en Bolivia y Ecuador*. FLACSO, Ecuador – Programa de las Naciones Unidas para el Desarrollo.

Correa, R. (2007). Es absurda la reelección indefinida. *El Universo*, 10 November. Retrieved February 28, 2023, from https://www.eluniverso.com/2007/11/10/0001/8/F275D24BD604403AA42BF797883984AD.html

Correa, R. (2014). INFORME A LA NACIÓN.

Correa, R. (2014a). Continuación del primer debate de la solicitud de enmienda constitucional. Archivo de la Asamblea Nacional del Ecuador, 2 December.

Correa, R. (2014b). Correa descartó reformar la Constitución para buscar reelección. *La Nación*, 20 January. Retrieved February 28, 2023, from https://www.lanacion.com.co/correa-descarto-reformar-la-constitucion-para-buscar-reeleccion/

Corte Constitucional del Ecuador. (2015). *Segundo debate de la solicitud de Enmiendas Constitucionales*. Archivo de la Asamblea Nacional del Ecuador, 3 December.

Dahl, R. (2003). *¿Es democrática la constitución de los Estados Unidos?* Fondo de Cultura Económica.

Donoso, P. (2014). *Continuación del primer debate de la solicitud de enmienda constitucional*. Archivo de la Asamblea Nacional del Ecuador, 2 December.

Eguiguren, M., Noboa, T., Saenz, J. (1869). Acta de instalación. Archivo de la Asamblea Nacional del Ecuador, 16 May.

El Jóven Conservador. (1869). *Candidaturas*. Pólit. (Retrieved: 8 January 2022).

El Universo. (2016). *Fernando Bustamante es el tercer asambleísta en dejar Alianza PAIS*. Retrieved February 9, 2023, from https://www.eluniverso.com/noticias/2016/01/28/nota/5373631/fernando-bustamante-es-tercer-asambleista-dejar-alianza-pais/

El Universo. (2017). *Rafael Correa, entre los cinco presidentes con más tiempo en el poder*. Retrieved February 24, 2023, from https://www.eluniverso.com/noticias/2017/05/22/nota/6195727/rafael-correa-cinco-presidentes-mas-tiempo-poder/

elDiario.es. (2015). Protestas en Ecuador contra enmiendas a Constitución y reelección indefinida. *elDiario.es*, 25 November. Retrieved February 28, 2023, from https://www.eldiario.es/politica/Protestas-Ecuador-Constitucion-reeleccion-indefinida_0_456005501.html

Enmienda S/N (Enmiendas a la Constitución de la República del Ecuador) (2015). *Cancillería del Ecuador*. Retrieved from https://www.cancilleria.gob.ec/wp-content/uploads/2016/01/enmiendas-a-la-constitucion-de-la-republica-del-ecuador.pdf

Escala, J. (2008). *Asamblea constituyente*. Archivo de la Asamblea Nacional del Ecuador, 25 June.

Espindola, E. (2016). *La construcción del Estado ecuatoriano y de su ciudadanía tributaria a la luz del diezmo*. E-book Retrieved January 24, 2023, from https://www.flacso.edu.ec/node/111?id=4283

Espindola, E. (2023). Making presidential re-elections indefinite: A psychoanalytic contribution to the case of the ecuadorian citizens' Revolution'. *Journal of Psychosocial Studies, 16*(2), 1–14. https://doi.org/10.1332/147867321X16763239991753

Espinosa, C. (2010). *Historia del Ecuador en contexto regional y global*. Lexus.

Evans, D. (1996). *An introductory dictionary of lacanian psychoanalysis*. Routledge.

Finlayson, A. (2007). From Beliefs to Arguments: Interpretive Methodology and Rhetorical Political Analysis. *British Journal of Politics & International, 9*, 545–563.

Finlayson, A. (2013). Ideology and Political Rhetoric. In *The oxford handbook of political ideologies*. Oxford University Press.

Freud, S. (1914) *On Narcissism*. The Standard Edition of the Complete Psychological Works of Sigmund Freud, Volume XIV (1914-1916): On the History of the Psycho-Analytic Movement, Papers on Metapsychology and Other Works, pp. 67–102. Retrieved February 28, 2023, from https://www.sas.upenn.edu/~cavitch/pdf-library/Freud_SE_On_Narcissism_complete.pdf

Freud, S. (1921/1959). *Group psychology and the analysis of the ego*. The Hogarth Press and The Institute of Psycho-Analysis.

Freud, S. (1959). *Group Psychology and The Analysis of The Ego*. The Hogarth Press and The Institute of Psycho-Analysis.

Freud, S. (1964a). Femininity, lecture XXXIII of the new introductory lectures on pyscho-analysis. In *The standard edition of the complete psychological works of Sigmund Freud* (Vol. XXII). The Hogarth Press and the Institute of Psycho-analysis.

Freud, S. (1964b). Moses and monotheism. In *The standard edition of the complete psychological works of Sigmund Freud* (Vol. XXIII). The Hogarth Press and the Institute of Psycho-analysis.

Freud, S. (1964c). The future of an illusion. In *The standard edition of the complete psychological works of Sigmund Freud* (Vol. XXI). The Hogarth Press and the Institute of Psycho-analysis.

Freud, S. (2015a). *Tótem y tabú*. Amorrortu Editores.

Freud, S. (2015b). *Moisés y la religión monoteísta*. Amorrortu Editores.

García Moreno, G. (1869). *Acta de instalación*. Archivo de la Asamblea Nacional del Ecuador, 16, 21 May, 9 August.
García Villegas, M. (2012). Constitucionalismo aspiracional: Derecho, Democracia Y Cambio social En América Latina. *Revista Análisis Político, 75*, 89–110.
Gargarella, R. (2015). El "Nuevo Constitucionalismo Latinoamericano". *Estudios Sociales, 48*, 169–173. Retrieved February 20, 2020, from https://bibliotecavirtual.unl.edu.ar/publicaciones/index.php/EstudiosSociales/article/view/5105/7752
Georgetown University. (2009). Republic of Ecuador. Chronology of Presidents. *Political Database of the Americas*. Retrieved February 28, 2023, from https://pdba.georgetown.edu/Executive/Ecuador/pres.html
Glynos, J. (2008). Self-transgressive enjoyment as a freedom fetter. *Political Studies, 56*, 679–704.
Glynos, J. (2021). Critical fantasy studies. *Journal of Language and Politics, 20*(1), 95–111.
Glynos, J., & Howarth, D. (2007). *Logics of critical explanation in social and political theory*. Routledge.
Grefa, C. (2007). *Asamblea constituyente*. Archivo de la Asamblea Nacional del Ecuador, 27 December.
Grijalva, A., & Castro-Montero, J. L. (2019). Reelección presidencial indefinida y reforma constitucional en América Latina: análisis comparado de los casos de Venezuela, Nicaragua, Ecuador y Bolivia. In M. C. Fuchs & M. Schaffler (Eds.), *Anuario de Derecho Constitucional Latinoamericano 2019* (pp. 222–244). Bogotá. Retrieved February 28, 2023, from https://www.scielo.cl/pdf/estconst/v18n1/0718-5200-estconst-18-01-9.pdf
Guamangate, L. (2008). *Asamblea constituyente*. Archivo de la Asamblea Nacional del Ecuador, 24 June.
Hernández, V. (2008). *Asamblea constituyente*. Archivo de la Asamblea Nacional del Ecuador, 13 May.
Hirschorn, L. (1990). Work and reparation. In *The workplace within: Psychodynamics of organisational life*. MIT Press.
Hook, D. (2008). Articulating psychoanalysis and psychosocial studies: Limitations and possibilities. *Psychoanalysis, Culture & Society, 13*, 397–405.
Hook, D. (2017). What is "enjoyment as a political factor"? *Political Psychology, 38*(4), 605–620.
Hook, D. (2018a). Racism and jouissance: Evaluating the "racism as (the theft of) enjoyment" hypothesis. *Psychoanalysis, Culture & Society, 23*, 244–266.
Hook, D. (2018b). *Six moments in Lacan. Communication and identification in psychology and psychoanalysis*. Routledge.
Howarth, D. (1997). Complexities of identity/difference: Black Consciousness ideology in South Africa. *Journal of Political Ideologies, 2*(1), 51–78.

Hurtado, L. (2007). *Asamblea constituyente*. Archivo de la Asamblea Nacional del Ecuador, 13 December.

Ibarra, H. (2010). *Visión histórico-política de la Constitución del 2008*. Centro Andino de Acción Popular.

Instituto Latinoamericano de Investigaciones Sociales – Revista La Tendencia. (2008). *Análisis Nueva Constitución*. Retrieved February 28, 2023, from https://library.fes.de/pdf-files/bueros/quito/05700.pdf

Instituto Nacional de Estadística y Censos (INEC). (2006) *La Población Indígena Del Ecuador. Análisis De Estadísticas Socio-Demográficas*. Retrieved February 28, 2023, from https://www.acnur.org/fileadmin/Documentos/Publicaciones/2009/7015.pdf

International Labour Organization. (n.d.). www.ilo.org

Issa, N. (2014). *Continuación del primer debate de la solicitud de enmienda constitucional*. Archivo de la Asamblea Nacional del Ecuador, 2 December.

King, A. (2011). *The British Constitution*. Oxford Scholarship Online. oxford.universitypressscholarship.com

La Estrella de Mayo (1869). Convencion De 1869, 24 May. Quito: Biblioteca Aurelio Espinosa Pólit.

La Nación. (2014). Correa descartó reformar la Constitución para buscar reelección. Retrieved February 28, 2023, from https://www.lanacion.com.co/correa-descarto-reformar-la-constitucion-para-buscar-reeleccion/

Lacan, J. (1938). Family complexes in the formation of the individual. Paris: Encyclopédie française (A. de Monzie, Editor), Vol. 8, translated by Cormac Gallagher.

Lacan, J. (1981). *The four fundamental concepts of psychoanalysis (Book XI)*. London.

Lacan, J. (1991). *Freud's Papers on Technique 1953-1954. Book I*. Norton.

Lacan, J. (1997). *The ethics of psychoanalysis 1959-1960. Book VII*. Norton.

Lacan, J. (1999). *Las formaciones del inconsciente 1957-1958. Libro 5*. Paidós.

Lacan, J. (2000). *The Psychoses 1955–1956. Book III*. Norton.

Lacan, J. (2016). *La Relación de objeto. seminario 4*. Paidós.

Laclau, E. (2005/2007). *On populist reason*. Verso.

Lagache, D. (1961). *El psicoanálisis y la estructura de la personalidad*. Asociación Psicoanalítica del Uruguay – Revista Uruguaya de Psicoanálisis.

Laplanche, J., & Pontalis, J.-B. (1973). *The Language of Psycho-analysis*. Norton.

Lavanguardia. (2015). *Parlamento de Ecuador aprueba enmiendas que incluyen reelección indefinida*. Retrieved February 28, 2023, from https://www.lavanguardia.com/politica/20151203/30580201267/parlamento-de-ecuador-aprueba-enmiendas-que-incluyen-la-reeleccion-indefinida.html

Lazo, M. A. (1869). *Sesión del 28 de Junio*. Archivo de la Asamblea Nacional del Ecuador, 28 June.

Lexico (English Dictionary). (n.d.). https://www.lexico.com/definition/latifundium

Lijphart, A. (1999). *Patterns of democracy. Government forms and performance in thirty-six countries.* Yale University Press.

Locke, J. (2002). *Segundo ensayo sobre el gobierno civil.* Editorial Losada.

Martin, J. (2014). *Politics and rhetoric: A critical introduction.* Routledge. Available at: University of Essex (E-book).

Martin, J. (2016). Capturing desire: Rhetorical strategies and the affectivity of discourse. *The British Journal of Politics and International Relations, 18*(1), 143–160.

Martin, J. (2019). *Psycho-politics of speech. Uncivil discourse and the excess of desire.* Transcript.

Martínez, M. (2008). *Asamblea constituyente.* Archivo de la Asamblea Nacional del Ecuador, 9 June.

Martínez, M. A. (1869). *Sesión del 19 de Mayo.* Archivo de la Asamblea Nacional del Ecuador, 19, 21, 28 May, 3 June.

Masaquiza, V. (2008). *Asamblea constituyente.* Archivo de la Asamblea Nacional del Ecuador, 7 July.

McLean, I., & Alistair, M. M. (2003). *Oxford concise dictionary of politics.* Oxford University Press.

Mendoza, N. T. (2008). *Asamblea constituyente.* Archivo de la Asamblea Nacional del Ecuador, 8 May.

Ministerio de Relaciones Exteriores y Movilidad Humana. (2015). *Enmienda S/N (Enmiendas a la Constitución de la República del Ecuador).* Retrieved February 28, 2023, from https://www.cancilleria.gob.ec/wp-content/uploads/2016/01/enmiendas-a-la-constitucion-de-la-republica-del-ecuador.pdf

Misión de Observación Electoral de la Unión Europea. (2007). *Informe Final.* https://aceproject.org/ero-en/regions/americas/EC/ecuador-final-report-constituent-assembly-eu-2007-1/view

Muldoon, P. (2017). A reconciliation most desirable: Shame, narcissism, justice and apology. *International Political Science Review, 38*(2), 213–226.

National Assembly. (1869). *Sesión ordinaria del 2 de Junio.* Archivo de la Asamblea Nacional del Ecuador, 2 June.

Negretto, G. L. (2008) The durability of constitutions in changing environments: explaining constitutional replacements in Latin America. Kellogg Institute, working paper 350 (pp. 1–34). Retrieved February 7, 2020, from https://kellogg.nd.edu/documents/1658

Negretto, G. L. (2013). Making constitutions. In *Presidents, parties, and institutional choice in Latin America.* Cambridge University Press.

Noboa, N. N. (1869). *Sesión del 31 de Mayo.* Archivo de la Asamblea Nacional del Ecuador, 31 May.

Notimérica. (2007). *Ecuador.- Tribunal Electoral aprueba la propuesta de Correa y convoca a una consulta popular para el 15 de abril.* Retrieved February 28, 2023, from https://www.notimerica.com/politica/noticia-ecuador-tribunal-

electoral-aprueba-propuesta-correa-convoca-consulta-popular-15-abril-20070302185318.html
O'Donnell, G. (2007). *Disonancias. Críticas democráticas a la democracia*. Prometeo Libros.
Oleas, J. (2018). *Ecuador 1972-1999: del boom del petróleo a la pérdida del signo monetario (o los costos del cambio de régimen de desarrollo)*. Editorial IAEN.
Ordónez, M. A. (1869). *Acta de instalación*. Archivo de la Asamblea Nacional del Ecuador, 3 June.
Ovid. (1977). *Metamorphoses, Book III (Narcissus and Echo)*. Harvard University Press. translation by Frank Justus Miller.
Paredes, P. (2008). *Asamblea constituyente*. Archivo de la Asamblea Nacional del Ecuador, 8 May.
Payne, M., & Allamand, A. (2007). The effects of presidential election systems on democratic governability. In J. M. Payne, G. Zovatto, & M. Mateo (Eds.), *Democracies in development. Politics and reform in Latin America*. Inter-American Development Bank.
Peters, R. (2010). The riddle of charisma. *Society, 47*, 516–520.
Pierson, P. (2004). *Politics in time. History, institutions, and social analysis*. Princeton University Press.
Pilamunga, C. (2007, 2008). *Asamblea constituyente*. Archivo de la Asamblea Nacional del Ecuador, 11 December 2007; 5 March, 7 June 2008.
Presidencia de la República. (2014). *Informe A La Nación*. Retrieved February 28, 2023, from https://www.presidencia.gob.ec/wp-content/uploads/downloads/2014/05/2014-15-24-INFORME-A-LA-NACIÓN-Segunda-Parte.pdf
Primer debate de la Solicitud de Enmienda Constitucional. (2014). Archivo de la Asamblea Nacional del Ecuador, 1 December.
Reporte de la mayoría. (2008). *Asamblea constituyente*. Archivo de la Asamblea Nacional del Ecuador, 8 May.
Richards, B. (2018). Exploring malignancies: Narcissism and paranoia today. *Psychoanalysis, Culture & Society, 23*, 15–27.
Roldós, M. (2008). *Asamblea constituyente*. Archivo de la Asamblea Nacional del Ecuador, 28 January, 25 June.
Rousseau, J.-J. (2005). *El Contrato social*. Editorial Losada.
Rueschemeyer, D., Huber Stephens, E., & Stephens, J. (1992). *Capitalist development and democracy*. University of Chicago Press.
Salazar, F. (2008). *Asamblea constituyente*. Archivo de la Asamblea Nacional del Ecuador, 8 May.
Salazar, V. (1869). Debates de la Convención Nacional, Archivo de la Asamblea Nacional del Ecuador, 19, 21 May.
Salvador Lara, J. (2005). *Breve historia contemporánea del Ecuador*. Fondo de Cultura Económica.

Sanders, E. (2009). Historical Institutionalism. In S. Binder, R. Rhodes, & B. Rockman (Eds.), *The oxford handbook of political institutions.* Oxford University Press. E-Book retrieved from the University of Essex Library. https://doi.org/10.1093/oxfordhb/9780199548460.003.0003

Sarango, J. (2008). *Asamblea constituyente.* Archivo de la Asamblea Nacional del Ecuador, 9 June.

Sarrade, M. A. (1869). *Sesión del 19 de Mayo.* 'Sesión del 4 de Junio. Archivo de la Asamblea Nacional del Ecuador, 19 May, 4 June, 28 July (b).

Sartori, G. (2003). *Ingeniería constitucional comparada.* Fondo de Cultura Económica.

Secretary of the Convention. (2008). *Asamblea constituyente.* Archivo de la Asamblea Nacional del Ecuador, 5 March, 9, 29 April, 8 May, 7, 24 June.

Secretary of the Treasury. (1869a). *Sesión del 1º de Junio, por la noche.* Archivo de la Asamblea Nacional del Ecuador, 1 June.

Secretary of the Treasury. (1869b). *Sesión del 4 de Junio.* Archivo de la Asamblea Nacional del Ecuador, 4 June.

Secretary of War. (1869). *Sesión extraordinaria del 2 de Junio.* Archivo de la Asamblea Nacional del Ecuador, 2 June.

Segundo Debate de la Solicitud de enmiendas Constitucionales. (2015) Archivo de la Asamblea Nacional del Ecuador, 3 December.

Sesión del 21 de Agosto. (1869). Debates de la Convención Nacional, Archivo de la Asamblea Nacional del Ecuador, 21 August.

Sesión del 24 de Agosto. (1869). Debates de la Convención Nacional, Archivo de la Asamblea Nacional del Ecuador, 24 August.

Sesión del 27 de Agosto por la noche. (1869). Debates de la Convención Nacional, Archivo de la Asamblea Nacional del Ecuador, 27 August.

Sesión del 29 de Agosto. (1869). Debates de la Convención Nacional, Archivo de la Asamblea Nacional del Ecuador, 29 August.

Sesión del 6 de Agosto por la Noche. (1869). Debates de la Convención Nacional, Archivo de la Asamblea Nacional del Ecuador, 6 August.

Sesión Solemne en la Iglesia de la Compañía el 29 de Julio. (1869). Debates de la Convención Nacional, Archivo de la Asamblea Nacional del Ecuador, 29 July.

Sharoni, J. (2016). The failure of the parental metaphor: A Lacanian reading of James Joyce's "Eveline". *Journal of Modern Literature, 39*(4), 33–48.

Sjoberg, G., Williams, N., Vaughan, T., & Sjoberg, A. (1991). The case study approach in social research: Basic methodological issues. In J. Feagin, A. Orum, & G. Sjoberg (Eds.), *A case for the case study.* The University of North Carolina Press.

Stacey, R. (2016). Popular sovereignty and revolutionary constitution-making. In D. Dyzenhaus & M. Thorburn (Eds.), *Philosophical foundations of constitutional law.* Oxford University Press.

Stavrakakis, Y. (1999). *Lacan & the political.* Routledge.

Stavrakakis, Y. (2010). *La izquierda lacaniana. Psicoanálisis, teoría, política*. Fondo de Cultura Económica.

Taiano, V. (2007, 2008). *Asamblea constituyente*. Archivo de la Asamblea Nacional del Ecuador, 13 December 2007; 13 May, 25 June 2008.

The Britannica Dictionary. (n.d.). https://www.britannica.com/dictionary

The Carter Center (2008). *Informe sobre la Asamblea Constituyente de la República del Ecuador*. Retrieved February 28, 2023, from https://www.cartercenter.org/resources/pdfs/peace/americas/informe_final_ac_-_centro_carter_distribuido.pdf

Thurschwell, P. (2000). *Sigmund Freud*. Routledge Critical Thinkers.

Tiban, L. (2014). Primer debate de la Solicitud de Enmienda Constitucional. Archivo de la Asamblea Nacional del Ecuador.

Tully, J. (2002). The unfreedom of the moderns in comparison to their ideals of constitutional democracy. *The Modern Law Review, 65*(2), 204–228.

United Nations. (n.d.). www.un.org

Uquillas, M. A. (1869). *Sesión del 21 de Mayo*. Archivo de la Asamblea Nacional del Ecuador, 21 May.

Villacís, B., & Carrillo, D. (2012). *País atrevido: la nueva cara sociodemográfica del Ecuador*. INEC and Analitika. https://www.ecuadorencifras.gob.ec/wp-content/descargas/Libros/Economia/Nuevacarademograficadeecuador.pdf

Villacreces, O. (2014). Continuación del primer debate de la solicitud de enmienda constitucional. Archivo de la Asamblea Nacional del Ecuador.

Viteri, L. (2007, 2008). *Asamblea constituyente*. Archivo de la Asamblea Nacional del Ecuador, 13 December 2007; 8 May 2008.

Weber, M. (2005/1992). *Economía y sociedad. Esbozo de sociología comprensiva*. Fondo de Cultura Económica.

Zambrano, E. (2008). *Asamblea constituyente*. Archivo de la Asamblea Nacional del Ecuador, 13 May.

Žižek, S. (1990). Eastern Europe's Republics of Gilead. *New Left Review* (I/183, September-October).

Žižek, S. (2005). Beyond Discourse Analysis. In *Interrogating the real*. Bloomsbury Publishing Plc.

Žižek, S. (2008). *The sublime object of ideology*. Verso.

Zolo, D. (2007). The rule of law: A critical reappraisal. In P. Costa & D. Zolo (Eds.), *The rule of Law. History, theory and criticism* (Vol. 80). Springer.

Zúñiga, N. (2004). Un estudio de caso: Los derechos de los pueblos indígenas en Ecuador. In F. Mariño & D. Oliva (Eds.), *Avances en la protección de los derechos de los pueblos indígenas*. Dykinson.

Zúñiga, N. (2014). Indigenous struggles over recognition in bolivia: Contesting Evo morales's discourse of international decolonization. PhD Thesis. Colchester: University of Essex.

Index

E. Espindola, *The Paternal Imago in Ruins*, The Palgrave Lacan Series, https://doi.org/10.1007/978-3-032-07507-9

GPSR Compliance
The European Union's (EU) General Product Safety Regulation (GPSR) is a set of rules that requires consumer products to be safe and our obligations to ensure this.

If you have any concerns about our products, you can contact us on

ProductSafety@springernature.com

In case Publisher is established outside the EU, the EU authorized representative is:

Springer Nature Customer Service Center GmbH
Europaplatz 3
69115 Heidelberg, Germany

www.ingramcontent.com/pod-product-compliance
Lightning Source LLC
Chambersburg PA
CBHW052341210126
38614CB00004B/53
9783032075062

PLANETARY NEBULAE

PLANETARY NEBULAE

A Practical Guide and Handbook for Amateur Astronomers

Includes 253 finder charts and a catalog of 1340 objects

STEVEN J. HYNES

Published by:

Willmann–Bell, Inc.

P.O. Box 35025
Richmond, Virginia 23235 ☎ (804)
United States of America 320-7016

Publishers and Booksellers

Serving Astronomers Worldwide
Since 1973

Published by Willmann-Bell, Inc.
P.O. Box 35025, Richmond, Virginia 23235

First published 1991

Printed in the United States of America

Library of Congress Cataloging-in-Publication Data.

Hynes, Steven J.
Planetary nebulae : a practical guide and handbook for amateur astronomers / Steven J. Hynes.
p. cm.
Includes bibliographical references and index.
ISBN 0-943396-30-1
1. Planetary nebulae. 2. Planetary nebulae – Amateurs' manuals.
I. Title.
QB855.5.H96 1991 90-25545
523.1'135–dc20 CIP

91 92 93 94 95 96 97 98 9 8 7 6 5 4 3 2

Preface

Scattered among the millions of stars that spangle the heavens, the astronomer will find small, seemingly insignificant balls of hazy light, likened by the early observers to the faint, distant outer planets, and called *planetary nebulae.* For many years their nature remained a mystery and they were considered to be little more than a curiosity, a comparatively rare phenomenon which for the most part seemed to be associated with tiny, centrally situated stars.

A little over a century ago, however, the English amateur astronomer William Huggins, using early spectroscopic equipment, was able to show that the nebulous shells were genuinely of a gaseous nature, the greatly extended atmospheres of the central stars. In the early decades of the twentieth century, American astronomers Campbell and Moore made observations which were to show that planetary nebulae were expanding at a rate indicating an age no greater than a few tens of thousands of years, very small on the timescale of cosmic events. The apparent rarity of these objects was shown to be merely an artefact of their transient nature and their true significance was soon revealed; they represent the penultimate stage in the life of a medium-mass star. After a comparatively tranquil existence of many thousands of millions of years on the main sequence, such a star will become unstable as its fuel runs low and expands to the vast size of a red giant, engulfing any inner planets in its system, before shedding its distended outer layers as planetary nebula. The core of the star now settles down as a tiny white dwarf, perhaps only the size of the Earth, yet so dense and massive and with such a high surface gravity that a small coin such as a U.S. Quarter Dollar would weigh over 2 tonnes! Thus will be the fate of our own star, the Sun.

The purpose of this book is to describe for the amateur astronomer the scientific processes by which our understanding of planetary nebulae has been derived and explore the way in which the threads of observation and theoretical research have been drawn together to produce our present day picture. The story is not straightforward, however; a variety of other celestial objects can mimic the characteristics of planetary nebulae and many of these interlopers are not only difficult to root out but are also interesting in their own right; these deserve a chapter of their own.

A major part of this book is devoted to a catalogue of planetary nebulae, with notes about objects of particular in interest and finder charts based on photographic sources. The widespread use of large-aperture Dobsonian mounted reflectors has brought within reach of the amateur astronomer many objects which only a decade ago would have been considered the sole province of the professional astronomer. The selection of objects in the catalogue takes account of the ever-increasing size of telescope available to amateurs but also provides for the user of small and medium aperture instruments. In many cases the planetary nebulae are still not well studied and even basic parameters are poorly determined but they all represent a challenge to observers. In addition, many references have been provided to enable the advanced amateur, with access to professional journals, to pursue his research further.

Acknowledgements

The preparation of this work has been greatly aided by a number of individuals and institutions. I would like to thank David A. Allen, Edmund S. Barker, and Steve Gottleib for some useful and interesting correspondence and conversations, and Keith Lowe, proprietor of Dark Star Telescopes (U.K.), for use of his facilities. Of particular value, though, has been the numerous contributions of Brian A. Skiff. Much of the research was carried out at the libraries of the Royal Astronomical Society, the University of Keele, and the Nuffield Radio Astronomy Laboratories, Jodrell Bank. I am indebted to the authorities of these institutions, but would like especially to thank Peter Hingley at the R.A.S. and Joan Adams of Jodrell Bank for their help and hospitality. Barry N. Rappaport provided computer programming expertise at several stages of this book's preparation which was particularly valuable. Finally, a special mention must be given to Perry W. Remaklus, President and Publisher of Willman-Bell Inc., for his help, ideas and support.

Steven J. Hynes

Table of Contents

Chapter 1

The Discovery of Planetary Nebulae

1.1 Historical Perspective

Even before the invention of the telescope, observers of the sky recognized that among the "fixed stars" were also tiny, hazy patches of light called "nebulae" (little clouds). Such nebulae can be seen in the constellations of Orion, Sagittarius, Cancer, and Andromeda, and by 1609, when Galileo first applied his diminutive "optick tube" to the heavens, perhaps eight or nine were known.

Galileo presented his early observations in his book *Sidereus Nuncius* (The Starry Messenger), which was published in March 1610. Clearly, he had been astonished by what he had seen:

> I have observed the nature and material of the Milky Way. With the aid of the telescope this has been examined so directly and with such ocular certainty that all the disputes which have vexed philosophers through so many ages have been resolved, and we are at last freed from wordy debates about it. The galaxy is, in fact, nothing but innumerable stars grouped together in clusters. Upon whatever part of it the telescope is directed, a vast crowd of stars is immediately presented to view. Many are large and bright, while the number of smaller ones is quite incalculable.

Having resolved the structure of the Milky Way, he examined the nebulae:

> But it is not only in the Milky Way that whitish clouds are seen; several patches of similar aspect shine with faint light here and there throughout the aether, and if the telescope is turned upon any of them we are confronted by a tight mass of stars. And what is even more remarkable, the stars which have been called "nebulous" by every astronomer to this time turn out to be a group of very small stars arranged in a wonderful manner. Although each star separately escapes our sight on account of its smallness, or the immense distance from us, the mingling

of their rays gives rise to that glow which was formerly believed to be some denser part of the aether that was capable of reflecting rays from stars or from the Sun.

The Galilean view that all nebulae could ultimately be resolved into stars was, of course, incorrect, but persisted for some time, even though some, such as that in the Sword of Orion, refused to be broken down into individual components. Scant attention was paid to the nebulae for over a century and even then only because they were found to be a nuisance to comet-hunters.

Even now, there is a certain prestige attached to the discovery of a new comet and in the eighteenth century it was a sure way of achieving recognition and reward. A comet-hunter of particular renown was the Frenchman, Charles Messier, born in 1730. In 1750 he went to Paris to become apprenticed to the prominent astronomer Delisle; he soon became a proficient observer and eventually discovered 13 comets. Telescopically, comets often appear as hazy patches of light, distinguished from the nebulae only by their movement across the sky. Messier found that his attempts to increase his tally of discoveries were continually frustrated by the realization that objects he believed to be comets were, in fact, fixed among the stars. For his own benefit and the benefit of other observers, he decided to catalogue these objects, later with the assistance of Pierre Mechain, and between them 110 were eventually recorded. The 27th entry in the catalogue, found on 1764 July 12, was the first discovered member of the class of objects later to be known as "planetary nebulae."

1.2 The Observations of William Herschel

The discoveries of Messier and Mechain greatly increased the known number of nebulae and excited the interest of amateur astronomer William Herschel, living in England. Born in 1738 in the German city of Hanover, Herschel became a musician in the regimental band of the Foot-Guards, joining his father and brother Jacob. In 1757 at Hastenbeck, he faced battle and found that in such circumstances the safety of musicians was not a military priority. He managed to obtain a discharge and went to Hamburg, where he and Jacob (who had been in hiding to avoid conscription) took a boat for England. After two years, Jacob returned home to Hanover but William stayed on, pursuing his love of music. Eventually, he set up home in Bath, and in 1772 was joined by his sister Caroline who herself became an astronomer of no small repute. On 1773 May 10, at the age of 35, he found his interest in astronomy after buying a copy of Ferguson's *Astronomy*, a popular text of the time.

It is possible that neither before nor since has a simple book purchase had such a dramatic effect on the direction of astronomy. With his ever increasing enthusiasm he became the leading telescope-maker of his time and the discoverer of the planet Uranus on 1781 March 13. In recognition of the latter, the first discovery of a major planet of the Solar System in recorded history, he was elected into the Royal Society on 1781 December 7, and subsequently awarded an annual stipend of £200 by King George III. This enabled him to give up music as a career and concentrate on astronomy.

On the day of his election to the Royal Society his friend, Dr. William Watson, sent him a copy of the new catalogue of nebulae recently published by Messier and Mechain. This clearly stimulated his imagination and he resolved to look for more—he was to discover some 2300 within a period of just seven years! With this significant database of observational material, he began to classify the objects he found and placed them in eight categories:

I Bright nebulae
II Faint nebulae
III Very faint nebulae
IV Planetary nebulae
V Very large nebulae
VI Very compressed, rich clusters of stars
VII Compressed clusters of small and large stars
VIII Coarsely scattered clusters of stars

Herschel gave the name "planetary nebulae" to the fourth category of objects because their small, well defined, sometimes greenish discs reminded him of the appearance of the planet Uranus. He seems to have felt that these characteristics identified them as being different from the other types to the extent that perhaps they were not even true nebulae. On the other hand, if they were stars of large enough diameter for the disc to be detectable, he could not account for their comparative faintness. At one point he considered the possibility that they were in fact star clusters rendered nebulous in appearance because of the faintness of the components and the high degree of compression; he speculated that they were in the process of coming together under gravity to "unite into a new body," adding "Perhaps the extraordinary and sudden blaze of a new star in Cassiopeia's chair of 1572 might possibly be of such a nature."

On the night of 1790 November 13 he discovered a new planetary nebula (now known as NGC 1514) which caused him to completely rethink his ideas on these objects. His original observation reads as follows:

> A most singular phenomenon! A star of about the 8th magnitude with a faint luminous atmosphere, of circular form, and about 3 minutes in diameter. The star is perfectly in the center, and the atmosphere is so delicate, faint and equal throughout that there can be no surmise of its consisting of stars; nor can there be a doubt of the evident connection between the atmosphere and the star. Another star, not much less in brightness and in the same field with the above, was perfectly free from any such appearance.

This observation, together with his conclusions, was published in a paper called "Nebulous Stars, properly so called," in the *Philosophical Transactions* of the Royal Society in 1791. Herschel reasoned that, since the star was so exactly centrally situated in the nebula, it was unlikely to be just a chance superposition and they were therefore part of the same system at the same distance. For the nebula to have been composed of unresolved stars they would have had to have been so faint in comparison with the central star that such a situation was beyond belief. He concluded that:

> We therefore have a central body which is not a star, or have a star which is involved in a shining fluid of a nature totally unknown to us.

Preferring to accept the latter explanation, Herschel went on to develop the implications of his conclusion:

> But what a field of novelty is here opened to our conceptions! A shining fluid of a brightness sufficient to reach from the remote regions of a star of the 8th, 9th, 10th, 11th and 12th magnitude, and of an extent so considerable as to take up 3, 4, 5 or 6 minutes in diameter... We may now explain that very extensive nebulosity, expanded over more than sixty degrees of the heavens, about the constellation of Orion; a luminous matter accounting much better for it than clustering of stars at a distance.

1.3 The Discovery of Spectroscopy

The nature of Herschel's "shining fluid" remained mysterious until the middle of the nineteenth century, when the spectroscope was first applied to celestial objects. This became possible following the work of Joseph von Fraunhofer who, in 1814, found that if sunlight was passed through a long, narrow slit in front of a prism, the spectrum produced was crossed by a number of dark lines. Eventually, he was able to map as many as 574 against the colored band. Fraunhofer did not know the cause of the lines, nor was he the first to observe them, since Wollaston had also seen some as indefinite shadings in 1802, but he had apparently dismissed them as vague divisions between the colors. However, Fraunhofer's systematic observations were of such a quality and precision that the lines are still called "Fraunhofer lines" in some textbooks, and the alphabetical sequence he devised to identify the more prominent is still used (e.g., the "D" line of sodium).

In the 1850's a number of scientists were involved in research on the Fraunhofer lines, and of particular importance is the work of Anders Ångström in Sweden and Kirchhoff and Bunsen in Germany. Ångström actually anticipated much of the work of the German scientists but his memoir of 1853 was published in Swedish and was overlooked by most of the scientific community. It was not until 1859 and 1860 that Kirchhoff and Bunsen published the results of their work and the true significance of the Fraunhofer lines became apparent. In their experiments they had made observations of the spectra of incandescent substances and found that this produced "bright line" spectra, and moreover, it was possible to match up the positions of certain lines in the spectrum against specific elements. It soon became clear that the positions of the dark lines found by Fraunhofer were also indicative of known elements.

Soon, this amazing discovery, by which the chemical composition of objects could be determined by messages encoded in light, was applied to the heavens. By visual observation of the solar spectrum, Kirchhoff was able to identify the elements sodium, magnesium, calcium, iron, nickel, copper, zinc, and barium. Another noteworthy discovery around this time was that of the spectral lines of hydrogen, this by Ångström in 1862.

In more general terms, Kirchhoff was able to derive the basic laws which determine the type of spectrum observed in any particular circumstances:

1. **Continuous spectrum**—produced by an incandescent solid or liquid or very dense gas.
2. **Emission (bright line) spectrum**—produced by a luminous but rarefied gas.
3. **Absorption (dark line) spectrum**—produced by the presence of a gas between the observer and a hotter source of continuous spectrum light.

1.4 Huggins and "Nebulium"

The discoveries made by Kirchhoff stimulated the imagination of many scientists but in particular the English amateur astronomer William Huggins. Huggins, like many of the Victorian "gentleman scientists," was a man of wide-ranging interests and occupied himself with chemistry, physics, and microscopical research, as well as astronomy. However, around 1853 he decided to concentrate on observational astronomy and in 1856 built an observatory attached to his house at Tulse Hill, south of London. This he equipped with a 12.7-cm Dollond equatorially-mounted refractor and an 8.25-cm transit-circle. In 1858 he bought a fine 20.3-cm Alvan Clark lens from the Rev. W. R. Dawes, and had it mounted by the well-known telescope makers, Cooke of York.

Huggins' early observations were undirected and he recorded details of stellar occultations and features on the planets. However, when he read of Kirchhoff's work in 1862 he decided that the most useful scientific work he could employ himself with would be the application of spectroscopy to the stars. With the assistance of his friend and neighbor, William A. Miller, professor of chemistry at King's College, he built a spectroscope suitable for this purpose and published his first report in the *Proceedings of the Royal*

Society the following year. A more comprehensive report was produced in 1864 and he concluded that:

> ...in plan of structure the stars, or at least the brightest of them, resemble the Sun. Their light, like that of the Sun, emanates from intensely white-hot matter, and passes through an atmosphere of absorbent vapours. With this unity of general plan of structure there exists a great diversity amongst the individual stars. Star differs from star in chemical constitution.

Soon, Huggins turned his telescope and spectroscope towards the nebulae, and in particular, towards the planetary nebula NGC 6543 in Draco. He later described his remarkable observation in the *Nineteenth Century Review* of June 1897:

> I looked into the spectroscope. No spectrum such as I expected. A single bright line only! At first I suspected some displacement of the prism, and that I was looking at a reflection of the illuminated slit from one of its faces. This thought was scarcely more than momentary; then the true interpretation flashed upon me. The light of the nebula was monochromatic, and so, unlike any other light I had as yet subjected to prismatic examination, could not be extended out to form a complete spectrum. After passing through the two prisms it remained concentrated into a single bright line, having a width corresponding to the width of the slit, and occupying in the instrument at that part of the spectrum to which its light belongs in refrangibility. A little closer looking showed two other bright lines on the side towards the blue, all the three lines being separated by intervals of relatively dark.
>
> The riddle of the nebulae was solved. The answer, which had come to us in the light itself, read: Not an aggregation of stars, but a luminous gas. Stars after the order of our own Sun, and of the brighter stars, would give a different spectrum; the light of this nebula had clearly been emitted by a luminous gas. With an excess of caution, at the moment I did not venture to go further than to point out that we had here to do with bodies of an order quite different from that of the stars.

A few days later, Huggins observed the Andromeda Nebula and found a continuous spectrum, correctly concluding that this object was formed of innumerable faint stars. Over the next four years, he spectroscopically examined about seventy nebulae, finding that about a third exhibited a "bright line" spectrum. In each case, the brightest line was in the green part of the spectrum, at a wavelength of 500.7 nm; this line was known as the "Chief Nebular Line" but the element which its existence proclaimed remained a mystery. It was presumed that it must be some previously unknown substance, called "nebulium." This was to be proved incorrect, but not for another 60 years. Meanwhile, the spectroscope remained a highly effective tool for the classification of nebulae, to the extent that of the 67 planetary nebulae listed in the *New General Catalogue* (NGC) of 1888, 57 are still accepted as such today.

1.5 Early 20th Century Studies

Of course, the larger and totally unrelated diffuse nebulae also exhibited a similar spectrum to the planetary nebulae but they were differentiated on the basis of their morphology, as explained by Heber D. Curtis in a classic treatise on planetary nebulae in *Lick Observatory Publications*, Volume XIII, 1918:

> Greater differences of form and structure could scarcely exist than obtain between the small, clear-cut planetaries, and the enormous, tenuous, highly-irregular and cloud-like diffuse nebulosities. Many small masses of diffuse nebulosity are associated with stars more or less centrally placed within the nebula, but there is never in such cases, any resemblance to the typical planetary form, nor is there any doubt as to the group of nebulae with which such objects should be classified.

In 1918, less than 100 planetary nebulae were known and it was apparent that they were comparatively rare objects. Curtis concluded that they were either the manifestation of some genuinely exotic evolutionary process, or a phase in stellar evolution of relatively brief duration which many stars passed through. Although the latter is now known to be the case, Curtis, on the basis of the limited data available to him, was unable to accept this possibility:

> ... it would seem much more reasonable to regard them as merely sporadic cases of stellar evolution, presumably of cataclysmic origin.

Interestingly, the observations which ultimately proved Curtis wrong were also published in the same work. W.W. Campbell and J.H. Moore had made high-resolution spectroscopic studies of 43 planetary nebulae and found evidence of internal motions in 23. The spectral lines were broadened, in a few cases to the extent that they were split; the lines were also tilted. Campbell and Moore suggested that this phenomenon was the result of the rotation of the nebulae; however, within a few years, C.D. Perrine and H. Zanstra had shown that it could more simply be explained by nebular expansion. Having made measurements of the size of the nebulae and their expansion rates, it then became possible to estimate their ages, which turned out to be in the order of a few tens of thousands of years, clearly indicating that the planetary nebulae are objects of comparatively recent formation. Since it would be reasonable to assume that as the nebulae expand the density of the gas falls and surface brightness diminishes, it was apparent that within a fairly short period of time they would fade into oblivion.

Discoveries of planetary nebulae grew slowly; the catalogue produced by Vorontsov-Velyaminov in 1934, for example, listed just 134 objects. However, some significant advances were made in understanding the astrophysics of planetary nebulae. Of particular importance was the work of Ira S. Bowen of the California Institute of Technology, who in 1927 was able to identify Huggins' mysterious "nebulium" lines.

It is well known that spectral lines arise when electrons in an atom "jump" (i.e., make a "transition") from one energy level to another. Some transitions are more probable than others and clearly, those transitions which are most probable will give rise to the strongest lines. Bowen knew that there was no place for a new element in the Periodic Table so the unidentified lines at 500.7 nm and 495.9 nm must have been a known element for which the transitions were improbable under terrestrial laboratory conditions. Such lines are called "forbidden lines." Having given further consideration to the matter, Bowen realized that the energy differences between the two energy levels calculated for doubly-ionized oxygen corresponded exactly to the frequencies of the nebulium lines and therefore they were the forbidden lines of doubly-ionized oxygen [O III].

The fact that [O III] lines were so difficult to reproduce in the laboratory yet dominated the spectra of planetary nebulae indicated that the conditions which exist in these objects are quite remarkable. In the laboratory the excited level is heavily depopulated by electron collision, greatly reducing the intensity of any [O III] emission. On the other hand, in an extremely low density environment, such as can be found in planetary nebulae, de-excitation by this means is much less important.

Once this phenomenon was understood it became possible to identify a large number of other lines and from these, the chemical composition and physical processes occurring in planetary nebulae.

Another interesting development at this time was the discovery by Zanstra, in 1931, of a method for determining the temperature of a planetary nebula nucleus (or indeed, any star involved in a low density nebula). This enables one to "count" the number of ionizing photons emitted by the star, the temperature being found by comparing this with the number of photons emitted at visual wavelengths. "Zanstra temperatures" are often quoted in the professional literature.

1.6 Modern Discoveries of Planetary Nebulae

Although there have been many great advances in understanding the astrophysics of planetary nebulae since 1945—some of which will be discussed in later sections—perhaps the post-war years might be considered as characterized by an ever-increasing rate of planetary nebula discoveries.

In 1946, Rudolf Minkowski published his first catalogue of new emission-line objects, found on objective-prism survey plates obtained by W.C. Miller with a 25.4 cm telescope. He subsequently classified 80 of these objects as planetary nebulae on the basis of more detailed spectra or their appearance on direct photographs obtained at the Newtonian focus of the Mount Wilson

1.5-meter and 2.5-meter reflectors. This first list was soon followed by lists in 1947 (56 objects) and 1948 (55 objects).

During the early 1960's, several catalogues of note were produced; in particular, those of B.A. Vorontsov-Velyaminov in the Soviet Union and Karl G. Henize in the U.S.A. In 1961, the latter produced a short list of 7 objects (He 1-) found in the Cygnus-Vulpecula region during the course of obtaining objective-prism plates to compare the limiting magnitude with that obtained during his greatly more extensive southern Hα survey. The southern survey (He 2-), eventually published in 1967, listed 468 objects, many of which are planetary nebulae.

Undoubtedly the greatest impetus to the discovery of planetary nebulae, however, came from the publication of the *National Geographic Society-Palomar Observatory Sky Survey* (P.O.S.S.). This was carried out using a 1.2-meter Schmidt telescope and covered the entire northern sky down to Declination $-33°$.

The P.O.S.S. consists of 935 pairs of plates—one blue sensitive (Kodak 103a-O plates) and one red-sensitive (Kodak 103a-E + red plexiglass)—each covering a field of 6° x 6° at a scale of 1 mm = 67″. The limiting stellar magnitude is 21 in the blue and 20 in the red.

Using these plates a number of investigators, notably Lubos Kohoutek and George Abell, have found a considerable number of new nebulae. In the case of Abell, 86 objects were recorded (although a small number have been found to be misclassifications). Even in very recent years, searches of the P.O.S.S. plates have proved fruitful; for example, Weinberger reported 12 new planetary nebulae in 1977 and Dengl *et al.* found 5 in 1980. A complete reference list of planetary nebulae is given in Appendix A.

1.7 The "P&K"

Until 1967, astronomers studying planetary nebulae were hampered by the lack of a "general catalogue" to act as a database. Observations, finder charts, and individual listings were scattered through many publications produced over a long period of time. Short lists, such as the two by Merrill which contained only 2 objects each, could easily be overlooked. This major gap in the literature was corrected with the publication of the *Catalogue of Galactic Planetary Nebulae* (CGPN) by Academia, the publishing house of the Czechoslovak Academy of Sciences. The catalogue was compiled by Lubos Perek and Lubos Kohoutek, and contains 1036 entries, covering all discoveries up to 1965. Despite quite a number of misclassifications, the "P&K"—as it is often known—remains the standard reference catalogue.

This catalogue introduced a new system of identifying objects which has been extended to cover all subsequent discoveries and has now been adopted as the standard way of listing planetary nebulae. However, although the P&K numbering is the preferred listing system, it is generally used in conjunction with personal designations rather than in place of them. The system is based on galactic co-ordinates rather than the traditional R.A. and Dec. The order of listing is in one-degree strips of galactic longitude and from the north to the south galactic pole inside each strip; the number is formed by truncating the galactic longitude and latitude to integer degrees and then allocating serial numbers from north to south within each $1^\circ \times 1^\circ$ compartment. New objects are slotted into the system by assigning the next free serial number in the particular compartment. For example, the planetary nebula Pu1, reported by A. Purgathofer in 1978 (ref. 1), lies at galactic co-ordinates $l = 181\overset{\circ}{.}7$, $b = +1\overset{\circ}{.}3$; in the P&K system this becomes PK181+1°1. The same astronomer found Pu2 in 1980 (ref. 2); this lies at galactic co-ordinates $l = 173\overset{\circ}{.}5$, $b = +3\overset{\circ}{.}2$ and would be designated as PK173+3°1.

The *Catalogue of Galactic Planetary Nebulae* contains much valuable positional and other data and is particularly useful for its selection of finder charts. All but two of the objects in the catalogue are represented, but the charts are not a homogeneous set and vary greatly in scale, depth, and quality.

1.8 Recent Planetary Nebula Discoveries

Recently, many discoveries of new planetary nebulae have occurred in the southern hemisphere, having been found on the blue *ESO-SERC Southern Sky Survey* plates, obtained with the 1.2-meter U.K. Schmidt Telescope at Siding Spring, Australia. This survey has used Kodak IIIa-J plates plus a Schott GG 395 filter; this is a particularly useful combination for recording planetary nebulae as the [O III] lines at 500.7 nm and 495.9 nm, and the Hβ line at 486.1 nm are all covered by the passband.

Lists of new planetary nebulae discovered on the *Southern Sky Survey* plates have been published by, among others, A.J. Longmore (17 objects), and A.J. Longmore and S.B. Tritton (11 objects). In addition, Holmberg *et al.* have published several extensive lists of new objects of all kinds, which include planetary nebulae, based on the *ESO(B) Atlas*.

These and other new discoveries of planetary nebulae are being included in the new *Strasbourg-ESO Catalogue of Planetary Nebulae* (SEC) and great care has been taken by the authors, Agnes Acker and her co-workers, to eliminate objects which have previously been misclassified. The SEC seems destined to replace P&K as the standard planetary nebula catalogue, although the numbering system will remain the same. A full account of the proposed scope of the SEC was given by Acker in 1987 (ref. 3).

As far as future discoveries are concerned, it seems likely that more new planetary nebulae will be found on the *Southern Sky Survey* plates and also on the forthcoming *Second Palomar Observatory Sky Survey*, which is being prepared using the improved emulsions which have become available since the original was published in the mid-1950's. However, it does seem certain that most of the future discoveries will be of objects of low surface brightness. Further discoveries might also be expected through objective-prism surveys specifically for this purpose or photographic surveys of small sections of the Milky Way at high resolution.

1.9 Extragalactic Planetary Nebulae

The small size and comparative faintness of planetary nebulae makes them a difficult subject for study at the great distances of even the nearby galaxies. Despite this, considerable progress has been made in this field during recent years, although in fact the first "extragalactic" planetary nebula could be said to be that discovered by Pease in the globular cluster M 15 in 1928.

The importance of the extragalactic planetary nebulae is largely that, being essentially at the same distance, their parameters can be compared with more precision than those in the Galaxy, whose distances are not well known. In addition, their chemical composition reflects to some extent the chemistry of the parent galaxy, so it can shed light on this aspect of astrophysics.

Obviously, extragalactic planetary nebulae are not likely to be recognized by their morphology—even in the closest galaxies the largest are not likely to be larger than $3''$—therefore, spectroscopic techniques must be the primary detection method. Candidates must be stellar (or virtually so), with strong emission lines including [O III] and [O II], and little or no continuum.

The Magellanic Clouds, in the southern hemisphere, are the nearest galaxies in which a large number of planetary nebulae can be identified and studied in detail. As a result of several surveys since the mid-1950's, a total of 51 planetary nebulae have been discovered in the SMC and 137 in the LMC; estimates of the total number in the Clouds are about 300 and 1000 respectively. Spectroscopic analysis of the Magellanic Clouds planetary nebulae shows that the helium and carbon abundance is comparable to that in the Milky Way but oxygen, nitrogen, and neon are significantly underabundant. Overall, the indications are of metal deficiency in the interstellar medium of the Clouds, with the SMC having slightly lower abundances than the LMC. If this is correct, it may be concluded that the Clouds have been chemically enriched only in the last few thousand million years, perhaps as a result of a burst of star formation having occurred (ref. 4). The brightest LMC planetary nebulae are listed in Table 1–1.

Table 1–1
LMC planetary nebulae with $m_{5007} > 15.0$

Name	R.A. (2000) Dec.	m_{5007}	Notes
SMP 25	05 06.7 −69 03	14.84	L124, BE 206
SMP 38	05 11.8 −70 01	14.99	N110, LM 1-25, WS 15
SMP 47	05 20.4 −69 30	14.94	N122, LM 1-28, WS 18
SMP 52	05 21.7 −68 35	14.81	N124, LM 1-33, WS 21
SMP 62	05 25.5 −71 32	14.41	N201, LM 1-38, WS 25
SMP 63	05 25.8 −68 55	14.89	N141, LM 1-39, WS 26
SMP 73	05 31.8 −70 40	14.66	N208, LM 1-45, WS 29
SMP 78	05 34.7 −68 57	14.76	N153, LM 1-49, WS 33
SMP 81	05 36.3 −73 54	14.91	N211, LM 1-51, WS 34
SMP 89	05 43.2 −70 08	14.91	N178, LM 1-56, WS 38
SMP 92	05 47.5 −69 26	14.80	N170, LM 1-58, WS 39
SMP 98	06 18.4 −73 10	14.52	LM 1-62, WS 41
SMP 99	06 19.6 −71 34	14.70	N221, LM 1-63, WS 42

Table 1–1 Notes:
1. Identifications from: Sanduleak, N. (*et al.*); *P.A.S.P. 90, 621, 1978.*
2. m_{5007} data from: Jacoby, G.H.; Ap.J. *365*, 471, 1990.
3. Abbreviations:
   BE— Bohannan, B. & Epps, H.W.; *Astron. Astrophys. Supp. Ser.*, **18**, 47, 1974.
   L— Lindsay, E.M.; *Irish A.J.*, **6**, 127, 1963.
   LM 1-#—Lindsay, E.M. & Mullan, D.J.; *Irish A.J.* **6**, 51, 1963 (Table 1).
   N—Henize, K.G.; *Ap.J. Supp.*, **2**, 315, 1956.
   WS—Westerlund, B.E. & Smith, L.F.; *M.N.R.A.S.*, **127**, 449, 1964.

Beyond the Magellanic Clouds, the great spiral in Andromeda, M 31, has come in for scrutiny on a number of occasions. For example, David G. Lawrie and Holland C. Ford (ref. 5) have studied the central region of the galaxy using a velocity modulating camera (VMC); this consists of a temperature-tuned interference filter of extremely narrow passband, centered on the [O III] line at 500.7 nm, together with a cooled two-stage image intensifier and a calibrating photomultiplier, attached to the f/17.5 Cassegrain focus of the Shane 3.0-meter telescope. By this means 42 planetary nebulae were found within 250pc of the nucleus of M 31, 19 of these being new identifications. These investigators conclude that there are probably some $21,000 \pm 2,600$ planetary nebulae within 8 magnitudes of the brightest within M 31. Taking into account other surveys, a total of 371 planetary nebulae have been found to be associated with this galaxy.

Surveys of other Local Group galaxies have revealed 58 in M 33, 8 in NGC 6822, and 7 in M 32. Individual planetary nebulae have also been found in the dwarf galaxies NGC 185, IC 10, Fornax, Leo A, Sextans A, Pegasus, and

WLM (ref. 6). Beyond the Local Group, increasing numbers of planetary nebulae are being found and under good conditions, existing ground-based telescopes should be able to identify these objects in galaxies as distant as 15 Mpc. Among the galaxies which have been surveyed to mid-1990 are NGC's 300, 404, 3031 (M 81), 3115, the members of the NGC 3379 group, NGC's 5102, 5128, and 5457 (M 101). As a result, the number of planetary nebulae known in external galaxies exceeds the number known in our own galaxy and provides a good data base for statistical analysis.

The most significant development from this is that the [O III] magnitudes of the brightest planetary nebulae have been found to be excellent "standard candles," or distance indicators, for external galaxies (ref. 7). The planetary nebula luminosity function (PNLF) has a sharp bright-end cutoff near [O III] magnitude $M = -4.48$, which is apparently due to the small range in masses of planetary nebula central stars in combination with the rapid evolution of the more massive stars, which pass through their most luminous phase so quickly as to make a negligible impact on the statistics. This determination of the PNLF makes planetary nebulae particularly valuable as extragalactic distance indicators, because not only can they be detected over a similar distance range to Cepheids but they are also found in all Hubble types. They are derived from a population insensitive to internal reddening and can be measured using simple and accurate photometric methods at a wavelength that virtually isolates them against otherwise potentially confusing backgrounds.

The forthcoming new generation of large ground-based telescopes (8-meter and larger) and space-based telescopes should be able to extend the range of planetary nebula detection out to around 25 Mpc, thus rendering them even more valuable to astronomers.

1.10 References

1. Purgathofer, A.; *Astron. Astrophys.*, **70**, 589, 1978.
2. Purgathofer, A.; *Astron. Astrophys.*, **88**, 275, 1980.
3. Acker, A.; *Planetary and Protoplanetary Nebulae: from IRAS to ISO*, A. Preite-Martinez (ed.), D. Reidel Publ. Co., 1987 (p. 35).
4. Jacoby, G.H.; "Planetary Nebulae in the Magellanic Clouds," in *Planetary Nebulae* (ed. D.R. Flower), IAU Symposium 103, D. Reidel Publ. Co., 1983 (p. 427).
5. Lawrie, D.G. & Ford, H.C., Ap.J., **256**, 120, 1982.
6. Ford, H.C.; "Planetary Nebulae in Local Group Galaxies," in *Planetary Nebulae* (ed. D.R. Flower), IAU Symposium 103, D. Reidel Publ. Co., 1983 (p. 443).
7. Jacoby, G.H. *et al.*; "Planetary Nebulae as Distance Indicators" in *The Extragalactic Distance Scale* (ed. S. van den Berg & C. Pritchet), A.S.P. Conference Series, **4**, 42, 1988.

Chapter 2

The Astrophysics of Planetary Nebulae

2.1 The Distances of Planetary Nebulae

The distance to planetary nebulae is perhaps the single most important parameter to be determined; on the accuracy of this depends the accuracy of calculations of nebular size, mass, absolute luminosity, birthrate, and determinations of the size, mass, luminosity, and stability of the central star. Estimates of the galactic distribution of planetary nebulae are also affected.

Unfortunately, it has to be admitted that the distances of most planetary nebulae are poorly known and such determinations are beset with difficulties. Trigonometric parallax methods cannot normally be applied because of the great distances involved, although Ianna and McAlister have obtained a parallax of $0''.020 \pm 0''.006$ for NGC 7293 (ref. 1).

Because of the impracticability of direct methods of distance measurement, indirect and statistical methods are used instead; these include the following:

1. **Spectroscopic parallax:** This is of limited value but can be applied to cases where the central star of a planetary nebula has a binary companion which has a "normal" spectrum. The binary need not necessarily be a visual pair; the method can be used with spectroscopic binaries as long as the spectrum of the "normal" star is dominant. Theoretically, the method could be used for perhaps 15% of planetary nebulae but only a handful of cases have been investigated in detail; these include NGC's 246, 1514, 2346, 3132, and Abell 35. Distances obtained this way may have errors of about ±30%.

2. **Radial expansion:** The expansion of planetaries can be established from characteristics of the emission lines in the spectrum and the calculated expansion velocity can be compared with direct angular expansion measurements, taken from plates exposed over a period of time. The distance is then calculated from the formula:

$$d = \frac{100v}{4.74\theta} pc$$

where v is the radial velocity (km/s) and θ is the angular expansion rate (arc sec/century). This method has been used for a number of nebulae, including, NGC's 246, 3242, 3587, 6572, 6720, 7009, and 7662.

3. **Interstellar extinction:** A nebula in a field of stars may well be obscured to some degree by clouds of interstellar gas and dust, particularly if it is close to the galactic plane. If the distances of some of the stars are known (say, from the spectra or photometric color) the amount by which they are affected by extinction can be calculated. If enough measurements of individual stars have been made, covering a wide enough range of distances, then the extinction as a function of distance in the direction of the nebula is known, and the degree of obscuration of the object itself will reveal its distance. Although producing fairly accurate distance determinations, the limitation of this method is that there is often insufficient data available on enough field stars and obtaining this information is very time consuming.

   Important work on the determination of planetary nebulae distances by the interstellar extinction method has been carried out by R. Gathier (see, for example, ref. 2).

4. **21cm hydrogen absorption line measurements:** This method is similar in principle to that described in (3), above, being dependent for its effectiveness on the density of the interstellar medium. It can be applied to any fairly compact object which radiates 21cm continuum emission; neutral hydrogen between the source and the observer will absorb some of the line radiation and an approximate distance can be derived from the strength of the absorption line.

5. **The "Shklovskii Method":** This statistical distance determination method is perhaps the one most commonly referred to in professional papers. It was first proposed by I.S. Shklovskii (ref. 3) and the basic assumption of this is that all planetary nebula shells are completely ionized and have a mass of about $0.2M\odot$. Of course, the expansion of the nebula results in a fall in the mean electron density and the radius

(r_N) increases according to the law:

$$\frac{4\pi}{3} r_N^3 Ne = \text{constant}.$$

Therefore, if the electron density can be measured, the radius can also be determined; if the angular radius is then measured, its distance follows.

The electron density can be derived through observing the effects of collisional de-excitation in the emission spectrum.

This is achieved by a comparison of the intensity of two lines of the same ion, emitted by different levels with nearly the same excitation energy. Those lines most commonly employed in this technique are those of [O II] 372.9 nm/372.6 nm and [S II] 671.6 nm/673.1 nm. If there is difficulty in obtaining this data the mean Hβ surface brightness can also be used to determine the electron density.

Maciel and Pottasch (ref. 4) have investigated the accuracy of the Shklovskii method by analyzing the results of Milne and Aller (ref. 5) who applied it in their 5 GHz survey of 165 southern planetary nebulae. Maciel and Pottasch found that, assuming no systematic error in the angular radii determinations, there was a clear correlation between the physical size of the objects and their distances. That is, all the larger objects were close and all the smaller objects further away—a somewhat unlikely situation which can be attributed to a failure of the Shklovskii method. However, this method is still quite attractive because of the ease with which it can be applied. Therefore, it was considered whether some variation on the theme could be employed. Unfortunately, there is no direct way of measuring the mass of a planetary nebula shell. Even so, using accurately derived electron densities for a number of galactic planetary nebulae, the authors established an empirical mass-radius relation from which distances could be determined; these seemingly represent an improvement over those obtained from the basic model and in their paper, Maciel and Pottasch use it to calculate the distances of 121 objects.

2.2 The Spectrum of a Planetary Nebula

Huggins' discovery of the emission line spectra of planetary nebulae (described in Chapter 1) established that they are formed of a low-density gas, and it is from a detailed investigation of the spectrum that clues can be gleaned about the physical conditions which exist in these objects. In particular, information can be obtained about the temperature, electron density, and chemical composition.

The spectrum of a planetary nebula, however, is rather complex and made up of a number of components:

1. Forbidden lines of oxygen, neon, and other abundant elements, in various states of ionization.

2. Permitted lines of hydrogen and helium, the two most abundant elements in the atmosphere of the progenitor star, plus a few of the stronger lines of other common elements, especially carbon, nitrogen, and oxygen.

3. Fluorescence lines of O III in nebulae showing a strong line of singly ionized helium (He II) at 468.6 nm.

4. An underlying continuous emission spectrum, resulting from the interaction between electrons and hydrogen and helium ions. The brightest components of a planetary nebula spectrum are shown in Figure 2–1.

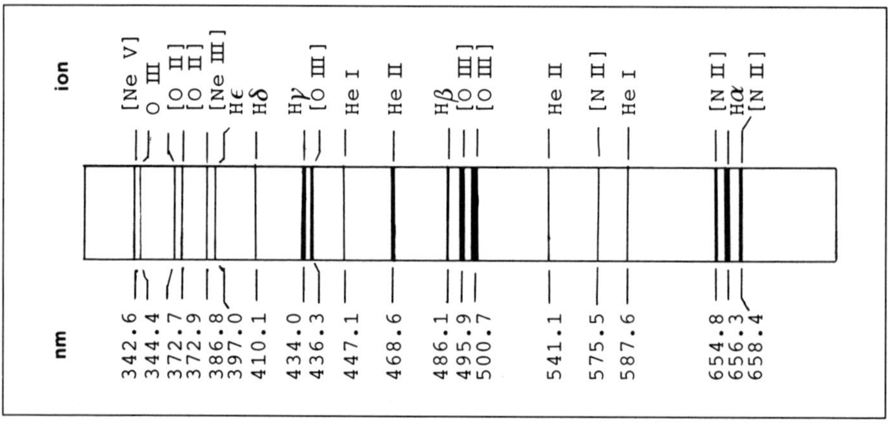

Figure 2–1. *The brightest components of a planetary nebula spectrum.*

It is the forbidden lines, particularly those of oxygen in the green part of the visible spectrum at 500.7 nm and 495.9 nm, which most influence the visual perception of planetary nebulae. Because of their strength—most planetary nebulae have 90–95% of visible energy in the [O III] lines—and because, coincidentally, these lines lie close to the eye's peak sensitivity (about 550 nm), many of the brighter objects of this class can actually be visually observed to glow with a green or blue-green light.

Another particularly important set of lines is the Balmer series of hydrogen lines. These are named after the German physicist, Johann Balmer, who, in

1885, recognized that the wavelengths of the spectral lines of hydrogen could be calculated from the simple formula:

$$\frac{1}{\lambda} = \left(\frac{1}{2^2} - \frac{1}{n^2}\right).$$

The lines begin with Hα at 656.3 nm (in the red part of the spectrum) and the wavelength of the other lines is computed by substituting $n = 3, 4, 5$, etc. R is the Rydberg Constant. By this means, other hydrogen lines can be shown to lie at 486.1 nm (Hβ), 434.0 nm (Hγ), 410.1 nm (Hδ). The lines eventually converge at 364.6 nm (the Balmer Limit) which is arrived at when $n = \infty$ in the formula.

The Hα line is especially significant in photographic representations of planetary nebulae; color emulsions have a tendency to be red-sensitive and certainly pick up Hα more easily than the dark-adapted eye. 656.3 nm is near the eye's limit of sensitivity. However, the Hβ line in the blue, with a strength of about one-third the Hα line, makes a more significant contribution to the visual brightness of the nebula.

An additional series of hydrogen lines was found by Lyman in the ultraviolet part of the spectrum, beginning at 121.6 nm. This line is called "Lymanα" and the other lines in the series are identified by the same use of the Greek alphabet as found in the Balmer series. Series of hydrogen lines were discovered by Paschen and also by Brackett in the infrared; other series are also known. With slight modifications to the Balmer formula, it can be used to predict the positions of spectral lines in other series.

In the visual part of the spectrum the principal emission lines are:

Wavelength (nm)	Ion	Notes
372.7	[O II]	Often very strong
386.9	[Ne III]	
434.0	H I	Hγ. Strength about 0.4 × Hβ
468.6	He II	
486.1	H I	Hβ. Strength about 0.25 × $H\alpha$
495.9	[O III]	Strength about 0.3 × 500.7 nm line
500.7	[O III]	Strongest line, 2 × Hα
630.2	[O I]	
654.8	[N II]	
656.3	H I	Hα
658.4	[N II]	

Because the ratio of line strengths is roughly similar, and because only a few lines contribute significantly to the visible brightness of a planetary nebula, it is possible to calculate the visual integrated magnitudes of these objects in a consistent, reproducible, and standardized manner. For amateur purposes, of course, visual magnitudes are much more valuable than the usually quoted photographic values—and can differ significantly. Important work on the computation of integrated visual magnitudes of planetary nebulae from line ratios has been carried out by Jack B. Marling, and he reports that empirically, his method produces magnitudes very close to visual estimates, and are probably accurate to about 0.15 magnitude.

2.3 The Origin of Planetary Nebulae

Planetary nebulae are believed to represent a late stage in the evolution of middle-weight, main-sequence stars, such as the Sun. A typical star is powered by nuclear fusion reactions at the center which convert hydrogen into helium. This "hydrogen-burning" stage may continue for 10 thousand million years or more but inevitably, the fuel will be consumed and the proportion of helium in the core will increase.

The conversion rate is not constant because as the hydrogen burns, the core gradually contracts and becomes hotter, increasing the burning rate. During this hydrogen-burning period, which may be 90% of the star's lifetime, it remains close to the main sequence and variations in luminosity are comparatively minor.

When the hydrogen fuel is used up, the core, now almost entirely helium, plus a small quantity of heavy elements, begins to contract releasing gravitational energy. The region of hydrogen burning moves outwards, forming a shell around the core. Of course, a star in equilibrium is balancing the forces of nuclear energy pushing outwards and the mass of the outer layers falling inwards. Once the mass of the core has increased to between 10% and 15% of the mass of the star, a point is reached where the core is unable to support the outer regions and it begins to contract. As the core contracts it becomes hotter. The thermal and gravitational balance of the star is restructured, causing the envelope to expand considerably. In this situation, the outer layers of the envelope become more rarified, cooler and redder. The star has now become a "red giant" and made a fairly rapid journey across the Hertzsprung-Russell (HR) diagram from the main sequence to the top right-hand side: the exact time scale of this process depends on the mass of the star.

For stars of roughly solar mass, the density of the core has become so great that the electron gas no longer obeys the normal laws which relate gas pressure and temperature. It is said to have become "degenerate." As a result of this, the continually contracting core becomes increasingly hot, due to the release of gravitational energy, so that eventually the helium is ignited. Although there is a considerable increase in energy production and, consequently, in temperature, the degeneracy of the core material does not allow it to expand and there is no reduction in the rate of energy release, which therefore continues at a runaway rate. The core temperature becomes so great (helium burning—to carbon, then oxygen—begins at a temperature of about 100 million K) that the material becomes non-degenerate and expands explosively. This phenomenon is called the "helium flash" or "thermal pulse."

Obviously, the helium fuel in the core also has a finite lifetime and when a significant fraction of it has been converted to carbon and oxygen, a further contraction occurs. Again, the envelope expands and the star ascends the giant branch. The degenerate carbon-oxygen (C-O) core at the center is now more-or-less dead but, during the core's helium burning stage, hydrogen-burning has continued in a shell surrounding it. Once the formation of the C-O core has been completed, helium-burning spreads into this region and hydrogen-burning commences in another shell around this. Red giant stars with a degenerate C-O core are described as being on the "asymptotic giant branch" (AGB), since the track of this second ascent of the giant branch shadows, or is roughly parallel to the first.

Such red giant stars are of vast dimensions, typically having a radius of 100 to 200 times that of the Sun. The resulting escape velocity at the surface is comparatively low, in the order of 10 km/s, which fits in with the known expansion velocities of planetary nebulae. However, there are problems in predicting the track an AGB star will follow at this point. This is primarily because the size and surface temperature of a star of a given luminosity is highly dependent on the effectiveness of the convection processes which transport fresh fuel into the nuclear burning region. Unfortunately, the physics of these convection processes are little understood.

The nuclear fusion processes around the C-O core are also fairly complex. As the star starts to ascend the AGB, the helium-burning occurs in a thick shell but, as the fuel becomes exhausted, the mass of the outer layers of the star compresses and reignites the hydrogen in the surrounding shell. Obviously, hydrogen fusion will occur at the greatest rate at the boundary between the shells where the pressure and temperature is the greatest. Helium is again the product of these reactions and once more, a point is reached when the mass of accumulated helium is such that fusion can restart in a thermal pulse event. The process continues with the result that the size and mass of the dead C-O core increases and the shells of helium-burning and hydrogen-burning migrate outwards.

Clearly, there is scope for the thermal pulse phenomenon to recur a number of times, dependent on the mass of the star. Typically, though, it is expected that about ten might take place, separated by intervals of a few hundred thousand years. When the thermal pulse events first start, it is likely that they would not be detectable at the surface because of the mass of the overlying envelope. However, as the core spreads outwards and the envelope thins, the effect of the events should become apparent, although there have not yet been any positively identified cases where this has been observed.

For stars with an initial main sequence mass of less than 9M$\odot$, the eventual mass of the core will normally be less than the critical limit of 1.4M$\odot$, and typically 0.6 to 0.8M$\odot$.

While the core has been evolving, mass loss from the surface of the red giant has been taking place at an ever-increasing rate. This is particularly important in the case of the Mira long-period variables, which are believed to be the immediate precursors of planetary nebulae. These have unstable atmospheres, a fact evidenced by the great visual magnitude range of the stars, and highly complex spectra which include emission-line features.

Observations of Mira stars at optical, IR, millimeter and radio wavelengths all show evidence of considerable mass loss. In the longer wavelengths it has also been shown that many are surrounded by dust shrouds, so dense in some cases that the star is totally obscured in the visible. There is also evidence that this phenomenon becomes more pronounced as the period of the star increases. While most of the visible mira variables have periods in the range of 100 to 500 days, some detected only in the IR have been found to have periods of 600 to 2000 days.

A further stage in the evolution of Mira stars is believed to be represented by the OH/IR stars. These emit strongly in the OH (hydroxyl) radio lines and the infrared due to the presence of the dust-rich circumstellar envelope. They are also associated with maser emission. Additional evidence that they are objects related to planetary nebulae can be found in their similar galactic distribution; also, the large range of radial velocities near the galactic center is comparable with the characteristics of planetary nebulae. By examining the largest OH/IR sources and dividing their size by the expansion velocity, it has been established that this phase does not normally last longer than about 10,000 years. Compared to the Mira stage, OH/IR stars are characterized by yet a further increase in the rate of mass loss.

In the transition phase from red giant to planetary nebula proper—protoplanetary nebulae (PPN)—the dust shroud obscures the activity occurring beneath and makes them difficult to identify and study, especially at visible wavelengths. One reasonable assumption, however, might be that they would exhibit spectra combining the features of a late-type star and a much hotter star. Unfortunately, the unrelated group of so-called "symbiotic stars" also do this and can sometimes be difficult to differentiate. Indeed, the classification of several objects once considered firm examples of PPN (such as V1016 Cyg, HM Sge, and V1329 Cyg) is now in doubt and there are very few cases, in the visible at least, where such identification can be made with confidence.

Through steady mass-loss from the progenitor and increasingly disruptive thermal pulse events, as the star reaches the top of the AGB, much of the envelope is removed. The core thus exposed may have a mass only 20%

that of the progenitor and it evolves quickly to the left-hand side of the HR diagram where, once it has achieved a surface temperature of about 28,000 K, the intensity of the UV radiation begins to ionize the expanding new-born planetary nebula.

2.4 Morphology and Classification of Planetary Nebulae

From what has been said about the origin of planetary nebulae it might be supposed that the structure of these objects should be fairly simple. Unfortunately, this is not the case. There are a number of complicating factors which may come into play in individual objects; these include the structure of the dust prior to the ejection of the circumstellar envelope, the presence of a binary companion, the strength of magnetic fields, and the respective masses of the nebula and core. However, the primary agent in determining the morphology of a planetary nebula is thought to be the interaction of stellar winds of various speeds and densities.

During the red giant stage, the progenitor star gives off a low-mass, low-velocity wind, and as it climbs the asymptotic giant branch, it ejects about $0.2M_\odot$ as a dense "superwind," with a slightly greater speed (about 10 km/s). The density of the red giant wind is sufficient, in the short term, to confine the superwind enabling hydrodynamic waves to form at the interface, redistributing the mass in the shell. The morphology of some nebulae suggests that more than one superwind event may occur, separated by intervals of several thousand years.

Once the hot nucleus has formed it emits, in addition to ionizing UV radiation, a tenuous fast wind at about 1000 km/s. This causes a shockwave to form at the interface with the slower moving superwind. The visible effect of this is the appearance of a cavity around the star, bordered by a bright rim. A small number of planetary nebulae, such as Abell 30, Abell 33, and Abell 39, exhibit no such features, suggesting that some central stars may not go through the fast wind phase.

Morphologies of individual nebulae can be explained by varying the time scale and duration over which these events occur or invoking multiple mass ejection events. A detailed review of the formation of planetary nebulae structures is given in ref. 10 and other references therein.

A planetary nebulae classification scheme based on these phenomena, and taking into account the symmetry of individual objects, is described by Bruce Balick (ref. 6) and illustrated in Table 2–1. This also has a parallel scheme for classifying many non-symmetrical objects by introducing a parameter called "density contrast," the ratio of equatorial to polar density in the ejected red giant envelope. Although seemingly comprehensive, even this classification is simplistic, assuming, for example, that the outflow from the star is uniform.

Table 2–1
Planetary Nebulae Categories

Spherical (Type S)	Non-spherical (Type N)
S1—Initial Ejection A red giant ejects its outer layers, which consist largely of neutral gas with some dust and simple molecules. This is driven outwards by radiation pressure at 10-15 km/s^{-1}.	**N1—Initial Ejection** As S1 but because of rapid rotation or the gravitational influence of a companion, material is preferentially ejected from the equatorial plane of the star.
S2—Bubble Formation The now smaller, hotter central star blows a high-speed, low mass wind which forms a "bubble" inside the nebula.	**N2—Bubble Formation** The stellar wind meets resistance from the greater density of equatorial material but pushes outward at a greater rate in the direction of the poles.
S3—The Snowplow Effect As the wind velocity increases to about 2000 km/s it exceeds the speed of sound in the gas and a shock wave is formed, pushing the gas ahead of it into a thin, very hot, bright, "Snowplow" (*e.g.*, NGC 6720).	**N3—The Snowplow Effect** **Moderate Density Contrast** The variation in density causes the Snowplow to develop an oval form, perhaps with a constricted minor axis (*e.g.*, NGC 7662). **High Density Contrast** If the density of the equatorial region is high, the wind may blow through the polar gas, leaving a thick equatorial disc, heated by the wind, which would also deflect the wind outward along the polar axis (*e.g.*, NGC 2346).
S4—Penetration The nebula breaks up into clumps when the Snowplow reaches the edge. The wind and hot gas inside escapes.	**N4—Penetration** **Moderate Density Contrast** The nebula is penetrated at the poles, focussing the wind. The puncture hole grows and the wind and gas escapes in a bipolar flow (*e.g.*, NGC 7009). **High Density Contrast** The equatorial disc is gradually eaten away by the stellar wind, but induces considerable turbulence in its flow (*e.g.*, NGC 6894).
S5—Fossil nebula The nebula has been reduced to irregular filaments and a new bubble may eventually be formed as the wind and outflowing gas interacts with any older ejecta (*e.g.*, Abell 30).	

This is certainly not the case; and increasing number of planetary nebulae (e.g., NGC 1535, NGC 2392) are known to have central stars producing bipolar jets of gas. Other planetary nebulae (e.g., NGC 2346) have dense patches of dust orbiting close to the central star which not only produce eclipse-type phenomena but must also surely interfere with the flow of the stellar wind. Furthermore, the expanding planetary nebula shell must interact with the interstellar medium, the density and uniformity of which will be different in every case.

Based purely on observational criteria, Khromov and Kohoutek (ref. 11) have suggested a classification scheme which they believe can account for 90% of planetary nebulae:

1. Round or ring-shaped nebulae of uniform surface brightness.
2. Elliptical nebulae with brightness maxima at each end of the minor axis.
3. Nebulae with two brightness maxima symmetrically placed with respect to the nebular center.

However, the most commonly used classification system is that devised by Vorontsov-Velyaminov, also based on observational criteria. This is more descriptive and can be quickly and simply applied:

I	Stellar	
II	Smooth disc	
		(a) brighter towards the center
		(b) uniform brightness
		(c) traces of ring structure
III	Irregular disc	
		(a) very irregular brightness distribution
		(b) traces of ring structure
IV	Ring structure	
V	Irregular form	
VI	Anomalous form	

In this system, more complex forms can be described by using a combination of these type numbers (for example, NGC 650-1 is classified as type III+VI). It is this system of Vorontsov-Velyaminov which will be employed in the Catalogue section of this book.

The classification schemes discussed above describe the main body of a planetary nebulae but it is becoming increasingly apparent that many are significantly larger than was formerly thought. Deep photographs often show large halo structures at great distances from the "main body" of the nebula. These generally seem to consist of irregular loops and filaments and may be present in up to 50% of all planetary nebulae. The first example of this phenomenon (around NGC 6720) was reported by Duncan in 1937 (ref. 7) but many more are now known, including NGC's 6543, 6826, 7009, 7027, 7293, and 7662. These are listed in more detail in Table 2–2 and examples are illustrated in Figures 2–2 and 2–3.

Planetary nebulae haloes are important because the material concerned is obviously ejecta from the red giant star which pre-dates the main nebula-forming event, or, less likely, material accelerated at a greater rate during the formation of the planetary nebula. Calculations indicate that the mass of the halo is often greater than that of the "main nebula."

2.5 Planetary Nebulae Central Stars

The evolution of a planetary nebula up to the ejection of the red giant envelope has already been described, but what of the core? Although the unusual spectra of these objects perhaps makes it a little inappropriate to plot them on an HR diagram, to do so can be quite instructive and the result is shown in Figure 2–4.

PNN are located to the left of the main sequence but above the normal range of white dwarf stars. They are therefore extremely hot objects, and a more detailed examination of the group reveals that the youngest stars seem to be on the right-hand side; they evolve towards the left, becoming hotter, though remaining approximately constant in luminosity, before cooling and becoming fainter (though still from 10 to 1000 times brighter than the Sun!). This sequence of events normally takes less than 40,000 years, and in this short period the radius of the star decreases by a factor of 100 with a consequent increase of perhaps 10 million in the internal density of the star.

The temperature range of PNN is tremendous, the coolest being about 25,000°K. The temperature of the hottest stars is uncertain because as a star of constant luminosity becomes hotter, a greater proportion of the radiation is emitted at wavelengths shorter than the Lyman limit (91.2 nm). This results in the nebula brightening relative to the central star so that, at visible wavelengths, it is almost impossible to identify within the enveloping nebulosity, still less measure its characteristics. However, using a CCD camera at the prime focus of the AAT, together with a 1 nm-wide filter centered at 478.8 nm (chosen to exclude any known nebular emission lines), P.D. Atherton *et al.* (ref. 8) managed to observe the nucleus of the planetary nebula NGC 2440. They measured the visual magnitude as being 18.9 ± 0.2 and derived an effective temperature of an amazing 350,000°K.

Figure 2–2. *NGC 6543 showing halo structure. The main body of the nebula has a diameter of around 20″ but in this long exposure it is seen to have a diameter of over 300″. Courtesy of Lick Observatory.*

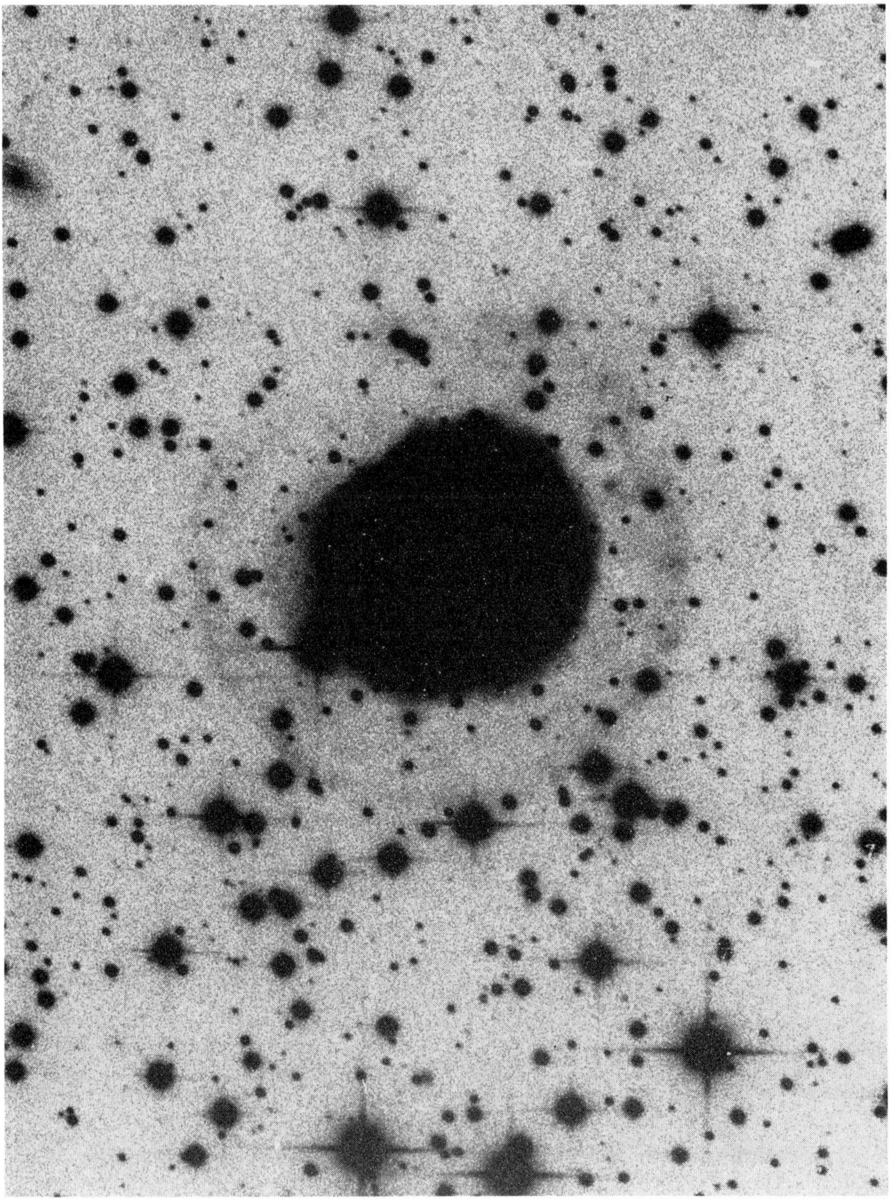

Figure 2–3. *NGC 2438 showing halo structure. The stars are part of the open cluster NGC2437. Anglo-Australian Observatory photograph by David Malin.*

Table 2–2
Some Planetary Nebulae With Halo Structures

Name	PK	Con	PN Diam(″)	Halo Diam(″)	Ref.
NGC 650-1	130-10.1	Per	65	290	7
NGC 1535	206-40.1	Eri	18	44	1
NGC 2440	234+02.1	Pup	14	32	1
M 1-18	231+04.1	Pup	32	130	1
K 1-2	253+10.1	Pyx	69	110	3
NGC 3242	261+32.1	Hya	16	1250	1
NGC 4361	294+43.1	Crv	45	110	1
Abell 36	318+41.1	Vir	293	400	1
IC 972	326+42.1	Vir	48	52	2
He 2-111	315-00.1	Cen	18	610	5
IC 4593	025+40.1	Her	12	120	1
NGC 6072	342+10.1	Sco	40	70	1
NGC 6309	009+14.1	Oph	32	90	2
NGC 6369	002+05.1	Oph	34	68	2
NGC 6445	008+03.1	Sgr	36	212	2
NGC 6543	096+29.1	Dra	20	386	7
M 3-28	021-00.1	Sct	8	28	2
M 1-64	064+15.1	Lyr	18	30	2
NGC 6720	063+13.1	Lyr	74	216	4
IC 1295	025-04.2	Sct	90	130	2
IC 1297	358-21.1	CrA	13	2	8
Ap 2-1	035-00.1	Aql	28	38	2
Sh 2-71	036-10.1	Aql	134	388	
NGC 6772	033-06.1	Aql	74	108	2
NGC 6781	041-02.1	Aql	120	158	2
NGC 6804	045-04.1	Aql	31	66	1
NGC 6826	083+12.1	Cyg	36	138	2
NGC 6842	065+00.1	Vul	26	58	2
He 1-4	068+01.2	Cyg	22	28	2
NGC 6853	060-03.1	Vul	350	907	7
M 1-75	068-00.1	Cyg	16	42	2
NGC 6891	054-12.1	Del	12	74	1
NGC 6894	069-02.1	Cyg	40	62	2
NGC 6905	061-09.1	Del	46	100	1
NGC 7008	093+05.2	Cyg	80	120	2
NGC 7009	037-34.1	Aqr	36	100	1
NGC 7026	089+00.1	Cyg	21	40	2
NGC 7048	088-01.1	Cyg	70	108	2
Abell 75	101+08.1	Cep	36	70	2
M 2-51	103+00.1	Cep	32	76	2
NGC 7293	036-57.1	Aqr	960	1680	6
NGC 7354	107+02.1	Cep	20	42	2
NGC 7662	106-17.1	And	30	130	1
Abell 82	114-04.1	Cas	84	106	2

References to Table 2–2

1. Hirshfeld, A. & Sinnot, R.W. (ed.); *Sky Catalogue 2000.0*: Vol. 2, Cambridge University Press, 1985.
2. Jewitt, D.C. *et al.*; *Ap.J.*, **302**, 727, 1986.
3. Kohoutek, L. & Schnur, G.; *M.N.R.A.S.*, **201**, 21, 1982.
4. Moreno, M. & Lopez, J.; *Astron. Astrophys.*, **178**, 319, 1987.
5. Webster, H.L.; *M.N.R.A.S.*, **185**, 45P, 1978.
6. Personal estimate measured from AAT and ESO photographs.
7. Millikan, A.G.; *Astron. J.*, **79**, 1259, 1974.
8. Aller, L.H. *et al.*; *Ap.J.*, **311**, 930, 1986.

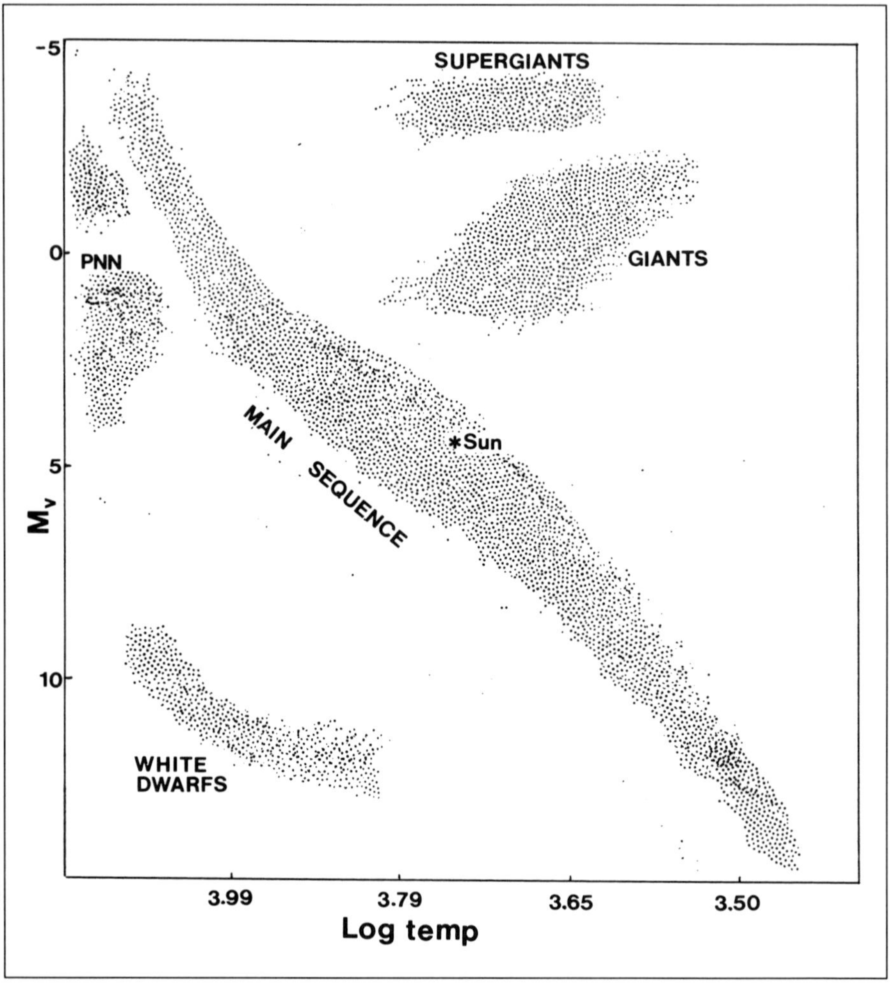

Figure 2–4. *H-R diagram showing relative positions of planetary nebula nuclei (PNN) and white dwarf stars.*

The spectra of PNN are similar to ordinary hot stars in the Galaxy. Of course, there is no real comparison as they are less than 5% the mass of hot main sequence stars, and their apparent similarity is just indicative of comparable temperatures in the stellar atmospheres. Even so, the classification system for these objects is based on the likenesses with their classical analogues. There are seven generally recognized categories of PNN spectra:

- **Wolf-Rayet:** WR stars lose mass by strong stellar winds and so exhibit broad emission lines, or even P Cygni characteristics. The dominant lines are of H, He, C, N, and O. Interestingly, stars of the WN subtype are unknown among PNN; only the WC group are represented.

- **Of:** Similar to the above but with emission lines of H, He II, N III, and usually C III.
- **WR+Of:** These stars have a combination spectrum and do not have an analogue in the normal range of main sequence stars.
- **OVI:** These exceptionally hot objects also have no main sequence analogue and are characterized by prominent OVI emission lines at 381.1 nm and 383.4 nm. Carbon lines are also strongly represented in these stars.
- **O:** Characterized by the normal absorption lines found in main sequence O stars, especially H and He II.
- **sdO:** Subdwarf O stars with absorption lines broader than in the above.
- **cont:** "Continuous spectrum" stars are probably an erroneous categorization. Most have been found as a result of low dispersion spectra at visual wavelengths or are faint or otherwise poorly observed. In many cases, more detailed or extended spectra have revealed some features; for example, the central stars of NGC's 7009 and 7662, which have not shown any absorption features in the visible spectrum, exhibit strong P Cygni profiles of C IV and NV when observed in the far-UV with the IUE.

From Figure 2–4 it can be seen that the white dwarfs appear to form an extension to the PNN sequence, and there is in fact every reason to suppose that this relationship is genuine. Certainly, the independently derived formation rates for white dwarfs and planetary nebulae are comparable (although the class of hot subdwarfs does also contribute towards the white dwarf population).

White dwarf stars are remarkable objects in their own right and significant for being the evolutionary terminal point of the bulk of the stars in the Galaxy. They are tiny objects—no larger than the Earth—but have a mass of typically 0.5 to 0.7 $M_\odot$. This implies a tremendous surface gravity, perhaps 200,000 times that of the Earth; as a consequence, the atmosphere of the star is stratified, leaving the lightest gas, hydrogen, as the outer layer. Because of this, hydrogen features dominate the spectrum, giving the impression that these stars are virtually pure hydrogen. About 80% of all white dwarf stars (classified as "DA") display only hydrogen absorption lines in their spectra; most of the remainder (classified "DB") exhibit only helium lines.

In the early stages of their evolution, vast quantities of neutrinos are produced in the interior of these degenerate of white dwarf stars; these evanescent particles hardly interact with matter at all; however, they carry away a considerable amount of energy and are the primary cooling agent during the first few million years. In addition, a number of hot white dwarfs are known to be variable as a result of atmospheric pulsation. The pulsation period is believed to be related to the cooling rate, and observations of the rate of change in the prototype, PG1159–035, confirm that the star is cooling as predicted by theory.

After perhaps 10 million years, the white dwarf has cooled from over 100,000°K to about 30,000°K and faded to a luminosity of about 0.1 Sun (ref. 9).

Unlike a normal star which is held in equilibrium by the balancing of thermal and gravitational forces, a white dwarf counteracts collapse by a quantum-mechanical effect known as electron degeneracy pressure. In this remarkable state, the constituent atoms have lost their electrons and the matter which makes up the star is composed of atomic nuclei crushed together, with the free electrons moving around within the mass. The degenerate electrons play a significant part in determining the thermal characteristics of a white dwarf, conducting heat through the interior and levelling out temperature gradients so that these objects are virtually isothermal. The surface layers of the star consist of material with more normal properties and energy is transported by radiation and convective processes.

As the white dwarf cools, convection in the outer layers becomes the more significant of the heat transfer processes and extends more deeply into the interior, mixing the hydrogen in the surface layer with the helium below. It is therefore found that the DA white dwarfs are hotter than the DB variety, the latter becoming dominant as the surface temperature falls to about 10,000°K.

The cooling process may take over a thousand million years and in the final stages, the attractive electrical forces dominate the kinetic energy of the gas, causing the ions to clump together, forming a "Coulomb liquid." Eventually, increasing amounts of matter become bound together in a symmetric, solid lattice, spreading outwards from the center until the entire star has become a solid crystal and able to evolve no further.

2.6 References

1. Ianna, P.A. & McAlister, H.A.; *Astron. J.*, **79**, 1314, 1974.
2. Gathier, R.; *Astron. Astrophys. Supp. Ser.*, **60**, 399, 1985.
3. Shkovskii, I.S.; *Sov. Astron. J.*, **33**, 315, 1956.
4. Maciel, W.J. & Pottasch, S.R.; *Astron. Astrophys.*, **88**, 1, 1980.
5. Milne, D.K. & Aller, L.H.; *Astron. Astrophys.*, **38**, 183, 1975.
6. Balick, H.; *Sky & Telescope*, February 1987, p. 125.
7. Duncan, J.D.; *Ap.J.*, **86**, 496, 1937.

8. Atherton, P.D. *et al.*; *Nature*, **320**, 423, 1986.
9. Kawaler, S.D. & Winget, D.E.; *Sky & Telescope*, August 1987.
10. Frank, A. *et al.*; *Astron. J.*, **100**, 1903, 1990.
11. Khromov, G.S. & Kohoutek, L.; *Bull. Astr. Inst. Cat.*, **19**, 1, 1968.

Chapter 3

Planetary Nebula Mimics

3.1 Introduction

In Chapter 1 it was observed that planetary nebulae are commonly identified as a result of objective-prism surveys or examination of photographic plates; however, a number of other types of emission line objects are revealed by objective-prism surveys, and a number of other types of object bear some visual similarity to planetary nebulae on photographic plates. If thorough spectroscopic and photographic studies are not performed on each object discovered, it is inevitable that incorrect classifications will occur. In addition, even when individual objects are investigated in depth, some can still give confusing signals as to their nature. It may, therefore, be the case that catalogues of planetary nebulae are plagued by more varieties of interloper than catalogues of any other object. This may have led to the following exchange between astronomers at an IAU Symposium (ref. 1):
David S. Evans

> It is essential to have a practical definition for a planetary nebula... The practical definition now in use seems to be that a planetary nebula is an object which appears in a catalogue of planetary nebulae.

Rudolf L. Minkowski

> ...there is no better way than to accept any object in a catalogue of planetary nebulae if nobody has serious objections.

Perhaps this more reflects the exasperation of professional astronomers in trying to define exactly what does constitute the specific characteristics of a planetary nebula, to the exclusion of other objects. The range of other types of celestial inhabitant which can sometimes mimic the characteristics of a planetary nebula is surprisingly large. At a more recent IAU Symposium (ref. 2), these were discussed by Lubos Kohoutek, who listed the following as possible sources of error:

1. Emission line galaxies
2. Supernova remnants
3. Reflection nebulae
4. Classical H II regions
5. Compact H II regions
6. Nebulae associated with Wolf-Rayet stars
7. Symbiotic stars
8. Slow novae
9. Be and related stars
10. Late-type stars with emission lines
11. Pre-main sequence emission objects
12. T Tauri stars
13. Herbig Ae, Be stars
14. Herbig-Haro objects

Since many of these types can also be divided into discrete subgroups, the potential size of the problem is considerable. However, a great deal of work is now being done to weed out the misclassified planetary nebulae. In a recent compilation (ref. 3), Agnes Acker and her co-workers have identified 266 objects which they believe have been incorrectly listed as planetary nebulae. This paper indicates that symbiotic stars are the most common source of error and account for about one quarter of all misclassified planetary nebulae. Reflection nebulae, H II regions, and galaxies are also substantially represented groups.

Although the main purpose of this book is to discuss planetary nebulae themselves, many of the mimics are interesting in their own right and it might be useful to take a look at some of the more commonly mistaken objects, listing some examples.

3.2 Symbiotic Stars

Objective-prism surveys are designed to identify emission line objects, which include planetary nebulae, but a number of varieties of stars also exhibit emission lines, and those which most closely mimic the features of stellar planetary nebulae are the symbiotic stars.

The definition of a symbiotic star is a little vague, reflecting the fact that much remains to be discovered about these objects. However, most models account for them in terms of interacting binaries, one component being a giant of spectral type G or later and the other considerably hotter, presenting emission lines of high excitation, such as He II and [Fe II]. The emission lines are in some cases broad and structured and in other cases unresolved, indicating a wide variety of conditions existing in these systems, as detailed in the extensive investigations by David A. Allen (ref. 4).

Symbiotic stars are generally variable, the variations being characterized by nova-like outbursts, *e.g.*, AG Peg and V1016 Cyg. In some instances, eclipses are also observed, *e.g.*, CI Cyg, SY Mus, and AR Pav.

Some symbiotic stars, such as V1016 Cyg, V1329 Cyg (= HBV 475), and HM Sge, have until recently been classified as proto-planetary nebulae (see, for example, ref. 5). Spectroscopic observations of V1016 Cyg at very high spectral and spatial resolution reveal a compact bipolar nebula, consisting of two lobes separated by 1.″40 in space and 51 km/s in radial velocity (ref. 6). HM Sge exhibits a similar phenomenon (ref. 7). In both cases this is taken to indicate bipolar mass flow of about 100–200 km/s with perhaps a slowly expanding equatorial ring structure. Analysis of the geometric and kinematical structure of HM Sge is found to be in agreement with the model of a binary consisting of a mass-losing M-type giant and a compact companion accreting part of the mass from the giant through an accretion disc.

Objects once considered to be planetary nebulae but now regarded as symbiotic stars include:

Ap 1-8, Ap 1-9, Ap 1-10, Ap 1-11, Ap 3-1
Bl 3-11, Bl L
CnMy 17
H 2-2 (= V455 Sco), H 2-4, H 2-5, H 2-28, H 2-38
He 2-38, He 2-87, He 2-106 (= V835 Cen), He 2-127, He 2-134,
He 2-147, He 2-171, He 2-173, He 2-176, He 2-177, He 2-294,
He 2-370, He 2- 374, He 2-390, He 2-417, He 2-467, He 2-468.
K 4-12
M 1-21, M 3-18.
Pe 2-16.
Th 3-7, Th 3-17, Th 3-18, Th 3-20, Th 3-30, Th 3-31.

3.3 Bipolar Nebulae

Bipolar nebulae consist of two, usually symmetrical lobes with either a visible star or an infrared source between the lobes. The standard model, which explains most cases, is that the light from a central star, which is more-or-less obscured by a dense equatorial disc or torus, is scattered from a surrounding gas and dust cloud, producing two apparent reflection nebulae and right-angles to the disc.

During recent years it has become evident that this morphological phenomenon is largely associated with a range of young objects, but also appears occasionally among genuine planetary nebulae (*e.g.*, NGC 2346) and proto-planetary nebulae.

A related phenomenon is the "cometary nebula," typified by NGC 2261 (Hubble's variable nebula); this object has been shown by Canto *et al.* (ref. 8) to be the visible half of a bipolar nebula, the second lobe being hidden by dust. However, it should be noted that "cometary nebulae" are not related to "cometary globules."

A survey by Neckel and Staude (ref. 9) of 20 bipolar and cometary nebulae, mostly new discoveries, showed that the illuminating stars were generally of spectral types O or B; however, the authors point out that this might be just a selection effect since only stars earlier than B3 can produce conspicuous emission nebulae, and only luminous stars can give origin to reflection nebulae sufficiently bright and extended to be detected at great distances. The visual extinction of the central stars varies greatly, from about 2.5 mag to values as great as 25 mag. Approximately half of the objects studied exhibited IR excesses, indicative of emission temperatures of 500–1300°K. All linear dimensions were found to lie in the range 0.1pc to 1.3pc, almost identical to that found for the high velocity bipolar molecular flows.

Some bipolar nebulae are listed below; however, since the precise classification of some remains unclear (some could be genuine planetary nebulae), I have not attempted to discriminate between them:

CRL 618, CRL 2688 (= IV Zw 67, = Cygnus Egg Nebula).
HD 44179 (= "The Red Rectangle").
LK Hα 208, Lk Hα 233.
M 1-91, M 1-92 (= "Minkowski"s Footprint').
Sharpless 106, Sharpless 175, Sharpless 270.

3.4 Compact H II Regions

H II regions are normally distinguished from planetary nebulae by being considerably larger and more irregular in shape; there could be no mistaking the Orion Nebula or NGC 3372 for a planetary nebula! However, there are cases where these distinctive features are not strongly presented and the object may be quite small and round, resembling a planetary nebula. However, even in these circumstances, the nebular spectrum may show evidence of being ionized by more than one star, which would tend to indicate that the object is an H II region. Another differentiating feature is that the star ionizing a planetary nebula is almost always considerably hotter than that responsible for ionizing an H II region; an identifying feature in this instance might be lines of He II in the spectrum, rarely found in H II regions. In addition, the gas in a planetary nebula is usually very much more dense and less clumpy than in an H II region.

Objects now classified as H II regions which were originally classified as planetary nebulae include:

H 2-3, H 2-6.
K 1-18, K 3-50, K 4-60.
NGC 1985, NGC 6857.
RCW 65, RCW 87, RCW 88, RCW 99.
Sh2-20 (= Bl 3-4), Sh2-61 (= VV1-8), Sh2-267 (= VV1-5).

3.5 Be Stars

Of all the stars of spectral type B, from the main sequence to the giant region, about 20% exhibit hydrogen emission lines in the visible spectrum. To distinguish them from the more plentiful absorption line B stars, these are called Be stars. Originally discovered by Fr. Angelo Secchi in 1866, over 3000 are now known.

Many of these stars exhibit an IR excess to a greater or lesser degree, and in addition, a number have forbidden emission lines; this group is usually identified as Bep or B[e] stars and is generally among the fainter members of the Be group.

Observations of early-type emission line stars and related objects by David A. Allen (ref. 10) showed that the B[e] stars were those most likely to have the largest excesses—greater than 1 magnitude at 2–3 μm—which has been interpreted as thermal radiation re-emitted by circumstellar dust particles.

It is this group of B[e] stars with strong IR excesses and forbidden emission lines in the spectrum which can be the source of some confusion in classification. These features are also present in planetary nebulae, and although in some cases it is comparatively easy to differentiate between them, because of the weaker emission spectra of the B[e] stars (say, just Balmer and FeII and perhaps, [O I] lines), a few do have spectral features showing higher ionization states, like [O III] and [Ne III]. Similarities between B[e] stars and planetary nebulae can also be found in the radio spectrum.

Be stars which have previously been included in catalogues of planetary nebulae include the following:

Ap 1-9.
Bl 3-19.
H 1-49.
He 2-58, He 2-79, He 2-80, He 2-91, He 2-174.
M 1-11.
Pe 2-9.

3.6 Ring Nebulae Associated with Wolf-Rayet Stars

Wolf-Rayet stars were identified as a distinct class in 1867 and are exceptionally hot, massive, and luminous objects. The spectra contain broad emission lines of He, C, N, and O against a continuous spectrum like that of O or B type stars. P Cygni profiles are in evidence, indicative of strong stellar winds. There are two subgroups, WC stars and WN stars, in which the spectra are dominated by lines from ions of carbon and nitrogen, respectively.

Some WR stars are associated with nebulous rings or arcs, the origin of which are believed to be due to interaction between the star and the interstellar medium. There are three means by which this can happen: stellar

UV radiation, stellar ejecta, and stellar winds. In his introductory paper on the classification of WR ring nebulae, You-Hua Chu (ref. 11) used these three processes as the basis of his scheme. The nebulae are divided into three categories:

R—radiatively excited H II regions
  Ra: amorphous H II regions
  Rs: shell-structured objects
E—stellar ejecta
W—wind-blown bubble.

Some of these WR ring nebulae show characteristics of structure which would make it difficult for any confusion to arise between them and planetary nebulae, for example, NGC's 2359, 3199, and 6888 (although the last of these was thought to be a supernova remnant at one time). Ring nebulae tend to exhibit a more filamentary structure than planetary nebulae and are usually significantly larger and more massive. However, in a few cases, the situation is less clear; for example, before being recognized as a WR ring nebula, M1-67 had been classified as an H II region and later, a planetary nebula. In a detailed study by Chu and Treffers (ref. 12), it was found that the kinematics were not consistent with that of a stellar wind-blown bubble but could be explained as material ejected from the central star at two distinct epochs about 10^4 to 10^5 years ago. The ejected material has been subsequently braked by interaction with the interstellar material and displaced by it.

A related phenomenon to the WR ring nebulae may be the shells around the small Ofpe/WN9 subgroup of stars. These are extremely massive, hot stars and, although the surrounding ring nebulae have apparently been ejected by the star, the mechanism is by no means clear. The rarity of these objects (only two have been identified in our own Galaxy, AG Car (= PK 289-0°1) and He 3-519, although more are known in the LMC) makes it difficult to draw statistically based conclusions; however, Stahl (ref. 13) finds that they typically have a linear size of 1pc, a kinematic age of 10^4 years and an ionized mass in the order of 1 solar mass. Clearly, they are significantly larger and more massive than typical planetary nebulae. The author suggests that these nebulae may result from violent S Dor outbursts of the central star. An amateur orientated discussion of these objects, with particular reference to AG Car, is given by Hynes (ref. 14).

3.7 Galaxies

That there could ever be any confusion between galaxies and planetary nebulae might seem unlikely, yet this has occurred. As one might expect, the problems tend to arise with objects which have been comparatively poorly studied. In many cases, the confusion is the result of morphological or spectral similarities; Abell 76 is an example of the former category and He2-10 an example of the latter.

Abell 76 was described by its discoverer as a regular, symmetrical planetary nebula, 13″ in diameter, having the appearance of a ring with gaps. However, in 1971, Chopinet (ref. 15) found the radial velocity of the object to be 3240±40 km/s, indicating a distance of about 32 Mpc and an absolute magnitude of Mv = −17. A more detailed investigation of the nature of Abell 76 was carried out by D.L. Talent *et al.* (ref. 16), who found it to be a small but beautiful morphological member of the ring-galaxy class, most likely of type RKO, in which a "nucleus" is seen projected against the ring. The presence of extensive optical line emission, high surface brightness, and pronounced blue continuum suggests the object is currently experiencing a very high rate of star formation.

He 2-10 was classified as a planetary nebula following its discovery as a source of strong Hα emission and subsequently, its nonstellar appearance. However, it was also listed as an elliptical galaxy in the *Morphological Catalogue of Galaxies* (ref. 17) as MCG-4-21-5. A thorough study by David A. Allen *et al.* (ref. 18) confirmed it as a galaxy and resulted in a distance determination of about 14 Mpc and Mv = −18. In addition, they found a number of remarkable features: non-thermal radio continuum, prominent IR excess, WR bands in the visible spectrum, and a high surface density of neutral hydrogen. The most recent investigation, by L. Johansson (ref. 19), has indicated a distance of 6 Mpc and suggests that He 2-10 consists of two separate dwarf galaxies undergoing a close encounter, or possibly merger. The two galaxies have had massive neutral hydrogen envelopes which are now falling towards the center of the system, triggering a burst of star formation. This scenario could also explain the WR emission and the non-thermal continuum.

A list of galaxies previously misclassified as planetary nebulae is given below:

Abell 76.
ESO 426-13, ESO 493-13, ESO 429-04, ESO 367-03, ESO 089-05, ESO 126-01, ESO 100-07, ESO 100-12, ESO 100-16, ESO 450-16, ESO 390-05, ESO 289-19.
He 2-10.
IC 4662.
K 1-5.
M 4-1 (= MCG 5-18-2)
NGC 5408.

Before completing this section, it is interesting to note that reverse misclassifications have also occurred; as recently as 1987 the object NGC 2242 was identified as a planetary nebula after previously having been listed as a galaxy (refs. 20 & 21).

Many planetary nebulae, particularly young objects, can now be identified with less ambiguity using a method devised by Pottasch *et al.* (ref. 22). The primary criterion is the infrared color as measured by IRAS; a color-color plot of the ratio of the flux density at 12μm to that at 25μm (in Jy) is plotted against the 25μm to 60μm flux density ratio. On this basis, planetary nebulae form a fairly discrete grouping, but with some overlap with OH/IR stars which can be separated out by checking for the presence of continuous thermal radio emission, a feature expected to be found only in planetary nebulae. This method is of particular value for identifying planetary nebulae in the direction of the galactic center, which are heavily obscured at optical wavelengths.

3.8 References

1. Osterbrock, D. & O'Dell, C.R. (ed.); *Planetary Nebulae*, IAU Symposium 34, Reidel, 1968 (p. 290).
2. Flower, D.R. (ed.); *Planetary Nebulae*, IAU Symposium 103, Reidel, 1983 (p. 17–30).
3. Acker, A. *et al.*; *Astron. Astrophys. Supp. Ser.*, **71**, 163, 1987.
4. Allen, D.A.; *Astrophys. & Sp. Sci.*, **99**, 101, 1984.
5. Feibelman, W.A.; *Ap.J.*, **258**, 548, 1982.
6. Solf, J.; *Ap.J.*, **266**, L113, 1983.
7. Solf, J.; *Astron. Astrophys.*, **139**, 296, 1984.
8. Canto, J. *et al.*; *Ap.J.*, **244**, 102, 1981.
9. Neckel, T. & Staude, H.J.; *Astron. Astrophys.* **131**, 200, 1984.
10. Allen, D.A.; *M.N.R.A.S.*, **161**, 145, 1973.
11. Chu, Y-H.; *Ap.J.*, **249**, 195, 198l.
12. Chu, Y-H & Treffers, R.R.; *Ap.J.*, **249**, 586, 1981.
13. Stahl, O.; *Astron. Astrophys.*, **182**, 229, 1987
14. Hynes, S.J.; *W.S.Q.J.* No. 67, 13, 1987.
15. Chopinet, M.; C.R. *Acad. Sci.* Paris, **272**, 290, 1971.
16. Talent, D.L. *et al.*; *Ap.J.*, **260**, 488, 1982.
17. Vorontsov-Velyaminov, B.A. & Arkhipova, B.A. *Morphological Catalogue of Galaxies*, Moscow, 1968.
18. Allen, D.A. *et al.*; *M.N.R.A.S.*, **177**, 91, 1976.
19. Johansson, L.; *Astron. Astrophys.* **182**, 179, 1987.
20. Shaw, R.A. & Bidelman, W.P.; *P.A.S.P.*, **99**, 27, 1987.
21. Maehara, H. *et al.*; *Astron. Astrophys.*, **178**, 221, 1987.
22. Pottasch, S.R. *et al.*; *Astron. Astrophys.* **205**, 248, 1988.

Chapter 4

Amateur Observation of Planetary Nebulae

4.1 Learning to See

Planetary nebulae are not the easiest objects to observe. While a number are fairly large and bright, most are small and comparatively faint. Therefore, practice is required to become a skilled observer. This was emphasized by perhaps the greatest of all visual observers, William Herschel:

> Seeing is in some respects, an art which must be learned. Many a night I have been practicing to see, and it would be strange if one did not acquire a certain dexterity by such constant practice.

First, one should be aware of fundamental factors which can contribute towards a successful observation. Sky conditions are particularly significant. One should be mindful of the relevance of "seeing" and "transparency" and how even minor variations in these parameters can result in success or failure. "Seeing" is the steadiness of the atmosphere. Seeing can be judged from the degree of scintillation or "twinkling" of the stars. "Transparency" is the clarity of the atmosphere and may be judged from naked-eye limiting magnitude estimates.

Biological and physiological factors are also important. The following should be particularly noted:

1. **Dark adaptation:** The eye is a remarkably versatile instrument. It is capable of operating over a wide range of light intensities. However, it does take time to adjust to a sudden, dramatic change in intensity. Everybody is familiar with the discomfort of leaving a darkened cinema and emerging into bright sunlight. For the astronomer the situation is reversed. While there is seldom discomfort when leaving a brightly

lit room and emerging into the dark of night, the eye takes time to adjust. Most authorities believe that the eye becomes adapted to the dark in about 15 minutes. However, there is some evidence that the greatest dark adaptation is reached after 30 minutes. Whatever the time it takes you to become dark adapted, it should be apparent that, having achieved a high level of dark adaptation, one does not want to ruin it during a few seconds of carelessness by switching on a bright light, say, to make notes or a drawing. Therefore, since the eye is less sensitive to red light most astronomers use a faint red light for these purposes. I use a small red LED flashlight, which enables me to write or draw but has only a minimal effect on my dark adaptation.

2. **Averted vision:** One characteristic of the eye is that it is not equally sensitive to light over its entire surface. The cells that make up the retina are of two types: "cones" and "rods." Cones are sensitive to color and high levels of illumination. Rods are sensitive to faint light but are comparatively poor detectors of color. Cones are tightly packed in the fovea centralis, which is a small area around the eye's optical axis. Rods surround the fovea centralis. Under normal daylight conditions, the clearest vision is obtained when the light is focussed on the fovea centralis. For optimum visibility of faint deep-sky objects, the image needs to be focussed away from the fovea centralis; this is achieved by aiming the eye at one point while concentrating attention to one side: this technique is called "averted vision." For best results the object under study should be placed to the nose side of the point where the eye is aimed; this also minimizes the possibility that the image will fall on the "blind spot." Averted vision, used by an experienced observer, is a formidable technique and can make objects visible and show detail well beyond that which can be seen by just looking straight at the object.

3. **Physiology:** Night vision can be improved or impaired by one's physical state. In particular, high blood sugar levels seem to have a positive effect on visual acuity, but fatigue, reduced oxygen levels in the blood (say, due to smoking), and alcohol seem to have a negative effect.

4.2 Telescopes

Practically any telescope can be used to observe planetary nebulae, but all things being equal, a larger instrument will enable you to see more. Since most observers will be restricted by how much they can spend, the best value is almost certainly the Newtonian reflector. Whatever advantages the refractor or Schmidt-Cassegrain telescopes have are outweighed by the Newtonian's lower cost per cm of aperture. Deep-sky observation has been revolutionized during recent years by the introduction of the Dobsonian mount. The

"Dobsonian," invented by John Dobson of the San Francisco Sidewalk Astronomers, is a simple alt-azimuth mounting that is sturdy, inexpensive, and easy to make. Since the Dobsonian mount costs less to make, more money can be put into increasing the size of the optics. Today, telescopes of 30 to 40 cm are now commonplace. Clearly, the result of this revolution has been to bring to amateur astronomers the capability to see fainter objects and resolve greater detail, factors which are particularly relevant for the study of planetary nebulae.

Table 4–1
Theoretical Light Grasp of Reflector Telescopes[1]

Aperture (cm)	Limiting Magnitude
15	13.7
20	14.3
25	14.8
30	15.2
40	15.8
50	16.3

Calculations of the limiting magnitudes reached by reflectors of a particular aperture have been made. Typical are those listed in Table 4–1; however, it should be noted that these should not be applied too strictly. For one thing, the figures apply to point sources, not extended objects, and the experience of many competent deep-sky observers has shown that they are perhaps too conservative—under a good sky the range of visibility can be extended by a magnitude or more. Therefore, it is important to establish the capabilities of your telescope through your own experience. Do not be put off trying for faint objects just because they *appear* to be beyond the "theoretical" limits of the instrument.

Finally, it is important to remember that the value of a quality instrument can easily be wasted if it is used with an inferior eyepiece. Great care should be taken in the selection of oculars. The ideal ocular has a flat, wide field and good definition across its diameter. Further, it should be free from internal reflections (which might produce "ghost" images) and any evidence of spherical or chromatic aberration. In practice, it will be necessary to compromise on some of these features, and the observer is nevertheless faced with the problem that some of the undesirable characteristics might not be evident without a detailed examination and use over time. Probably the best protection against disappointment is to obtain eyepieces from a reputable, well-established dealer.

[1]Adapted from *The Amateur Astronomer's Handbook*, by J.B. Sidgwick (rev. J. Muirden); Pelham Books, 1979.

A good eyepiece is important for the observation of any object, but perhaps particularly so for nebulae because of the often faint and subtle detail which they exhibit. Some types of eyepiece which might generally be recommended for such use include the following:

1. **Orthoscopic** There are several variants on the basic design, which consists of a plano-convex eye lens and a cemented triplet field lens, the outer lenses being made of tough crown glass. Fields are generally in the range of 35° to 50° and light transmission is high, perhaps 90%.
2. **Plössl** These consist of two symmetrical, or nearly symmetrical, achromatic doublets, their crown surfaces facing inwards and nearly touching. They generally have a wide, flat field of about 50° and a transmission level comparable to orthoscopics.
3. **Erfle** These are 5 or 6 element oculars with the lenses arranged in three groups. They provide a field from about 60° to 80°. The larger-field variants tend to have problems with astigmatism at the edges. The eye lenses are normally faced with less resistant flint glass, which may become abraded over time if not handled with particular care. Erfles tend to have lower transmission than Orthoscopics or Plössls, typically 80 to 85%.
4. **Nagler** These highly regarded eyepieces have a complex 7 or 8 element system of lenses with a flat 82° apparent field and sharp images across the field of view.

When not in use, eyepieces should be kept in dust-proof containers. In use eyepieces tend to "dew up" and there is great temptation to dry them by wiping off the condensation. This can lead to scratches. It is always better to allow them to clear naturally or by placing them in a warmer environment. Portable hair dryers are an effective way of safely drying an eyepiece while at the telescope.

4.3 Star Charts

Because many planetary nebulae are small and faint, they can be quite difficult to locate. Accurate and detailed star charts make the job much easier. The charts provided in this volume will enable you to identify a planetary nebulae once you have the object in your field of view, but their comparatively small field means that a good, general purpose star atlas is still a requirement.

For the larger, brighter objects, *Atlas Coeli* (equinox 1950.0) or *Sky Atlas 2000.0* are more than adequate, but for many planetary nebulae a more detailed reference is needed. There are a number of such references. Some are readily available, others are very expensive, and still others are out-of-print. Nevertheless, even the expensive or out-of-print atlas may be available through a local or university library, fellow amateur, or an astronomical society.

Some of the star atlases which may be found to be of particular value to the student of planetary nebulae include the following:

1. *Uranometria 2000.0*, by Wil Tirion, Barry Rappaport, and George Lovi, 1987–8. This hardbound, 2-volume atlas covers the entire sky down to about magnitude 9.5. The scale is good ($1° = 1.85$ cm) and the charts are highly detailed. Well over 500 planetary nebulae are shown. The surrounding field stars aid considerably in the location of many individual objects. Indeed, one will often find that the brighter stars on the charts in the atlas section of this book are also plotted in *Uranometria 2000.0.* All planetary nebulae are denoted by a unique symbol, and non-NGC/IC planetary nebulae are labeled with their PK number.
2. *True Visual Magnitude Photographic Star Atlas* (equinox 2000.0), by C.E. Scovil and C. Papadopoulos, 1969–80. This is a photographic star atlas reproduced as line-work. It covers the entire sky down to about visual magnitude 13.5 on 456 loose charts in three volumes. The charts show a field 33 cm square, equivalent to 11° on a side. They were made from photographs filtered to give a view of the sky as near as possible like that obtained by the eye. The large plate scale, many faint stars, and its accuracy make this a particularly good atlas when searching for small or faint planetary nebulae. The major problem with this work is that objects are not actually identified. Transparent grid overlays are provided, and a nice touch is the inclusion of a set of circles representing eyepiece fields from 10′ diameter up to 1°. Since this is reproduced as line-work, extended objects are reproduced as irregular, dark blobs. When it was in-print this atlas sold for nearly $1,000.
3. *Smithsonian Astrophysical Observatory Star Atlas of Reference Stars and non-Stellar objects* (equinox 1950.0). The SAO shows some 260,000 stars down to magnitude 9.0 on 152 loose charts. These are detailed enough to provide a valuable reference, and the individual charts are convenient for use at the telescope. Unfortunately, the scale of the charts is rather small, and although deep-sky objects are shown, none are identified, neither is any other object nor even constellation boundaries. Further, this atlas has been out-of-print since about 1970 and used copies are seldom offered for sale.
4. *Atlas Eclipticalis/Borealis/Australis* (equinox 1950.0). This series of atlases is on a larger scale than the *SAO Atlas* or *Uranometria* and are presented in a spiral-bound form. No deep-sky objects are shown,

but stars and constellation boundaries are identified. Stars down to magnitude about 11 are included, which makes it useful for plotting objects. This atlas is now out-of-print.

5. *AAVSO Variable Star Atlas* (equinox 1950.0). Based on the *SAO*, this work shows stars down to about visual magnitude 9.5 on 178 loose charts. The advantage of the *AAVSO Atlas* is that the scale is somewhat better than that of the *SAO*, and many deep-sky objects, including planetary nebulae, are shown. However, none are labeled. Unfortunately, there is no transparent grid overlay, making it difficult to accurately plot objects oneself.
6. *Atlas Stellarum* (equinox 1950.0), by Hans Vehrenberg. Like the "True Visual Magnitude" atlas, this is a photographic star atlas reproduced as line-work, with the consequence that extended objects are poorly rendered. It is also in blue light so the comparative magnitudes of stars will differ from those observed visually. In 2 volumes, it covers the entire sky in 486 charts (including overlap). Stars down to fainter than visual magnitude 14 are recorded at a scale of 2 arcminutes per millimeter. Again, no objects are identified, but a series of grid overlays are provided to aid identification.
7. *National Geographic-Palomar Observatory Sky Survey*, by the Staff of Palomar Observatory, 1954. This magnificent photographic star atlas consists of 935 pairs of loose red and blue sensitive photographic prints (or glass plates), as described in section 1.6. Both sets have a limiting magnitude well beyond that of normal amateur equipment and are presented at a large scale, so this should cover the requirements of most astronomers. These charts have formed the resource material for several surveys of new objects, such as that of George Abell, and even now occasional additional discoveries are made. Many planetary nebulae are seen on the prints which, although rather large, can be used as finding charts in their own rights. Although most amateurs would find the purchase of the entire set prohibitively expensive, POSS charts can be bought individually, and many observatory and university libraries have a set to which the amateur may be able to gain access. The plate centers are based on the BD survey (equinox 1855.0), but a transparent grid overlay, marked with equinox 1950.0 co-ordinates, has been produced at Ohio State University. This labels every nonstellar object known up to 1975, approximately 186,000 objects. A second survey, using the same Schimdt telescope but with improved, higher-resolution emulsions, is now in process.
8. *ESO-SERC Southern Sky Survey*, by the Staff of the European Southern Observatory and Siding Spring Observatory. This southern hemisphere

survey was undertaken with 1-meter and 1.2-meter Schmidt telescopes, similar to that on Mount Palomar, using the modern emulsions with which the second Palomar survey is being carried out. Both blue and red atlases are complete but are only available as film copies, not paper prints. A second-epoch survey is underway at Siding Spring, and infrared plates are also being taken.

In addition to the above large-scale atlases, there are two sources for planetary nebulae finder charts: The *P & K* and *Catalogue of Central Stars of True and Possible Planetary Nebulae.* The *P & K* was described in section 1.7. Generally, this work contains finding charts for all but three of the 1036 objects included in the *P & K Catalogue.* Since it is now more than 25 years old, many of objects identified as planetaries are no longer considered to be true planetary nebulae. The charts, which for the most part are quite small, are taken from a wide variety of sources and are of variable depth and quality. In some cases, the charts are quite confused, and the identification of the object unclear. Indeed, a small number actually misidentify the planetary nebulae; the following charts are affected by this problem: B1 B, B1 3-6, B1 3-11, H 1-43, H 2-14, H 2-20, He 1-3, He 2-25, He 2-34, He 2-133, He 2-275, He 2-370, He 2-376, M 4-7, Sa 3-24, Th 3-11, and Th 3-34. Nevertheless, the *P & K* remains a primary source of planetary nebulae finding charts. Since this work has been long out-of-print, it will probably only be found in a specialized astronomical library.

The second source of finder charts is the *Catalogue of Central Stars of True and Possible Planetary Nebulae*, by Agnes Acker *et al.*, published by the Centre Donées Stellaires (CDS) at Strasbourg Observatory, France. This work is composed of a catalogue and an atlas. The catalogue contains much valuable photometric and other data about the central stars of planetary nebulae. The atlas is made up of 456 planetary nebulae finder charts. The charts are mostly taken from POSS or *Southern Sky Survey* prints and reproduced as line work. The prints chosen are generally in blue light; these tend to enhance the visibility of the central star at the expense of the surrounding nebulosity. Since this work was published in 1981, it includes objects from more recent listings than *P & K.* The scale and detail of the charts is excellent for use at the telescope. Since the charts are based on fewer sources, they are more homogeneous and directly comparable. Unfortunately, this useful publication is not widely available, and access to it will almost certainly require visiting a specialized astronomical library.

From the above, my own recommendation would be for the observer to obtain copies of *Uranometria 2000.0* as the best general-purpose atlas. It identifies a large number of planetary nebulae and is available at a reasonable cost. It can also be used in conjunction with the charts found in this book or, POSS prints, *P & K* charts, or the charts found with the *Catalogue of*

Central Stars. This selection of references should enable the observer to go through the range of "star-hopping" from the large scale down to the immediate neighborhood of almost any planetary nebula. As final confirmation of identification, an [O III] filter might usefully be employed.

4.4 Observing Procedure

When making observations one should follow a set procedure. While this requires self-discipline, it is the most sure way to obtain consistent results. When strictly adhered to your observational records become more valuable because they are more consistent and hence can be compared with your other work and that of other careful observers.

I recommend that you first make a drawing of the object; no matter how detailed one's written description, it never seems to do full justice to the visual appearance. In addition, since it takes more time to make a sketch, and the sketch can be directly compared to the object while at the telescope, it is more likely to include more detail than a written description. I find that long periods of visual observation causes eye fatigue and that I can miss faint detail if I rely only on note taking. Sketching allows me to shift my concentration between the eyepiece and the drawing. The result is that I become less fatigued even though I spend more total time observing each object.

While drawing may not appear to be as accurate in recording information as a photograph, there are some compensations. Not only does it provide "on-line data reduction," but the responsiveness of the eye to varying light levels obviates a common problem with photography, that is, the limited dynamic range of emulsions.

Because planetary nebulae come in a tremendous range of sizes and surface brightness, there cannot be a single standardized drawing technique. We will have to generalize. First, one might start at low-to-medium power and sketch the position and orientation of the nebula against the stellar background. Next, switch to high power to record nebular detail. If the object is apparently stellar you should check for the presence of any "fuzziness." A myth has arisen among amateur astronomers that the use of high powers is counterproductive as it "spreads the light" and reduces the object's contrast. However, if the magnification does not exceed about 20 times per cm of telescope aperture you are likely to find high power extremely valuable. The reason is that the resolving capability of the eye is much reduced in dim light. Therefore, details in very faint objects can only be resolved if they are large. You can establish you own optimum range of powers by experimentation.

Your drawings should record the field's orientation and scale, details about your telescope, eyepiece, and any accessories, especially nebular filters. Detailed notes supplement your field drawing and make it easier to make comparisons with other observations later. Seldom does a drawing suffer from too much information. Perhaps the inexperienced observer might be well advised to start with a check-list of points to look out for, but the procedure will soon become automatic. Ask yourself a series of questions:

1. How large is the object? A specific estimate in arcmin or arcsec is preferable to vague terms like "very small" or "large." To be able to do this you will have to know the sizes of your eyepiece fields. This can be done by viewing starfields and comparing them with an accurate atlas, or by timing a star's drift across your eyepiece field.
2. Is it round? If not, what shape is it (e.g., oval, irregular, dumbbell, stellar)? What is the Position Angle (P.A.) of any elongation?
3. How bright is the object? Can its brightness be compared with nearby stars? A good procedure is to "calibrate" your visual estimates by estimating the "comparison stars" that variable star observers use to make their magnitude estimates. The *AAVSO Star Atlas* provides this information.
4. Is the nebula of uniform surface brightness? If not, what are the irregularities (e.g., is it brighter in the center? Is it darker in the center? Are the edges well defined or does it fade gradually into the background? Are there any "knots" in the structure?)?
5. Is there any trace of nebulosity beyond the main body of the planetary nebulae?
6. Does the nebula exhibit any color? If so, which?
7. Is there a visible central star?
8. Are there any other stars involved in the nebulosity?
9. When using different kinds of filter, what kind of contrast gain/loss can be seen?

Needless to say, it is important at all times to make observations as objectively as possible. Having seen photographs, or drawings and descriptions by other people, it is easy to be influenced by the memory of what should be there. Record only what is visible; if a feature is only suspected, make sure this is clear in your notes.

Finally, to illustrate some of the features which might be observed in planetary nebulae, I present some of my own observations in Figures 4–1 through 4–14. With the exception of Abell 4, these observations were made without the aid of filters and give some indication of the range of features which might be seen with small to moderate aperture instruments. The effect of filters is described in section 4.6.

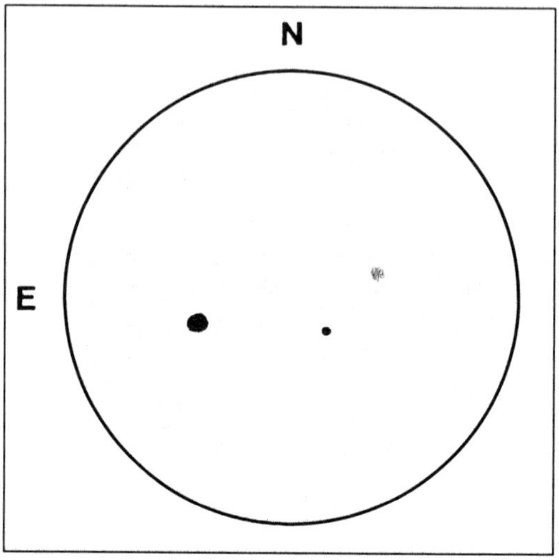

Figure 4–1. *Abell 4, 25.4 cm., ×232 + [O III] filter, Field 10′. This planetary nebula lies on the outskirts of the open cluster M.34, in Perseus. It is in an easily identifiable field but, using a 25.4 cm reflector, I am unable to detect any trace of it without using an [O III] filter. Once this filter is employed, the nebula, although very faint, is clearly visible with averted vision and often held with direct vision.*

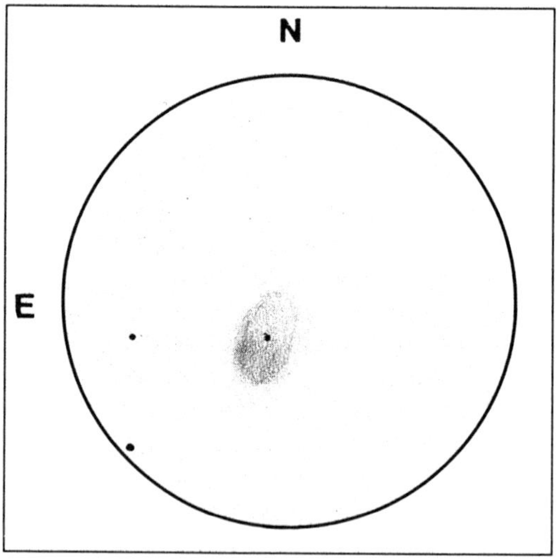

Figure 4–2. *NGC 1360, 10.5 cm., ×50, Field 30′. Using a 10.5 cm RFT from Malta, NGC 1360 appears as a fairly large, hazy object, centered on a distinct though not especially bright star. The nebulosity is oval, the major axis being about 5′ in length and oriented roughly N-S. The outline of the object is not well defined and the nebulosity is distinctly brighter to the south of the central star.*

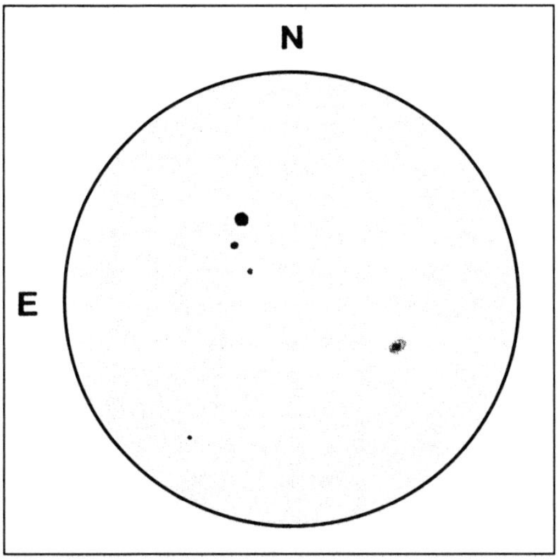

Figure 4–3. *IC 351 25.4 cm, ×155, Field 8′. Close to a distinctive triangle of stars, this planetary nebula is only barely nonstellar at ×155 and is of about magnitude 12. No obvious elongation or color.*

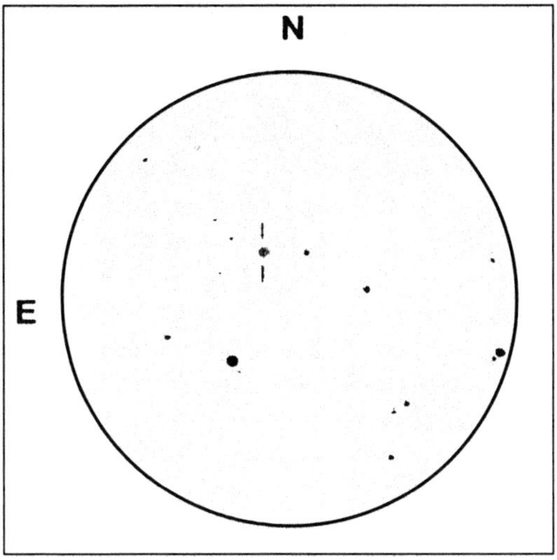

Figure 4–4. *J320, 25.4 cm, ×155, Field 12′. Another small planetary nebula, obviously nonstellar at ×155 but size difficult to gauge. Easily found because of distinctive starfield.*

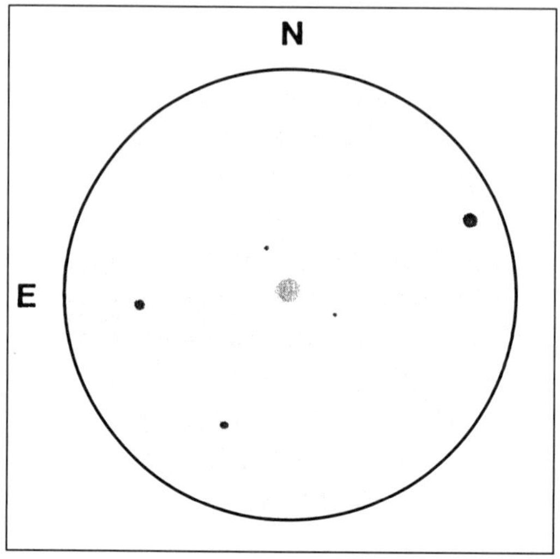

Figure 4–5. *NGC 2022, 25.4 cm, ×155, Field 15′. A soft, round nebula, about 20″ to 25″ in diameter. It is of uniform surface brightness and has a slightly diffuse boundary. No evidence of any central star.*

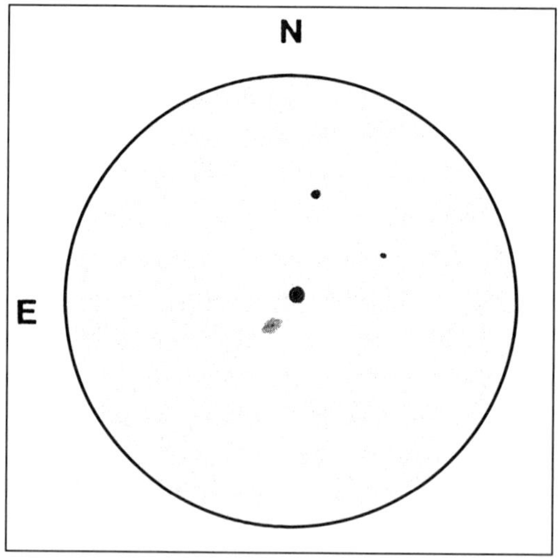

Figure 4–6. *M 1-7, 25.4cm, ×232, Field 10′. Easily found, close S.f. a bright star, this planetary nebula is seen as a small spot of hazy light. It is elongated N.p.-S.f. and is about 10″ in its greatest extent.*

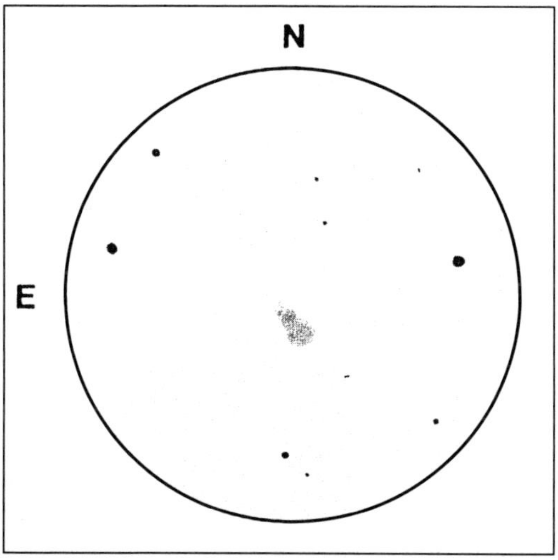

Figure 4–7. *NGC 2371-2, 25.4 cm, ×155, Field 15′. A fairly bright planetary nebula, easily resolved into two lobes, elongated N.f.-S.p. The S.p. element is the largest and brightest of the lobes. Being rather diffuse, the extent of the nebula is difficult to judge, but is about 90″ × 60″. No central star is visible.*

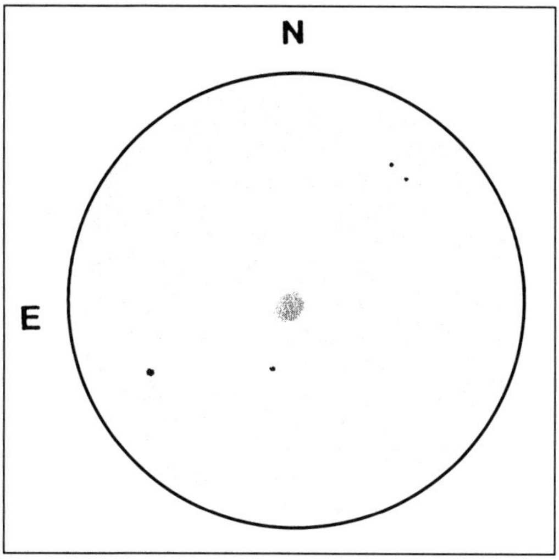

Figure 4–8. *NGC 3242, 25.4 cm, ×155, Field 15′. A very bright, pale green, almost circular object, about 30″ across. There is a slight elongation N.p.-S.f. The disc appears uniformly bright, with no sign of a central star, and is surrounded by a small but distinct halo.*

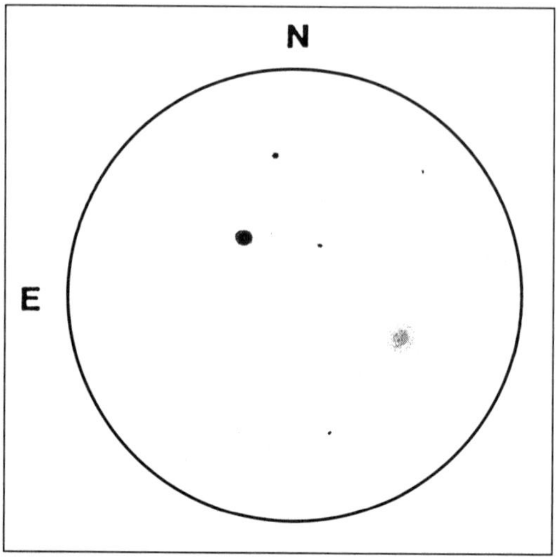

Figure 4–9. *NGC 6210, 25.4 cm, ×232, Field 10′. Bright, easily visible at low power (×78) as a slightly hazy star forming the p. apex of an isosceles triangle. The main body of the nebula is slightly elongated N.p.-S.f., slightly spindle shaped, and very bright. This seems to be surrounded by a very faint circular envelope.*

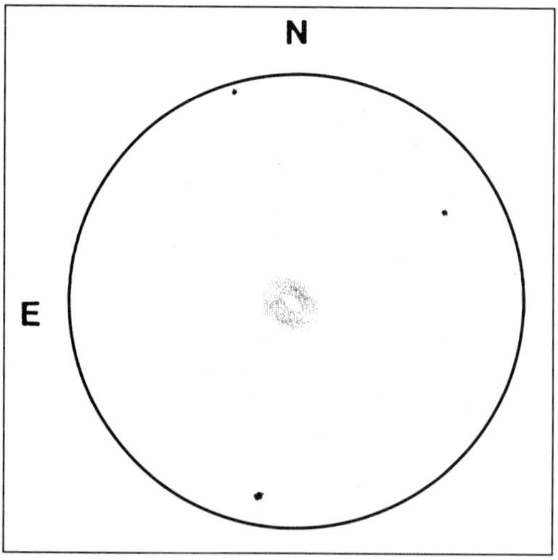

Figure 4–10. *NGC 6720 (M.57), 21.6 cm, ×154, Field 10′. A bright planetary nebula, easily identifiable from the stellar background even at a low power (×77) because of its diffuse appearance. At ×154, it is distinctly annular with a dusky center. The extremities of the major axis are distinctly less bright and less well defined than the extremities of the minor axis. No central star is detected within the nebula, which is about 60″ across.*

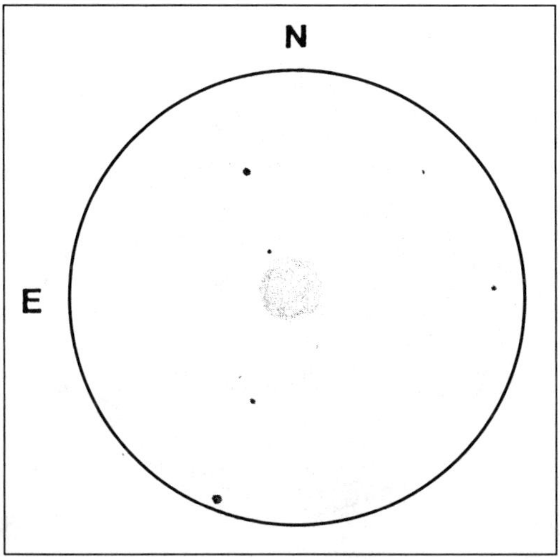

Figure 4–11. *NGC 6781, 25.4 cm, ×232, Field 10′. At ×78, this object appears as a fairly large circular haze, about 2′ in diameter, easily visible with direct vision. It is located in quite a rich starfield. At ×232, the annular nature of the nebula is faintly visible as an enhancement of the well-defined periphery; this is particularly clear on the eastern and southern sides. A faint star is visible close to the N.N.f. edge. No evidence of any central star was found, nor any sign of color.*

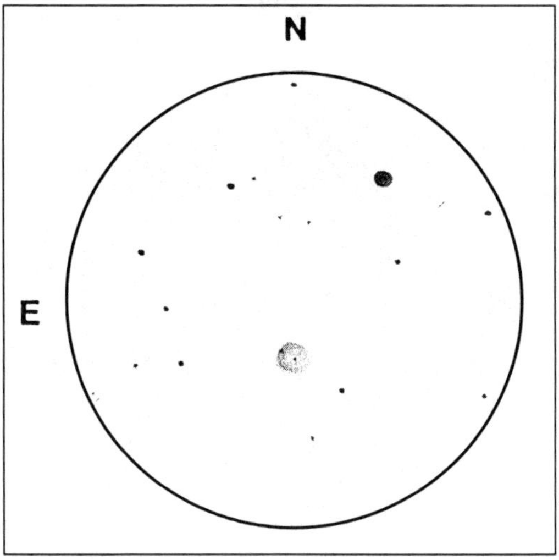

Figure 4–12. *NGC 6804, 25.4 cm, ×232, Field 10′. At ×78, NGC 6804 is clearly visible in a rich starfield. It appears as a fairly bright, irregular spot on one of the sides of a triangle of bright stars. At ×232, the object is seemingly almost circular. It is not of even brightness, the following edge of nebulosity is distinctly brighter. There is a star just within the N.f. edge of the nebula and a fainter one at the center.*

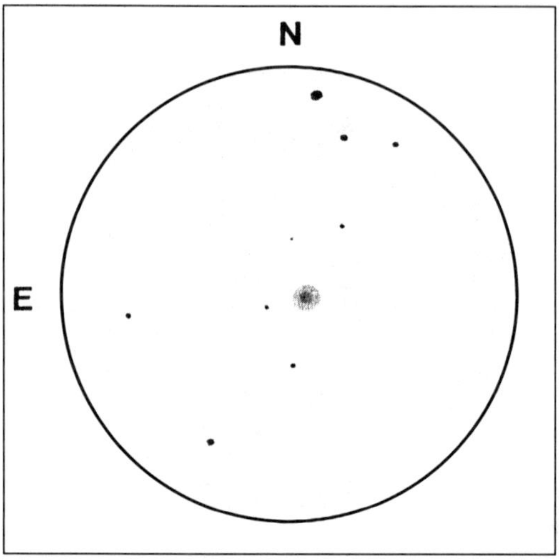

Figure 4–13. *NGC 6826, 25.4 cm,* $\times$*155, Field* 10′. *A bright round disc with a brighter center, but not obviously a central star. At* $\times$*78 the object seems to have a pale blue color but at* $\times$*155 it seems more blue-green.*

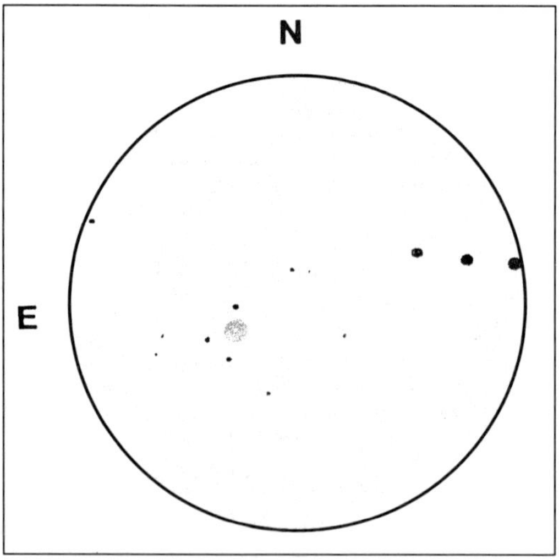

Figure 4–14. *NGC 6905, 25.4 cm,* $\times$*155, Field* 15′. *A bright, apparently round planetary nebula about* 1′ *in diameter. There is no obvious internal structure and no central star seen. NGC 6905 is closely enclosed by three stars and the general starfield is fairly rich.*

4.5 Prism Observations

Since many planetary nebulae are stellar, or nearly so, they can be difficult to identify against the background of stars. Of course, finder charts are helpful, but they may not always be available. Another method to locate a planetary nebulae relies upon a simple prism. A diffraction grating or slitless direct vision spectroscope would work equally well, but the former are easily damaged and the latter expensive and not readily available.

While small planetary nebulae are difficult to visually differentiate from stars, their emission line spectra, as opposed to the continuous spectra of stars, is quite distinctive when observed through a prism. The field stars will appear as tiny spectra but the planetary nebula will usually remain stellar.

Using a prism is straightforward; only a little practice is required. The prism is carefully held against the eyepiece, as shown in Figure 4–15. The observer then places one eye almost in contact with the prism at one corner, so that, in effect, one is looking almost at right-angles to the axis of the eyepiece. Obviously, a certain amount of adjustment will be required to the positioning and angle of the prism and the eye to achieve the best effect. In addition, the characteristics of the individual prism will need to be taken into account to achieve the optimum balance of clarity and dispersion.

The British observer Edmund S. Barker, a long standing proponent of this technique, also recommends the use of a head cover to eliminate stray light, particularly when fainter objects are involved (which is probably a good idea for all visual observing!).

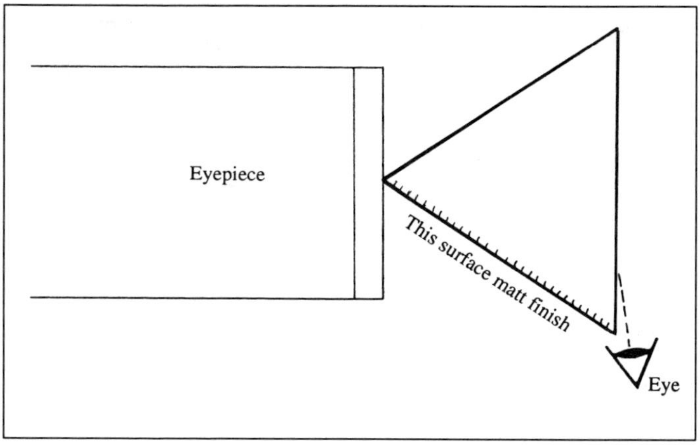

Figure 4–15. *Approximate observing angle for prism observations.*

4.6 Nebular Filters

Any discussion of filters in a standard astronomy text of the 1970's would probably have been limited to the use of colored filters, such as the Kodak Wratten series, which are used in the observation of planets. There was little application of filters to the study of objects commonly viewed by the deep-sky enthusiast. In recent years, however, new types filters has been developed specifically for the deep sky observer. These are called "nebular filters" and much of the credit for this innovation must go to Jack B. Marling of the U.S. Lumicon Company.

Nebular filters are a development of the Fabry-Perot interference filters. They are made up of a series of thin film dielectric coatings on optically flat glass. For some filters, over 30 layers may be required, each on the order of one wavelength of light thick. The filter is then mounted so that it can be screwed into the rear of an eyepiece. These filters isolate specific sections of the spectrum, suppressing background skylight of all types, natural and artificial. Because of this, they enhance the contrast of nebulous objects even when observing from sites free of anthropogenic sources of light. To some extent, they are also useful as thin cirrus "cloud filters."

The transmission characteristics of filters vary considerably between the different types. Therefore, it is important in any observation report to specify the make and type of filter used. There are four basic kinds of nebular filters:

1. **LPR (light-pollution reduction) filter** This is the most commonly available and least specialized filter. It is produced by a number of manufacturers. The transmission characteristics of different models vary slightly but essentially they are designed to eliminate the light from low-pressure sodium vapor, and mercury vapor lamps, together with the emission lines of naturally occurring "airglow." Note, though, that the light from modern high-pressure sodium lamps is not greatly attenuated by nebular filters, as their emission covers virtually all of the visible spectrum. As one might imagine, the use of this type of filter under properly dark sky conditions results in comparatively small contrast gain.

Most of the remaining types of filter are produced solely by Lumicon and do not presently have any counterpart; therefore, the names used are those given by that company:

2. **UHC filter** Another general purpose device, the Ultra-High Contrast filter has a 24 nm bandpass which encompasses the [O III] lines at 500.7 nm and 495.9 nm, and also the Hβ line at 486.1 nm. Therefore, in addition to rejecting light pollution emission, much of the remainder of the continuum is also eliminated, greatly enhancing the contrast of

diffuse and planetary nebulae. The Orion "Ultrablock," DayStar, Parks, and Celestron nebular filters have similar passbands to the UHC filter.

3. **Hβ filter** This specialized filter has a bandpass of 9 nm, centered on the 486.1 nm Hβ line, of which about 90% is transmitted. Because this line is a prominent feature in the spectra of diffuse nebulae, and because so much of the rest of the visible spectrum is rejected, the Hβ filter is particularly useful for the observation of faint diffuse nebulae. It has little application in the observation of planetary nebulae; however, a very small number of low-excitation objects (e.g., SwSt 1 and Campbell's Star) do show a reasonably good contrast gain.
4. **[O III] filter** This is undoubtedly the filter for the planetary nebula specialist, having an 11 nm bandpass covering the two primary [O III] emission lines at 500.7 nm and 495.9 nm. This considerably enhances the contrast of most planetary nebulae but, like the Hβ filter, the narrow passband means that much starlight is rejected, greatly reducing their brightness. As a result, a starfield observed with an [O III] filter will differ significantly from that observed without one. This may cause some disorientation, and if you are making a drawing you may want to first draw the field, then insert the filter to sketch the nebula. A useful technique for identifying stellar planetary nebulae with the [O III] filter is "blinking." This simply involves passing the filter between the eye and the eyepiece and observing which of the stars stands out against the background to a greater degree than the rest. By rapidly moving the filter across the field, the planetary nebula will appear to flash "on and off" and the stars virtually disappear. Figure 4–16 shows the effect of observing a planetary nebula field with and without an [O III] filter. The object, IC 2149, is small. At low power it is difficult to distinguish from the starfield. However, with an [O III] filter inserted it is no longer the fifth brightest "star" in a field of many, but the second brightest in a field of only seven, making its identification much easier.

In addition to making planetary nebulae much easier to identify, filters can also reveal a considerable amount of detail in larger, brighter objects, which would otherwise go unobserved. Examples of this are given in Figures 4–17 through 4–21. The sketches are of bright planetary nebulae made with my 25.4 cm reflector. Three sets of sketches are provided: with no filter, with a UHC filter, and with an [O III] filter. Each set of sketches was made on the same night and one after the other, about 20 minutes being spent on each observation. Therefore, even though in some instances the seeing and transparency conditions were not ideal, the observations are otherwise directly comparable.

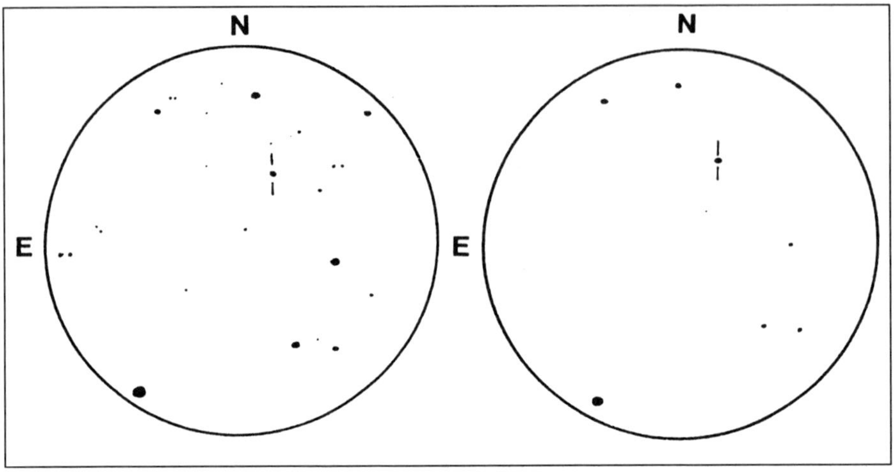

Figure 4–16. *IC 2149 viewed with a 25.4 cm telescope at ×78, field = 30″.* **Left:** *no filter.* **Right:** *[O III] filter.*

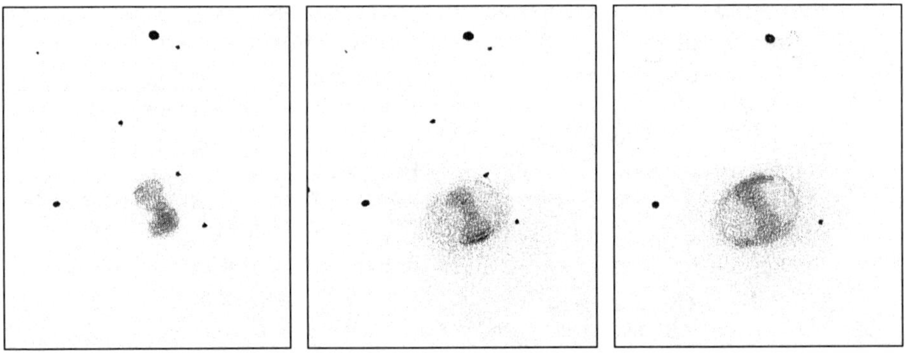

Figure 4–17. *NGC 650-1 (M.76) with a 25.4 cm telescope, ×155, Field = 30′.* **Left with no filter:** *A bright, irregular bar about 2′ long with brightness enhancements at both ends. The bar has a "waist" which gives a double lobe impression. S.f. lobe is the larger and brighter.* **Center with a UHC filter:** *The bar is now seen to cross the center of a bright oval nebula. The bar is still larger and brighter at the S.f. end but the filter seems to have evened out the difference a little. Starfield much as before.* **Right with an [O III] filter:** *The bar seems a little thicker overall and more uniform in thickness and brightness. From the N end a bright "spur" is seen extending westward and from the S end a similar, though fainter, spur extends eastward. The oval nebulosity around the bar is brighter and with averted vision there is the suggestion of the spurs extending into loops defining the outline of the oval.*

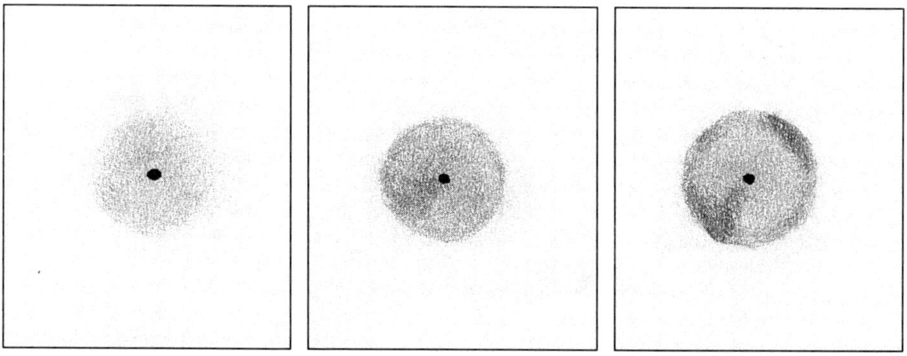

Figure 4–18. *NGC 1514, with 25.4 cm telescope, ×155.* **Left with no filter:** *The nebula appears as a 3′ diameter circular, faintish haze of uniform surface brightness around a bright star. The starfield is sparse but there is a slightly brighter star than that in the nebula about 8′ north.* **Center with a UHC filter:** *The nebulosity is considerably stronger, with the hint of a ring defining the outer edge and a brighter patch S.f. the center star.* **Right with an [O III] filter:** *The brightness of the nebulosity is enhanced to an even greater degree. A thick ring clearly defines the outer edge; this is of irregular brightness and is quite prominent N.p. and S.f. the star. There is also an obvious bright patch S.f. the star which spreads down to and merges with the S.f. enhancement of the ring.*

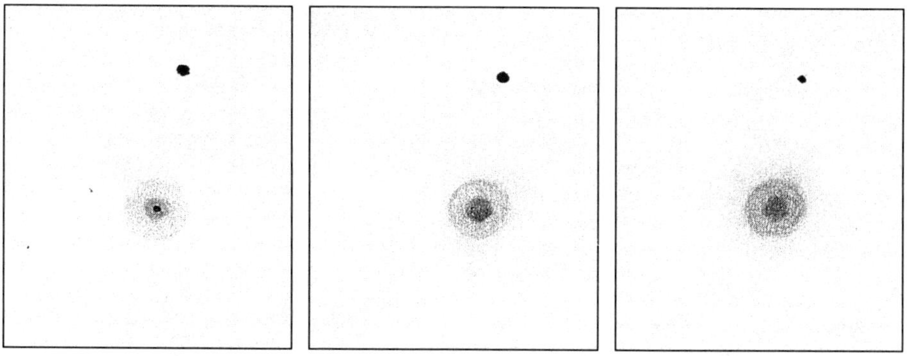

Figure 4–19. *NGC 2392 with a 25.4 cm telescope, ×232.* **Left with no filter:** *A small, bright object about 40″ in diameter. It appears to be perfectly circular and is well defined. It is generally of uniform surface brightness but at the center is a small nucleus with a mag 10 star at the center. With low power the object forms a double with a star of similar mag, 1′.5 S.* **Center with an UHC filter:** *The nebulosity now appears much brighter and the star is no longer visible, having been replaced by a very bright, more diffuse nucleus. Slight evidence of ring structure detected around the edge of the nebula.* **Right with an [O III] filter:** *The object now seems slightly larger and is certainly stronger. The ring structure is marginally more apparent and the feature seems to be quite thick. The star to the south is considerably fainter than the nebula.*

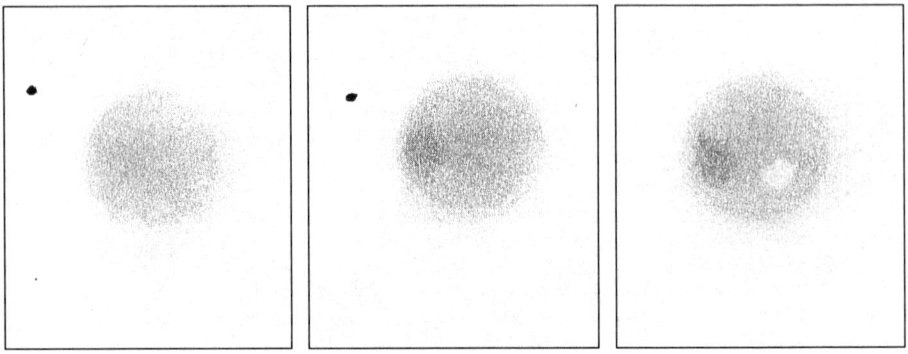

Figure 4–20. *NGC 3587 (M.97) with a 25.4 cm telescope , ×155.* **Left with no filter:** *A low surface brightness, circular haze of ill-defined extent, but of perhaps 3′ to 4′ diameter. No structure or central star noted. Star slightly N.f.* **Center with an UHC filter:** *Image stronger than when unfiltered and the nebulosity seems to have a mottled texture and is more well defined. There is a slight brightness enhancement on the f. side of the nebula, almost facing the star.* **Right with an [O III] filter:** *Image about as strong as with UHC filter but the nebula has a more distinct mottled appearance. Specific surface brightness variations are elusive, with two exceptions: the brightness enhancement on the f. side, which is now fairly prominent, and a slight brightness decrement S.p. the center. No sign of nearby star.*

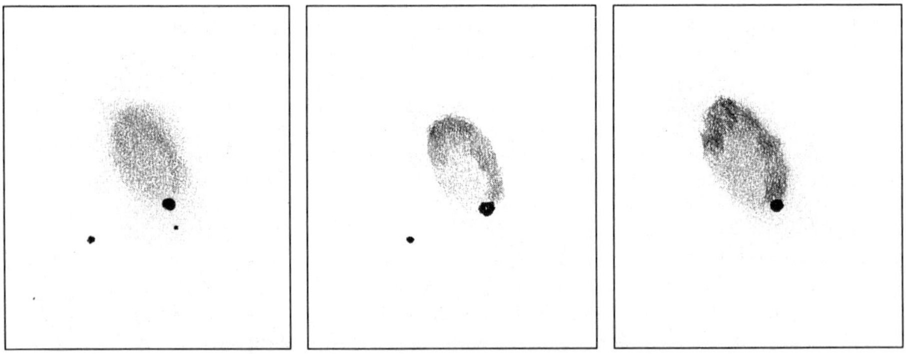

Figure 4–21. *NGC 7008 with a 25.4 cm telescope, ×155.* **Left no filter:** *A bright oval nebula about 2′ × 1′ with a conspicuous star at the more southerly end. The nebulosity is of roughly uniform surface brightness except for an enhancement at the northern end. Also, the p. edge seems much better defined.* **Center with a UHC filter:** *Northern end of the nebula now very bright and the p. edge is seen as a broad, irregular arc joining the northern enhancement and the star at the southern end.* **Right with an [O III] filter:** *The enhancement at the northern end of the nebula is large and quite pronounced. The arc forming the p. edge is thick and bright with a brighter knot roughly midway along; a couple of other knots are also apparent. (One of the knots in this object was at one time incorrectly classified as a separate planetary nebula, K 4-44).*

In addition to those filters already in common use, the possibility exists for the development of others, but, of course, the limiting factor is their commercial prospects. For example, one could envision a filter to enhance the visibility of planetary nebula central stars by rejecting the nebula lines of [O III] and Hβ—in fact, a virtual reverse of the UHC filter!

4.7 Astrophotography

Basic astrophotography is not difficult. Pleasing widefield shots of Milky Way regions can be obtained with quite simple equipment. A camera may have its own simple drive or it can be "piggybacked" on a telescope with a clock drive. These methods can also be used to obtain images of large, diffuse nebulae and open clusters. However, the photography of planetary nebulae is a more demanding task, primarily because of the small image size and faintness of most of the potential targets. Entire books are available that deal with the various nuances of astrophotography. Since even the most expensive of these books costs no more than 4 or 5 roles of processed and printed color film, purchase is highly recommended. In this section, therefore, I will merely discuss some of the more important considerations that have a bearing on the astrophotography of planetary nebulae.

1. **Collimation** The optics must be accurately aligned. This applies equally to visual and photographic work. Because the objective element in a refractor is usually mounted in a cell machined to exact tolerances, it is seldom subject to mis-alignment. Reflectors are much more prone to mis-alignment and must be constantly checked. If the correct alignment is not effected, images will be blurred or streaked.

2. **Guiding** Faint objects will require long exposures—from a few minutes to several hours. If the image does not remain stationary on the film, the image will blur. How well one is able to maintain a steady image on the film depends on the following:

    (a) **Polar alignment** The importance of this factor is strongly affected by the length of the exposure. Simple polar alignment techniques exist which produce quite satisfactory images during a period of from 5 to 10 minutes. Such exposures seldom show evidence of trailing or field rotation. Longer exposures will require more rigorous polar alignment methods, such as those described in Chapter 16 of Sidgwick's *Amateur Astronomer's Handbook*.

    (b) **Periodic errors in the gear train** While most telescope drive units are well made, nevertheless, few are able to track the sky with absolute smoothness. It is usually necessary to monitor the accuracy of the tracking and make manual corrections though a drive corrector.

(c) **Telescope flexure** This is not normally a problem with small instruments, but larger aperture Newtonians, particularly those with lightweight tubes, can be affected by this problem. As the telescope changes orientation, the loading (i.e., guidescope, camera etc.) stresses the tube by varying amounts and in different places. This can be alleviated somewhat by using off-axis guiding systems rather than a tube-mounted guidescope.

(d) **Power fluctuations** The frequency (50 or 60 Hertz) of main power supplies is fairly stable; however, fluctuations do occur, and at unpredictable intervals.

3. **Extrinsic factors** Atmospheric refraction and wind can create problems. Changes in the density of the air mass between the telescope and the object will change its apparent position. Gusts of wind can make the telescope tremble. The latter is a particular problem for telescopes not sited in an observatory. The effects of gusting wind can be reduced by a windbreak, or by interrupting the exposure temporarily (this also is a method of dealing with another hazard for the astrophotographer—aircraft passing through the field of view).

4. **Personal comfort** Even under the best of circumstances, long-exposure guiding stretches the individual's ability to concentrate, but doing so in a position which is uncomfortable is extremely difficult. A seated position is normally better than standing and, where possible, postures which strain the neck and back should be avoided. However, when guiding from a seated position, check that the seat will not obstruct the rotation of the telescope during the exposure.

5. **Focussing** There should be few problems with focus slippage from a well-constructed focussing mount; but it should be remembered that during the course of an exposure, the temperature can change markedly and alter the telescope tube length, shifting the focus point slightly.

6. **Film choice** The range of commercially available photographic emulsions seems to be expanding at an ever-increasing rate and many can be adopted for use in astrophotography. High-speed films have been developed using new silver halide crystallization techniques which match in grain size standard slow films of, say, the 1970's. Modern slow, high resolution films now have truly microscopic grain. It would be impractical to discuss in depth the characteristics of such a large number of films, together with their characteristics when hypersensitized, cooled, and push processed; however, some of the films most commonly used in

astrophotography have been reviewed in the amateur astronomy press, and these reviews are listed in Table 4–2.

Table 4–2
Reviews of some films commonly used in amateur astrophotography

Film	Reviewer	Magazine	Issue & Page
Black & White			
Kodak Tech Pan 2415	Everhart	Sky & Tel.	1981 Feb., p. 100
Kodak Tech Pan 2415	Hooley	Astronomy	1986 July, p. 76
Color Slide			
3M 1000	Di Cicco	*Sky & Tel.*	1983 Dec., p. 506
Color Print			
Konica SR-V 3200	DiCicco	*Sky & Tel.*	1987 Nov., p. 558
Konica SR-V 3200	Berry	*Astronomy*	1987 Nov., p. 78
Kodak Ektar 1000	Quirk	*Sky & Tel.*	1991 Mar., p. 328
Kodacolor Gold 1600	Quirk	*Sky & Tel.*	1991 Mar., p. 328
Kodak VR 1000	di Cicco	*Sky & Tel.*	1983 Mar., p. 215
Various	di Cicco	*Sky & Tel.*	1988 Aug., p. 207
Various	Marling	*Sky & Tel.*	1984 June, p. 582

From the list in Table 4–2, the following are worthy of particular mention:

1. **Kodak Technical Pan 2415** Referred to in older magazine articles and books as SO-115, this is without doubt the most popular film for amateur black and white astrophotography. It is extremely fine grained and produces high contrast images of extraordinarily high resolution. While it is sensitive to all visible wavelengths, it is especially red sensitive. Under normal daylight conditions it is a fairly slow film, rated at 25 to 125 ISO depending on development chemistry and times. It really comes into its own for astrophotography when gas hypersensitized. This procedure removes water vapor and oxygen from the emulsion. This treatment reduces reciprocity failure.[2]

   Gas hypering kits are commercially available from a number of sources. The process involves exposing the film (usually called "soaking" or "baking") to a forming gas (normally 92% nitrogen, 8% hydrogen) at particular values of temperature and pressure for specific times. The exact "recipe" to a forming gas will vary with individual manufacturers' instructions.

   Developing 2415 is straightforward: 4 to 5 minutes in D-19 at 20°C, followed by a 30 second stop-bath, a 2 minute fix and a 5 to 10 minute wash in running water.

[2]Reciprocity failure is a characteristic of most films where the exposures are greater than 1 second. Unlike shorter duration exposures, longer exposures do not produce proportionally greater image build-up on the film.

2. **3M 1000** This slide film is a good choice for a beginner. Not only is it fast but, being a slide film, the processing is a simple matter. The standard E6 3 or 4 bath chemistry works well and avoids the printing stage. The film is a little grainy, which is of particular relevance in the photography of small, extended objects. Sky backgrounds also tend to have a greenish cast. Nevertheless, 3M 1000 does provide excellent color rendition of nebulae. It should be noted that 3M provides film stock for a number of independent retailers. In the U.K. the 1000 ISO film sold by Boots stores is 3M stock.
3. **Konica SR-V 3200** This is the fastest color print film currently available. It is, of course, grainy by comparison with slower films. However, the grain compares favorably to other fast films and still allows for fairly substantial enlargements. For deep-sky purposes, its sensitivity to both blue and red light is a useful characteristic. It has comparatively few problems with reciprocity failure, but this can be reduced still further since the film responds well to hypersensitizing and cooling. These techniques generate speed gains of two or three times and also increase its sensitivity to blue light.

Finally, whatever one reads about the characteristics or value of a particular film for astrophotography purposes, it should be remembered that manufacturers are continually striving to improve their emulsions and, with seemingly increasing regularity, make unannounced changes to their formulations. Of course, the changes are designed to improve performance under normal daylight conditions and may not necessarily benefit specialist users, such as astrophotographers.

Chapter 5

Catalogue and Atlas of Planetary Nebulae

5.1 Introduction

The following sections provide observational information on galactic planetary nebulae in both northern and southern hemispheres. The objects included cover a wide variety of systems from the small to the large and from the faint to the bright. Some objects are visible with all but the smallest instruments and have been studied thoroughly by professional astronomers, while others are so obscure that little is known about them beyond their position. Many have never been observed visually. As a result of this range, there should be something of interest for all observers, whatever their experience and instrumentation.

This chapter is divided into three sections, the Catalogue, Extended Notes, and the Atlas.

Extended Notes This Section is designed to provide more detailed information on a number of planetary nebulae of particular interest. Each set of notes is individually provided with references.

Catalogue This Section is a more-or-less complete catalogue of planetary nebulae as of May 1990. Each object is listed by PK number, constellation, and most commonly used other designation. This is followed by positional information for 1950.0 and 2000.0. Other physical data is given as follows: *Nebula*—type (according to the system of Vorontsov-Velyaminov), mean diameter of the main body of the nebula, photographic magnitude, and visual magnitude. *Star*—spectral type, V magnitude (except where otherwise specified), and any name for the star (in the HD survey, some compact nebulae were recorded as stars and this identification is given here also). Additional Notes detail some alternative designations and other points of interest. In a small number of cases, I have identified objects in general compilations of planetary nebulae for which I can find no provenance; these are marked with "identity?" in the Notes column and may possibly be nonexistent. Finally, it should be remarked that for some objects, not even basic parameters such as magnitude have been determined and the classification as planetary nebulae must be considered tentative.

Atlas The charts included in the Atlas are hand-produced interpretations of planetary nebulae fields based on a variety of photographic sources. These include the Palomar Observatory Sky Survey, the ESO/SERC Southern Sky Survey, and the photographic finder charts of P&K; in addition, finder charts from individual articles in the various astronomical journals have also been used. Of course, the number of sources employed means that the depth and scale of individual charts is variable, but, in many cases, the brighter stars in each field will also be found on some of the better star atlases, such as *Uranometria 2000.0*. It should also be noted that the relative brightness of some stars on the charts will differ from that observed visually due to the red or blue bias of the source material concerned. Where possible, I have tried to compensate for this by personal visual examination of the field or examination of prints at both ends of the color range.

The charts are orientated with North at the top and East to the left, and the planetary nebulae are indicated by circles showing the position and approximate extent of the nebulosity. In a few cases, where the nebula is strongly asymmetric or elongated, it may be shown by a different symbol; for example, Abell 21 is shown as an east-facing crescent because the eastern half is comparatively bright, whereas the western half is virtually invisible and unlikely to be detected by normal visual or photographic methods. Where, at the scale of the chart, the nebula appears more-or-less stellar, it is shown by a star symbol and identified by tick marks.

5.2 Source Material

The framework of the Catalogue section is largely based on the *Strasbourg Catalogue of Galactic Planetary Nebulae* by Acker *et al.*, and the *Catalogue of Galactic Planetary Nebulae* by Perek and Kohoutek. However, it has been significantly modified by the deletion of misclassified objects and the addition of new discoveries. The primary data sources are listed in the Bibliography and the discovery papers are given in Appendix A. Many of the more recent papers include photographic finder charts which have been useful in the compilation of the Atlas section.

In addition, the following articles have been found useful:

1. Acker, A. *et al.*; *Astron. Astrophys. Supp. Ser.*, **71**, 163, 1987.
2. Acker, A. *et al.*; *Astron. Astrophys. Supp. Ser.*, **77**, 487, 1989.

3. Acker, A. *et al.*; *Astron. Astrophys. Supp. Ser.*, **86**, 219, 1990.
4. Calabretta, M.R.; *M.N.R.A.S.*, **199**, 141, 1982.
5. Gathier, R.; *Astron. Astrophys Supp. Ser.*, **60**, 399, 1985.
6. Gottlieb, S. & Marling, J.B.; *W.S.Q.J.*, No. 82, 17, 1990.
7. Hynes, S.J.; *W.S.Q.J.*, No. 72, 9, 1988.
8. Hynes, S.J.; *W.S.Q.J.*, No. 78, 1, 1989.
9. Hynes, S.J.; *W.S.Q.J.*, No. 80, 9, 1990.
10. Kaler, J.B.; *Ap.J.*, **226**, 947, 1978.
11. Kaler, J.B.; *Ap.J.*, **250**, L31, 1981.
12. Kaler, J.B.; *Ap.J.*, **271**, 188, 1983.
13. Kaler, J.B. & Shaw, R.A.; *Ap.J.*, **295**, 537, 1985.
14. Marling, J.B.; *Deep Sky*, **4**, 8, 1986.
15. Marling, J.B. & Gottlieb, S.; *W.S.Q.J.*, No. 65, 14, 1986.
16. Marling, J.B. & Gottlieb, S.; *W.S.Q.J.*, No. 66, 20, 1986.
17. Marling, J.B. & Gottlieb, S.; *W.S.Q.J.*, No. 68, 6, 1987.
18. Marling, J.B. & Gottlieb, S.; *W.S.Q.J.*, No. 73, 34, 1988.
19. Schonberner, D. & Napiwotzki, R.; *Astron. Astrophys.*, **231**, L33, 1990.
20. Shaw, R.A. & Kaler, J.B.; *Ap.J. Supp.*, **69**, 495, 1989.
21. Tylenda, R. *et al.*; *Astron. Astrophys. Supp. Ser.*, **77**, 39, 1989.
22. Zijlstra, A. *et al.*; *Kapteyn Institute Preprint No. 018*, 1989.

5.3 Extended Notes

NGC 40

Curtis (1918) described NGC 40 thus:

> The nebula resembles a truncated ring, from the ends of which extend much fainter wisps. The brighter central portion is $18'' \times 35''$ in P.A. 14°, while the total length along this axis is about $60''$.

This basic description is still valid today. Curtis mentioned the existence of faint wisps beyond the main body of the nebula; one of these is particularly noteworthy, extending at a tangent in an easterly direction from the N end of the nebula. This feature is especially prominent on red-light photographs.

Work by Sabbadin & Hamzaoglu (ref. 2) indicates that the main body of the nebula is in the form of a shell $30''$ in diameter and $5''$ thick. A particularly interesting photograph of this object, taken in Hα + [N II] and [O III] wavelengths can be found in a paper by Louise (ref. 3), which also reports evidence of matter ejected from the central star at a velocity in excess of 200 km/s.

References

1. Gathier, R.. & Pottasch, S.R.; *Astron. Astrophys.* **197**, 266, 1988.
2. Sabbadin, F. & Hamzaoglu, E.; *Astron. Astrophys.* **109**, 131, 1982.
3. Louise, R.; *Astron. Astrophys.* **102**, 303, 1981.

NGC 246

NGC 246 is one of the brighter planetary nebulae and lies at a high galactic latitude ($b = -74°$) so it is easily studied because of the minimal level of interstellar extinction. A detailed study has been made by Heap (ref. 1), confirming the previous work by Aller that the central star has one of the most excited spectra of any PNN, the only lines definitely present being those of C IV and O VI, although lines of He II are probably also present. Nitrogen lines were not found in any ionization state. An effective temperature of 200,000°K was derived for the star.

Heap estimated an age of about 15,000 years for NGC 246. This is a fairly good age for this type of object and is given some support by the comparatively low nebular density. Using the evolutionary model of planetary nebulae described by Paczynski (ref. 2) and a central star mass slightly greater than 0.6 that of the Sun, it was found that the star is near the point of exhausting its nuclear fuels and will soon contract from its present radius of 0.05 to 0.08 Sun down to a white dwarf radius of 0.013 Sun.

References

1. Heap, S.R.; *Ap.J.*, **196**, 195, 1975.
2. Paczynski, H.E.; *Acta Astr.*, **21**, 417, 1971

NGC 650-1

Discovered by Mechain on 1780 September 5, this object was included by Messier as number 76 in his list of nebulae and star clusters. Subsequently, it was included in the NGC as two objects in contact. It has an unusual form, consisting of a broad, dense bar, narrowing in the center and brighter at the ends, with considerably fainter irregular wisps looping between the ends—not unlike the appearance of a bar magnet surrounded by iron filings. Several investigators have proposed possible explanations of its morphology, beginning in 1891 when Isaac Roberts, a pioneer astrophotographer, suggested that the central bar was probably a broad ring seen edge-on. A number of more modern theories have also been based on this idea; for example, Minkowski & Osterbrock (ref. 1) suggested that the nebula has a flattened ring-like form, surrounded by a thin shell centered approximately on the center of the ring.

A three-dimensional model for NGC 650-1 has been derived by Sabbadin & Hamazaoglu (ref. 2) based on expansion velocities measured from spectra obtained with an echelle spectrograph. By this means the bright bar was found to be a slightly elliptical ring, the plane of which makes an angle of just a few degrees with the line of sight and which is expanding at a velocity of about 42 km/s. The outer, less dense envelope consists of two partial half-shells centered approximately on the exciting star; these may be made up of material ejected by the star earlier than that forming the bar or, more probably, material produced at the same time but with a greater velocity.

Several mechanisms could account for this situation; however, Sabbadin & Hamzaoglu suggest that the red-giant progenitor of the planetary nebula released a shell of gas which was denser in the equatorial plane. The central star evolved rapidly, becoming hotter, and as a result the gas was accelerated by radiation pressure but at a greater rate further away from the denser equatorial part. The nebula then became both optically thin and the dominant factor of acceleration thermal diffusion into the vacuum.

References

1. Minkowski, R. & Osterbrock, D.; *Ap.J.*, **131**, 537, 1960.
2. Sabbadin, F. & Hamzaoglu, E. ; *M.N.R.A.S.*, 197, 363, 1981.

NGC 1535

In 1918 Curtis described NGC 1535 as

> a somewhat irregular elliptical ring about 20″ × 17″, with its major axis in P.A. 35° Outside this is an oval disc of much fainter matter, not quite symmetrical with the nucleus, with very vague traces of a ring formation on the southeast.

Modern high resolution CCD images have been obtained by Louise & Pascoli (ref. 1); they infer from these, and other spectroscopic studies, that NGC 1535 consists of two isothermal shells which are approximately represented by 3-axis ellipsoids. According to Sabbadin *et al.* (ref. 2) the optical appearance and the observed velocity distribution suggests that it consists of two coaxial prolate spheroids (ellipses rotated about their major axes) of moderate ellipticity. The internal shell is the brighter and is also expanding the more quickly. This object is believed to be in a rather early evolutionary phase and optically thick.

C.A. Clayton (ref. 3) reports that the inner shell has revealed a bi-polar expansion with velocities of over 20km/s. This feature was unexpected because of the object's round morphology; however, it is proposed that the bipolarity is most likely caused by a ring of dense material in the equatorial plane of the central star which has led to a faster expansion in the directions along the polar axis. Evidence for this ring of material is revealed in emission-line images of NGC 1535.

References

1. Louise, R. & Pascoli, R.; *Astron. Astrophys.*, **150**, 285, 1985.
2. Sabbadin, F. *et al.*; *Astron. Astrophys.*, **136**, 193, 1984.
3. Clayton, C.A.; *Astron. Astrophys.*, **195**, 263, 1988.

IC 418

IC 418, in the constellation of Lepus, is a small, symmetrical oval nebula, relatively bright but not necessarily easy to observe because of the comparative brightness of the central star.

Because of its apparently simple structure it has been well studied both observationally and theoretically. As early as 1951, Wilson & Aller (ref. 1) made spectroscopic observations and were able to deduce the distribution of the major ions. However, their finding of an H I density enhancement in the center is now discounted and recent models assume a shell-like distribution of gas.

The structure of IC 418 has been examined by, among others, Flower (ref. 2), Buerger (ref. 3), and Reay & Worswick (ref. 4). The last of these have undertaken a programme of electronographic observations through narrow-band interference filters. They conclude that the main features of the nebula can be accounted for in terms of an expanding oblate spheroid model where there is a region of reduced gas density around the central star. Overlap in the spatial distribution of ions of differing ionization potential is interpreted as implying unresolved filamentary structure within the shell.

References

1. Wilson, O.C. & Aller, L.H.; *Ap.J.*, **114**, 421, 1951.
2. Flower, D.R.. *M.N.R.A.S.*, **146**, 243, 1969.
3. Buerger, E.G.; *Ap.J.*, **180**, 817, 1973.
4. Reay, N.K. & Worswick, S.P.; *Astron. Astrophys.*, **66**, 31, 1978.

NGC 2022

This double-shell nebula was described by Curtis (1918) as:

> ... an elliptical ring $22'' \times 17''$ in outside dimensions, in P.A. 29° Outside this is an oval disc of fainter matter $28'' \times 27''$ The brightest parts are the two masses at the ends of the major axis of the inner ring.

Sabbadin *et al.* (ref. 1) have derived the following model for NGC 2022: the main part of the nebula is a prolate spheroid of moderate ellipticity, with the major/minor axis ratio being 1.2 and the angle between the line of sight and the major axis being $45°(\pm 15°)$ in P.A. 30°. This is then surrounded by an almost spherical, fainter emitting region which is not expanding as fast as the central part. At an assumed distance of 2.1kpc, the diameter of NGC 2022 is given as 0.2 pc.

References

1. Sabbadin, F. *et al.*; *Astron. Astrophys.*, **136**, 193, 1984.

NGC 2346

NGC 2346 is a high-excitation nebula with a bipolar form, and observations of the radial velocity structure by J.R. Walsh (ref. 1) indicate a cylindrical geometry, or possibly two cavities with the ionized material in the form of thin sheets.

The most remarkable feature of NGC 2346, however, is its central star. What appears to be the central star is of spectral type A but this is not hot enough to be the object responsible for ionizing the nebula; the observed He II nebular emission line at 468.6nm, for example, requires an ionizing source with a temperature of at least 45,000°K. In 1973, Kohoutek & Senkbeil (ref. 2) suggested that the central star was a binary (A+sdO); this was subsequently confirmed by Mendez & Niemela in 1981 and they also derived an orbital period of 15.995±0.025 days for this single-lined spectroscopic binary.

In 1974 Kohoutek began a search for variability and in seven observing runs up until 1980 found no significant changes from the normal brightness. However, during January-February 1982, light variations of over 2 magnitudes were found, containing evidence of two consecutive minima (ref. 4). Initially, this was interpreted as an eclipse phenomenon but subsequent observations of the spectrum and radial velocity ruled this out. In 1982, Mendez *et al.* (ref. 5) suggested that the variations were caused by a dust cloud passing through the line of sight to the central star. In January 1983, further variations were found, but the light curve was significantly different in terms of shape and duration; this behavior is not compatible with the simple model of Mendez *et al.* but even so, there seems little doubt about the correctness of the theory that dust, circulating close to the star, is the cause of the light variations. This is also supported by IR observations: the object has been found to exhibit an appreciable near-IR excess.

References

1. Walsh, J.R.; in *IAU Symposium No. 103: Planetary Nebulae* (ed. D.R. Flower), D. Reidel, 1983 (p. 57).
2. Kohoutek, L. & Senkbeil, R.; *Mem. Soc. Roy. Sci.* Liege, 6^{e} Ser., 485, 1973.
3. Mendez, R. & Niemela, V.S.; *Ap.J.*, **250**, 240, 1981.
4. Kohoutek, L.; *IBVS*, No. 2113, 1982.
5. Mendez, R. *et al.*; *Astron. Astrophys.*, **116**, L5, 1982.

NGC 2371-2

This object was first recognized as a planetary nebula by Curtis in 1918. The main body of the nebula consists of two irregular lobes, the northernmost being the brightest. It is believed to be relatively close by, at a distance of 0.5kpc, and its size indicates that it is probably quite old (about 10,000 years). It is likely that the nucleus of NGC 2371-2, which has a temperature of about 100,000°K, is composed of a CNO core surrounded by a hydrogen-rich envelope of 10^{-3} to 10^{-5} M☉. Pottasch *et al.* (ref. 1), during the course of an investigation of the UV spectrum to determine the relative abundance of carbon, nitrogen, and oxygen (important for understanding the processes which occurred in the progenitor star prior to the ejection of the nebula), have calculated an upper limit to the rate of mass loss from the central star. This works out to be in the order of 10^{-7} solar mass per year so that the envelope will be lost from the star in a comparatively short period of time.

References

1. Pottasch, S.R. *et al.*; *Astron. Astrophys.*, **102**, 237, 1981.

Abell 21

This planetary nebula was first reported by Abell (ref. 1) and independently found by H.M. Johnson (ref. 2) in his survey of "symmetric galactic nebulae." There was initially some confusion over its classification and both Minkowski (ref. 3) and Vorontsov-Velyaminov identified it as a supernova remnant. As a result of this it was omitted from the Perek & Kohoutek *Catalogue of Galactic Planetary Nebulae.* Morphologically there are certainly some similarities between this object and an SNR, particularly, the filamentary structure of this apparent half-shell of nebulosity. However, there is no evidence of any non-thermal source associated with it, and the mean expansion velocity is too low for an SNR, though typical of a planetary nebula (ref. 4: this also includes a particularly clear photograph of Abell 21, reproduced from the red P.O.S.S. print). The age of the nebula, as estimated from the expansion rate, is 6800 years. The chemical composition and physical conditions of the nebula also point to its correct classification, being that of a planetary nebula (ref. 5 & 6). The morphology and the enhanced helium and nitrogen abundances—relative to solar and Orion Nebula values—are taken to indicate a comparatively massive progenitor star (ref. 6).

References

1. Abell, G.O.; *P.A.S.P.*, **67**, 253, 1955.
2. Johnson, H.M.; *Ap.J.*, **121**, 604, 1955.
3. Minkowski, R.; *Rev. Modern Phys.* **30**, 1048, 1958.
4. Recillas-Cruz, E. & Pismis, P.; *Astron. Astrophys.*, **97**, 398, 1981.
5. Leibowitz, E.M.; *Ap.J.*, **196**, 191, 1975.
6. Kwitter, K.H. *et al.*; in *IAU Symposium No. 103: Planetary Nebulae* (ed. D.R. Flower), D. Reidel, 1983 (p. 523).

Figure 5–1. *NGC 2392 showing double-shell morphology. Photograph courtesy of Lick Observatory.*

NGC 2392

This bright planetary nebula was found by William Herschel in 1787 and consists of a bright star centrally situated in an interesting double-shell nebula. The inner, brighter shell is about $13''$ in diameter and the outer shell about $46''$. In [O III] light (500.7nm) the envelopes are fairly uniform, but in Hα (656.3nm) the light distribution is somewhat more irregular and has been compared with a human face, staring out through a furry "collar," hence its popular name, the "Eskimo Nebula."

A detailed study of the morphology of NGC 2392 has been made by Louise (ref. 1) using monochromatic photographs, and a three-dimensional model of the nebula has been derived by Reay *et al.* (ref. 2) using observations made with the TAURUS Fabry-Perot interferometer. This latter work indicates that this planetary nebula consists of two concentric spheroidal shells, viewed along their major axes. The inner shell has an axial ratio of 2:1 and is expanding with a velocity of 65km/s; the outer shell is more nearly circular and has a maximum expansion velocity of around 75km/s.

A bipolar mass flow of high velocity and high collimation has been discovered in NGC 2392 by Gieskinq *et al.* (ref. 3). This flow appears to have occurred during a long period within the last 1500 years.

References

1. Louise, R.; *Astrophys. & Sp. Sci.*, **79**, 229, 1981.
2. Reay, N.K. *et al.*; *M.N.R.A.S.*, **203**, 1087, 1983.
3. Gieseking, F., *et al.*; *Ap.J.*, **295**, L17, 1985.

NGC 2440

NGC 2440 is an irregular planetary nebula of very complex appearance, centered on two bright condensations 7″ apart in P.A. 153°, within a chaotically structured envelope about 30″ in its greatest extent. Two smaller condensations are also found at the ends of the major axis. An excellent series of CCD images which reveal the complexity of this object have been obtained by Louise & Pascoli (ref. 1); these include a long exposure Hα (656.3nm) photograph which shows two faint, extended lobes on either side of the main body of the nebula, making the form of a butterfly. The inner and outer structure is sufficiently different in appearance and orientation that it suggests they were formed either by different mechanisms and/or at different epochs.

A further indication of the complexity of this object is found in the schematic diagram given by Condal (ref. 2). This paper also provides a study of the chemical abundances in the nebula, as does an earlier paper by Shields *et al.* (ref. 3).

References

1. Louise, R. & Pascoli, R.; *Astron. Astrophys.* **150**, 285, 1985.
2. Condal, A.R.; *Astron. Astrophys.* 112, **124**, 1982.
3. Shields, G.A. *et al.*; *Ap.J.* **248**, 569, 1981.

Abell 30

Abell 30 is a large (diameter 130″) and, therefore, presumably old planetary nebula. Photographically, it is smooth and uniform and centered on a

Figure 5–2. *Abell 30. The irregular appearance of the central star is due to the presence of the ansae. Anglo-Australian Observatory photograph by David Malin.*

star of magnitude V = 14.31. In 1979, Jacoby (ref. 1) found that there were two pairs of ansae symmetrically situated about the central star within a radius of 10 arcsec. Hazard *et al.* (ref. 2) subsequently made spectroscopic observations of these knots and established that three of the four consisted of highly processed hydrogen-deficient material, suggesting a model in which ejection of the hydrogen envelope of the star during the formation of the planetary nebula resulted in processed He-rich material being exposed at the stellar surface. Support for this theory was provided by Reay *et al.* (ref. 3), who measured an expansion velocity of 40 km/s for the main envelope, with an age of 10^4 to 10^5 years, assuming a distance of 1.4 kpc. The ansae were measured as moving at a velocity of 22-25 km/s relative to the star and their age was estimated at 1500 years, consistent with ejection at a late epoch from an evolved star.

Cohen *et al.* (ref. 4) made a particular study of the star and central region of the nebula, recording high-excitation emission lines strongly resembling those of Wolf-Rayet stars of the carbon sequence; OVI, He II, and CIV were noted as being particularly strong. A stellar temperature of 80,000° K was determined and a luminosity of 500 times that of the Sun. The authors also found that within a 10 arcsec radius of the star was strong IR emission suggestive of thermal emission from cool dust.

References

1. Jacoby, G.H.; *P.A.S.P.*, **91**, 754, 1979.
2. Hazard, C. *et al.*; *Nature*, **285**, 463, 1980.
3. Reay, N.K. *et al.*; *M.N.R.A.S.*, **203**, 1079, 1983.
4. Cohen, M. *et al.*; *M.N.R.A.S.*, **233**, 1977.

K 1–2

This object was classified as a planetary nebula by Kohoutek in 1962 (ref. 1) from its appearance on P.O.S.S. prints. A more detailed photograph was obtained by Kohoutek & Schuur (ref. 2) using the E.S.O. 3.6-meter reflector; it was found that the main body of the nebula is $69'' \times 53''$, elongated in P.A. 95°, the outer parts being brighter than the central region. There is also fainter peripheral structure extending the size to about $110'' \times 53''$, in P.A. 90°. At the estimated distance of 2.4 kpc this gives the greatest extent of the nebula as 1.3 pc.

The nucleus, which is located in the center of the nebula, was found to be variable in 1964 by Kohoutek (ref. 3), who noted its differing brightness on the overlapping portion of two P.O.S.S. prints. Further investigation by Liller & Shao (ref. 4), through a search of the Harvard plate archive, revealed that the star had varied from $m(pg)$ 15.7 to 17.4 between the years 1898 and 1952.

More recently, Bond (ref. 5) has obtained B (blue-band) photometry showing variations from 16.4 to 17.8 with a period of 0.6707 days. In an interview with *Astronomy* magazine (ref. 6), he explains the variations as being due to the heating effect of a hot subdwarf on a late-type companion. The tidal force exerted by the subdwarf has slowed down the rotation of the companion so that it probably keeps the same face turned towards the primary; these same forces have also distorted the companion into an egg-shape. The intense radiation from the subdwarf heats the side of the companion which faces it to perhaps 12,000°K, and when the companion is on the far side of its orbit the heated side faces us and the whole system, which is unresolved from Earth, appears to brighten.

These so-called "reflection effect" variables seem to form one of the major groupings of variable planetary nebulae central stars. These, together with examples of other types, are listed in Table 5.3.

Table 5–3
Some Planetary Nebulae with Variable Central Stars

PK Name	Alternate Name	Central Star	Type	Period	Range	Notes
009+03.2	Th 4-4					(1)
009+10.1	Abell 41	MT Ser	ref eff.	$2^{h}.717$	±15.95	
037-05.1	Abell 58	V605 Aql			±19.4	(2)
050-03.1	K 4-31	V998 Aql			15–16:	
053-03.1	Abell 63	UU Sge	EA	$0^{d}.465$	14.7–19.0	(3)
055+16.1	Abell 46	V477 Lyr	EA	$0^{h}.4717294$	14.87–?	
060-07.1	He 1-5	FG Sge		irr.	8.9–13.6	(4)
094+27.1	K 1-16	DS Dra	GW Vir	$0^{h}.4717$	15.04±0.01	(5)
133-08.1	M 1-2	V471 Per	EA	$4^{h}.0002$	13.1±0.06	(6)
136+05.1	HFG 1	V664 Cas	ref. eff.	$13^{h}.95$	±15::	
174-14.1	H 3-29	GL Tau			±18.6	
215+03.1	NGC 2346	V651 Mon		irr.	11.16–15.3	(7)
253+10.1	K 1-2	VW Pyx	ref. eff.	$0^{d}.6707$	16.5–17.7B	
283+09.1	DS 1	KV Vel	ref. eff.	$8^{h}.571$	11.8–12.3	(8)
303+40.1	Abell 35	LW Hya	ref. eff.	$10^{h}.383$	±9.63	(9)
339+88.1	LoTr 5	IN Com	ref. eff.	$5^{h}.922$	8.8–8.9	(10)

Notes: (1) Possible peculiar Be star; (2) Nova-like outburst in 1919. Helium-shell flash? (3) Spec. dK+sdO; (4) Spectrum variable; (5) Period variable. GW Vir stars are multiperiodic, hydrogen deficient, white dwarf pulsators. (6) Spec. G2 II+sdO; (7) V651 Mon is a 16-day spec. bin. but light variations appear to be due to dust circulating close to the star; (8) KV Vel = LSS 2018; (9) Spec. G8 III-IV+sdO; (10) Spec. G5 III+sdO?.

References

1. Kohoutek, L.; *Bull. Astr. Inst. Csl.*, **13**, 220, 1962.
2. Kohoutek, L. & Schuur, G.; *M.N.R.A.S.*, **201**, 1982.
3. Kohoutek, L.; *Bull. Astr. Inst. Cls.*, **15**, 161, 1964.

4. Liller, W. & Shao, C.; in *IAU Symposium No. 34: Planetary Nebulae* (ed. D.E. Osterbrock & C.R. O'Dell), D. Reidel, 1968.
5. Bond, H.; in *IAU Colloquium No. 53*, D. Reidel, 1979 (p. 266)
6. ....; *Astronomy* (September 1988), p.12.

NGC 2818

NGC 2818 was discovered by John Herschel in the field of an inconspicuous open cluster, NGC 2818A, and it is unique in being the only planetary nebula known to be physically associated with such a cluster (the more well-known case of the planetary nebula NGC 2438 in the cluster NGC 2437 is only a projection effect). Evidence for the association was first provided by Tifft *et al.* (ref. 1), based on radial velocity measurements, and the fact of the relationship makes it possible to determine the distance and hence other nebular parameters independently of the problems which normally bedevil such matters. In this case, the distance is calculated at 3.5kpc.

The nebula itself has been studied in detail by Dufour (ref. 2), who described it as having a filamentary structure, consisting of a bright, bipolar "hourglass" oriented north-south and larger, fainter "wings" oriented east-west, centered on a faint star. The distance of NGC 2818 indicates that it is exceptionally large, about 2.2×1.0 pc. Taking into account the expansion velocity, an age of perhaps 10,000 years is implied for the "hourglass" and 22,000 years for the "wings." Dufour calculates that the mass of the nebula is 0.6 solar mass and the mass of the progenitor star 2.2 solar masses. Chemically, the nebula is similar to NGC 2440 and is rich in helium and nitrogen.

The brightness of the central star has been the subject of some discussion with a considerable amount of variation in the determinations; however, the detailed photographic photometry of Kohoutek *et al.* (ref. 3) yields $V = 18.5$ mag., $B - V = +0.1$ mag., $U - B = -1.22$ mag.

References

1. Tifft, W.G. *et al.*; *M.N.R.A.S.*, **158**, 47, 1972.
2. Dufour, R.J.; *Ap.J.*, **287**, 341, 1984.
3. Kohoutek, L. *et al.*; *Astron. Astrophys.*, **162**, 232, 1986.

NGC 3132

NGC 3132 is a bright southern planetary nebula of slightly distorted structure, near the center of which is the mag V = 10.07 star HD 87892. This star has been shown to have a spectrum of type A2V, not hot enough to ionize the nebula by itself, indicating that the apparent central star probably has an unseen companion. Kohoutek & Laustsen (ref. 1) have made a search for such an object, using the 3.6-meter telescope at E.S.O. A star was indeed found, at P.A. 226°.3, Sep. 1″.65. This tiny 16th magnitude star has a spectral type earlier than the primary and lies more precisely on the axis of symmetry, and is therefore almost certainly the exciting star.

Kohoutek & Laustsen suggested that HD 87892 and the hot, apparent companion probably form a binary pair. This was also considered by Sahu & Desai (ref. 2) during their study of the velocity structure of the nebula. Using a Fabry-Perot spectrometer, [O III] 500.7 nm line profiles were obtained at 5 positions across the nebula. The velocity structure thus determined shows that NGC 3132 has an ellipsoidal structure with a velocity asymmetry which could be explained by a binary star hypothesis for the nucleus of the nebula.

A more recent study by J.L. Juguet *et al.* (ref. 3) has given additional consideration to the morphology of NGC 3132 by obtaining spectrophotometric and CCD observations of the nebula at a number of different wavelengths. By this means the authors conclude that this object consists of an inner oblate shell, with a density enhancement towards the polar region, surrounded by a faint outer shell. The major axes of the shells are not precisely aligned, and the authors note that the nucleus is not located at the center of the ellipses but about 2″.5 distant.

References

1. Kohoutek, L. & Laustsen, S.; *Astron. Astrophys.*, **61**, 761, 1977.
2. Sahu, K.C. & Desai, J.N.; *Astron. Astrophys.*, **161**, 357, 1986.
3. Juguet, J.L. *et al.*; *Astron. Astrophys.*, **205**, 267, 1988.

NGC 3587 (M97)

NGC 3587, popularly known as the "Owl Nebula," is one of the most well-known planetaries and was discovered by Pierre Mechain on 1781 February 16. In 1858 it was described by John Herschel thus:

> The light of this stupendous globe is perfectly equable (except just at the edge where it is slightly softened), and of considerable brightness. Such an appearance would not be by a globular space filled with stars or luminous matter, which structure would necessarily give rise to an apparent increase of brightness towards the center in proportion to the thickness traversed by the visual ray. We might, therefore, be induced to conclude its real constitution to be either that of a hollow spherical shell or of a flat disc, presented to us (by a highly improbable coincidence) in a plane precisely perpendicular to the visual ray.

Of course, it is now known that the visible disc is not entirely smooth; indeed, it is the appearance of two darkish patches, symmetrically placed against it which have reminded some of an owl's face and given rise to its popular name. Even so, compared to many other planetary nebulae, the structure is quite

Figure 5–3. *NGC 3587 (M97). Photograph Courtesy of Juhani Salmi.*

smooth, lacking significant stratification or clumpy or filamentary structure (see Figure 5–3).

Herschel was fairly correct in his reasoning about the cause of the Owl Nebula's appearance, although the hypothesis of a simple shell will not work. Minkowski & Aller (ref. 1) interpreted the object as a globe with two smooth, bright condensations placed symmetrically on opposite sides of the central star, within the shell. On the basis of isophotic contours, Proisy (ref. 2) concluded that the nebula is a spherical shell with an inner belt twice as thick and having a greater emission density. More recently, Sabbadin *et al.* (ref. 3) have reached a similar conclusion after studying the kinematical properties of the gas in the brighter nebular emission lines ([O III], Hα and [N II]). The main part of the nebula consists of an inhomogeneous shell whose density and thickness are greater in a belt passing through the two bright condensations. The shell is enveloped in a fainter, low-ionization nebula. The total mass of the nebulosity has been estimated at 0.15 solar mass and the dynamical age 6000 years.

The 16th magnitude central star is a little more massive than most planetary nebula nuclei at about 0.7 solar mass.

References

1. Minkowski, R. & Aller, L.H.; *Ap.J.* **120**, 261, 1954.
2. Pròisy, P.; *Astron. Astrophys.* **20**, 115, 1972.
3. Sabbadin, F. *et al.*; *M.N.R.A.S.* **217**, 539, 1985.

Abell 35

This large, low surface brightness nebula was discovered on P.O.S.S. plates by Abell (ref. 1). On the red plate the morphology of the nebula is dominated by two parallel linear features oriented N.E.-S.W. and about $3'$ south of the geometric center of the nebula.

The structure of Abell 35 has been studied in detail by Jacoby (ref. 2), based on a series of Hα and [O III] plates. On the latter the object exhibits a quite remarkable form; at the center is a bright star which is within the apex of a parabola-shaped nebula making it appear almost comet-like. The morphology bears some comparison to distorted interstellar bubbles (ref. 3). Abell 35 is apparently an extremely large object, with a diameter of 1.6 pc at its estimated distance of 360 pc.

The apparent central star is of spectral type G8 III-IV and is far too cool to ionize the nebula; however, its association is clear enough since it lies at the apex of the parabola, and its proper motion is in the direction of the axis of symmetry of the parabola. There are no other obvious nearby candidates for the central star, so Jacoby considers the possibility that there may be an unseen companion to the G8 star. Evidence for the existence of such a companion appears to have been found in $B-V$ and $U-B$ measurements, which show an excess of "blueness" in the apparent primary. This is suggestive of the presence of a hot, compact star of V mag. = 14.2. The interpretation of the morphology of Abell 35 is believed to involve the effects of a stellar wind from the binary, interacting with the nebular shell.

References

1. Abell, G.O.; *Ap.J.* **144**, 259, 1966.
2. Jacoby, G.H.; Ap.J. **244**, 903, 1981.
3. Weaver, R. *et al.*; Ap.J. **218**, 377, 1977.

NGC 5189

Inaccessible to most northern observers because of its southerly declination of −66°, NGC 5189 is nevertheless one of the most remarkable planetary nebulae because of its strange and complex morphology and has thus been the subject of several investigations. Campbell & Moore (ref. 1) evidently thought it to be a group of nebulae.

> Nebulous field about 1.′3 in length. Composed of three nebulae. NGC 5189, the following one of the three, is about 20″ in diameter, and slightly fainter than the spindle-shaped nebula in the center ...

A more recent description and drawing has been obtained by Buta (ref. 2):

> This is a very fine object in the 24-inch telescope. I saw a large, irregular nebula that bears a striking resemblance to an S-shaped barred spiral galaxy. The "bar" is diffuse and splits on one side. The "arms" are patchy and quite extensive, and they arch sharply off the ends of the bar ... I assume that the catalogues are correct in referring to it as a galactic nebulosity. It looked more like a barred galaxy than some real galaxies I have seen!

A photograph of NGC 5189 can be found in an article by Evans & Thackeray (ref. 3).

Phillips & Reay (ref. 4) have obtained isophotometric contour maps which confirm the complexity of this object and suggest the presence of at least five sets of low-excitation ansae. Another recent investigation, by Reay *et al.* (ref. 5), expands on this, and provides a model in which a ring of condensations around the central star is expanding at 25 km/s in a plane the normal to which subtends an angle of 78° with the line of sight. At greater distance from the star are other pairs of condensations, symmetrically placed to either side of the star and expanding radially away from it. The whole system is enveloped in two lobes of tenuous, patchy material.

Although other planetary nebulae are also known to have these pairs of condensations (ansae)—the most well-known of which is NGC 7009—the structure of NGC 5189 is perhaps the most complex and its evolutionary history is little understood. Obviously though, symmetric outbursts from the central star are implied.

References

1. Campbell, W.W. & Moore, J.H.; Publ. Lick Obs. **13**, 77, 1918.
2. Buta, R.J.; W.S.Q.J. No. 66, 1, 1986.
3. Evans, D. & Thackeray, D.A.; *M.N.R.A.S.* **110**, 429, 1950.
4. Phillips, J.P. & Reay, N.K.; *Astron. Astrophys.* **117**, 33, 1983.
5. Reay, N.K. *et al.*; M.N.R..A.S. **206**, 71, 1984.

He2-111

Discovered by Karl G. Henize during his extensive survey of southern Hα objects, He2-111 is an irregular planetary nebula about $26'' \times 10''$. In 1978 Webster (ref. 1) reported that surrounding the main body was a faint, regular, giant halo. The projected shape of the shell is that of a fairly regular figure of eight, with dimensions of about $10\rlap{.}'2 \times 4\rlap{.}'7$; at an assumed distance of 2.4 kpc this translates into an actual size of 7.1×3.3 pc. The most remarkable feature of this shell, however, is its velocity range of 400 km/s, greater than that observed in any other planetary nebula. It is suggested that both the main body and the outer shell were ejected in the same event, but the lower density material forming the halo was subsequently accelerated more strongly.

Webster points out that there is some positional coincidence between He2-111 and the "new star" event of A.D. 185, recorded by the Chinese. Clark & Stephenson (ref. 2) have concluded that this object was probably a supernova and suggested RCW 86 (G 315.4-2.3) as the likely remnant, although some reservations were expressed because of an apparent positional disparity. However, making some assumptions about the structure and dynamics of the object, the age of He2-111 can be made to fit in with the date of the "new star."

References

1. Webster, H.L.; *M.N.R.A.S.* **185**, 45P, 1978.
2. Clarke, D.H. & Stephenson, F.R.; *The Historical Supernovae*, Pergamon Press, 1977.

Cn 1-1

Cn 1-1 is a peculiar object exhibiting some characteristics of both a symbiotic star and a planetary nebula. It is stellar, with the absorption spectrum of an F5 III-IV star but emission lines indicative of high-density planetary nebula. It has strong IR emission longward of 2 μm, particularly around 3.3 μm and 11.3 μm. There is no history of variability.

Ultraviolet and optical spectra of Cn 1-1 have been obtained by Lutz (ref. 1), who concluded that the object appears to have characteristics which favour its classification as a planetary nebula; she suggests a model whereby Cn 1-1 is a dense planetary nebula involved in a binary system with a star of spectral type F5 III-IV, the nebula itself having arisen from a fairly massive star.

Making use of far-infrared IRAS data and other observational material, Bhatt & Mallik (ref. 2) conclude that over 90% of the radiation from the central star of Cn1-1 is absorbed by dust in the nebula and re-emitted in the far-IR. The luminosity of this star is about 63 times that of the Sun, abnormally low for a young PNN (implied by the high density of the nebula), and the effective temperature could be as high as 250,000°K. Cn1-1 is suggested here to be a Type I proto-planetary nebula evolving in a binary system and the two distinct components of IR emitting dust, indicative of the F-type star being embedded in the nebular dust.

References

1. Lutz, J.H.; *Ap.J.*, **279**, 714, 1984.
2. Bhatt, H.C. & Mallik, D.C. V.; *Astron. Astrophys.*, **168**, 248, 1986.

NGC 6302

This remarkable nebula is often included in lists of planetary nebulae but its actual classification is still open to question; it is certainly not a typical member of the class. The system comprises two lobes of luminous gas separated by a relatively dark lane. It was first described in any real detail by Barnard (ref. 1), who also published a drawing of it. The visual appearance is suggestive of a violent outburst from a central star, though none has ever been detected. It is highly elongated along an approximately E-W axis and almost 4 arcmin in its greatest extent. Minkowski & Johnson (ref. 2) examined its complex structure, based on photographs in Hα and [N II] obtained with the Palomar Observatory 200-inch (5-meter) reflector, and, mystified by its kinematics, concluded that NGC 6302 must be "an example of a hitherto unrecognized kind of expanding nebulae."

The existence of the double lobe structure suggests that, despite the many peculiar features, the basic morphology may be similar to other bipolar objects. If so, the absence of a detectable central star could be explained by its obscuration in a dense disc (or torus) of gas and dust, the lobes being the product of an intense stellar wind escaping at right-angles to the disc. Elliott & Meaburn (ref. 3) have obtained Hα and [N II] line profiles from the ionized material of the nebula, and [OI] from the neutral gas, for many positions across the nebula. These observations have shown that neutral and ionized material is flowing out from the core. Direct evidence for such a wind has been found by Meaburn & Walsh (ref. 4), who have observed an 800km/s wide wing on profiles of the [NeV] line at 324.6nm.

The actual lobes may be the walls of cavities, blown out by the stellar wind into an hourglass-like form and maintained by standing shocks. Energized by the star, sheets of ionized material "flow" along these walls at an ever-increasing velocity as they reach less dense parts of the nebula.

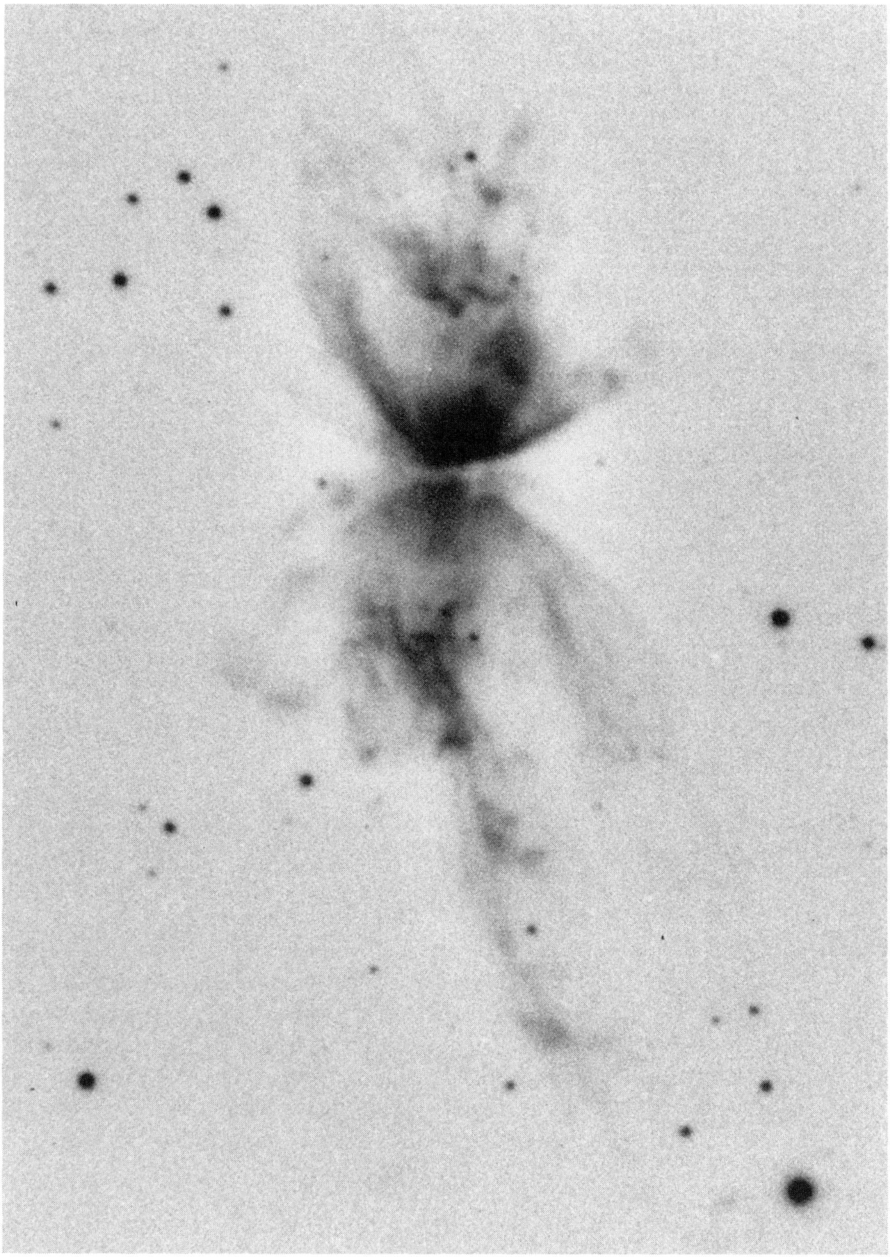

Figure 5–4. *NGC 6302. The complex filamentary structure of this high-excitation nebula is revealed in this unsharp mask print. Anglo-Australian Observatory photograph by David Malin.*

In addition to the complex morphology of NGC 6302, its chemical composition is also poorly understood. An investigation by Aller *et al.* (ref. 5), using IUE data and visible wavelength spectroscopic data obtained through the 3.9-m. Anglo-Australian Telescope (AAT), shows that the chemical abundances are by no means typical of a normal planetary nebula, with excesses of helium and, especially, nitrogen.

References

1. Barnard, E.E.; *Astr. Nach.*, 173, 123, 1906.
2. Minkowski, R. & Johnson, N.M.; *Ap.J.*, **148**, 659, 1967.
3. Elliott, K.H. & Meaburn, J.; *M.N.R.A.S.*, **181**, 499, 1977.
4. Meaburn, J. & Walsh, J.R.; *M.N.R.A.S.*, **191**, 5P, 1980.
5. Aller, L.H. *et al.*; *M.N.R.A.S.*, **197**, 95, 1981.

NGC 6543

The first nebulous object determined to be of a gaseous nature, by Huggins in 1864, NGC 6543 has been the subject of numerous studies because of its complex structure and extended halo. Feibelman (ref. 1) found the size of the bright main body of the nebula to be $23''.4 \times 19''.7$; however, immediately surrounding this, Coleman *et al.* (ref. 2) found a faint halo of $35''$ diameter. The giant outer halo extends its size to a diameter of $4'$.

A particularly detailed study of the structure of NGC 6543 has been carried out by Phillips *et al.* (ref. 3) using electronographic equipment to obtain isophotal maps at seven different wavelengths. It was found that the apparently complex internal structure might easily be explained in terms of an intrinsically simple model with three axes of differing lengths. In three of the maps (Hα, He I and [O III]), there is an apparent compression of the outer isophotes in the northeastern sector, closely matched by a similar displacement of the northeastern poles of the forbidden line maps. This northeastern pole is also brighter. On the opposite side of the nebula, and particularly clear in radio maps, is a slight "tail." These observations are interpreted in terms of the nebula interacting with the interstellar medium.

References

1. Feibelman, W.A.; *J. Roy. Astr. Soc. Can.*, **65**, 25, 1971.
2. Coleman, C.I. *et al.*; *M.N.R.A.S.*, **171**, 415, 1975.
3. Phillips, J.P. *et al.*; *Astron. Astrophys.*, **61**, 695, 1977.

K 1-16

Discovered by Kohoutek (ref. 1) in 1963, this faint planetary nebula is of particular interest because of the variability of its 15th magnitude central star. High-speed photometry of the star by Grauer & Bond (ref. 2) has shown it to be a low-amplitude pulsating variable. The dominant period is 28.3 minutes, with a semi-amplitude of 0.01 magnitude; however, this behavior is not consistent, as additional periods appear and sometimes no variations at all occur. Such "mode switching" activity is typical of some of the ZZ Ceti variables, which are white dwarf nonradial pulsators. However, the central star of Kl-16 with an effective temperature in excess of 80,000°K is much too hot to be included in this class. It is more similar to the GW Vir class of variables, the prototype of which is also known as PG 1159-035.

References

1. Kohoutek, L.; Hull. *Astr. Inst. Csl.*, **14**, 70, 1963.
2. Grauer, A.D. & Bond, H.E.; *Ap.J.*, **277**, 211, 1984.

SwSt 1

This object was first described by Swings & Struve (ref. 1) in 1940. They drew attention to the complex spectrum which they explained as being produced by a combination of carbon emission lines from a Wolf-Rayet type exciting star and sharp lines of nebular origin. The central star has since been classified as being of type WC 10 by Cohen (ref. 2), a conclusion also reached by Carlson & Henize (ref. 3).

An optical study of SwSt 1 has been made by de Freitas Pacheco & Veliz (ref. 4), who concluded that this object is a compact, dense, and young planetary nebula at a distance of about 1.2 kpc and about 150 pc below the galactic plane. The progenitor star is suggested to have been of 1.5 to 2.0 times the mass of the Sun. In the nebular shell, elements such as C, N, and O are underabundant with respect to cosmic values by a factor of 2. The central star 0.89 M$\odot$ and is losing mass at a rate of about $6^{-7} \times 10^{-8}$ solar mass per year.

References

1. Swings, P. & Struve, O.; *Proc. Nat. Acad. Sci.*, **26**, 454, 1940.
2. Cohen, M.; *M.N.R.A.S.*, **173**, 489, 1975.
3. Carlson, J. & Henize, K.G.; *Vistas Astr.*, **23**, 213, 1979.
4. de Freitas Pacheco, J. & Veliz, J.G.; *M.N.R.A.S.*, **227**, 773, 1987.

NGC 6720 (M57)

M57, the "Ring Nebula," with its distinctive annular form, may be considered the archetypal planetary nebula. It was discovered in January 1779 by Antoine Darquier, and independently by Charles Messier, while they were following a comet. In 1785 it was observed by William Herschel, who described it as:

> ... a nebula that has a regular concentric dark spot in the middle and is probably a ring of stars.

A little later he had reconsidered his views on the nature of nebulae and concluded that they were formed from a "luminous fluid" as described in Chapter 1. Perhaps the best of the early descriptions was that of John Herschel:

> It is small, and particularly well defined, so as in fact to have much more the appearance of a flat oval solid ring than of a nebula. The axes of the ellipse are to each other in the proportion of about 4 to 5, and the opening occupies about half its diameter: its light is not quite uniform but has something of a curdled appearance, particularly at the exterior edge, the central opening is not entirely dark but is filled up with a faint hazy light, uniformly spread over it like a fine gauze stretched over a hoop.

John Herschel's meticulous, descriptive style could well be emulated by modern observers and records precisely the appearance of NGC 6720 as viewed in a moderate-to-large aperture telescope.

Many studies have been made of the structure and morphology of NGC 6720 (see, for example, refs. 1, 2, and 3). These show that the basic annular form, more chaotically structured at the extremities of the major axis, is the product of a 3-dimensional ellipsoidal shell compressed into two dimensions. However, the detail of the structure is much more complex and, like many planetaries, changes dramatically at different wavelengths (see Figure 5–5). This, of course, is due to the fact that not only does the distribution of matter in the shell affect its appearance but also the decreasing ionization potential of the central star with increasing distance. Color photographs illustrate this quite dramatically; the faint nebulosity near the center shows up well in green light, while in red light the annulus predominates and the center is essentially dark. Close to the star, the intense UV emission ionizes oxygen and nitrogen quite strongly and, since their primary emission lines are in the green part of the spectrum, this color is most apparent. Further out the intensity of the radiation is reduced by the distance and other factors and is capable of ionizing only the more easily excited hydrogen gas, which emits primarily in the red Hα line.

The familiar structure is by no means the greatest extent of the nebula however, as a very faint extended halo was discovered by Duncan (ref. 4) as long ago as 1937. Excellent images of this structure have been obtained by a number of investigators (see, for example, refs. 5 & 6) but even beyond this, very deep photographs, using narrow-band Hα and [N II] filters, have revealed the presence of additional extended filamentary structure (ref. 7). These give NGC 6720 an overall diameter of about 216″ which, adopting a distance of 400 pc, translates into a linear diameter of 0.42 pc. These dimensions for the faint halo make it likely that its mass is at least as great as that contained in the "main body" of the nebula.

The central star of NGC 6720 has been the source of some controversy in the past. Discovered in 1800 by F. von Hahn, its visibility seems to depend quite critically on atmospheric conditions and the size, power and quality of the optics used. Some observers claim to have seen it in quite small instruments while users of significantly larger telescopes have failed. This led to some speculation that its brightness might be variable; however, this is now pretty well discounted and its brightness is now taken as about 15.0 (ref. 8).

References

1. Phillips, J.P. & Reay, N.K.; *Astrophys. Lett.*, **21**, 47, 1980.
2. Proisy, P.E.; *Astron. Astrophys.*, **35**, 71, 1974.
3. Louise, R.; *Astron. Astrophys.*, **30**, 189, 1974.
4. Duncan, J.C.; *Ap.J.*, **86**, 496, 1937.
5. Minkowski, R. & Osterbrock, D.; *Ap.J.*, **131**, 537, 1960.
6. Jewett, D.C. *et al.*; *Ap.J.*, **302**, 727, 1986.
7. Moreno, M.A. & Lopez, J.A.; *Astron. Astrophys.*, **178**, 319, 1987.
8. Kaler, J.B.; *Ap.J.*, **271**, 188, 1983.

BD +30° 3639

The emission-line nature of BD +30° 3639 was first reported by W.W. Campbell in 1894 and it is still often referred to as "Campbell's Star." It is a small, symmetric planetary nebula of high surface brightness, centered on a Wolf-Rayet nucleus. The object shows low excitation characteristics (ref. 1) having very weak [O III] lines but strong [N II] and [O II] lines; the latter features, when combined with a high degree of reddening, give the nebula an unusual red appearance when visually observed through a large telescope (ref. 2).

Infrared images of BD +30° 3639 have been obtained by Bentley *et al.* (ref. 3). They conclude that the unidentified emission features at 8.6 μm and 11.3 μm, which are stronger towards the edge of the nebula, must both belong to the same dust population because of the similarity in distribution, and are probably the result of patches where the composition of the dust grains is different. A similar phenomenon has also been noted in NGC 7027. A model

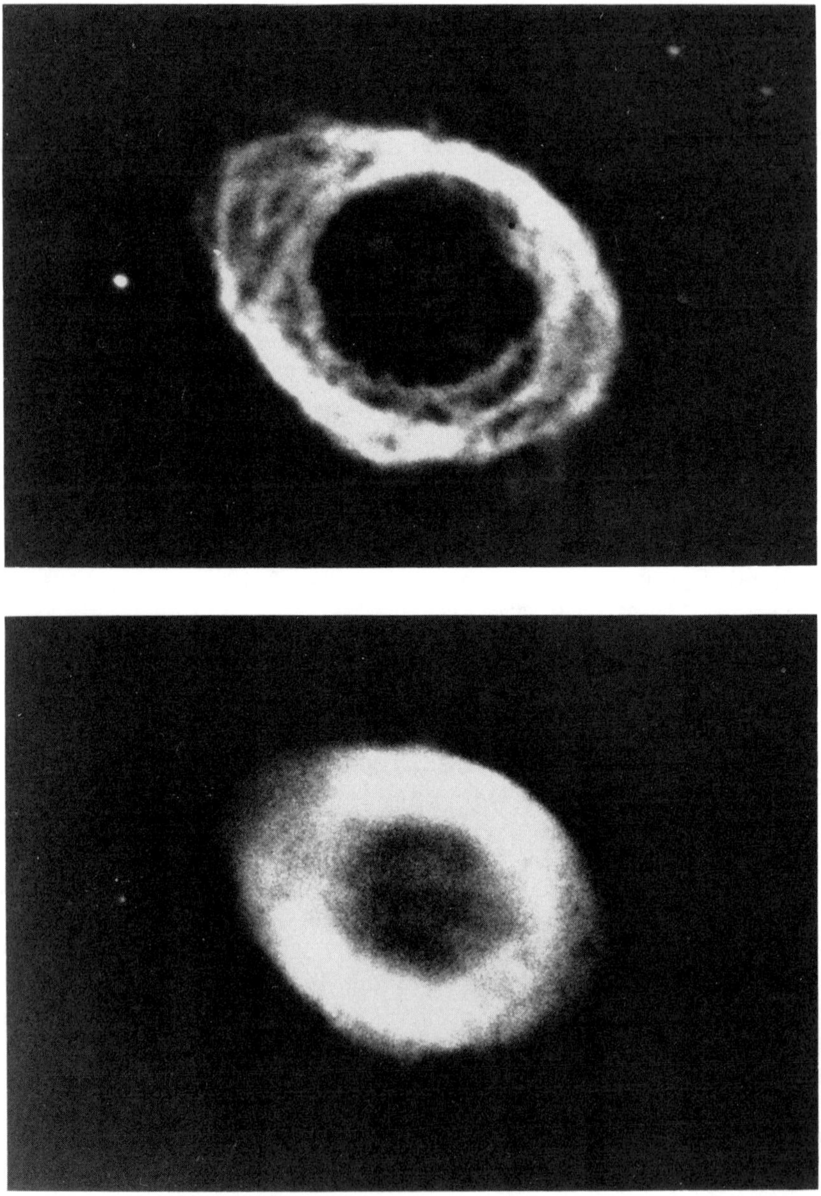

Figure 5–5 (above and facing page). *Four views of the Ring Nebula, NGC 6720, taken at four different wavelengths (above top λ6300, bottom λ5007, facing page top λ4861, and bottom λ4686). The use of photographic plates sensitive to*

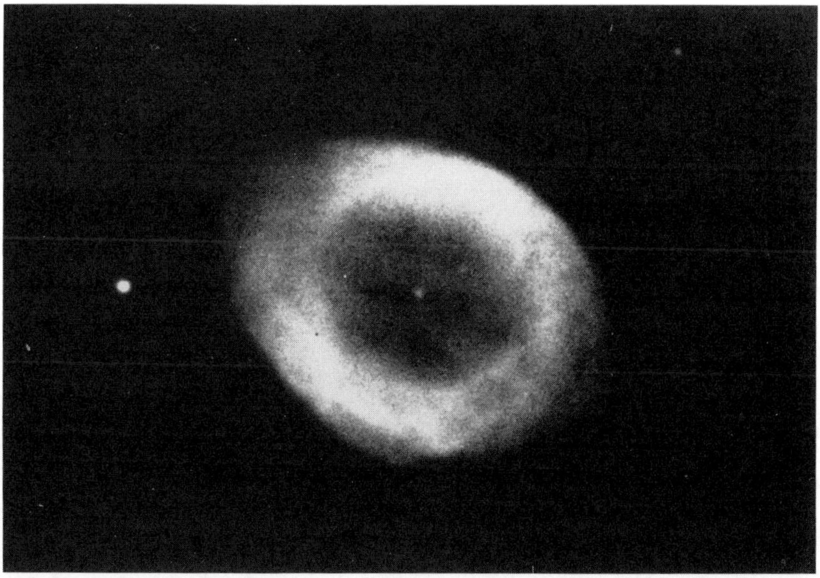

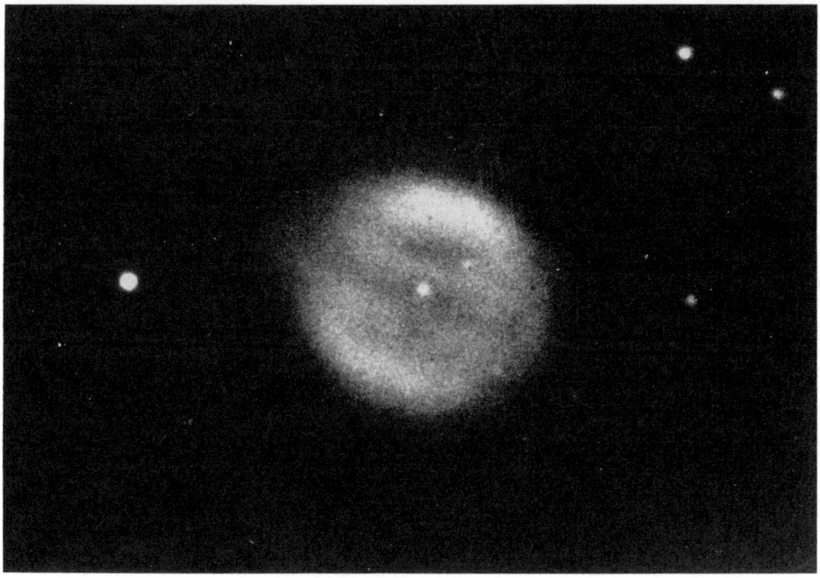

different wavelengths enables astronomers to study the distributions of different elements in the nebulae. Kitt Peak National Observatory, 2.1-meter photographs. Courtesy National Optical Astronomy Observatories.

is proposed whereby graphite grains, coextensive with the ionized hydrogen nebula, produce a background continuum at 10 μm. Nearer to the edges of the nebula, some of the graphite grains are coated by a volatile mantle which survives because of the partial shielding provided by the interior material. This gives rise to the emission peaks at 8.6 μm and 11.3 μm. The nature of additional emission at 20 μm and 23 μm is not yet fully understood.

References

1. Wilson, O.C.; *Ap.J.* **111**, 279, 1950.
2. O'Dell, C.R. & Terzian, Y.; *Ap.J.* **160**, 915, 1970.
3. Bentley, A.F. *et al.*; *Ap.J.* **278**, 665. 1984.

Abell 63

Abell 63 is a large, low surface brightness nebula first reported as object 51 in the 1955 catalogue of George Abell (ref. 1); however, its usual designation derives from its listing as object 63 in his revised, enlarged catalogue of 1966 (ref. 2). The nebula itself, though little studied, seems to be fairly unremarkable, but the main point of interest about this object is its variable central star, UU Sge.

The variability of this star was discovered by D. Hoffleit in 1932, but it was not until 1976 that Bond (ref. 3) noticed the coincidence of the star and the nebula. In 1978 Bond *et al.* (ref. 4) were able "to present observations establishing UU Sge as the first known eclipsing nucleus of a planetary nebula."

Bond *et al.* constructed a photoelectric B light-curve showing that UU Sge is an eclipsing binary with an orbital period of 0.465 days. The primary minima, which are 4.3 magnitudes deep, are due to total eclipses of the hot white dwarf primary star by a cooler main sequence K star. The observational material is consistent with a system containing an sdO primary just a little less massive than the Sun, together with a larger but somewhat less massive (0.7 solar mass) dK secondary, the pair being separated by just 3 solar radii. Because of this proximity the white dwarf heats the side of the secondary which faces it to about 10,000°K.

The authors consider that UU Sge is following the same line of evolution as that proposed by Paczynski (ref. 5) for the remarkable binary in the Hyades, V471 Tau. It is proposed that as the primary expanded into its red giant phase, its envelope engulfed the low mass secondary, which spiralled inwards, transferring its angular momentum to the envelope until this was ejected to form the planetary nebula. The resulting binary consists of the hot, degenerate core of the red giant plus a cool main-sequence star of somewhat increased mass, surrounded by the ejected envelope which is, of course, ionized by the hotter star. It is suggested that ultimately the system will evolve to become an interacting, cataclysmic variable binary.

References

1. Abell, G.O.; *P.A.S.P.*, **67**, 258, 1955.
2. Abell, G.O.; *Ap.J.*, **144**, 259, 1966.
3. Bond, H.E.; *P.A.S.P.*, **88**, 192, 1976.
4. Bond, H.E. *et al.*; *Ap.J.*, **223**, 252, 1978.
5. Paczynski, H.; in *IAU Symposium No. 73* (ed. P. Eggleton, S. Mitton & J. Whelan), D. Reidel, 1976 (p.75).

NGC 6853 (M27)

Discovered by Charles Messier on 1764 July 12, this was the first to be found in the class of objects later to be known as "planetary nebulae." With his small refractor he was unable to see much detail and described it thus:

> ...it appears to have an oval form and does not contain any star.

The main body of the nebula appears to consist of two broad, wedge-shaped lobes, joined together at the center, where it is narrowest; it is from this structure that the nebula derives its popular name, the "Dumbbell Nebula" (see Figure 5–6). To either side of this main body, however, is more tenuous nebulosity, as noted by John Herschel:

> ...faint luminosity fills the lateral concavities of the body and converts them into protuberances so as to render the general outline of the whole nebula a regular ellipse.

The brightness of the nebula and its large size (350″) indicate that NGC 6853 is quite close and several distance determinations, using different methods, have given a value of 250 pc (ref. 1). As a result of its proximity, the sdO central star is not too difficult to detect at magnitude V = $13^{\text{m}}_{.}82$ (ref. 2).

Several studies have focussed on the ionization and chemical structure of the nebula (see, for example, refs. 3, 4, & 5). Based on observations made in the UV, IR, and visible regions of the spectrum, these show that NGC 6853 is a fairly typical object of its class, although not entirely without its peculiarities. In particular, it shows significant enhancements of the elements O, N, Ne, and C, implying some mixing of nuclear processed material into the red giant envelope prior to the ejection of the planetary nebulae (ref. 4).

References

1. Pottasch, S.R. ; *Planetary Nebulae*, D. Reidel, 1984.
2. Kaler, J.B.; *Ap.J.*, **271**, 188, 1983.
3. Hawley, S.A. & Miller, J.S.; *P.A.S.P.* **90**, 39, 1978.
4. Barker, T.; *Ap.J.*, **284**, 589, 1984.

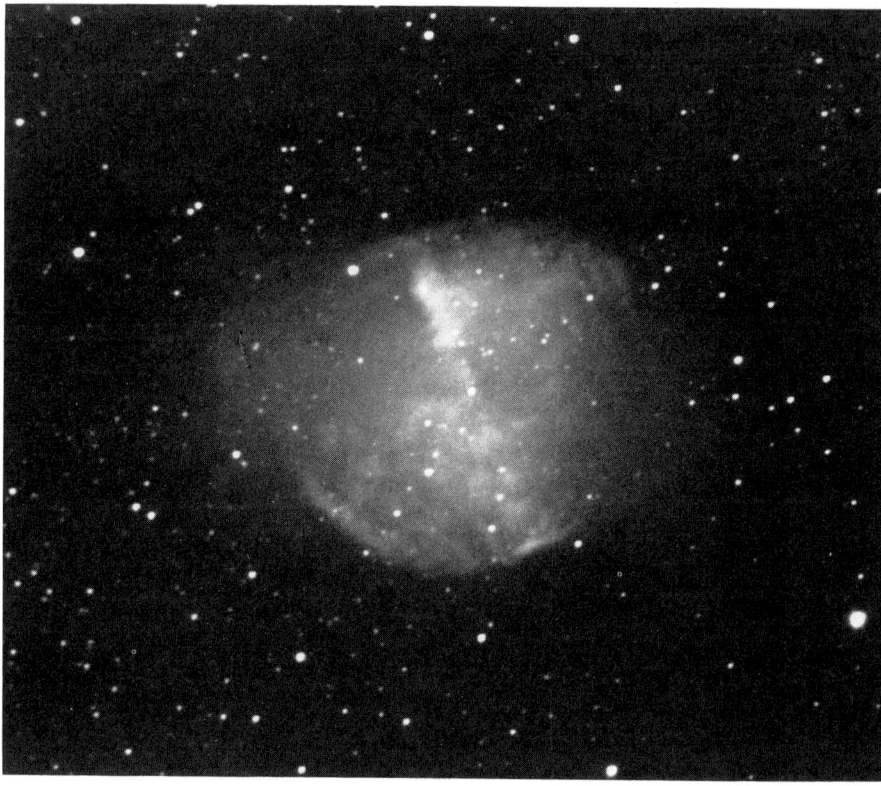

Figure 5–6. *NGC 6853 (M27). Photo courtesy of Juhani Salmi*

5. Zhang, C.Y. *et al.*; *Astron. Astrophys.*, **178**, 247, 1987.

He 1-5

This faint planetary nebula was discovered by Henize in 1955 and described in the notes to his first listing (ref. 1). The diameter of the nebula at its greatest extent is about 36″; the inner 28″ of this appears as a uniformly bright, featureless disc and the peripheral region is fainter.

The nebulosity itself seems to bear the characteristics of a normal planetary nebula, but this system is remarkable for the behavior of its central star which, from $m(pg)$ 13.6 in 1894, rose steadily in brightness to about $m(pg)$ 8.9 around 1970, before starting to fade. At the present time (mid 1990), the star is irregularly variable between $m(v)$ 9.0 to 9.5. With the brightness changes in the star, there has also been a continuous change in the spectral and corresponding effective temperature $(T_{\rm eff})12,000°K$, but by the early 1980's this had fallen to 4500°K. Projecting backwards to the start of the changes Pottasch (ref. 2), finds an effective temperature of 50,000°K and a luminosity of 2000 Suns, values which would place it on the HR diagram with the central stars of other planetary nebulae.

Herbig & Boyarchuk (ref. 3) note that the emission nebula certainly predates the brightening of the star. Examination of the image of the star on plates taken in 1894, 1910, and 1916 shows it to be distinctly "soft" and, within the uncertainties of such comparisons, the nebula has the same dimensions as when subsequently measured on a blue plate of 1960, made with the 3-meter reflector at Lick Observatory.

The variable, named FG Sagittae, has a mag 14 companion at a distance of 8.″1, in P.A. 100°. Since the two would not have been resolved on the early plates, the brightness estimates at this time (say, up to about 1910) would have been strongly influenced by its presence and the degree of brightness increase underestimated.

The literature on FG Sge is quite extensive, but of particular interest are those at refs. 4, 5, and 6 which detail spectroscopic and photometric changes which occurred in the decade either side of the star reaching its peak brightness. Of particular note is the discovery of Langer *et al.* (ref. 4) that from about 1964 there began an incredible increase in the abundance of the so-called s-process elements (particularly, La, Ce, Ha, Y, and Zr) from approximately solar values before this time to about 25 times solar abundance in 1972.

References

1. Henize, K.G.; *P.A.S.P.*, **73**, 159, 196l.
2. Pottasch, S.R.; *Planetary Nebulae*, D. Reidel, 1984.
3. Herbig, G & Boyarchuk, A.A.; *Ap.J.*, **153**, 397, 1968.
4. Langer, G.E. *et al.*; *Ap.J.*, **189**, 509, 1974.
5. Stone, R.P.; *P.A.S.P.*, **91**, 389, 1979.
6. Cohen, J.G. & Phillips, A.C.; *Ap.J.*, **237**, 99, 1980.

NGC 7009

This bright, elliptical object was discovered by Sir William Herschel in 1782. It was named the "Saturn Nebula" by Lord Rosse because of the extensions, or "ansae," which project from the ends of the major axis; these give NGC 7009 the look of a planet with an almost edge-on ring system.

High-resolution photographs show that the structure of the nebula is highly complex with a significant degree of stratification (see Figure 5–7).

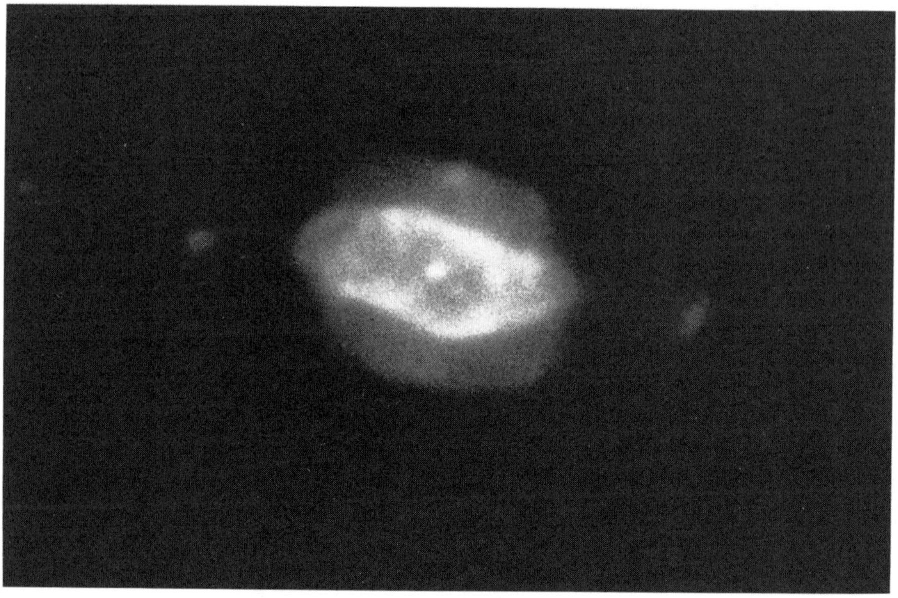

Figure 5–7. *NGC 7009 showing structure and ansae. Photograph courtesy of Lick Observatory*

Around the central star is a broad, elliptical (3:1) ring of irregular structure; contained within this ring, at the ends of the major axis, are a pair of condensations similar to but larger than those which can be seen at the ends of the ansae. The nature of the two pairs of condensations is by no means clear, but theoretical considerations indicate that they must be comparatively cool and quite dense. Enveloping the inner structure is a less elliptical (1.5:1) but more broken ring, which in some places appears to be composed of individual irregular condensations or beads.

The kinematics of the nebula have been investigated by Reay & Atherton (ref. 1), using the TAURUS Fabry-Perot interferometer in conjunction with the AAT. They find that the line containing the outer ansae and the central star is at an angle of about 84° to the line of sight, i.e., almost in the plane of the sky. Adopting a distance of 740 pc, the kinematic age of the outer condensations is determined as about 1500 years and the inner pair about 1100 years.

IUE observations of the central star (ref. 2) show that the spectrum exhibits P Cygni profiles, implying mass loss, and indicative of a stellar wind velocity of around 2000 km/s. It may be that many of the visible features of the nebula can be explained by the dynamical effect of the stellar wind on the envelope. UV radiation pressure probably also plays an important role, preferentially accelerating condensations in the envelope.

References

1. Reay, N.K. & Atherton, P.D.; *M.N.R.A.S.*, **215**, 233, 1985.
2. Koppen, J. & Werthse, R.; *Astron. Astrophys.*, **85**, 1, 1980.

NGC 7027

Discovered by the Rev. T.W. Webb in 1879, this is not only one of the very brightest planetary nebulae but also one of the most unusual, reflected by the fact that it has inspired more papers in the professional journals than any other object of this kind (730 references from 1965 to 1987). Despite the attention, however, it is by no means thoroughly understood.

NGC 7027 is believed to be a very young planetary nebula with the remnants of a red giant circumstellar envelope surrounding the central ionized region, which is extremely dense. By comparing the outer molecular envelope with the inner ionized material, Jura (ref. 1) suggests that during the past 1000 years the mass loss rate has decreased by a factor of at least 3, and probably a factor of 10. If correct, this would suggest that the luminosity of the central star has also decreased by a substantial amount over the same period, consistent with the model proposed by Paczynski (ref. 2) for the very rapid evolution of the more massive post-AGB stars.

From the morphological point of view, there are significant differences between the appearance of NGC 7027 at visual and at radio wavelengths. Comparative observations have been made by, for example, Hicks *et al.* (ref. 3), where it is shown that in [O III] and Hβ light the object is an irregular oval, gradually brightening to an off-center peak. However, at 5 GHz, as observed by Scott (ref. 4), NGC 7027 exhibits a highly symmetrical annular form, strongly reminiscent of NGC 6720, the "Ring Nebula" in Lyra. This apparent anomaly is believed to be due to highly variable absorption due to dust across the face of the nebula, which affects our perception of the object in the visible part of the spectrum; however, at longer wavelengths its true morphology is revealed.

The spectrum of NGC 7027 is also quite remarkable. It emits a rich variety of atomic lines, both via recombination of electrons and forbidden transitions. Molecular line emission has also been detected, indicating the presence of simple, up to fairly complex molecules. Unidentified features occur throughout the spectrum and include strong band emissions, probably due to some solid material. Because of the density of the nebula, the central star has always proved difficult to detect and study; however, in 1988, both G. Jacoby (ref. 5) and N.A. Walton *et al.* (ref. 6) reported unambiguous identifications and secured brightness measurements. Jacoby obtained a value of m(v) = 16.32±0.35 and Walton *et al.* obtained 17.0±0.2. From the value he obtained, and using a distance of 900 pc, Jacoby calculates a temperature of 180,000°K, a mass of 0.65 to 0.70 M⊙, and a luminosity of 4900 L⊙.

References

1. Jura, M.; *Ap.J.*, **286**, 630, 1984.
2. Paczynski, H.; *Acta Astr.*, **21**, 417, 1971.
3. Hicks, T.R. *et al.*; *M.N.R.A.S.*, **176**, 409, 1976.
4. Scott, P.F.; *M.N.R.A.S.*, **161**, 35, 1973.
5. Jacoby, G.H.; *Ap.J.*, **333**, 193, 1988.
6. Walton, N.A. *et al.*; *Astron. Astrophys.*, **200**, L21, 1988.

Hu1-2

This 12th magnitude planetary nebula was found by Humason in 1921. High-resolution images show that the brightest part of the nebula appears as an irregular rectangle about 7″ long and 2″ across, the major axis lying in P.A. 45°. Fainter projections from the ends of the major axis give the object an overall Z-shaped form, making it similar in appearance to the more well-known NGC 650-1. This main body is then enveloped in a fainter, roughly oval nebulosity, about 18″ in greatest extent, with its major axis at approximately right-angles to the major axis of the brightest part.

High-resolution spectroscopy by Sabbadin *et al.* (ref. 1) seems to indicate that the bright "rectangle" is, in fact, a very irregular and patchy, thick equatorial ring or torus, seen edge-on. This presents two bright lobes, symmetrically located with respect to the central star, the N.E. lobe receding and the S.W. lobe approaching.

The position of the star on the HR diagram, together with chemical overabundances of He and N and its small dynamical age of about 2500 years, points to the progenitor star being quite massive. This is also given some support by the present mass of the exciting star—about 0.65 M⊙—which is a little greater than the mean value normally assumed for PN nuclei.

References

1. Sabbadin, F. *et al.*; *Astron. Astrophys.*, **182**, 305, 1987.

NGC 7293

NGC 7293, the "Helix Nebula," is one of the largest planetary nebulae in apparent diameter and therefore, presumably, one of the closest. As a consequence, it has been the target of several attempts to obtain a parallax, the first being that of van Maanen, who obtained a value of $0\farcs038$, corresponding to a distance of 26 pc. More recently, Ianna & McAlister (ref. 1) have obtained $0\farcs020 \pm 0\farcs006$, equivalent to about 50 pc.

The popular name of the nebula derives from its photographic appearance, where the annulus gives the impression of being made from two overlapping circles, or a helix viewed at a slight angle. Consideration has been given to the possibility that this apparent helical structure might be genuine, and the means by which it could occur, however, it is now believed that the appearance is illusory. A study by Warner & Rubin (ref. 2) produced photographs in the light of [O III] 500.7nm, [OI] 630.0nm, Hα 656.3nm, and [N II] 658.4nm, using narrow passband interference filters. In the light of neutral oxygen, in particular, the picture which emerges is of two concentric circles, the outer one being broken on the N.W. and S.E. edges. Filamentary structure does complicate interpretation, however. Anomalies in the electron temperatures, derived from the observations, indicate that the nebula contains compact pockets of comparatively cold, neutral material, and work by Meaburn & Walsh (ref. 3) suggests the presence of stellar wind-driven flows around such objects, which may be revealed by the appearance of condensations and radial streaks.

The material contained within the annulus is by no means the full extent of NGC 7293. A huge outer halo has been discovered by Araya *et al.* (ref. 4), and the full complexity of this outer structure has only been revealed by photographic amplification techniques employed by Malin (ref. 5) on a red image of the nebula.

IRAS observations (ref. 6) show the pattern of 12μm emission (atomic line emission) follows the general outline of the optical nebula but does not show any trace of the extended halo. The 60μm and 100μm emission due to dust also fails to show evidence of the halo.

References

1. Ianna, P.A. & McAlister, H.A.; *Astron.J.*, **79**, 1314, 1974.
2. Warner, J.W. & Rubin, V.C.; *Ap.J.*, **198**, 593, 1975.
3. Meaburn, J. & Walsh, J.R.; *Astrophys. Lett.*, **21**, 53, 1980.
4. Araya, G. *et al.*; *P.A.S.P.*, **84**, 70, 1972.
5. Malin, D. & Murdin, P.; *Colours of the Stars*, Cambridge University Press, 1984 (p. 100).
6. Leene, A. & Pottasch, S.R.; *Astron. Astrophys.*, **173**, 145, 1987.

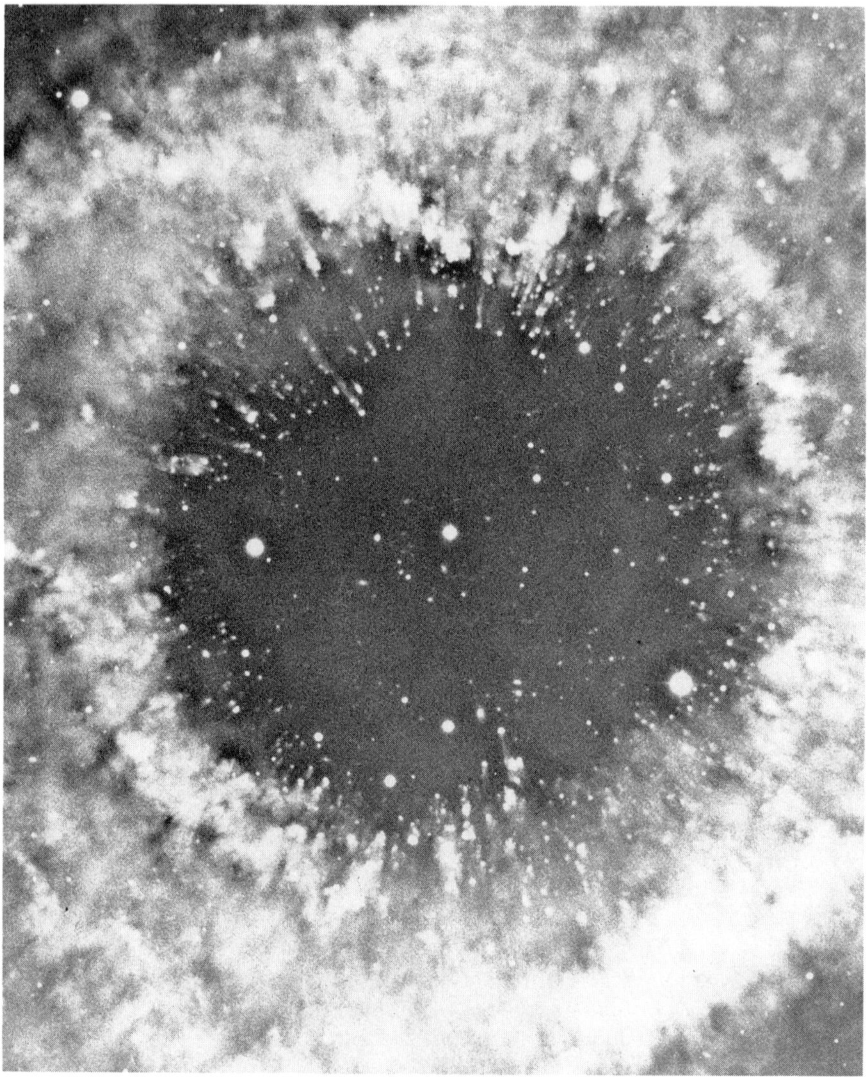

Figure 5–8. *Inner regions of NGC 7293 showing central stars, condensations, and radial streaks. The angular size of condensations is in the range 1″ to 3″. Anglo-Australian Observatory photograph by David Malin.*

5.4
Cross Index of Planetary Nebulae by Name

Cross Index of Planetary Nebulae by Name

Name		Name		Name		Name	
19 W 32	17 39.1	ARO 109	20 12.72	ARO 231	07 14.82	ARO 371	22 20.52
A 06-09	21 05.8	ARO 110	20 16.42	ARO 233	07 19.35	ARO 372	22 26.33
ARO 2	01 42.36	ARO 112	21 32.50	ARO 234	07 21.25	ARO 373	22 31.70
ARO 3	05 27.51	ARO 113	22 56.28	ARO 235	07 24.24	ARO 374	22 32.34
ARO 4	10 24.81	ARO 114	23 45.85	ARO 236	07 26.58	ARO 375	22 34.73
ARO 5	16 44.50	ARO 115	23 47.68	ARO 237	07 27.94	ARO 376	22 42.59
ARO 6	17 58.58	ARO 116	01 58.78	ARO 239	07 37.32	ARO 380	23 22.96
ARO 7	18 12.13	ARO 117	19 58.41	ARO 240	07 40.37	ARO 381	23 26.29
ARO 8	18 54.63	ARO 119	18 31.20	ARO 242	07 49.67	ARO 382	23 31.87
ARO 9	18 53.56	ARO 120	19 21.02	ARO 243	07 50.22	ARO 384	23 39.14
ARO 11	19 34.76	ARO 121	07 57.78	ARO 244	08 02.48	ARO 385	23 46.76
ARO 12	19 43.96	ARO 122	05 28.96	ARO 246	08 06.72	ARO 386	23 56.60
ARO 13	19 44.85	ARO 123	05 46.86	ARO 248	17 21.07	ARO 387	18 27.94
ARO 14	19 59.56	ARO 124	06 04.84	ARO 250	17 27.34	ARO 388	07 29.01
ARO 15	20 19.94	ARO 125	06 11.19	ARO 252	17 29.72	ARO 389	17 47.93
ARO 16	21 04.22	ARO 126	06 35.74	ARO 253	17 33.62	ARO 500	16 12.98
ARO 17	22 29.63	ARO 127	06 37.35	ARO 254	17 35.97	ARO 501	16 31.51
ARO 19	03 47.51	ARO 129	06 53.52	ARO 255	17 38.50	ARO 502	17 13.73
ARO 20	23 25.91	ARO 130	06 59.94	ARO 256	17 39.91	ARO 503	18 12.04
ARO 21	04 09.25	ARO 131	07 05.31	ARO 257	17 40.12	ARO 504	10 07.00
ARO 22	04 14.24	ARO 132	07 22.99	ARO 258	17 40.30	ARO 505	15 16.84
ARO 23	05 56.32	ARO 133	07 36.11	ARO 259	17 48.62	ARO 506	09 07.11
ARO 24	07 29.16	ARO 134	07 51.71	ARO 260	17 50.46	ARO 507	09 12.44
ARO 25	11 14.78	ARO 136	18 24.71	ARO 262	17 50.96	ARO 509	09 21.42
ARO 26	12 24.50	ARO 137	18 27.78	ARO 263	17 52.38	ARO 510	09 38.79
ARO 27	16 12.25	ARO 138	18 35.36	ARO 265	17 54.41	ARO 511	10 09.50
ARO 29	17 55.60	ARO 139	18 41.11	ARO 266	17 55.95	ARO 512	10 17.84
ARO 30	18 25.71	ARO 140	18 43.04	ARO 267	18 00.15	ARO 513	11 00.33
ARO 31	19 02.02	ARO 141	18 54.75	ARO 268	18 04.47	ARO 514	11 50.30
ARO 32	19 18.44	ARO 142	18 56.55	ARO 269	18 05.96	ARO 515	13 33.52
ARO 33	19 23.23	ARO 143	18 58.13	ARO 270	18 12.15	ARO 516	13 51.06
ARO 34	19 31.60	ARO 144	19 04.52	ARO 272	18 19.42	ARO 517	14 22.43
ARO 35	12 18.35	ARO 146	19 13.11	ARO 273	18 20.14	ARO 518	15 51.68
ARO 36	19 46.59	ARO 147	19 13.58	ARO 275	18 21.40	ARO 519	17 20.77
ARO 37	20 15.15	ARO 148	19 13.68	ARO 276	18 23.13	ARO 520	18 00.20
ARO 38	20 20.19	ARO 149	19 17.06	ARO 277	18 26.66	ARO 521	18 18.53
ARO 39	21 00.56	ARO 150	19 18.33	ARO 278	18 30.19	ARO 522	18 45.84
ARO 40	21 07.07	ARO 151	19 24.38	ARO 279	18 31.02	ARO 523	18 55.63
ARO 41	21 14.19	ARO 152	19 27.77	ARO 280	18 31.88	ARO 529	12 46.45
ARO 42	21 19.11	ARO 153	19 28.24	ARO 281	18 32.69	ARO 530	13 39.58
ARO 43	00 47.01	ARO 154	19 32.94	ARO 282	18 33.26	ARO 531	15 34.28
ARO 44	04 07.01	ARO 155	19 33.37	ARO 283	18 33.97	ARO 532	15 54.84
ARO 45	07 25.55	ARO 156	19 36.50	ARO 284	18 34.22	ARO 533	15 12.85
ARO 47	07 41.92	ARO 158	19 41.19	ARO 285	18 34.23	ARO 534	07 02.83
ARO 48	17 42.53	ARO 159	19 41.54	ARO 286	18 39.37	ARO 535	07 18.24
ARO 49	16 04.42	ARO 160	19 42.01	ARO 287	18 40.34	ARO 536	07 19.12
ARO 50	17 01.56	ARO 161	19 42.15	ARO 288	18 41.25	ARO 538	07 27.98
ARO 51	17 29.34	ARO 162	19 42.29	ARO 289	18 43.34	ARO 539	07 28.89
ARO 52	18 05.21	ARO 163	19 45.66	ARO 290	18 45.42	ARO 540	07 37.37
ARO 53	19 02.60	ARO 164	19 48.46	ARO 291	18 47.53	ARO 541	07 41.97
ARO 54	21 45.92	ARO 165	19 51.92	ARO 293	18 49.75	ARO 542	07 43.27
ARO 55	22 40.37	ARO 166	20 00.18	ARO 294	18 51.67	ARO 543	07 46.78
ARO 56	12 32.94	ARO 167	20 00.63	ARO 295	18 53.03	ARO 544	07 56.13
ARO 57	20 10.37	ARO 168	20 04.78	ARO 297	18 56.33	ARO 545	08 08.96
ARO 58	01 37.31	ARO 169	20 11.92	ARO 298	18 57.29	ARO 546	08 14.56
ARO 59	21 06.32	ARO 171	20 17.33	ARO 299	19 00.57	ARO 547	08 15.88
ARO 60	05 05.56	ARO 172	20 21.08	ARO 300	19 01.02	ARO 549	17 14.71
ARO 61	05 42.14	ARO 173	20 50.06	ARO 301	19 01.61	ARO 552	17 44.34
ARO 62	06 21.71	ARO 174	21 35.56	ARO 303	19 04.86	ARO 553	08 40.67
ARO 64	08 33.39	ARO 175	05 08.11	ARO 305	19 12.08	ARO 554	11 28.60
ARO 65	09 39.13	ARO 176	05 31.80	ARO 307	19 14.30	ARO 555	12 09.03
ARO 66	17 14.06	ARO 179	12 59.41	ARO 308	19 14.03	ARO 556	16 08.98
ARO 67	17 49.25	ARO 180	16 27.52	ARO 309	19 14.66	Abell 2	00 45.60
ARO 68	18 11.87	ARO 181	17 53.55	ARO 312	19 16.47	Abell 3	02 12.19
ARO 69	18 13.75	ARO 183	19 06.74	ARO 314	19 19.29	Abell 4	02 45.43
ARO 70	18 16.28	ARO 184	19 08.71	ARO 315	19 19.00	Abell 5	02 52.28
ARO 71	18 33.91	ARO 185	19 11.14	ARO 318	19 21.94	Abell 6	02 58.88
ARO 72	19 18.41	ARO 186	19 13.06	ARO 321	19 23.46	Abell 7	05 03.16
ARO 73	19 31.28	ARO 187	19 13.90	ARO 322	19 27.03	Abell 8	05 06.64
ARO 74	19 34.56	ARO 188	19 23.76	ARO 323	19 27.75	Abell 9	05 28.96
ARO 75	20 22.43	ARO 189	19 26.66	ARO 325	19 33.80	Abell 10	05 31.80
ARO 76	03 56.40	ARO 190	19 50.48	ARO 326	19 35.89	Abell 12	06 02.35
ARO 80	07 09.40	ARO 191	19 59.26	ARO 327	19 37.11	Abell 13	06 04.84
ARO 81	07 55.18	ARO 192	20 19.60	ARO 328	19 39.27	Abell 14	06 11.19
ARO 82	18 49.99	ARO 193	21 16.83	ARO 330	19 45.72	Abell 15	06 27.04
ARO 83	19 03.59	ARO 194	21 36.91	ARO 331	19 46.46	Abell 16	06 43.90
ARO 84	19 18.69	ARO 195	23 35.89	ARO 334	19 50.00	Abell 17	06 48.58
ARO 85	22 23.90	ARO 201	00 40.33	ARO 337	19 53.14	Abell 18	06 56.21
ARO 86	03 10.35	ARO 202	00 45.60	ARO 338	19 54.02	Abell 19	06 59.94
ARO 87	03 53.49	ARO 203	01 53.75	ARO 339	19 57.55	Abell 20	07 22.99
ARO 88	15 22.31	ARO 204	02 12.19	ARO 340	20 02.56	Abell 21	07 29.01
ARO 89	21 33.11	ARO 205	02 45.43	ARO 341	20 03.37	Abell 22	07 36.11
ARO 91	01 57.63	ARO 206	02 52.28	ARO 342	20 04.37	Abell 23	07 43.27
ARO 92	06 25.92	ARO 207	02 58.88	ARO 343	20 05.01	Abell 24	07 51.71
ARO 93	07 47.44	ARO 208	03 33.33	ARO 345	20 06.94	Abell 25	08 06.72
ARO 94	17 41.88	ARO 209	03 41.74	ARO 346	20 09.06	Abell 26	08 08.96
ARO 95	17 48.33	ARO 211	04 13.28	ARO 347	20 13.93	Abell 27	08 31.81
ARO 96	17 55.12	ARO 214	04 37.35	ARO 348	20 21.94	Abell 28	08 41.64
ARO 97	18 17.56	ARO 215	05 03.16	ARO 351	20 31.57	Abell 29	08 40.24
ARO 98	17 44.99	ARO 216	05 06.64	ARO 352	20 32.41	Abell 30	08 46.83
ARO 99	18 22.90	ARO 218	05 40.70	ARO 357	21 14.05	Abell 31	08 54.19
ARO 100	18 49.75	ARO 220	06 02.35	ARO 359	21 26.41	Abell 33	09 39.13
ARO 101	19 05.92	ARO 221	06 27.04	ARO 362	21 31.88	Abell 34	09 45.62
ARO 102	19 14.60	ARO 222	06 43.90	ARO 363	21 32.17	Abell 35	12 53.57
ARO 103	19 16.47	ARO 223	06 48.58	ARO 365	21 37.01	Abell 36	13 40.63
ARO 104	19 39.17	ARO 224	06 56.21	ARO 366	21 39.22	Abell 37	14 04.44
ARO 105	19 49.73	ARO 225	07 02.78	ARO 367	21 43.30	Abell 38	16 23.29
ARO 106	19 55.01	ARO 227	07 06.93	ARO 368	21 57.74	Abell 39	16 27.52
ARO 107	20 10.48	ARO 229	07 11.28	ARO 369	22 16.09	Abell 40	16 48.57
ARO 108	20 10.84	ARO 230	07 12.46	ARO 370	22 20.30	Abell 41	17 29.03

Cross Index of Planetary Nebulae by Name							
Abell 42	17 31.52	DS 3	09 52.7	ESO 170-07	11 33.29	ESO 289-19	22 21.12
Abell 43	17 53.55	Dd 1	20 08.72	ESO 170-06	11 28.60	ESO 312-05	08 28.46
Abell 44	18 30.19	DdDm 1	16 40.27	ESO 170-01	11 24.02	ESO 313-01	08 30.93
Abell 45	18 30.29	DeHt 1	17 06.9	ESO 170-13	11 50.30	ESO 313-05	08 37.13
Abell 46	18 31.20	DeHt 1	05 55.1	ESO 173-04	13 05.80	ESO 313-17	08 53.51
Abell 47	18 35.36	DeHt 2	17 41.7	ESO 173-01	13 00.68	ESO 316-27	10 07.00
Abell 48	18 42.82	DeHt 3	19 17.1	ESO 173-12	13 24.37	ESO 320-28	11 52.5
Abell 49	18 53.49	DeHt 4	19 26.4	ESO 175-07	14 20.81	ESO 328-34	15 12.85
Abell 50	18 59.35	DeHt 5	22 19.6	ESO 176-01	14 41.60	ESO 330-02	15 53.20
Abell 51	19 01.02	ESO 019-02	10 09.50	ESO 176-12	15 05.98	ESO 330-08	16 02.22
Abell 52	19 04.52	ESO 033-33	05 57.03	ESO 176-10	15 05.28	ESO 331-06	16 31.51
Abell 53	19 06.74	ESO 040-11	13 34.24	ESO 177-05	15 25.54	ESO 331-08	16 42.56
Abell 54	19 08.71	ESO 041-03	14 15.51	ESO 177-03	15 23.71	ESO 331-01	16 19.38
Abell 55	19 10.51	ESO 046-03	19 33.79	ESO 177-01	15 11.94	ESO 332-01	16 46.75
Abell 56	19 13.11	ESO 063-18	11 39.18	ESO 177-02	15 22.32	ESO 332-07	16 54.46
Abell 57	19 17.06	ESO 068-08	15 37.17	ESO 177-04	15 23.60	ESO 332-02	16 49.53
Abell 58	19 18.33	ESO 070-01	17 01.28	ESO 177-10	15 41.98	ESO 332-04	16 50.65
Abell 59	19 18.69	ESO 092-11	10 07.40	ESO 178-07	16 00.99	ESO 332-03	16 50.42
Abell 60	19 19.29	ESO 092-23	10 35.77	ESO 178-05	15 59.96	ESO 332-18	17 04.56
Abell 61	19 19.17	ESO 093-04	11 00.33	ESO 178-04	15 58.13	ESO 332-15	16 57.39
Abell 62	19 33.37	ESO 094-07	11 48.65	ESO 178-10	16 10.67	ESO 332-21	17 05.18
Abell 63	19 42.15	ESO 094-03	11 31.75	ESO 178-14	16 14.41	ESO 332-24	17 10.45
Abell 64	19 45.66	ESO 094-14	12 08.42	ESO 178-15	16 14.53	ESO 333-05	17 22.26
Abell 65	19 46.59	ESO 094-12	12 04.22	ESO 178-16	16 15.35	ESO 333-12	17 32.37
Abell 66	19 57.55	ESO 095-08	12 23.03	ESO 179-05	16 24.63	ESO 333-11	17 32.87
Abell 67	19 58.41	ESO 095-01	12 09.03	ESO 179-06	16 27.84	ESO 333-13	17 32.79
Abell 68	20 00.18	ESO 095-09	12 28.78	ESO 179-07	16 29.89	ESO 334-01	17 36.50
Abell 69	20 19.94	ESO 095-11	12 30.12	ESO 179-04	16 24.35	ESO 334-05	17 42.90
Abell 70	20 31.57	ESO 095-17	12 46.45	ESO 179-08	16 30.00	ESO 334-06	17 45.11
Abell 71	20 32.41	ESO 095-12	12 30.41	ESO 179-03	16 22.23	ESO 334-09	17 50.74
Abell 72	20 50.06	ESO 095-13	12 30.51	ESO 179-11	16 37.71	ESO 334-10	18 00.20
Abell 73	20 56.51	ESO 096-07	13 19.51	ESO 179-10	16 35.34	ESO 335-01	18 04.94
Abell 74	21 16.83	ESO 096-02	13 08.79	ESO 180-04	17 11.75	ESO 337-20	19 17.39
Abell 75	21 26.41	ESO 096-09	13 22.55	ESO 180-07	17 22.60	ESO 344-05	21 59.53
Abell 77	21 32.17	ESO 096-16	13 33.52	ESO 182-04	18 09.50	ESO 364-25	06 02.11
Abell 78	21 35.56	ESO 097-01	13 39.58	ESO 182-02	18 00.98	ESO 368-10	07 43.27
Abell 79	22 26.33	ESO 097-08	13 52.51	ESO 209-01	07 47.33	ESO 369-02	07 52.96
Abell 80	22 34.73	ESO 097-09	13 53.95	ESO 209-19	08 11.53	ESO 369-05	08 08.96
Abell 81	22 42.59	ESO 097-16	14 18.74	ESO 209-15	08 05.2	ESO 369-04	08 04.24
Abell 82	23 45.85	ESO 097-11	14 05.61	ESO 211-04	08 54.30	ESO 370-09	08 20.90
Abell 83	23 46.76	ESO 099-01	15 10.69	ESO 212-08	09 31.40	ESO 370-18	08 36.27
Abell 84	23 47.68	ESO 100-03	15 56.03	ESO 212-14	09 41.62	ESO 371-06	08 41.16
Al 1	18 34.92	ESO 101-16	16 54.58	ESO 212-13	09 41.23	ESO 372-13	09 16.03
Al 2-A	!7 26.94	ESO 126-01	09 12.61	ESO 213-07	10 13.26	ESO 378-01	11 26.73
Al 2-B	17 27.8	ESO 126-06	09 19.46	ESO 213-01	09 47.41	ESO 382-63	13 25.62
Al 2-D	17 29.5	ESO 126-08	09 21.42	ESO 215-04	10 54.7	ESO 389-07	16 01.35
Al 2-E	17 30.2	ESO 127-03	10 03.83	ESO 215-35	11 13.84	ESO 389-09	16 03.36
Al 2-F	17 30.5	ESO 127-12	10 15.58	ESO 216-02	11 18.17	ESO 389-16	16 13.46
Al 2-G	17 32.4	ESO 127-16	10 23.15	ESO 217-11	11 53.06	ESO 389-15	16 12.98
Al 2-H	17 33.3	ESO 127-15	10 17.84	ESO 221-11	13 51.06	ESO 389-14	16 08.44
Al 2-I	17 34.2	ESO 127-18	10 09.34	ESO 221-31	14 11.86	ESO 390-07	16 34.07
Al 2-J	17 35.5	ESO 127-22	10 28.54	ESO 221-36	14 18.14	ESO 391-01	16 39.46
Al 2-K	17 36.3	ESO 128-09	10 44.53	ESO 222-13	14 40.52	ESO 391-08	17 02.31
Al 2-L	17 46.03	ESO 128-19	10 54.59	ESO 223-10	15 01.67	ESO 391-07	17 01.10
Al 2-M	17 47.8	ESO 128-18	10 53.99	ESO 224-03	15 25.13	ESO 391-03	16 48.90
Al 2-O	17 51.8	ESO 128-29	11 03.94	ESO 225-02	15 51.68	ESO 392-01	17 03.78
Al 2-P	17 51.75	ESO 128-20	10 55.99	ESO 225-05	16 08.98	ESO 392-05	17 13.73
Al 2-Q	17 53.4	ESO 129-22	11 28.79	ESO 225-01	15 51.26	ESO 392-02	17 04.60
Al 2-R	17 53.6	ESO 129-21	11 27.96	ESO 225-08	16 15.33	ESO 392-06	17 14.71
Ap 1-2	18 58.13	ESO 129-29	11 41.68	ESO 225-03	15 54.84	ESO 392-12	17 26.40
Ap 1-12	18 11.58	ESO 129-26	11 35.18	ESO 225-09	16 17.23	ESO 393-01	17 28.46
Ap 4-1	19 28.24	ESO 130-07	12 09.16	ESO 226-15	16 34.22	ESO 393-06	17 33.01
BV 2	00 40.33	ESO 131-08	12 28.72	ESO 227-05	17 06.24	ESO 393-16	17 44.23
BV 3	01 53.75	ESO 131-01	12 23.89	ESO 227-02	17 01.62	ESO 393-19	17 44.34
Baade 1	03 53.49	ESO 131-15	12 45.92	ESO 227-06	17 09.60	ESO 393-26	17 47.82
Bl 2-1	22 20.30	ESO 132-01	13 09.60	ESO 227-01	16 59.60	ESO 393-21	17 45.54
Bl 3-8	17 55.60	ESO 133-02	13 43.99	ESO 228-01	17 20.77	ESO 393-29	17 49.23
Bl 3-10	17 55.33	ESO 133-08	13 58.23	ESO 228-06	17 36.11	ESO 393-27	17 48.96
Bl 3-12	17 56.40	ESO 133-01	13 42.63	ESO 229-06	18 07.27	ESO 393-24	17 46.76
Bl 3-13	17 56.04	ESO 134-07	14 33.29	ESO 247-13	02 56.97	ESO 393-23	17 46.10
Bl 3-14	17 52.40	ESO 135-02	15 04.14	ESO 256-19	07 14.82	ESO 393-35	17 50.75
Bl 3-15	17 52.58	ESO 135-04	15 08.71	ESO 259-06	08 24.12	ESO 393-31	17 49.80
Bl B	17 36.99	ESO 135-03	15 06.03	ESO 259-03	08 21.07	ESO 393-37	17 51.21
Bl C	17 45.96	ESO 135-11	15 34.28	ESO 259-04	08 20.67	ESO 393-33	17 49.80
Bl E	17 47.93	ESO 136-01	15 38.02	ESO 259-10	08 34.1	ESO 393-32	17 49.84
Bl F	17 50.30	ESO 136-03	15 47.68	ESO 260-08	08 48.64	ESO 394-07	17 53.35
Bl G	17 50.39	ESO 136-05	15 52.18	ESO 260-05	08 43.47	ESO 394-04	17 52.58
Bl M	17 53.78	ESO 136-11	15 59.14	ESO 261-04	09 16.16	ESO 394-05	17 52.98
Bl O	17 53.82	ESO 137-09	16 15.69	ESO 263-02	10 05.77	ESO 394-06	17 53.28
Bl Q	17 54.58	ESO 137-22	16 23.51	ESO 268-12	12 30.88	ESO 394-02	17 51.85
BlDz 1	11 53.06	ESO 137-30	16 29.51	ESO 272-06	14 22.43	ESO 394-08	17 53.63
Bn 0808+11	08 11.2	ESO 166-07	09 18.02	ESO 273-16	15 06.23	ESO 394-13	17 57.32
Bn 0950+13	09 53.0	ESO 166-02	09 08.67	ESO 274-07	15 16.84	ESO 394-14	17 57.42
CRL 618	04 42.88	ESO 166-05	09 13.88	ESO 276-04	16 30.43	ESO 394-15	17 58.24
CTIO 1230-275	12 33.2	ESO 166-06	09 15.13	ESO 276-03	16 23.88	ESO 394-10	17 54.55
CTS 1	18 07.0	ESO 166-13	09 27.04	ESO 277-17	16 53.50	ESO 394-16	17 58.55
CTS 2	19 19.3	ESO 166-18	09 30.81	ESO 278-04	17 06.98	ESO 394-17	18 00.31
CTSS 1	19 02.2	ESO 166-19	09 30.91	ESO 278-09	17 26.20	ESO 394-19	18 01.71
CTSS 2	18 50.7	ESO 166-10	09 24.76	ESO 278-08	17 19.53	ESO 394-18	18 01.37
CTSS 3	19 03.1	ESO 166-21	09 31.45	ESO 278-01	17 05.60	ESO 394-25	18 04.09
CTSS 4	19 06.4	ESO 167-02	09 40.89	ESO 278-03	17 06.37	ESO 394-22	18 02.53
Cn 1-1	15 51.26	ESO 167-03	09 43.43	ESO 278-05	17 11.45	ESO 394-26	18 04.49
Cn 1-3	17 26.20	ESO 168-06	10 31.56	ESO 278-10	17 27.81	ESO 394-27	18 04.94
Cn 1-4	17 27.81	ESO 168-05	10 31.53	ESO 279-04	17 39.33	ESO 394-24	18 03.89
Cn 1-5	18 29.19	ESO 168-08	10 34.31	ESO 279-06	17 45.48	ESO 394-20	18 02.05
Cn 1-6	18 55.63	ESO 168-12	10 39.55	ESO 279-07	17 45.59	ESO 394-21	18 02.54
Cn 2-1	17 54.55	ESO 168-13	10 41.33	ESO 279-01	17 35.69	ESO 394-31	18 09.82
Cn 3-1	18 17.56	ESO 168-10	10 38.47	ESO 279-12	17 56.56	ESO 394-33	18 12.04
DS 1	10 54.7	ESO 169-03	10 48.73	ESO 279-14	17 59.61	ESO 394-35	18 14.84
DS 2	15 43.0	ESO 170-05	11 27.40	ESO 280-08	18 18.53	ESO 395-07	18 27.80

Cross Index of Planetary Nebulae by Name

Name		Name		Name		Name	
ESO 396-02	18 45.84	ESO 456-54	18 07.10	ESO 559-06	07 21.25	H 1-23	17 32.78
ESO 397-02	19 05.59	ESO 456-58	18 08.06	ESO 559-03	07 19.35	H 1-24	17 33.62
ESO 397-07	19 14.39	ESO 456-52	18 06.09	ESO 559-11	07 27.94	H 1-26	17 36.50
ESO 398-07	19 32.11	ESO 456-57	18 07.90	ESO 560-09	07 41.92	H 1-27	17 40.30
ESO 422-58	17 52.58	ESO 456-68	18 11.49	ESO 560-16	07 50.22	H 1-28	17 42.90
ESO 427-19	06 55.2	ESO 456-69	18 11.58	ESO 561-16	08 08.73	H 1-29	17 44.23
ESO 431-14	08 31.81	ESO 456-67	18 11.08	ESO 563-09	08 40.24	H 1-30	17 45.11
ESO 432-14	08 57.82	ESO 456-71	18 12.40	ESO 568-05	10 24.81	H 1-31	17 45.54
ESO 436-41	10 34.51	ESO 456-76	18 13.30	ESO 573-19	12 24.50	H 1-32	17 46.10
ESO 452-01	16 23.29	ESO 456-74	18 12.56	ESO 577-24	13 40.63	H 1-33	17 47.82
ESO 452-12	16 41.72	ESO 456-70	18 11.87	ESO 586-03	16 48.57	H 1-34	17 48.13
ESO 453-09	16 53.62	ESO 456-75	18 12.79	ESO 586-01	16 43.82	H 1-35	17 49.23
ESO 453-02	16 44.82	ESO 456-80	18 15.10	ESO 587-07	17 21.29	H 1-36	17 49.80
ESO 453-06	16 50.28	ESO 457-04	18 17.61	ESO 587-01	17 01.56	H 1-37	17 50.74
ESO 453-10	16 55.78	ESO 457-05	18 17.68	ESO 588-05	17 33.62	H 1-38	17 50.75
ESO 453-16	17 04.31	ESO 457-07	18 18.69	ESO 588-08	17 35.16	H 1-39	17 53.35
ESO 453-18	17 05.51	ESO 457-06	18 17.66	ESO 588-03	17 28.96	H 1-40	17 55.60
ESO 453-17	17 05.23	ESO 457-03	18 16.32	ESO 588-09	17 35.35	H 1-41	17 57.32
ESO 454-01	17 14.11	ESO 457-08	18 18.64	ESO 588-02	17 24.80	H 1-42	17 57.42
ESO 454-09	17 19.32	ESO 457-02	18 16.21	ESO 588-14	17 38.95	H 1-43	17 58.24
ESO 454-07	17 18.87	ESO 457-10	18 22.57	ESO 588-15	17 39.91	H 1-44	17 58.18
ESO 454-05	17 17.27	ESO 457-12	18 29.19	ESO 588-17	17 41.61	H 1-45	17 58.36
ESO 454-11	17 20.55	ESO 457-16	18 32.52	ESO 588-11	17 37.37	H 1-46	17 59.04
ESO 454-19	17 24.57	ESO 458-01	18 39.42	ESO 588-10	17 36.38	H 1-47	18 00.63
ESO 454-14	17 21.52	ESO 458-04	18 44.23	ESO 588-12	17 38.19	H 1-50	18 03.89
ESO 454-16	17 23.41	ESO 458-09	18 55.63	ESO 588-13	17 38.50	H 1-51	18 04.49
ESO 454-18	17 24.44	ESO 459-17	19 22.17	ESO 588-16	17 40.30	H 1-52	18 04.94
ESO 454-13	17 21.07	ESO 490-01	06 27.04	ESO 589-02	17 45.52	H 1-53	18 05.96
ESO 454-28	17 27.40	ESO 493-19	07 49.67	ESO 589-01	17 43.48	H 1-54	18 07.11
ESO 454-27	17 27.34	ESO 494-02	07 55.18	ESO 589-06	17 47.63	H 1-55	18 07.65
ESO 454-24	17 25.31	ESO 514-12	15 22.31	ESO 589-03	17 46.24	H 1-56	18 07.90
ESO 454-23	17 25.10	ESO 518-11	17 05.77	ESO 589-04	17 46.27	H 1-57	18 09.82
ESO 454-26	!7 26.94	ESO 519-07	17 10.70	ESO 589-05	17 47.57	H 1-58	18 09.23
ESO 454-25	17 25.99	ESO 519-14	17 22.42	ESO 589-07	17 48.62	H 1-59	18 11.49
ESO 454-22	17 24.87	ESO 519-16	17 24.03	ESO 589-09	17 49.25	H 1-60	18 12.42
ESO 454-21	17 24.68	ESO 519-17	17 25.72	ESO 589-11	17 50.48	H 1-61	18 12.57
ESO 454-34	17 28.66	ESO 519-18	17 25.73	ESO 589-16	17 52.69	H 1-62	18 13.30
ESO 454-36	17 28.84	ESO 519-19	17 28.06	ESO 589-10	17 50.46	H 1-63	18 16.32
ESO 454-31	17 27.55	ESO 519-12	17 19.22	ESO 589-15	17 52.38	H 1-64	18 18.39
ESO 455-06	17 30.38	ESO 519-10	17 12.65	ESO 589-12	17 50.96	H 1-65	18 20.14
ESO 455-02	17 29.67	ESO 519-13	17 21.18	ESO 589-14	17 52.08	H 1-66	18 24.95
ESO 455-03	17 29.72	ESO 520-09	17 34.91	ESO 589-19	17 53.61	H 1-67	18 25.08
ESO 455-09	17 30.81	ESO 520-06	17 30.92	ESO 589-20	17 55.12	H 2-1	17 04.60
ESO 455-05	17 30.04	ESO 520-03	17 29.34	ESO 589-23	17 57.11	H 2-7	17 23.41
ESO 455-12	17 31.13	ESO 520-01	17 28.62	ESO 589-21	17 55.95	H 2-8	17 24.80
ESO 455-10	17 30.97	ESO 520-02	17 29.39	ESO 589-25	18 00.15	H 2-10	17 27.55
ESO 455-13	17 31.15	ESO 520-08	17 34.45	ESO 590-05	18 11.81	H 2-11	17 29.43
ESO 455-16	17 32.78	ESO 520-05	17 30.78	ESO 590-01	18 05.21	H 2-13	17 31.13
ESO 455-21	17 35.25	ESO 520-04	17 29.43	ESO 590-08	18 13.75	H 2-14	17 32.87
ESO 455-20	17 35.24	ESO 520-15	17 40.21	ESO 590-02	18 08.43	H 2-15	17 34.45
ESO 455-24	17 35.80	ESO 520-17	17 41.88	ESO 590-18	18 23.13	H 2-16	17 39.91
ESO 455-28	17 38.67	ESO 520-16	17 40.47	ESO 590-12	18 16.28	H 2-17	17 40.12
ESO 455-26	17 36.99	ESO 520-14	17 40.12	ESO 591-09	18 36.53	H 2-18	17 43.48
ESO 455-27	17 37.76	ESO 520-10	17 35.97	ESO 591-03	18 29.49	H 2-20	17 45.66
ESO 455-34	17 46.03	ESO 520-18	17 41.95	ESO 591-02	18 29.18	H 2-22	17 47.57
ESO 455-33	17 45.96	ESO 520-28	17 48.13	ESO 591-04	18 30.00	H 2-23	17 48.96
ESO 455-48	17 50.39	ESO 520-23	17 45.66	ESO 591-08	18 35.80	H 2-24	17 48.60
ESO 455-47	17 50.30	ESO 520-29	17 48.60	ESO 591-05	18 30.57	H 2-25	17 49.01
ESO 455-42	17 47.93	ESO 520-22	17 45.61	ESO 591-07	18 33.35	H 2-26	17 49.84
ESO 455-55	17 52.40	ESO 520-30	17 49.01	ESO 591-13	18 41.93	H 2-27	17 51.85
ESO 455-54	17 51.75	ESO 521-14	18 03.20	ESO 591-15	18 44.03	H 2-29	17 53.28
ESO 455-51	17 51.31	ESO 521-17	18 03.65	ESO 591-10	18 36.56	H 2-31	17 56.04
ESO 455-53	17 52.10	ESO 521-15	18 03.30	ESO 591-16	18 45.58	H 2-32	17 56.40
ESO 456-08	17 30.73	ESO 521-27	18 06.68	ESO 591-11	18 37.18	H 2-33	17 58.20
ESO 456-07	17 53.76	ESO 521-24	18 05.96	ESO 592-06	18 55.51	H 2-35	18 00.31
ESO 456-02	17 52.77	ESO 521-30	18 07.89	ESO 594-10	19 40.54	H 2-36	18 04.13
ESO 456-15	17 55.10	ESO 521-34	18 09.23	ESO 595-04	19 57.55	H 2-37	18 04.47
ESO 456-17	17 55.60	ESO 522-06	18 13.26	El 0103+73	01 07.2	H 2-39	18 08.06
ESO 456-10	17 53.78	ESO 522-02	18 12.42	El 0419+72	04 25.2	H 2-40	18 08.43
ESO 456-19	17 56.04	ESO 522-03	18 12.42	El 1647+64	16 47.6	H 2-41	18 12.40
ESO 456-14	17 54.58	ESO 522-07	18 13.68	Fg 1	11 28.60	H 2-42	18 12.42
ESO 456-11	17 53.82	ESO 522-08	18 14.47	Fg 2	17 39.33	H 2-43	18 12.79
ESO 456-18	17 56.04	ESO 522-04	18 12.57	Fg 3	18 00.20	H 2-44	18 13.68
ESO 456-12	17 54.41	ESO 522-14	18 18.22	G339.2-0.4	16 45.5	H 2-45	18 14.47
ESO 456-16	17 55.33	ESO 522-12	18 17.27	Gr 0155+10	01 58.0	H 2-46	18 18.69
ESO 456-27	17 58.36	ESO 522-13	18 17.79	Gum 27	09 27.04	H 2-48	18 46.59
ESO 456-20	17 56.40	ESO 522-17	18 19.42	Gum 47	13 33.52	H 3-29	04 37.35
ESO 456-22	17 57.81	ESO 522-11	18 16.29	Gum 60	17 13.73	H 3-75	05 40.70
ESO 456-23	17 58.18	ESO 522-18	18 20.14	H 1-1	16 13.46	H 4-1	12 59.41
ESO 456-21	17 56.43	ESO 522-10	18 16.18	H 1-2	16 48.90	HFG 1	03 03.7
ESO 456-25	17 58.20	ESO 522-15	18 18.39	H 1-3	16 53.50	HFG 2	07 42.4
ESO 456-26	17 58.31	ESO 522-25	18 25.08	H 1-4	16 53.62	Hb 1	03 10.35
ESO 456-24	17 58.16	ESO 522-24	18 24.95	H 1-5	16 57.39	Hb 3	16 12.98
ESO 456-36	18 01.16	ESO 522-20	18 22.02	H 1-6	17 06.98	Hb 4	17 41.88
ESO 456-35	18 00.63	ESO 522-27	18 27.99	H 1-7	17 10.45	Hb 5	17 47.93
ESO 456-32	17 59.32	ESO 522-23	18 32.58	H 1-8	17 14.71	Hb 6	17 55.12
ESO 456-30	17 58.51	ESO 522-22	18 22.90	H 1-9	17 21.52	Hb 7	18 55.63
ESO 456-39	18 02.31	ESO 522-26	18 25.71	H 1-10	17 22.26	Hb 8	19 05.59
ESO 456-31	17 59.04	ESO 522-21	18 22.53	H 1-11	17 21.29	Hb 9	21 14.19
ESO 456-34	18 01.70	ESO 522-31	18 31.88	H 1-12	17 26.40	Hb 12	23 26.29
ESO 456-44	18 03.88	ESO 523-09	18 48.20	H 1-13	17 28.46	HbDS 1	09 52.7
ESO 456-49	18 05.04	ESO 523-07	18 46.59	H 1-14	17 28.06	He 1-1	19 23.76
ESO 456-40	18 02.77	ESO 523-02	18 34.92	H 1-15	17 28.62	He 1-2	19 26.66
ESO 456-45	18 04.13	ESO 523-06	18 44.68	H 1-16	17 29.39	He 1-3	19 48.46
ESO 456-43	17 59.94	ESO 523-01	18 33.91	H 1-17	17 29.67	He 1-4	19 59.26
ESO 456-46	18 04.47	ESO 523-03	18 34.86	H 1-18	17 29.72	He 1-5	20 11.92
ESO 456-59	18 08.43	ESO 523-10	18 50.43	H 1-19	17 30.04	He 1-6	20 17.33
ESO 456-55	18 07.11	ESO 526-03	19 46.59	H 1-20	17 30.73	He 1-7	20 19.60
ESO 456-50	18 05.43	ESO 558-11	07 06.93	H 1-21	17 32.79	He 1-48	18 02.31
ESO 456-56	18 07.65	ESO 558-14	07 11.28	H 1-22	17 32.37	He 2-1	07 02.83

Cross Index of Planetary Nebulae by Name							
He 2-2	07 14.82	He 2-116	15 06.03	He 2-229	17 28.62	He 2-340	18 05.21
He 2-3	07 28.89	He 2-117	15 05.98	He 2-230	17 28.56	He 2-341	18 07.27
He 2-4	07 47.44	He 2-118	15 06.23	He 2-231	17 29.39	He 2-342	18 05.96
He 2-5	07 47.33	He 2-119	15 10.69	He 2-232	17 29.34	He 2-344	18 06.09
He 2-6	08 02.48	He 2-120	15 11.94	He 2-233	17 29.67	He 2-345	18 06.68
He 2-7	08 11.53	He 2-121	15 12.85	He 2-234	17 29.72	He 2-346	18 07.11
He 2-8	08 20.67	He 2-122	15 16.84	He 2-235	17 28.96	He 2-347	18 07.65
He 2-9	08 28.46	He 2-123	15 22.32	He 2-236	17 29.03	He 2-348	18 07.10
He 2-11	08 37.13	He 2-124	15 23.71	He 2-237	17 30.04	He 2-350	18 07.89
He 2-12	08 40.67	He 2-125	15 23.60	He 2-238	17 30.73	He 2-351	18 07.51
He 2-13	08 43.47	He 2-126	15 22.31	He 2-239	17 30.78	He 2-352	18 08.43
He 2-15	08 53.51	He 2-128	15 25.13	He 2-240	17 31.15	He 2-353	18 09.82
He 2-16	08 54.30	He 2-129	15 25.54	He 2-241	17 32.37	He 2-359	18 11.08
He 2-18	09 08.67	He 2-130	15 34.28	He 2-242	17 32.78	He 2-360	18 11.58
He 2-19	09 07.11	He 2-131	15 37.17	He 2-244	17 33.62	He 2-361	18 12.04
He 2-20	09 12.44	He 2-132	15 38.02	He 2-246	17 35.69	He 2-362	18 11.87
He 2-21	09 13.88	He 2-133	15 41.98	He 2-248	17 36.11	He 2-363	18 11.81
He 2-22	09 15.13	He 2-135	15 47.68	He 2-249	17 34.45	He 2-364	18 12.57
He 2-23	09 16.03	He 2-136	15 52.18	He 2-250	17 34.91	He 2-365	18 12.56
He 2-24	09 16.16	He 2-137	15 51.68	He 2-252	17 35.16	He 2-366	18 12.79
He 2-25	09 18.02	He 2-138	15 56.03	He 2-253	17 36.50	He 2-367	18 13.30
He 2-26	09 19.46	He 2-140	15 58.13	He 2-254	17 35.35	He 2-368	18 13.26
He 2-27	09 21.42	He 2-141	15 59.14	He 2-255	17 36.38	He 2-369	18 13.75
He 2-28	09 22.11	He 2-142	15 59.96	He 2-256	17 37.37	He 2-371	18 14.84
He 2-29	09 24.76	He 2-143	16 00.99	He 2-257	17 39.33	He 2-372	18 15.10
He 2-30	09 27.04	He 2-144	16 01.35	He 2-258	17 38.19	He 2-375	18 18.14
He 2-31	09 30.81	He 2-145	16 08.98	He 2-259	17 38.50	He 2-377	18 16.21
He 2-32	09 30.91	He 2-146	16 10.67	He 2-260	17 38.95	He 2-378	18 16.18
He 2-33	09 38.79	He 2-148	16 12.98	He 2-261	17 39.91	He 2-379	18 16.29
He 2-34	09 41.23	He 2-149	16 14.41	He 2-262	17 40.21	He 2-380	18 16.32
He 2-35	09 41.62	He 2-150	16 14.53	He 2-263	17 40.12	He 2-381	18 16.28
He 2-36	09 43.43	He 2-151	16 15.69	He 2-264	17 40.47	He 2-382	18 17.27
He 2-37	09 47.41	He 2-152	16 15.33	He 2-265	17 40.30	He 2-383	18 18.53
He 2-39	10 03.83	He 2-153	16 17.23	He 2-266	17 41.88	He 2-384	18 17.61
He 2-40	10 07.00	He 2-154	16 17.23	He 2-267	17 41.95	He 2-385	18 17.68
He 2-41	10 07.40	He 2-155	16 19.38	He 2-268	17 42.90	He 2-386	18 18.39
He 2-42	10 09.34	He 2-157	16 22.23	He 2-270	17 44.23	He 2-387	18 18.64
He 2-43	10 13.26	He 2-158	16 23.51	He 2-271	17 44.34	He 2-388	18 19.42
He 2-44	10 09.50	He 2-159	16 24.35	He 2-272	17 45.11	He 2-389	18 20.14
He 2-45	10 15.58	He 2-160	16 23.88	He 2-273	17 45.48	He 2-391	18 22.02
He 2-46	10 17.84	He 2-161	16 24.63	He 2-274	17 45.59	He 2-392	18 22.57
He 2-47	10 23.15	He 2-162	16 27.84	He 2-276	17 45.54	He 2-393	18 22.53
He 2-48	10 31.53	He 2-163	16 29.51	He 2-277	17 45.96	He 2-394	18 22.90
He 2-49	10 31.56	He 2-164	16 29.89	He 2-278	17 46.10	He 2-395	18 23.13
He 2-50	10 34.31	He 2-165	16 30.00	He 2-279	17 45.52	He 2-397	18 24.95
He 2-51	10 35.77	He 2-166	16 30.43	He 2-280	17 46.76	He 2-398	18 25.08
He 2-52	10 38.47	He 2-167	16 31.51	He 2-281	17 46.24	He 2-399	18 25.71
He 2-53	10 39.55	He 2-169	16 34.22	He 2-282	17 46.27	He 2-400	18 27.99
He 2-54	10 44.53	He 2-170	16 35.34	He 2-283	17 47.82	He 2-401	18 27.94
He 2-55	10 48.73	He 2-171	16 34.07	He 2-284	17 46.91	He 2-402	18 29.19
He 2-56	10 54.59	He 2-172	16 37.71	He 2-285	17 47.63	He 2-403	18 29.18
He 2-57	10 55.99	He 2-175	16 39.46	He 2-286	17 47.93	He 2-404	18 29.49
He 2-59	11 00.33	He 2-178	16 42.56	He 2-287	17 48.33	He 2-406	18 31.88
He 2-60	11 03.94	He 2-180	16 43.82	He 2-288	17 49.23	He 2-407	18 32.52
He 2-62	11 17.72	He 2-181	16 48.90	He 2-289	17 49.80	He 2-408	18 32.58
He 2-63	11 24.02	He 2-182	16 54.58	He 2-290	17 49.25	He 2-409	18 33.35
He 2-64	11 27.40	He 2-184	16 55.78	He 2-291	17 50.74	He 2-410	18 33.91
He 2-65	11 27.96	He 2-185	17 01.28	He 2-292	17 50.30	He 2-411	18 33.48
He 2-66	11 28.60	He 2-186	16 59.60	He 2-293	17 50.48	He 2-412	18 35.80
He 2-67	11 28.79	He 2-187	17 01.62	He 2-295	17 52.98	He 2-413	18 36.14
He 2-68	11 31.75	He 2-188	17 01.10	He 2-296	17 52.77	He 2-414	18 36.56
He 2-69	11 33.29	He 2-189	17 01.56	He 2-297	17 52.58	He 2-415	18 37.77
He 2-70	11 35.18	He 2-190	17 02.31	He 2-298	17 52.08	He 2-416	18 39.42
He 2-71	11 39.18	He 2-191	17 03.78	He 2-299	17 52.69	He 2-418	18 44.23
He 2-72	11 41.68	He 2-192	17 04.31	He 2-300	17 53.35	He 2-419	18 44.03
He 2-73	11 48.65	He 2-193	17 05.18	He 2-301	17 53.63	He 2-420	18 44.68
He 2-74	11 50.30	He 2-194	17 04.60	He 2-302	17 53.76	He 2-421	18 45.84
He 2-75	12 04.22	He 2-195	17 06.24	He 2-303	17 54.55	He 2-422	18 46.59
He 2-76	12 08.42	He 2-196	17 05.23	He 2-304	17 54.41	He 2-423	18 48.20
He 2-77	12 09.03	He 2-197	17 05.51	He 2-305	17 55.12	He 2-424	18 50.43
He 2-78	12 09.16	He 2-198	17 06.37	He 2-306	17 56.56	He 2-425	18 55.63
He 2-81	12 23.03	He 2-199	17 06.98	He 2-307	17 56.43	He 2-426	19 05.59
He 2-82	12 23.89	He 2-200	17 10.45	He 2-308	17 57.32	He 2-428	19 13.06
He 2-83	12 28.72	He 2-201	17 11.75	He 2-309	17 56.33	He 2-429	19 13.68
He 2-84	12 28.78	He 2-202	17 10.70	He 2-310	17 57.42	He 2-430	19 14.03
He 2-85	12 30.12	He 2-203	17 12.65	He 2-311	17 57.11	He 2-431	19 17.39
He 2-86	12 30.51	He 2-204	17 13.73	He 2-313	17 58.24	He 2-432	19 23.46
He 2-88	13 05.80	He 2-205	17 14.11	He 2-314	17 58.18	He 2-433	19 23.76
He 2-89	13 08.79	He 2-206	17 14.06	He 2-315	17 58.16	He 2-434	19 33.79
He 2-90	13 09.60	He 2-207	17 19.53	He 2-316	17 58.55	He 2-435	19 26.66
He 2-92	13 22.55	He 2-208	17 20.77	He 2-318	17 59.04	He 2-436	19 32.11
He 2-95	13 39.58	He 2-209	17 19.22	He 2-319	17 59.32	He 2-437	19 32.94
He 2-96	13 42.63	He 2-210	17 20.55	He 2-320	18 00.20	He 2-438	19 34.76
He 2-97	13 45.38	He 2-211	17 21.07	He 2-321	17 58.98	He 2-439	19 36.50
He 2-98	13 51.06	He 2-212	17 21.18	He 2-322	18 00.15	He 2-440	19 38.18
He 2-99	13 52.51	He 2-213	17 21.52	He 2-323	18 00.63	He 2-441	19 39.17
He 2-100	13 53.95	He 2-214	17 21.29	He 2-324	18 01.37	He 2-443	19 41.19
He 2-102	13 58.23	He 2-215	17 22.26	He 2-326	18 01.70	He 2-444	19 41.54
He 2-103	14 05.61	He 2-216	17 22.42	He 2-327	18 02.05	He 2-445	19 42.29
He 2-104	14 11.86	He 2-217	17 24.03	He 2-328	18 02.54	He 2-447	19 45.37
He 2-105	14 15.51	He 2-218	17 24.57	He 2-329	18 02.53	He 2-448	19 48.46
He 2-107	14 18.74	He 2-219	17 24.87	He 2-330	18 02.77	He 2-449	19 50.48
He 2-108	14 18.14	He 2-220	17 26.20	He 2-332	18 03.20	He 2-450	19 51.92
He 2-109	14 20.81	He 2-221	17 25.72	He 2-333	18 03.30	He 2-451	19 55.01
He 2-110	14 22.43	He 2-222	17 26.40	He 2-334	18 03.89	He 2-452	19 59.56
He 2-111	14 33.29	He 2-223	17 25.99	He 2-335	18 03.88	He 2-453	19 59.26
He 2-112	14 40.52	He 2-224	17 27.81	He 2-336	18 03.65	He 2-454	20 04.78
He 2-113	14 59.89	He 2-225	17 27.34	He 2-337	18 04.94	He 2-455	20 10.48
He 2-114	15 04.14	He 2-226	17 27.55	He 2-338	18 05.04	He 2-456	20 10.84
He 2-115	15 05.28	He 2-227	17 28.46	He 2-339	18 05.43	He 2-457	20 11.92

Cross Index of Planetary Nebulae by Name							
He 2-458	20 12.72	IRAS 21282+5050	21 30.0	K 3-63	21 39.22	LoTr 2	08 24.12
He 2-459	20 13.93	IsWe 1	03 49.2	K 3-64	04 13.45	LoTr 3	08 34.1
He 2-460	20 16.42	IsWe 2	22 13.3	K 3-65	04 15.91	LoTr 4	11 52.5
He 2-462	20 17.33	J 320	05 05.56	K 3-66	04 36.62	LoTr 5	12 55.5
He 2-463	20 19.60	J 900	06 25.92	K 3-67	04 39.80	LoTr 7	14 15.3
He 2-464	20 20.19	JE 1	07 57.78	K 3-68	05 31.59	LoTr 8	14 22.0
He 2-465	20 21.08	Jones 1	23 35.89	K 3-69	05 41.37	LoTr 9	14 41.3
He 2-466	20 22.43	K 1-1	08 31.81	K 3-70	05 58.76	LoTr 10	14 46.4
He 3-358	10 02.04	K 1-2	08 57.82	K 3-71	06 13.92	LoTr 11	15 21.2
He 3-519	10 53.99	K 1-3	16 23.29	K 3-72	06 23.91	M 1-1	01 37.31
He 3-1223	16 37.71	K 1-4	17 40.47	K 3-73	20 03.98	M 1-2	01 58.78
He 3-1312	17 03.04	K 1-6	20 04.46	K 3-74	20 08.72	M 1-3	03 33.33
He 3-1489	17 48.96	K 1-7	05 31.80	K 3-75	20 15.37	M 1-4	03 41.74
Hf 4	10 15.58	K 1-10	07 12.46	K 3-76	20 35.09	M 1-5	05 46.86
Hf 2-1	17 51.21	K 1-11	07 36.11	K 3-77	20 29.31	M 1-6	06 35.74
Hf 2-2	18 32.52	K 1-12	07 50.22	K 3-78	20 45.37	M 1-7	06 37.35
Hf 38	10 54.59	K 1-13	08 06.72	K 3-79	20 53.23	M 1-8	06 53.52
Hf 39	10 53.99	K 1-14	17 42.53	K 3-80	21 07.67	M 1-9	07 05.31
Hf 48	11 03.94	K 1-15	17 44.99	K 3-81	21 22.28	M 1-10	07 09.40
Hf 69	11 41.68	K 1-16	18 21.85	K 3-82	21 30.87	M 1-11	07 11.28
HtDe 1	01 07.2	K 1-17	19 03.59	K 3-83	21 35.73	M 1-12	07 19.35
HtDe 2	03 11.0	K 1-18	20 00.63	K 3-84	21 38.81	M 1-13	07 21.25
HtDe 3	03 27.2	K 1-19	21 36.91	K 3-85	22 50.89	M 1-14	07 27.94
HtDe 4	05 38.0	K 1-20	23 39.14	K 3-86	22 54.76	M 1-16	07 37.32
HtDe 5	06 23.6	K 1-21	08 04.24	K 3-87	22 55.11	M 1-17	07 40.37
HtDe 6	06 40.2	K 1-22	11 26.73	K 3-88	23 12.25	M 1-18	07 42.05
HtDe 7	07 54.9	K 1-23	12 30.88	K 3-89	23 24.17	M 1-19	17 03.78
HtDe 8	17 31.9	K 1-24	14 38.27	K 3-90	01 24.98	M 1-20	17 28.96
HtDe 10	19 05.7	K 1-25	18 33.17	K 3-91	01 58.60	M 1-22	17 35.16
HtDe 11	19 31.3	K 1-26	02 56.97	K 3-92	02 03.67	M 1-23	17 37.37
HtDe 12	19 57.2	K 1-27	05 57.03	K 3-93	02 26.50	M 1-24	17 38.19
HtDe 13	22 30.2	K 1-28	10 34.51	K 3-94	03 36.12	M 1-25	17 38.50
HtTr 1	12 16.5	K 1-29	13 25.62	K 4-1	18 16.53	M 1-26	17 45.96
HtTr 2	15 30.3	K 1-30	15 42.22	K 4-5	18 45.58	M 1-27	17 46.76
HtTr 3	16 39.6	K 1-31	15 53.20	K 4-8	18 54.33	M 1-28	17 47.63
HtTr 4	16 45.0	K 1-32	16 03.36	K 4-9	18 53.67	M 1-29	17 50.30
HtTr 5	17 01.5	K 1-33	16 08.44	K 4-10	18 59.06	M 1-30	17 52.98
HtTr 6	17 51.9	K 2-1	05 08.11	K 4-16	19 04.86	M 1-31	17 52.69
HtTr 7	17 54.2	K 2-2	06 52.55	K 4-19	19 13.40	M 1-32	17 56.33
HtTr 8	17 55.9	K 2-3	07 06.93	K 4-20	19 13.52	M 1-33	17 58.98
HtTr 9	18 09.0	K 2-4	12 18.35	K 4-28	19 30.29	M 1-34	18 01.37
HtTr 10	18 50.4	K 2-5	17 54.41	K 4-29	19 30.62	M 1-35	18 03.65
HtTr 11	19 03.0	K 2-6	18 41.11	K 4-30	19 33.13	M 1-36	18 03.30
HtTr 12	19 03.8	K 2-7	19 40.54	K 4-31	19 37.11	M 1-37	18 05.43
HtTr 13	19 08.0	K 2-10	19 13.03	K 4-33	19 45.72	M 1-38	18 06.09
HtTr 14	19 09.2	K 2-11	19 14.30	K 4-34	19 46.46	M 1-39	18 07.51
HtWe 3	03 16.6	K 2-12	06 02.11	K 4-37	19 50.97	M 1-40	18 08.43
HtWe 5	03 45.5	K 2-16	16 44.82	K 4-39	19 53.14	M 1-42	18 11.08
HtWe 7	06 23.6	K 2-17	17 09.60	K 4-41	19 56.55	M 1-43	18 11.81
HtWe 8	06 40.2	K 3-1	18 23.39	K 4-47	04 20.75	M 1-44	18 16.29
HtWe 9	06 54.4	K 3-2	18 25.01	K 4-48	06 39.93	M 1-45	18 23.13
HtWe 10	07 54.9	K 3-3	18 27.14	K 4-51	20 12.40	M 1-46	18 27.94
HtWe 12	19 05.7	K 3-4	18 31.02	K 4-52	20 17.25	M 1-47	18 29.18
HtWe 13	19 31.3	K 3-5	18 31.78	K 4-53	20 42.26	M 1-48	18 29.49
HtWe 14	19 57.2	K 3-6	18 33.26	K 4-55	20 45.16	M 1-50	18 33.35
HtWe 15	22 30.2	K 3-7	18 34.23	K 4-56	20 55.73	M 1-51	18 33.48
Hu 1-2	21 33.11	K 3-8	18 34.86	K 4-57	22 48.58	M 1-52	18 33.97
Hu 2-1	18 49.75	K 3-11	18 41.12	K 4-58	22 49.03	M 1-53	18 35.80
IC 289	03 10.35	K 3-12	18 44.74	K 4-59	01 30.54	M 1-54	18 36.14
IC 351	03 47.51	K 3-13	18 45.42	KFL 1	17 59.2	M 1-55	18 36.56
IC 418	05 27.51	K 3-14	18 48.56	KFL 2	18 01.0	M 1-56	18 37.77
IC 972	14 04.44	K 3-15	18 51.67	KFL 3	18 02.8	M 1-57	18 40.34
IC 1295	18 54.63	K 3-16	18 53.03	KFL 4	18 02.8	M 1-58	18 44.10
IC 1297	19 17.39	K 3-17	18 56.33	KFL 5	18 03.9	M 1-59	18 43.34
IC 1454	22 42.59	K 3-18	19 00.57	KFL 7	18 06.8	M 1-60	18 43.63
IC 1747	01 57.63	K 3-19	19 01.61	KFL 9	18 07.4	M 1-61	18 45.91
IC 2003	03 56.40	K 3-20	19 02.17	KFL 10	18 08.0	M 1-62	18 50.43
IC 2149	05 56.32	K 3-21	19 02.69	KFL 11	18 10.2	M 1-63	18 51.51
IC 2165	06 21.71	K 3-24	19 12.08	KFL 12	18 10.5	M 1-64	18 49.99
IC 2448	09 07.11	K 3-26	19 14.66	KFL 13	18 12.7	M 1-65	18 56.55
IC 2501	09 38.79	K 3-27	19 14.48	KFL 14	18 13.0	M 1-66	18 58.43
IC 2553	10 09.34	K 3-29	19 15.50	KFL 15	18 14.3	M 1-68	19 11.14
IC 2621	11 00.33	K 3-30	19 16.47	KFL 16	18 16.9	M 1-69	19 13.90
IC 3568	12 32.94	K 3-31	19 19.00	KFL 19	18 23.1	M 1-70	19 24.38
IC 4191	13 08.79	K 3-33	19 22.47	Kj 2-1	20 17.40	M 1-71	19 36.50
IC 4274	13 33.52	K 3-34	19 24.07	KjPn 1	20 12.40	M 1-72	19 41.54
IC 4406	14 22.43	K 3-35	19 27.75	KjPn 2	20 15.37	M 1-73	19 41.19
IC 4593	16 12.25	K 3-36	19 32.63	KjPn 3	20 17.25	M 1-74	19 42.29
IC 4634	17 01.56	K 3-37	19 33.80	KjPn 4	20 28.81	M 1-75	20 04.78
IC 4637	17 05.18	K 3-38	19 35.35	KjPn 5	20 29.31	M 1-77	21 19.11
IC 4642	17 11.75	K 3-39	19 35.89	KjPn 6	22 49.03	M 1-79	21 37.01
IC 4663	17 45.48	K 3-40	19 36.32	KjPn 8	23 24.17	M 1-80	22 56.28
IC 4673	18 03.30	K 3-41	19 39.27	KtRe 1	16 19.3	M 2-2	04 13.28
IC 4699	18 18.53	K 3-42	19 39.59	LSA 1	19 13.9	M 2-4	17 01.10
IC 4732	18 33.91	K 3-43	19 40.42	Lo 1	02 56.97	M 2-5	17 02.31
IC 4776	18 45.84	K 3-45	19 46.21	Lo 3	07 14.82	M 2-6	17 04.31
IC 4846	19 16.47	K 3-46	19 50.00	Lo 4	10 05.77	M 2-7	17 05.23
IC 4997	20 20.19	K 3-48	19 52.15	Lo 5	11 13.84	M 2-8	17 05.51
IC 5117	21 32.50	K 3-49	19 54.02	Lo 6	12 00.73	M 2-9	17 05.63
IC 5148-50	21 59.53	K 3-51	20 02.56	Lo 7	12 46.45	M 2-10	17 14.11
IC 5217	22 23.90	K 3-52	20 03.20	Lo 8	13 25.62	M 2-11	17 20.55
IRAS 15154-5258	15 19.2	K 3-53	20 03.37	Lo 9	15 42.22	M 2-12	17 24.03
IRAS 16455-3455	16 48.8	K 3-54	20 05.01	Lo 10	15 49.54	M 2-13	17 28.56
IRAS 17516-2525	17 54.7	K 3-55	20 06.96	Lo 11	16 03.36	M 2-14	17 41.95
IRAS 18042-0855	18 07.0	K 3-56	20 06.94	Lo 12	16 08.44	M 2-15	17 46.91
IRAS 18059-3211	18 09.2	K 3-57	20 12.83	Lo 13	16 09.73	M 2-16	17 52.58
IRAS 18333-2357	18 36.3	K 3-58	20 21.94	Lo 16	17 35.67	M 2-17	17 52.08
IRAS 18599+1013	19 02.2	K 3-60	21 27.48	Lo 17	18 27.80	M 2-18	17 53.63
IRAS 1912+172PO9	19 15.0	K 3-61	21 30.01	Lo 18	19 09.75	M 2-19	17 53.76
IRAS 19170+1706	19 19.3	K 3-62	21 31.88	LoTr 1	05 55.1	M 2-20	17 54.41

Cross Index of Planetary Nebulae by Name							
M 2-21	17 58.16	M 4-12	19 13.06	NGC 6543	17 58.58	PK 000+12.1	17 01.56
M 2-22	17 58.55	M 4-13	19 13.68	NGC 6563	18 12.04	PK 000+17.1	16 43.82
M 2-23	18 01.70	M 4-14	19 21.02	NGC 6565	18 11.87	PK 001−01.2	17 54.58
M 2-24	18 02.05	M 4-15	19 32.94	NGC 6567	18 13.75	PK 001−01.3	17 56.04
M 2-25	18 02.77	M 4-17	20 09.06	NGC 6572	18 12.13	PK 001−01.1	17 53.78
M 2-26	18 03.20	M 4-18	04 25.83	NGC 6578	18 16.28	PK 001−01.4	17 54.86
M 2-27	18 03.88	M.27	19 59.56	NGC 6620	18 22.90	PK 001+01.1	17 40.47
M 2-28	18 05.04	M.57	18 53.56	NGC 6629	18 25.71	PK 001−02.2	17 58.43
M 2-29	18 06.68	M.76	01 42.36	NGC 6644	18 32.58	PK 001+02.1	17 40.21
M 2-30	18 12.56	M.97	11 14.78	NGC 6720	18 53.56	PK 001−03.4	18 03.0
M 2-31	18 13.26	MWC 574	07 48.06	NGC 6741	19 02.60	PK 001−03.9	18 05.1
M 2-32	18 14.84	MWC AS 201	08 31.71	NGC 6742	18 59.35	PK 001−03.6	18 03.6
M 2-33	18 15.10	Ma 2	18 15.2	NGC 6751	19 05.92	PK 001−03.8	18 04.0
M 2-34	18 17.27	Ma 3	18 17.8	NGC 6765	19 11.14	PK 001−03.1	18 00.63
M 2-35	18 17.61	Ma 13	18 30.5	NGC 6772	19 14.60	PK 001−03.7	18 03.9
M 2-36	18 17.68	MaC 1-4	17 26.6	NGC 6778	19 18.41	PK 001−03.0	18 03.9
M 2-37	18 18.64	MaC 1-9	17 55.8	NGC 6781	19 18.44	PK 001−03.3	18 02.5
M 2-38	18 19.42	MaC 1-10	18 09.2	NGC 6790	19 23.23	PK 001−04.2	18 07.90
M 2-39	18 22.02	MaC 1-11	18 14.8	NGC 6803	19 31.28	PK 001−04.1	18 07.65
M 2-40	18 21.40	MaC 1-12	18 21.3	NGC 6804	19 31.60	PK 001+05.1	17 28.06
M 2-41	18 22.57	MaC 1-14	18 41.2	NGC 6807	19 34.56	PK 001+05.2	17 28.62
M 2-42	18 22.53	MaC 1-15	18 57.3	NGC 6818	19 43.96	PK 001−06.2	18 16.21
M 2-43	18 26.66	MaC 1-16	19 01.4	NGC 6826	19 44.85	PK 002−01.1	17 58.51
M 2-44	18 37.61	MaC 1-17	19 13.0	NGC 6833	19 49.73	PK 002+01.1	17 45.66
M 2-45	18 39.37	MaC 2-1	05 03.6	NGC 6842	19 55.01	PK 002+01.2	17 46.11
M 2-46	18 46.57	MaC 2-2	05 28.9	NGC 6852	20 00.63	PK 002−02.1	17 58.36
M 2-47	19 13.58	MaC 2-3	05 38.3	NGC 6853	19 59.56	PK 002−02.3	18 01.16
M 2-48	19 50.48	Me 1-1	19 39.17	NGC 6879	20 10.48	PK 002−02.2	17 59.32
M 2-49	21 43.30	Me 2-1	15 22.31	NGC 6881	20 10.84	PK 002−02.5	18 01.0
M 2-50	21 57.74	Me 2-2	22 31.70	NGC 6884	20 10.37	PK 002−02.4	18 01.70
M 2-51	22 16.09	MrWe 1-1	08 53.5	NGC 6886	20 12.72	PK 002−03.5	18 06.09
M 2-52	22 20.52	MrWe 1-2	10 14.4	NGC 6891	20 15.15	PK 002−03.6	18 08.06
M 2-53	22 32.34	MrWe 1-3	13 28.1	NGC 6894	20 16.42	PK 002−03.2	18 04.47
M 2-55	23 31.87	MrWe 1-4	14 17.5	NGC 6905	20 22.43	PK 002−03.7	18 04.08
M 2-56	23 56.60	MrWe 1-5	14 46.5	NGC 7008	21 00.56	PK 002−03.3	18 05.43
M 3-1	07 02.83	MrWe 1-6	16 31.1	NGC 7009	21 04.22	PK 002−04.1	18 07.11
M 3-2	07 14.82	MrWe 1-7	16 48.0	NGC 7026	21 06.32	PK 002−04.2	18 11.08
M 3-3	07 26.58	MrWe 1-8	16 48.7	NGC 7027	21 07.07	PK 002+04.1	17 35.97
M 3-4	07 55.18	MrWe 1-9	16 57.5	NGC 7048	21 14.19	PK 002+05.1	17 29.34
M 3-5	08 02.48	MrWe 1-10	17 34.4	NGC 7094	21 36.91	PK 002−05.2	18 13.0
M 3-6	08 40.67	MrWe 1-11	17 52.7	NGC 7139	21 45.92	PK 002−06.1	18 15.10
M 3-7	17 24.57	MrWe 2-1	08 20.8	NGC 7293	22 29.63	PK 002−06.2	18 16.32
M 3-8	17 24.87	MrWe 2-2	09 58.2	NGC 7354	22 40.37	PK 002−07.1	18 22.57
M 3-9	17 25.72	MrWe 2-3	11 56.7	NGC 7662	23 25.91	PK 002+08.1	17 21.29
M 3-10	17 27.34	MrWe 2-4	14 01.2	Na 1	17 12.86	PK 002−09.1	18 29.19
M 3-11	17 35.35	MrWe 2-5	16 34.8	Na 2	19 18.32	PK 002−13.1	18 45.84
M 3-12	17 36.38	My 56	10 09.50	Ns 238	08 20.90	PK 002−52.1	21 59.53
M 3-13	17 41.61	My 118	18 18.14	PB 1	07 02.78	PK 003−02.4	18 02.8
M 3-14	17 44.34	MyCn 18	13 39.58	PB 2	08 20.67	PK 003−02.2	18 03.20
M 3-15	17 45.52	MyCn 26	16 55.78	PB 3	08 54.30	PK 003−02.1	18 03.65
M 3-16	17 52.77	Mz 1	15 34.28	PB 4	09 15.13	PK 003−02.3	18 03.30
M 3-17	17 56.43	Mz 2	16 14.53	PB 5	09 16.16	PK 003+02.1	17 41.88
M 3-19	17 58.31	Mz 3	16 17.23	PB 6	10 13.26	PK 003−03.2	18 06.8
M 3-20	17 59.32	NGC 246	00 47.01	PB 7	10 31.56	PK 003+03.1	17 40.12
M 3-21	18 02.54	NGC 650-1	01 42.36	PB 8	11 33.29	PK 003+03.2	17 41.95
M 3-22	18 02.31	NGC 1360	03 33.33	PB 9	19 27.77	PK 003−04.5	18 11.87
M 3-23	18 07.10	NGC 1501	04 07.01	PB 10	19 28.24	PK 003−04.9	18 12.79
M 3-24	18 07.89	NGC 1514	04 09.25	PC 11	16 37.71	PK 003−04.7	18 11.58
M 3-25	18 15.28	NGC 1535	04 14.24	PC 12	16 43.82	PK 003−04.1	18 10.5
M 3-26	18 16.18	NGC 2022	05 42.14	PC 13	16 50.28	PK 003−04.3	18 11.49
M 3-27	18 27.78	NGC 2242	06 34.2	PC 14	17 06.24	PK 003−04.4	18 12.40
M 3-28	18 32.69	NGC 2346	07 09.40	PC 15	17 26.20	PK 003−04.8	18 12.56
M 3-29	18 39.42	NGC 2371-2	07 25.55	PC 16	17 27.81	PK 003+05.1	17 34.45
M 3-30	18 41.25	NGC 2392	07 29.16	PC 17	17 35.69	PK 003−06.1	18 17.68
M 3-31	18 44.03	NGC 2438	07 41.84	PC 19	18 24.71	PK 003+07.1	17 24.80
M 3-32	18 44.68	NGC 2440	07 41.92	PC 20	18 43.04	PK 003−07.1	18 23.1
M 3-33	18 48.20	NGC 2452	07 47.44	PC 21	18 45.58	PK 003−14.1	18 55.63
M 3-34	19 27.03	NGC 2610	08 33.39	PC 22	19 42.01	PK 003−17.1	19 05.59
M 3-35	20 21.08	NGC 2792	09 12.44	PC 23	19 51.92	PK 004+00.1	17 54.7
M 3-36	17 12.65	NGC 2818	09 16.03	PHL 932	00 59.96	PK 004+01.1	17 48.60
M 3-37	17 19.22	NGC 2867	09 21.42	PM 1-89	15 19.2	PK 004+02.1	17 49.01
M 3-38	17 21.07	NGC 2899	09 27.04	PM 1-166	17 39.1	PK 004−02.1	18 05.96
M 3-39	17 21.18	NGC 3132	10 07.00	PM 1-213	18 09.2	PK 004−03.1	18 06.68
M 3-40	17 22.42	NGC 3195	10 09.50	PM 1-226	18 21.3	PK 004+03.1	17 41.65
M 3-41	17 25.99	NGC 3211	10 17.84	PM 1-276	19 02.2	PK 004−03.2	18 08.0
M 3-42	17 27.00	NGC 3242	10 24.81	PK 000−01.1	17 50.39	PK 004−03.3	18 10.2
M 3-43	17 50.39	NGC 3587	11 14.78	PK 000−01.7	17 53.4	PK 004+04.1	17 38.50
M 3-44	17 51.31	NGC 3699	11 27.96	PK 000−01.6	17 54.41	PK 004−04.1	18 12.42
M 3-45	17 52.10	NGC 3918	11 50.30	PK 000−01.5	17 53.76	PK 004−04.2	18 16.29
M 3-46	17 55.10	NGC 4071	12 04.22	PK 000−01.4	17 52.40	PK 004−05.1	18 16.18
M 3-47	17 57.81	NGC 4361	12 24.50	PK 000−01.3	17 53.82	PK 004−05.3	18 17.66
M 3-48	17 59.94	NGC 5189	13 33.52	PK 000−01.2	17 52.58	PK 004−05.5	18 18.64
M 3-49	18 02.53	NGC 5307	13 51.06	PK 000+02.1	17 35.5	PK 004+06.2	17 33.62
M 3-50	18 04.09	NGC 5315	13 53.95	PK 000−02.3	17 56.40	PK 004−11.2	18 44.23
M 3-51	18 04.94	NGC 5873	15 12.85	PK 000−02.5	17 57.81	PK 004−11.1	18 39.42
M 3-52	18 10.47	NGC 5882	15 16.84	PK 000−02.6	17 58.31	PK 004−22.1	19 32.11
M 3-53	18 24.13	NGC 5979	15 47.68	PK 000−02.2	17 55.33	PK 005+02.1	17 48.13
M 3-54	18 33.06	NGC 6026	16 01.35	PK 000−02.1	17 56.04	PK 005−02.1	18 07.89
M 3-55	18 33.26	NGC 6058	16 04.42	PK 000−02.4	17 58.16	PK 005−02.2	18 09.2
M 3-57	17 31.9	NGC 6072	16 12.98	PK 000+03.1	17 34.91	PK 005−03.2	18 12.42
M 4-2	07 28.89	NGC 6153	16 31.51	PK 000−03.2	17 59.2	PK 005−03.3	18 12.7
M 4-3	17 10.70	NGC 6210	16 44.50	PK 000−03.1	18 02.31	PK 005+03.1	17 45.61
M 4-4	17 28.84	NGC 6302	17 13.73	PK 000−04.1	18 05.04	PK 005−03.1	18 09.23
M 4-5	17 34.91	NGC 6309	17 14.06	PK 000−04.3	18 04.73	PK 005−04.1	18 13.68
M 4-6	17 35.24	NGC 6326	17 20.77	PK 000+04.2	17 29.39	PK 005+04.1	17 40.30
M 4-7	17 51.75	NGC 6337	17 22.26	PK 000−04.2	18 07.10	PK 005−04.2	18 16.9
M 4-8	18 12.15	NGC 6369	17 29.34	PK 000+04.1	17 29.43	PK 005+04.2	17 41.61
M 4-9	18 14.31	NGC 6439	17 48.33	PK 000−05.1	18 08.43	PK 005−05.1	18 19.42
M 4-10	18 34.22	NGC 6445	17 49.25	PK 000−07.1	18 17.61	PK 005+05.2	17 39.91
M 4-11	18 54.29	NGC 6537	18 05.21	PK 000−07.2	18 18.69	PK 005+05.1	17 36.38

Cross Index of Planetary Nebulae by Name	
PK 005−06.1	18 22.90
PK 005+06.1	17 35.35
PK 005−08.1	18 32.52
PK 005−18.1	19 14.39
PK 006+01.1	17 55.9
PK 006+02.4	17 53.61
PK 006+02.1	17 48.62
PK 006+02.3	17 52.38
PK 006+02.5	17 52.69
PK 006−03.1	18 12.57
PK 006+03.1	17 47.57
PK 006−03.4	18 14.3
PK 006−03.3	18 13.26
PK 006−03.2	18 14.47
PK 006+03.2	17 47.63
PK 006−04.1	18 18.22
PK 006+04.2	17 45.52
PK 006+04.1	17 43.48
PK 006+08.1	17 28.96
PK 006−08.1	18 34.92
PK 006−19.1	19 22.17
PK 006−41.1	21 05.8
PK 007+01.1	17 55.12
PK 007−03.1	18 17.27
PK 007−03.2	18 17.79
PK 007+04.1	17 46.27
PK 007−04.1	18 20.14
PK 007+06.1	17 37.37
PK 007−06.2	18 27.99
PK 007+06.2	17 38.19
PK 007−06.1	18 24.95
PK 007+07.1	17 35.16
PK 007+10.1	17 26.6
PK 008−01.1	18 08.43
PK 008−02.1	18 14.8
PK 008−03.1	18 18.39
PK 008+03.2	17 50.46
PK 008+03.1	17 49.25
PK 008−04.2	18 22.53
PK 008−04.1	18 22.02
PK 008+05.1	17 46.24
PK 008+06.1	17 38.95
PK 008−07.1	18 31.88
PK 008−07.2	18 32.58
PK 009+02.1	17 55.95
PK 009−04.1	18 25.08
PK 009+04.1	17 50.48
PK 009+04.2	17 50.96
PK 009−05.1	18 25.71
PK 009−07.1	18 36.3
PK 009−08.1	18 37.5
PK 009−09.1	18 44.68
PK 009+10.1	17 29.03
PK 009−10.1	18 48.20
PK 009+14.1	17 14.06
PK 010+00.1	18 05.21
PK 010−01.1	18 16.28
PK 010+03.1	17 57.11
PK 010+04.1	17 52.08
PK 010−06.2	18 34.86
PK 010−06.1	18 33.91
PK 010+07.1	17 42.05
PK 010−09.1	18 40.3
PK 010+18.2	17 05.63
PK 011−00.1	18 11.81
PK 011−00.2	18 13.75
PK 011+02.1	18 00.15
PK 011+04.1	17 56.33
PK 011+05.1	17 48.33
PK 011−05.1	18 29.18
PK 011+06.1	17 46.91
PK 011−06.1	18 36.56
PK 011+07.1	17 44.69
PK 011−09.1	18 46.59
PK 011+11.1	17 28.56
PK 011−14.1	19 05.7
PK 011+17.1	17 06.9
PK 012−02.1	18 23.13
PK 012−09.1	18 50.43
PK 013−02.1	18 26.0
PK 013−03.1	18 29.49
PK 013+04.1	17 58.98
PK 013−04.2	18 30.57
PK 013−04.1	18 30.00
PK 013+05.2	17 55.8
PK 013+05.1	17 55.78
PK 013−07.2	18 41.93
PK 013−07.1	18 45.58
PK 013−10.1	18 55.51
PK 013+32.1	16 21.06
PK 014−04.1	18 33.35
PK 014+04.1	18 01.12
PK 014−05.2	18 37.18
PK 014−05.1	18 36.53
PK 014+06.1	17 54.41
PK 014−07.1	18 44.03
PK 014−11.1	19 02.3
PK 014−25.1	19 57.2
PK 015−03.1	18 30.19
PK 015+03.1	18 07.51
PK 015−04.1	18 35.80
PK 015−08.1	18 49.14
PK 016−01.1	18 27.94
PK 016−02.1	18 29.33
PK 016−04.1	18 36.14
PK 016−04.2	18 37.77
PK 016+13.1	17 31.52
PK 017−02.1	18 33.97
PK 017−04.1	18 41.25
PK 017−10.1	19 01.02
PK 017−21.1	19 46.59
PK 018−02.1	18 33.06
PK 018+03.1	18 12.15
PK 018+04.1	18 10.47
PK 018+20.1	17 12.86
PK 019+00.1	18 24.13
PK 019−02.1	18 34.22
PK 019+03.1	18 15.28
PK 019−04.1	18 43.63
PK 019−05.1	18 45.91
PK 019+05.1	18 07.0
PK 019−08.1	18 57.3
PK 019−13.1	19 17.1
PK 019−19.1	19 40.54
PK 019−23.1	19 57.55
PK 020−00.1	18 30.29
PK 020−03.1	18 41.2
PK 020−05.1	18 50.73
PK 021−00.2	18 33.26
PK 021−00.1	18 32.69
PK 021−01.1	18 33.48
PK 021+02.1	18 21.3
PK 021−03.1	18 44.12
PK 021−05.1	18 51.51
PK 022−02.1	18 40.34
PK 022−03.1	18 44.10
PK 022+04.1	18 15.2
PK 023+01.1	18 30.5
PK 023−01.2	18 41.12
PK 023−02.1	18 43.34
PK 023+04.1	18 17.8
PK 023−07.1	19 01.4
PK 024−02.1	18 46.57
PK 024−03.1	18 47.81
PK 024+03.1	18 21.40
PK 024+05.1	18 14.31
PK 024−05.1	18 54.29
PK 025−00.1	18 42.09
PK 025−02.1	18 46.41
PK 025−04.2	18 54.63
PK 025−04.1	18 54.33
PK 025−11.1	19 19.29
PK 025−17.1	19 43.96
PK 025+40.1	16 12.25
PK 026−01.1	18 45.58
PK 026−01.2	18 45.50
PK 026−02.3	18 49.75
PK 026−02.1	18 47.53
PK 026−11.1	19 18.32
PK 027+00.1	18 39.37
PK 027−02.1	18 48.78
PK 027−03.2	18 54.03
PK 027−03.1	18 53.49
PK 027+04.1	18 26.66
PK 027−09.1	19 16.47
PK 027+16.1	17 41.7
PK 028+01.1	18 37.61
PK 028+02.1	18 34.23
PK 028−03.1	18 57.83
PK 028−04.1	18 57.29
PK 028+05.1	18 25.01
PK 028+10.1	18 06.1
PK 029+00.1	18 42.82
PK 029−05.1	19 05.92
PK 029−07.1	19 13.9
PK 030+03.1	18 35.36
PK 030+04.1	18 33.26
PK 030+06.1	18 24.9
PK 030−07.1	19 13.0
PK 030+08.1	18 16.53
PK 031−00.1	18 50.7
PK 031−00.2	18 50.4
PK 031+01.1	18 43.04
PK 031+05.1	18 27.14
PK 031−10.1	19 27.03
PK 032−02.1	18 58.43
PK 032−02.2	19 01.61
PK 032−03.2	19 02.17
PK 032−03.1	19 00.57
PK 032+05.1	18 31.02
PK 032−06.1	19 13.03
PK 032+07.2	18 24.71
PK 032+07.1	18 23.39
PK 032−08.1	19 21.94
PK 033−01.1	18 58.84
PK 033−02.1	19 02.60
PK 033−05.1	19 10.51
PK 033−06.1	19 14.60
PK 034+02.1	18 45.42
PK 034+06.1	18 31.78
PK 034−06.1	19 18.41
PK 034−10.1	19 31.3
PK 034+11.1	18 12.13
PK 035−00.1	18 58.13
PK 035−05.1	19 14.66
PK 035+05.1	18 34.86
PK 036−01.1	19 02.02
PK 036−01.2	19 03.0
PK 036−02.1	19 08.0
PK 036+17.1	17 53.55
PK 036+20.1	17 43.0
PK 036+21.1	17 38.4
PK 036−57.1	22 29.63
PK 037−03.2	19 13.11
PK 037+04.1	18 44.74
PK 037−05.1	19 18.33
PK 037−06.1	19 23.23
PK 037−34.1	21 04.22
PK 038−00.1	19 03.8
PK 038+02.1	18 54.75
PK 038−03.2	19 13.90
PK 038−03.3	19 14.30
PK 038−03.1	19 13.40
PK 038+07.1	18 33.17
PK 038+12.1	18 17.56
PK 038−25.1	20 31.57
PK 039+02.1	18 56.33
PK 039−02.1	19 13.58
PK 040−00.1	19 06.74
PK 040−03.1	19 16.47
PK 041−00.1	19 09.2
PK 041−02.1	19 18.44
PK 041+04.1	18 51.67
PK 042−01.1	19 13.52
PK 042+05.1	18 48.56
PK 042−06.1	19 34.56
PK 042−14.1	20 00.63
PK 043+02.1	19 02.2
PK 043−03.1	19 21.02
PK 043+03.1	18 56.55
PK 043+11.1	18 27.78
PK 043−13.1	19 58.41
PK 043+37.1	16 44.50
PK 044+05.2	18 50.7
PK 044+05.1	18 53.03
PK 044−05.1	19 32.63
PK 044−09.1	19 45.66
PK 044+10.1	18 34.1
PK 045−01.1	19 22.47
PK 045−02.1	19 24.38
PK 045−04.1	19 31.60
PK 045+24.1	17 42.53
PK 046+02.1	19 06.4
PK 046−03.1	19 27.77
PK 046+03.1	19 03.1
PK 046−04.1	19 31.28
PK 047+04.1	19 02.69
PK 047−04.1	19 33.37
PK 047+42.1	16 27.52
PK 048−01.1	19 26.4
PK 048+01.1	19 13.68
PK 048+01.2	19 15.50
PK 048+02.1	19 12.08
PK 048−02.1	19 28.24
PK 048+04.2	19 04.86
PK 049+02.1	19 13.06
PK 049+88.1	12 59.41
PK 050−01.1	19 30.29
PK 050−03.1	19 37.11
PK 050+05.1	19 04.52
PK 051+01.1	19 19.3
PK 051+02.1	19 15.0
PK 051+03.1	19 14.03
PK 051−03.1	19 41.19
PK 051−04.1	19 42.01
PK 051+06.1	19 03.59
PK 051+09.1	18 49.75
PK 051+25.1	17 44.99
PK 052−02.2	19 39.17
PK 052+02.1	19 19.00
PK 052−02.1	19 39.27
PK 052−04.1	19 42.29
PK 052+07.1	18 59.06
PK 053−01.1	19 35.35
PK 053−03.1	19 42.15
PK 053+03.1	19 18.69
PK 053+24.1	17 54.37
PK 054−02.1	19 41.54
PK 054−03.1	19 46.46
PK 054−12.1	20 15.15
PK 055−00.1	19 36.50
PK 055−01.1	19 40.42
PK 055+02.2	19 23.76
PK 055+02.3	19 26.66
PK 055+02.1	19 23.46
PK 055+06.1	19 08.71
PK 055+16.1	18 31.20
PK 056−00.1	19 39.59
PK 056+02.1	19 27.75
PK 056−06.1	20 02.56
PK 056+14.1	18 41.11
PK 057+01.1	19 33.13
PK 057−01.1	19 45.37
PK 057+02.1	19 30.62
PK 057−08.1	20 10.48
PK 058+01.1	19 36.32
PK 058−05.1	20 01.7
PK 058+06.1	19 17.06
PK 058−10.1	20 20.19
PK 058+12.1	18 53.67
PK 059−01.1	19 48.46
PK 059−01.2	19 48.87
PK 059+02.2	19 35.89
PK 059+02.1	19 33.80
PK 059+04.1	19 24.07
PK 059−18.1	20 50.06
PK 060−00.1	19 46.21
PK 060+01.1	19 38.18
PK 060−02.1	19 53.14
PK 060−03.1	19 59.56
PK 060−04.1	20 00.18
PK 060−07.1	20 11.92
PK 060−07.2	20 12.72
PK 061+03.1	19 32.94
PK 061+08.1	19 14.48
PK 061−09.1	20 22.43
PK 061+41.1	16 40.27
PK 062−00.1	19 50.48
PK 062+09.1	19 11.14
PK 063+00.1	19 52.15
PK 063−03.1	20 05.01
PK 063+13.1	18 53.56
PK 064−02.1	20 03.37
PK 064+02.1	19 45.72
PK 064+05.1	19 34.76
PK 064+15.1	18 49.99
PK 064+48.1	16 04.42
PK 065+00.1	19 55.01
PK 065−03.1	20 09.07
PK 065−05.1	20 17.33
PK 065−27.1	21 30.02
PK 066+02.1	19 50.97
PK 066−05.1	20 19.60
PK 066−28.1	21 36.91
PK 067−00.1	20 03.20
PK 068−00.1	20 04.78
PK 068+01.1	19 56.55
PK 068+01.2	19 59.26
PK 068−02.1	20 13.93
PK 068+03.1	19 51.92
PK 068+14.1	19 00.4
PK 069+00.1	20 06.96
PK 069−02.1	20 16.42
PK 069+02.1	19 54.02
PK 069−03.1	20 21.94
PK 069+03.1	19 50.00
PK 071−02.1	20 21.08
PK 072+00.1	20 12.83
PK 072−17.1	21 16.83
PK 073−02.1	20 35.09
PK 074+02.1	20 10.84
PK 075+04.1	20 04.37
PK 075+05.1	19 57.1
PK 075+35.1	17 13.8
PK 076+01.2	20 17.25
PK 076+01.1	20 19.94
PK 077+02.1	20 17.40
PK 077+03.1	20 12.40
PK 077+03.2	20 15.37
PK 077+14.1	19 19.17
PK 078+00.1	20 29.31
PK 078−02.1	20 42.26
PK 078+05.1	20 08.72
PK 078+18.1	18 59.35
PK 079+00.1	20 28.81
PK 079+05.1	20 09.06
PK 079+06.1	20 06.94
PK 081−14.1	21 35.56
PK 082+07.1	20 10.37
PK 082+11.1	19 49.73
PK 083−08.1	21 22.28
PK 083+12.1	19 44.85
PK 084+01.1	20 45.16
PK 084−03.1	21 07.07
PK 084−04.1	21 07.67
PK 084+09.1	20 03.98
PK 085+04.1	20 32.41
PK 086+00.1	20 55.73
PK 086+05.1	20 31.88
PK 086−08.1	21 33.11
PK 087−03.1	21 18.12
PK 088−01.1	21 14.19
PK 088+04.1	20 45.37
PK 089+00.1	21 06.32
PK 089−00.1	21 14.05
PK 089−02.1	21 19.11
PK 089−05.1	21 32.50
PK 091+01.1	21 10.87
PK 091−04.1	21 38.81
PK 092+05.1	20 53.23

Cross Index of Planetary Nebulae by Name							
PK 093−00.1	21 30.87	PK 160−00.1	04 46.71	PK 239+13.1	08 33.39	PK 274+03.3	09 48.24
PK 093−02.1	21 37.01	PK 161−14.1	03 56.40	PK 240−07.1	07 14.82	PK 274+09.1	10 05.77
PK 093+05.2	21 00.56	PK 163−00.1	04 54.53	PK 240+07.1	08 10.69	PK 275−01.1	09 30.81
PK 094−00.1	21 35.73	PK 164+31.1	07 57.78	PK 241+02.1	07 55.18	PK 275−02.1	09 22.11
PK 094−00.2	21 30.0	PK 165−06.1	04 39.80	PK 242−06.1	07 24.24	PK 275−02.2	09 24.76
PK 094+27.1	18 21.85	PK 165−15.1	04 09.25	PK 242−11.1	07 02.83	PK 275−03.2	09 24.53
PK 094+38.1	16 47.6	PK 166−06.1	04 42.88	PK 242−37.1	05 03.1	PK 275−03.1	09 18.02
PK 095+00.1	21 31.88	PK 166+10.1	05 56.32	PK 243−00.1	07 49.67	PK 275−04.2	09 13.88
PK 095−02.1	21 43.30	PK 167−00.1	05 06.64	PK 243−01.1	07 47.44	PK 275−04.1	09 15.13
PK 095+07.1	20 56.51	PK 167−09.1	04 36.62	PK 243−25.1	06 02.11	PK 275+72.1	12 18.35
PK 096+02.1	21 30.01	PK 170+04.1	05 41.37	PK 244−04.1	07 37.37	PK 277−03.2	09 31.45
PK 096+29.1	17 58.58	PK 170+15.1	06 34.2	PK 244−06.2	07 28.04	PK 277+03.1	09 58.2
PK 097−02.1	21 57.74	PK 171−25.1	03 53.49	PK 244−06.1	07 27.98	PK 277−03.1	09 27.04
PK 097+03.1	21 32.17	PK 172+00.1	05 28.96	PK 244+12.1	08 40.24	PK 277−07.1	09 12.61
PK 098+02.1	21 39.22	PK 173+02.1	05 40.9	PK 245+01.1	08 02.48	PK 278+00.1	09 52.06
PK 098+04.1	21 27.48	PK 173−05.1	05 08.11	PK 245+05.1	08 15.76	PK 278−04.1	09 30.91
PK 099−08.1	22 30.2	PK 174−14.1	04 37.35	PK 245−08.1	07 19.12	PK 278+05.1	10 13.26
PK 100−05.1	22 23.90	PK 175+06.1	06 02.6	PK 246−04.1	07 41.97	PK 278−05.1	09 21.42
PK 100−08.1	22 31.70	PK 178−02.1	05 31.59	PK 247−04.1	07 42.4	PK 278−06.1	09 19.46
PK 101+08.1	21 26.41	PK 181+00.1	05 52.81	PK 247−08.1	07 26.27	PK 278−06.3	09 19.63
PK 102−02.1	22 26.33	PK 183+05.1	06 16.2	PK 247−10.1	07 18.24	PK 278−06.2	09 23.25
PK 102−05.1	22 34.73	PK 184+00.1	05 58.76	PK 248−04.1	07 46.78	PK 279+01.1	09 59.68
PK 103+00.1	22 16.09	PK 184−02.1	05 46.86	PK 248−08.1	07 28.89	PK 279−03.2	09 40.89
PK 103+00.2	22 20.52	PK 184+04.1	06 13.92	PK 248+29.1	09 45.62	PK 279−03.1	09 43.43
PK 104+00.1	22 20.30	PK 189+07.1	06 37.35	PK 249−05.1	07 43.27	PK 279−08.1	09 13.67
PK 104−01.1	22 32.34	PK 189+19.1	07 25.55	PK 249+06.1	08 31.71	PK 280−00.1	10 02.89
PK 104+07.1	21 45.92	PK 190−17.1	05 05.56	PK 250+00.1	08 08.96	PK 280+02.1	10 12.00
PK 104−29.1	23 35.89	PK 192+07.1	06 40.2	PK 251+00.1	08 14.56	PK 281−05.1	09 38.79
PK 106−04.1	22 54.76	PK 193−09.1	05 40.70	PK 251−01.1	08 04.24	PK 282−02.1	10 02.26
PK 106−17.1	23 25.91	PK 194+02.1	06 25.92	PK 251+01.1	08 15.88	PK 282+03.1	10 31.53
PK 107−00.1	22 48.58	PK 196−10.1	05 42.14	PK 251−03.1	07 56.13	PK 282−07.1	09 37.06
PK 107+02.1	22 40.37	PK 197−03.1	06 11.19	PK 252+04.1	08 31.81	PK 282−10.1	09 16.79
PK 107−02.1	22 56.28	PK 197−06.1	05 59.4	PK 252−04.1	07 52.96	PK 283−01.2	10 14.4
PK 107−02.2	22 55.11	PK 197−14.1	05 31.80	PK 253+00.1	08 20.8	PK 283−01.1	10 15.58
PK 107+07.1	22 13.3	PK 197+17.1	07 29.16	PK 253+10.1	08 57.82	PK 283+02.1	10 31.56
PK 107−13.1	23 22.96	PK 198−06.1	06 02.35	PK 254+00.1	08 20.90	PK 283+03.1	10 34.31
PK 107+21.1	20 04.46	PK 200+08.1	06 59.94	PK 254+05.1	08 40.67	PK 283−04.1	10 03.83
PK 108+00.1	22 50.89	PK 201+02.1	06 39.93	PK 255+03.1	08 36.27	PK 283−07.1	09 39.95
PK 110−01.1	23 13.1	PK 201−04.1	06 14.56	PK 255−59.1	02 56.97	PK 283+09.1	10 54.7
PK 110−12.1	23 39.14	PK 203−18.1	05 28.9	PK 256+03.1	08 41.16	PK 283+25.1	11 26.73
PK 111−02.1	23 26.29	PK 204−03.1	06 23.91	PK 256−11.1	07 35.39	PK 284−05.1	10 02.04
PK 111−03.1	23 22.35	PK 204+04.1	06 52.55	PK 257−00.1	08 27.57	PK 285−01.2	10 29.29
PK 111+06.1	22 49.03	PK 204−08.1	06 04.84	PK 257+00.1	08 30.93	PK 285+01.2	10 39.55
PK 111+11.1	22 19.6	PK 204−16.1	05 38.3	PK 258−00.1	08 28.46	PK 285+01.1	10 38.47
PK 112−00.1	23 24.17	PK 205+14.1	07 29.01	PK 258−06.1	08 03.17	PK 285−01.1	10 28.54
PK 112+03.1	23 12.25	PK 205−26.1	05 03.6	PK 258−15.1	07 14.82	PK 285−02.1	10 23.15
PK 112−10.1	23 47.68	PK 206−40.1	04 14.24	PK 259+00.2	08 37.95	PK 285+02.1	10 41.33
PK 113−06.1	23 46.76	PK 208+33.1	08 46.83	PK 259+00.1	08 37.13	PK 285−05.1	10 09.34
PK 114−04.1	23 45.85	PK 210+01.1	06 53.52	PK 259−07.1	07 59.52	PK 285−09.1	09 46.32
PK 116+00.1	23 52.33	PK 210+03.1	07 00.46	PK 259−09.1	07 52.77	PK 285+11.1	11 09.15
PK 116+08.1	23 31.87	PK 211−03.1	06 35.74	PK 259−09.2	07 52.49	PK 285−14.1	09 07.11
PK 117+18.1	22 42.59	PK 211+18.1	07 54.9	PK 260−03.1	08 23.71	PK 286−02.1	10 26.69
PK 118+08.1	23 56.60	PK 211+22.1	08 11.2	PK 261+02.1	08 53.51	PK 286+02.1	10 48.73
PK 118−74.1	00 47.01	PK 212+04.1	07 05.31	PK 261+04.1	08 56.24	PK 286−04.1	10 17.84
PK 121+00.1	00 40.33	PK 214+07.1	07 22.99	PK 261−04.1	08 21.07	PK 286−06.1	10 07.40
PK 122−04.1	00 45.60	PK 215+03.1	07 09.40	PK 261+08.1	09 16.03	PK 286−06.2	10 06.92
PK 123+34.1	12 32.94	PK 215+11.1	07 36.11	PK 261−08.1	08 01.40	PK 286+11.1	11 13.84
PK 124−07.1	01 00.9	PK 215−24.1	05 27.51	PK 261−08.2	07 59.54	PK 286−29.1	05 57.03
PK 124+10.1	01 07.2	PK 215−30.1	05 03.16	PK 261+32.1	10 24.81	PK 287+10.1	11 17.08
PK 125−47.1	00 59.96	PK 216−00.1	06 56.21	PK 262−04.1	08 24.12	PK 288+00.1	10 54.59
PK 126+03.1	01 24.98	PK 216−04.1	06 41.58	PK 262−08.1	08 02.70	PK 288−00.1	10 53.99
PK 127−01.1	01 30.54	PK 217+02.1	07 06.80	PK 262−10.1	07 55.61	PK 288−02.1	10 44.53
PK 128−04.1	01 30.6	PK 217+14.1	07 51.71	PK 263+00.1	08 48.64	PK 288−05.1	10 35.77
PK 129−02.1	01 42.64	PK 218−10.1	06 23.6	PK 263−05.1	08 20.67	PK 288+08.1	11 18.17
PK 129+04.1	01 58.60	PK 219+07.1	07 29.9	PK 263−08.1	08 05.2	PK 289−01.1	10 55.99
PK 130+01.1	01 57.63	PK 219+31.1	08 54.19	PK 263−09.1	08 00.42	PK 289+07.1	11 24.02
PK 130+03.1	02 03.67	PK 220−53.1	03 33.33	PK 264−03.1	08 34.48	PK 289−08.1	10 21.05
PK 130−10.1	01 42.36	PK 221−04.1	06 48.58	PK 264+03.1	09 07.12	PK 290−00.1	11 03.94
PK 130−11.1	01 37.31	PK 221+05.2	07 26.5	PK 264+08.1	09 24.50	PK 290+07.1	11 28.60
PK 131+02.1	02 12.19	PK 221+05.1	07 26.58	PK 264−08.1	08 11.53	PK 290+27.1	11 56.7
PK 131−05.1	01 53.75	PK 221−12.1	06 21.71	PK 264−12.1	07 47.33	PK 291+03.1	11 27.40
PK 132+04.1	02 26.50	PK 221+46.1	09 53.0	PK 265−02.1	08 43.47	PK 291−04.1	11 00.33
PK 133−08.1	01 58.78	PK 224+01.1	07 17.43	PK 265−04.1	08 34.1	PK 291+19.1	11 52.5
PK 136+04.1	02 58.88	PK 224+15.1	08 06.72	PK 265+04.1	09 12.44	PK 292−01.1	11 23.23
PK 136+05.1	03 03.7	PK 225+00.1	07 16.13	PK 265−09.1	08 08.37	PK 292+01.3	11 30.82
PK 137+16.1	04 25.2	PK 225−02.1	07 06.74	PK 266−00.1	08 56.61	PK 292+01.2	11 28.79
PK 138+02.1	03 10.35	PK 226−03.1	07 02.78	PK 266+08.1	09 32.74	PK 292+01.1	11 27.96
PK 138+04.1	03 11.0	PK 226+05.1	07 37.32	PK 267−03.1	08 43.49	PK 292+04.1	11 33.29
PK 141−07.1	02 52.28	PK 228+05.1	07 40.37	PK 268+02.1	09 16.16	PK 292+10.1	11 47.63
PK 142+03.1	03 36.12	PK 228−22.1	05 55.1	PK 268−03.1	08 46.61	PK 293+01.1	11 35.18
PK 144+06.1	04 07.01	PK 229−02.1	07 12.46	PK 268−14.1	07 51.45	PK 293+05.1	11 45.70
PK 144−15.1	02 45.43	PK 231+04.2	07 41.84	PK 269−03.1	08 54.30	PK 293+10.1	11 53.06
PK 146+07.1	04 25.83	PK 231+04.1	07 42.05	PK 269−13.1	07 59.26	PK 294−00.1	11 41.68
PK 147−02.1	03 41.74	PK 232−01.1	07 21.25	PK 270−02.1	09 05.94	PK 294+00.1	11 44.57
PK 147+04.1	04 13.28	PK 232−04.1	07 11.28	PK 270−04.1	08 52.73	PK 294+04.1	11 50.30
PK 147−09.1	03 16.6	PK 232+05.1	07 48.06	PK 270−05.1	08 50.79	PK 294−04.1	11 31.75
PK 148−48.1	01 58.0	PK 233−10.1	06 50.7	PK 270+24.1	10 34.51	PK 294+12.1	12 00.18
PK 148+57.1	11 14.78	PK 233−16.1	06 27.04	PK 271−05.1	08 53.5	PK 294+14.1	12 00.73
PK 149−03.1	03 49.2	PK 234+02.1	07 41.92	PK 271−08.1	08 34.8	PK 294+43.1	12 24.50
PK 149+04.1	04 20.75	PK 234−06.1	07 06.93	PK 272+00.1	09 24.12	PK 295+04.1	11 56.30
PK 149−09.1	03 27.2	PK 235−01.1	07 27.94	PK 272+12.1	10 07.00	PK 295+06.1	11 56.23
PK 151+00.1	04 13.45	PK 235−03.1	07 19.35	PK 273−03.1	09 08.67	PK 295+07.1	12 03.46
PK 153−01.1	04 15.91	PK 235+04.1	07 50.0	PK 273+06.1	09 52.7	PK 295−09.1	11 17.72
PK 153+22.1	06 43.90	PK 236+03.1	07 50.22	PK 274−00.1	09 31.40	PK 295−09.2	11 18.08
PK 156+12.1	05 38.0	PK 236−10.1	06 54.4	PK 274+01.1	09 37.99	PK 296−03.1	11 48.65
PK 156−13.1	03 45.5	PK 237−65.1	02 39.82	PK 274+02.1	09 41.23	PK 296−06.1	11 39.18
PK 158+00.1	04 45.0	PK 238+07.2	08 08.73	PK 274+02.2	09 41.62	PK 296−06.2	11 39.29
PK 158+17.1	06 19.6	PK 238+07.1	08 09.23	PK 274+02.3	09 38.56	PK 296+10.1	12 10.08
PK 158+37.1	08 41.64	PK 238+34.1	09 39.13	PK 274+03.2	09 46.85	PK 296−20.1	10 09.50
PK 159−15.1	03 47.51	PK 239−12.1	06 55.2	PK 274+03.1	09 47.41	PK 297+03.1	12 09.16

Cross Index of Planetary Nebulae by Name							
PK 297−03.1	12 00.39	PK 322−06.1	15 52.18	PK 342−06.1	17 27.81	PK 356+03.1	17 25.10
PK 297+07.1	12 17.36	PK 322+14.1	14 38.27	PK 342+10.1	16 12.98	PK 356−03.1	17 49.84
PK 297+13.1	12 16.52	PK 323−02.1	15 38.02	PK 342−14.1	18 07.27	PK 356−03.4	17 49.80
PK 298−00.1	12 09.03	PK 323+02.1	15 22.32	PK 342+15.1	15 58.78	PK 356−04.2	17 57.32
PK 298−01.2	12 08.42	PK 323−07.1	16 04.50	PK 342+27.1	15 22.31	PK 356+04.2	17 21.07
PK 298−04.1	12 04.22	PK 324−01.1	15 41.98	PK 343−00.1	17 01.5	PK 356+04.1	17 20.55
PK 298+34.1	12 33.2	PK 324+02.1	15 23.60	PK 343−01.1	17 05.60	PK 356−04.1	17 54.55
PK 299−01.1	12 23.03	PK 324+03.1	15 19.2	PK 343+03.1	16 44.3	PK 356+05.1	17 17.27
PK 299+02.1	12 23.89	PK 324+09.1	15 01.67	PK 343−07.1	17 35.69	PK 356−05.1	18 00.31
PK 299−04.1	12 16.5	PK 325−01.1	15 51.3	PK 343+11.1	16 13.46	PK 356−05.2	18 02.05
PK 299+18.1	12 30.88	PK 325+03.1	15 25.54	PK 344+00.1	16 57.39	PK 356−06.1	18 02.53
PK 300+00.1	12 28.72	PK 325+04.3	15 24.75	PK 344−01.1	17 06.98	PK 356−06.2	18 04.49
PK 300−00.1	12 28.78	PK 325+04.1	15 25.13	PK 344+02.1	16 50.65	PK 356−06.3	18 03.74
PK 300−01.1	12 30.12	PK 325−04.1	15 59.14	PK 344+03.1	16 49.53	PK 356−07.2	18 09.82
PK 300−02.2	12 28.63	PK 325−07.1	16 15.85	PK 344+04.1	16 42.56	PK 356−11.1	18 27.80
PK 300−02.1	12 30.51	PK 325−12.1	16 54.58	PK 344−06.1	17 30.07	PK 357−01.1	17 44.16
PK 300−03.1	12 30.41	PK 326−01.2	15 53.0	PK 345+00.1	17 05.18	PK 357+01.1	17 32.78
PK 302−00.3	12 48.52	PK 326−03.1	15 59.76	PK 345−01.1	17 10.45	PK 357+01.2	17 33.3
PK 302−00.2	12 46.45	PK 326−06.1	16 15.69	PK 345+03.2	16 54.46	PK 357+01.3	17 35.7
PK 302+02.1	12 45.92	PK 326+42.1	14 04.44	PK 345+03.1	16 50.42	PK 357+02.6	17 31.13
PK 303+01.1	12 53.25	PK 327−01.1	16 00.99	PK 345+04.1	16 46.75	PK 357+02.8	17 29.5
PK 303+40.1	12 53.57	PK 327−01.2	15 58.13	PK 345−04.1	17 26.20	PK 357+02.4	17 29.72
PK 304−04.1	13 08.79	PK 327−02.1	15 59.96	PK 345+06.1	16 39.46	PK 357+02.7	17 30.81
PK 304+05.2	13 00.68	PK 327−05.1	16 19.3	PK 345−08.1	17 45.59	PK 357−02.1	17 47.8
PK 304+05.1	13 05.80	PK 327−06.1	16 23.51	PK 345−10.1	17 52.7	PK 357+02.5	17 28.84
PK 305+01.1	13 09.60	PK 327−07.1	16 29.51	PK 345−11.1	17 59.61	PK 357−03.2	17 52.58
PK 305+03.2	13 10.33	PK 327+10.1	15 16.84	PK 345−13.1	18 10.59	PK 357+03.1	17 24.57
PK 305−03.1	13 19.51	PK 327+13.1	15 06.23	PK 345+15.1	16 09.73	PK 357+03.4	17 27.00
PK 305−13.1	13 34.24	PK 328+01.1	15 49.54	PK 346−04.1	17 29.17	PK 357+03.5	17 27.40
PK 306−00.1	13 22.55	PK 328−02.1	16 10.67	PK 346−06.1	17 39.33	PK 357−03.4	17 53.63
PK 306−00.2	13 26.22	PK 329+01.1	15 54.84	PK 346+08.1	16 34.07	PK 357+03.2	17 25.99
PK 307+01.1	13 26.19	PK 329−02.1	16 14.41	PK 346−08.1	17 45.48	PK 357−03.3	17 53.28
PK 307−01.2	13 37.68	PK 329−02.2	16 14.53	PK 346+12.1	16 23.29	PK 357−04.2	17 58.55
PK 307−03.1	13 33.52	PK 329+02.1	15 51.68	PK 346+22.1	15 49.90	PK 357−04.4	17 58.40
PK 307−04.1	13 39.58	PK 330−02.2	16 15.35	PK 347+01.1	17 04.56	PK 357+04.1	17 23.41
PK 307+05.1	13 24.37	PK 330−02.3	16 16.90	PK 347+05.1	16 48.90	PK 357−04.3	17 58.24
PK 307−09.1	13 45.38	PK 330−02.1	16 17.23	PK 348−04.1	17 32.79	PK 357−04.1	17 57.42
PK 308+00.2	13 40.37	PK 330−03.1	16 24.35	PK 348+06.1	16 48.8	PK 357−05.1	18 01.37
PK 308+00.1	13 37.67	PK 330+04.1	15 51.26	PK 348−09.1	17 56.56	PK 357−06.1	18 04.09
PK 308+07.1	13 28.1	PK 330+04.2	15 51.33	PK 348−13.1	18 18.53	PK 357+07.1	17 10.70
PK 308−12.2	14 15.58	PK 330+05.1	15 42.22	PK 349+01.1	17 13.73	PK 358+00.1	17 41.58
PK 308−12.1	14 15.51	PK 331+00.1	16 08.98	PK 349−01.1	17 22.26	PK 358−00.2	17 45.96
PK 309+00.1	13 42.63	PK 331−01.1	16 17.23	PK 349−03.1	17 32.87	PK 358+01.1	17 35.24
PK 309+01.1	13 43.99	PK 331−02.1	16 22.23	PK 349−04.1	17 35.67	PK 358+01.4	17 36.99
PK 309−04.2	13 53.95	PK 331−02.2	16 24.63	PK 349+04.1	17 01.10	PK 358−01.1	17 46.03
PK 309−04.1	13 52.51	PK 331+03.1	15 53.47	PK 350−02.2	17 34.33	PK 358+02.2	17 30.38
PK 310−02.1	14 05.61	PK 331−03.1	16 27.84	PK 350−02.1	17 32.37	PK 358+02.5	17 31.9
PK 310−03.1	14 00.36	PK 331−03.2	16 30.00	PK 350−03.1	17 36.50	PK 358−02.1	17 51.75
PK 310−05.1	14 15.3	PK 331−05.1	16 37.71	PK 350+04.1	17 04.60	PK 358−02.4	17 51.8
PK 310+06.1	13 43.98	PK 331−13.1	17 25.13	PK 350−05.1	17 42.90	PK 358+02.4	17 30.5
PK 310+24.1	13 25.62	PK 331+16.1	15 12.85	PK 351−01.1	17 33.01	PK 358−02.5	17 53.6
PK 311−00.1	14 08.77	PK 332+03.1	16 00.37	PK 351+04.1	17 03.78	PK 358−03.1	17 58.18
PK 311+02.1	13 58.23	PK 332−03.1	16 29.89	PK 351+05.1	17 02.31	PK 358+03.8	17 31.15
PK 311+02.2	13 55.75	PK 332−04.1	16 35.34	PK 351−06.1	17 50.74	PK 358+03.7	17 29.67
PK 311−02.1	14 11.71	PK 332−16.1	17 51.9	PK 351+07.1	16 53.62	PK 358+03.1	17 27.34
PK 311−06.1	14 18.99	PK 332−16.2	17 54.2	PK 351+09.1	16 50.28	PK 358+03.4	17 30.04
PK 312−01.1	14 18.74	PK 333+01.1	16 15.33	PK 351−10.1	18 12.90	PK 358+03.3	17 28.66
PK 312+10.1	13 51.06	PK 333−04.1	16 39.6	PK 351−10.2	18 09.0	PK 358+03.2	17 27.55
PK 313+01.1	14 18.92	PK 334−01.1	16 31.1	PK 352−00.1	17 28.46	PK 358+03.6	17 30.73
PK 313+04.1	14 08.79	PK 334−07.1	17 03.04	PK 352+00.2	17 24.92	PK 358+03.9	17 27.8
PK 313−05.1	14 40.88	PK 334−09.1	17 11.75	PK 352+00.1	17 26.40	PK 358−04.1	17 59.04
PK 313−12.1	15 21.2	PK 335−01.1	16 34.22	PK 352+03.2	17 14.71	PK 358−04.2	17 59.91
PK 314−00.1	14 33.08	PK 335−03.2	16 48.0	PK 352+04.1	17 10.22	PK 358+04.3	17 26.9
PK 314+10.1	14 01.2	PK 335−03.1	16 45.0	PK 352−04.1	17 45.11	PK 358+04.2	!7 26.94
PK 315−00.1	14 33.29	PK 335−04.1	16 48.7	PK 352+05.1	17 05.51	PK 358+04.1	17 24.87
PK 315−01.1	14 41.3	PK 335+09.1	15 53.20	PK 352−07.1	18 00.20	PK 358−05.1	18 01.71
PK 315−04.1	14 52.61	PK 335+12.1	15 43.0	PK 352−09.1	18 10.59	PK 358−05.3	18 03.89
PK 315+05.2	14 22.0	PK 336−01.1	16 38.2	PK 352+11.1	16 41.72	PK 358+05.2	17 22.42
PK 315+05.1	14 20.81	PK 336+01.1	16 23.88	PK 352+11.2	16 44.82	PK 358+05.1	17 21.18
PK 315+08.1	14 17.5	PK 336−02.1	16 42.1	PK 353−04.1	17 49.80	PK 358−05.4	18 04.94
PK 315+09.1	14 11.86	PK 336−05.1	16 59.60	PK 353−05.1	17 50.75	PK 358−07.1	18 12.04
PK 315−13.1	15 37.17	PK 336−06.1	17 06.24	PK 353+06.1	17 05.23	PK 358+07.1	17 12.65
PK 315+59.1	13 16.9	PK 336−07.1	17 09.60	PK 353+06.2	17 04.31	PK 358+09.1	17 05.77
PK 316−01.1	14 46.4	PK 336+08.1	16 02.22	PK 353+08.1	16 55.78	PK 358−21.1	19 17.39
PK 316+08.1	14 18.14	PK 336−11.1	17 34.4	PK 353−12.1	18 26.69	PK 359−00.1	17 47.93
PK 317+03.1	14 41.60	PK 337+01.1	16 30.43	PK 353−55.1	22 21.12	PK 359+01.3	17 39.1
PK 317−05.1	15 10.69	PK 337−04.1	16 57.5	PK 354−02.1	17 40.62	PK 359−01.3	17 52.10
PK 318−02.3	15 05.54	PK 337−05.1	17 01.62	PK 354+03.1	17 18.87	PK 359−01.2	17 51.31
PK 318−02.1	15 04.14	PK 337−09.1	17 22.60	PK 354+04.1	17 14.11	PK 359−01.1	17 50.30
PK 318−02.2	15 06.03	PK 337−18.1	18 18.14	PK 354−07.1	18 04.94	PK 359+01.1	17 38.67
PK 318+03.1	14 43.74	PK 338+05.1	16 19.38	PK 355−02.2	17 44.23	PK 359−02.3	17 55.60
PK 318−03.1	15 08.71	PK 338−08.1	17 20.77	PK 355−02.1	17 44.34	PK 359+02.6	17 34.2
PK 318+41.1	13 40.63	PK 339−00.1	16 45.5	PK 355+02.3	17 24.44	PK 359+02.5	17 32.4
PK 319+06.1	14 40.52	PK 339+09.1	16 08.49	PK 355−02.3	17 46.10	PK 359−02.2	17 52.77
PK 319+15.1	14 22.43	PK 339+29.1	15 08.35	PK 355+02.2	17 24.68	PK 359+02.3	17 35.80
PK 320−09.1	15 56.03	PK 339+88.1	12 55.5	PK 355−02.4	17 45.54	PK 359−02.4	17 55.10
PK 320−28.1	19 33.79	PK 340+03.1	16 34.8	PK 355−03.2	17 48.96	PK 359+02.4	17 35.25
PK 321−00.1	15 19.48	PK 340−04.1	17 11.45	PK 355+03.3	17 19.32	PK 359+02.7	17 36.3
PK 321−00.2	15 21.11	PK 340+10.1	16 08.44	PK 355+03.2	17 21.52	PK 359−03.1	17 56.43
PK 321+01.1	15 11.94	PK 340+12.1	16 03.36	PK 355−03.1	17 47.82	PK 359−03.2	17 58.20
PK 321−01.1	15 26.91	PK 340−14.1	18 00.98	PK 355−03.3	17 49.23	PK 359+03.2	17 30.78
PK 321+02.2	15 05.98	PK 341+05.1	16 31.51	PK 355−04.2	17 52.98	PK 359+03.4	17 30.2
PK 321+02.1	15 05.28	PK 341−09.1	17 36.11	PK 355−04.1	17 51.21	PK 359+03.1	17 30.92
PK 321−03.1	15 30.3	PK 341+13.1	16 01.35	PK 355−06.1	18 02.54	PK 359−04.3	18 02.77
PK 321+03.1	14 59.89	PK 341−15.1	18 09.50	PK 356−00.1	17 37.76	PK 359−04.2	18 03.88
PK 321+08.1	14 46.5	PK 341−24.1	19 09.75	PK 356+01.2	17 30.97	PK 359−04.4	18 04.13
PK 321−16.1	17 01.28	PK 342+00.1	16 53.50	PK 356+02.1	17 25.31	PK 359−04.1	17 59.94
PK 322−00.1	15 23.71	PK 342−02.1	17 06.37	PK 356−02.2	17 46.76	PK 359+04.1	17 25.73
PK 322−02.1	15 34.28	PK 342−02.2	17 07.50	PK 356−03.2	17 51.85	PK 359−04.5	18 02.8
PK 322−05.1	15 47.68	PK 342−04.1	17 19.53	PK 356−03.3	17 53.35	PK 359−05.1	18 07.4

Cross Index of Planetary Nebulae by Name							
PK 359+05.1	17 24.03	Sa 2-62	10 34.31	Sa 2-237	17 44.69	Sa 3-34	16 08.98
PK 359+05.2	17 25.72	Sa 2-63	10 35.77	Sa 2-242	17 46.91	Sa 3-36	16 34.22
PK 359−06.2	18 09.2	Sa 2-66	10 41.33	Sa 2-248	17 49.25	Sa 3-37	16 49.53
PK 359−06.1	18 13.30	Sa 2-68	10 48.73	Sa 2-250	17 50.30	Sa 3-38	16 53.50
PK 359+06.1	17 19.22	Sa 2-70	11 00.33	Sa 2-260	17 52.69	Sa 3-39	16 57.39
PK 359−07.1	18 14.84	Sa 2-72	11 17.72	Sa 2-265	17 55.33	Sa 3-41	17 07.50
PK 359+15.1	16 48.57	Sa 2-76	11 28.79	Sa 2-266	17 55.60	Sa 3-42	17 17.27
PP 40	05 40.9	Sa 2-78	11 35.18	Sa 2-267	17 56.56	Sa 3-44	17 18.87
PRTM-1	05 03.1	Sa 2-80	11 48.65	Sa 2-268	17 56.33	Sa 3-45	17 19.32
PTH-1	18 40.3	Sa 2-81	11 50.30	Sa 2-275	17 58.98	Sa 3-47	17 24.44
Pe 1-0	17 51.21	Sa 2-84	12 28.78	Sa 2-277	18 00.20	Sa 3-48	17 24.68
Pe 1-1	10 38.47	Sa 2-85	12 30.12	Sa 2-278	18 00.98	Sa 3-49	17 25.10
Pe 1-2	10 39.55	Sa 2-86	12 30.51	Sa 2-280	18 01.71	Sa 3-50	17 25.73
Pe 1-3	10 44.53	Sa 2-88	13 05.80	Sa 2-286	18 03.30	Sa 3-52	17 27.00
Pe 1-4	16 08.98	Sa 2-90	13 09.60	Sa 2-290	18 04.09	Sa 3-53	17 27.40
Pe 1-5	16 15.33	Sa 2-91	13 19.51	Sa 2-292	18 04.94	Sa 3-56	17 28.84
Pe 1-6	16 23.88	Sa 2-93	13 24.37	Sa 2-294	18 05.21	Sa 3-58	17 30.97
Pe 1-7	16 30.43	Sa 2-97	13 42.63	Sa 2-299	18 07.90	Sa 3-59	17 31.13
Pe 1-8	17 06.37	Sa 2-98	13 45.38	Sa 2-301	18 08.06	Sa 3-62	17 32.87
Pe 1-9	17 45.61	Sa 2-99	13 51.06	Sa 2-303	18 09.23	Sa 3-65	17 35.24
Pe 1-11	18 01.71	Sa 2-100	13 53.95	Sa 2-304	18 10.59	Sa 3-67	17 35.80
Pe 1-12	18 17.66	Sa 2-101	13 58.23	Sa 2-306	18 11.49	Sa 3-68	17 40.21
Pe 1-13	18 34.86	Sa 2-103	14 05.61	Sa 2-307	18 11.87	Sa 3-71	17 45.61
Pe 1-14	18 42.09	Sa 2-104	14 20.81	Sa 2-308	18 12.04	Sa 3-75	17 47.57
Pe 1-15	18 46.41	Sa 2-105	14 22.43	Sa 2-309	18 12.40	Sa 3-77	17 48.60
Pe 1-16	18 47.53	Sa 2-106	14 33.29	Sa 2-310	18 12.42	Sa 3-79	17 49.84
Pe 1-17	18 47.81	Sa 2-108	14 52.61	Sa 2-311	18 12.90	Sa 3-81	17 50.75
Pe 1-18	18 48.78	Sa 2-109	15 04.14	Sa 2-314	18 13.75	Sa 3-82	17 51.31
Pe 1-19	18 49.75	Sa 2-111	15 05.54	Sa 2-315	18 14.47	Sa 3-83	17 51.85
Pe 1-20	18 57.29	Sa 2-112	15 05.28	Sa 2-318	18 15.28	Sa 3-84	17 52.10
Pe 1-21	18 57.83	Sa 2-114	15 06.23	Sa 2-322	18 16.28	Sa 3-87	17 53.28
Pe 2-4	09 30.81	Sa 2-115	15 10.69	Sa 2-323	18 18.14	Sa 3-89	17 53.78
Pe 2-5	10 28.54	Sa 2-116	15 11.94	Sa 2-326	18 18.53	Sa 3-90	17 53.82
Pe 2-7	10 41.33	Sa 2-117	15 12.85	Sa 2-327	18 18.69	Sa 3-91	17 54.58
Pe 2-8	15 23.71	Sa 2-118	15 16.84	Sa 2-328	18 19.42	Sa 3-92	17 54.86
Pe 2-10	17 53.61	Sa 2-119	15 22.32	Sa 2-332	18 22.90	Sa 3-93	17 55.10
Pe 2-11	17 58.51	Sa 2-120	15 22.31	Sa 2-335	18 25.71	Sa 3-94	17 56.04
Pe 2-12	18 01.16	Sa 2-121	15 25.13	Sa 2-340	18 30.00	Sa 3-95	17 56.04
Pe 2-13	18 18.22	Sa 2-122	15 25.54	Sa 2-341	18 30.57	Sa 3-96	17 55.78
Pe 2-14	18 30.00	Sa 2-125	15 51.33	Sa 2-345	18 33.91	Sa 3-98	17 56.40
Pe 2-15	18 45.50	Sa 2-126	15 52.18	Sa 2-346	18 33.97	Sa 3-100	17 57.81
Ps 1	21 30.02	Sa 2-128	15 53.47	Sa 2-347	18 34.22	Sa 3-101	17 58.18
Pt 1	17 41.65	Sa 2-129	15 59.14	Sa 2-348	18 34.86	Sa 3-102	17 58.20
Pu 1	05 52.81	Sa 2-130	16 00.99	Sa 2-350	18 36.14	Sa 3-103	17 58.31
Pu 2	06 02.6	Sa 2-132	16 02.22	Sa 2-352	18 37.18	Sa 3-104	17 58.43
PuWe 1	06 19.6	Sa 2-133	16 10.67	Sa 2-353	18 37.77	Sa 3-106	17 58.51
RCW 21	08 30.93	Sa 2-135	16 13.46	Sa 2-354	18 37.61	Sa 3-107	17 59.91
RCW 43	09 27.04	Sa 2-136	16 14.41	Sa 2-356	18 40.34	Sa 3-108	17 59.94
RCW 44	09 31.45	Sa 2-138	16 15.35	Sa 2-357	18 44.10	Sa 3-109	18 00.31
RCW 70	12 46.45	Sa 2-141	16 19.38	Sa 2-358	18 43.34	Sa 3-110	18 01.16
RCW 77	13 39.58	Sa 2-142	16 23.51	Sa 2-359	18 43.63	Sa 3-111	18 01.12
RCW 90	15 05.98	Sa 2-143	16 24.35	Sa 2-360	18 44.23	Sa 3-114	18 04.13
RCW 93	15 34.28	Sa 2-144	16 24.63	Sa 2-363	18 45.84	Sa 3-115	18 04.08
RCW 100	15 51.68	Sa 2-145	16 29.51	Sa 2-364	18 45.58	Sa 3-116	18 04.49
RCW 112	16 31.51	Sa 2-146	16 29.89	Sa 2-365	18 45.91	Sa 3-117	18 04.73
RCW 135	17 45.96	Sa 2-147	16 30.00	Sa 2-366	18 47.53	Sa 3-120	18 08.43
RCW 136	17 58.18	Sa 2-149	16 35.34	Sa 2-368	18 49.75	Sa 3-123	18 12.15
RCW 181	18 54.75	Sa 2-150	16 39.46	Sa 2-370	18 50.73	Sa 3-124	18 13.68
RWT 152	07 29.9	Sa 2-151	16 42.56	Sa 2-371	18 51.51	Sa 3-125	18 14.31
S 22	01 30.6	Sa 2-154	16 50.42	Sa 2-372	18 54.03	Sa 3-128	18 17.79
Sa 1-3	16 02.22	Sa 2-155	16 50.28	Sa 2-373	18 54.29	Sa 3-129	18 18.22
Sa 1-4	16 15.35	Sa 2-156	16 50.65	Sa 2-374	18 54.33	Sa 3-132	18 24.13
Sa 1-5	17 11.45	Sa 2-157	16 54.58	Sa 2-376	18 55.51	Sa 3-133	18 26.66
Sa 1-6	18 00.98	Sa 2-158	16 53.62	Sa 2-377	18 57.29	Sa 3-134	18 29.33
Sa 1-7	18 36.53	Sa 2-159	16 54.46	Sa 2-378	18 58.43	Sa 3-136	18 32.69
Sa 1-8	18 50.73	Sa 2-161	16 59.60	Sa 2-379	19 01.61	Sa 3-137	18 33.06
Sa 2-1	06 21.71	Sa 2-162	17 01.28	Sa 2-380	19 02.60	Sa 3-138	18 33.26
Sa 2-2	07 02.78	Sa 2-164	17 01.56	Sa 2-382	19 05.92	Sa 3-140	18 34.23
Sa 2-4	07 06.74	Sa 2-167	17 04.56	Sa 2-383	19 14.39	Sa 3-141	18 39.37
Sa 2-6	07 14.82	Sa 2-172	17 05.77	Sa 2-384	19 14.60	Sa 3-143	18 41.25
Sa 2-8	07 26.58	Sa 2-175	17 10.70	Sa 2-385	19 16.47	Sa 3-144	18 41.12
Sa 2-11	07 37.32	Sa 2-176	17 11.75	Sa 2-387	19 18.32	Sa 3-145	18 46.41
Sa 2-12	07 40.37	Sa 2-177	17 11.45	Sa 2-388	19 18.41	Sa 3-146	18 46.57
Sa 2-15	07 42.05	Sa 2-179	17 12.86	Sa 2-389	19 22.17	Sa 3-147	18 47.81
Sa 2-17	07 47.33	Sa 2-183	17 19.53	Sa 2-390	19 27.03	Sa 3-148	18 48.78
Sa 2-18	07 52.96	Sa 2-185	17 20.77	Sa 2-391	19 32.11	Sa 3-150	18 57.83
Sa 2-21	08 08.73	Sa 2-187	17 21.07	Sa 2-392	19 43.96	Sa 3-151	18 58.84
Sa 2-22	08 10.69	Sa 2-191	17 22.26	Sa 3-1	06 35.74	Sa 3-152	19 00.57
Sa 2-25	08 21.07	Sa 2-192	17 23.41	Sa 3-4	07 18.24	Sa 3-153	19 02.17
Sa 2-26	08 28.46	Sa 2-193	17 25.13	Sa 3-7	08 43.49	Sa 4-1	17 13.8
Sa 2-27	08 33.39	Sa 2-195	17 26.20	Sa 3-9	09 30.91	SaSt 1-1	08 31.71
Sa 2-28	08 36.27	Sa 2-197	17 27.81	Sa 3-10	09 31.45	SaSt 1-2	09 18.02
Sa 2-30	08 41.16	Sa 2-198	17 27.34	Sa 3-11	09 40.89	SaSt 2-3	07 48.06
Sa 2-31	08 43.47	Sa 2-200	17 28.06	Sa 3-13	10 55.99	SaSt 2-5	10 23.15
Sa 2-32	08 53.51	Sa 2-202	17 29.17	Sa 3-15	12 08.42	SaSt 2-6	11 31.75
Sa 2-35	09 08.67	Sa 2-203	17 28.56	Sa 3-16	12 09.03	SaSt 2-7	11 39.18
Sa 2-37	09 13.88	Sa 2-205	17 29.03	Sa 3-17	12 09.16	SaSt 2-8	14 18.14
Sa 2-41	09 19.46	Sa 2-207	17 29.34	Sa 3-18	12 23.03	SaSt 2-9	15 37.17
Sa 2-44	09 24.76	Sa 2-208	17 30.07	Sa 3-19	12 23.89	SaSt 2-10	15 56.03
Sa 2-47	09 38.79	Sa 2-210	17 29.72	Sa 3-20	12 28.63	SaSt 2-11	15 59.96
Sa 2-48	09 41.62	Sa 2-213	17 32.79	Sa 3-21	12 28.72	SaSt 2-12	17 03.04
Sa 2-49	09 43.43	Sa 2-215	17 33.01	Sa 3-23	13 52.51	SaSt 2-15	17 38.95
Sa 2-50	09 47.41	Sa 2-218	17 36.11	Sa 3-24	14 15.51	SaSt 2-20	18 17.56
Sa 2-51	10 02.04	Sa 2-224	17 38.50	Sa 3-25	14 18.99	Sd 1	20 29.31
Sa 2-52	10 03.83	Sa 2-226	17 39.91	Sa 3-26	14 18.74	Sh 1-89	21 14.05
Sa 2-53	10 07.00	Sa 2-227	17 40.30	Sa 3-27	15 06.03	Sh 2-52	19 46.59
Sa 2-54	10 07.40	Sa 2-228	17 41.88	Sa 3-29	15 23.60	Sh 2-68	18 24.9
Sa 2-56	10 12.00	Sa 2-230	17 42.05	Sa 3-30	15 38.02	Sh 2-71	19 02.02
Sa 2-59	10 17.84	Sa 2-232	17 43.48	Sa 3-31	15 41.98	Sh 2-78	19 03.1
Sa 2-60	10 31.53	Sa 2-234	17 44.34	Sa 3-32	16 00.37	Sh 2-116	20 32.41

Cross Index of Planetary Nebulae by Name							
Sh 2-128	21 32.17	TrJu 21	17 35.7	Wra 16-24	08 37.95	Wra 17-20	08 34.48
Sh 2-179	00 40.33	V-V 1-9	19 02.02	Wra 16-26	08 41.16	Wra 17-27	09 16.79
Sh 2-188	01 30.6	V-V 3-1	11 26.73	Wra 16-20	08 23.71	Wra 17-30	09 24.53
Sh 2-189	02 12.19	V-V 3-2	12 30.88	Wra 16-29	08 50.79	Wra 17-33	09 38.56
Sh 2-200	03 11.0	V-V 3-3	14 38.27	Wra 16-31	08 52.73	Wra 17-38	09 59.68
Sh 2-216	04 45.0	V1016 Cyg	19 57.1	Wra 16-42	09 19.63	Wra 17-37	09 48.24
Sh 2-290	08 54.19	VB 1	16 45.5	Wra 16-45	09 24.12	Wra 17-31	09 31.45
Sh 2-313	12 53.57	VB 2	15 51.3	Wra 16-50	09 32.74	Wra 17-32	09 37.06
ShWi 1	18 02.5	VB 3	15 53.0	Wra 16-56	09 41.23	Wra 17-39	10 02.89
ShWi 2	18 03.0	VBRC 1	08 30.93	Wra 16-53	09 37.99	Wra 17-34	09 39.95
ShWi 4	18 03.6	VBRC 2	09 31.45	Wra 16-58	09 46.85	Wra 17-36	09 46.32
ShWi 5	18 03.9	VBRC 3	09 40.89	Wra 16-61	09 52.06	Wra 17-40	10 06.92
ShWi 6	18 04.0	VBRC 4	12 46.45	Wra 16-63	10 02.26	Wra 17-43	10 26.69
ShWi 7	18 05.1	VBRC 5	13 43.99	Wra 16-89	11 27.40	Wra 17-48	11 45.70
Sn 1	16 21.06	VBRC 6	14 41.60	Wra 16-87	11 18.08	Wra 17-44	10 29.29
Sp 1	15 51.68	VBRC 7	15 54.84	Wra 16-93	11 30.82	Wra 17-49	11 47.63
Sp 2	17 11.75	VLA 4	17 26.9	Wra 16-99	11 39.29	Wra 17-46	11 23.23
Sp 3	18 07.27	Vd 1-1	16 42.56	Wra 16-102	11 56.23	Wra 17-47	11 44.57
SrWe 1	06 50.7	Vd 1-2	16 46.75	Wra 16-103	12 00.18	Wra 17-42	10 21.05
SrWe 2	17 26.9	Vd 1-3	16 49.53	Wra 16-113	12 28.63	Wra 17-57	12 53.25
SrWe 3	18 26.0	Vd 1-4	16 50.42	Wra 16-120	12 45.92	Wra 17-52	12 03.46
SrWe 4	19 02.3	Vd 1-5	16 50.65	Wra 16-122	13 00.68	Wra 17-53	12 10.08
St 3-1	07 06.80	Vd 1-6	16 54.46	Wra 16-129	13 26.19	Wra 17-59	13 19.51
St 4-1	19 00.4	Vd 1-8	17 04.56	Wra 16-134	13 43.98	Wra 17-54	12 16.52
StWr 1-4	11 17.72	Vd 1-9	17 05.60	Wra 16-140	13 53.95	Wra 17-56	12 48.52
StWr 1-6	13 45.38	Ve 59	17 52.69	Wra 16-146	14 11.71	Wra 17-58	13 10.33
StWr 2-18	19 22.17	Ve 60	17 55.12	Wra 16-145	14 08.79	Wra 17-50	11 56.30
StWr 2-21	19 14.39	VeRa 104	16 42.1	Wra 16-143	14 00.36	Wra 17-51	12 00.39
StWr 2-28	18 12.90	VeRa 90	16 38.2	Wra 16-150	14 18.99	Wra 17-55	12 17.36
StWr 2-37	18 10.59	Vy 1-2	17 54.37	Wra 16-155	14 33.08	Wra 17-64	14 08.77
StWr 2-43	16 37.71	Vy 1-4	18 54.03	Wra 16-158	14 52.61	Wra 17-66	14 18.92
StWr 2-48	17 25.13	Vy 2-1	18 27.99	Wra 16-161	15 05.54	Wra 17-67	14 40.88
Ste 2-1	10 12.00	Vy 2-2	19 24.38	Wra 16-179	15 24.75	Wra 17-60	13 26.22
Ste 2-4	17 49.80	Vy 2-3	23 22.96	Wra 16-174	15 19.48	Wra 17-62	13 37.67
SuWt 1	13 43.99	We 1-2	04 46.71	Wra 16-189	15 51.33	Wra 17-63	13 40.37
SuWt 2	13 55.75	We 1-3	04 54.53	Wra 16-199	16 00.37	Wra 17-61	13 37.68
SuWt 3	16 44.3	We 1-4	06 14.56	Wra 16-192	15 53.47	Wra 17-69	15 21.11
SwSt 1	18 16.21	We 1-5	06 41.58	Wra 16-197	15 59.76	Wra 17-65	14 15.58
Tc 1	17 45.59	We 1-6	07 17.43	Wra 16-203	16 08.49	Wra 17-76	16 44.82
Th 1-A	18 37.61	We 1-7	18 44.12	Wra 16-231	16 42.56	Wra 17-75	16 16.90
Th 1-D	18 48.78	We 1-8	19 48.87	Wra 16-255	17 10.22	Wra 17-70	15 26.91
Th 1-E	18 54.03	We 1-9	20 09.07	Wra 16-251	17 07.50	Wra 17-72	16 04.50
Th 1-H	18 57.83	We 1-10	20 31.88	Wra 16-266	17 22.60	Wra 17-73	16 15.85
Th 2-A	13 22.55	We 1-11	21 10.87	Wra 16-269	17 24.92	Wra 17-71	15 49.90
Th 3-1	17 05.77	We 2-5	01 42.64	Wra 16-278	17 30.07	Wra 17-80	17 27.00
Th 3-2	17 10.70	We 2-34	07 00.46	Wra 16-287	17 34.33	Wra 17-93	17 40.12
Th 3-3	17 17.27	We 2-37	07 16.13	Wra 16-295	17 40.62	Wra 17-96	17 41.58
Th 3-4	17 18.87	We 2-245	21 18.12	Wra 16-298	17 44.16	Wra 17-104	17 58.40
Th 3-6	17 19.32	We 2-260	23 22.35	Wra 16-344	17 59.91	Wra 17-107	18 04.08
Th 3-10	17 24.68	We 2-262	23 52.33	Wra 16-363	18 04.73	Y-C 2-1	07 52.49
Th 3-11	17 24.44	We 3-1	18 34.1	Wra 16-376	18 10.59	Y-C 2-2	07 52.77
Th 3-12	17 25.10	We a	03 27.2	Wra 16-385	18 12.90	Y-C 2-3	07 59.52
Th 3-13	17 25.31	We b	05 38.0	Wra 16-411	18 26.69	Y-C 2-4	08 09.23
Th 3-14	17 25.73	We c	06 40.2	Wra 17-7	07 37.37	Y-C 2-5	08 10.69
Th 3-15	!7 26.94	We d	07 54.9	Wra 17-8	07 49.67	Y-C 2-7	11 09.15
Th 3-16	17 27.40	We e	19 31.3	Wra 17-6	07 35.39	Y-C 2-9	11 17.08
Th 3-19	17 28.66	We f	19 57.2	Wra 17-5	07 28.04	Y-C 2-10	11 24.02
Th 3-23	17 30.38	WeDe 1	05 59.4	Wra 17-2	07 18.24	Y-C 2-11	11 28.60
Th 3-24	17 30.81	WeSb 1	01 00.9	Wra 17-3	07 19.12	Y-C 2-15	14 40.52
Th 3-25	17 30.78	WeSb 2	06 16.2	Wra 17-9	07 51.45	Y-C 2-17	15 08.35
Th 3-26	17 31.15	WeSb 3	18 06.1	Wra 17-4	07 26.27	Y-C 2-19	15 58.78
Th 3-27	17 35.97	WeSb 4	18 50.7	Wra 17-14	08 01.40	Y-C 2-25	18 37.18
Th 3-28	17 30.92	WeSb 5	20 01.7	Wra 17-13	08 00.42	Y-C 2-26	18 41.93
Th 3-32	17 35.25	WeSb 6	23 13.1	Wra 17-10	07 56.13	Y-C 2-29	18 49.14
Th 3-33	17 35.80	Wra 15-126	14 59.89	Wra 17-17	08 15.88	Y-C 2-32	18 55.51
Th 3-34	17 37.76	Wra 15-490	10 02.04	Wra 17-19	08 27.57	Y-C 2-37	07 26.5
Th 3-35	17 38.67	Wra 16-7	07 46.78	Wra 17-15	08 14.56	Y-C 2-40	07 50.0
Th 4-1	17 46.27	Wra 16-9	07 55.61	Wra 17-11	07 59.54	Y-C 2-41	08 34.8
Th 4-2	17 46.24	Wra 16-3	07 27.98	Wra 17-16	08 15.76	Y-C 2-43	13 16.9
Th 4-3	17 48.62	Wra 16-6	07 41.97	Wra 17-12	07 59.26	Y-C 2-44	17 38.4
Th 4-4	17 50.46	Wra 16-2	07 24.24	Wra 17-18	08 24.12	Y-C 2-45	17 43.0
Th 4-5	17 50.48	Wra 16-14	08 08.37	Wra 17-29	09 24.50	Y-C 2-47	18 37.5
Th 4-6	17 50.96	Wra 16-19	08 21.07	Wra 17-21	08 46.61	YM 15	18 24.9
Th 4-7	17 52.38	Wra 16-11	08 02.70	Wra 17-23	09 05.94	YM 16	18 54.75
Th 4-9	17 55.95	Wra 16-12	08 03.17	Wra 17-24	09 07.12	YM 22	04 45.0
Th 4-10	17 57.11	Wra 16-22	08 36.27	Wra 17-28	09 23.25	YM 28	06 04.84
Th 4-11	18 00.15	Wra 16-23	08 37.13	Wra 17-22	08 56.24	YM 29	07 29.01
TrBr 4	17 35.7	Wra 16-28	08 43.49	Wra 17-26	09 13.67		

5.5
Misclassified Planetary Nebulae

MISCLASSIFIED PLANETARY NEBULAE

PK Name	2000.0 R.A. (h m)	2000.0 Dec. (° ′)	1950.0 R.A. (h m)	1950.0 Dec. (° ′)
000−00.1	17 47.17	−28 46.4	17 44.00	−28 45.4
000−00.2	17 47.04	−29 01.0	17 43.86	−28 59.9
001+00.1	17 45.97	−26 58.1	17 42.84	−26 57.0
001−00.1	17 48.23	−28 00.8	17 45.08	−27 59.8
001−00.2	17 49.55	−27 45.9	17 46.4	−27 45.
001−00.3	17 51.75	−27 47.7	17 48.6	−27 47.
001−00.4	17 49.58	−27 40.8	17 46.44	−27 39.9
001−01.5	17 54.86	−28 48.9	17 51.69	−28 48.4
001−02.1	17 58.47	−28 33.7	17 55.30	−28 33.5
001−03.2	18 01.50	−29 19.5	17 58.31	−29 19.5
001−06.1	18 15.41	−30 31.9	18 12.19	−30 32.9
002+02.1	17 39.23	−25 38.1	17 36.14	−25 36.5
002−03.1	18 04.49	−28 21.6	18 01.33	−28 21.8
002−03.4	18 06.01	−28 17.1	18 02.85	−28 17.4
002−05.1	18 14.57	−29 49.4	18 11.37	−29 50.3
003−01.1	18 01.10	−26 21.4	17 57.99	−26 21.4
003−03.1	18 06.50	−27 44.4	18 03.35	−27 44.8
003−04.1	18 10.73	−27 57.8	18 07.58	−27 58.5
003−04.2	18 10.48	−28 07.7	18 07.32	−28 08.3
003−04.6	18 11.03	−28 32.7	18 07.86	−28 33.4
004+06.1	17 30.59	−21 28.2	17 27.6	−21 26.
004−05.2	18 15.77	−27 53.8	18 12.62	−27 54.8
004−05.4	18 18.75	−28 06.7	18 15.6	−28 08.
005−05.2	18 20.98	−26 48.5	18 17.86	−26 49.9
006+02.2	17 51.02	−22 19.6	17 48.00	−22 18.8
006+07.1	17 34.29	−19 09.4	17 31.34	−19 07.4
006−02.1	18 09.50	−24 12.3	18 06.44	−24 12.9
007+01.2	17 57.26	−21 41.5	17 54.26	−21 41.2
008−06.1	18 28.85	−24 32.0	18 25.78	−24 34.0
009−02.1	18 15.51	−21 35.4	18 12.51	−21 36.4
009−21.1	19 32.44	−29 24.6	19 29.3	−29 31.
010+18.1	17 05.55	−10 06.0	17 02.8	−10 02.
010−03.1	18 23.49	−21 53.1	18 20.48	−21 54.7
011−11.1	18 53.28	−24 22.9	18 50.23	−24 26.6
012−07.1	18 42.55	−21 17.8	18 39.56	−21 20.8
018−01.1	18 30.22	−13 54.0	18 27.38	−13 56.1
023−01.1	18 40.40	−08 43.8	18 37.67	−08 46.6
026+01.1	18 33.36	−04 58.1	18 30.70	−05 00.4
026−02.2	18 48.59	−06 41.2	18 45.90	−06 44.6
028−02.1	18 50.15	−05 15.0	18 47.49	−05 18.5
028−04.2	18 58.86	−05 21.9	18 56.2	−05 26.
029−02.1	18 54.17	−04 38.9	18 51.52	−04 42.7
033−04.1	19 09.40	−01 09.1	19 06.82	−01 14.0
035−02.1	19 04.64	+01 22.6	19 02.1	+01 18.
036−06.1	19 22.46	+00 12.8	19 19.9	+00 07.
037−02.1	19 10.61	+02 50.0	19 08.1	+02 45.
037−03.1	19 12.11	+02 38.1	19 09.6	+02 33.
037−03.3	19 13.52	+02 18.2	19 11.0	+02 13.
037−04.1	19 15.32	+02 33.3	19 12.8	+02 28.
037−06.2	19 23.55	+00 37.9	19 21.0	+00 32.
038+04.1	18 44.23	+06 47.1	18 41.8	+06 44.
038−04.1	19 17.81	+02 49.5	19 15.3	+02 44.
042+01.1	19 03.60	+08 44.5	19 01.2	+08 40.
043+01.1	19 04.17	+10 10.5	19 01.8	+10 06.
044+01.1	19 09.75	+11 04.9	19 07.4	+11 00.
044+08.1	18 40.08	+14 11.8	18 37.8	+14 09.
045+01.1	19 09.44	+12 00.9	19 07.1	+11 56.
045−00.1	19 14.46	+10 51.2	19 12.1	+10 46.
047−03.1	19 30.35	+11 23.3	19 28.0	+11 17.
048+04.1	19 03.75	+16 26.5	19 01.5	+16 22.
048−00.1	19 21.20	+14 06.7	19 18.9	+14 01.
049+00.1	19 18.58	+14 59.5	19 16.3	+14 54.
050+03.1	19 11.54	+16 52.1	19 09.3	+16 47.
050−36.1	21 30.10	−02 47.8	21 27.5	−03 01.
053−03.2	19 41.95	+16 44.7	19 39.69	+16 37.6
055−01.2	19 40.92	+18 45.0	19 38.7	+18 38.
056+04.1	19 19.63	+22 34.6	19 17.5	+22 29.
057−02.1	19 48.90	+20 07.6	19 46.7	+20 00.
059−00.1	19 44.13	+23 27.3	19 42.0	+23 20.
060+00.1	19 42.10	+24 30.1	19 40.0	+24 23.
061+02.1	19 39.66	+26 31.0	19 37.6	+26 24.
062−01.1	19 54.21	+24 57.9	19 52.1	+24 50.
063−03.2	20 06.72	+25 00.7	20 04.6	+24 52.
063−12.1	20 36.04	+20 10.4	20 33.8	+20 00.
064+00.1	19 50.43	+28 11.7	19 48.4	+28 04.
065−27.2	21 30.02	+12 10.2	21 27.6	+11 57.
069+01.1	20 00.93	+33 16.3	19 59.	+33 08.
070+01.1	20 01.72	+33 33.0	19 59.8	+33 24.6
070+01.2	20 01.83	+33 32.4	19 59.9	+33 24.
074+01.1	20 16.46	+37 06.3	20 14.6	+36 57.
075−04.1	20 41.37	+34 43.8	20 39.4	+34 33.
077−05.1	20 51.02	+35 34.9	20 49.04	+35 23.6
080−06.1	21 02.31	+36 41.6	21 00.33	+36 29.7
081+03.1	20 25.20	+43 52.8	20 23.5	+43 43.
088+06.1	20 35.57	+51 33.4	20 34.1	+51 23.
093+01.1	21 20.75	+51 53.8	21 19.1	+51 41.
093+05.1	21 00.46	+54 32.8	20 59.0	+54 21.
104−06.1	22 51.64	+51 50.9	22 49.5	+51 35.
108−05.1	23 09.31	+54 45.3	23 07.1	+54 29.
110−00.1	23 12.20	+59 36.0	23 10.04	+59 19.7
113+05.1	23 09.18	+66 48.3	23 07.2	+66 32.0
113+06.1	23 07.66	+66 59.4	23 05.7	+66 43.1
114+10.1	22 56.65	+71 28.0	22 55.0	+71 12.
118+02.1	00 07.63	+64 57.7	00 05.0	+64 41.
121−02.1	00 38.68	+60 16.5	00 35.8	+60 00.
132−00.1	02 08 08	+60 46.0	02 04.48	+60 31.8
149−01.1	03 51.64	+51 29.0	03 47.9	+51 20.
151+02.1	04 19.80	+53 06.2	04 15.9	+52 59.
169−00.1	05 18.20	+37 36.2	05 14.8	+37 33.
176+00.1	05 37.75	+31 58.7	05 34.5	+31 57.
195−00.1	06 18.86	+15 16.7	06 16.0	+15 18.
196−01.1	06 15.84	+14 15.9	06 13.0	+14 17.
196−12.1	05 37.32	+08 15.7	05 34.6	+08 14.
197−02.1	06 15.21	+12 22.0	06 12.4	+12 23.
197−02.2	06 12.81	+12 23.2	06 10.	+12 24.
208+01.1	06 47.07	+04 37.3	06 44.42	+04 40.6
210−00.1	06 44.63	+01 19.6	06 42.04	+01 22.7
210−00.2	06 44.62	+01 19.0	06 42.03	+01 22.1
219+01.1	07 07.27	−05 09.7	07 04.8	−05 05.
221+45.1	09 47.96	+13 16.7	09 45.25	+13 30.7
223−02.1	07 03.36	−10 34.5	07 01.0	−10 30.
227+33.1	09 16.41	+03 53.4	09 13.8	+04 06.
233−00.1	07 28.27	−17 56.8	07 26.04	−17 50.6
234−00.1	07 31.82	−19 27.5	07 29.62	−19 21.1
235+01.1	07 41.22	−18 59.4	07 39.00	−18 52.3
241−07.1	07 16.52	−29 19.4	07 14.55	−29 14.0

MISCLASSIFIED PLANETARY NEBULAE									
PK Name	2000.0		1950.0		PK Name	2000.0		1950.0	
	R.A.	Dec.	R.A.	Dec.		R.A.	Dec.	R.A.	Dec.
	h m	° ′	h m	° ′		h m	° ′	h m	° ′
246+02.1	08 08.59	−27 41.2	08 06.52	−27 32.4	327−04.1	16 14.01	−56 59.5	16 09.93	−56 51.9
247−21.1	06 25.48	−39 51.8	06 23.84	−39 50.0	328−00.1	15 59.60	−53 45.9	15 55.73	−53 37.4
248+08.1	08 36.25	−26 24.6	08 34.12	−26 14.1	328−17.1	17 47.14	−64 38.1	17 42.24	−64 37.0
252−00.1	08 11.77	−35 21.3	08 09.87	−35 12.3	331+00.2	16 11.74	−51 17.8	16 07.95	−51 10.1
258−03.1	08 14.20	−41 42.5	08 12.47	−41 33.3	332+01.1	16 06.95	−49 26.6	16 03.25	−49 18.6
266+00.1	08 59.26	−45 35.5	08 57.51	−45 23.8	332−00.2	16 19.47	−50 37.8	16 15.69	−50 30.6
266+01.1	09 04.20	−44 33.0	09 02.4	−44 21.	334+00.1	16 24.92	−48 43.9	16 21.2	−48 37.
266+02.1	09 10.33	−44 24.3	09 08.5	−44 12.	336−00.1	16 33.88	−48 06.9	16 30.17	−48 00.6
266+02.2	09 09.02	−44 17.2	09 07.2	−44 05.	336−08.1	17 17.16	−53 36.3	17 13.12	−53 33.1
266−01.1	08 52.00	−46 18.0	08 50.29	−46 06.7	338+01.1	16 38.47	−45 23.6	16 34.86	−45 17.7
271+03.1	09 33.50	−46 34.7	09 31.64	−46 21.3	338+05.2	16 21.13	−42 23.9	16 17.65	−42 16.8
276−18.1	07 50.62	−64 15.7	07 50.10	−64 08.0	339+00.1	16 41.52	−45 13.0	16 37.91	−45 07.3
277−01.1	09 39.65	−54 53.6	09 38.0	−54 40.	339+00.2	16 43.27	−46 00.7	16 39.62	−45 55.1
280−02.1	09 54.73	−57 18.9	09 53.07	−57 04.7	341−00.1	16 53.41	−44 52.8	16 49.79	−44 47.9
280−02.2	09 52.99	−57 25.5	09 51.35	−57 11.3	342+05.1	16 36.41	−39 51.7	16 32.98	−39 45.6
281−04.1	09 48.35	−59 32.0	09 46.82	−59 18.0	344−08.1	17 41.08	−47 03.3	17 37.33	−47 01.8
283+12.1	10 57.27	−46 10.5	10 55.03	−45 54.4	345−00.1	17 09.56	−41 36.2	17 06.04	−41 32.4
284−39.1	04 03.16	−70 14.9	04 03.32	−70 23.0	347+03.1	16 57.47	−37 06.6	16 54.1	−37 02.
287−02.1	10 35.64	−60 38.9	10 33.79	−60 23.3	348−00.1	17 18.39	−39 19.2	17 14.93	−39 16.1
288+00.2	10 59.67	−59 01.1	10 57.60	−58 45.0	349−10.1	18 04.53	−43 23.8	18 00.92	−43 24.0
288+05.1	11 06.51	−54 48.5	11 04.32	−54 32.3	351+03.1	17 07.36	−34 05.2	17 04.07	−34 01.3
289+01.1	11 03.26	−58 27.5	11 01.15	−58 11.3	351−04.1	17 45.23	−38 17.4	17 41.79	−38 16.2
289+10.1	11 31.44	−49 58.6	11 29.05	−49 42.0	351−05.1	17 45.51	−38 39.8	17 42.06	−38 38.6
289−00.1	10 56.18	−60 27.2	10 54.16	−60 11.2	352+03.1	17 12.21	−32 37.8	17 08.95	−32 34.2
289−00.2	11 00.95	−60 49.1	10 58.9	−60 33.	354+02.1	17 22.85	−32 13.8	17 19.6	−32 11.
292−03.1	11 10.52	−63 43.2	11 08.45	−63 26.9	354+04.2	17 15.31	−31 34.1	17 12.08	−31 30.7
294−00.2	11 38.08	−62 15.9	11 35.73	−61 59.3	355+00.1	17 36.33	−33 26.1	17 33.04	−33 24.3
295−13.1	11 02.72	−74 53.3	11 01.18	−74 37.1	355+02.1	17 23.98	−31 01.9	17 20.76	−30 59.2
298−01.1	12 15.35	−63 39.2	12 12.65	−63 22.5	355+03.1	17 19.02	−30 54.1	17 15.8	−30 51.
299−00.1	12 22.36	−60 17.2	12 19.62	−60 00.6	355+04.1	17 17.92	−30 01.8	17 14.73	−29 58.6
299−00.2	12 19.96	−62 55.3	12 17.22	−62 38.7	355+11.1	16 51.34	−26 00.4	16 48.26	−25 55.4
301+01.1	12 34.91	−61 39.0	12 32.05	−61 22.5	356+01.1	17 30.01	−30 37.3	17 26.8	−30 35.
302+00.1	12 48.47	−62 49.5	12 45.47	−62 33.1	356+04.3	17 21.08	−29 21.9	17 17.9	−29 19.
302−00.1	12 45.79	−63 00.5	12 42.81	−62 44.1	356−02.1	17 47.38	−32 50.0	17 44.1	−32 49.
302−05.1	12 43.35	−68 12.6	12 40.29	−67 56.2	356−07.1	18 07.66	−36 06.4	18 04.29	−36 06.8
305+03.1	13 14.51	−58 51.8	13 11.37	−58 35.9	357+02.1	17 28.87	−29 07.4	17 25.7	−29 05.
305−00.1	13 10.08	−63 11.5	13 06.87	−62 55.5	357+02.2	17 29.08	−29 14.4	17 25.9	−29 12.
307−01.1	13 28.64	−63 49.7	13 25.24	−63 34.2	357+02.3	17 29.10	−29 43.4	17 25.91	−29 41.0
308−01.1	13 41.08	−64 15.7	13 37.55	−64 00.5	357+03.3	17 27.52	−29 02.9	17 24.35	−29 00.4
309+00.2	13 49.55	−61 31.8	13 46.06	−61 16.9	357−03.1	17 51.75	−32 55.0	17 48.47	−32 54.3
309+01.1	13 43.99	−60 49.7	13 40.57	−60 34.6	358+01.2	17 34.28	−29 29.2	17 31.09	−29 27.2
310+02.1	13 53.42	−58 57.7	13 50.00	−58 42.9	358+01.3	17 35.36	−29 45.3	17 32.17	−29 43.4
311+03.1	13 54.94	−58 27.3	13 51.52	−58 12.6	358+02.1	17 31.26	−28 24.2	17 28.1	−28 22.
312−02.1	14 14.15	−63 25.7	14 10.38	−63 11.7	358+02.3	17 32.47	−29 05.1	17 29.29	−29 03.0
314−00.2	14 31.11	−61 20.9	14 27.32	−61 07.6	358+03.1	17 28.70	−28 27.3	17 25.54	−28 24.9
317+19.1	14 03.31	−41 23.3	14 00.25	−41 08.9	358+03.5	17 28.44	−28 38.6	17 25.28	−28 36.2
319−04.1	15 27.45	−62 31.1	15 23.22	−62 20.7	358−00.1	17 42.31	−30 27.4	17 39.1	−30 26.
319−09.1	15 47.18	−66 29.3	15 42.50	−66 20.0	358−01.2	17 50.28	−30 57.5	17 47.05	−30 56.7
320+00.1	15 05.30	−57 31.6	15 01.49	−57 20.0	358−01.3	17 46.04	−31 03.6	17 42.81	−31 02.5
320+00.2	15 07.14	−57 48.3	15 03.3	−57 36.8	358−02.2	17 52.95	−31 19.3	17 49.71	−31 18.7
320−01.1	15 18.19	−59 38.9	15 14.2	−59 28.	358−03.2	17 56.27	−32 37.4	17 53.0	−32 37.
320−01.2	15 18.35	−59 38.1	15 14.36	−59 27.2	358−05.2	18 03.40	−32 42.4	18 00.12	−32 42.5
321−09.1	16 01.32	−64 47.9	15 56.72	−64 39.5	359+01.2	17 39.37	−28 47.6	17 36.2	−28 46.
321−11.1	16 12.39	−66 39.1	16 07.55	−66 31.4	359+02.1	17 33.71	−28 07.3	17 30.56	−28 05.3
321−11.2	16 17.11	−66 38.0	16 12.25	−66 30.6	359+02.2	17 33.16	−28 21.1	17 30.0	−28 19.
326+00.1	15 45.03	−54 02.4	15 41.2	−53 53.	359+03.3	17 32.13	−27 05.1	17 29.0	−27 03.
326−01.1	15 54.74	−55 29.6	15 50.81	−55 20.8	359−02.1	17 53.21	−30 18.0	17 50.00	−30 17.4
326−10.1	16 44.58	−62 37.4	16 40.00	−62 31.8	359−07.2	18 12.19	−33 10.5	18 08.90	−33 11.3

5.6
The Catalogue of Planetary Nebulae

CATALOGUE OF PLANETARY NEBULAE—TABLE 1

PK Name	Alternate Name	2000.0 R.A. (h m)	2000.0 Dec. (° ′)	1950.0 R.A. (h m)	1950.0 Dec. (° ′)	Con	Nebula Type	Nebula Diam. (″)	Nebula Mag. p	Nebula Mag. v	Star Spectra	Star Mag. V	Star Name	Notes
118+08.2	Abell 86	00 01.57	+70 42.7	23 59.0	+70 26.	Cep	IIc	70	16.7					
119+06.1	Abell 1	00 12.60	+69 10.7	00 09.9	+68 54.	Cep	IIb	44	18.3			19.9		ARO 198
120+09.1	NGC 40	00 13.04	+72 31.7	00 10.3	+72 15.	Cep	IIIb+III	>37	10.7	12.3	WC8	11.61	HD 826	ARO 1
118−08.1	Vy 1-1	00 18.68	+53 52.7	00 16.0	+53 36.	Cas		5		12.5		14.1		ARO 90
119+00.1	BV 1	00 19.94	+62 58.6	00 17.2	+62 42.	Cas				14.7				ARO 199
119−06.1	Hu 1-1	00 28.25	+55 57.9	00 25.5	+55 41.3	Cas	II	5	13.3	12.3				ARO 18
120−05.1	Sh 2-176	00 31.7	+57 17.	00 28.9	+57 01.	Cas								
108−76.1	BoBn 1	00 37.30	−13 42.2	00 34.78	−13 58.7	Cet								galactic halo object
121+03.1	We 1-1	00 38.89	+66 23.7	00 35.92	+66 07.2	Cas		19				>20.		
121+00.1	BV 2	00 40.33	+62 51.5	00 37.4	+62 35.	Cas				15.4				ARO 201, Sh 2-179
122−04.1	Abell 2	00 45.60	+57 57.4	00 42.7	+57 41.	Cas	IIc	31	16.3	14.1		19.8		ARO 202
118−74.1	NGC 246	00 47.01	−11 52.6	00 44.5	−12 09.	Cet	IIIb	225	8.0	10.9	OVI	11.95		ARO 43
125−47.1	PHL 932	00 59.96	+15 44.2	00 57.32	+15 28.	Psc		270						
124−07.1	WeSb 1	01 00.9	+55 03.	00 57.9	+54 47.	Cas		155						
124+10.1	El 0103+73	01 07.2	+73 33.	01 03.6	+73 17.	Cas	V	240				16.35		HtDe 1
126+03.1	K 3-90	01 24.98	+65 38.6	01 21.55	+65 23.0	Cas		<12						
127−01.1	K 4-59	01 30.54	+60 31.4	01 27.24	+60 15.9	Cas		<5						
128−04.1	Sh 2-188	01 30.6	+58 22.	01 27.4	+58 07.	Cas						17.44		S 22
130−11.1	M 1-1	01 37.31	+50 28.3	01 34.2	+50 13.	And		6		14.1				ARO 58
130−10.1	NGC 650-1	01 42.36	+51 34.1	01 39.2	+51 19.	Per	III+VI	>65	12.2	10.1		15.87		M.76, ARO 2
129−02.1	We 2-5	01 42.64	+60 10.1	01 39.25	+59 55.	Cas		194						
131−05.1	BV 3	01 53.75	+56 24.7	01 50.4	+56 10.	Cas				14.2				ARO 203
130+01.1	IC 1747	01 57.63	+63 19.6	01 54.0	+63 05.	Cas	IIIb	13	13.6	12.0	WC4	15.8	HD 11758	ARO 91
148−48.1	Gr 0155+10	01 58.0	+10 57.	01 55.3	+10 43.	Ari		210						
129+04.1	K 3-91	01 58.60	+66 34.1	01 54.79	+66 19.5	Cas		11						
133−08.1	M 1-2	01 58.78	+52 53.6	01 55.5	+52 39.	Per		<1				13.var	V471 Per	ARO 116
130+03.1	K 3-92	02 03.67	+64 57.6	01 59.91	+64 43.2	Cas		12						
131+02.1	Abell 3	02 12.19	+64 09.1	02 08.4	+63 55.	Cas	IIIb	60	18.2			17.6		ARO 204, Sh 2-189
132+04.1	K 3-93	02 26.50	+65 47.9	02 22.49	+65 34.4	Cas		10						
237−65.1		02 39.82	−34 32.8	02 37.75	−34 45.6	For								identity?
144−15.1	Abell 4	02 45.43	+42 32.6	02 42.2	+42 20.	Per	IIIb	22	16.7	14.4		19.3		ARO 205
141−07.1	Abell 5	02 52.28	+50 36.3	02 48.8	+50 24.	Per	IV	128	>16.			21.4		ARO 206
255−59.1	K 1-26	02 56.97	−44 10.3	02 55.16	−44 22.3	Eri		373						Lo 1, ESO 247-13
136+04.1	Abell 6	02 58.88	+64 30.0	02 54.7	+64 18.	Cas	IIb	185	>15.5	14.3		18.3		ARO 207
136+05.1	HFG 1	03 03.7	+64 54.	02 59.5	+64 43.	Cas		900				15.::	V664 Cas	
138+02.1	IC 289	03 10.35	+61 19.4	03 06.3	+61 08.	Cas	IV+II	>34	12.3	13.2		16.8		ARO 86, Hb 1

CATALOGUE OF PLANETARY NEBULAE—TABLE 2

PK Name	Alternate Name	2000.0 R.A. (h m)	2000.0 Dec. (° ′)	1950.0 R.A. (h m)	1950.0 Dec. (° ′)	Con	Nebula Type	Nebula Diam. (″)	Nebula Mag. p	Nebula Mag. v	Star Spectra	Star Mag. V	Star Name	Notes
138+04.1	Sh 2-200	03 11.0	+62 48.	03 06.9	+62 37.	Cas								HtDe 2
147−09.1	HtWe 3	03 16.6	+46 54.	03 13.1	+46 43.	Per	IV	30				17.68		
149−09.1	We a	03 27.2	+45 25.	03 23.8	+45 14.	Per		480				17.05		HtDe 3
220−53.1	NGC 1360	03 33.33	−25 51.0	03 31.2	−26 01.	For	III	390		9.4	sdO	10.98		ARO 208, M 1-3
142+03.1	K 3-94	03 36.12	+60 03.7	03 32.01	+59 53.8	Cam		<12						
147−02.1	M 1-4	03 41.74	+52 16.6	03 38.0	+52 07.	Per		4		13.6				ARO 209
156−13.1	HtWe 5	03 45.5	+37 48.	03 42.2	+37 39.	Per		36						
159−15.1	IC 351	03 47.51	+35 03.2	03 44.3	+34 54.	Per	IIa	7	12.4	11.9	WC	15.		ARO 19
149−03.1	IsWe 1	03 49.2	+50 00.	03 45.5	+49 51.	Per		780			PG 1159	16.56		
171−25.1	Baade 1	03 53.49	+19 27.8	03 50.6	+19 19.	Tau	IV	40	13.9	15.1		17.2		ARO 87
161−14.1	IC 2003	03 56.40	+33 51.7	03 53.2	+33 43.	Per	II	7	12.6	11.4	WC7	15.3		ARO 76
144+06.1	NGC 1501	04 07.01	+60 55.0	04 02.7	+60 47.	Cam	III	52	13.3	11.5	WC7	14.45		ARO 44
165−15.1	NGC 1514	04 09.25	+30 46.9	04 06.1	+30 39.	Tau	III+II	>114	10.	10.9	A0+sd0	9.40	HD 281679	ARO 21
147+04.1	M 2-2	04 13.28	+56 56.6	04 09.2	+56 49.	Cam	III	12		13.7				ARO 211
151+00.1	K 3-64	04 13.45	+51 51.0	04 09.63	+51 43.4	Per		8						
206−40.1	NGC 1535	04 14.24	−12 44.5	04 11.9	−12 52.	Eri	IV+IIc	>18	9.6	9.6		11.59	HD 26847	ARO 22
153−01.1	K 3-65	04 15.91	+48 49.6	04 12.21	+48 42.2	Per		2						
149+04.1	K 4-47	04 20.75	+56 18.1	04 16.68	+56 11.0	Cam								
137+16.1	El 0419+72	04 25.2	+72 48.	04 19.4	+72 42.	Per		130						
146+07.1	M 4-18	04 25.83	+60 06.8	04 21.5	+60 00.	Cam				15.8				
167−09.1	K 3-66	04 36.62	+33 39.5	04 33.37	+33 33.4	Per								
174−14.1	H 3-29	04 37.35	+25 03.0	04 34.3	+24 57.	Tau		20		15.1		18.6v	GL Tau	ARO 214
165−06.1	K 3-67	04 39.80	+36 45.7	04 36.46	+36 39.9	Per								
166−06.1	CRL 618	04 42.88	+36 06.8	04 39.56	+36 01.2	Aur		12			B0-O9			PPN?
158+00.1	Sh 2-216	04 45.0	+46 49.	04 41.3	+46 44.	Per								YM 22
160−00.1	We 1-2	04 46.71	+44 28.0	04 43.12	+44 22.6	Per		92				20.87		
163−00.1	We 1-3	04 54.53	+42 16.6	04 51.00	+42 11.8	Aur		116				21.0		
242−37.1	PRTM-1	05 03.1	−39 45.0	05 01.4	−39 49.9	Cae		23				15.47		
215−30.1	Abell 7	05 03.16	−15 35.8	05 00.9	−15 40.	Lep		770	13.2			15.5		ARO 215
205−26.1	MaC 2-1	05 03.6	−06 09.	05 01.2	−06 14.	Eri						16.7:		
190−17.1	J 320	05 05.56	+10 42.0	05 02.8	+10 38.	Ori	II+IV	>7	12.9	11.9	cont	14.31		ARO 60
167−00.1	Abell 8	05 06.64	+39 08.0	05 03.2	+39 04.	Aur	IIb	60	16.6			19.7		ARO 216
173−05.1	K 2-1	05 08.11	+30 47.9	05 04.9	+30 44.	Aur	III	132						ARO 175
215−24.1	IC 418	05 27.51	−12 41.6	05 25.2	−12 44.	Lep	IV	12	10.7	9.3	O7f	10.17	HD 35914	ARO 3
203−18.1	MaC 2-2	05 28.9	−00 40.	05 26.4	−00 43.	Ori								
172+00.1	Abell 9	05 28.96	+36 02.4	05 25.6	+36 00.	Aur	IV	37	>18.9			23.5		ARO 122
178−02.1	K 3-68	05 31.59	+28 58.7	05 28.42	+28 56.5	Aur		11						

CATALOGUE OF PLANETARY NEBULAE—TABLE 3

PK Name	Alternate Name	2000.0 R.A.	2000.0 Dec.	1950.0 R.A.	1950.0 Dec.	Con	Nebula Type	Nebula Diam.	Nebula Mag. p	Nebula Mag. v	Star Spectra	Star Mag. V	Star Name	Notes
		h m	° ′	h m	° ′			″	p	v		V		
197−14.1	Abell 10	05 31.80	+06 56.1	05 29.1	+06 54.	Ori	III	35	15.2	14.7		19.6		ARO 176, K 1-7
156+12.1	We b	05 38.0	+55 32.	05 33.8	+55 30.	Aur		90				17.::		HtDe 4
204−16.1	MaC 2-3	05 38.3	+00 14.	05 35.7	+00 13.	Ori								
193−09.1	H 3-75	05 40.70	+12 20.5	05 37.9	+12 19.	Ori		24		13.9				ARO 218
173+02.1	PP 40	05 40.9	+35 42.	05 37.5	+35 41.	Aur		30						
170+04.1	K 3-69	05 41.37	+39 15.1	05 37.90	+39 13.6	Aur								
196−10.1	NGC 2022	05 42.14	+09 05.4	05 39.4	+09 04.	Ori	IV+II	>18	12.4	11.6	cont	14.9		ARO 61
184−02.1	M 1-5	05 46.86	+24 22.1	05 43.8	+24 21.0	Tau		2		14.6				ARO 123
181+00.1	Pu 1	05 52.81	+28 06.4	05 49.65	+28 05.8	Tau						21.16		
228−22.1	DeHt 1	05 55.1	−22 53.	05 53.0	−22 54.	Lep		128						LoTr 1
166+10.1	IC 2149	05 56.32	+46 07.4	05 52.6	+46 07.	Aur	IIIb+II	>8	11.2	10.6		7.5p		ARO 23
286−29.1	K 1-27	05 57.03	−75 40.3	05 58.83	−75 40.5	Men								ESO 033-33
184+00.1	K 3-70	05 58.76	+25 18.7	05 55.67	+25 18.5	Gem		2						
197−06.1	WeDe 1	05 59.4	+10 41.	05 56.6	+10 41.	Ori		930				17.4		
243−25.1	K 2-12	06 02.11	−37 25.5	06 00.40	−37 25.4	Col		52						ESO 364-25
198−06.1	Abell 12	06 02.35	+09 38.9	05 59.6	+09 39.	Ori		37	13.9	12.0		19.1		ARO 220
175+06.1	Pu 2	06 02.6	+36 07.	05 59.2	+36 08.	Aur		20				20.::		2′ S. HD 37737
204−08.1	Abell 13	06 04.84	+03 56.7	06 02.2	+03 57.	Ori	IV	154	>16.0	15.3		18.8		ARO 124, YM 28
197−03.1	Abell 14	06 11.19	+11 46.3	06 08.4	+11 47.	Ori	IIc	34	>18.2			15.0		ARO 125
184+04.1	K 3-71	06 13.92	+26 52.9	06 10.79	+26 53.8	Gem		3						
201−04.1	We 1-4	06 14.56	+07 34.5	06 11.85	+07 35.5	Ori		40				>20.		
183+05.1	WeSb 2	06 16.2	+28 21.	06 13.0	+28 23.	Aur		135						
158+17.1	PuWe 1	06 19.6	+55 36.	06 15.4	+55 38.	Lyn	III	1200	11.2			15.::		c.s. double (5″.1, 120°)
221−12.1	IC 2165	06 21.71	−12 59.2	06 19.40	−12 57.7	CMa	IIIb	4	12.9	10.5	cont	14.99:		ARO 62, Sa 2-1
218−10.1	HtDe 5	06 23.6	−10 12.	06 21.2	−10 11.	Mon		94				16.8		HtWe 7
204−03.1	K 3-72	06 23.91	+05 30.2	06 21.24	+05 31.8	Mon		23						
194+02.1	J 900	06 25.92	+17 47.2	06 23.0	+17 49.	Gem	IIIb+II	>8	12.4	11.7		16.5:		ARO 92
233−16.1	Abell 15	06 27.04	−25 22.9	06 25.0	−25 21.	CMa	IV	34	16.3	15.6	sdO	16.4		ARO 221, ESO 490-01
170+15.1	NGC 2242	06 34.2	+44 46.	06 30.5	+44 49.	Aur		22		15.0		15.2		galactic halo object?
211−03.1	M 1-6	06 35.74	+00 00.6	06 33.18	−00 03.1	Mon		<5				15.8		ARO 126, Sa 3-1
189+07.1	M 1-7	06 37.35	+24 00.4	06 34.3	+24 03.	Gem	II	29		13.0				ARO 127
201+02.1	K 4-48	06 39.93	+11 06.5	06 37.15	+11 09.3	Mon								
192+07.1	We c	06 40.2	+21 25.	06 37.2	+21 28.	Gem		72				19.::		HtDe 6, HtWe 8
216−04.1	We 1-5	06 41.58	−05 02.6	06 39.11	−04 59.7	Mon		15				18.2		
153+22.1	Abell 16	06 43.90	+61 47.0	06 39.3	+61 50.	Lyn	IIb	148	15.9	14.5		17.4		ARO 222

CATALOGUE OF PLANETARY NEBULAE—TABLE 4

PK Name	Alternate Name	2000.0 R.A.	2000.0 Dec.	1950.0 R.A.	1950.0 Dec.	Con	Nebula Type	Nebula Diam.	Nebula Mag. p	Nebula Mag. v	Star Spectra	Star Mag. V	Star Name	Notes
		h m	° ′	h m	° ′			″						
221−04.1	Abell 17	06 48.58	−09 32.4	06 46.2	−09 29.	Mon	IIc	44	>18.5			19.9		ARO 223
233−10.1	SrWe 1	06 50.7	−22 26.	06 48.6	−22 23.	CMa	IV	55						
204+04.1	K 2-2	06 52.55	+09 58.3	06 49.8	+10 02.	Mon	III	414				15.0		
210+01.1	M 1-8	06 53.52	+03 12.2	06 50.9	+03 16.	Mon		19		14.5				ARO 129
236−10.1	HtWe 9	06 54.4	−25 20.	06 52.4	−25 17.	CMa	V	148				19.8		
239−12.1	ESO 427-19	06 55.2	−29 06.	06 53.2	−29 03.	CMa								
216−00.1	Abell 18	06 56.21	−02 53.0	06 53.7	−02 49.	Mon	IIb	75	17.5			20.90		ARO 224
200+08.1	Abell 19	06 59.94	+14 36.8	06 57.1	+14 41.	Gem	IIb	69	17.0					ARO 130
210+03.1	We 2-34	07 00.46	+04 20.7	06 57.82	+04 25.	Mon		232						
226−03.1	PB 1	07 02.78	−13 42.5	07 00.48	−13 38.1	CMa				14.0		16.0		ARO 225, Sa 2-2
242−11.1	M 3-1	07 02.83	−31 35.5	07 00.93	−31 31.0	CMa		12		12.3:		15.77		ARO 534, He 2-1
212+04.1	M 1-9	07 05.31	+02 47.4	07 02.7	+02 52.	Mon	I			13.4		15.5		ARO 131
225−02.1	Sa 2-4	07 06.74	−11 45.7	07 04.4	−11 41.	CMa								
217+02.1	St 3-1	07 06.80	−03 04.7	07 04.3	−03 00.	Mon								
234−06.1	K 2-3	07 06.93	−22 01.7	07 04.8	−21 57.	CMa	III	65		14.5:		>21.		ARO 227, ESO 558-11
215+03.1	NGC 2346	07 09.40	+00 38.6	07 06.83	−00 43.5	Mon	IIIb+VI	>55		11.6	A5+?	11.16v	V651 Mon	ARO 80, M 1-10
232−04.1	M 1-11	07 11.28	−19 51.0	07 09.10	−19 46.0	CMa	I			15.5		14.07		ARO 229, ESO 558-14
229−02.1	K 1-10	07 12.46	−16 08.1	07 10.2	−16 03.	CMa	IIIb	66				>21.		ARO 230
240−07.1	M 3-2	07 14.82	−27 50.4	07 12.82	−27 45.1	CMa	IIIb			14.7		16.96		ARO 231, He 2-2
258−15.1	Lo 3	07 14.82	−46 58.2	07 13.39	−46 52.9	Pup								ESO 256-19, Sa 2-6
225+00.1	We 2-37	07 16.13	−10 53.0	07 13.77	−10 47.6	Mon		29						
224+01.1	We 1-6	07 17.43	−10 10.7	07 15.06	−10 05.2	Mon		62				16.4		
247−10.1	Sa 3-4	07 18.24	−34 54.6	07 16.41	−34 49.1	Pup								ARO 535, Wra 17-2
245−08.1	Wra 17-3	07 19.12	−32 35.2	07 17.23	−32 29.6	CMa								ARO 536
235−03.1	M 1-12	07 19.35	−21 43.9	07 17.21	−21 38.3	CMa						14.08		ARO 233, ESO 559-03
232−01.1	M 1-13	07 21.25	−18 08.6	07 19.03	−18 02.9	CMa		10		12.6				ARO 234, ESO 559-06
214+07.1	Abell 20	07 22.99	+01 46.2	07 20.4	+01 52.	CMi	IIc	64	16.3	14.3		15.7		ARO 132
242−06.1	Wra 16-2	07 24.24	−28 59.4	07 22.25	−28 53.5	CMa								ARO 235
189+19.1	NGC 2371-2	07 25.55	+29 29.0	07 22.4	+29 35.	Gem	IIIa+VI	>55	13.0	11.2		14.80		ARO 45
247−08.1	Wra 17-4	07 26.27	−34 57.0	07 24.43	−34 50.9	Pup								
221+05.2	Y-C 2-37	07 26.5	−05 22.	07 24.0	−05 16.	Mon								
221+05.1	M 3-3	07 26.58	−05 21.8	07 24.11	−05 15.7	Mon	IV	13		14.8				ARO 236, Sa 2-8

CATALOGUE OF PLANETARY NEBULAE—TABLE 5

PK Name	Alternate Name	2000.0 R.A. (h m)	2000.0 Dec. (° ′)	1950.0 R.A. (h m)	1950.0 Dec. (° ′)	Con	Nebula Type	Nebula Diam. (″)	Nebula Mag. p	Nebula Mag. v	Star Spectra	Star Mag. V	Star Name	Notes
235−01.1	M 1-14	07 27.94	−20 13.4	07 25.76	−20 07.2	Pup				13.5		14.09		ARO 237, ESO 559-11
244−06.1	Wra 16-3	07 27.98	−30 42.1	07 26.03	−30 35.9	Pup								ARO 538
244−06.2	Wra 17-5	07 28.04	−30 45.5	07 26.09	−30 39.3	Pup								
248−08.1	M 4-2	07 28.89	−35 45.3	07 27.07	−35 39.0	Pup		6		13.2				ARO 539, He 2-3
205+14.1	Abell 21	07 29.01	+13 14.8	07 26.2	+13 21.	Gem				10.3:				ARO 388, YM 29
197+17.1	NGC 2392	07 29.16	+20 54.8	07 26.2	+21 01.	Gem	IIIb+III	>15	9.9	9.1	O7f	10.5	HD 59088	ARO 24,
219+07.1	RWT 152	07 29.9	−02 06.	07 27.4	−02 00.	Mon		24						
256−11.1	Wra 17-6	07 35.39	−44 01.1	07 33.81	−43 54.4	Pup								
215+11.1	Abell 22	07 36.11	+02 42.3	07 33.5	+02 49.	CMi	III	87	15.4			19.1		ARO 133, K 1-11
226+05.1	M 1-16	07 37.32	−09 38.8	07 34.93	−09 32.0	Mon	?+VI	>3		13.0		16.94		ARO 239, Sa 2-11
244−04.1	Wra 17-7	07 37.37	−30 07.5	07 35.40	−30 00.7	Pup								ARO 540
228+05.1	M 1-17	07 40.37	−11 32.5	07 38.01	−11 25.5	Pup		3		14.0				ARO 240, Sa 2-12
231+04.2	NGC 2438	07 41.84	−14 44.2	07 39.54	−14 37.1	Pup	IV+II	>66	10.1	10.8	cont	17.5		in front of cluster M.46
234+02.1	NGC 2440	07 41.92	−18 12.5	07 39.69	−18 05.4	Pup	V+III	>14	10.8	9.4		18.9		ARO 47, ESO 560-09
246−04.1	Wra 16-6	07 41.97	−31 46.4	07 40.03	−31 39.3	Pup								ARO 541
231+04.1	M 1-18	07 42.05	−14 21.2	07 39.75	−14 14.1	Pup	IIb	32		15.0		19.1		Sa 2-15
247−04.1	HFG 2	07 42.4	−32 48.	07 40.5	−32 41.	Pup		155		15.::		17.::		
249−05.1	Abell 23	07 43.27	−34 45.2	07 41.4	−34 38.	Pup		54		13.1				ARO 542, ESO 368-10
248−04.1	Wra 16-7	07 46.78	−33 25.8	07 44.88	−33 18.4	Pup								ARO 543
264−12.1	He 2-5	07 47.33	−51 15.1	07 46.01	−51 07.6	Car		<10				14.74		Sa 2-17, ESO 209-01
243−01.1	NGC 2452	07 47.44	−27 20.1	07 45.39	−27 12.6	Pup	IV+III	>19	12.6	12.0	WC3	16.11		ARO 93, He 2-4
232+05.1	SaSt 2-3	07 48.06	−14 07.7	07 45.75	−14 00.2	Pup								MWC 574
243−00.1	Wra 17-8	07 49.67	−27 35.5	07 47.62	−27 27.9	Pup								ARO 242, ESO 493-19
235+04.1	Y-C 2-40	07 50.0	−17 51.	07 47.8	−17 44.	Pup								
236+03.1	K 1-12	07 50.22	−19 17.7	07 48.0	−19 10.	Pup	II	37				>21.		ARO 243, ESO 560-16
268−14.1	Wra 17-9	07 51.45	−55 42.0	07 50.33	−55 34.2	Car								
217+14.1	Abell 24	07 51.71	+03 00.3	07 49.1	+03 08.	CMi	IV+III	>229	13.6	13.5:		16.5		ARO 134
259−09.2	Y-C 2-1	07 52.49	−45 50.9	07 50.94	−45 43.1	Pup								
259−09.1	Y-C 2-2	07 52.77	−45 12.0	07 51.20	−45 04.2	Pup								
252−04.1	Sa 2-18	07 52.96	−36 43.8	07 51.13	−36 36.0	Pup								ESO 369-02
211+18.1	We d	07 54.9	+09 35.	07 52.2	+09 43.	CMi	V	90				17.7:		HtDe7. HtWe 10
241+02.1	M 3-4	07 55.18	−23 38.3	07 53.05	−23 30.3	Pup	IV	14						ARO 81, ESO 494-02
262−10.1	Wra 16-9	07 55.61	−48 49.7	07 54.16	−48 41.7	Pup								

CATALOGUE OF PLANETARY NEBULAE—TABLE 6

PK Name	Alternate Name	2000.0 R.A. (h m)	2000.0 Dec. (° ′)	1950.0 R.A. (h m)	1950.0 Dec. (° ′)	Con	Nebula Type	Nebula Diam. (″)	Nebula Mag. p	Nebula Mag. v	Star Spectra	Star Mag. V	Star Name	Notes
251−03.1	Wra 17-10	07 56.13	−35 42.1	07 54.27	−35 34.1	Pup								ARO 544
164+31.1	JE 1	07 57.78	+53 24.9	07 53.9	+53 33.	Lyn	IV	399	14.	12.1	PG 1159	16.8		ARO 121
269−13.1	Wra 17-12	07 59.26	−55 36.6	07 58.11	−55 28.3	Car								
259−07.1	Y-C 2-3	07 59.52	−44 44.0	07 57.91	−44 35.7	Pup								
261−08.2	Wra 17-11	07 59.54	−47 02.1	07 58.01	−46 53.8	Pup								
263−09.1	Wra 17-13	08 00.42	−48 30.9	07 58.95	−48 22.6	Pup								
261−08.1	Wra 17-14	08 01.40	−46 57.0	07 59.87	−46 48.6	Pup								
245+01.1	M 3-5	08 02.48	−27 41.9	08 00.42	−27 33.5	Pup	IV	7		14.2		17.9		ARO 244, He 2-6
262−08.1	Wra 16-11	08 02.70	−47 57.5	08 01.2	−47 49.	Pup								
258−06.1	Wra 16-12	08 03.17	−42 53.5	08 01.5	−42 45.	Pup								
251−01.1	K 1-21	08 04.24	−34 16.1	08 02.33	−34 07.5	Pup		29						ESO 369-04
263−08.1	ESO 209-15	08 05.2	−48 23.	08 03.7	−48 15.	Pup								
224+15.1	Abell 25	08 06.72	−02 51.7	08 04.2	−02 43.	Mon	IIIb	168	15.4			17.8		ARO 246, K 1-13
265−09.1	Wra 16-14	08 08.37	−50 32.7	08 06.95	−50 23.9	Car								
238+07.2	Sa 2-21	08 08.73	−19 13.8	08 06.5	−19 05.	Pup		40						ESO 561-16
250+00.1	Abell 26	08 08.96	−32 39.8	08 07.0	−32 31.	Pup	II	34	18.1					ARO 545, ESO 369-05
238+07.1	Y-C 2-4	08 09.23	−18 41.7	08 06.99	−18 32.8	Pup								
240+07.1	Y-C 2-5	08 10.69	−20 31.5	08 08.48	−20 22.6	Pup		8						Sa 2-22
211+22.1	Bn 0808+11	08 11.2	+10 57.	08 08.5	+11 06.	Cnc		180				13.83		
264−08.1	He 2-7	08 11.53	−48 43.3	08 10.03	−48 34.3	Vel		46	12.4	12.4		16.6:		ESO 209-19
251+00.1	Wra 17-15	08 14.56	−33 46.9	08 12.62	−33 37.7	Pup								ARO 546
245+05.1	Wra 17-16	08 15.76	−25 58.6	08 13.65	−25 49.3	Pup								
251+01.1	Wra 17-17	08 15.88	−33 15.8	08 13.92	−33 06.5	Pup								ARO 547
263−05.1	He 2-8	08 20.67	−46 23.0	08 19.06	−46 13.4	Vel		<10						PB 2, ESO 259-04
253+00.1	MrWe 2-1	08 20.8	−35 16.	08 18.9	−35 07.	Pup	IIa	20						Poss PN
254+00.1	Ns 238	08 20.90	−36 12.6	08 19.0	−36 03.	Pup								ESO 370-09
261−04.1	Sa 2-25	08 21.07	−44 23.8	08 19.40	−44 14.2	Vel								ESO 259-03, Wra 16-19
260−03.1	Wra 16-20	08 23.71	−43 12.7	08 22.0	−43 03.	Vel								
262−04.1	LoTr 2	08 24.12	−45 26.9	08 22.47	−45 17.1	Vel	IV							ESO 259-06, Wra 17-18
257−00.1	Wra 17-19	08 27.57	−38 53.8	08 25.73	−38 43.8	Vel								
258−00.1	He 2-9	08 28.46	−39 23.7	08 26.63	−39 13.7	Vel		<10		14.8		16.25		ESO 312-05, Sa 2-26
257+00.1	VBRC 1	08 30.93	−38 19.9	08 29.06	−38 09.7	Vel								ESO 313-01, RCW 21
249+06.1	SaSt 1-1	08 31.71	−27 45.5	08 29.61	−27 35.3	Pyx								MWC AS 201
252+04.1	Abell 27	08 31.81	−32 05.2	08 29.8	−31 55.	Pyx	IIIb	49	>17.9			>21.		ESO 431-14, K 1-1
239+13.1	NGC 2610	08 33.39	−16 09.0	08 31.08	−15 58.7	Hya	IV+II	>37	13.6	12.7	cont	15.90		ARO 64, Sa 2-27

CATALOGUE OF PLANETARY NEBULAE—TABLE 7

PK Name	Alternate Name	2000.0 R.A. (h m)	2000.0 Dec. (° ′)	1950.0 R.A. (h m)	1950.0 Dec. (° ′)	Con	Nebula Type	Nebula Diam. (″)	Nebula Mag. p	Nebula Mag. v	Star Spectra	Star Mag. V	Star Name	Notes
265−04.1	ESO 259-10	08 34.1	−47 16.	08 32.5	−47 06.	Vel								LoTr 3
264−03.1	Wra 17-20	08 34.48	−46 25.7	08 32.83	−46 15.3	Vel								
271−08.1	Y-C 2-41	08 34.8	−55 03.	08 33.5	−54 53.	Vel								
255+03.1	Sa 2-28	08 36.27	−35 15.9	08 34.32	−35 05.4	Pyx								ESO 370-18, Wra 16-22
259+00.1	He 2-11	08 37.13	−39 26.4	08 35.28	−39 15.9	Vel		65		14.1		18.92:		ESO 313-05, Wra 16-23
259+00.2	Wra 16-24	08 37.95	−39 44.6	08 36.1	−39 34.	Vel								
244+12.1	Abell 29	08 40.24	−20 53.7	08 38.0	−20 43.	Pyx	IV	393	14.3			17.8		ESO 563-09
254+05.1	M 3-6	08 40.67	−32 22.5	08 38.65	−32 11.8	Pyx	IIa	9		10.9:		13.9		ARO 553, He 2-12
256+03.1	Sa 2-30	08 41.16	−36 02.6	08 39.22	−35 51.9	Pyx								ESO 371-06, Wra 16-26
158+37.1	Abell 28	08 41.64	+58 13.3	08 37.7	+58 24.	UMa	IIb	284	>14.6	13.5		16.1		
265−02.1	He 2-13	08 43.47	−46 06.7	08 41.78	−45 55.8	Vel		<5						ESO 260-05, Sa 2-31
267−03.1	Sa 3-7	08 43.49	−48 54.8	08 41.89	−48 43.9	Vel								Wra 16-28
268−03.1	Wra 17-21	08 46.61	−49 21.3	08 45.02	−49 10.2	Vel								
208+33.1	Abell 30	08 46.83	+17 53.0	08 44.0	+18 04.	Cnc	IIc	109	15.6		OVI	14.3		
263+00.1	K 2-15	08 48.64	+42 53.8	08 46.85	−42 42.6	Vel								ESO 260-08
270−05.1	Wra 16-29	08 50.79	−52 36.3	08 49.3	−52 25.	Vel								
270−04.1	Wra 16-31	08 52.73	−51 41.4	08 51.2	−51 30.	Vel								
271−05.1	MrWe 1-1	08 53.5	−54 05.	08 52.1	−53 54.	Vel	II	96				19.::		
261+02.1	He 2-15	08 53.51	−40 03.6	08 51.63	−39 52.2	Vel		20		12.9:		17.8		ESO 313-17, Sa 2-32
219+31.1	Abell 31	08 54.19	+08 54.6	08 51.5	+09 06.	Cnc	IIIa	>980	12.2	12.0	sdO	15.5		Sh 2-290
269−03.1	He 2-16	08 54.30	−50 32.4	08 52.72	−50 20.9	Vel		<25		13.6				ESO 211-04, PB 3
261+04.1	Wra 17-22	08 56.24	−39 02.2	08 54.33	−38 50.6	Vel								
266−00.1		08 56.61	−46 24.0	08 54.89	−46 12.4	Vel								identity?
253+10.1	K 1-2	08 57.82	−28 56.6	08 55.7	−28 45.	Pyx	II	59				16.8v	VW Pyx	ESO 432-14. ‘Ref. effect’ var., P = $0^{d}.6707$.
270−02.1	Wra 17-23	09 05.94	−50 19.2	09 04.30	−50 07.1	Vel								
285−14.1	IC 2448	09 07.11	−69 56.6	09 06.63	−69 44.4	Car	IIb	8	11.5	10.4		14.09		ARO 506, He 2-19
264+03.1	Wra 17-24	09 07.12	−42 15.4	09 05.25	−42 03.3	Vel								
273−03.1	He 2-18	09 08.67	−53 19.2	09 07.12	−53 07.0	Vel		<255						ESO 166-02, Sa 2-35
265+04.1	NGC 2792	09 12.44	−42 25.7	09 10.56	−42 13.3	Vel	IV	11	13.5	11.6		15.74:		ARO 507, He 2-20
277−07.1	ESO 126-01	09 12.61	−58 50.5	09 11.28	−58 38.1	Car		39						
279−08.1	Wra 17-26	09 13.67	−60 46.0	09 12.43	−60 33.5	Car								
275−04.2	He 2-21	09 13.88	−55 28.3	09 12.39	−55 15.8	Vel		<10						ESO 166-05, Sa 2-37

CATALOGUE OF PLANETARY NEBULAE—TABLE 8

PK Name	Alternate Name	2000.0 R.A. (h m)	2000.0 Dec. (° ′)	1950.0 R.A. (h m)	1950.0 Dec. (° ′)	Con	Nebula Type	Nebula Diam. (″)	Nebula Mag. p	Nebula Mag. v	Star Spectra	Star Mag. V	Star Name	Notes
275−04.1	He 2-22	09 15.13	−54 52.7	09 13.61	−54 40.2	Vel		<10		12.8		16.15		ESO 166-06, PB 4
261+08.1	NGC 2818	09 16.03	−36 37.8	09 14.01	−36 25.2	Pyx	IIIb	38	13.0	11.6				ESO 372-13, He 2-23 Open cluster member
268+02.1	He 2-24	09 16.16	−45 28.8	09 14.34	−45 16.2	Vel	I	<5				18.67		ESO 261-04, PB 5
282−10.1	Wra 17-27	09 16.79	−64 58.2	09 15.78	−64 45.6	Car								
275−03.1	He 2-25	09 18.02	−54 39.5	09 16.48	−54 26.8	Vel		5				16.96::		ESO 166-07, SaSt 1-2
278−06.1	He 2-26	09 19.46	−59 12.0	09 18.10	−58 59.3	Car		<10				16.7:		ESO 126-06, Sa 2-41
278−06.3	Wra 16-42	09 19.63	−59 03.8	09 18.26	−58 51.1	Car								
278−05.1	NGC 2867	09 21.42	−58 18.7	09 20.01	−58 05.9	Car	IV	11	9.7	9.7	WC	15.0::		ARO 509, ESO 126-08, He 2-27
275−02.1	He 2-28	09 22.11	−54 09.7	09 20.53	−53 56.8	Vel		<25						
278−06.2	Wra 17-28	09 23.25	−58 52.0	09 21.85	−58 39.1	Car								
272+00.1	Wra 16-45	09 24.12	−50 15.1	09 22.4	−50 02.2	Vel								
264+08.1	Wra 17-29	09 24.50	−38 36.7	09 22.50	−38 23.7	Vel								
275−03.2	Wra 17-30	09 24.53	−54 46.6	09 22.96	−54 33.6	Vel								
275−02.2	He 2-29	09 24.76	−54 36.3	09 23.18	−54 23.3	Vel		20		13.3				ESO 166-10, Sa 2-44
277−03.1	NGC 2899	09 27.04	−56 06.5	09 25.50	−55 53.4	Vel		120		11.8		15.9:		ESO 166-13, He 2-30, Gum 27, RCW 43
275−01.1	He 2-31	09 30.81	−53 09.9	09 29.15	−52 56.7	Vel		<10						ESO 166-18, Pe 2-4
278−04.1	He 2-32	09 30.91	−57 36.9	09 29.41	−57 23.6	Car		40						ESO 166-19, Sa 3-9
274−00.1	ESO 212-08	09 31.40	−52 07.3	09 29.70	−51 54.0	Vel		24						
277−03.2	VBRC 2	09 31.45	−56 17.7	09 29.90	−56 04.4	Vel	IV	160				18.1		ESO 166-21, RCW 44, Sa 3-10, Wra 17-31
266+08.1	Wra 16-50	09 32.74	−39 33.9	09 30.73	−39 20.6	Ant								
282−07.1	Wra 17-32	09 37.06	−62 27.1	09 35.74	−62 13.6	Car								
274+01.1	Wra 16-53	09 37.99	−50 09.6	09 36.2	−49 56.	Vel								
274+02.3	Wra 17-33	09 38.56	−49 45.8	09 36.76	−49 32.2	Vel								
281−05.1	IC 2501	09 38.79	−60 05.5	09 37.35	−59 51.9	Car	I	<25	11.3	10.4		14.48:		ARO 510, He 2-33, Sa 2-47
238+34.1	Abell 33	09 39.13	−02 47.6	09 36.6	−02 34.	Hya	IIb	268	13.4	12.6	sdO	15.66		ARO 65
283−07.1	Wra 17-34	09 39.95	−63 12.4	09 38.65	−62 58.7	Car								
279−03.2	VBRC 3	09 40.89	−56 58.1	09 39.31	−56 44.4	Vel		35						ESO 167-02, Sa 3-11
274+02.1	He 2-34	09 41.23	−49 22.7	09 39.41	−49 09.0	Vel		<10				16.5:		ESO 212-13, Wra 16-56
274+02.2	He 2-35	09 41.62	−49 57.9	09 39.81	−49 44.2	Vel		5		14.3		16.2:		ESO 212-14, Sa 2-48

CATALOGUE OF PLANETARY NEBULAE—TABLE 9

PK Name	Alternate Name	2000.0 R.A. h m	2000.0 Dec. ° ′	1950.0 R.A. h m	1950.0 Dec. ° ′	Con	Nebula Type	Nebula Diam. ″	Nebula Mag. p	Nebula Mag. v	Star Spectra	Star Mag. V	Star Name	Notes
279−03.1	He 2-36	09 43.43	−57 16.9	09 41.84	−57 03.1	Car		<25		11.8	A2+?	11.37		ESO 167-03, Sa 2-49
248+29.1	Abell 34	09 45.62	−13 09.9	09 43.2	−12 56.	Hya	IIb	288	14.5	12.9		16.2		
285−09.1	Wra 17-36	09 46.32	−65 43.1	09 45.12	−65 29.2	Car								
274+03.2	Wra 16-58	09 46.85	−49 23.6	09 45.0	−49 09.7	Vel								
274+03.1	He 2-37	09 47.41	−48 58.1	09 45.55	−48 44.2	Vel		30		14.:				ESO 213-01, Sa 2-50
274+03.3	Wra 17-37	09 48.24	−48 33.4	09 46.37	−48 19.4	Vel								
278+00.1	Wra 16-61	09 52.06	−53 34.1	09 50.3	−53 20.	Vel								
273+06.1	DS 3	09 52.7	−46 17.	09 50.8	−46 03.	Vel	IV	90			sdO	12.47	LSS 1362	HbDS 1
221+46.1	Bn 0950+13	09 53.0	+13 44.	09 50.3	+13 59.	Leo		720				16.00		
277+03.1	MrWe 2-2	09 58.2	−50 39.	09 56.3	−50 25.	Vel		20						Poss PN
279+01.1	Wra 17-38	09 59.68	−53 28.2	09 57.87	−53 13.8	Vel								
284−05.1	He 3-358	10 02.04	−61 57.3	10 00.51	−61 42.8	Car								Sa 2-51, Wra 15-490
282−02.1	Wra 16-63	10 02.26	−58 13.8	10 00.58	−57 59.3	Car								
280−00.1	Wra 17-39	10 02.89	−55 49.5	10 01.13	−55 35.0	Vel								
283−04.1	He 2-39	10 03.83	−60 43.8	10 02.23	−60 29.2	Car		<25						ESO 127-03, Sa 2-52
274+09.1	Lo 4	10 05.77	−44 18.8	10 03.73	−44 04.2	Vel		48			GW Vir	16.6±		ESO 263-02
286−06.2	Wra 17-40	10 06.92	−64 21.8	10 05.46	−64 07.1	Car								
272+12.1	NGC 3132	10 07.00	−41 26.7	10 04.91	−41 12.0	Vel	IV+II	>47	8.2	9.2	A2V+sdO	10.07	HD 87892	ARO 504, He 2-40, ESO 316-27, Sa 2-53
286−06.1	He 2-41	10 07.40	−63 54.5	10 05.91	−63 39.8	Car		<10						ESO 092-11, Sa 2-54
285−05.1	IC 2553	10 09.34	−62 36.8	10 07.78	−62 22.0	Car		4	13.0	10.3		15.51:		He 2-42, ESO 127-18
296−20.1	NGC 3195	10 09.50	−80 51.8	10 10.1	−80 37.	Cha	III	38		11.6		15.3		ARO 511, He 2-44, ESO 019-02, My 56
280+02.1	Ste 2-1	10 12.00	−52 39.1	10 10.10	−52 24.3	Vel								Sa 2-56
278+05.1	He 2-43	10 13.26	−50 20.0	10 11.30	−50 05.1	Vel		<25		12.8				ESO 213-07, PB 6
283−01.2	MrWe 1-2	10 14.4	−58 11.	10 12.6	−57 57.	Car	IV	264				19.::		
283−01.1	He 2-45	10 15.58	−58 51.2	10 13.83	−58 36.2	Car		30						ESO 127-12, Hf 4
286−04.1	NGC 3211	10 17.84	−62 40.2	10 16.21	−62 25.2	Car	IIb	12	11.8	10.7		15.50:		ARO 512, ESO 127-15, He 2-46, Sa 2-59
289−08.1	Wra 17-42	10 21.05	−67 31.9	10 19.62	−67 16.8	Car								
285−02.1	He 2-47	10 23.15	−60 32.7	10 21.40	−60 17.5	Car		<5				12.96		ESO 127-16, SaSt 2-5

CATALOGUE OF PLANETARY NEBULAE—TABLE 10

PK Name	Alternate Name	2000.0 R.A. (h m)	2000.0 Dec. (° ′)	1950.0 R.A. (h m)	1950.0 Dec. (° ′)	Con	Nebula Type	Nebula Diam. (″)	Nebula Mag. p	Nebula Mag. v	Star Spectra	Star Mag. V	Star Name	Notes
261+32.1	NGC 3242	10 24.81	−18 38.2	10 22.4	−18 23.	Hya	IV+IIIb	>16	8.6	7.7		12.10	HD 90255	ARO 4, ESO 568-05
286−02.1	Wra 17-43	10 26.69	−60 55.6	10 24.92	−60 40.3	Car								
285−01.1	Pe 2-5	10 28.54	−59 03.4	10 26.7	−58 48.	Car								ESO 127-22
285−01.2	Wra 17-44	10 29.29	−59 49.7	10 27.47	−59 34.3	Car								
282+03.1	He 2-48	10 31.53	−53 33.4	10 29.54	−53 18.0	Vel		30						ESO 168-05, Sa 2-60
283+02.1	He 2-49	10 31.56	−55 20.8	10 29.61	−55 05.4	Vel		<10		13.3		16.87:		ESO 168-06, PB 7
283+03.1	He 2-50	10 34.31	−53 41.1	10 32.31	−53 25.6	Vel		<25						ESO 168-08, Sa 2-62
270+24.1	K 1-28	10 34.51	−29 11.2	10 32.18	−28 55.7	Hya								ESO 436-41
288−05.1	He 2-51	10 35.77	−64 19.2	10 34.04	−64 03.6	Car		10	14.2	13.8		15.62		ESO 092-23, Sa 2-63
285+01.1	Pe 1-1	10 38.47	−56 47.1	10 36.50	−56 31.5	Vel		<5						ESO 168-10, He 2-52
285+01.2	Pe 1-2	10 39.55	−57 06.3	10 37.58	−56 50.6	Vel		<10						ESO 168-12, He 2-53
285+02.1	Pe 2-7	10 41.33	−56 09.3	10 39.33	−55 53.6	Vel								ESO 168-13, Sa 2-66
288−02.1	Pe 1-3	10 44.53	−61 39.7	10 42.64	−61 23.9	Car		<25						ESO 128-09, He 2-54
286+02.1	He 2-55	10 48.73	−56 03.2	10 46.68	−55 47.3	Vel		<25						ESO 169-03, Sa 2-68
288−00.1	Hf 39	10 53.99	−60 26.7	10 51.99	−60 10.7	Car		72				10.5		ESO 128-18, He 3-519
288+00.1	Hf 38	10 54.59	−59 09.7	10 52.56	−58 53.7	Car	IV	33						ESO 128-19, He 2-56
283+09.1	DS 1	10 54.7	−48 47.	10 52.5	−48 31.	Vel	IV	180			sdO	11.8-12	KV Vel	ESO 215-04. Ref. effect var. P = 8ʰ.571
289−01.1	He 2-57	10 55.99	−61 27.0	10 54.0	−61 11.	Car		<25						ESO 128-20, Sa 3-13
291−04.1	IC 2621	11 00.33	−65 14.9	10 58.40	−64 58.8	Car	I	5		11.2		15.39:		ARO 513, ESO 093-04, He 2-59, Sa 2-70
290−00.1	Hf 48	11 03.94	−60 36.0	11 01.86	−60 19.8	Car	III	28						ESO 128-29, He 2-60
285+11.1	Y-C 2-7	11 09.15	−48 02.9	11 06.87	−47 46.6	Cen								
286+11.1	Lo 5	11 13.84	−48 05.5	11 11.53	−47 49.2	Cen		216						ESO 215-35
148+57.1	NGC 3587	11 14.78	+55 00.6	11 11.9	+55 17.	UMa	IIIa	194	12.0	9.9		13.2		M.97, ARO 25
287+10.1	Y-C 2-9	11 17.08	−49 12.1	11 14.76	−48 55.7	Cen								
295−09.1	He 2-62	11 17.72	−70 49.5	11 15.75	−70 33.1	Car		<10						Sa 2-72, StWr 1-4
295−09.2	Wra 16-87	11 18.08	−70 38.4	11 16.1	−70 22.	Car								
288+08.1	ESO 216-02	11 18.17	−52 10.1	11 15.87	−51 53.7	Cen		36						
292−01.1	Wra 17-46	11 23.23	−62 20.4	11 21.02	−62 03.9	Cen								
289+07.1	Y-C 2-10	11 24.02	−52 51.4	11 21.69	−52 34.9	Cen		<10						ESO 170-01, He 2-63
283+25.1	K 1-22	11 26.73	−34 22.2	11 24.28	−34 05.7	Hya		181		12.1:				ESO 378-01, V-V 3-1
291+03.1	He 2-64	11 27.40	−57 17.9	11 25.09	−57 01.4	Cen		<10						ESO 170-05, Wra 16-89

CATALOGUE OF PLANETARY NEBULAE—TABLE 11

PK Name	Alternate Name	2000.0 R.A. (h m)	2000.0 Dec. (° ′)	1950.0 R.A. (h m)	1950.0 Dec. (° ′)	Con	Nebula Type	Nebula Diam. (″)	Nebula Mag. p	Nebula Mag. v	Star Spectra	Star Mag. V	Star Name	Notes
292+01.1	NGC 3699	11 27.96	−59 57.4	11 25.67	−59 40.9	Cen		67		11.3				ESO 129-21, He 2-65
290+07.1	Fg 1	11 28.60	−52 56.1	11 26.25	−52 39.6	Cen	III+VI	>25		11.4				ARO 554, ESO 170-06, He 2-66, Y-C 2-11
292+01.2	He 2-67	11 28.79	−60 06.6	11 26.50	−59 50.1	Cen		<5		13.8				ESO 129-22, Sa 2-76
292+01.3	Wra 16-93	11 30.82	−59 17.6	11 28.5	−59 01.	Cen								
294−04.1	He 2-68	11 31.75	−65 58.2	11 29.51	−65 41.6	Mus		<10						ESO 094-03, SaSt 2-6
292+04.1	He 2-69	11 33.29	−57 06.3	11 30.94	−56 49.7	Cen		<10		12.8		13.55		ESO 170-07, PB 8
293+01.1	He 2-70	11 35.18	−60 17.2	11 32.84	−60 00.6	Cen		30						ESO 129-26, Sa 2-78
296−06.1	He 2-71	11 39.18	−68 52.1	11 36.89	−68 35.5	Mus		<5						ESO 063-18, SaSt 2-7
296−06.2	Wra 16-99	11 39.29	−68 46.6	11 37.0	−68 30.	Mus								
294−00.1	Hf 69	11 41.68	−62 28.6	11 39.3	−62 12.	Cen		69						ESO 129-29, He 2-72
294+00.1	Wra 17-47	11 44.57	−61 11.7	11 42.15	−60 55.0	Cen								
293+05.1	Wra 17-48	11 45.70	−56 20.9	11 43.25	−56 04.2	Cen								
292+10.1	Wra 17-49	11 47.63	−51 28.2	11 45.15	−51 11.5	Cen								
296−03.1	He 2-73	11 48.65	−65 08.6	11 46.22	−64 51.9	Mus		<5				16.11:		ESO 094-07, Sa 2-80
294+04.1	NGC 3918	11 50.30	−57 11.0	11 47.82	−56 54.3	Cen	IIb	12	8.4	8.1		13.24		ARO 514, ESO 170-13, He 2-74, Sa 2-81
291+19.1	ESO 320-28	11 52.5	−42 17.	11 50.0	−42 01.	Cen								LoTr 4
293+10.1	BlDz 1	11 53.06	−50 50.7	11 50.55	−50 34.	Cen		82						ESO 217-11
295+06.1	Wra 16-102	11 56.23	−55 32.7	11 53.7	−55 16.	Cen								
295+04.1	Wra 17-50	11 56.30	−57 12.3	11 53.78	−56 55.6	Cen								
290+27.1	MrWe 2-3	11 56.7	−34 25.	11 54.2	−34 09.	Hya	V	66				17.::		Poss PN
294+12.1	Wra 16-103	12 00.18	−49 26.0	11 57.62	−49 09.3	Cen								
297−03.1	Wra 17-51	12 00.39	−65 47.5	11 57.84	−65 30.8	Mus								
294+14.1	Lo 6	12 00.73	−47 33.2	11 58.17	−47 16.5	Cen		63						
295+07.1	Wra 17-52	12 03.46	−54 24.5	12 00.88	−54 07.8	Cen								
298−04.1	NGC 4071	12 04.22	−67 18.3	12 01.62	−67 01.6	Mus		75		13.0		19.15:		ESO 094-12, He 2-75
298−01.2	He 2-76	12 08.42	−64 12.2	12 05.79	−63 55.5	Cru		<25						ESO 094-14, Sa 3-15
298−00.1	He 2-77	12 09.03	−63 16.1	12 06.39	−62 59.4	Cru								ARO 555, ESO 095-01, Sa 3-16
297+03.1	He 2-78	12 09.16	−58 42.6	12 06.54	−58 25.9	Cru		<5						ESO 130-07, Sa 3-17
296+10.1	Wra 17-53	12 10.08	−51 46.5	12 07.46	−51 29.8	Cen								
299−04.1	HtTr 1	12 16.5	−66 45.	12 13.8	−66 29.	Mus		80						
297+13.1	Wra 17-54	12 16.52	−49 11.6	12 13.87	−48 54.9	Cen								
297+07.1	Wra 17-55	12 17.36	−54 35.8	12 14.69	−54 19.1	Cen								

CATALOGUE OF PLANETARY NEBULAE—TABLE 12

PK Name	Alternate Name	2000.0 R.A. (h m)	2000.0 Dec. (° ′)	1950.0 R.A. (h m)	1950.0 Dec. (° ′)	Con	Nebula Type	Nebula Diam. (″)	Nebula Mag. p	Nebula Mag. v	Star Spectra	Star Mag. V	Star Name	Notes
275+72.1	K 2-4	12 18.35	+11 02.3	12 15.8	+11 19.	Vir		690				17.7		ARO 35. Not PN? QSO lies behind.
299−01.1	He 2-81	12 23.03	−64 01.8	12 20.25	−63 45.2	Cru		<25						ESO 095-08, Sa 3-18
299+02.1	He 2-82	12 23.89	−60 13.2	12 21.14	−59 56.6	Cru		30						ESO 131-01, Sa 3-19
294+43.1	NGC 4361	12 24.50	−18 47.6	12 21.9	−18 31.	Crv	IIIa+II	>45	10.3	10.9		13.18		ARO 26, ESO 573-19
300−02.2	Sa 3-20	12 28.63	−65 19.3	12 25.78	−65 02.7	Mus								Wra 16-113
300+00.1	He 2-83	12 28.72	−62 05.6	12 25.91	−61 49.0	Cru		<25						ESO 131-08, Sa 3-21
300−00.1	He 2-84	12 28.78	−63 44.6	12 25.95	−63 28.0	Cru								ESO 095-09, Sa 2-84
300−01.1	He 2-85	12 30.12	−63 53.0	12 27.28	−63 36.4	Cru		<10				16.59		ESO 095-11, Sa 2-85
300−03.1	ESO 095-12	12 30.41	−66 14.4	12 27.53	−65 57.8	Mus		18						
300−02.1	He 2-86	12 30.51	−64 52.1	12 27.65	−64 35.5	Cru		<5				18.4::		ESO 095-13, Sa 2-86
299+18.1	K 1-23	12 30.88	−44 14.4	12 28.18	−43 57.8	Cen		62						ESO 268-12, V-V 3-2
123+34.1	IC 3568	12 32.94	+82 33.5	12 31.6	+82 50.	Cam	II+IIa	>6	11.6	10.6	O5f	11.4	HD 109540	ARO 56
298+34.1	CTIO 1230-275	12 33.2	−27 48.	12 30.6	−27 32.	Hya								
302+02.1	ESO 131-15	12 45.92	−60 20.2	12 42.98	−60 03.8	Cru		12						Wra 16-120
302−00.2	Lo 7	12 46.45	−63 24.5	12 43.46	−63 08.1	Cru								ARO 529, ESO 095-17, RCW 70, VBRC 4
302−00.3	Wra 17-56	12 48.52	−63 50.0	12 45.50	−63 33.6	Cru		45						
303+01.1	Wra 17-57	12 53.25	−61 46.2	12 50.23	−61 29.9	Cru								
303+40.1	Abell 35	12 53.57	−22 52.3	12 50.9	−22 36.	Hya	IIIa	709	12.0	12.7	G8IV+sdO	9.63	LW Hya	Sh 2-313
339+88.1	LoTr 5	12 55.5	+25 53.	12 53.1	+26 10.	Com		525			G5+sdo	8.7-8	IN Com	P = $5^{d}922$, ref. effect
049+88.1	H 4-1	12 59.41	+27 37.8	12 57.0	+27 54.	Com			16.0	15.0				ARO 179
304+05.2	ESO 173-01	13 00.68	−56 53.6	12 57.68	−56 37.5	Cen		36						Wra 16-122
304+05.1	He 2-88	13 05.80	−57 39.3	13 02.75	−57 23.3	Cen		<10				15.26		ESO 173-04, Sa 2-88
304−04.1	IC 4191	13 08.79	−67 38.7	13 05.45	−67 22.7	Mus	II	5	12.0	10.6		16.4::		ESO 096-02, He 2-89
305+01.1	He 2-90	13 09.60	−61 19.6	13 06.45	−61 03.6	Cen		<10				15.3		ESO 132-01, Sa 2-90
305+03.2	Wra 17-58	13 10.33	−59 45.2	13 07.21	−59 29.2	Cen								
315+59.1	Y-C 2-43	13 16.9	−03 03.	13 14.3	−02 48.	Vir								
305−03.1	ESO 096-07	13 19.51	−66 09.1	13 16.11	−65 53.4	Mus		24						Sa 2-91, Wra 17-59
306−00.1	He 2-92	13 22.55	−63 20.8	13 19.23	−63 05.1	Cen		25				14.48		ESO 096-09, Th 2-A
307+05.1	Sa 2-93	13 24.37	−57 31.3	13 21.19	−57 15.7	Cen		18						ESO 173-12
310+24.1	Lo 8	13 25.62	−37 45.2	13 22.75	−37 29.6	Cen		115						ESO 382-63, K 1-29
307+01.1	Wra 16-129	13 26.19	−61 15.6	13 22.9	−61 00.	Cen								
306−00.2	Wra 17-60	13 26.22	−63 34.4	13 22.86	−63 18.8	Cen								
308+07.1	MrWe 1-3	13 28.1	−54 41.	13 25.0	−54 26.	Cen	IV	20				17.::		

CATALOGUE OF PLANETARY NEBULAE—TABLE 13

PK Name	Alternate Name	2000.0 R.A. (h m)	2000.0 Dec. (° ′)	1950.0 R.A. (h m)	1950.0 Dec. (° ′)	Con	Nebula Type	Nebula Diam. (″)	Nebula Mag. p	Nebula Mag. v	Star Spectra	Star Mag. V	Star Name	Notes
307−03.1	NGC 5189	13 33.52	−65 58.6	13 29.99	−65 43.2	Mus	V	153	10.3		OVI	14.0	HD 117622	ARO 515, ESO 096-16, Gum 47, IC 4274
305−13.1	ESO 040-11	13 34.24	−75 46.5	13 29.98	−75 31.1	Mus		72						
308+00.1	Wra 17-62	13 37.67	−61 48.1	13 34.27	−61 32.8	Cen								
307−01.2	Wra 17-61	13 37.68	−64 00.7	13 34.20	−63 45.4	Cen								
307−04.1	He 2-95	13 39.58	−67 22.8	13 35.92	−67 07.6	Mus		<25	12.2	12.9		13.9:		ARO 530, ESO 097-01, MyCn 18, RCW 77
308+00.2	Wra 17-63	13 40.37	−62 06.5	13 36.94	−61 51.3	Cen								
318+41.1	Abell 36	13 40.63	−19 53.2	13 37.9	−19 38.	Vir	IIIb+IIIa		13.0		sdO	11.51		ESO 577-24
309+00.1	He 2-96	13 42.63	−61 23.1	13 39.2	−61 08.	Cen		<10						ESO 133-01, Sa 2-97
310+06.1	Wra 16-134	13 43.98	−55 19.6	13 40.73	−55 04.5	Cen								
309+01.1	SuWt 1	13 43.99	−60 49.7	13 40.57	−60 34.6	Cen								ESO 133-02, VBRC 5
307−09.1	He 2-97	13 45.38	−71 28.9	13 41.38	−71 13.9	Mus		<5				15.4		Sa 2-98, StWr 1-6
312+10.1	NGC 5307	13 51.06	−51 12.3	13 47.86	−50 57.5	Cen	III	13	12.1	11.2		14.58		ARO 516, ESO 221-11, He 2-98, Sa 2-99
309−04.1	He 2-99	13 52.51	−66 23.4	13 48.77	−66 08.6	Cir		25				13.84		ESO 097-08, Sa 3-23
309−04.2	NGC 5315	13 53.95	−66 30.8	13 50.19	−66 16.1	Cir	II	5	13.0	9.8	WC6	14.3:		ESO 097-09, He 2-100, Sa 2-100, Wra 16-140
311+02.2	SuWt 2	13 55.75	−59 22.7	13 52.3	−59 08.	Cen		68						
311+02.1	He 2-102	13 58.23	−58 54.5	13 54.77	−58 39.9	Cen		<10				17.25		ESO 133-08, Sa 2-101
310−03.1	Wra 16-143	14 00.36	−65 25.5	13 56.6	−65 11.	Cir								
314+10.1	MrWe 2-4	14 01.2	−50 40.	13 58.0	−50 26.	Cen		360				19.::		Poss PN
326+42.1	IC 972	14 04.44	−17 15.3	14 01.7	−17 01.	Vir	IIc	43	14.9	13.9		17.7		Abell 37
310−02.1	He 2-103	14 05.61	−64 40.7	14 01.85	−64 26.4	Cen		20		14.0				ESO 097-11, Sa 2-103
311−00.1	Wra 17-64	14 08.77	−62 29.9	14 05.09	−62 15.7	Cen								
313+04.1	Wra 16-145	14 08.79	−57 04.5	14 05.33	−56 50.3	Cen								
311−02.1	Wra 16-146	14 11.71	−64 17.4	14 07.91	−64 03.3	Cen								
315+09.1	He 2-104	14 11.86	−51 26.4	14 08.55	−51 12.3	Cen		75				15.::		ESO 221-31, PN binary with 400d Mira var.
310−05.1	LoTr 7	14 15.3	−67 31.	14 11.3	−67 18.	Cir		16						
308−12.1	He 2-105	14 15.51	−74 13.0	14 10.8	−73 59.0	Aps		35				14.73		ESO 041-03, Sa 3-24
308−12.2	Wra 17-65	14 15.58	−74 07.0	14 10.89	−73 53.0	Aps								
315+08.1	MrWe 1-4	14 17.5	−52 25.	14 14.1	−52 12.	Cen		54				19.::		
316+08.1	He 2-108	14 18.14	−52 10.6	14 14.78	−51 56.8	Cen		<25		13.9		12.83		ESO 221-36, SaSt 2-8
312−01.1	He 2-107	14 18.74	−63 07.1	14 14.95	−62 53.3	Cen		<25				15.11		ESO 097-16, Sa 3-26

CATALOGUE OF PLANETARY NEBULAE—TABLE 14

PK Name	Alternate Name	2000.0 R.A. h	m	Dec. °	′	1950.0 R.A. h	m	Dec. °	′	Con	Nebula Type	Diam. ″	Mag. p	v	Star Spectra	Mag. V	Name	Notes
313+01.1	Wra 17-66	14	18.92	−59	52.6	14	15.28	−59	38.8	Cen								
311−06.1	Sa 3-25	14	18.99	−67	29.2	14	14.93	−67	15.4	Cir								Wra 16-150
315+05.1	He 2-109	14	20.81	−55	28.1	14	17.33	−55	14.4	Lup		<10				18.9		ESO 175-07, Sa 2-104
315+05.2	LoTr 8	14	22.0	−55	02.	14	18.5	−54	49.	Lup		19						
319+15.1	IC 4406	14	22.43	−44	09.4	14	19.25	−43	55.8	Lup	IV+III	>28	10.6	10.2	WC	14.7	HD 125720	ARO 517, ESO 272-06, He 2-110, Sa 2-105
314−00.1	Wra 16-155	14	33.08	−60	55.2	14	29.3	−60	42.	Cen								
315−00.1	He 2-111	14	33.29	−60	49.6	14	29.51	−60	36.4	Cen	V+V	30		14.::		16.7::		ESO 134-07, Sa 2-106
322+14.1	K 1-24	14	38.27	−44	12.9	14	35.03	−44	00.0	Lup		48						V-V 3-3
319+06.1	Y-C 2-15	14	40.52	−52	35.0	14	37.03	−52	22.1	Lup		<25				17.1::		ESO 222-13, He 2-112
313−05.1	Wra 17-67	14	40.88	−65	50.8	14	36.74	−65	38.0	Cir								
315−01.1	LoTr 9	14	41.3	−61	19.	14	37.4	−61	07.	Cen		28						
317+03.1	VBRC 6	14	41.60	−56	15.1	14	37.97	−56	02.3	Nor		45						ESO 176-01
318+03.1		14	43.74	−56	17.7	14	40.1	−56	05.	Cir								identity?
316−01.1	LoTr 10	14	46.4	−61	13.	14	42.5	−61	01.	Cir		54						
321+08.1	MrWe 1-5	14	46.5	−50	23.	14	43.1	−50	11.	Lup		30				20.::		
315−04.1	Sa 2-108	14	52.61	−64	02.3	14	48.51	−63	50.0	Cir								Wra 16-158
321+03.1	He 2-113	14	59.89	−54	18.1	14	56.25	−54	06.2	Lup						12.16		Wra 15-126
324+09.1	ESO 223-10	15	01.67	−48	21.0	14	58.23	−48	09.2	Lup		18						
318−02.1	He 2-114	15	04.14	−60	53.3	15	00.16	−60	41.6	Cir		30						ESO 135-02, Sa 2-109
321+02.1	He 2-115	15	05.28	−55	11.1	15	01.57	−54	59.5	Lup		<5				16.24		ESO 176-10, Sa 2-112
318−02.3	Sa 2-111	15	05.54	−60	48.8	15	01.55	−60	37.2	Cir								Wra 16-161
321+02.2	He 2-117	15	05.98	−55	59.2	15	02.24	−55	47.6	Cir		<5				17.9		ESO 176-12, RCW 90
318−02.2	He 2-116	15	06.03	−61	21.4	15	02.01	−61	09.8	Cir		45						ESO 135-03, Sa 3-27
327+13.1	He 2-118	15	06.23	−43	00.0	15	02.92	−42	48.4	Lup		<5		12.6		16.1		ESO 273-16, Sa 2-114
339+29.1	Y-C 2-17	15	08.35	−23	14.8	15	05.44	−23	03.4	Lib								
318−03.1	ESO 135-04	15	08.71	−61	44.1	15	04.65	−61	32.6	Cir		42						
317−05.1	He 2-119	15	10.69	−64	40.4	15	06.41	−64	29.0	TrA		50						ESO 099-01, Sa 2-115
321+01.1	He 2-120	15	11.94	−55	39.8	15	08.18	−55	28.5	Cir		30						ESO 177-01, Sa 2-116
331+16.1	NGC 5873	15	12.85	−38	07.5	15	09.64	−37	56.3	Lup	II	3	13.3	11.0		15.52:		ARO 533, ESO 328-34, He 2-121, Sa 2-117
327+10.1	NGC 5882	15	16.84	−45	38.9	15	13.42	−45	27.9	Lup		7	10.5	9.4		13.62		ARO 505, ESO 274-07, He 2-122, Sa 2-118
324+03.1	IRAS 15154-5258	15	19.2	−53	08.	15	15.5	−52	58.	Lup		27		16.0	WC 4	16.2		PM 1-89

CATALOGUE OF PLANETARY NEBULAE—TABLE 15

PK Name	Alternate Name	2000.0 R.A.	2000.0 Dec.	1950.0 R.A.	1950.0 Dec.	Con	Nebula Type	Nebula Diam.	Nebula Mag.		Star Spectra	Star Mag.	Star Name	Notes
		h m	° ′	h m	° ′			″	p	v		V		
321−00.1	Wra 16-174	15 19.48	−57 21.9	15 15.6	−57 11.	Cir								
321−00.2	Wra 17-69	15 21.11	−57 57.0	15 17.20	−57 46.2	Cir								
313−12.1	LoTr 11	15 21.2	−72 13.	15 16.0	−72 03.	Aps		112				19.0		
342+27.1	Me 2-1	15 22.31	−23 37.6	15 19.38	−23 26.9	Lib	II	7		11.6		16.03		ARO 88, ESO 514-12, He 2-126, Sa 2-120
323+02.1	He 2-123	15 22.32	−54 08.1	15 18.58	−53 57.4	Lup		<25				16.84:		ESO 177-02, Sa 2-119
324+02.1	He 2-125	15 23.60	−53 51.4	15 19.87	−53 40.8	Lup		<25						ESO 177-04, Sa 3-29
322−00.1	Pe 2-8	15 23.71	−57 09.3	15 19.82	−56 58.7	Cir		<10						ESO 177-03, He 2-124
325+04.3	Wra 16-179	15 24.75	−51 36.6	15 21.1	−51 26.	Lup								
325+04.1	He 2-128	15 25.13	−51 19.6	15 21.49	−51 09.1	Lup		<5						ESO 224-03, Sa 2-121
325+03.1	He 2-129	15 25.54	−52 50.6	15 21.84	−52 40.1	Lup		<10						ESO 177-05, Sa 2-122
321−01.1	Wra 17-70	15 26.91	−58 58.7	15 22.91	−58 48.2	Cir								
321−03.1	HtTr 2	15 30.3	−61 01.	15 26.2	−60 51.	TrA		12						
322−02.1	Mz 1	15 34.28	−59 09.1	15 30.23	−58 59.1	Nor	IV+VI	>26	12.5	12.1				ARO 531, ESO 135-11, He 2-130, RCW 93
315−13.1	He 2-131	15 37.17	−71 54.9	15 31.88	−71 45.0	Aps	II	5		11.6		11.08	HD 138403	ESO 068-08, SaSt 2-9
323−02.1	He 2-132	15 38.02	−58 44.5	15 33.98	−58 34.7	Nor		<25				17.04		ESO 136-01, Sa 3-30
324−01.1	He 2-133	15 41.98	−56 36.4	15 38.04	−56 26.8	Nor		<10						ESO 177-10, Sa 3-31
330+05.1	Lo 9	15 42.22	−47 40.8	15 38.66	−47 31.2	Lup		106						K 1-30
335+12.1	DS 2	15 43.0	−39 19.	15 39.7	−39 10.	Lup	IV	180			sdO	12.38	LSE 125	
322−05.1	NGC 5979	15 47.68	−61 13.1	15 43.44	−61 03.9	TrA		<25		11.5		15.29		ESO 136-03, He 2-135
328+01.1	Lo 10	15 49.54	−52 30.5	15 45.77	−52 21.4	Nor		12						
346+22.1	Wra 17-71	15 49.90	−24 25.6	15 46.92	−24 16.5	Sco								
330+04.1	Cn 1-1	15 51.26	−48 44.9	15 47.63	−48 35.9	Nor	I					11.14		ESO 225-01
325−01.1	VB 2	15 51.3	−56 21.	15 47.3	−56 12.	Nor								
330+04.2	Sa 2-125	15 51.33	−48 26.1	15 47.71	−48 17.1	Nor								Wra 16-189
329+02.1	Sp 1	15 51.68	−51 31.5	15 47.94	−51 22.5	Nor	IV	76	13.6	12.6	cont	14.03		ARO 518, ESO 225-02, He 2-137, RCW 100
322−06.1	He 2-136	15 52.18	−62 30.8	15 47.82	−62 21.8	TrA		<10		12.5		16.6:		ESO 136-05, Sa 2-126
326−01.2	VB 3	15 53.0	−56 23.	15 49.0	−56 15.	Nor								
335+09.1	K 1-31	15 53.20	−41 50.5	15 49.80	−41 41.6	Lup		36						ESO 330-02
331+03.1	Sa 2-128	15 53.47	−48 43.4	15 49.84	−48 34.5	Nor								Wra 16-192

CATALOGUE OF PLANETARY NEBULAE—TABLE 16

PK Name	Alternate Name	2000.0 R.A. (h m)	2000.0 Dec. (° ′)	1950.0 R.A. (h m)	1950.0 Dec. (° ′)	Con	Nebula Type	Nebula Diam. (″)	Nebula Mag. p	Nebula Mag. v	Star Spectra	Star Mag. V	Star Name	Notes
329+01.1	VBRC 7	15 54.84	−51 22.5	15 51.1	−51 13.7	Nor								ARO 532, ESO 225-03
320−09.1	He 2-138	15 56.03	−66 09.0	15 51.33	−66 00.3	TrA		<25		13.2		10.98		ESO 100-03, SaSt 2-10
327−01.2	He 2-140	15 58.13	−55 41.9	15 54.17	−55 33.3	Nor		<5				17.2:		ESO 178-04
342+15.1	Y-C 2-19	15 58.78	−32 00.3	15 55.62	−31 51.8	Lup								
325−04.1	He 2-141	15 59.14	−58 23.8	15 55.03	−58 15.3	Nor		<25		12.2				ESO 136-11, Sa 2-129
326−03.1	Wra 16-197	15 59.76	−57 29.5	15 55.7	−57 21.	Nor								
327−02.1	He 2-142	15 59.96	−55 55.6	15 55.98	−55 47.1	Nor		<5						ESO 178-05, SaSt 2-11
332+03.1	Sa 3-32	16 00.37	−48 15.5	15 56.73	−48 07.1	Nor								Wra 16-199
327−01.1	He 2-143	16 00.99	−55 05.6	15 57.05	−54 57.2	Nor		<25						ESO 178-07, Sa 2-130
341+13.1	NGC 6026	16 01.35	−34 32.4	15 58.13	−34 24.0	Lup	IV	45		12.9		13.29		ESO 389-07, He 2-144
336+08.1	Sa 1-3	16 02.22	−41 33.5	15 58.80	−41 25.2	Lup								ESO 330-08, Sa 2-132
340+12.1	Lo 11	16 03.36	−36 00.8	16 00.10	−35 52.6	Lup		59						ESO 389-09, K 1-32
064+48.1	NGC 6058	16 04.42	+40 40.9	16 02.7	+40 49.	Her	III+II	>23	13.3	12.9	O9	13.6		ARO 49
323−07.1	Wra 17-72	16 04.50	−62 22.7	16 00.09	−62 14.5	TrA								
340+10.1	Lo 12	16 08.44	−37 08.8	16 05.14	−37 00.9	Sco		79						ESO 389-14, K 1-33
339+09.1	Wra 16-203	16 08.49	−39 02.8	16 05.14	−38 54.9	Sco								
331+00.1	Pe 1-4	16 08.98	−51 02.0	16 05.21	−50 54.1	Nor		<25						ARO 556, ESO 225-05, He 2-145, Sa 3-34
345+15.1	Lo 13	16 09.73	−30 54.0	16 06.58	−30 46.2	Sco		71						
328−02.1	He 2-146	16 10.67	−54 57.5	16 06.71	−54 49.7	Nor		20						ESO 178-10, Sa 2-133
025+40.1	IC 4593	16 12.25	+12 04.4	16 09.9	+12 12.	Her	II+II	>12	10.9	10.7	O7f	11.13	HD 145649	ARO 27
342+10.1	NGC 6072	16 12.98	−36 13.7	16 09.69	−36 06.1	Sco	IIIa	40	14.1	11.7		18.47:		ARO 500, ESO 389-15, He 2-148, Hb 3
343+11.1	H 1-1	16 13.46	−34 35.6	16 10.22	−34 28.0	Sco		2		14.5		17.30		ESO 389-16, Sa 2-135
329−02.1	He 2-149	16 14.41	−54 47.7	16 10.44	−54 40.1	Nor		<5				16.1:		ESO 178-14, Sa 2-136
329−02.2	Mz 2	16 14.53	−54 57.0	16 10.56	−54 49.5	Nor	IV+III	27	12.6					ESO 178-15, He 2-150
333+01.1	Pe 1-5	16 15.33	−49 13.4	16 11.62	−49 05.9	Nor		<5						ESO 225-08, He 2-152
330−02.2	Sa 1-4	16 15.35	−53 51.6	16 11.43	−53 44.1	Nor								ESO 178-16, Sa 2-138
326−06.1	He 2-151	16 15.69	−59 54.0	16 11.42	−59 46.5	Nor		<5				13.07		ESO 137-09
325−07.1	Wra 17-73	16 15.85	−61 02.5	16 11.49	−60 55.0	TrA								
330−02.3	Wra 17-75	16 16.90	−53 24.6	16 13.00	−53 17.2	Nor								
331−01.1	Mz 3	16 17.23	−51 59.3	16 13.39	−51 51.9	Nor	VI	24			O9	16.0:		ESO 225-09, He 2-154

CATALOGUE OF PLANETARY NEBULAE—TABLE 17

PK Name	Alternate Name	2000.0 R.A. (h m)	2000.0 Dec. (° ′)	1950.0 R.A. (h m)	1950.0 Dec. (° ′)	Con	Nebula Type	Nebula Diam. (″)	Nebula Mag. p	Nebula Mag. v	Star Spectra	Star Mag. V	Star Name	Notes
330−02.1	He 2-153	16 17.23	−53 32.1	16 13.32	−53 24.7	Nor		20						
327−05.1	KtRe 1	16 19.3	−57 58.	16 15.1	−57 51.	Nor		14				19.3		in field of NGC 6087
338+05.1	He 2-155	16 19.38	−42 15.6	16 15.91	−42 08.4	Nor		<25				16.26:		ESO 331-01, Sa 2-141
013+32.1	Sn 1	16 21.06	+00 02.9	16 18.5	−00 10.	Ser				12.8		14.69		
331−02.1	He 2-157	16 22.23	−53 40.8	16 18.30	−53 33.8	Nor		<5						ESO 179-03
346+12.1	Abell 38	16 23.29	−31 44.9	16 20.1	−31 38.	Nor	VI	92	>15.7			20.		ESO 452-01, K 1-3
327−06.1	He 2-158	16 23.51	−58 19.4	16 19.31	−58 12.4	Nor		<5						ESO 137-22, Sa 2-142
336+01.1	Pe 1-6	16 23.88	−46 42.3	16 20.25	−46 35.4	Nor	II	12		16.1				ESO 276-03, He 2-160
330−03.1	He 2-159	16 24.35	−54 36.0	16 20.36	−54 29.1	Nor		<25						ESO 179-04, Sa 2-143
331−02.2	He 2-161	16 24.63	−53 22.5	16 20.71	−53 15.6	Nor		<25						ESO 179-05, Sa 2-144
047+42.1	Abell 39	16 27.52	+27 54.4	16 25.5	+28 01.	Her	IIc	170	13.7	13.0		15.6		ARO 180
331−03.1	He 2-162	16 27.84	−54 01.5	16 23.88	−53 54.8	Nor		<5				13.43		ESO 179-06
327−07.1	He 2-163	16 29.51	−59 09.7	16 25.24	−59 03.1	Nor		<25						ESO 137-30, Sa 2-145
332−03.1	He 2-164	16 29.89	−53 23.1	16 25.95	−53 16.6	Nor		<25						ESO 179-07, Sa 2-146
331−03.2	He 2-165	16 30.00	−54 09.4	16 26.02	−54 02.9	Nor		35						ESO 179-08, Sa 2-147
337+01.1	Pe 1-7	16 30.43	−46 02.8	16 26.81	−45 56.3	Nor		<5				17.1:		ESO 276-04, He 2-166
334−01.1	MrWe 1-6	16 31.1	−50 27.	16 27.3	−50 21.	Nor	IV	20						
341+05.1	NGC 6153	16 31.51	−40 15.1	16 28.08	−40 08.7	Sco	IV	25	11.5	10.9		15.39		ARO 501, ESO 331-06, He 2-167, RCW 112
346+08.1	He 2-171	16 34.07	−35 05.4	16 30.78	−34 59.2	Sco		<10						ESO 390-07
335−01.1	He 2-169	16 34.22	−49 21.2	16 30.46	−49 15.0	Nor		<25		17.4				ESO 226-15, Sa 3-36
340+03.1	MrWe 2-5	16 34.8	−42 04.	16 31.3	−41 58.	Sco	IIb	20						Poss PN
332−04.1	He 2-170	16 35.34	−53 50.2	16 31.37	−53 44.0	Nor		<5						ESO 179-10, Sa 2-149
331−05.1	He 2-172	16 37.71	−55 42.4	16 33.63	−55 36.4	Ara		<5				12.67		ESO 179-11, PC 11, He 3-1223, StWr 2-43
336−01.1	VeRa 90	16 38.2	−49 44.	16 34.4	−49 39.	Ara	I					15.58		
345+06.1	He 2-175	16 39.46	−36 34.2	16 36.13	−36 28.3	Sco		<5		15.0				ESO 391-01, Sa 2-150
333−04.1	HtTr 3	16 39.6	−52 48.	16 35.7	−52 43.	Ara		42						
061+41.1	DdDm 1	16 40.27	+38 42.0	16 38.55	+38 47.8	Her						14.71		galactic halo object
352+11.1	ESO 452-12	16 41.72	−27 58.7	16 38.6	−27 53.	Sco								
336−02.1	VeRa 104	16 42.1	−49 44.	16 38.3	−49 39.	Ara						15.58		
344+04.1	He 2-178	16 42.56	−38 54.6	16 39.15	−38 48.9	Sco		<10		12.:				ESO 331-08, Sa 2-151, Vd 1-1, Wra 16-231
000+17.1	He 2-180	16 43.82	−18 56.5	16 40.9	−18 51.	Oph	I	5		13.9		15.26		ESO 586-01, PC 12

CATALOGUE OF PLANETARY NEBULAE—TABLE 18

PK Name	Alternate Name	2000.0 R.A. h	2000.0 R.A. m	2000.0 Dec. °	2000.0 Dec. ′	1950.0 R.A. h	1950.0 R.A. m	1950.0 Dec. °	1950.0 Dec. ′	Con	Nebula Type	Nebula Diam. ″	Nebula Mag. p	Nebula Mag. v	Star Spectra	Star Mag. V	Star Name	Notes
351+07.1	H 1-4	16	53.62	−31	40.6	16	50.40	−31	35.7	Sco	I							ESO 453-09, Sa 2-158
343+03.1	SuWt 3	16	44.3	−40	03.	16	40.9	−39	58.	Sco		20				20.::		
043+37.1	NGC 6210	16	44.50	+23	48.5	16	42.4	+23	54.	Her	II+IIIb	>14	9.3	8.8		13.7	HD 151121	ARO 5
352+11.2	K 2-16	16	44.82	−28	04.1	16	41.70	−27	58.6	Sco								ESO 453-02, Wra 17-76
335−03.1	HtTr 4	16	45.0	−51	12.	16	41.1	−51	07.	Ara		24						
339−00.1	VB 1	16	45.5	−46	08.	16	41.8	−46	03.	Ara								G339.2-0.4
345+04.1	Vd 1-2	16	46.75	−38	37.0	16	43.35	−38	31.6	Sco								ESO 332-01
094+38.1	El 1647+64	16	47.6	+64	12.	16	47.2	+64	18.	Dra		900						
335−03.2	MrWe 1-7	16	48.0	−50	42.	16	44.1	−50	37.	Ara	IV	6				21.::		
359+15.1	Abell 40	16	48.57	−21	01.2	16	45.6	−20	56.	Oph	IIb	29	16.8			19.6		ESO 586-03
335−04.1	MrWe 1-8	16	48.7	−51	09.	16	44.8	−51	04.	Ara		24				20.::		
348+06.1	IRAS 16455-3455	16	48.8	−35	01.	16	45.5	−34	56.	Sco		9		12.7		18.2		
347+05.1	H 1-2	16	48.90	−35	47.1	16	45.58	−35	41.9	Sco		<5						ESO 391-03, He 2-181
344+03.1	Vd 1-3	16	49.53	−39	20.2	16	46.1	−39	15.	Sco								ESO 332-02, Sa 3-37
351+09.1	PC 13	16	50.28	−30	19.9	16	47.10	−30	14.8	Sco				14.0				ESO 453-06, Sa 2-155
345+03.1	Vd 1-4	16	50.42	−39	08.3	16	47.00	−39	03.2	Sco								ESO 332-03, Sa 2-154
344+02.1	Vd 1-5	16	50.65	−40	03.1	16	47.2	−39	58.	Sco				14.8				ESO 332-04, Sa 2-156
342+00.1	H 1-3	16	53.50	−42	39.4	16	49.96	−42	34.5	Sco		16						ESO 277-17, Sa 3-38
345+03.2	Vd 1-6	16	54.46	−38	44.1	16	51.04	−38	39.3	Sco								ESO 332-07, Sa 2-159
325−12.1	He 2-182	16	54.58	−64	14.6	16	49.82	−64	09.7	TrA		<10				13.47		ESO 101-16, Sa 2-157
353+08.1	He 2-184	16	55.78	−29	50.3	16	52.61	−29	45.6	Oph	I	<5	12.8	12.8				ESO 453-10, MyCn 26
344+00.1	H 1-5	16	57.39	−41	37.9	16	53.88	−41	33.3	Sco	II	5						ESO 332-15, Sa 3-39
337−04.1	MrWe 1-9	16	57.5	−49	46.	16	53.7	−49	42.	Ara		15				22.::		
336−05.1	He 2-186	16	59.60	−51	42.1	16	55.68	−51	37.6	Ara		<25				16.62		ESO 227-01, Sa 2-161
349+04.1	M 2-4	17	01.10	−34	49.7	16	57.79	−34	45.3	Sco		<5		14.0		16.9:		ESO 391-07, He 2-188
321−16.1	He 2-185	17	01.28	−70	06.0	16	55.76	−70	01.6	TrA		<10				16.46:		ESO 070-01, Sa 2-162
343−00.1	HtTr 5	17	01.5	−43	06.	16	57.9	−43	02.	Sco		120						
000+12.1	IC 4634	17	01.56	−21	49.5	16	58.57	−21	45.2	Oph	IIa+III	>9	10.7	10.9		13.95	HD 153655	ARO 50, ESO 587-01, He 2-189, Sa 2-164
337−05.1	He 2-187	17	01.62	−50	23.0	16	57.76	−50	18.7	Ara		<10				12.78		ESO 227-02
351+05.1	M 2-5	17	02.31	−33	10.1	16	59.05	−33	05.8	Sco	II	5				16.0		ESO 391-08, He 2-190
334−07.1	He 3-1312	17	03.04	−53	55.8	16	59.00	−53	51.5	Ara								SaSt 2-12
351+04.1	M 1-19	17	03.78	−33	29.8	17	00.51	−33	25.6	Sco		<10		14.5				ESO 392-01, He 2-191

CATALOGUE OF PLANETARY NEBULAE—TABLE 19

PK Name	Alternate Name	2000.0 R.A. (h m)	2000.0 Dec. (° ′)	1950.0 R.A. (h m)	1950.0 Dec. (° ′)	Con	Nebula Type	Nebula Diam. (″)	Nebula Mag. p	Nebula Mag. v	Star Spectra	Star Mag. V	Star Name	Notes
353+06.2	M 2-6	17 04.31	−30 53.4	17 01.10	−30 49.3	Sco		<10		14.5				ESO 453-16, He 2-192
347+01.1	Vd 1-8	17 04.56	−37 53.2	17 01.16	−37 49.1	Sco								ESO 332-18, Sa 2-167
350+04.1	H 2-1	17 04.60	−33 59.3	17 01.31	−33 55.2	Sco	II	5		13.6		13.27		ESO 392-02, He 2-194
345+00.1	IC 4637	17 05.18	−40 53.2	17 01.68	−40 49.1	Sco	III	19	13.6	12.5		12.47	HD 154072	ESO 332-21, He 2-193
353+06.1	M 2-7	17 05.23	−30 32.3	17 02.03	−30 28.2	Sco	II	8				13.92		ESO 453-17, He 2-196
352+05.1	M 2-8	17 05.51	−32 32.1	17 02.26	−32 28.1	Sco		4		14.7				ESO 453-18, He 2-197
343−01.1	Vd 1-9	17 05.60	−43 56.1	17 02.0	−43 52.	Sco								ESO 278-01
010+18.2	M 2-9	17 05.63	−10 08.4	17 02.88	−10 04.4	Oph	?+VI	20		14.6		15.65		
358+09.1	Th 3-1	17 05.77	−25 24.0	17 02.7	−25 20.	Oph								ESO 518-11, Sa 2-172
336−06.1	He 2-195	17 06.24	−52 30.0	17 02.27	−52 26.0	Ara		<10				16.51		ESO 227-05, PC 14
342−02.1	Pe 1-8	17 06.37	−44 13.2	17 02.76	−44 09.2	Sco	IV	20		14.0				ESO 278-03, He 2-198
011+17.1	DeHt 1	17 06.9	−09 46.	17 04.2	−09 43.	Oph								
344−01.1	H 1-6	17 06.98	−42 41.2	17 03.42	−42 37.2	Sco	IV	12						ESO 278-04, He 2-199
342−02.2	Sa 3-41	17 07.50	−44 22.7	17 03.88	−44 18.8	Sco								Wra 16-251
336−07.1	K 2-17	17 09.60	−52 13.1	17 05.64	−52 09.3	Ara								ESO 227-06
352+04.1	Wra 16-255	17 10.22	−32 58.8	17 06.96	−32 55.1	Sco								
345−01.1	H 1-7	17 10.45	−41 52.8	17 06.92	−41 49.1	Sco	II	8		13.5				ESO 332-24, He 2-200
357+07.1	M 4-3	17 10.70	−27 08.8	17 07.58	−27 05.1	Oph		<10		13.5				ESO 519-07, He 2-202, Sa 2-175, Th 3-2
340−04.1	Sa 1-5	17 11.45	−47 24.9	17 07.71	−47 21.3	Ara								ESO 278-05, Sa 2-177
334−09.1	IC 4642	17 11.75	−55 23.9	17 07.62	−55 20.3	Ara	IV	21	13.4			15.66:	HD 154952	ESO 180-04, He 2-201, Sa 2-176, Sp 2
358+07.1	M 3-36	17 12.65	−25 43.6	17 09.56	−25 40.1	Oph	II	4		15.3				ESO 519-10, He 2-203
018+20.1	Na 1	17 12.86	−03 15.9	17 10.24	−03 12.4	Oph			13.4	13.4		16.25		Sa 2-179
349+01.1	NGC 6302	17 13.73	−37 06.2	17 10.35	−37 02.7	Sco	VI	50	12.8	9.6	OVI	16.0:	HD 155520	ARO 502, ESO 392-05, He 2-204, Gum 60
075+35.1	Sa 4-1	17 13.8	+49 15.	17 12.5	+49 19.	Her		13		13.:				
009+14.1	NGC 6309	17 14.06	−12 54.6	17 11.25	−12 51.2	Oph	IIIb+VI	>16	10.8	11.5	cont	13.	HD 155752	ARO 66, He 2-206
354+04.1	M 2-10	17 14.11	−31 19.7	17 10.89	−31 16.3	Sco	II	4						ESO 454-01, He 2-205
352+03.2	H 1-8	17 14.71	−33 24.8	17 11.43	−33 21.4	Sco	II	3						ARO 549, ESO 392-06
356+05.1	Th 3-3	17 17.27	−28 59.2	17 14.1	−28 56.	Oph								ESO 454-05, Sa 3-42
354+03.1	Th 3-4	17 18.87	−31 39.1	17 15.63	−31 36.0	Sco								ESO 454-07, Sa 3-44
359+06.1	M 3-37	17 19.22	−25 17.3	17 16.14	−25 14.2	Oph	IIa	10						ESO 519-12, He 2-209
355+03.3	Th 3-6	17 19.32	−31 11.1	17 16.1	−31 08.	Sco								ESO 454-09, Sa 3-45
342−04.1	He 2-207	17 19.53	−45 53.3	17 15.84	−45 50.2	Ara		35		12.:				ESO 278-08, Sa 2-183

CATALOGUE OF PLANETARY NEBULAE—TABLE 20

PK Name	Alternate Name	2000.0 R.A. (h m)	2000.0 Dec. (° ′)	1950.0 R.A. (h m)	1950.0 Dec. (° ′)	Con	Nebula Type	Nebula Diam. (″)	Nebula Mag. p	Nebula Mag. v	Star Spectra	Star Mag. V	Star Name	Notes
356+04.1	M 2-11	17 20.55	−29 00.7	17 17.38	−28 57.7	Oph		<10		14.:				ESO 454-11, He 2-210
338−08.1	NGC 6326	17 20.77	−51 45.2	17 16.82	−51 42.2	Ara	IIIb	14	12.2			15.53	HD 156531	ARO 519, ESO 228-01, He 2-208, Sa 2-185
356+04.2	M 3-38	17 21.07	−29 03.0	17 17.90	−29 00.1	Oph		<25		15.5				ARO 248, ESO 454-13, He 2-211, Sa 2-187
358+05.1	M 3-39	17 21.18	−27 11.5	17 18.06	−27 08.6	Oph	III+II	16		15.2				ESO 519-13, He 2-212
002+08.1	H 1-11	17 21.29	−22 18.5	17 18.28	−22 15.6	Oph	II	4						ESO 587-07, He 2-214
355+03.2	H 1-9	17 21.52	−30 20.8	17 18.32	−30 17.9	Sco		<10				15.8		ESO 454-14, He 2-213
349−01.1	NGC 6337	17 22.26	−38 29.1	17 18.83	−38 26.2	Sco	IV	48		12.3		14.90		ESO 333-05, He 2-215, Sa 2-191, H 1-10
358+05.2	M 3-40	17 22.42	−27 08.8	17 19.3	−27 06.	Oph		<10				17.2:		ESO 519-14, He 2-216
337−09.1	ESO 180-07	17 22.60	−52 46.6	17 18.60	−52 43.7	Ara		18						Wra 16-266
357+04.1	H 2-7	17 23.41	−28 59.1	17 20.24	−28 56.3	Oph	II	4				20.		ESO 454-16, Sa 2-192
359+05.1	M 2-12	17 24.03	−25 59.4	17 20.93	−25 56.7	Oph		<5				14.74		ESO 519-16, He 2-217
355+02.3	Th 3-11	17 24.44	−31 43.3	17 21.20	−31 40.6	Sco								ESO 454-18, Sa 3-47
357+03.1	M 3-7	17 24.57	−29 24.3	17 21.39	−29 21.6	Oph	II	5		15.7		16.5		ESO 454-19, He 2-218
355+02.2	Th 3-10	17 24.68	−30 52.0	17 21.46	−30 49.3	Sco								ESO 454-21, Sa 3-48
003+07.1	H 2-8	17 24.80	−21 33.7	17 21.8	−21 31.	Oph	II	4				>21.		ESO 588-02
358+04.1	M 3-8	17 24.87	−28 06.0	17 21.72	−28 03.3	Oph	II	5				16.7		ESO 454-22, He 2-219
352+00.2	Wra 16-269	17 24.92	−34 41.7	17 21.6	−34 39.	Sco								
356+03.1	Th 3-12	17 25.10	−29 45.2	17 21.91	−29 42.6	Oph								ESO 454-23, Sa 3-49
331−13.1	Sa 2-193	17 25.13	−59 32.3	17 20.70	−59 29.6	Ara								StWr 2-48
356+02.1	Th 3-13	17 25.31	−30 40.6	17 22.1	−30 38.	Sco								ESO 454-24
359+05.2	M 3-9	17 25.72	−26 11.9	17 22.62	−26 09.3	Oph	III	16		15.:		18.		ESO 519-17, He 2-221
359+04.1	Th 3-14	17 25.73	−26 57.8	17 22.61	−26 55.2	Oph						15.87		ESO 519-18, Sa 3-50
357+03.2	M 3-41	17 25.99	−29 21.9	17 22.81	−29 19.3	Oph		4						ESO 454-25, He 2-223
345−04.1	Cn 1-3	17 26.20	−44 11.4	17 22.57	−44 08.8	Sco		<5						ESO 278-09, He 2-220, PC 15, Sa 2-195
352+00.1	H 1-12	17 26.40	−35 01.8	17 23.07	−34 59.2	Sco	II	7						ESO 392-12, He 2-222
007+10.1	Mac 1-4	17 26.6	−16 48.	17 23.7	−16 46.	Oph	I							
358+04.3	SrWe 2	17 26.9	−27 36.	17 23.8	−27 38.	Oph	IV	72						VLA 4
358+04.2	Th 3-15	!7 26.94	−27 43.5	17 23.8	−27 41.	Oph								Al 2-A, ESO 454-26
357+03.4	M 3-42	17 27.00	−29 15.5	17 23.82	−29 13.0	Oph	II	6						Sa 3-52, Wra 17-80
358+03.1	M 3-10	17 27.34	−28 27.9	17 24.18	−28 25.4	Oph		3		13.6				ARO 250, ESO 454-27, He 2-225, Sa 2-198
357+03.5	Th 3-16	17 27.40	−29 21.2	!7 24.22	−29 18.7	Oph								ESO 454-28, Sa 3-53
358+03.2	H 2-10	17 27.55	−28 31.2	17 24.39	−28 28.7	Oph		<5						ESO 454-31, He 2-226

CATALOGUE OF PLANETARY NEBULAE—TABLE 21

PK Name	Alternate Name	2000.0 R.A. (h m)	2000.0 Dec. (° ′)	1950.0 R.A. (h m)	1950.0 Dec. (° ′)	Con	Nebula Type	Nebula Diam. (″)	Nebula Mag. p	Nebula Mag. v	Star Spectra	Star Mag. V	Star Name	Notes
358+03.9	Al 2-B	17 27.8	−28 11.	17 24.6	−28 09.	Oph								
342−06.1	Cn 1-4	17 27.81	−46 55.7	17 24.07	−46 53.2	Sco		<10						ESO 278-10, He 2-224, PC 16, Sa 2-197
001+05.1	H 1-14	17 28.06	−24 25.3	17 25.0	−24 22.9	Oph	II	7						ESO 519-19, Sa 2-200
352−00.1	H 1-13	17 28.46	−35 07.5	17 25.12	−35 05.1	Sco	IV	10						ESO 393-01, He 2-227
011+11.1	M 2-13	17 28.56	−13 26.3	17 25.74	−13 23.9	Ser		<10		14.7		18.8:		He 2-230, Sa 2-203
001+05.2	H 1-15	17 28.62	−24 51.1	17 25.55	−24 48.7	Oph	II	5						ESO 520-01, He 2-229
358+03.3	Th 3-19	17 28.66	−28 26.4	17 25.5	−28 24.	Oph								ESO 454-34
357+02.5	M 4-4	17 28.84	−30 07.8	17 25.64	−30 05.4	Sco	II	7				>21.		ESO 454-36, Sa 3-56
006+08.1	M 1-20	17 28.96	−19 15.9	17 26.01	−19 13.5	Oph	I	<10		13.:		17.1		ESO 588-03, He 2-235
009+10.1	Abell 41	17 29.03	−15 13.1	17 26 17	−15 10.7	Ser	III+II	12	17.2			15.95v	MT Ser	He 2-236, Sa 2-205
346−04.1	Sa 2-202	17 29.17	−42 32.4	17 25.6	−42 30.	Sco								
002+05.1	NGC 6369	17 29.34	−23 45.6	17 26.29	−23 43.3	Oph	IV+II	>30	12.9	11.4	WC	15.56	HD 158269	ARO 51, ESO 520-03, He 2-232, Sa 2-207
000+04.2	H 1-16	17 29.39	−26 26.1	17 26.28	−26 23.8	Oph		<5						ESO 520-02, He 2-231
000+04.1	H 2-11	17 29.43	−25 49.1	17 26.34	−25 46.8	Oph	I					>21.		ESO 520-04
357+02.8	Al 2-D	17 29.5	−29 47.	17 26.3	−29 45.	Oph								
358+03.7	H 1-17	17 29.67	−28 40.4	17 26.51	−28 38.1	Oph		<5		15.5				ESO 455-02, He 2-233
357+02.4	H 1-18	17 29.72	−29 32.8	17 26.53	−29 30.5	Oph	I	<25						ARO 252, ESO 455-03, He 2-234, Sa 2-210
358+03.4	H 1-19	17 30.04	−27 59.3	17 26.89	−27 57.0	Oph	I	<25						ESO 455-05, He 2-237
344−06.1	Sa 2-208	17 30.07	−45 22.8	17 26.39	−45 20.5	Sco								Wra 16-278
359+03.4	Al 2-E	17 30.2	−27 30.	17 27.1	−27 28.	Oph								
358+02.2	Th 3-23	17 30.38	−29 10.3	17 27.2	−29 08.	Oph								ESO 455-06
358+02.4	Al 2-F	17 30.5	−28 36.	17 27.3	−28 34.	Oph								
358+03.6	H 1-20	17 30.73	−28 04.1	17 27.58	−28 01.9	Oph	II	4						ESO 456-08, He 2-238
359+03.2	Th 3-25	17 30.78	−27 06.0	17 27.65	−27 03.8	Oph		<10						ESO 520-05, He 2-239
357+02.7	Th 3-24	17 30.81	−30 17.2	17 27.6	−30 15.	Sco								ESO 455-09
359+03.1	Th 3-28	17 30.92	−26 59.2	17 27.8	−26 57.	Oph								ESO 520-06
356+01.2	Sa 3-58	17 30.97	−31 01.1	17 27.75	−30 58.9	Sco								ESO 455-10
357+02.6	H 2-13	17 31.13	−30 10.5	17 27.93	−30 08.3	Sco	I							ESO 455-12, Sa 3-59
358+03.8	Th 3-26	17 31.15	−28 14.8	17 28.00	−28 12.6	Oph		<25						ESO 455-13, He 2-240
016+13.1	Abell 42	17 31.52	−08 19.2	17 28.8	−08 17.	Oph	IIb	58	17.8			19.8		
358+02.5	HtDe 8	17 31.9	−28 41.	17 28.7	−28 39.	Oph	III	37						M 3-57
350−02.1	H 1-22	17 32.37	−37 57.3	17 28.95	−37 55.2	Sco		<25						ESO 333-12, He 2-241

CATALOGUE OF PLANETARY NEBULAE—TABLE 22

PK Name	Alternate Name	2000.0 R.A.	2000.0 Dec.	1950.0 R.A.	1950.0 Dec.	Con	Nebula Type	Nebula Diam.	Nebula Mag. p	Nebula Mag. v	Star Spectra	Star Mag.	Star Name	Notes
		h m	° ′	h m	° ′			″	p	v		V		
359+02.5	Al 2-G	17 32.4	−28 14.	17 29.2	−28 12.	Oph	I							
357+01.1	H 1-23	17 32.78	−30 00.3	17 29.58	−29 58.2	Oph	II	3						ESO 455-16, He 2-242
348−04.1	H 1-21	17 32.79	−40 58.5	17 29.27	−40 56.4	Sco								ESO 333-13, Sa 2-213
349−03.1	H 2-14	17 32.87	−39 52.4	17 29.39	−39 50.3	Sco								ESO 333-11, Sa 3-62
351−01.1	Sa 2-215	17 33.01	−36 43.9	17 29.62	−36 41.8	Sco								ESO 393-06
357+01.2	Al 2-H	17 33.3	−30 26.	17 30.1	−30 24.	Sco								
004+06.2	H 1-24	17 33.62	−21 46.3	17 30.62	−21 44.3	Oph	II	9						ARO 253, ESO 588-05, He 2-244
359+02.6	Al 2-I	17 34.2	−27 55.	17 31.1	−27 54.	Oph								
350−02.2	Wra 16-287	17 34.33	−38 09.0	17 30.9	−38 07.	Sco								
336−11.1	MrWe 1-10	17 34.4	−54 29.	17 30.3	−54 27.	Ara	IV	60				19.::		
003+05.1	H 2-15	17 34.45	−22 53.3	17 31.42	−22 51.3	Oph	II	4						ESO 520-08, He 2-249
000+03.1	M 4-5	17 34.91	−26 36.0	17 31.80	−26 34.1	Oph	II	5						ESO 520-09, He 2-250
007+07.1	M 1-22	17 35.16	−18 34.4	17 32.23	−18 32.5	Oph	IV	9	13.3					ESO 588-08, He 2-252
358+01.1	M 4-6	17 35.24	−29 03.2	17 32.06	−29 01.3	Oph	I					>21.		ESO 455-20, Sa 3-65
359+02.4	Th 3-32	17 35.25	−28 06.9	17 32.1	−28 05.	Oph								ESO 455-21
005+06.1	M 3-11	17 35.35	−20 57.3	17 32.37	−20 55.4	Oph	II	10						ESO 588-09, He 2-254
000+02.1	Al 2-J	17 35.5	−27 23.	17 32.4	−27 22.	Oph								
349−04.1	Lo 16	17 35.67	−40 12.0	17 32.17	−40 10.1	Sco								
343−07.1	He 2-246	17 35.69	−46 59.8	17 31.94	−46 57.9	Ara		<5		14.1				ESO 279-01, PC 17
357+01.3	TrBr 4	17 35.7	−30 21.	17 32.5	−30 20.	Sco								TrJu 21
359+02.3	Th 3-33	17 35.80	−27 43.4	17 32.66	−27 41.5	Oph								ESO 455-24, Sa 3-67
002+04.1	Th 3-27	17 35.97	−24 25.5	17 32.91	−24 23.6	Oph								ARO 254, ESO 520-10
341−09.1	He 2-248	17 36.11	−49 25.7	17 32.26	−49 23.8	Ara		<5		15.5				ESO 228-06, Sa 2-218
359+02.7	Al 2-K	17 36.3	−28 00.	17 33.1	−27 59.	Oph								
005+05.1	M 3-12	17 36.38	−21 31.2	17 33.38	−21 29.4	Oph	II	6		15.3				ESO 588-10, He 2-255
350−03.1	H 1-26	17 36.50	−39 21.9	17 33.03	−39 20.1	Sco	IV	18		14.0				ESO 334-01, He 2-253
358+01.4	Bl B	17 36.99	−29 39.8	17 33.8	−29 38.	Oph								ESO 455-26
007+06.1	M 1-23	17 37.37	−18 46.8	17 34.43	−18 45.0	Oph	II	7		14.5				ESO 588-11, He 2-256
356−00.1	Th 3-34	17 37.76	−32 15.7	17 34.5	−32 14.	Sco								ESO 455-27
007+06.2	M 1-24	17 38.19	−19 37.7	17 35.23	−19 36.0	Oph	II	6		14.:		15.9		ESO 588-12, He 2-258
036+21.1	Y-C 2-44	17 38.4	+12 41.	17 36.1	+12 43.	Oph								
004+04.1	M 1-25	17 38.50	−22 08.6	17 35.49	−22 06.9	Oph	II	5		13.3		17.7:		ARO 255, ESO 588-13, He 2-259, Sa 2-224
359+01.1	Th 3-35	17 38.67	−28 42.7	17 35.5	−28 41.	Oph								ESO 455-28
008+06.1	He 2-260	17 38.95	−18 17.6	17 36.02	−18 16.0	Oph		<10		11.:		14.25		ESO 588-14, SaSt 2-15

CATALOGUE OF PLANETARY NEBULAE—TABLE 23

PK Name	Alternate Name	2000.0 R.A. (h m)	2000.0 Dec. (° ′)	1950.0 R.A. (h m)	1950.0 Dec. (° ′)	Con	Nebula Type	Nebula Diam. (″)	Nebula Mag. p	Nebula Mag. v	Star Spectra	Star Mag. V	Star Name	Notes
359+01.3	19 W 32	17 39.1	−28 56.	17 35.9	−28 55.	Oph								PM 1-166
346−06.1	Fg 2	17 39.33	−44 09.6	17 35.69	−44 08.0	Sco		<5						ESO 279-04, He 2-257
005+05.2	H 2-16	17 39.91	−21 14.1	17 36.92	−21 12.5	Oph	III	15						ARO 256, ESO 588-15, He 2-261, Sa 2-226
003+03.1	H 2-17	17 40.12	−24 25.7	17 37.06	−24 24.1	Oph	II	<25				>21.		ARO 257, ESO 520-14, He 2-263, Wra 17-93
001+02.1	He 2-262	17 40.21	−26 44.4	17 37.09	−26 42.8	Oph		<10						ESO 520-15, Sa 3-68
005+04.1	H 1-27	17 40.30	−22 19.2	17 37.28	−22 17.7	Oph	II	5		15.5				ARO 258, ESO 588-16, He 2-265, Sa 2-227
001+01.1	K 1-4	17 40.47	−27 01.1	17 37.34	−26 59.6	Oph	III	40				19.7		ESO 520-16, He 2-264
354−02.1	Wra 16-295	17 40.62	−34 30.5	17 37.3	−34 29.	Sco								
358+00.1	Wra 17-96	17 41.58	−30 06.7	17 38.38	−30 05.2	Sco								
005+04.2	M 3-13	17 41.61	−22 13.0	17 38.60	−22 11.6	Oph		<7						ESO 588-17
004+03.1	Pt 1	17 41.65	−23 34.4	17 38.6	−23 33.	Oph				16.::				3′ E & 0.′5 N of NGC 6401; member?
027+16.1	DeHt 2	17 41.7	+03 06.	17 39.2	+03 08.	Oph		94				14.2		
003+02.1	Hb 4	17 41.88	−24 42.1	17 38.81	−24 40.7	Oph	IIIb	6		13.0		17.0:		ARO 94, ESO 520-17, He 2-266, Sa 2-228
003+03.2	M 2-14	17 41.95	−24 11.2	17 38.89	−24 09.8	Oph		<25						ESO 520-18, He 2-267
010+07.1	Sa 2-230	17 42.05	−15 56.2	17 39.17	−15 54.8	Ser								
045+24.1	K 1-14	17 42.53	+21 26.7	17 40.4	+21 28.	Her	IV	48		15.1				ARO 48
350−05.1	H 1-28	17 42.90	−39 36.4	17 39.42	−39 35.0	Sco	II	8						ESO 334-05, He 2-268
036+20.1	Y-C 2-45	17 43.0	+12 20.	17 40.7	+12 22.	Oph								
006+04.1	H 2-18	17 43.48	−21 09.9	17 40.49	−21 08.6	Sgr	II	4		15.0				ESO 589-01, Sa 2-232
357−01.1	Wra 16-298	17 44.16	−32 01.3	17 40.9	−32 00.	Sco								
355−02.2	H 1-29	17 44.23	−34 17.6	17 40.91	−34 16.3	Sco		<10		14.3				ESO 393-16, He 2-270
355−02.1	M 3-14	17 44.34	−34 06.7	17 41.03	−34 05.4	Sco	IIa	8		15.0				ARO 552, ESO 393-19, He 2-271, Sa 2-234
011+07.1	Sa 2-237	17 44.69	−15 45.2	17 41.82	−15 44.0	Ser								
051+25.1	K 1-15	17 44.99	+27 18.8	17 43.0	+27 20.	Her		43				16.5:		ARO 98
352−04.1	H 1-30	17 45.11	−38 08.8	17 41.68	−38 07.6	Sco	II	5						ESO 334-06, He 2-272
346−08.1	IC 4663	17 45.48	−44 54.3	17 41.81	−44 53.1	Sco	IV	13	13.1	12.5				ESO 279-06, He 2-273
006+04.2	M 3-15	17 45.52	−20 58.2	17 42.53	−20 57.0	Sgr	II	4		14.5				ESO 589-02, He 2-279
355−02.4	H 1-31	17 45.54	−34 33.9	17 42.21	−34 32.7	Sco		<5						ESO 393-21, He 2-276
345−08.1	Tc 1	17 45.59	−46 05.2	17 41.88	−46 04.0	Ara	IV	10				11.38	HD 161044	ESO 279-07, He 2-274

CATALOGUE OF PLANETARY NEBULAE—TABLE 24

PK Name	Alternate Name	2000.0 R.A. (h m)	2000.0 Dec. (° ′)	1950.0 R.A. (h m)	1950.0 Dec. (° ′)	Con	Nebula Type	Nebula Diam. (″)	Nebula Mag. p	Nebula Mag. v	Star Spectra	Star Mag. V	Star Name	Notes
005+03.1	Pe 1-9	17 45.61	−23 02.5	17 42.58	−23 01.3	Sgr	II	12				>21.		ESO 520-22, Sa 3-71
002+01.1	H 2-20	17 45.66	−25 40.0	17 42.57	−25 38.8	Sgr	II	4						ESO 520-23
358−00.2	M 1-26	17 45.96	−30 12.0	17 42.75	−30 10.9	Sco	II	4		13.8		12.61	HD 316248	ESO 455-33, He 2-277, Bl C, RCW 135
358−01.1	Al 2-L	17 46.03	−31 04.1	17 42.8	−31 03.	Sco		13						ESO 455-34
355−02.3	H 1-32	17 46.10	−34 03.7	17 42.79	−34 02.6	Sco		<5		14.3				ESO 393-23, He 2-278
002+01.2		17 46.11	−26 11.1	17 43.	−26 10.	Sgr								identity?
008+05.1	Th 4-2	17 46.24	−18 40.1	17 43.3	−18 39.	Sgr								ESO 589-03, He 2-281
007+04.1	Th 4-1	17 46.27	−20 13.1	17 43.3	−20 12.	Sgr		<10						ESO 589-04, He 2-282
356−02.2	M 1-27	17 46.76	−33 08.6	17 43.47	−33 07.5	Sco		5				14.35		ESO 393-24, He 2-280
011+06.1	M 2-15	17 46.91	−16 17.5	17 44.02	−16 16.4	Sgr	II	5		14.6		18.2::		He 2-284, Sa 2-242
006+03.1	H 2-22	17 47.57	−21 47.4	17 44.56	−21 46.4	Sgr	II	6						ESO 589-05, Sa 3-75
006+03.2	M 1-28	17 47.63	−22 06.3	17 44.62	−22 05.3	Sgr	III+VI	18		17.:		20.8		ESO 589-06, He 2-285
357−02.1	Al 2-M	17 47.8	−32 21.	17 44.5	−32 20.	Sco								
355−03.1	H 1-33	17 47.82	−34 08.0	17 44.51	−34 07.0	Sco		<10		15.5				ESO 393-26, He 2-283
359−00.1	Hb 5	17 47.93	−29 59.7	17 44.73	−29 58.7	Sgr	II+VI	>13	13.6	11.8	cont		HD 316340	ARO 389, ESO 455-42, Bl E, He 2-286
005+02.1	H 1-34	17 48.13	−22 46.8	17 45.10	−22 45.8	Sgr								ESO 520-28
011+05.1	NGC 6439	17 48.33	−16 28.8	17 45.44	−16 27.8	Sgr	IIa	5	13.8	12.6		16.10:		ARO 95, He 2-287
004+01.1	H 2-24	17 48.60	−24 16.5	17 45.54	−24 15.6	Sgr		5						ESO 520-29, Sa 3-77
006+02.1	Th 4-3	17 48.62	−22 16.8	17 45.60	−22 15.9	Sgr								ARO 259, ESO 589-07
355−03.2	H 2-23	17 48.96	−34 21.9	17 45.64	−34 21.0	Sco				15.5				ESO 393-27, He 3-1489
004+02.1	H 2-25	17 49.01	−23 42.9	17 45.96	−23 42.0	Sgr		4						ESO 520-30
355−03.3	H 1-35	17 49.23	−34 22.9	17 45.91	−34 22.0	Sco		<5		13.1		15.3:		ESO 393-29, He 2-288
008+03.1	NGC 6445	17 49.25	−20 00.6	17 46.28	−19 59.7	Sgr	IIIb+III	>34	13.2	11.2	cont	19.		ARO 67, ESO 589-09, He 2-290, Sa 2-248
356−03.4	Ste 2-4	17 49.80	−33 32.1	17 46.50	−33 31.2	Sco								ESO 393-33
353−04.1	H 1-36	17 49.80	−37 01.5	17 46.40	−37 00.6	Sco		<10		12.1				ESO 393-31, He 2-289
356−03.1	H 2-26	17 49.84	−34 00.7	17 46.53	−33 59.8	Sco	II	5						ESO 393-32, Sa 3-79
359−01.1	M 1-29	17 50.30	−30 34.9	17 47.08	−30 34.1	Sco		7		14.7				ESO 455-47, He 2-292, Bl F, Sa 2-250
000−01.1	M 3-43	17 50.39	−29 24.8	17 47.2	−29 24.	Sgr	II	4				>21.		ESO 455-48, Bl G
008+03.2	Th 4-4	17 50.46	−19 52.8	17 47.5	−19 52.	Sgr						13.4-15		ARO 260, ESO 589-10
009+04.1	Th 4-5	17 50.48	−19 03.1	17 47.53	−19 02.3	Sgr		<10		14.7				ESO 589-11, He 2-293
351−06.1	H 1-37	17 50.74	−39 17.5	17 47.27	−39 16.7	Sco	II	9		15.:				ESO 334-09, He 2-291

CATALOGUE OF PLANETARY NEBULAE—TABLE 25

PK Name	Alternate Name	2000.0 R.A. (h m)	2000.0 Dec. (° ′)	1950.0 R.A. (h m)	1950.0 Dec. (° ′)	Con	Nebula Type	Nebula Diam. (″)	Nebula Mag. p	Nebula Mag. v	Star Spectra	Star Mag. V	Star Name	Notes
353−05.1	H 1-38	17 50.75	−37 23.9	17 47.34	−37 23.1	Sco	II	7						ESO 393-35, Sa 3-81
009+04.2	Th 4-6	17 50.96	−18 46.8	17 48.02	−18 46.0	Sgr								ARO 262, ESO 589-12
355−04.1	Pe 1-0	17 51.21	−34 55.4	17 47.87	−34 54.6	Sco	III	10		14.0				ESO 393-37, Hf 2-1
359−01.2	M 3-44	17 51.31	−30 23.9	17 48.10	−30 23.2	Sco	II	4		16.:				ESO 455-51, Sa 3-82
358−02.1	M 4-7	17 51.75	−31 35.7	17 48.5	−31 35.	Sco	II	5						Al2-P, ESO 455-54
358−02.4	Al 2-O	17 51.8	−32 02.	17 48.5	−32 02.	Sco								
356−03.2	H 2-27	17 51.85	−33 47.6	17 48.54	−33 46.9	Sco								ESO 394-02, Sa 3-83
332−16.1	HtTr 6	17 51.9	−60 23.	17 47.4	−60 23.	Pav		36						
010+04.1	M 2-17	17 52.08	−17 36.2	17 49.17	−17 35.5	Sgr	II	6		14.5				ESO 589-14, He 2-298
359−01.3	M 3-45	17 52.10	−30 05.3	17 48.89	−30 04.6	Sco	II	6		16.:				ESO 455-53, Sa 3-84
006+02.3	Th 4-7	17 52.38	−21 51.3	17 49.37	−21 50.6	Sgr								ARO 263, ESO 589-15
000−01.4	Bl 3-14	17 52.40	−29 45.7	17 49.2	−29 45.	Sgr								ESO 455-55
000−01.2	Bl 3-15	17 52.58	−29 06.7	17 49.4	−29 06.	Sgr								ESO 422-58
357−03.2	M 2-16	17 52.58	−32 45.9	17 49.30	−32 45.2	Sco	II	5		14.3				ESO 394-04, He 2-297
006+02.5	M 1-31	17 52.69	−22 21.9	17 49.67	−22 21.3	Sgr	I	<25		14.5		18.2::		ESO 589-16, He 2-299, Sa 2-260, Ve 59
345−10.1	MrWe 1-11	17 52.7	−46 41.	17 49.0	−46 41.	Ara	IV	54				18.::		
359−02.2	M 3-16	17 52.77	−30 49.6	17 49.54	−30 49.0	Sco	II	7		15.5				ESO 456-02, He 2-296
355−04.2	M 1-30	17 52.98	−34 38.4	17 49.65	−34 37.8	Sco		<5		14.7		16.3		ESO 394-05, He 2-295
357−03.3	H 2-29	17 53.28	−32 40.7	17 50.00	−32 40.1	Sco	II	7				>21.		ESO 394-06, Sa 3-87
356−03.3	H 1-39	17 53.35	−33 56.0	17 50.04	−33 55.4	Sco		<5						ESO 394-07, He 2-300
000−01.7	Al 2-Q	17 53.4	−29 16.	17 50.2	−29 16.	Sgr								
036+17.1	Abell 43	17 53.55	+10 37.4	17 51.2	+10 38.	Oph	IIc	156	14.7	14.6	O7f	14.7		ARO 181
358−02.5	Al 2-R	17 53.6	−31 25.	17 50.4	−31 25.	Sco								
006+02.4	Pe 2-10	17 53.61	−21 58.6	17 50.6	−21 58.	Sgr	II	4						ESO 589-19
013+05.2	MaC 1-9	17 55.8	−14 06.	17 53.0	−14 06.	Ser	I							
357−03.4	M 2-18	17 53.63	−32 58.8	17 50.35	−32 58.2	Sco		<5		15.0				ESO 394-08, He 2-301
000−01.5	M 2-19	17 53.76	−29 43.8	17 50.56	−29 43.2	Sgr	II	6		15.5				ESO 456-07, He 2-302
001−01.1	Sa 3-89	17 53.78	−28 27.3	17 50.62	−28 26.7	Sgr		4						ESO 456-10, Bl M
000−01.3	Sa 3-90	17 53.82	−28 59.3	17 50.64	−28 58.7	Sgr								ESO 456-11, Bl O
332−16.2	HtTr 7	17 54.2	−60 49.	17 49.6	−60 49.	Pav		190						
053+24.1	Vy 1-2	17 54.37	+27 59.5	17 52.4	+28 00.	Her	II	5		12.1				
014+06.1	K 2-5	17 54.41	−12 48.5	17 51.6	−12 48.	Ser	III	25				21.71		ARO 265
000−01.6	M 2-20	17 54.41	−29 36.2	17 51.22	−29 35.7	Sgr	I	<25		15.1				ESO 456-12, He 2-304

CATALOGUE OF PLANETARY NEBULAE—TABLE 26

PK Name	Alternate Name	2000.0 R.A. (h m)	2000.0 Dec. (° ′)	1950.0 R.A. (h m)	1950.0 Dec. (° ′)	Con	Nebula Type	Nebula Diam. (″)	Nebula Mag. p	Nebula Mag. v	Star Spectra	Star Mag. V	Star Name	Notes
356−04.1	Cn 2-1	17 54.55	−34 22.3	17 51.23	−34 21.8	Sco		<5	13.9	12.2				ESO 394-10, He 2-303
001−01.2	Sa 3-91	17 54.58	−28 12.7	17 51.42	−28 12.2	Sgr								ESO 456-14, Bl Q
004+00.1	IRAS 17516-2525	17 54.7	−25 26.	17 51.6	−25 26.	Sgr	I					22.::		
001−01.4	Sa 3-92	17 54.86	−28 48.9	17 51.69	−28 48.4	Sgr								
359−02.4	M 3-46	17 55.10	−31 12.4	17 51.86	−31 11.9	Sco	III	4						ESO 456-15, Sa 3-93
007+01.1	Hb 6	17 55.12	−21 44.7	17 52.11	−21 44.2	Sgr	II	6		12.0		14.72v	AS Sgr	ARO 96, ESO 589-20, He 2-305, Ve 60
000−02.2	Bl 3-10	17 55.33	−29 57.7	17 52.13	−29 57.2	Sgr								ESO 456-16, Sa 2-265
359−02.3	H 1-40	17 55.60	−30 33.5	17 52.38	−30 33.1	Sco								ARO 29, ESO 456-17, Bl 3-8, Sa 2-266
013+05.1	Sa 3-96	17 55.78	−15 02.6	17 52.92	−15 02.2	Ser								
006+01.1	HtTr 8	17 55.9	−22 59.	17 52.9	−22 59.	Sgr		12						
009+02.1	Th 4-9	17 55.95	−19 28.4	17 53.0	−19 28.	Sgr								ARO 266, ESO 589-21
001−01.3	H 2-31	17 56.04	−28 14.2	17 52.88	−28 13.8	Sgr	I							ESO 456-19, Sa 3-95
000−02.1	Bl 3-13	17 56.04	−29 11.3	17 52.86	−29 10.9	Sgr								ESO 456-18, Sa 3-94
011+04.1	M 1-32	17 56.33	−16 29.8	17 53.44	−16 29.4	Sgr	II	7						He 2-309, Sa 2-268
000−02.3	H 2-32	17 56.40	−29 38.1	17 53.21	−29 37.7	Sgr								Bl 3-12, ESO 456-20, Sa 3-98
359−03.1	M 3-17	17 56.43	−31 04.4	17 53.20	−31 04.0	Sco		<5						ESO 456-21, He 2-307
348−09.1	He 2-306	17 56.56	−43 03.3	17 52.96	−43 02.9	Sco		<5		14.0		16.0		ESO 279-12, Sa 2-267
010+03.1	Th 4-10	17 57.11	−18 06.7	17 54.18	−18 06.4	Sgr		<25						ESO 589-23, He 2-311
356−04.2	H 1-41	17 57.32	−34 09.8	17 54.00	−34 09.5	Sco	II	10				16.1		ESO 394-13, He 2-308
357−04.1	H 1-42	17 57.42	−33 35.7	17 54.12	−33 35.4	Sco		6	14.3	13.3		17.2:		ESO 394-14, He 2-310
000−02.5	M 3-47	17 57.81	−30 02.3	17 54.6	−30 02.	Sco								ESO 456-22, Sa 3-100
000−02.4	M 2-21	17 58.16	−29 44.4	17 54.96	−29 44.1	Sgr		<10		13.6		14.64		ESO 456-24, He 2-315
358−03.1	H 1-44	17 58.18	−31 43.0	17 54.93	−31 42.7	Sgr	II	4						ESO 456-23, He 2-314, RCW 136, Sa 3-101
359−03.2	H 2-33	17 58.20	−31 08.1	17 54.97	−31 07.9	Sgr	II	6				>21.		ESO 456-25, Sa 3-102
357−04.3	H 1-43	17 58.24	−33 47.6	17 54.93	−33 47.4	Sco	I	<25				15.53		ESO 394-15, He 2-313
000−02.6	M 3-19	17 58.31	−30 00.6	17 55.11	−30 00.4	Sgr	II	5				16.9:		ESO 456-26, Sa 3-103
002−02.1	H 1-45	17 58.36	−28 14.8	17 55.20	−28 14.6	Sgr	I							ESO 456-27, He 2-317
357−04.4	Wra 17-104	17 58.40	−33 04.3	17 55.11	−33 04.1	Sgr								
001−02.2	Sa 3-104	17 58.43	−29 20.8	17 55.24	−29 20.6	Sgr								
002−01.1	Pe 2-11	17 58.51	−27 37.1	17 55.37	−27 36.9	Sgr	II	5				>21.		ESO 456-30, Sa 3-106
357−04.2	M 2-22	17 58.55	−33 28.6	17 55.25	−33 28.4	Sgr	II	5				16.4:		ESO 394-16, He 2-316
096+29.1	NGC 6543	17 58.58	+66 37.9	17 58.6	+66 38.	Dra	IIIa+II	>18	8.8	8.1	O7+WR	10.9	HD 164963	ARO 6

CATALOGUE OF PLANETARY NEBULAE—TABLE 27

PK Name	Alternate Name	2000.0 R.A. (h m)	2000.0 Dec. (° ′)	1950.0 R.A. (h m)	1950.0 Dec. (° ′)	Con	Nebula Type	Nebula Diam. (″)	Nebula Mag. p	Nebula Mag. v	Star Spectra	Star Mag. V	Star Name	Notes
013+04.1	M 1-33	17 58.98	−15 32.3	17 56.11	−15 32.1	Ser	II	5		13.3				He 2-321, Sa 2-275
358−04.1	H 1-46	17 59.04	−32 21.8	17 55.77	−32 21.6	Sgr		<10		14.2				ESO 456-31, He 2-318
000−03.2	KFL 1	17 59.2	−30 03.	17 56.0	−30 03.	Sgr	II	5				19.2		
002−02.2	M 3-20	17 59.32	−28 13.9	17 56.16	−28 13.7	Sgr		<10		14.3				ESO 456-32, He 2-319
345−11.1	ESO 279-14	17 59.61	−46 38.9	17 55.87	−46 38.7	Ara		24						
358−04.2	Sa 3-107	17 59.91	−32 59.2	17 56.63	−32 59.1	Sgr								Wra 16-344
359−04.1	M 3-48	17 59.94	−31 54.4	17 56.69	−31 54.3	Sgr		6				>21.		ESO 456-43, Sa 3-108
011+02.1	Th 4-11	18 00.15	−17 40.8	17 57.23	−17 40.7	Sgr		<5						ARO 267, ESO 589-25, He 2-322
352−07.1	Fg 3	18 00.20	−38 49.8	17 56.74	−38 49.7	CrA	I	<25	11.4			14.3		ARO 520, ESO 334-10, He 2-320, Sa 2-277
356−05.1	H 2-35	18 00.31	−34 27.7	17 56.98	−34 27.6	Sgr		10						ESO 394-17, Sa 3-109
001−03.1	H 1-47	18 00.63	−29 21.8	17 57.44	−29 21.7	Sgr		<5						ESO 456-35, He 2-323
340−14.1	Sa 1-6	18 00.98	−52 44.3	17 56.96	−52 44.2	Ara								ESO 182-02, Sa 2-278
002−02.5	KFL 2	18 01.0	−28 16.	17 57.8	−28 16.	Sgr		4						
014+04.1	Sa 3-111	18 01.12	−14 30.3	17 58.27	−14 30.3	Ser								
002−02.3	Pe 2-12	18 01.16	−27 38.4	17 58.02	−27 38.4	Sgr	III	5						ESO 456-36, Sa 3-110
357−05.1	M 1-34	18 01.37	−33 17.7	17 58.08	−33 17.7	Sgr	II	12		13.3				ESO 394-18, He 2-324
002−02.4	M 2-23	18 01.70	−28 25.7	17 58.54	−28 25.7	Sgr		<10		12.4		16.7:		ESO 456-34, He 2-326
358−05.1	Pe 1-11	18 01.71	−33 15.4	17 58.42	−33 15.4	Sgr	II	9						ESO 394-19, Sa 2-280
356−05.2	M 2-24	18 02.05	−34 27.7	17 58.72	−34 27.7	Sgr	II	8		14.6				ESO 394-20, He 2-327
000−03.1	M 3-22	18 02.31	−30 14.4	17 59.10	−30 14.5	Sgr	IIc	6		15.1		17.8:		ESO 456-39, He 1-48
001−03.3	ShWi 1	18 02.5	−29 24.	17 59.3	−29 25.	Sgr		13						
356−06.1	M 3-49	18 02.53	−35 13.1	17 59.18	−35 13.2	Sgr	IV	10						ESO 394-22, He 2-329
355−06.1	M 3-21	18 02.54	−36 39.1	17 59.15	−36 39.2	Sgr		<5		12.7		15.34		ESO 394-21, He 2-328
359−04.3	M 2-25	18 02.77	−32 09.5	17 59.51	−32 09.6	Sgr	III	13		14.5				ESO 456-40, He 2-330
003−02.4	KFL 4	18 02.8	−27 40.	17 59.7	−27 41.	Sgr	I					21.8		
359−04.5	KFL 3	18 02.8	−31 23.	17 59.6	−31 24.	Sgr	II	10				18.7		
001−03.4	ShWi 2	18 03.0	−29 45.	17 59.8	−29 46.	Sgr	I							
003−02.2	M 2-26	18 03.20	−26 58.5	18 00.07	−26 58.6	Sgr	IIa	9		14.3				ESO 521-14, He 2-332
003−02.3	IC 4673	18 03.30	−27 06.4	18 00.17	−27 06.5	Sgr	IV	15		13.0		17.58		ESO 521-15, He 2-333, M 1-36, Sa 2-286
001−03.6	ShWi 4	18 03.6	−29 45.	18 00.4	−29 46.	Sgr	I							
003−02.1	M 1-35	18 03.65	−26 43.5	18 00.53	−26 43.7	Sgr	II	5		14.6				ESO 521-17, He 2-336
356−06.3		18 03.74	−34 53.0	18 00.40	−34 53.2	Sgr								identity?

CATALOGUE OF PLANETARY NEBULAE—TABLE 28

PK Name	Alternate Name	2000.0 R.A. (h m)	2000.0 Dec. (° ′)	1950.0 R.A. (h m)	1950.0 Dec. (° ′)	Con	Nebula Type	Nebula Diam. (″)	Nebula Mag. p	Nebula Mag. v	Star Spectra	Star Mag. V	Star Name	Notes
359−04.2	M 2-27	18 03.88	−31 17.7	18 00.64	−31 17.9	Sgr		<5		14.2				ESO 456-44, He 2-335
358−05.3	H 1-50	18 03.89	−32 41.6	18 00.61	−32 41.8	Sgr		<10	14.5	13.5		16.2:		ESO 394-24, He 2-334
001−03.0	KFL 5	18 03.9	−29 50.	18 00.7	−29 51.	Sgr	I	2				21.7		
001−03.7	ShWi 5	18 03.9	−29 51.	18 00.7	−29 52.	Sgr	I					16.55		
001−03.8	ShWi 6	18 04.0	−29 26.	18 00.8	−29 27.	Sgr	I							
002−03.7	Sa 3-115	18 04.08	−28 27.9	18 00.91	−28 28.1	Sgr								Wra 17-107
357−06.1	M 3-50	18 04.09	−34 28.6	18 00.76	−34 28.8	Sgr	II	5						ESO 394-25, Sa 2-290
359−04.4	H 2-36	18 04.13	−31 39.2	18 00.88	−31 39.4	Sgr								ESO 456-45, Sa 3-114
002−03.2	H 2-37	18 04.47	−28 37.7	18 01.30	−28 37.9	Sgr	II	5						ARO 268, ESO 456-46
356−06.2	H 1-51	18 04.49	−34 58.0	18 01.15	−34 58.2	Sgr	IV	13						ESO 394-26, Sa 3-116
000−04.3	Sa 3-117	18 04.73	−31 02.8	18 01.50	−31 03.0	Sgr								Wra 16-363
358−05.4	M 3-51	18 04.94	−32 54.0	18 01.66	−32 54.2	Sgr	II	10						ESO 394-27, He 2-337
354−07.1	H 1-52	18 04.94	−37 37.9	18 01.52	−37 38.1	CrA	II	11						ESO 335-01, Sa 2-292
000−04.1	M 2-28	18 05.04	−30 58.4	18 01.81	−30 58.6	Sgr	II	5						ESO 456-49, He 2-338
001−03.9	ShWi 7	18 05.1	−29 19.	18 01.9	−29 20.	Sgr		13						
010+00.1	NGC 6537	18 05.21	−19 50.5	18 02.25	−19 50.8	Sgr	IIa+VI	>9	12.5	11.6			HD 312582	ARO 52, ESO 590-01, He 2-340, Sa 2-294
002−03.3	M 1-37	18 05.43	−28 22.1	18 02.27	−28 22.4	Sgr	I	<25				14.98		ESO 456-50, He 2-339
004−02.1	H 1-53	18 05.96	−26 29.7	18 02.84	−26 30.0	Sgr	I	<25		15.3				ARO 269, ESO 521-24, He 2-342
002−03.5	M 1-38	18 06.09	−28 40.6	18 02.92	−28 40.9	Sgr		<5				14.42		ESO 456-52, He 2-344
028+10.1	WeSb 3	18 06.1	+00 22.	18 03.5	+00 22.	Oph		37						
004−03.1	M 2-29	18 06.68	−26 54.9	18 03.55	−26 55.3	Sgr	II	5						ESO 521-27, He 2-345
003−03.2	KFL 7	18 06.8	−27 06.	18 03.7	−27 07.	Sgr	I	2						
019+05.1	CTS 1	18 07.0	−08 56.	18 04.3	−08 56.	Ser	II	4						IRAS 18042-0855
000−04.2	M 3-23	18 07.10	−30 34.3	18 03.88	−30 34.7	Sgr	II	10		14.3				ESO 456-54, He 2-348
002−04.1	H 1-54	18 07.11	−29 13.1	18 03.93	−29 13.5	Sgr		<10		14.0		15.4		ESO 456-55, He 2-346
342−14.1	Sp 3	18 07.27	−51 01.5	18 03.33	−51 01.9	Ara		35	11.9					ESO 229-06, He 2-341
359−05.1	KFL 9	18 07.4	−31 42.	18 04.1	−31 43.	Sgr	II	11						
015+03.1	M 1-39	18 07.51	−13 28.9	18 04.68	−13 29.3	Ser		<10		15.8				He 2-351
001−04.1	H 1-55	18 07.65	−29 41.4	18 04.45	−29 41.8	Sgr		<5				16.57		ESO 456-56, He 2-347
005−02.1	M 3-24	18 07.89	−25 24.0	18 04.80	−25 24.5	Sgr	II	10						ESO 521-30, He 2-350
001−04.2	H 1-56	18 07.90	−29 44.5	18 04.7	−29 45.	Sgr	II	3		14.5				ESO 456-57, Sa 2-299
004−03.2	KFL 10	18 08.0	−26 53.	18 04.9	−26 54.	Sgr	II	5				19.8		

CATALOGUE OF PLANETARY NEBULAE—TABLE 29

PK Name	Alternate Name	2000.0 R.A.	2000.0 Dec.	1950.0 R.A.	1950.0 Dec.	Con	Nebula Type	Nebula Diam.	Nebula Mag. p	Nebula Mag. v	Star Spectra	Star Mag. V	Star Name	Notes
		h m	° ′	h m	° ′			″						
002−03.6	H 2-39	18 08.06	−28 23.5	18 04.9	−28 24.	Sgr								ESO 456-58, Sa 2-301
008−01.1	M 1-40	18 08.43	−22 16.8	18 05.41	−22 17.3	Sgr	II	5		14.8				ESO 590-02, He 2-352
000−05.1	H 2-40	18 08.43	−31 37.4	18 05.18	−31 37.9	Sgr	II	13				>21.		ESO 456-59, Sa 3-120
351−10.2	HtTr 9	18 09.0	−41 48.	18 05.4	−41 49.	CrA		160						
005−02.2	MaC 1-10	18 09.2	−25 04.	18 06.1	−25 05.	Sgr		10						PM 1-213
359−06.2	IRAS 18059-3211	18 09.2	−32 10.	18 05.9	−32 11.	Sgr		4		14.:				
005−03.1	H 1-58	18 09.23	−26 02.4	18 06.12	−26 03.0	Sgr	I					17.4:		ESO 521-34, Sa 2-303
341−15.1	ESO 182-04	18 09.50	−52 33.9	18 05.48	−52 34.4	Tel		72						
356−07.2	H 1-57	18 09.82	−35 43.9	18 06.46	−35 44.5	Sgr	II	12						ESO 394-31, He 2-353
004−03.3	KFL 11	18 10.2	−27 16.	18 07.1	−27 17.	Sgr	II	4				20.4		
018+04.1	M 3-52	18 10.47	−10 29.3	18 07.7	−10 30.	Ser		12						
003−04.11	KFL 12	18 10.5	−28 19.	18 07.3	−28 20.	Sgr	II	4				20.0		
352−09.1	Wra 16-376	18 10.59	−39 53.4	18 07.1	−39 54.	CrA								
345−13.1	Sa 2-304	18 10.59	−48 25.8	18 06.77	−48 26.4	Tel								StWr 2-37
002−04.2	M 1-42	18 11.08	−28 59.0	18 07.90	−28 59.7	Sgr	IV	8		13.8	WC	17.3:		ESO 456-67, He 2-359
003−04.3	H 1-59	18 11.49	−27 46.3	18 08.34	−27 47.0	Sgr	II	6		14.8				ESO 456-68, Sa 2-306
003−04.7	Ap 1-12	18 11.58	−28 22.6	18 08.42	−28 23.3	Sgr		12				13.27		ESO 456-69, He 2-360
011−00.1	M 1-43	18 11.81	−18 46.3	18 08.87	−18 47.1	Sgr	II	5				16.0		ESO 590-05, He 2-363
003−04.5	NGC 6565	18 11.87	−28 10.8	18 08.71	−28 11.5	Sgr	IV	9	13.2	11.6		15.88:	HD 166468	ARO 68, ESO 456-70,
														He 2-362, Sa 2-307
358−07.1	NGC 6563	18 12.04	−33 52.1	18 08.73	−33 52.9	Sgr	IIIa	48	13.8	11.0		15.38	HD 166449	ARO 503, ESO 394-33,
														He 2-361, Sa 2-308
034+11.1	NGC 6572	18 12.13	+06 50.8	18 09.7	+06 50.	Oph	IIa	8	9.0	8.1	Of+WR	12.88:	HD 166802	ARO 7
018+03.1	M 4-8	18 12.15	−10 43.0	18 09.38	−10 43.8	Ser								ARO 270, Sa 3-123
003−04.4	H 2-41	18 12.40	−27 52.2	18 09.25	−27 53.0	Sgr	IV	7			WC			ESO 456-71, Sa 2-309
005−03.2	H 2-42	18 12.42	−26 33.2	18 09.3	−26 34.	Sgr	IIIb	14				20.0		ESO 522-02
004−04.1	H 1-60	18 12.42	−27 29.3	18 09.28	−27 30.1	Sgr	II	4						ESO 522-03, Sa 2-310
003−04.8	M 2-30	18 12.56	−27 58.2	18 09.41	−27 59.0	Sgr		<10		13.2		17.1:		ESO 456-74, He 2-365
006−03.1	H 1-61	18 12.57	−24 50.0	18 09.49	−24 50.8	Sgr		<25						ESO 522-04, He 2-364
005−03.3	KFL 13	18 12.7	−25 44.	18 09.6	−25 45.	Sgr	IV	11				18.1		
003−04.9	H 2-43	18 12.79	−28 20.1	18 09.63	−28 20.9	Sgr	I	9						ESO 456-75, He 2-366
351−10.1	Sa 2-311	18 12.90	−41 30.4	18 09.35	−41 31.2	CrA								StWr 2-28, Wra 16-385
002−05.2	KFL 14	18 13.0	−29 25.	18 09.8	−29 26.	Sgr	IV	11						Poss H II region
006−03.3	M 2-31	18 13.26	−25 30.0	18 10.17	−25 30.9	Sgr		<5						ESO 522-06, He 2-368

CATALOGUE OF PLANETARY NEBULAE—TABLE 30

PK Name	Alternate Name	2000.0 R.A. (h m)	2000.0 Dec. (° ′)	1950.0 R.A. (h m)	1950.0 Dec. (° ′)	Con	Nebula Type	Nebula Diam. (″)	Nebula Mag. p	Nebula Mag. v	Star Spectra	Star Mag. V	Star Name	Notes
359−06.1	H 1-62	18 13.30	−32 19.7	18 10.03	−32 20.5	Sgr	I	<25				14.89		ESO 456-76, He 2-367
005−04.1	H 2-44	18 13.68	−26 08.6	18 10.57	−26 09.5	Sgr	II	8						ESO 522-07, Sa 3-124
011−00.2	NGC 6567	18 13.75	−19 04.6	18 10.80	−19 05.5	Sgr	IIa+II	>8	11.7	11.0	cont	14.43:	HD 166935	ARO 69, ESO 590-08, He 2-369, Sa 2-314
006−03.4	KFL 15	18 14.3	−25 21.	18 11.2	−25 22.	Sgr		6				20.7		
024+05.1	M 4-9	18 14.31	−04 59.4	18 11.65	−05 00.3	Ser	IV	42		14.1		19.7		Sa 3-125
006−03.2	H 2-45	18 14.47	−24 43.6	18 11.40	−24 44.5	Sgr	II	5						ESO 522-08, Sa 2-315
008−02.1	MaC 1-11	18 14.8	−22 44.	18 11.8	−22 45.	Sgr	I							
359−07.1	M 2-32	18 14.84	−32 36.8	18 11.57	−32 37.8	Sgr		<10		13.7		15.7		ESO 394-35, He 2-371
002−06.1	M 2-33	18 15.10	−30 15.5	18 11.89	−30 16.5	Sgr	II	4		14.0				ESO 456-80, He 2-372
022+04.1	Ma 2	18 15.2	−06 56.	18 12.5	−06 58.	Ser						18.0::		
019+03.1	M 3-25	18 15.28	−10 10.2	18 12.52	−10 11.2	Ser		4		14.3				Sa 2-318
004−05.1	M 3-26	18 16.18	−27 14.9	18 13.05	−27 16.0	Sgr	IV	7		14.2				ESO 522-10, He 2-378
001−06.2	SwSt 1	18 16.21	−30 52.1	18 12.98	−30 53.2	Sgr	I	<5	12.0	13.0	Of+WR	11.8	HD 167362	ESO 457-02, He 2-377
010−01.1	NGC 6578	18 16.28	−20 27.1	18 13.30	−20 28.2	Sgr	IIa	9	13.1	12.9		15.74		ARO 70, ESO 590-12, He 2-381, Sa 2-322
004−04.2	M 1-44	18 16.29	−27 04.5	18 13.16	−27 05.6	Sgr	II	4		16.5				ESO 522-11, He 2-379
002−06.2	H 1-63	18 16.32	−30 07.6	18 13.11	−30 08.7	Sgr		<5						ESO 457-03, He 2-380
030+08.1	K 4-1	18 16.53	+01 53.1	18 14.0	+01 52.	Oph								
005−04.2	KFL 16	18 16.9	−26 23.	18 13.8	−26 25.	Sgr		11				18.9		
007−03.1	M 2-34	18 17.27	−23 58.9	18 14.21	−24 00.0	Sgr	II	10						ESO 522-12, He 2-382
038+12.1	Cn 3-1	18 17.56	+10 09.2	18 15.2	+10 08.	Oph	II	5	12.4		WR	13.		ARO 97, SaSt 2-20
000−07.1	M 2-35	18 17.61	−31 56.6	18 14.36	−31 57.8	Sgr	I	<25		14.9				ESO 457-04, He 2-384
004−05.3	Pe 1-12	18 17.66	−28 16.8	18 14.5	−28 18.	Sgr	II	10						ESO 457-06
003−06.1	M 2-36	18 17.68	−29 08.3	18 14.50	−29 09.5	Sgr	II	7	13.0					ESO 457-05, He 2-385
007−03.2	Sa 3-128	18 17.79	−24 02.6	18 14.73	−24 03.8	Sgr								ESO 522-13
023+04.1	Ma 3	18 17.8	−06 48.	18 15.1	−06 50.	Ser						17.0::		
337−18.1	He 2-375	18 18.14	−57 11.2	18 13.86	−57 12.4	Pav		<10						Sa 2-323, My 118
006−04.1	Pe 2-13	18 18.22	−25 38.2	18 15.13	−25 39.4	Sgr		6		15.0				ESO 522-14, Sa 3-129
008−03.1	H 1-64	18 18.39	−23 25.0	18 15.35	−23 26.2	Sgr	II	7						ESO 522-15, He 2-386
348−13.1	IC 4699	18 18.53	−45 59.1	18 14.82	−46 00.3	Tel	II	<10	11.9	13.0		15.26:	HD 167672	ARO 521, ESO 280-08, He 2-383, Sa 2-326
004−05.5	M 2-37	18 18.64	−28 08.1	18 15.48	−28 09.3	Sgr	III	7						ESO 457-08, He 2-387

CATALOGUE OF PLANETARY NEBULAE—TABLE 31

PK Name	Alternate Name	2000.0 R.A. (h m)	2000.0 Dec. (° ′)	1950.0 R.A. (h m)	1950.0 Dec. (° ′)	Con	Nebula Type	Nebula Diam. (″)	Nebula Mag. p	Nebula Mag. v	Star Spectra	Star Mag. V	Star Name	Notes
000−07.2	H 2-46	18 18.69	−31 54.7	18 15.44	−31 55.9	Sgr	I			15.5				ESO 457-07, Sa 2-327
005−05.1	M 2-38	18 19.42	−26 35.4	18 16.30	−26 36.7	Sgr	IV	8						ARO 272, ESO 522-17, He 2-388, Sa 2-328
007−04.1	H 1-65	18 20.14	−24 15.0	18 17.08	−24 16.4	Sgr	I	<17				14.66		ARO 273, ESO 522-18, He 2-389
021+02.1	MaC 1-12	18 21.3	−08 31.	18 18.6	−08 33.	Ser	I							PM 1-226
024+03.1	M 2-40	18 21.40	−06 01.9	18 18.72	−06 03.4	Ser	II	5						ARO 275
094+27.1	K 1-16	18 21.85	+64 21.6	18 21.6	+64 20.	Dra	III	115		14.2	9W Vir	15.09v	DS Dra	
008−04.1	M 2-39	18 22.02	−24 10.7	18 18.96	−24 12.2	Sgr	II	3				15.8		ESO 522-20, He 2-391
008−04.2	M 2-42	18 22.53	−24 09.5	18 19.47	−24 11.0	Sgr	II	4						ESO 522-21, He 2-393
002−07.1	M 2-41	18 22.57	−30 43.5	18 19.35	−30 45.0	Sgr	IV	14		13.8				ESO 457-10, He 2-392
005−06.1	NGC 6620	18 22.90	−26 49.3	18 19.78	−26 50.9	Sgr	IIb	5	15.0	12.7		16.25		ARO 99, ESO 522-22, He 2-394, Sa 2-332
003−07.1	KFL 19	18 23.1	−29 43.	18 19.9	−29 45.	Sgr	II	5				17.0		
012−02.1	M 1-45	18 23.13	−19 17.1	18 20.18	−19 18.7	Sgr		<10						ARO 276, ESO 590-18, He 2-395
032+07.1	K 3-1	18 23.39	+03 36.6	18 20.9	+03 35.	Oph				14.3				
019+00.1	M 3-53	18 24.13	−11 06.7	18 21.35	−11 08.4	Sct	II	5						Sa 3-132
032+07.2	PC 19	18 24.71	+02 29.7	18 22.2	+02 28.	Ser				13.0				ARO 136
030+06.1	Sh 2-68	18 24.9	+00 51.	18 22.4	+00 50.	Ser		400		10.::		16.0::		YM 15
007−06.1	H 1-66	18 24.95	−25 41.9	18 21.86	−25 43.6	Sgr	IV	8		13.2				ESO 522-24, He2-397
028+05.1	K 3-2	18 25.01	−01 30.9	18 22.42	−01 32.6	Ser		3		14.5				
009−04.1	H 1-67	18 25.08	−22 34.9	18 22.06	−22 36.6	Sgr	II	6		13.7				ESO 522-25, He 2-398
009−05.1	NGC 6629	18 25.71	−23 12.1	18 22.67	−23 13.9	Sgr	IIa	15	11.6	11.3	O	12.82	HD 169460	ARO 30, ESO 522-26, He 2-399, Sa 2-335
013−02.1	SrWe 3	18 26.0	−18 12.	18 23.1	−18 14.	Sgr		115						
027+04.1	M 2-43	18 26.66	−02 43.0	18 24.05	−02 44.8	Ser	I			15.0				ARO 277, Sa 3-133
353−12.1	Wra 16-411	18 26.69	−40 29.9	18 23.18	−40 31.7	CrA								
031+05.1	K 3-3	18 27.14	+01 14.9	18 24.6	+01 13.	Ser	III	9						
043+11.1	M 3-27	18 27.78	+14 28.9	18 25.5	+14 27.	Her	I			13.9				ARO 137
356−11.1	Lo 17	18 27.80	−37 16.0	18 24.40	−37 17.9	CrA		104				16.2		ESO 395-07
016−01.1	M 1-46	18 27.94	−15 32.9	18 25.07	−15 34.8	Sct	IV+II	>11		15.4		12.83		ARO 387, He 2-401
007−06.2	Vy 2-1	18 27.99	−26 06.9	18 24.89	−26 08.8	Sgr	I	<9	13.3	13.1		17.6:		ESO 522-27, He 2-400

CATALOGUE OF PLANETARY NEBULAE—TABLE 32

PK Name	Alternate Name	2000.0 R.A.	2000.0 Dec.	1950.0 R.A.	1950.0 Dec.	Con	Nebula Type	Nebula Diam.	Nebula Mag. p	Nebula Mag. v	Star Spectra	Star Mag. V	Star Name	Notes
		h m	° ′	h m	° ′			″						
011−05.1	M 1-47	18 29.18	−21 46.9	18 26.18	−21 48.9	Sgr	II	5		13.5				ESO 591-02, He 2-403
002−09.1	Cn 1-5	18 29.19	−31 30.0	18 25.95	−31 32.0	Sgr		<5	12.6	11.9	WC	16.6:	HD 170124	ESO 457-12, He 2-402
016−02.1	Sa 3-134	18 29.33	−15 07.7	18 26.47	−15 09.7	Sct								
013−03.1	M 1-48	18 29.49	−19 05.8	18 26.55	−19 07.8	Sgr	II	5		14.8				ESO 591-03, He 2-404
013−04.1	Pe 2-14	18 30.00	−19 40.6	18 27.04	−19 42.7	Sgr	II	5		15.5				ESO 591-04, Sa 2-340
015−03.1	Abell 44	18 30.19	−16 44.9	18 27.3	−16 47.	Sgr	II	52	17.4					ARO 278
020−00.1	Abell 45	18 30.29	−11 36.9	18 27.5	−11 39.	Sct	IIIb	285				21.1		
023+01.1	Ma 13	18 30.5	−07 27.	18 27.8	−07 30.	Sct								
013−04.2	Sa 2-341	18 30.57	−19 14.8	18 27.62	−19 16.9	Sgr								ESO 591-05
032+05.1	K 3-4	18 31.02	+02 25.2	18 28.5	+02 23.	Ser	IIIb+II	>12		14.6				ARO 279
055+16.1	Abell 46	18 31.20	+26 55.2	18 29.2	+26 53.	Lyr	IIIb+II	>60	15.6	14.3		14.87v	V477 Lyr	ARO 119. Central star ecl. bin. P = $0^{d}471729$
034+06.1	K 3-5	18 31.78	+04 05.2	18 29.3	+04 03.	Ser	II	10						
008−07.1	He 2-406	18 31.88	−24 46.3	18 28.81	−24 48.5	Sgr		<25		15.6				ARO 280, ESO 522-31
005−08.1	Hf 2-2	18 32.52	−28 43.4	18 29.35	−28 45.6	Sgr	II	18		16.7		17.4		ESO 457-16, He 2-407
008−07.2	NGC 6644	18 32.58	−25 07.7	18 29.50	−25 10.0	Sgr	II	3	12.2	10.7		15.63:		ESO 522-23, He 2-408
021−00.1	M 3-28	18 32.69	−10 05.8	18 29.93	−10 08.1	Sct	II+III	>8	>14.3			20.1		ARO 281, Sa 3-136
018−02.1	M 3-54	18 33.06	−13 44.4	18 30.23	−13 46.7	Sct								Sa 3-137
038+07.1	K 1-25	18 33.17	+08 18.4	18 30.77	+08 16.1	Oph		20						
030+04.1	K 3-6	18 33.26	+00 12.3	18 30.7	+00 10.	Ser								
021−00.2	M 3-55	18 33.26	−10 15.4	18 30.50	−10 17.7	Sct	II	7				20.1		ARO 282, Sa 3-138
014−04.1	M 1-50	18 33.35	−18 16.7	18 30.42	−18 19.0	Sgr	II	5		13.3				ESO 591-07, He 2-409
021−01.1	M 1-51	18 33.48	−11 07.4	18 30.70	−11 09.7	Sct	III	<10						He 2-411
010−06.1	IC 4732	18 33.91	−22 38.6	18 30.89	−22 41.0	Sgr	I	3	13.3	12.1		16.9	HD 171131	ARO 71, ESO 523-01, He 2-410, Sa 2-345
017−02.1	M 1-52	18 33.97	−14 52.3	18 31.12	−14 54.7	Sct	II	6		14.7				ARO 283, Sa 2-346
044+10.1	We 3-1	18 34.1	+14 49.	18 31.8	+14 47.	Her								
019−02.1	M 4-10	18 34.22	−13 12.4	18 31.40	−13 14.8	Sct				14.3				ARO 284, Sa 2-347
028+02.1	K 3-7	18 34.23	−02 27.6	18 31.62	−02 30.0	Ser				15.6				ARO 285, Sa 3-140
035+05.1	K 3-8	18 34.86	+05 04.4	18 32.4	+05 02.	Ser								

CATALOGUE OF PLANETARY NEBULAE—TABLE 33

PK Name	Alternate Name	2000.0 R.A. (h m)	2000.0 Dec. (° ′)	1950.0 R.A. (h m)	1950.0 Dec. (° ′)	Con	Nebula Type	Nebula Diam. (″)	Nebula Mag. p	Nebula Mag. v	Star Spectra	Star Mag. V	Star Name	Notes
010−06.2	Pe 1-13	18 34.86	−22 43.3	18 31.84	−22 45.7	Sgr	II	7		14.7				ESO 523-03, Sa 2-348
006−08.1	Al 1	18 34.92	−27 06.4	18 31.79	−27 08.8	Sgr		14						ESO 523-02
030+03.1	Abell 47	18 35.36	+00 18.5	18 32.8	−00 16.	Ser		15	>20.9			20.4		ARO 138
015−04.1	M 1-53	18 35.80	−17 36.2	18 32.89	−17 38.7	Sgr	II	6		13.5		14.50		ESO 591-08, He 2-412
016−04.1	M 1-54	18 36.14	−17 00.0	18 33.24	−17 02.5	Sgr	III	14		13.5				He 2-413, Sa 2-350
009−07.1	IRAS 18333-2357	18 36.3	−23 55.5	18 33.3	−23 58.	Sgr		8	15.::					in g.c. M.22, 1′ S. of center
014−05.1	Sa 1-7	18 36.53	−19 19.5	18 33.58	−19 22.0	Sgr								ESO 591-09
011−06.1	M 1-55	18 36.56	−21 49.1	18 33.56	−21 51.6	Sgr		<25				13.99		ESO 591-10, He 2-414
014−05.2	Y-C 2-25	18 37.18	−19 02.4	18 34.24	−19 05.0	Sgr								ESO 591-11, Sa 2-352
009−08.1	Y-C 2-47	18 37.5	−24 26.	18 34.4	−24 29.	Sgr								
028+01.1	M 2-44	18 37.61	−03 06.0	18 34.99	−03 08.6	Ser	IV	8		13.5				Sa 2-354, Th 1-A
016−04.2	M 1-56	18 37.77	−17 05.8	18 34.87	−17 08.4	Sgr		<10		13.5				He 2-415, Sa 2-353
027+00.1	M 2-45	18 39.37	−04 19.8	18 36.72	−04 22.6	Sct	II	6				>21.		ARO 286, Sa 3-141
004−11.1	M 3-29	18 39.42	−30 40.7	18 36.21	−30 43.4	Sgr	II	8	13.1	13.8		15.55		ESO 458-01, He 2-416
010−09.1	PTH-1	18 40.3	−22 55.0	18 37.3	−22 57.5	Sgr		8		16.::	WC II	12.1-14	V348 Sgr	
022−02.1	M 1-57	18 40.34	−10 39.9	18 37.57	−10 42.7	Sct	II	8		13.7		16.3:		ARO 287, Sa 2-356
056+14.1	K 2-6	18 41.11	+26 54.9	18 39.1	+26 52.	Lyr	IV	16				>21.		ARO 139
023−01.2	K 3-11	18 41.12	−08 56.0	18 38.39	−08 58.9	Sct								Sa 3-144
020−03.1	MaC 1-14	18 41.2	−13 12.	18 38.4	−13 15.	Sct	I							
017−04.1	M 3-30	18 41.25	−15 33.7	18 38.38	−15 36.6	Sct	IV	17		14.8		16.0		ARO 288, Sa 3-143
013−07.2	Y-C 2-26	18 41.93	−20 32.3	18 38.96	−20 35.2	Sgr								ESO 591-13
025−00.1	Pe 1-14	18 42.09	−06 41.0	18 39.4	−06 44.	Sct		5		20.8				
029+00.1	Abell 48	18 42.82	−03 13.0	18 40.2	−03 16.	Aql	IV	42	>18.					
031+01.1	PC 20	18 43.04	+00 22.6	18 40.49	−00 19.6	Aql	I							ARO 140
023−02.1	M 1-59	18 43.34	−09 04.8	18 40.60	−09 07.8	Sct	II	4		12.5				ARO 289, Sa 2-358
019−04.1	M 1-60	18 43.63	−13 44.3	18 40.80	−13 47.4	Sct	I			14.0				Sa 2-359
014−07.1	M 3-31	18 44.03	−19 54.9	18 41.07	−19 58.0	Sgr		<10		14.2				ESO 591-15, He 2-419
022−03.1	M 1-58	18 44.10	−11 06.8	18 41.32	−11 09.9	Sct	II	6		13.0				Sa 2-357
021−03.1	We 1-7	18 44.12	−12 12.9	18 41.32	−12 16.0	Sct		17				>20.		
004−11.2	He 2-418	18 44.23	−30 19.6	18 41.03	−30 22.7	Sgr				14.0		16.0		ESO 458-04, Sa 2-360
009−09.1	M 3-32	18 44.68	−25 19.9	18 41.6	−25 23.	Sgr	II	6		13.3				ESO 523-06, He 2-420
037+04.1	K 3-12	18 44.74	+06 07.2	18 42.3	+06 04.	Oph								
034+02.1	K 3-13	18 45.42	+02 01.2	18 42.9	+01 58.	Aql								ARO 290
026−01.2	Pe 2-15	18 45.50	−06 56.8	18 42.8	−07 00.	Sct	II	3						
026−01.1	K 4-5	18 45.58	−06 18.8	18 42.9	−06 22.	Sct				14.2				

CATALOGUE OF PLANETARY NEBULAE—TABLE 34

PK Name	Alternate Name	2000.0 R.A. (h m)	2000.0 Dec. (° ′)	1950.0 R.A. (h m)	1950.0 Dec. (° ′)	Con	Nebula Type	Nebula Diam. (″)	Nebula Mag. p	Nebula Mag. v	Star Spectra	Star Mag. V	Star Name	Notes
013−07.1	PC 21	18 45.58	−20 35.0	18 42.61	−20 38.2	Sgr	?+III	14		14.0				ESO 591-16, Sa 2-364
002−13.1	IC 4776	18 45.84	−33 20.6	18 42.56	−33 23.8	Sgr	IIa	8	11.7	10.8	WC6	14.47:	HD 173283	ARO 522, ESO 396-02, He 2-421, Sa 2-363
019−05.1	M 1-61	18 45.91	−14 27.6	18 43.07	−14 30.8	Sct	I			12.8		16.8:		Sa 2-365
025−02.1	Pe 1-15	18 46.41	−07 14.5	18 43.71	−07 17.8	Sct	II+IIIb	5						Sa 3-145
024−02.1	M 2-46	18 46.57	−08 28.0	18 43.85	−08 31.3	Sct	III	5						Sa 3-146
011−09.1	H 2-48	18 46.59	−23 26.7	18 43.55	−23 30.0	Sgr		<5		14.0		13.37		ESO 523-07, He 2-422
026−02.1	Pe 1-16	18 47.53	−06 54.1	18 44.84	−06 57.4	Sct	IIb	7		14.3				ARO 291, Sa 2-366
024−03.1	Pe 1-17	18 47.81	−09 09.1	18 45.07	−09 12.5	Sct	III+II	6		14.8				Sa 3-147
009−10.1	M 3-33	18 48.20	−25 28.9	18 45.12	−25 32.3	Sgr	II	5		13.7		15.9		ESO 523-09, He 2-423
042+05.1	K 3-14	18 48.56	+10 35.4	18 46.2	+10 32.	Aql								
027−02.1	Pe 1-18	18 48.78	−05 56.1	18 46.10	−05 59.5	Sct	IIa	7						Sa 3-148, Th 1-D
015−08.1	Y-C 2-29	18 49.14	−19 34.1	18 46.19	−19 37.5	Sgr								
051+09.1	Hu 2-1	18 49.75	+20 50.5	18 47.6	+20 47.	Her		3	12.2	11.4	WR	13.4		ARO 100
026−02.3	Pe 1-19	18 49.75	−07 01.6	18 47.05	−07 05.1	Sct	II	4		14.5				ARO 293, Sa 2-368
064+15.1	M 1-64	18 49.99	+35 14.6	18 48.2	+35 11.	Lyr	IV	17		13.3	cont			ARO 82
031−00.2	HtTr 10	18 50.4	−01 40.	18 47.8	−01 44.	Aql		30						
012−09.1	M 1-62	18 50.43	−22 34.4	18 47.42	−22 37.9	Sgr	II	4		13.8				ESO 523-10, He 2-424
044+05.2	CTSS 2	18 50.7	−12 36.7	18 48.4	+12 33.0	Her								
031−00.1	WeSb 4	18 50.7	−00 03.	18 48.1	−00 07.	Aql		30						
020−05.1	Sa 1-8	18 50.73	−13 31.1	18 47.91	−13 34.7	Sct								Sa 2-370
021−05.1	M 1-63	18 51.51	−13 10.7	18 48.69	−13 14.3	Sct	II	4		13.8				Sa 2-371
041+04.1	K 3-15	18 51.67	+09 54.6	18 49.3	+09 51.	Aql								ARO 294
044+05.1	K 3-16	18 53.03	+12 15.7	18 50.7	+12 12.	Her								ARO 295
027−03.1	Abell 49	18 53.49	−06 29.2	18 50.8	−06 33.	Sct	IIc	35	16.7			>21.		
063+13.1	NGC 6720	18 53.56	+33 01.8	18 51.7	+32 58.	Lyr	IV+III	>71	9.7	8.8	cont	14.7		M.57, ARO 9
058+12.1	K 4-9	18 53.67	+28 31.8	18 51.7	+28 28.	Lyr								
027−03.2	Vy 1-4	18 54.03	−06 26.3	18 51.35	−06 30.1	Sct			13.4					Sa 2-372, Th 1-E
024−05.1	M 4-11	18 54.29	−10 05.2	18 51.54	−10 09.0	Sct	II	21		13.8		18.0		Sa 2-373
025−04.1	K 4-8	18 54.33	−08 47.6	18 51.60	−08 51.4	Sct				14.0				Sa 2-374
025−04.2	IC 1295	18 54.63	−08 50.2	18 51.9	−08 54.	Sct	IIIb+II	>86	15.0			15.		ARO 8
038+02.1	YM 16	18 54.75	+06 01.9	18 52.3	+05 58.	Ser	IIIb	308						ARO 141, RCW 181
013−10.1	Y-C 2-32	18 55.51	−21 49.6	18 52.51	−21 53.5	Sgr								ESO 592-06, Sa 2-376
003−14.1	Hb 7	18 55.63	−32 15.8	18 52.38	−32 19.7	Sgr	II	4	10.9		O	13.97	HD 175194	ARO 523, ESO 458-09, Cn 1-6, He 2-425

CATALOGUE OF PLANETARY NEBULAE—TABLE 35

PK Name	Alternate Name	2000.0 R.A. (h m)	2000.0 Dec. (° ′)	1950.0 R.A. (h m)	1950.0 Dec. (° ′)	Con	Nebula Type	Nebula Diam. (″)	Nebula Mag. p	Nebula Mag. v	Star Spectra	Star Mag. V	Star Name	Notes
039+02.1	K 3-17	18 56.33	+07 08.0	18 53.9	+07 04.	Aql	II	16						ARO 297
043+03.1	M 1-65	18 56.55	+10 52.0	18 54.2	+10 48.	Aql	II	4						ARO 142
028−04.1	Pe 1-20	18 57.29	−05 59.9	18 54.61	−06 03.9	Sct	IV	8		15.0				ARO 298, Sa 2-377
019−08.1	MaC 1-15	18 57.3	−15 28.	18 54.4	−15 33.	Sct	I							
028−03.1	Pe 1-21	18 57.83	−05 27.6	18 55.16	−05 31.7	Sct	IV	8						Sa 3-150, Th 1-H
035−00.1	Ap 1-2	18 58.13	+01 37.1	18 55.6	+01 33.	Aql								ARO 143
032−02.1	M 1-66	18 58.43	−01 03.8	18 55.85	−01 07.9	Aql	I			13.0				Sa 2-378
033−01.1	Sa 3-151	18 58.84	+00 41.3	18 56.29	−00 37.1	Aql								
052+07.1	K 4-10	18 59.06	+20 37.2	18 56.9	+20 33.	Sge				14.7				
078+18.1	NGC 6742	18 59.35	+48 28.2	18 58.0	+48 24.	Dra	IIc	30	15.0	13.4		19.4		Abell 50
068+14.1	St 4-1	19 00.4	+38 21.	18 58.7	+38 17.	Lyr	I	2						
032−03.1	K 3-18	19 00.57	−02 11.9	18 57.97	−02 16.2	Aql	II	5						ARO 299, Sa 3-152
017−10.1	Abell 51	19 01.02	−18 12.7	18 58.1	−18 17.	Sgr	IV	62	15.4	15.0	sdO	15.4		ARO 300
023−07.1	MaC 1-16	19 01.4	−11 58.	18 58.6	−12 03.	Aql		10						
032−02.2	K 3-19	19 01.61	−01 19.2	18 59.02	−01 23.5	Aql								ARO 301, Sa 2-379
036−01.1	Sh 2-71	19 02.02	+02 09.4	18 59.5	+02 05.	Aql	IIIb+III	>107		13.2		13.8		ARO 31, V-V 1-9
032−03.2	K 3-20	19 02.17	−01 48.7	18 59.57	−01 53.1	Aql								Sa 3-153
043+02.1	CTSS 1	19 02.2	+10 17.4	18 59.9	+10 13.0	Agl		14				18.5		PM 1-276, IRAS 18599+1013
014−11.1	SrWe 4	19 02.3	−21 26.	18 59.3	−21 31.	Sgr		85				20.::		
033−02.1	NGC 6741	19 02.60	+00 35.8	19 00.05	−00 31.4	Aql	IV	6	10.8	11.5		17.6:		ARO 53, Sa 2-380
047+04.1	K 3-21	19 02.69	+14 28.4	19 00.4	+14 24.	Aql		7						
036−01.2	HtTr 11	19 03.0	+03 02.	19 00.5	+02 58.	Aql		12						
046+03.1	Sh 2-78	19 03.1	+14 06.9	19 00.8	+14 02.5	Agl		10				17.78		CTSS 3
051+06.1	K 1-17	19 03.59	+19 21.5	19 01.4	+19 17.	Sge	IV	45		15.2		18.6		ARO 83
038−00.1	HtTr 12	19 03.8	+05 09.	19 01.3	+05 05.	Aql		55						
050+05.1	Abell 52	19 04.52	+17 57.6	19 02.3	+17 53.	Aql	IIIb	36	16.5			17.2		ARO 144
048+04.2	K 4-16	19 04.86	+15 47.6	19 02.6	+15 43.	Aql								ARO 303
003−17.1	Hb 8	19 05.59	−33 11.7	19 02.33	−33 16.3	Sgr	II	5	13.4	12.5				ESO 397-02, He 2-426
011−14.1	HtDe 10	19 05.7	−25 23.	19 02.6	−25 28.	Sgr	IIIb	27						HtWe 12
029−05.1	NGC 6751	19 05.92	−05 59.6	19 03.25	−06 04.2	Aql	III	20	12.5	11.9	WC6	15.44	HD 177656	ARO 101, Sa 2-382
046+02.1	CTSS 4	19 06.4	+13 44.6	19 04.1	+13 40.0	Aql		10				17.::		
040−00.1	Abell 53	19 06.74	+06 23.7	19 04.3	+06 19.	Aql	IV	31	16.9	15.5		20.3		ARO 183
036−02.1	HtTr 13	19 08.0	+02 21.	19 05.5	+02 17.	Aql		20						
055+06.1	Abell 54	19 08.71	+22 58.9	19 06.6	+22 54.	Vul	IIb	63	17.1					ARO 184

CATALOGUE OF PLANETARY NEBULAE—TABLE 36

PK Name	Alternate Name	2000.0 R.A. (h m)	2000.0 Dec. (° ′)	1950.0 R.A. (h m)	1950.0 Dec. (° ′)	Con	Nebula Type	Nebula Diam. (″)	Nebula Mag. p	Nebula Mag. v	Star Spectra	Star Mag. V	Star Name	Notes
041−00.1	HtTr 14	19 09.2	+07 05.	19 06.8	+07 01.	Aql		20						
341−24.1	Lo 18	19 09.75	−55 34.6	19 05.63	−55 39.5	Tel		43						
033−05.1	Abell 55	19 10.51	−02 21.0	19 07.9	−02 26.	Aql	III	41	15.4			19.2		
062+09.1	NGC 6765	19 11.14	+30 33.0	19 09.2	+30 28.	Lyr	V	38		12.9				ARO 185, M 1-68
048+02.1	K 3-24	19 12.08	+15 09.1	19 09.8	+15 04.	Aql	II	6						ARO 305
030−07.1	MaC 1-17	19 13.0	−05 20.	19 10.3	−05 26.	Aql	I							
032−06.1	K 2-10	19 13.03	−03 31.9	19 10.4	−03 37.	Aql	IV	22				>21.		
049+02.1	M 4-12	19 13.06	+15 47.2	19 10.8	+15 42.	Aql	IV+II	>9						ARO 186, He 2-428
037−03.2	Abell 56	19 13.11	+02 53.2	19 10.6	+02 48.	Aql	IV	188	>15.5					ARO 146
038−03.1	K 4-19	19 13.40	+03 25.2	19 10.9	+03 20.	Aql								
042−01.1	K 4-20	19 13.52	+07 27.2	19 11.1	+07 22.	Aql								
039−02.1	M 2-47	19 13.58	+04 38.2	19 11.1	+04 33.	Aql	II	8		14.5				ARO 147
048+01.1	M 4-13	19 13.68	+14 59.2	19 11.4	+14 54.	Aql	IV	4		15.0				ARO 148, He 2-429
029−07.1	LSA 1	19 13.9	+-6 18.	19 11.2	−06 24.	Aql		14						
038−03.2	M 1-69	19 13.90	+03 38.2	19 11.4	+03 33.	Aql	I			14.0				ARO 187
051+03.1	He 2-430	19 14.03	+17 31.2	19 11.8	+17 26.	Sge		<10		15.0				ARO 308
038−03.3	K 2-11	19 14.30	+03 35.2	19 11.8	+03 30.	Aql	IIIb	14				19.4		ARO 307
005−18.1	Sa 2-383	19 14.39	−32 34.3	19 11.15	−32 39.5	Sgr								ESO 397-07, StWr 2-21
061+08.1	K 3-27	19 14.48	+28 41.3	19 12.5	+28 36.	Lyr		16		14.3				
033−06.1	NGC 6772	19 14.60	−02 42.3	19 11.99	−02 47.6	Aql	IIIb+II	>62	14.2	12.7		18.2		ARO 102, Sa 2-384
035−05.1	K 3-26	19 14.66	+00 13.3	19 12.1	+00 08.	Aql				14.5				ARO 309
051+02.1	IRAS 1912+172PO9	19 15.0	+17 22.	19 12.8	+17 17.	Sge						13.4		c.s. binary
048+01.2	K 3-29	19 15.50	+14 04.3	19 13.2	+13 59.	Aql								
040−03.1	K 3-30	19 16.47	+05 13.4	19 14.0	+05 08.	Aql								ARO 312
027−09.1	IC 4846	19 16.47	−09 02.5	19 13.74	−09 07.9	Aql	II		12.7	11.9	Of	15.45	HD 180324	ARO 103, Sa 2-385
058+06.1	Abell 57	19 17.06	+25 37.4	19 15.0	+25 32.	Vul	IIIb	37	17.5	14.7		17.4		ARO 149
019−13.1	DeHt 3	19 17.1	−18 01.	19 14.2	−18 07.	Sgr		32						
358−21.1	IC 1297	19 17.39	−39 36.8	19 13.96	−39 42.2	CrA		7		10.7	WR	14.22		ESO 337-20, He 2-431
026−11.1	Na 2	19 18.32	−11 06.2	19 15.55	−11 11.7	Aql			13.3	13.5	WR	14.		Sa 2-387
037−05.1	Abell 58	19 18.33	+01 47.5	19 15.8	+01 42.	Aql		40	>18.8			19.4v	V605 Aql	ARO 150
034−06.1	NGC 6778	19 18.41	−01 35.8	19 15.82	−01 41.3	Aql	III+III	>16	13.3	12.3		14.8	HD 180871	ARO 72, Sa 2-388
041−02.1	NGC 6781	19 18.44	+06 32.5	19 16.0	+06 27.	Aql	IIIb+III	>109	11.8	11.4		16.2		ARO 32
053+03.1	Abell 59	19 18.69	+19 33.5	19 16.5	+19 28.	Sge	IIIb	86	17.2			21.15		ARO 84
052+02.1	K 3-31	19 19.00	+19 02.6	19 16.8	+18 57.	Sge								ARO 315
077+14.1	Abell 61	19 19.17	+46 14.6	19 17.7	+46 09.	Cyg	IIb	190	14.4	13.5		17.3		

CATALOGUE OF PLANETARY NEBULAE—TABLE 37

PK Name	Alternate Name	2000.0 R.A. (h m)	2000.0 Dec. (° ′)	1950.0 R.A. (h m)	1950.0 Dec. (° ′)	Con	Nebula Type	Nebula Diam. (″)	Nebula Mag. p	Nebula Mag. v	Star Spectra	Star Mag. V	Star Name	Notes
025−11.1	Abell 60	19 19.29	−12 16.4	19 16.5	−12 22.	Sgr	IIb	76	15.7	15.5		17.9		ARO 314
051+01.1	CTS 2	19 19.3	+17 12.	19 17.1	+17 06.	Sge	IV	20				15.1		IRAS 19170+1706
043−03.1	M 4-14	19 21.02	+07 36.7	19 18.6	+07 31.	Aql	IV+III	>8		15.3				ARO 120
032−08.1	ARO 318	19 21.94	−04 13.2	19 19.3	−04 19.	Aql								
006−19.1	Sa 2-389	19 22.17	−31 30.6	19 18.97	−31 36.4	Sgr								ESO 459-17, StWr 2-18
045−01.1	K 3-33	19 22.47	+10 41.8	19 20.1	+10 36.	Aql								
037−06.1	NGC 6790	19 23.23	+01 30.8	19 20.7	+01 25.	Aql	II	7	10.2	10.5	WR	15.5:	HD 182083	ARO 33
055+02.1	He 2-432	19 23.46	+21 07.9	19 21.3	+21 02.	Vul		<10		15.8				ARO 321
055+02.2	He 1-1	19 23.76	+21 06.9	19 21.6	+21 01.	Vul	II+III	>6						ARO 188, He 2-433
059+04.1	K 3-34	19 24.07	+25 18.9	19 22.0	+25 13.	Vul		9						
045−02.1	Vy 2-2	19 24.38	+09 53.9	19 22.0	+09 48.	Aql	I		12.7	12.7		14.45		ARO 151, M 1-70
048−01.1	DeHt 4	19 26.4	+13 20.	19 24.1	+13 14.	Aql		40						
055+02.3	He 1-2	19 26.66	+21 09.1	19 24.5	+21 03.	Vul		5						ARO 189, He 2-435
031−10.1	M 3-34	19 27.03	−06 35.1	19 24.35	−06 41.2	Aql	II	5		12.5		15.9:		ARO 322, Sa 2-390
056+02.1	K 3-35	19 27.75	+21 30.2	19 25.6	+21 24.	Vul								ARO 323
046−03.1	PB 9	19 27.77	+10 24.2	19 25.4	+10 18.	Aql	I			14.0				ARO 152
048−02.1	PB 10	19 28.24	+12 19.2	19 25.9	+12 13.	Aql				14.4				ARO 153, Ap 4-1
050−01.1	K 4-28	19 30.29	+14 47.3	19 28.0	+14 41.	Aql								
057+02.1	K 4-29	19 30.62	+23 04.4	19 28.5	+22 58.	Vul								
046−04.1	NGC 6803	19 31.28	+10 03.4	19 28.9	+09 57.	Aql	IIa	6	11.3	11.4	WR	14.	HD 183889	ARO 73
034−10.1	We e	19 31.3	−03 43.	19 28.7	−03 49	Aql	III	60				16.6		HtDe 11, HtWe 13
045−04.1	NGC 6804	19 31.60	+09 13.4	19 29.2	+09 07.	Aql	IV+II	>31	12.2	12.0	O9	14.4		ARO 34
004−22.1	He 2-436	19 32.11	−34 13.0	19 28.85	−34 19.4	Sgr		<10		14.5				ESO 398-07, Sa 2-391
044−05.1	K 3-36	19 32.63	+07 27.5	19 30.2	+07 21.	Aql								
061+03.1	M 4-15	19 32.94	+26 52.5	19 30.9	+26 46.	Vul		9						ARO 154, He 2-437
057+01.1	K 4-30	19 33.13	+22 58.5	19 31.0	+22 52.	Vul								
047−04.1	Abell 62	19 33.37	+10 37.5	19 31.0	+10 31.	Aql	IIc	156	14.8			18.2		ARO 155
320−28.1	He 2-434	19 33.79	−74 32.6	19 27.5	−74 39.	Pav		<10				14.45		ESO 046-03
059+02.1	K 3-37	19 33.80	+24 32.6	19 31.7	+24 26.	Vul				16.2				ARO 325
042−06.1	NGC 6807	19 34.56	+05 40.6	19 32.1	+05 34.	Aql	II		13.8	12.0				ARO 74
064+05.1	He 2-438	19 34.76	+30 30.6	19 32.8	+30 24.	Cyg	IV	8	9.6	11.3	WC9	10.00	HD 184738	ARO 11, Campbell's Star. BD+30°3639
053−01.1	K 3-38	19 35.35	+17 12.7	19 33.1	+17 06.	Sge		4						
059+02.2	K 3-39	19 35.89	+24 54.7	19 33.8	+24 48.	Vul								ARO 326
058+01.1	K 3-40	19 36.32	+23 39.7	19 34.2	+23 33.	Vul								
055−00.1	M 1-71	19 36.50	+19 42.8	19 34.3	+19 36.	Vul		4		13.9				ARO 156, He 2-439

CATALOGUE OF PLANETARY NEBULAE—TABLE 38

PK Name	Alternate Name	2000.0 R.A. h	m	2000.0 Dec. °	′	1950.0 R.A. h	m	1950.0 Dec. °	′	Con	Nebula Type	Diam. ″	Mag. p	Mag. v	Star Spectra	Mag. V	Name	Notes
050−03.1	K 4-31	19	37.11	+13	40.8	19	34.8	+13	34.	Aql						15.-16:	V998 Aql	ARO 327
060+01.1	He 2-440	19	38.18	+25	15.9	19	36.1	+25	09.	Vul		<25						
052−02.2	Me 1-1	19	39.17	+15	56.9	19	36.9	+15	50.	Aql	IV	<10	12.6	11.8				ARO 104, He 2-441
052−02.1	K 3-41	19	39.27	+16	20.9	19	37.0	+16	14.	Aql								ARO 328
056−00.1	K 3-42	19	39.59	+20	19.0	19	37.4	+20	12.	Vul		3						
055−01.1	K 3-43	19	40.42	+18	49.0	19	38.2	+18	42.	Sge	II	3						
019−19.1	K 2-7	19	40.54	−20	27.0	19	37.6	−20	34.	Sgr	IIIb	140				18.7		ESO 594-10
051−03.1	M 1-73	19	41.19	+14	57.1	19	38.9	+14	50.	Aql	II	5		14.0				ARO 158, He 2-443
054−02.1	M 1-72	19	41.54	+17	45.1	19	39.3	+17	38.	Sge		<10				17.6:		ARO 159, He 2-444
051−04.1	PC 22	19	42.01	+13	51.1	19	39.7	+13	44.	Aql				13.3				ARO 160
053−03.1	Abell 63	19	42.15	+17	05.1	19	39.9	+16	58.	Sge	II	34	17.1		sdO+dK	14.67v	UU Sge	ARO 161
052−04.1	M 1-74	19	42.29	+15	09.1	19	40.0	+15	02.	Aql	I	<10		12.9	WR	18.1:		ARO 162, He 2-445
025−17.1	NGC 6818	19	43.96	−14	09.2	19	41.14	−14	16.4	Sgr	IV	>17	9.9	9.3	WR	15.		ARO 12, Sa 2-392
083+12.1	NGC 6826	19	44.85	+50	31.3	19	43.5	+50	24.	Cyg	IIIa+II	>25	9.8	8.8	O6fp	10.6	HD 186924	ARO 13
057−01.1	He 2-447	19	45.37	+21	20.3	19	43.2	+21	13.	Vul		<25						
044−09.1	Abell 64	19	45.66	+05	34.3	19	43.2	+05	27.	Aql	III	35	15.3			18.1		ARO 163
064+02.1	K 4-33	19	45.72	+28	38.4	19	43.7	+28	31.	Vul								ARO 330
060−00.1	K 3-45	19	46.21	+24	11.4	19	44.1	+24	04.	Vul		7						
054−03.1	K 4-34	19	46.46	+17	01.4	19	44.2	+16	54.	Sge								ARO 331
017−21.1	Abell 65	19	46.59	−23	08.6	19	43.6	−23	16.	Sgr	IIa	104	15.2	13.2	Opk	15.9		ARO 36, ESO 526-03, Sh 2-52
059−01.1	He 1-3	19	48.46	+22	08.5	19	46.3	+22	01.	Vul	II	8		14.8				ARO 164, He 2-448
059−01.2	We 1-8	19	48.87	+22	25.2	19	46.72	+22	17.6	Vul		22				>20.		
082+11.1	NGC 6833	19	49.73	+48	57.6	19	48.3	+48	50.	Cyg	II	1	13.8	12.1	cont	14.8		ARO 105
069+03.1	K 3-46	19	50.00	+33	45.6	19	48.1	+33	38.	Cyg	IIIb+VI	>23						ARO 334
062−00.1	M 2-48	19	50.48	+25	54.7	19	48.4	+25	47.	Vul	III	8						ARO 190, He 2-449
066+02.1	K 4-37	19	50.97	+31	02.7	19	49.0	+30	55.	Cyg								
068+03.1	PC 23	19	51.92	+32	59.8	19	50.0	+32	52.	Cyg		<10						ARO 165, He 2-450
063+00.1	K 3-48	19	52.15	+27	18.8	19	50.1	+27	11.	Vul								
060−02.1	K 4-39	19	53.14	+23	13.8	19	51.0	+23	06.	Vul								ARO 337
069+02.1	K 3-49	19	54.02	+33	21.9	19	52.1	+33	14.	Cyg								ARO 338
065+00.1	NGC 6842	19	55.01	+29	17.0	19	53.0	+29	09.	Vul	IIIb	50	13.6	13.1		16.2		ARO 106, He 2-451

CATALOGUE OF PLANETARY NEBULAE—TABLE 39

PK Name	Alternate Name	2000.0 R.A. (h m)	2000.0 Dec. (° ′)	1950.0 R.A. (h m)	1950.0 Dec. (° ′)	Con	Nebula Type	Nebula Diam. (″)	Nebula Mag. p	Nebula Mag. v	Star Spectra	Star Mag. V	Star Name	Notes
068+01.1	K 4-41	19 56.55	+32 22.1	19 54.6	+32 14.	Cyg								
075+05.1	V1016 Cyg	19 57.1	+39 49.	19 55.3	+39 41.	Cyg	I							
014−25.1	We f	19 57.2	−26 39.	19 55.1	−26 31	Sgr		36				18.5:		HtDe 12, HtWe 14
019−23.1	Abell 66	19 57.55	−21 36.9	19 54.6	−21 45.	Sgr	IIIb	251	14.9			16.9		ARO 339, ESO 595-04
043−13.1	Abell 67	19 58.41	+03 03.2	19 55.9	+02 55.	Aql	IIb	66	16.0			18.3		ARO 117
068+01.2	He 1-4	19 59.26	+31 55.2	19 57.3	+31 47.	Cyg	IIIb	22		14.7:		21.07		ARO 191, He 2-453
060−03.1	NGC 6853	19 59.56	+22 43.3	19 57.4	+22 35.	Vul	III+II	>348	7.6	7.4	O7	13.8		M.27, ARO 14, He 2-452
060−04.1	Abell 68	20 00.18	+21 43.3	19 58.0	+21 35.	Vul	III	39	16.6	15.2		18.8		ARO 166
042−14.1	NGC 6852	20 00.63	+01 43.3	19 58.1	+01 35.	Aql	IV	28		12.6:		17.90		ARO 167, K 1-18
058−05.1	WeSb 5	20 01.7	+19 54.	19 59.5	+19 46.	Sge		152						
056−06.1	K 3-51	20 02.56	+17 36.4	20 00.3	+17 28.	Sge				14.4				ARO 340
067−00.1	K 3-52	20 03.20	+30 32.5	20 01.2	+30 24.	Cyg								
064−02.1	K 3-53	20 03.37	+27 00.5	20 01.3	+26 52.	Vul				16.0				ARO 341
084+09.1	K 3-73	20 03.98	+49 19.2	20 02.53	+49 10.6	Cyg		<17		15.0				
075+04.1	ARO 342	20 04.37	+39 34.6	20 02.6	+39 26.	Cyg		28						
107+21.1	K 1-6	20 04.46	+74 26.7	20 05.3	+74 18.	Dra	II	216				17.58		
068−00.1	M 1-75	20 04.78	+31 27.6	20 02.8	+31 19.	Cyg	IIIb+VI	>14		16.0		>21.		ARO 168, He 2-454
063−03.1	K 3-54	20 05.01	+25 26.6	20 02.9	+25 18.	Vul								ARO 343
079+06.1	K 3-56	20 06.94	+44 14.7	20 05.3	+44 06.	Cyg	II	4						ARO 345
069+00.1	K 3-55	20 06.96	+32 16.7	20 05.0	+32 08.	Cyg								
078+05.1	K 3-74	20 08.72	+42 30.1	20 07.02	+42 21.3	Cyg		22						Dd 1
079+05.1	M 4-17	20 09.06	+43 43.9	20 07.4	+43 35.	Cyg	IV+II	>19		13.7				ARO 346
065−03.1	We 1-9	20 09.07	+26 26.9	20 06.98	+26 18.0	Vul		25				>20.		
082+07.1	NGC 6884	20 10.37	+46 27.9	20 08.8	+46 19.	Cyg	IIb	6	12.6	10.9	WR	15.8		ARO 57
057−08.1	NGC 6879	20 10.48	+16 54.9	20 08.2	+16 46.	Sge	IIa	5	13.0	12.5	Of+WR	15.		ARO 107, He 2-455
074+02.1	NGC 6881	20 10.84	+37 25.0	20 09.0	+37 16.	Cyg	IIa+III	4	14.3	13.9				ARO 108, He 2-456
060−07.1	He 1-5	20 11.92	+20 20.0	20 09.7	+20 11.	Sge	III+II	>29		16.0	var	var.	FG Sge	ARO 169, He 2-457
077+03.1	K 4-51	20 12.40	+40 45.5	20 10.64	+40 36.4	Cyg		13						KjPn 1
060−07.2	NGC 6886	20 12.72	+19 59.1	20 10.5	+19 50.	Sge	II+III	4	12.2	11.4	cont	18.		ARO 109, He 2-458
072+00.1	K 3-57	20 12.83	+34 20.1	20 10.9	+34 11.	Cyg								
068−02.1	He 2-459	20 13.93	+29 34.2	20 11.9	+29 25.	Cyg		<10						ARO 347
054−12.1	NGC 6891	20 15.15	+12 42.2	20 12.8	+12 33.	Del	IIa+IIb	>14	11.7	10.5	O7	12.44	HD 192563	ARO 37
077+03.2	K 3-75	20 15.37	+40 34.7	20 13.60	+40 25.5	Cyg		14						KjPn 2

CATALOGUE OF PLANETARY NEBULAE—TABLE 40

PK Name	Alternate Name	2000.0				1950.0				Con	Nebula				Star			Notes
		R.A.		Dec.		R.A.		Dec.			Type	Diam.	Mag.		Spectra	Mag.	Name	
		h	m	°	′	h	m	°	′			″	p	v		V		
069−02.1	NGC 6894	20	16.42	+30	34.3	20	14.4	+30	25.	Cyg	IV+II	>42	14.4	12.3		17.6		ARO 110, He 2-460
076+01.2	K 4-52	20	17.25	+38	50.3	20	15.43	+38	40.9	Cyg		7						KjPn 3
065−05.1	He 1-6	20	17.33	+25	22.4	20	15.2	+25	13.	Vul	III+II	>17		14.8				ARO 171, He 2-462
077+02.1	Kj 2-1	20	17.40	+39	45.3	20	15.6	+39	35.9	Cyg								
066−05.1	He 1-7	20	19.60	+27	00.5	20	17.5	+26	51.	Vul		5						ARO 192, He 2-463
076+01.1	Abell 69	20	19.94	+38	24.5	20	18.1	+38	15.	Cyg		22	>20.1			>21.		ARO 15
058−10.1	IC 4997	20	20.19	+16	44.5	20	17.9	+16	35.	Sge	I	2	11.6	10.5	Of+WR	15.4:	HD 193538	ARO 38, He 2-464
071−02.1	M 3-35	20	21.08	+32	29.6	20	19.1	+32	20.	Cyg	I	<5		14.5		15.7		ARO 172, He 2-465
069−03.1	K 3-58	20	21.94	+29	59.6	20	19.9	+29	50.	Cyg	?+III	>8		16.::				ARO 348
061−09.1	NGC 6905	20	22.43	+20	06.7	20	20.2	+19	57.	Del	III+III	>39	11.9	11.1	WC6	15.5	HD 193949	ARO 75, He 2-466
079+00.1	KjPn 4	20	28.81	+40	24.7	20	27.0	+40	14.7	Cyg		7						
078+00.1	Sd 1	20	29.31	+40	15.4	20	27.50	+40	05.3	Cyg		10						K 3-77, KjPn 5
038−25.1	Abell 70	20	31.57	−07	05.8	20	28.9	−07	16.	Aql	IV	43	14.3	14.5		18.4		ARO 351
086+05.1	We 1-10	20	31.88	+48	52.6	20	30.32	+48	42.4	Cyg		191		15.1		18.7		
085+04.1	Abell 71	20	32.41	+47	21.3	20	30.8	+47	11.	Cyg	IIIb	157	15.2	14.0		19.0		ARO 352, Sh 2-116
073−02.1	K 3-76	20	35.09	+33	35.4	20	33.11	+33	25.0	Cyg		<9						
078−02.1	K 4-53	20	42.26	+37	40.5	20	40.35	+37	29.7	Cyg		21						
084+01.1	K 4-55	20	45.16	+44	39.3	20	43.43	+44	28.3	Cyg		28						
088+04.1	K 3-78	20	45.37	+50	22.7	20	43.82	+50	11.7	Cyg		<7						
059−18.1	Abell 72	20	50.06	+13	33.2	20	47.7	+13	22.	Del	IIIb	130	14.6	13.8		15.0		ARO 173
092+05.1	K 3-79	20	53.23	+53	45.7	20	51.77	+53	34.3	Cyg		12						
086+00.1	K 4-56	20	55.73	+46	33.2	20	54.02	+46	21.7	Cyg		<8						
095+07.1	Abell 73	20	56.51	+57	26.6	20	55.2	+57	15.	Cep	IV	73	>17.4	16.5		20.5		
093+05.2	NGC 7008	21	00.56	+54	32.8	20	59.1	+54	21.	Cyg	III	83	13.3	10.7	O7	13.2		ARO 39
037−34.1	NGC 7009	21	04.22	−11	22.0	21	01.5	−11	34.	Aqr	IV+VI	>25	8.3	8.0	cont	11.5	HD 200516	ARO 16
006−41.1	A 06-09	21	05.8	−37	07.	21	02.7	−37	20.	Mic		8				17.0		galactic halo object
089+00.1	NGC 7026	21	06.32	+47	51.1	21	04.6	+47	39.	Cyg	IIIa	21	12.7	10.9	WC	14.8	HD 201192	ARO 59
084−03.1	NGC 7027	21	07.07	+42	14.1	21	05.2	+42	02.	Cyg	IIIa	15	10.4	8.5		16.32		ARO 40
084−04.1	K 3-80	21	07.67	+40	58.0	21	05.77	+40	45.8	Cyg		<10						
091+01.1	We 1-11	21	10.87	+50	47.1	21	09.23	+50	34.8	Cyg		25				>20.		
089−00.1	Sh 1-89	21	14.05	+47	45.5	21	12.3	+47	33.	Cyg	III+VI	>35		14.8		19.1		ARO 357
088−01.1	NGC 7048	21	14.19	+46	16.5	21	12.4	+46	04.	Cyg	IIIb	61	11.3	12.1		18.		ARO 41, Hb 9

CATALOGUE OF PLANETARY NEBULAE—TABLE 41

PK Name	Alternate Name	2000.0 R.A. (h m)	2000.0 Dec. (° ′)	1950.0 R.A. (h m)	1950.0 Dec. (° ′)	Con	Nebula Type	Nebula Diam. (″)	Nebula Mag. p	Nebula Mag. v	Star Spectra	Star Mag. V	Star Name	Notes
072−17.1	Abell 74	21 16.83	+24 09.6	21 14.6	+23 57.	Vul	II	831	>12.2		sdO	17.1		ARO 193
087−03.1	We 2-245	21 18.12	+43 48.7	21 16.25	+43 36.0	Cyg		35						
089−02.1	M 1-77	21 19.11	+46 18.7	21 17.3	+46 06.	Cyg	IIa	7						ARO 42
083−08.1	K 3-81	21 22.28	+38 07.3	21 20.27	+37 54.4	Cyg		<11		15.5:				
101+08.1	Abell 75	21 26.41	+62 53.1	21 25.2	+62 40.	Cep	IIIb	57	17.0			17.4		ARO 359
098+04.1	K 3-60	21 27.48	+57 39.1	21 26.0	+57 26.	Cep				16.2				
094−00.2	IRAS 21282+5050	21 30.0	+51 04.	21 28.3	+50 51.	Cyg					WC 11	14.4		
096+02.1	K 3-61	21 30.01	+54 27.2	21 28.4	+54 14.	Cyg		6						
065−27.1	Ps 1	21 30.02	+12 10.2	21 27.6	+11 57.	Peg	I	3	14.9	15.5				in glob. cluster M.15
093−00.1	K 3-82	21 30.87	+50 00.1	21 29.11	+49 46.9	Cyg		<24		14.9:				
095+00.1	K 3-62	21 31.88	+52 34.3	21 30.2	+52 21.	Cyg				15.6				ARO 362
097+03.1	Abell 77	21 32.17	+55 53.3	21 30.6	+55 40.	Cep	IIIa+III	37	16.4					ARO 363, Sh 2-128
089−05.1	IC 5117	21 32.50	+44 35.3	21 30.6	+44 22.	Cyg	II	1	13.3	11.5	WR	17.2	HD 205211	ARO 112
086−08.1	Hu 1-2	21 33.11	+39 38.3	21 31.1	+39 25.	Cyg	II	5	12.7	12.0				ARO 89
081−14.1	Abell 78	21 35.56	+31 41.4	21 33.4	+31 28.	Cyg	IV	101	16.0	13.4	O5	12.3		ARO 174
094−00.1	K 3-83	21 35.73	+50 54.3	21 33.98	+50 40.8	Cyg		<9						
066−28.1	NGC 7094	21 36.91	+12 47.5	21 34.5	+12 34.	Peg	IV	95		13.4	O	13.73		ARO 194, K 1-19
093−02.1	M 1-79	21 37.01	+48 56.5	21 35.2	+48 43.	Cyg	IV	32		13.2				ARO 365
091−04.1	K 3-84	21 38.81	+46 00.5	21 36.92	+45 46.9	Cyg		<12						
098+02.1	K 3-63	21 39.22	+55 45.6	21 37.6	+55 32.	Cep	II	7		16.0				ARO 366
095−02.1	M 2-49	21 43.30	+50 24.8	21 41.5	+50 11.	Cyg	I			14.3				ARO 367
104+07.1	NGC 7139	21 45.92	+63 38.9	21 44.6	+63 25.	Cep	IIIb	78	<13.	13.3		18.1		ARO 54
097−02.1	M 2-50	21 57.74	+51 41.3	21 55.9	+51 27.	Cyg	II	4		14.7				ARO 368
002−52.1	IC 5148-50	21 59.53	−39 22.6	21 56.5	−39 37.	Gru	IV	120		11.::	cont			ESO 344-05
107+07.1	IsWe 2	22 13.3	+65 53.	22 11.9	+65 39.	Cep		900				17.71		
103+00.1	M 2-51	22 16.09	+57 29.0	22 14.3	+57 14.	Cep	II+III	>41		13.5				ARO 369
111+11.1	DeHt 5	22 19.6	+70 56.	22 18.4	+70 41.	Cep		526				15.3		
104+00.1	Bl 2-1	22 20.30	+58 14.1	22 18.5	+57 59.	Cep								ARO 370
103+00.2	M 2-52	22 20.52	+57 36.1	22 18.7	+57 21.	Cep	III	13		15.3				ARO 371
353−55.1	ESO 289-19	22 21.12	−43 52.9	22 18.10	−44 08.0	Gru		12						
100−05.1	IC 5217	22 23.90	+50 58.2	22 21.9	+50 43.	Lac	II	6	12.6	11.3		15.4		ARO 85
102−02.1	Abell 79	22 26.33	+54 49.3	22 24.4	+54 34.	Lac	IV+III	>59	15.8	15.0		17.6		ARO 372
036−57.1	NGC 7293	22 29.63	−20 47.6	22 26.9	−21 03.	Aqr	IV+III	>769		7.3	sdO	13.62		ARO 17
099−08.1	HtDe 13	22 30.2	+47 30.	22 28.1	+47 15.	Lac	III	178				18.1:		HtWe 15

CATALOGUE OF PLANETARY NEBULAE—TABLE 42

PK Name	Alternate Name	2000.0 R.A. (h m)	2000.0 Dec. (° ′)	1950.0 R.A. (h m)	1950.0 Dec. (° ′)	Con	Nebula Type	Nebula Diam. (″)	Nebula Mag. p	Nebula Mag. v	Star Spectra	Star Mag. V	Star Name	Notes
100−08.1	Me 2-2	22 31.70	+47 48.4	22 29.6	+47 33.	Lac	I	1		11.9				ARO 373
104−01.1	M 2-53	22 32.34	+56 10.5	22 30.4	+55 55.	Lac	IIIb	14		14.8	WR			ARO 374
102−05.1	Abell 80	22 34.73	+52 26.5	22 32.7	+52 11.	Lac	IV	132	15.2	16.0		19.61		ARO 375
107+02.1	NGC 7354	22 40.37	+61 16.7	22 38.5	+61 01.	Cep	IV+IIIb	>20	12.9	12.2	cont	16.1		ARO 55
117+18.1	IC 1454	22 42.59	+80 26.8	22 42.2	+80 11.	Cep	IV	33	14.8	14.:		18.0		ARO 376, Abell 81
107−00.1	K 4-57	22 48.58	+58 29.1	22 46.58	+58 13.2	Cep								
111+06.1	K 4-58	22 49.03	+67 01.7	22 47.27	+66 45.8	Cep		15						KjPn 6
108+00.1	K 3-85	22 50.89	+59 30.3	22 48.89	+59 14.4	Cep		<7						
106−04.1	K 3-86	22 54.76	+54 56.0	22 52.65	+54 40.0	Lac		10						
107−02.2	K 3-87	22 55.11	+56 42.5	22 53.03	+56 26.5	Lac		<7						
107−02.1	M 1-80	22 56.28	+57 09.3	22 54.2	+56 53.3	Cep	II	8	14.0	14.0	cont			ARO 113
112+03.1	K 3-88	23 12.25	+64 39.3	23 10.18	+64 23.0	Cep		<9						
110−01.1	WeSb 6	23 13.1	+59 17.	23 10.9	+59 01.	Cep		82						
111−03.1	We 2-260	23 22.35	+57 46.1	23 20.08	+57 29.6	Cas		140						
107−13.1	Vy 2-3	23 22.96	+46 54.5	23 20.6	+46 38.	And	II	5	13.9	13.6	cont			ARO 380
112−00.1	K 3-89	23 24.17	+60 57.5	23 21.93	+60 41.0	Cas		13						KjPn 8
106−17.1	NGC 7662	23 25.91	+42 32.5	23 23.5	+42 16.	And	IV+III	>12	9.2	8.3	cont	12.5	HD 220733	ARO 20
111−02.1	Hb 12	23 26.29	+58 10.5	23 24.0	+57 54.	Cas		1	14.0	11.9		15.		ARO 381
116+08.1	M 2-55	23 31.87	+70 22.6	23 29.7	+70 06.	Cep	III	40		14.2				ARO 382
104−29.1	Jones 1	23 35.89	+30 27.6	23 33.4	+30 11.	Peg	IIIb	332	15.1	12.1	PG 1159	16.1		ARO 195
110−12.1	K 1-20	23 39.14	+48 12.6	23 36.7	+47 56.	And	IV	34		16.::		20.1		ARO 384
114−04.1	Abell 82	23 45.85	+57 03.7	23 43.4	+56 47.	Cas	IIIb	95	15.2	12.7		14.92		ARO 114
113−06.1	Abell 83	23 46.76	+54 44.7	23 44.3	+54 28.	Cas	IIc	40	17.6			>20.0		ARO 385
112−10.1	Abell 84	23 47.68	+51 23.7	23 45.2	+51 07.	Cas	IIIb	126	14.4	13.0		18.0		ARO 115
116+00.1	We 2-262	23 52.33	+62 30.7	23 49.85	+62 14.	Cas		130						
118+08.1	M 2-56	23 56.60	+70 48.7	23 54.1	+70 32.	Cep	I			12.0		>21.		ARO 386

The Atlas of Planetary Nebulae

See page 261 for Index to Charts

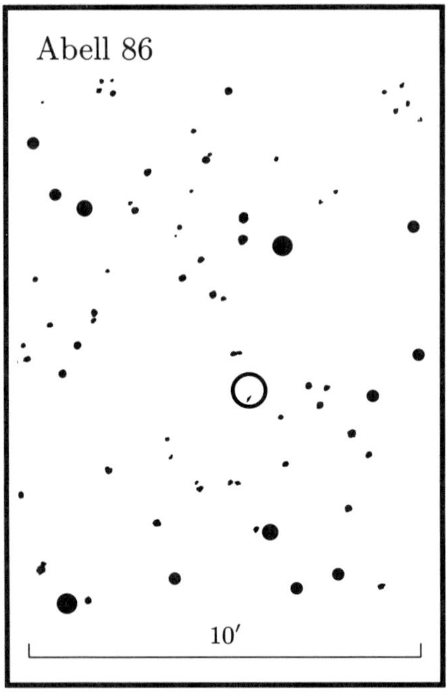
Abell 86
10′

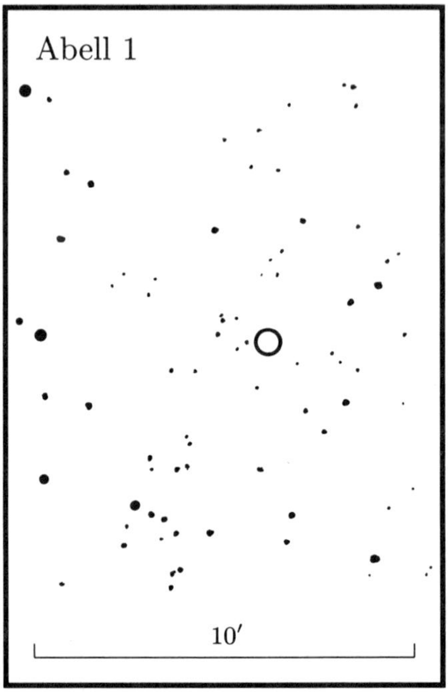
Abell 1
10′

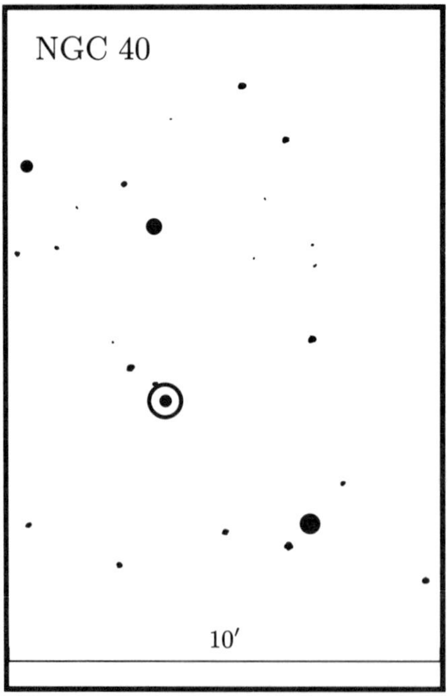
NGC 40
10′

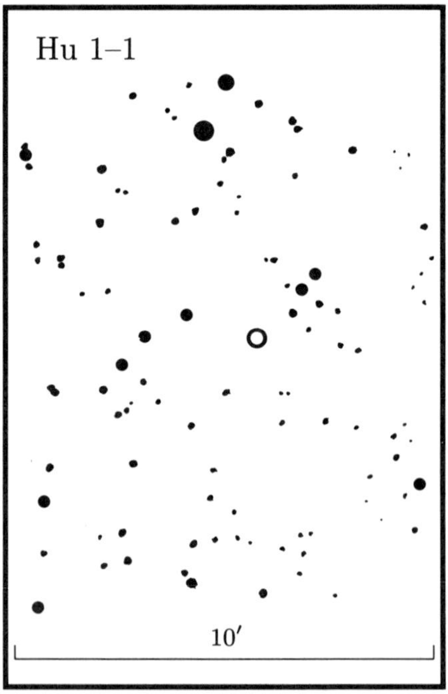
Hu 1–1
10′

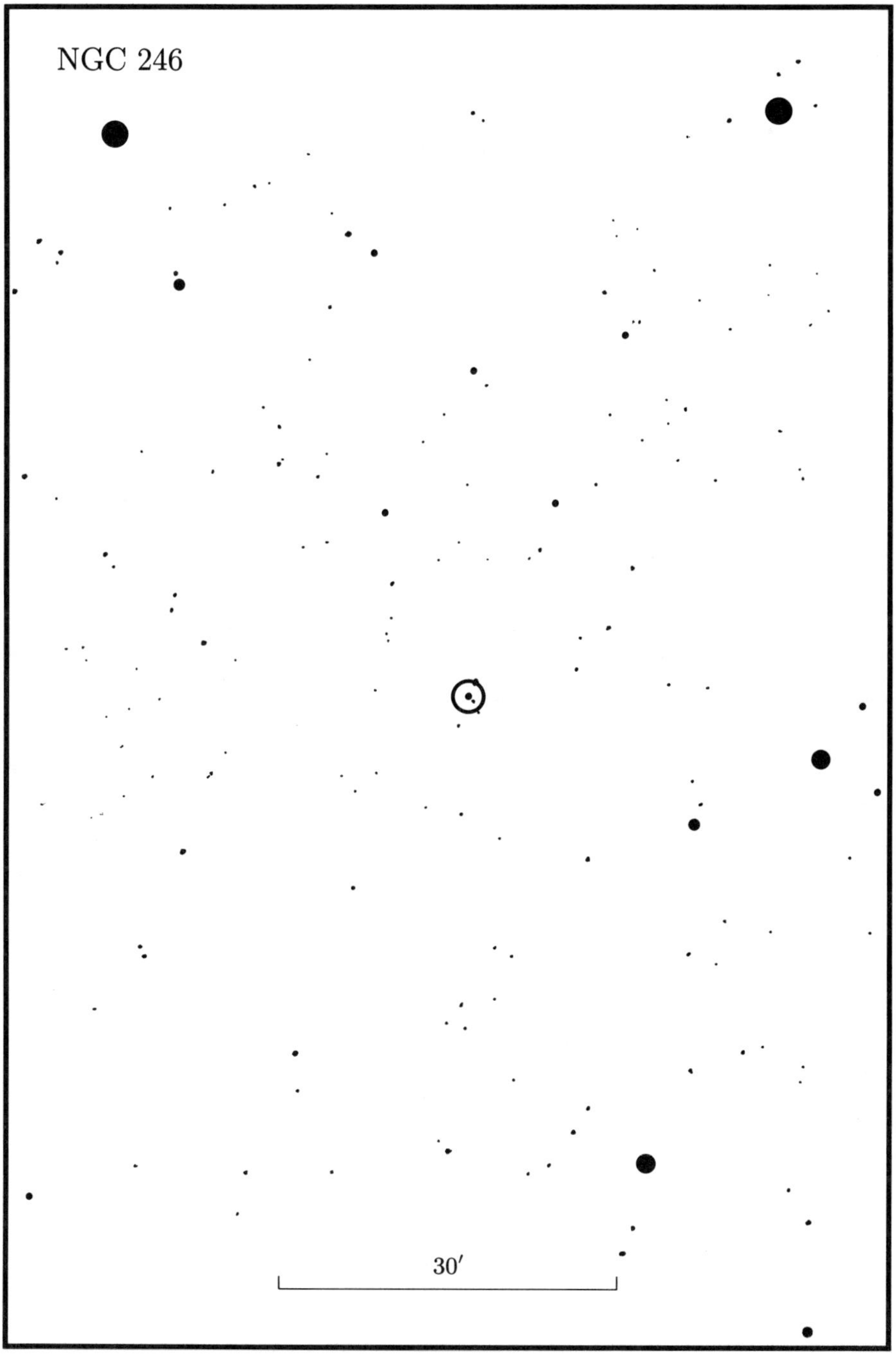
NGC 246
30′

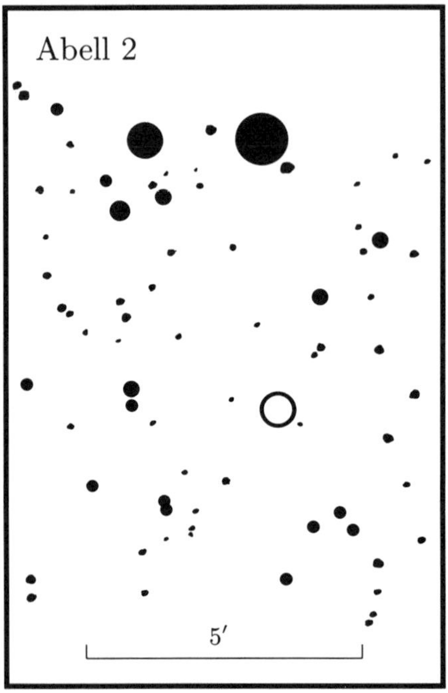
Abell 2
5′

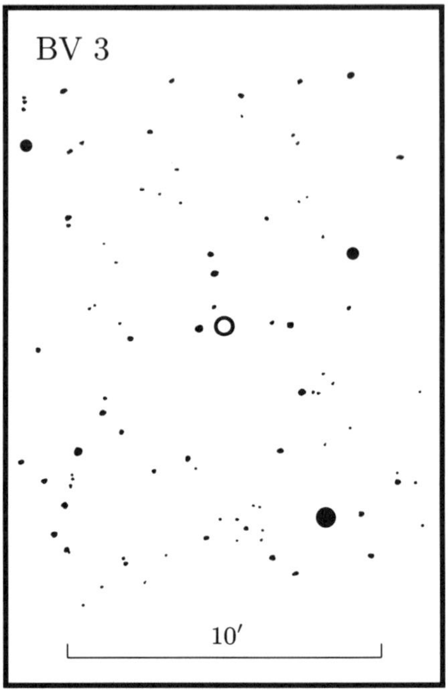
BV 3
10′

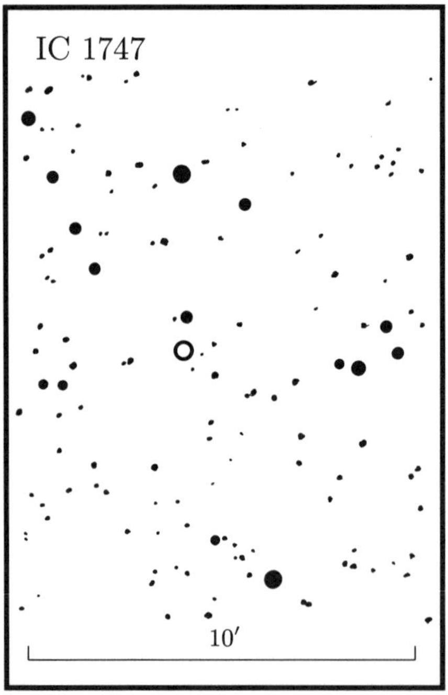
IC 1747
10′

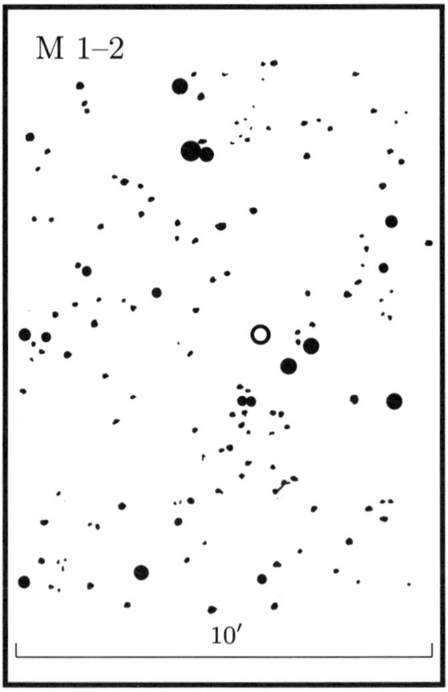
M 1–2
10′

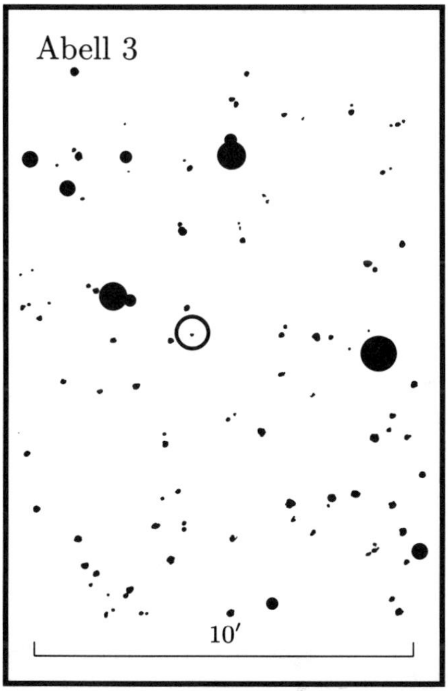
Abell 3
10′

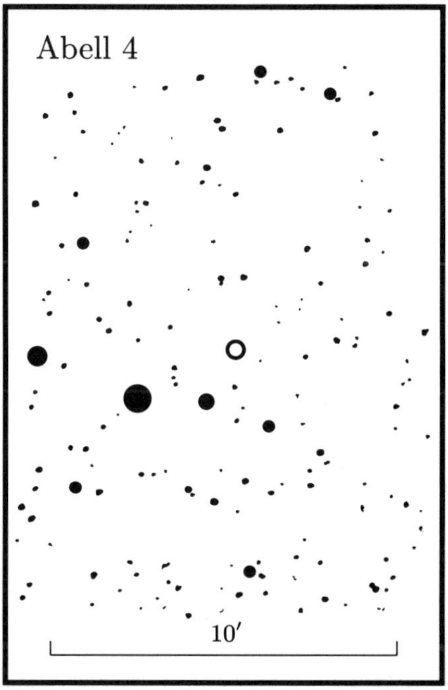
Abell 4
10′

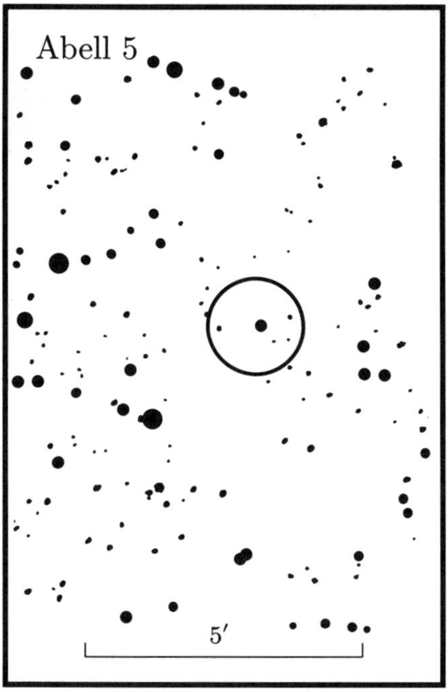
Abell 5
5′

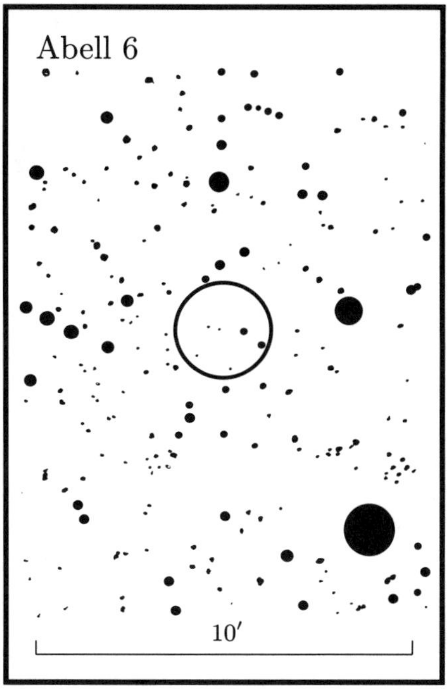
Abell 6
10′

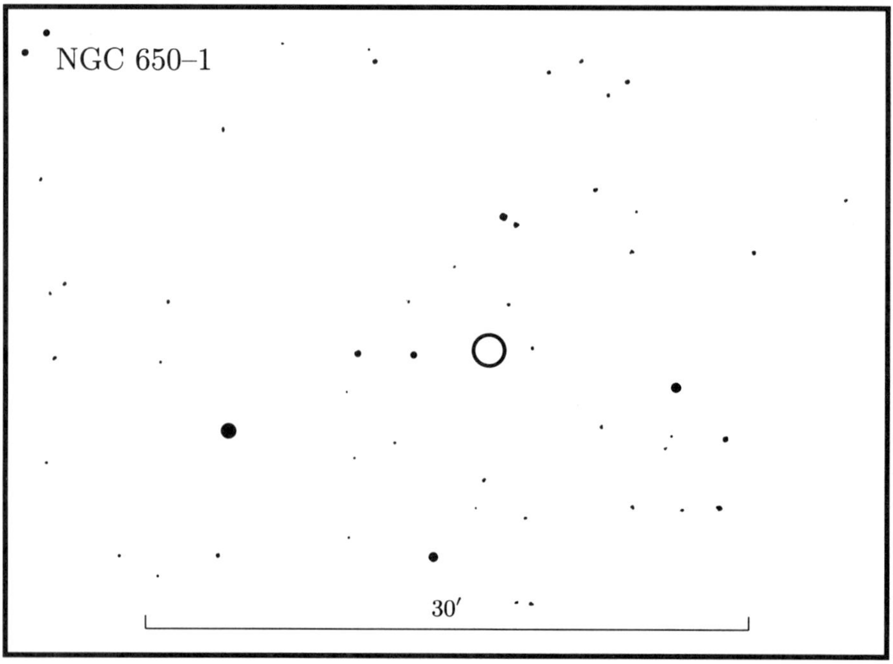
NGC 650–1
30′

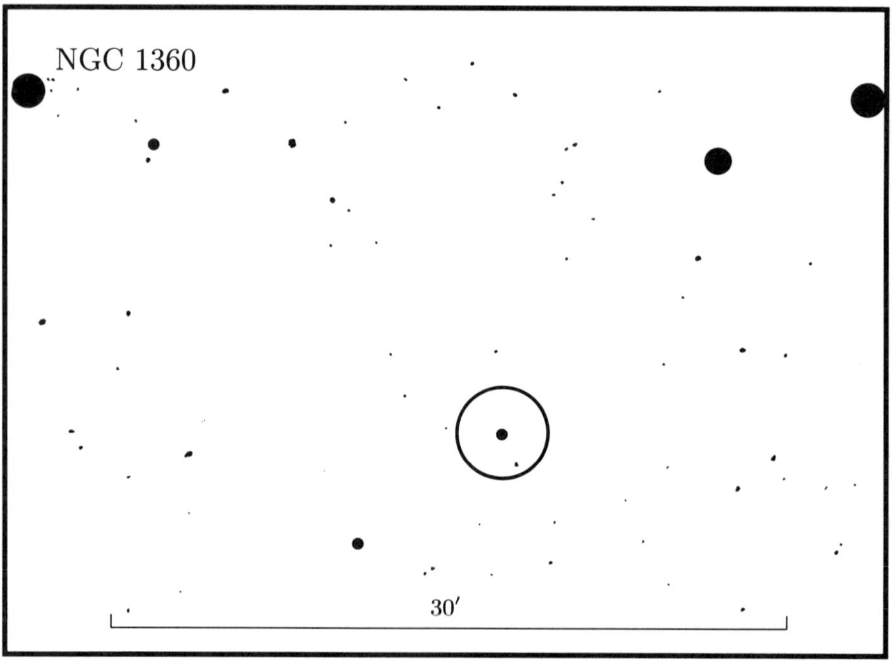
NGC 1360
30′

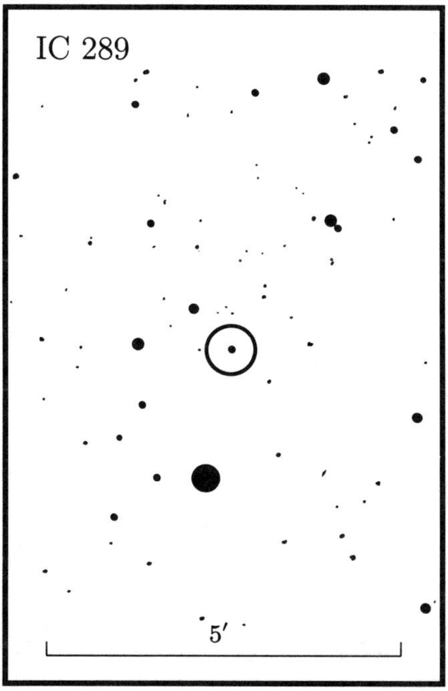
IC 289
5′

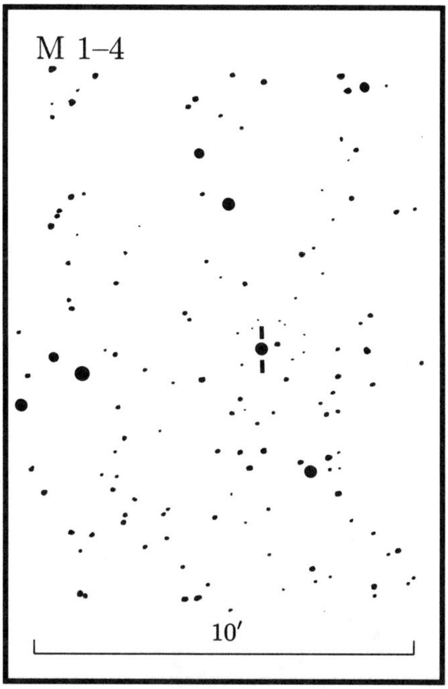
M 1–4
10′

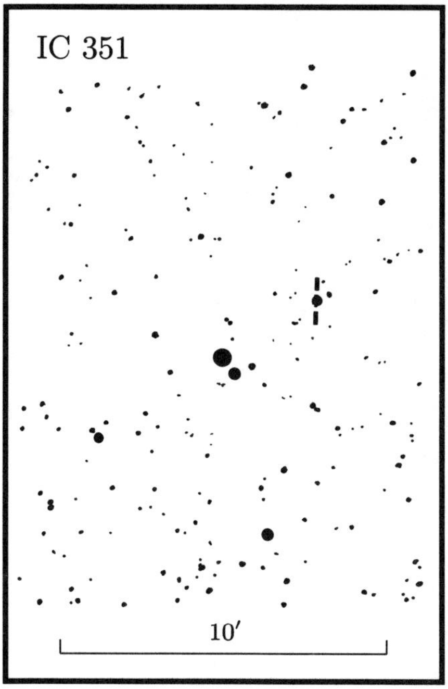
IC 351
10′

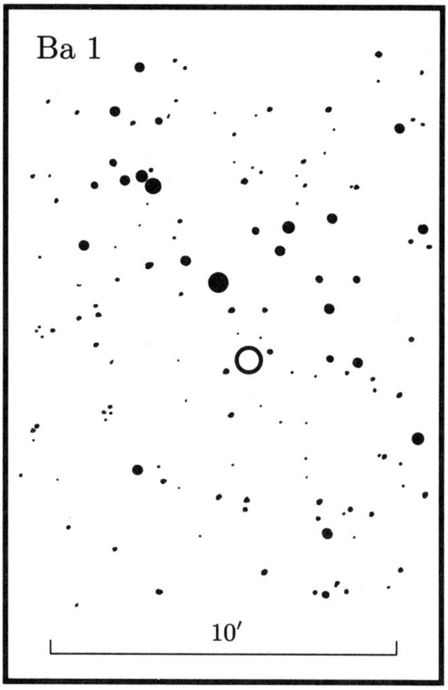
Ba 1
10′

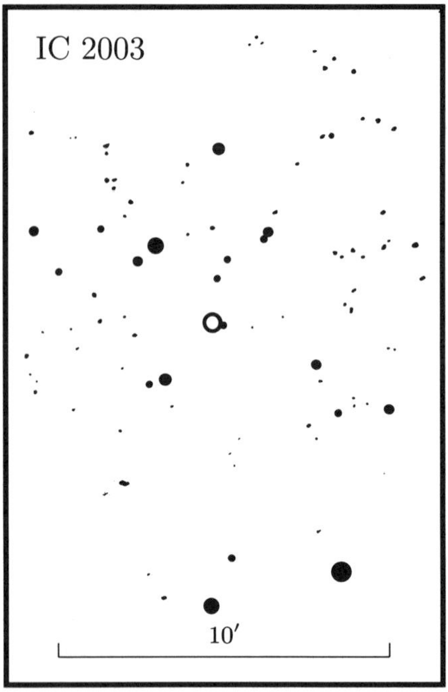
IC 2003
10′

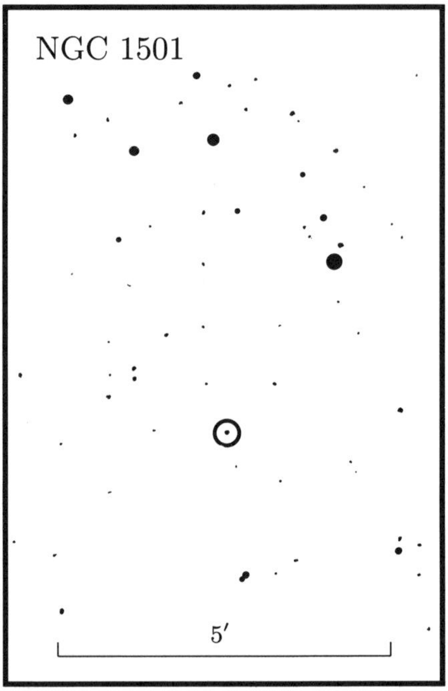
NGC 1501
5′

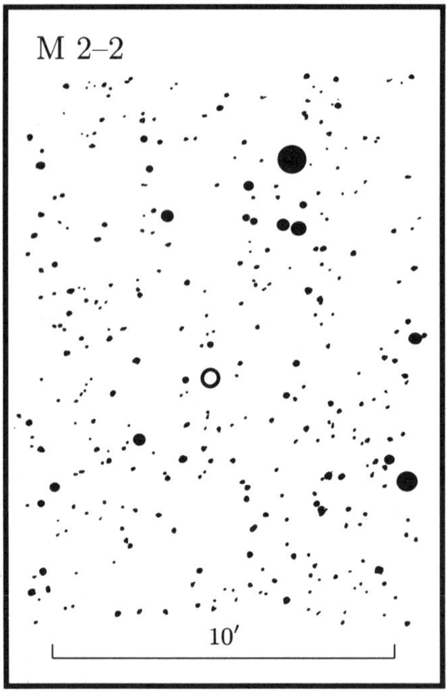
M 2–2
10′

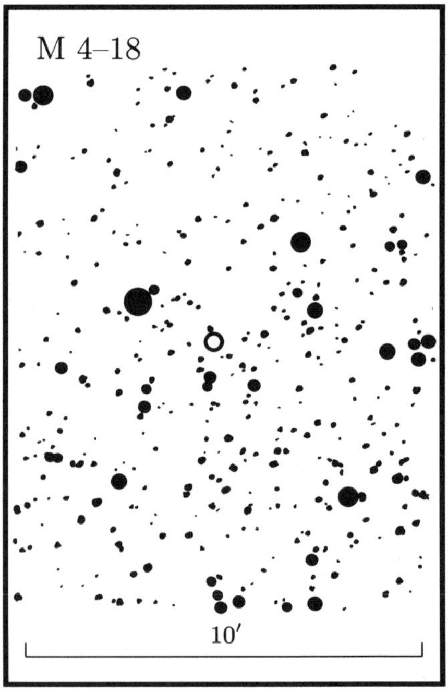
M 4–18
10′

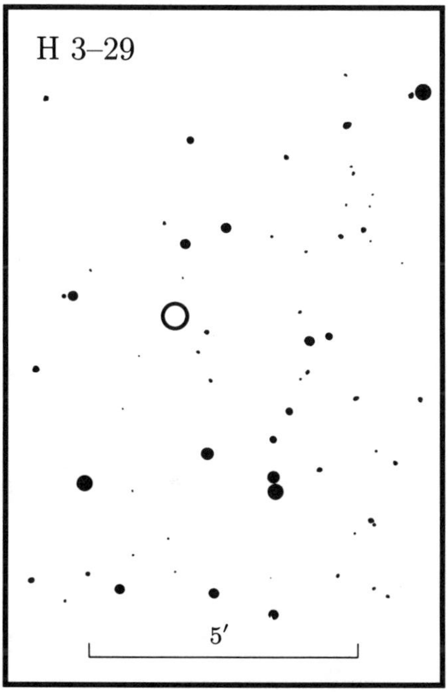
H 3–29
5′

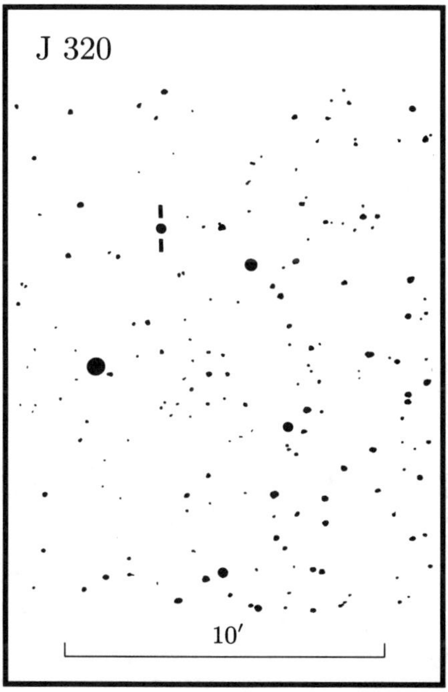
J 320
10′

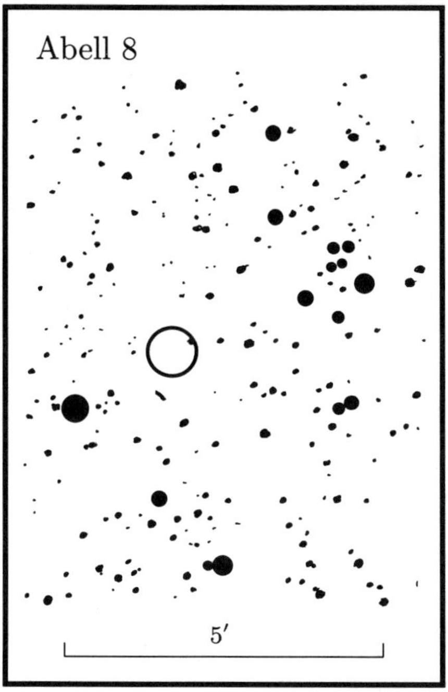
Abell 8
5′

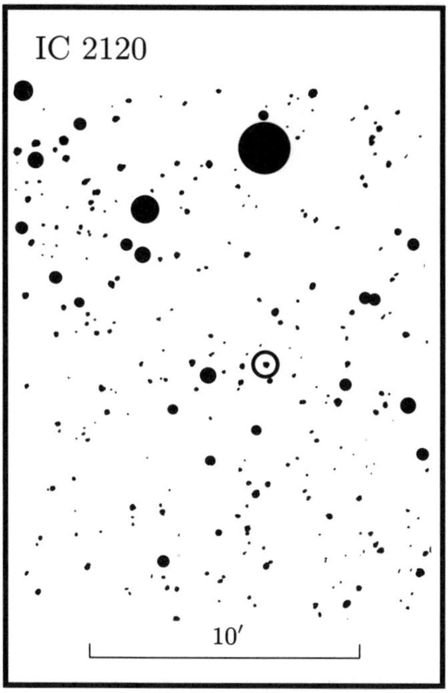
IC 2120
10′

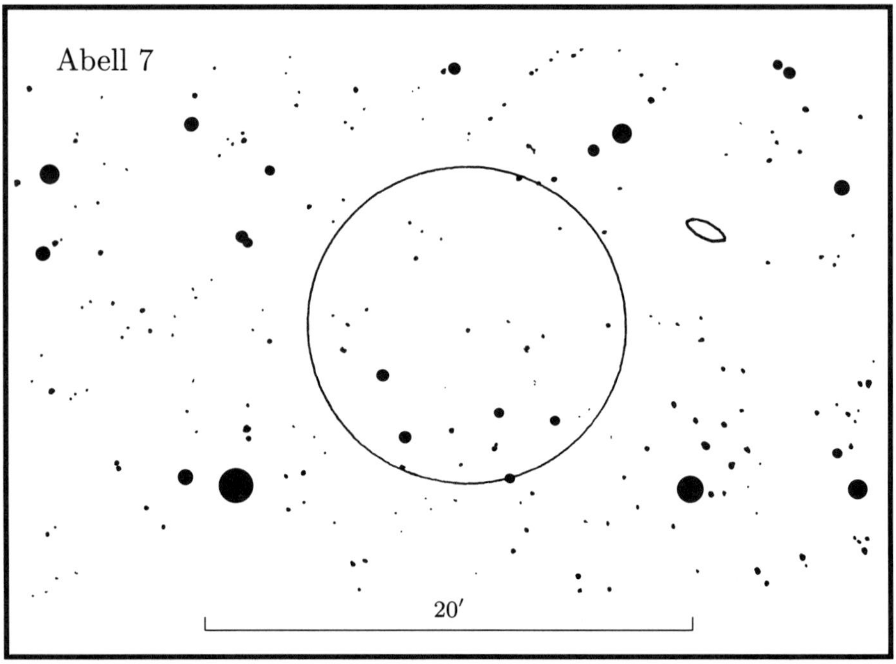
Abell 7
20′

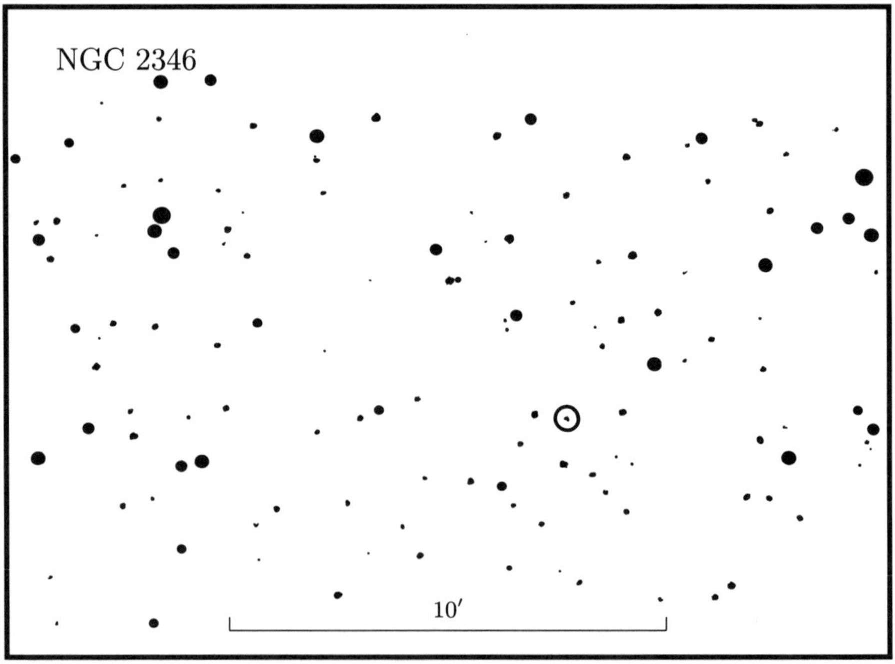
NGC 2346
10′

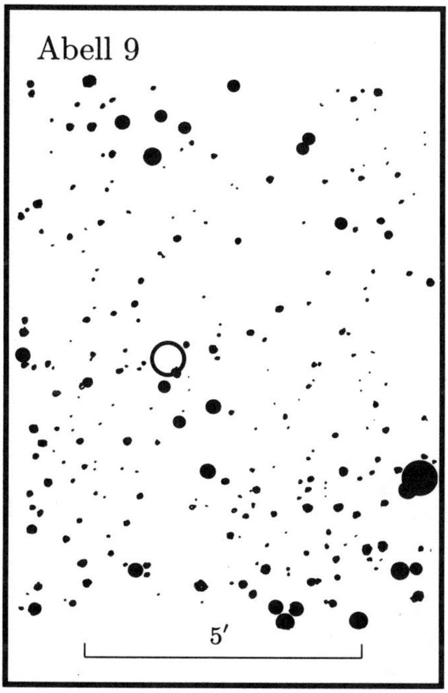
Abell 9
5′

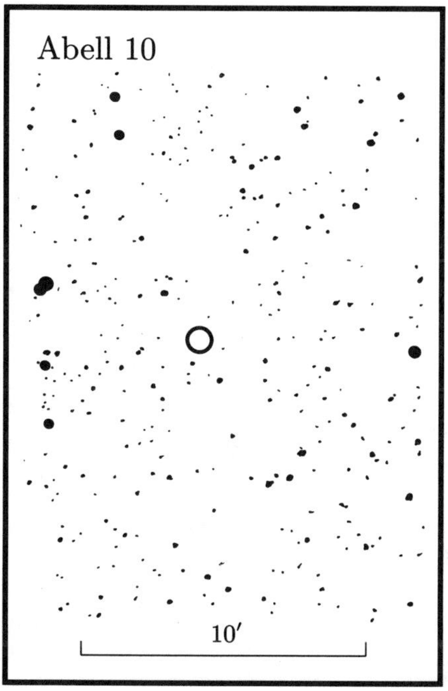
Abell 10
10′

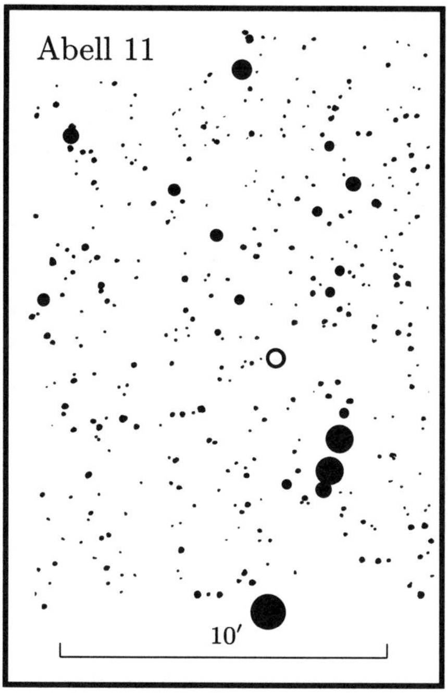
Abell 11
10′

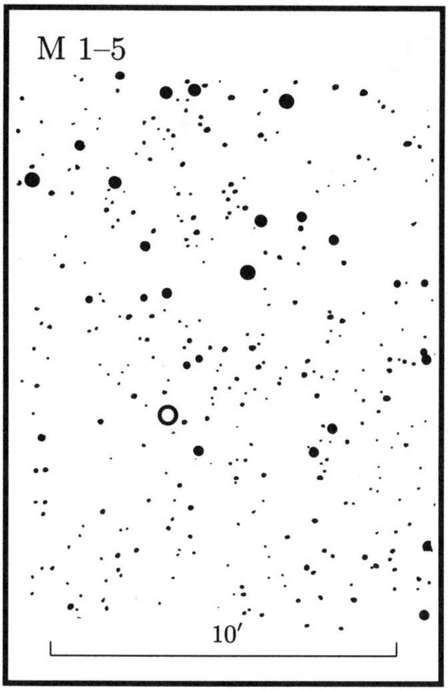
M 1–5
10′

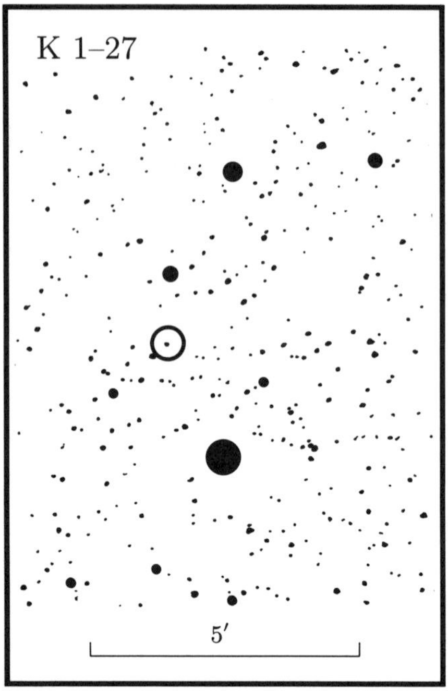
K 1–27
5′

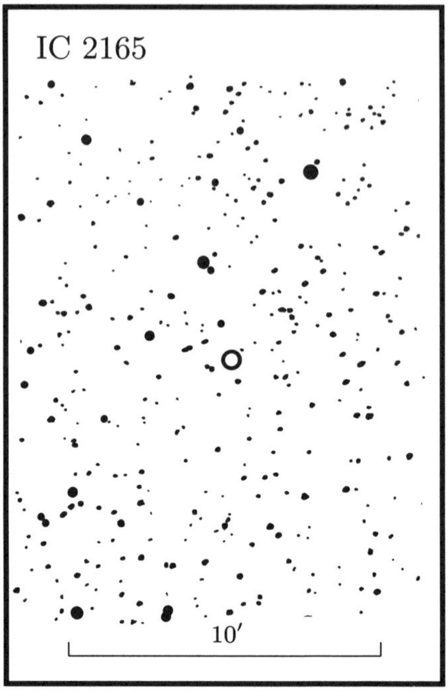
IC 2165
10′

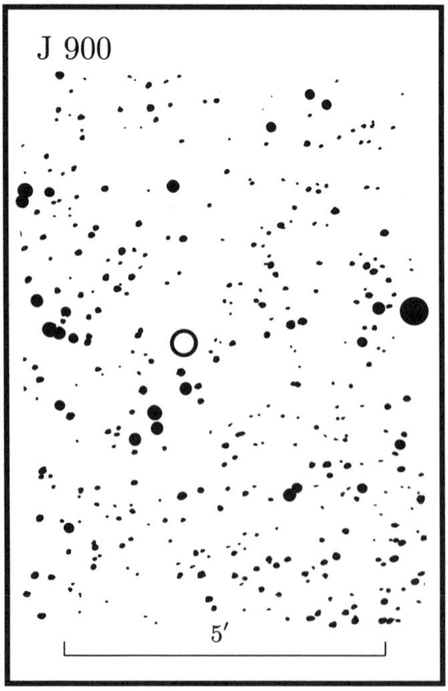
J 900
5′

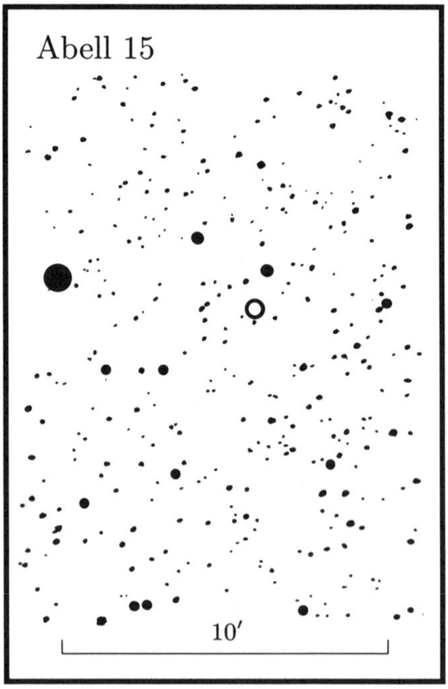
Abell 15
10′

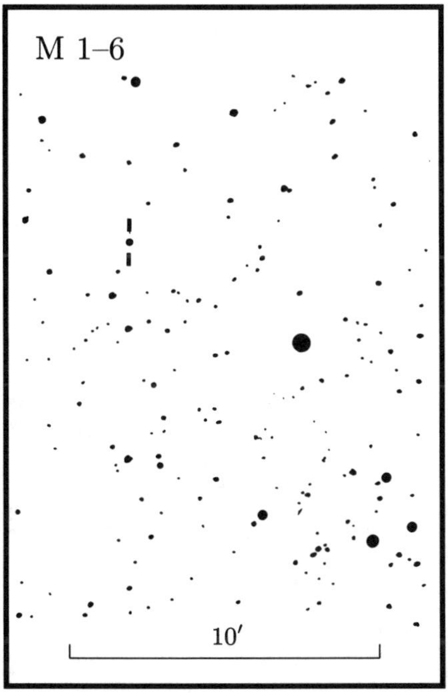
M 1–6
10′

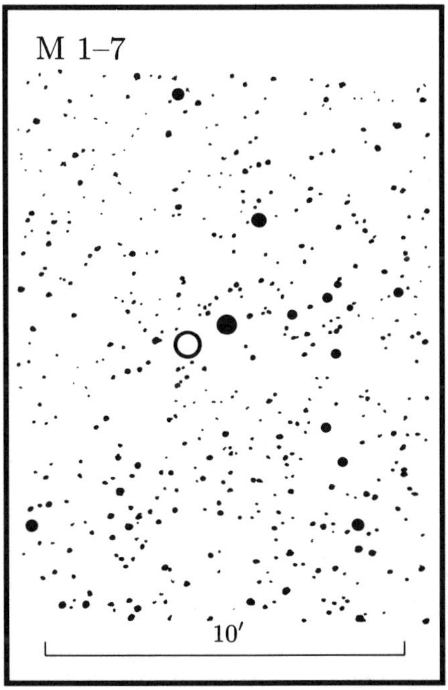
M 1–7
10′

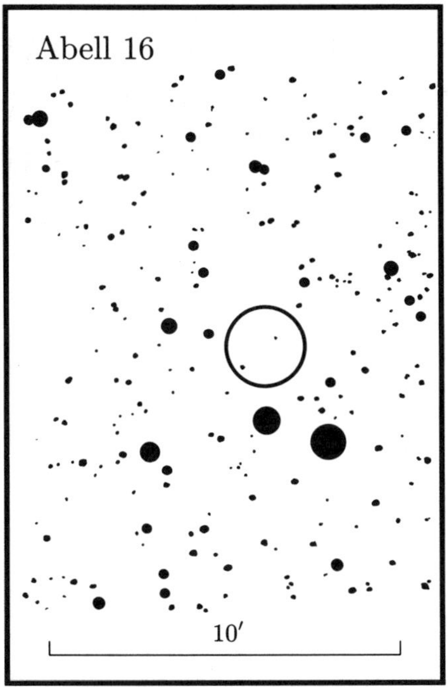
Abell 16
10′

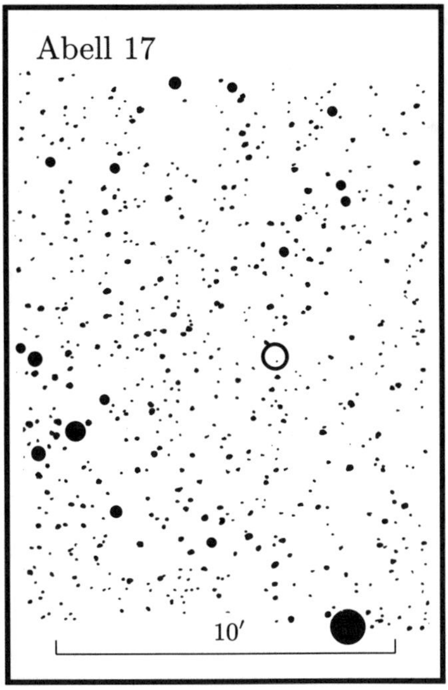
Abell 17
10′

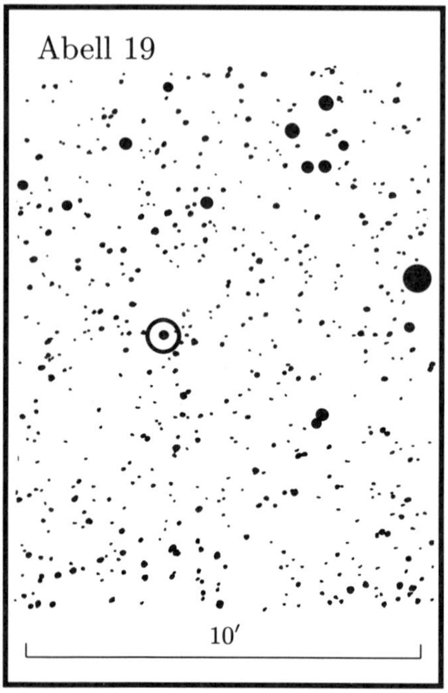
Abell 19
10′

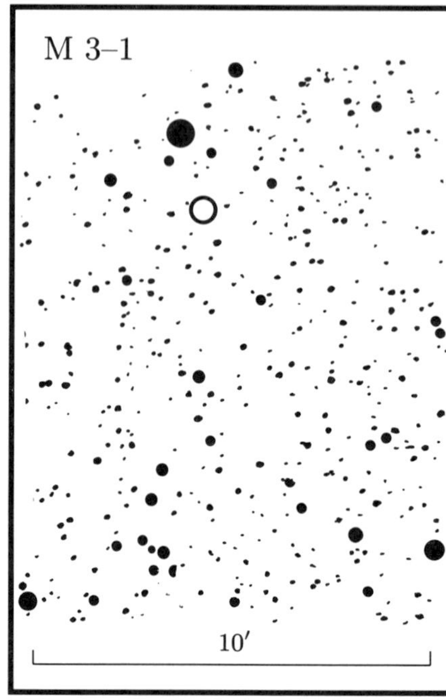
M 3–1
10′

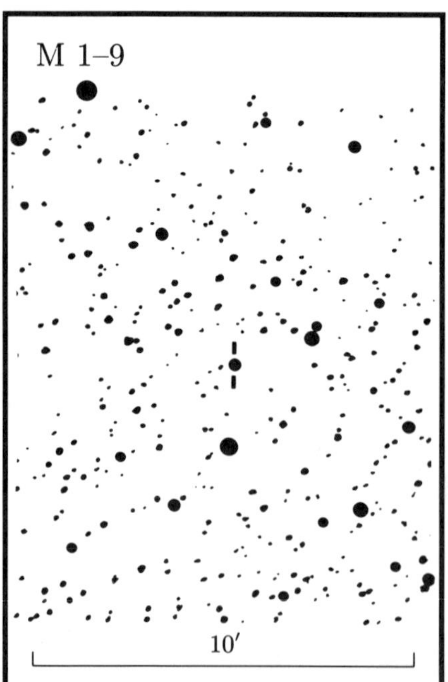
M 1–9
10′

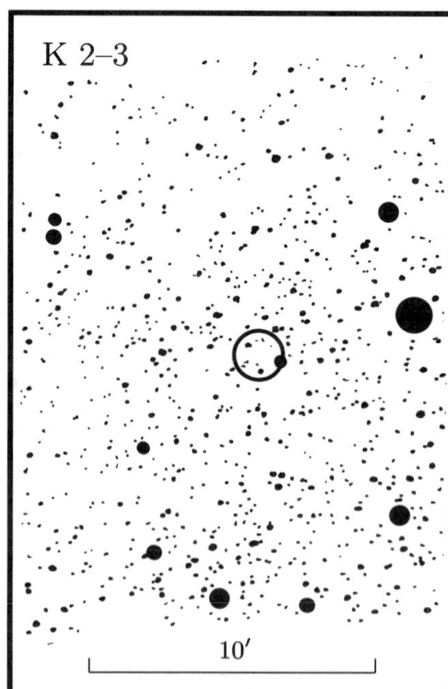
K 2–3
10′

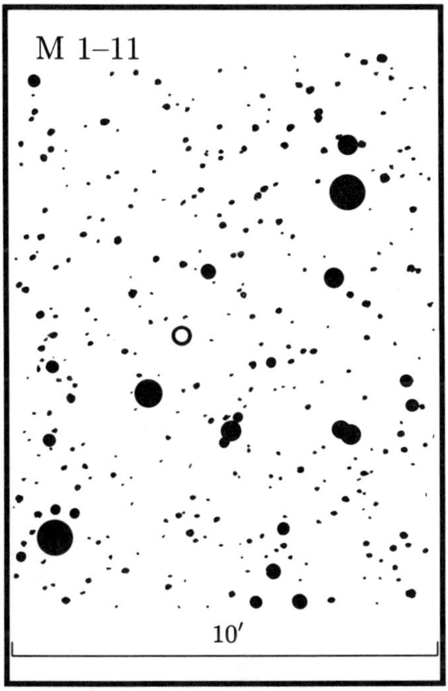
M 1–11
10′

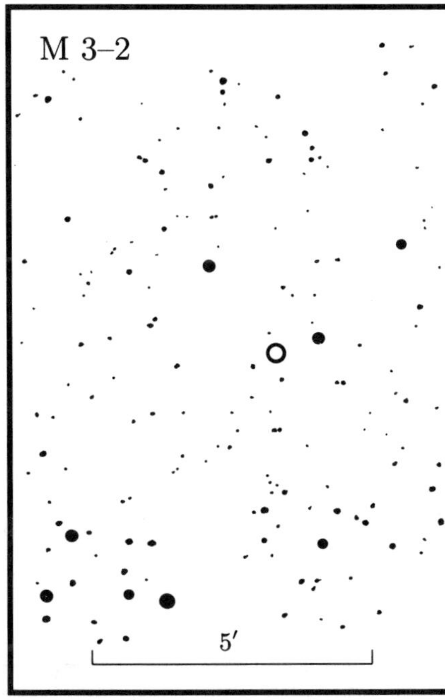
M 3–2
5′

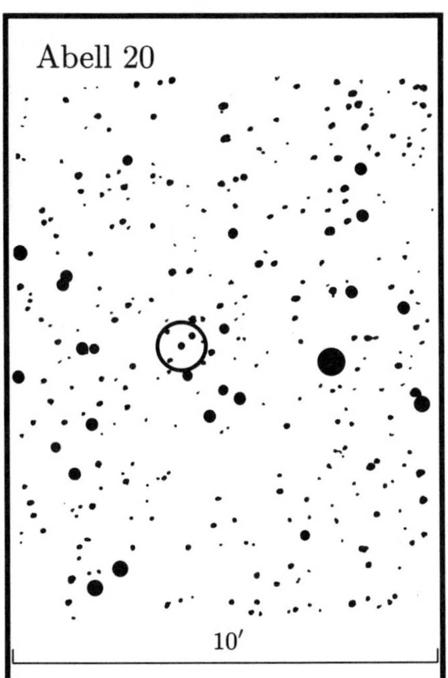
Abell 20
10′

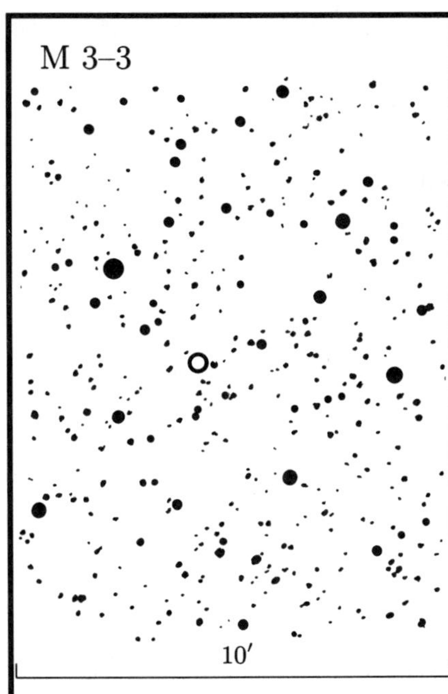
M 3–3
10′

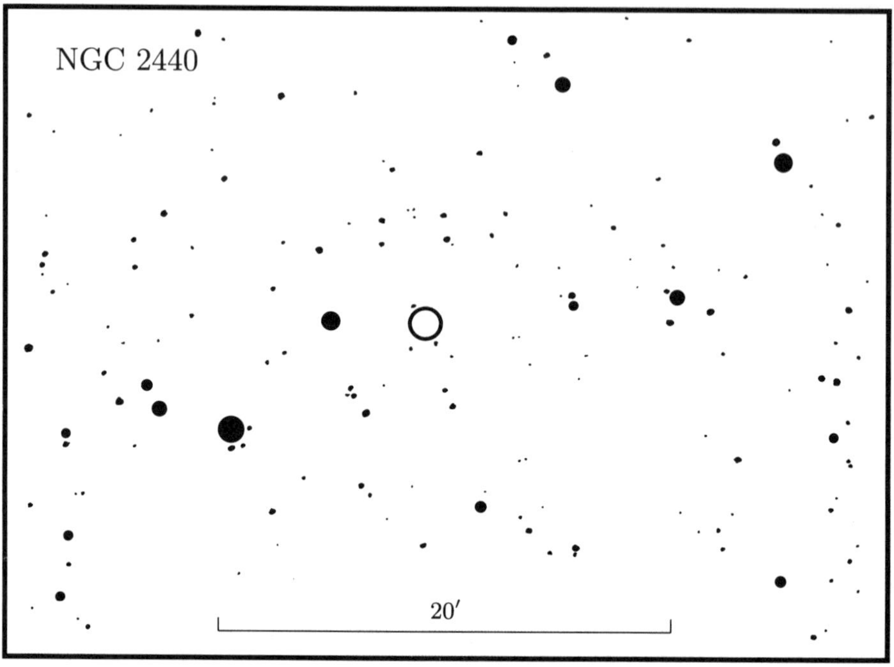
NGC 2440
20′

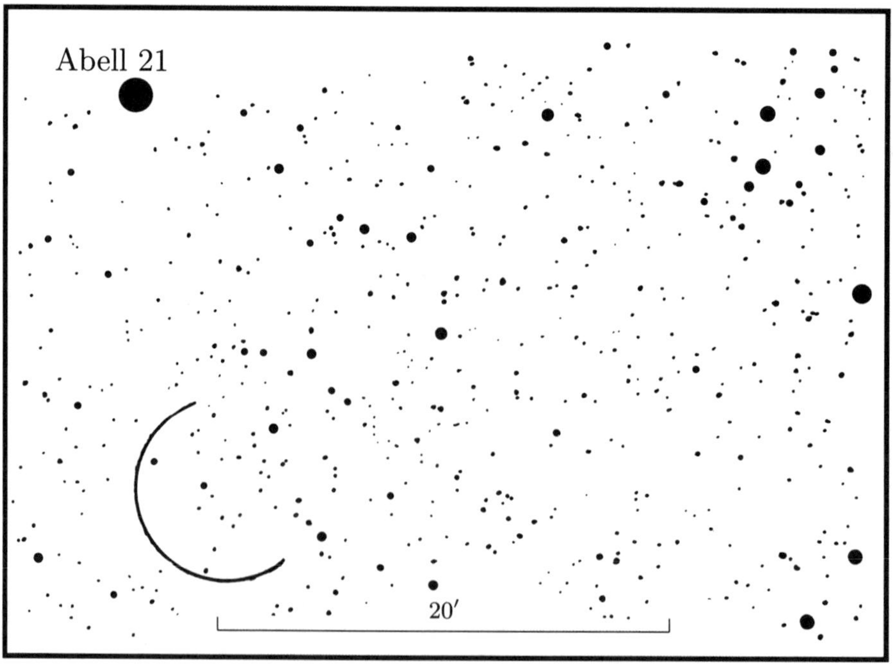
Abell 21
20′

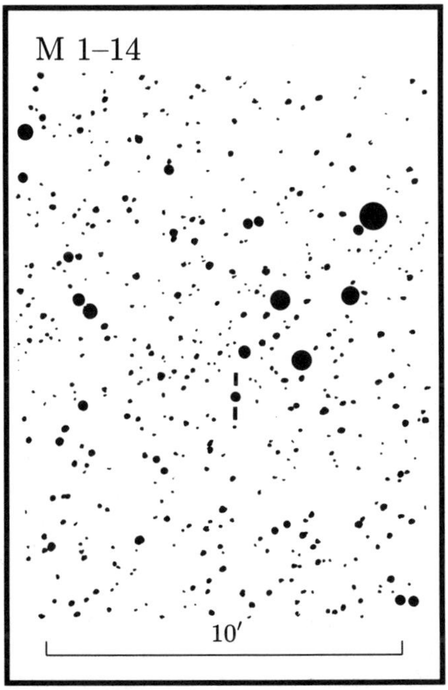
M 1–14
10′

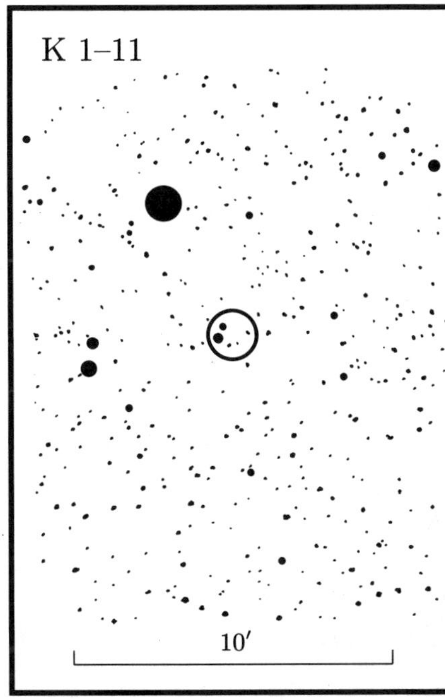
K 1–11
10′

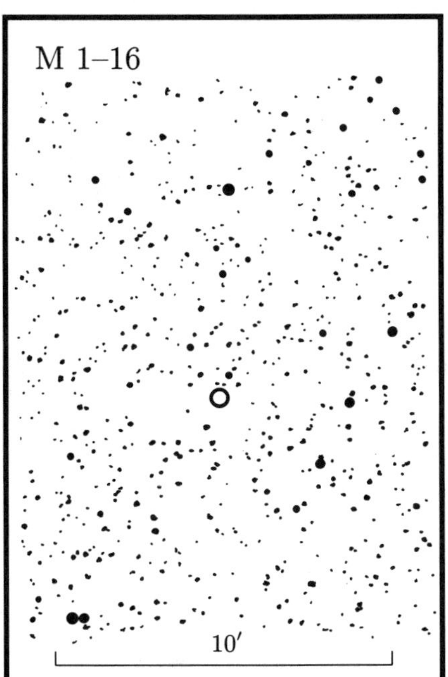
M 1–16
10′

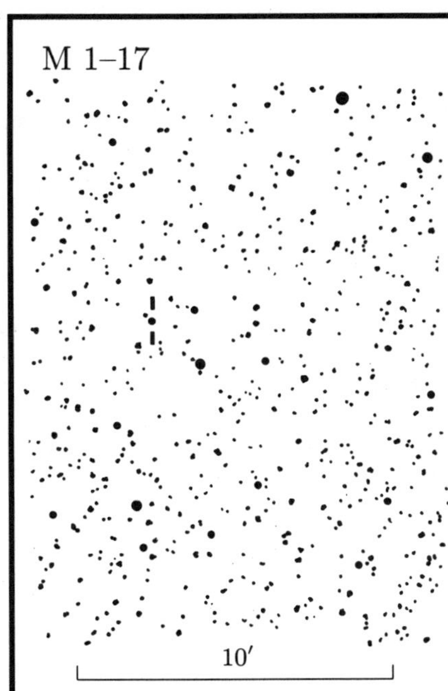
M 1–17
10′

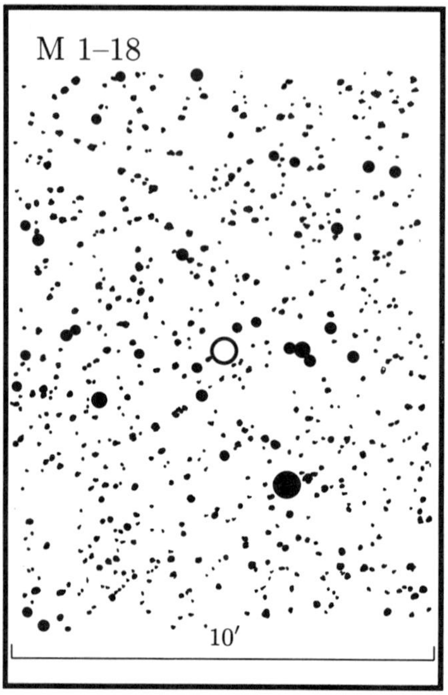
M 1–18
10′

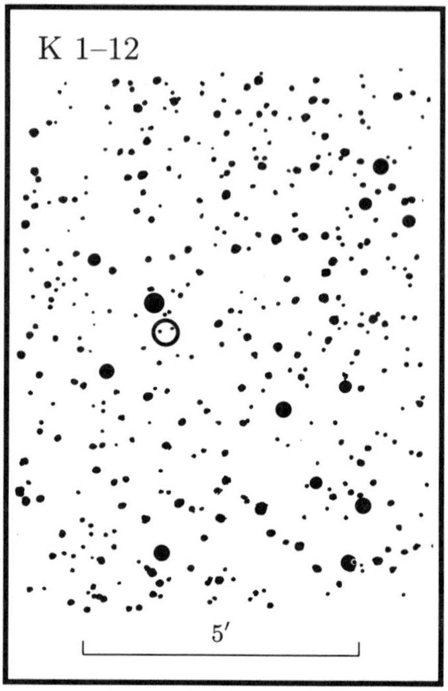
K 1–12
5′

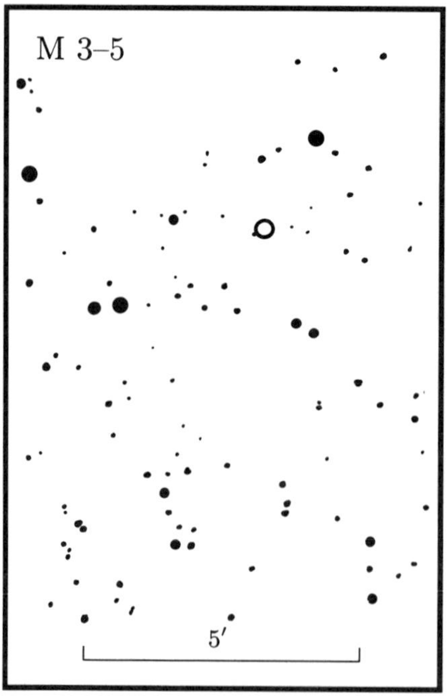
M 3–5
5′

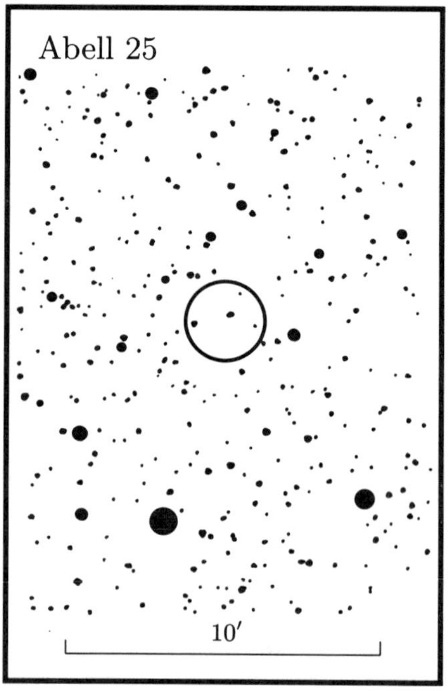
Abell 25
10′

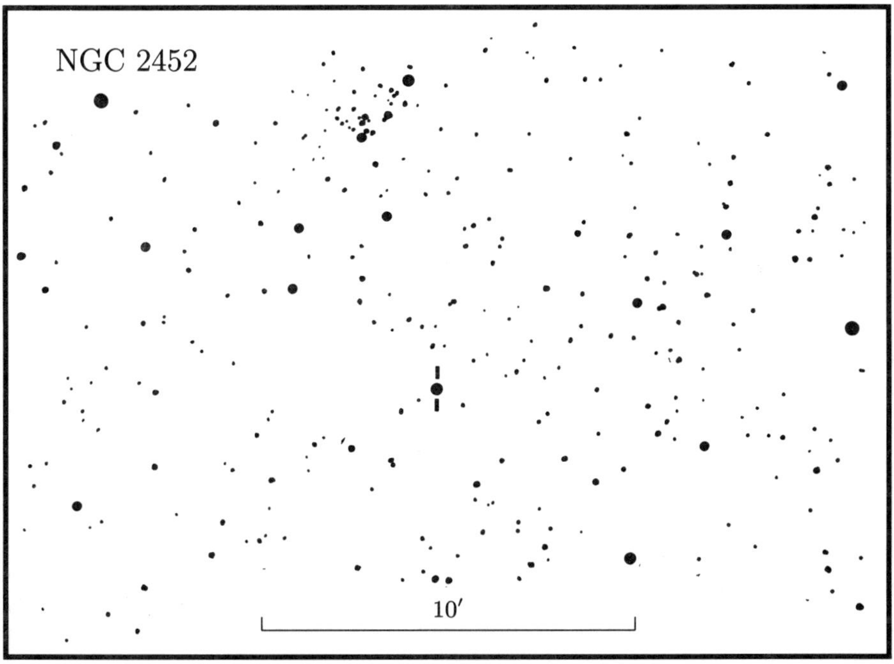
NGC 2452
10′

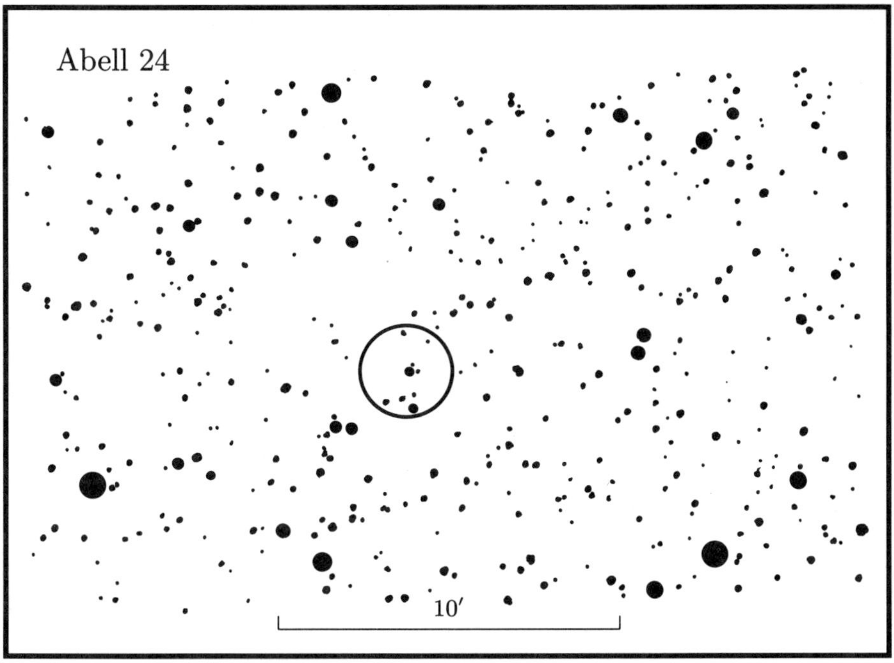
Abell 24
10′

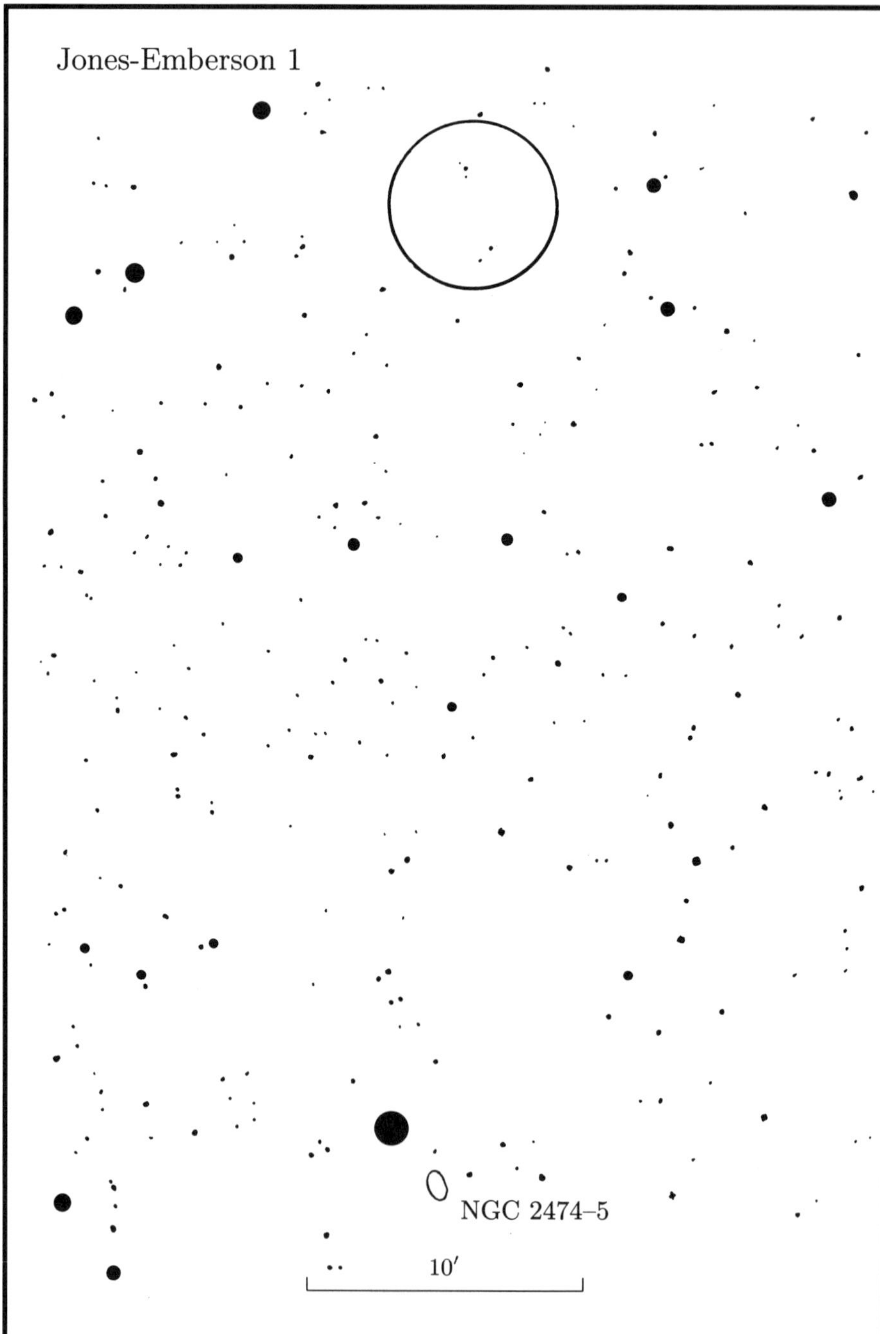
Jones-Emberson 1
NGC 2474–5
10′

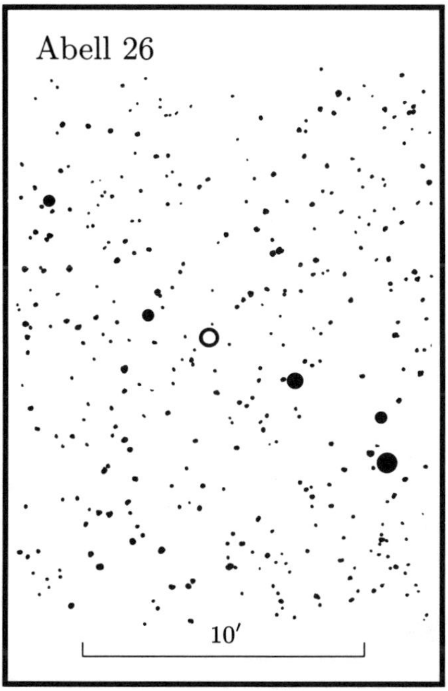
Abell 26
10′

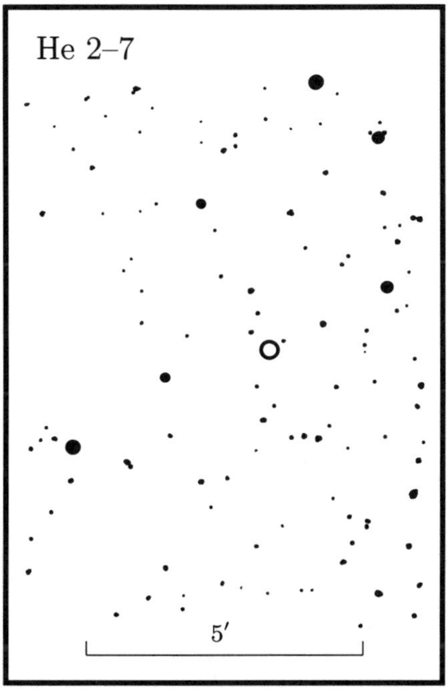
He 2–7
5′

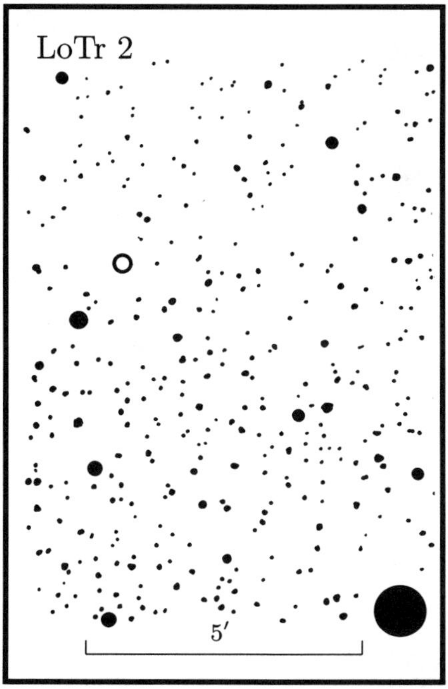
LoTr 2
5′

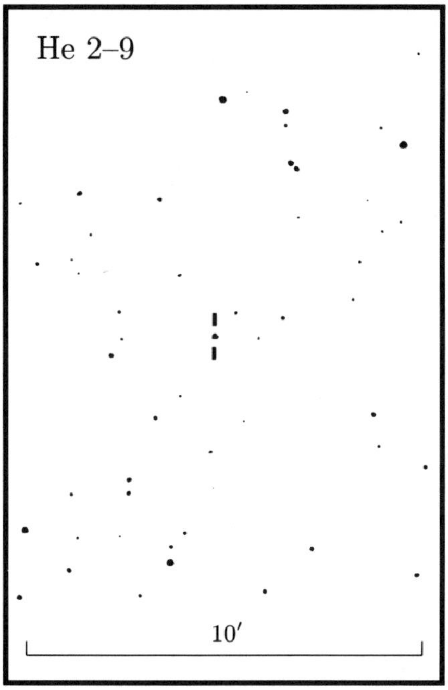
He 2–9
10′

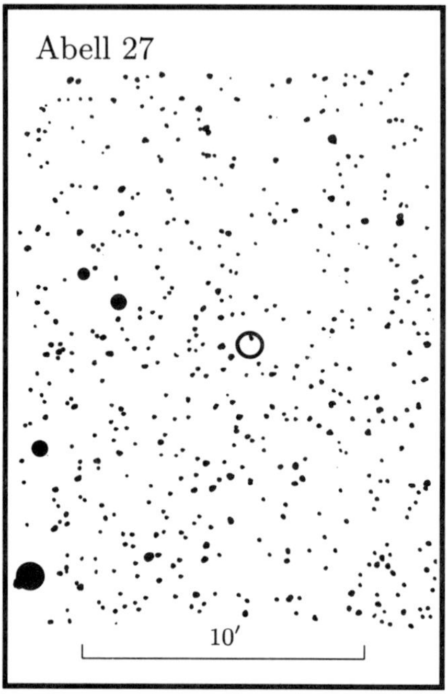
Abell 27
10′

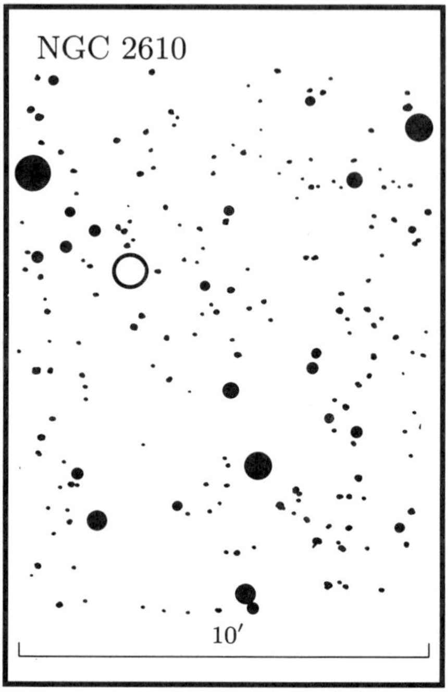
NGC 2610
10′

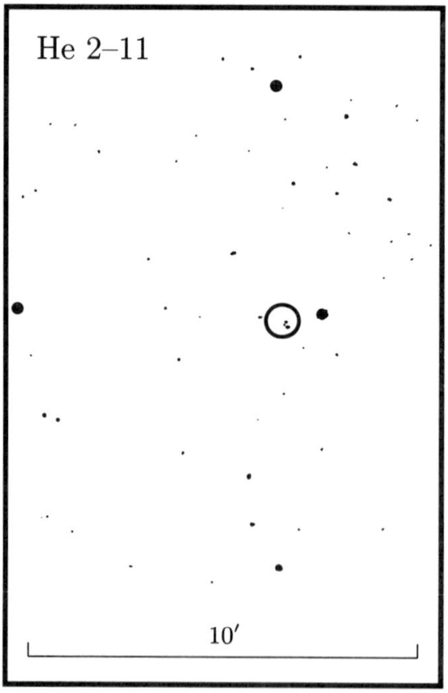
He 2–11
10′

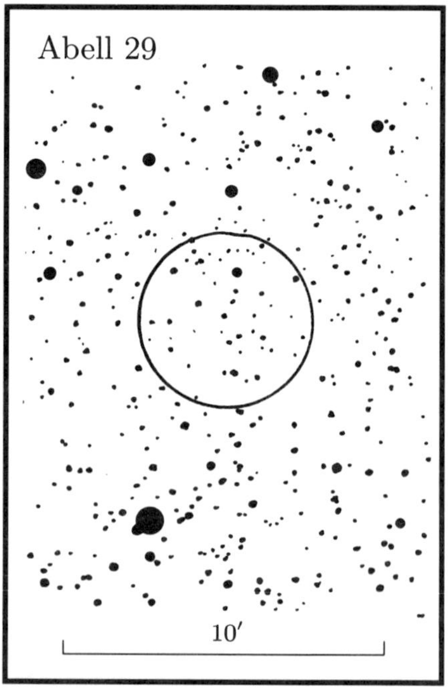
Abell 29
10′

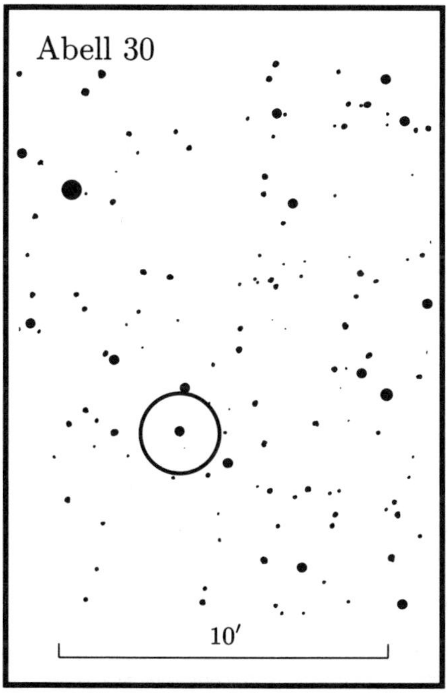
Abell 30
10′

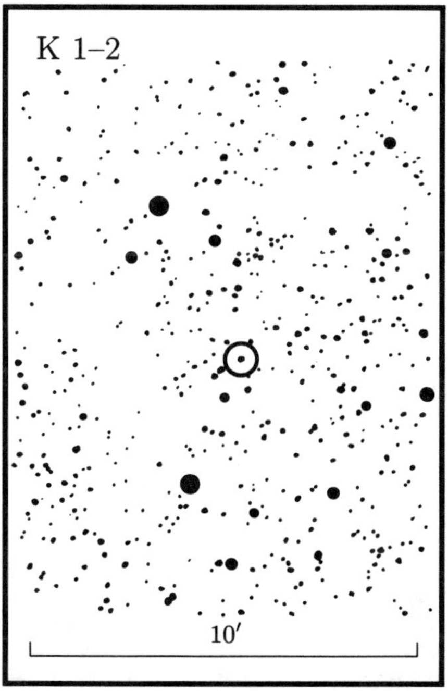
K 1–2
10′

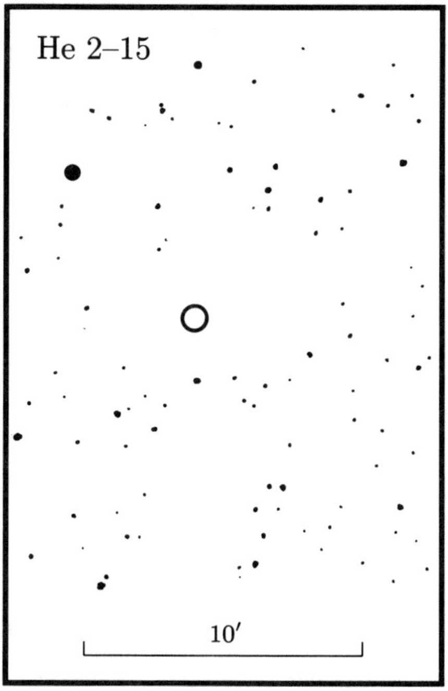
He 2–15
10′

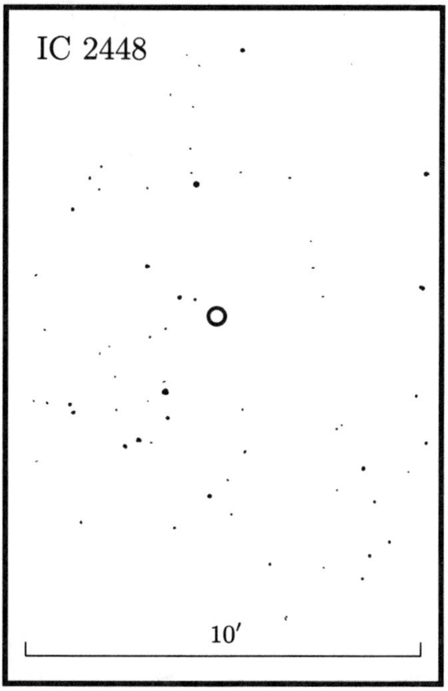
IC 2448
10′

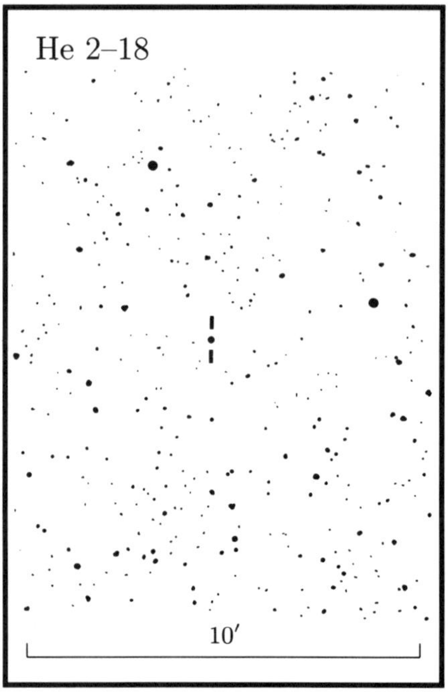
He 2–18
10′

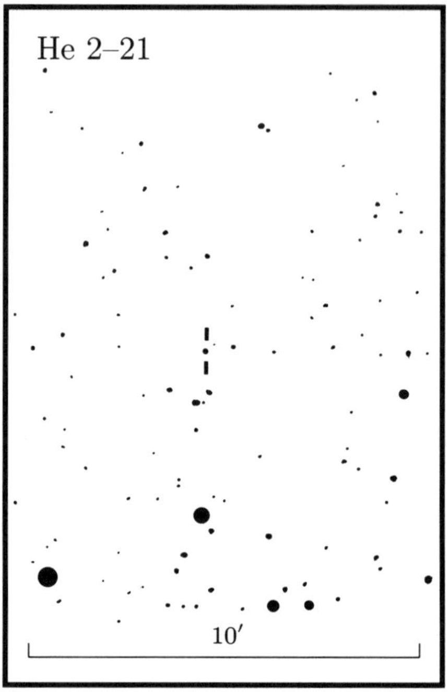
He 2–21
10′

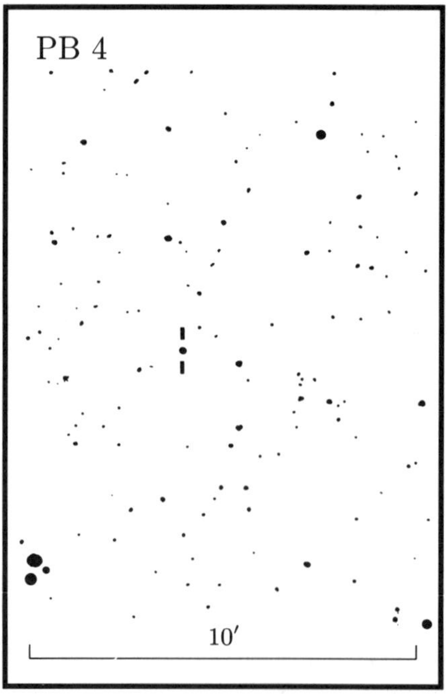
PB 4
10′

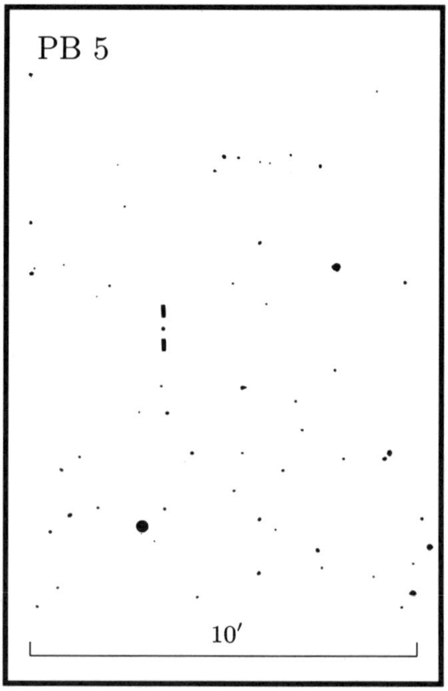
PB 5
10′

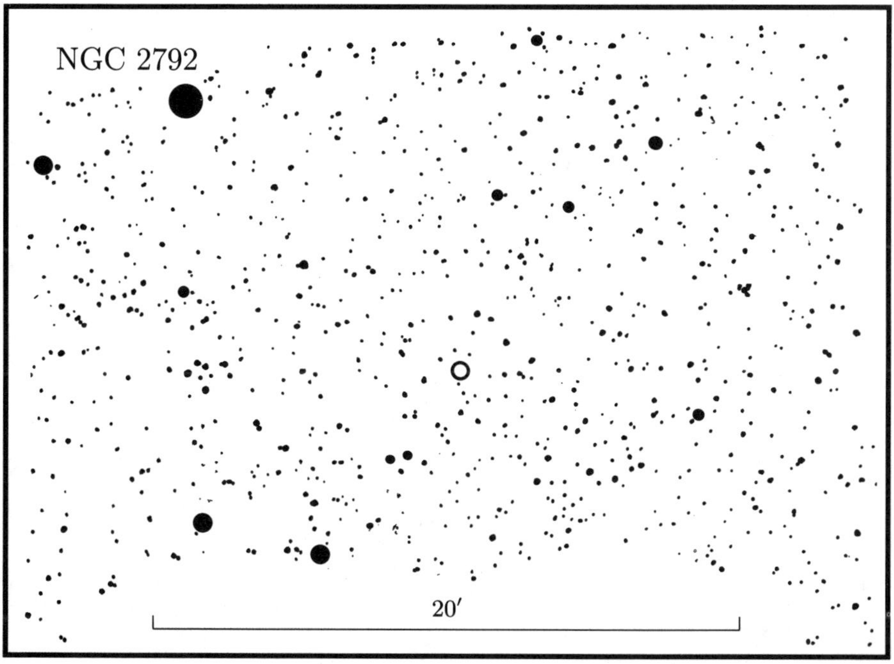
NGC 2792
20′

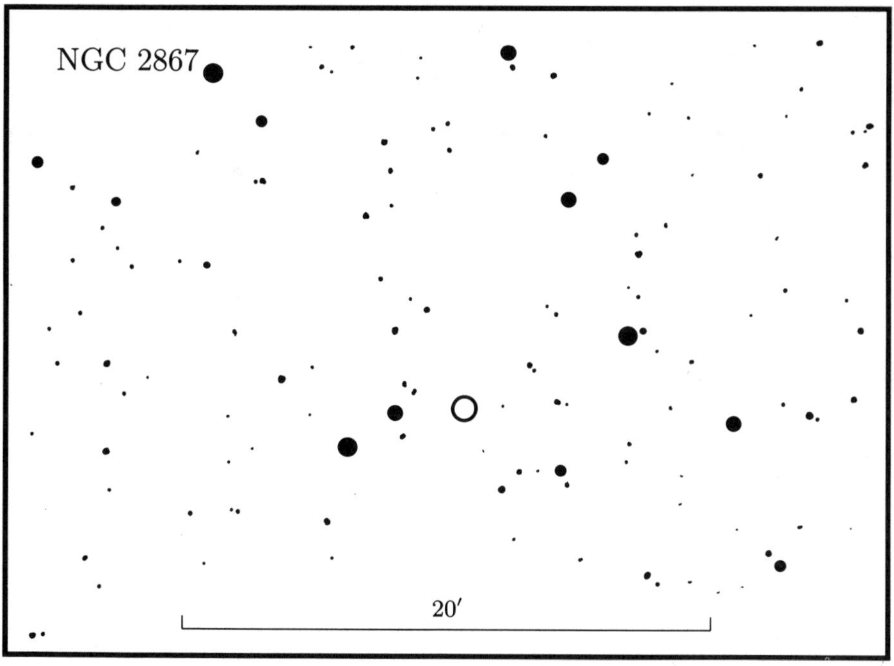
NGC 2867
20′

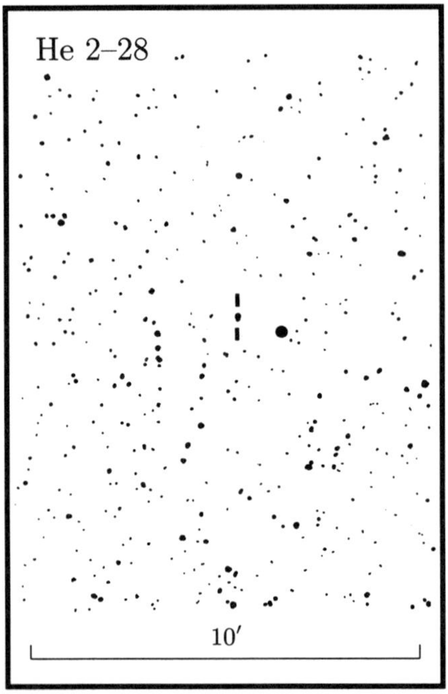
He 2–28
10′

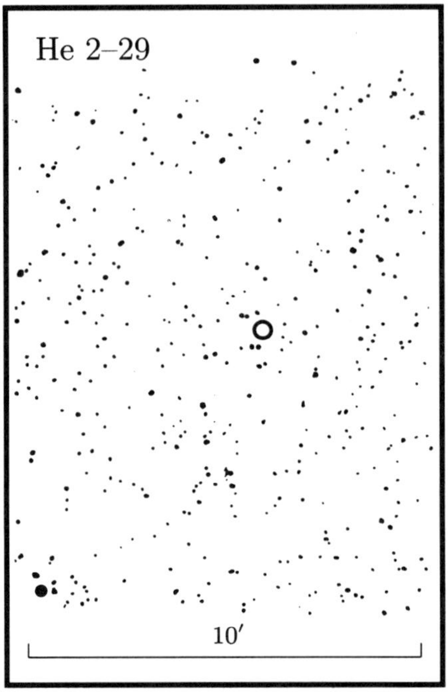
He 2–29
10′

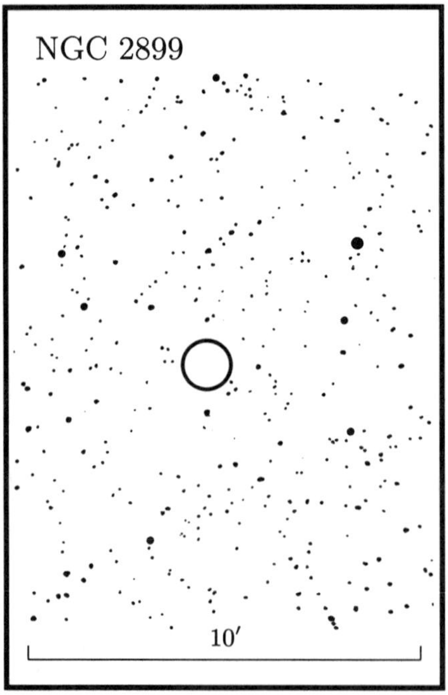
NGC 2899
10′

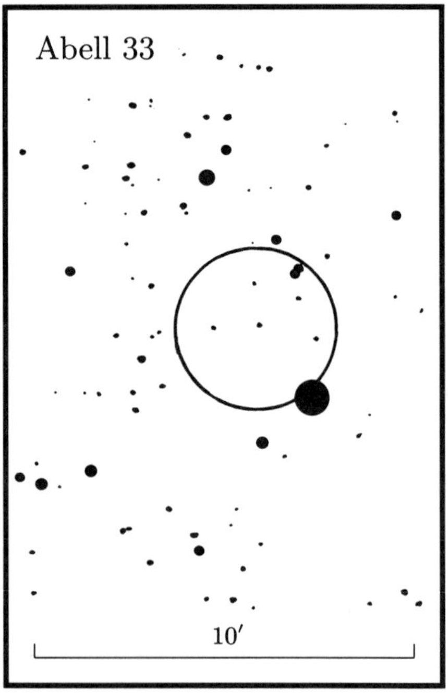
Abell 33
10′

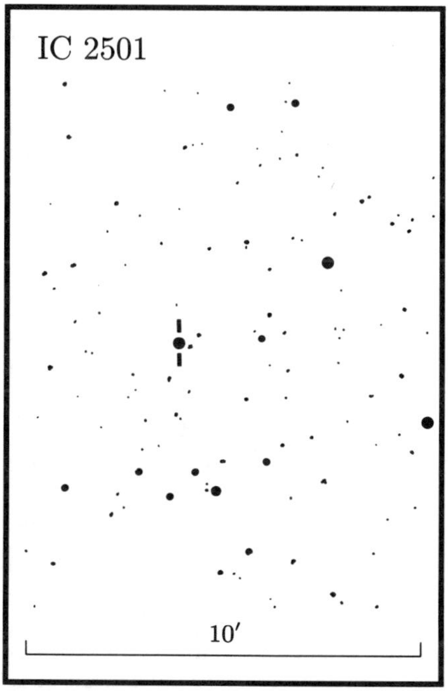
IC 2501
10′

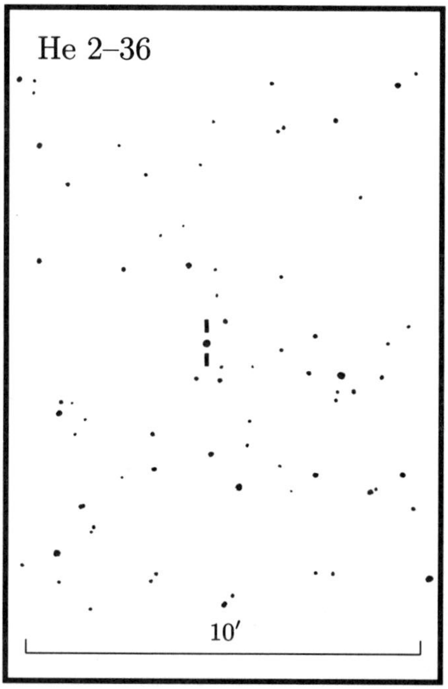
He 2–36
10′

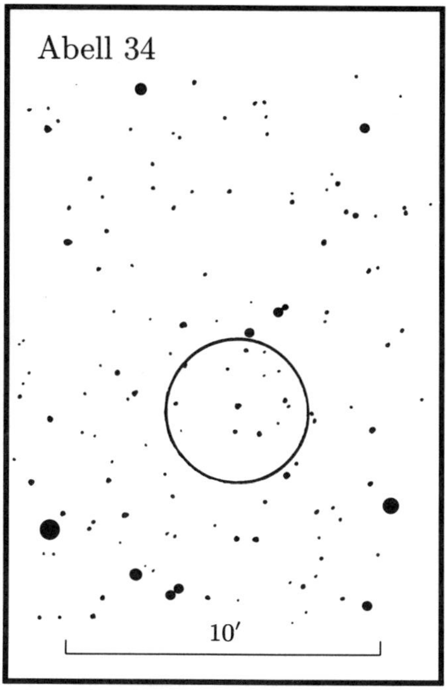
Abell 34
10′

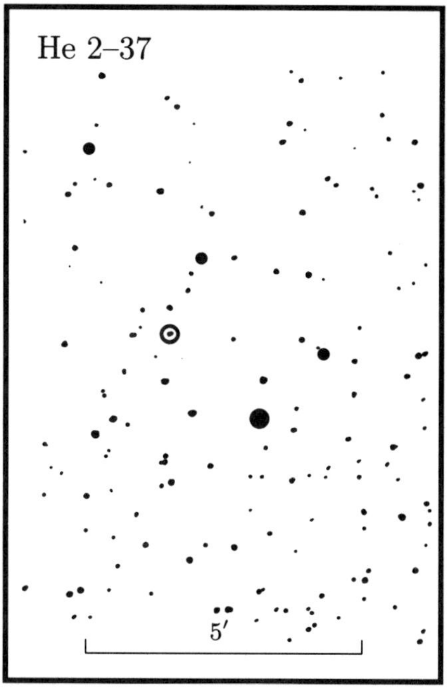
He 2–37
5′

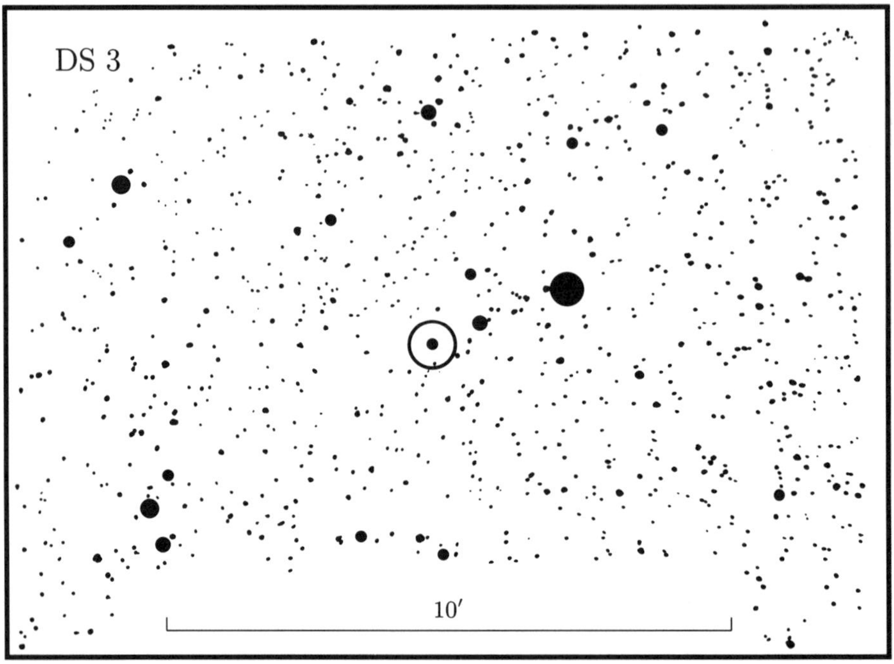
DS 3
10′

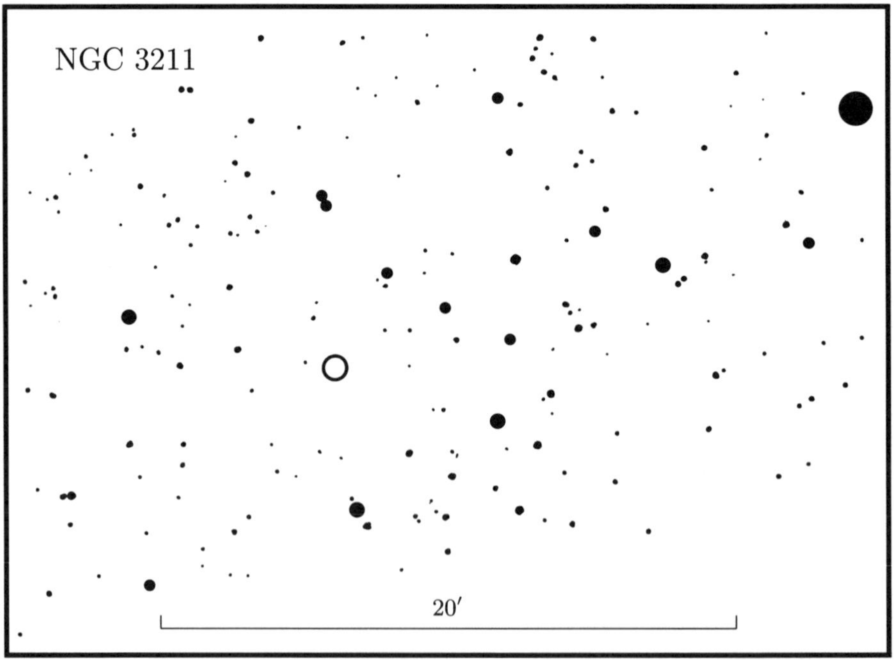
NGC 3211
20′

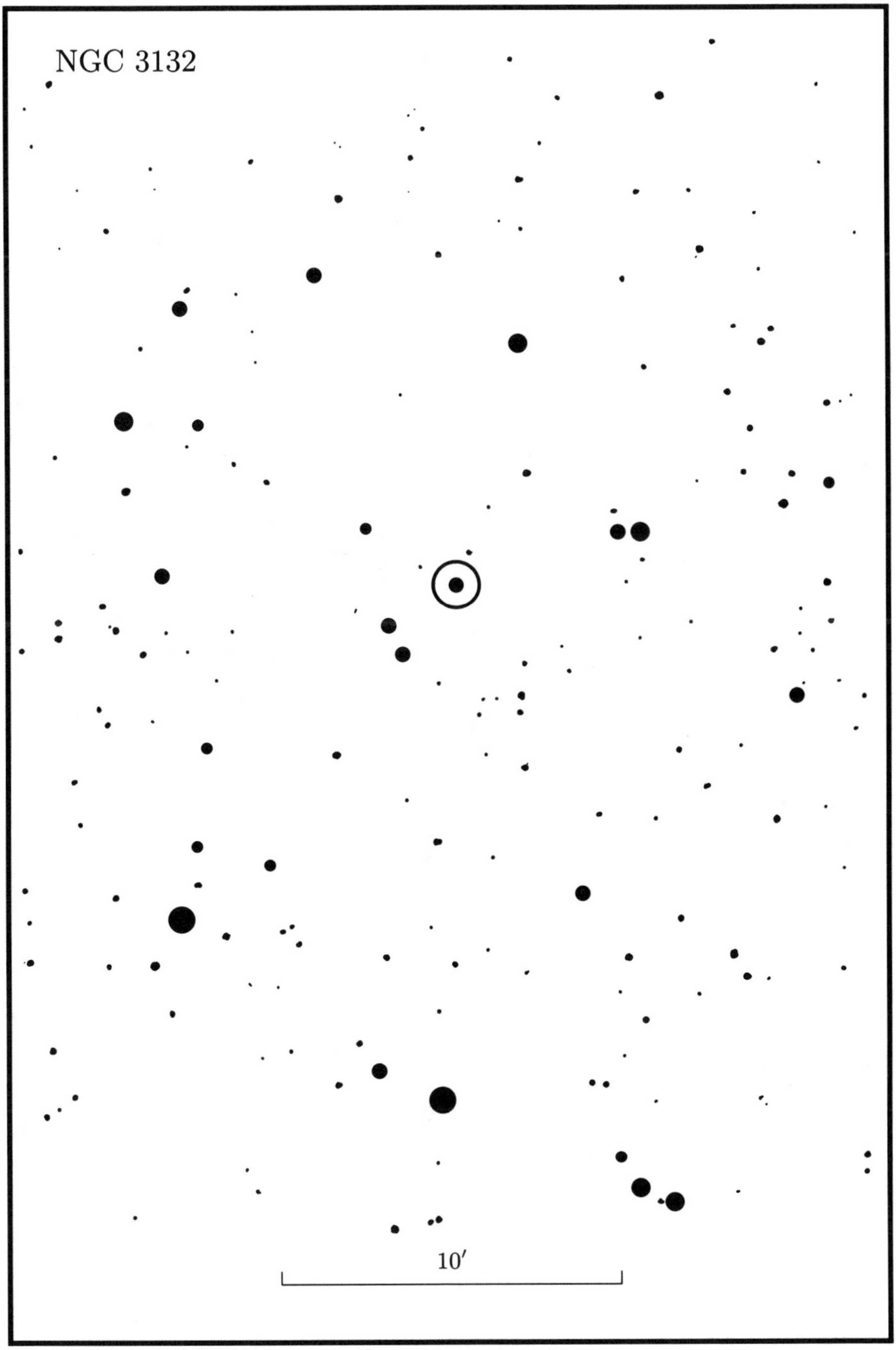
NGC 3132
10′

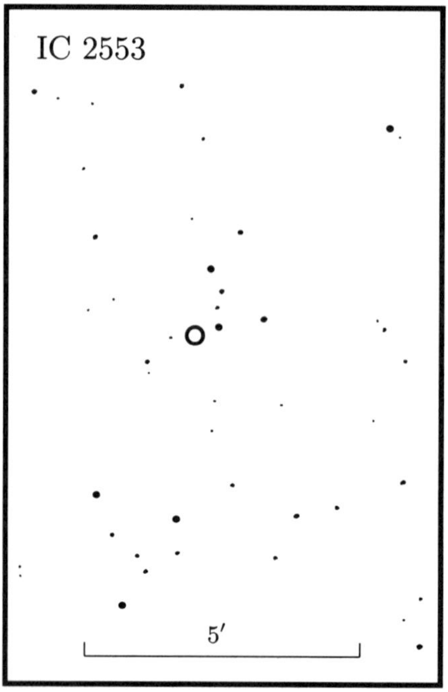
IC 2553
5′

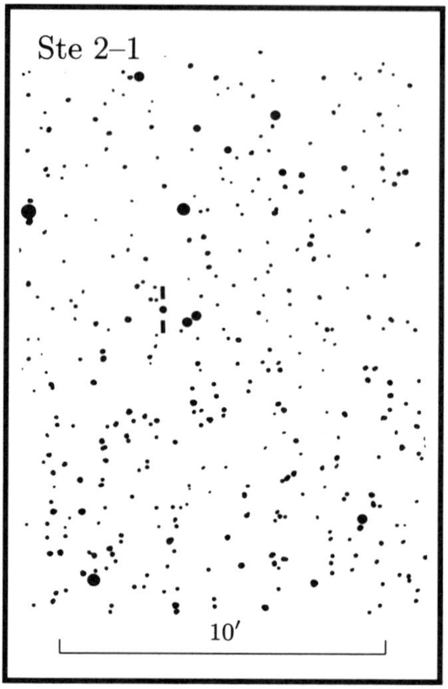
Ste 2–1
10′

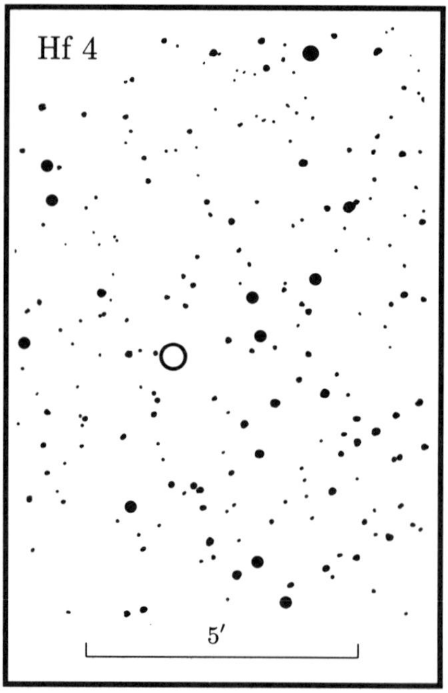
Hf 4
5′

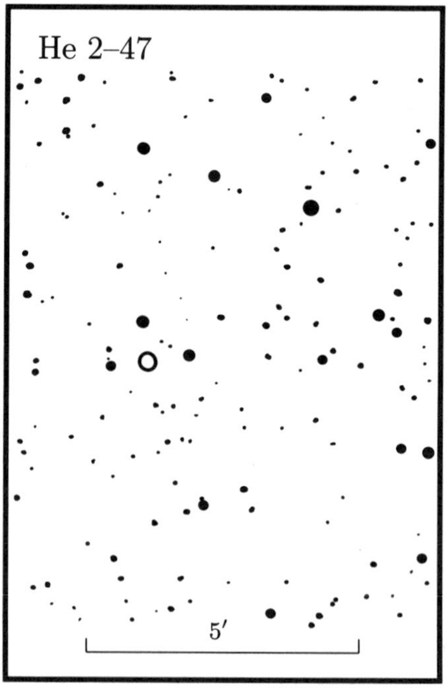
He 2–47
5′

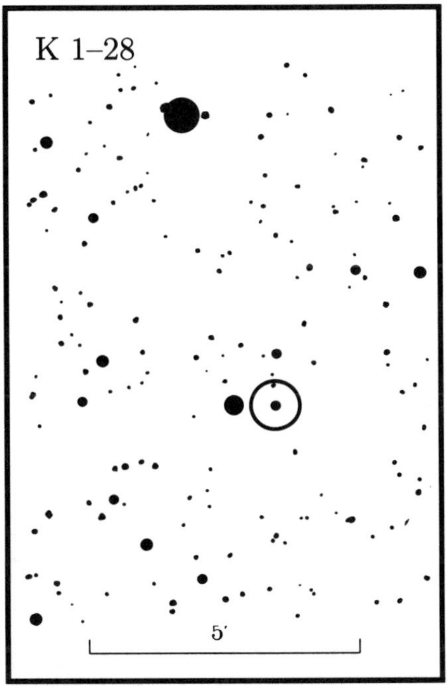
K 1–28
5′

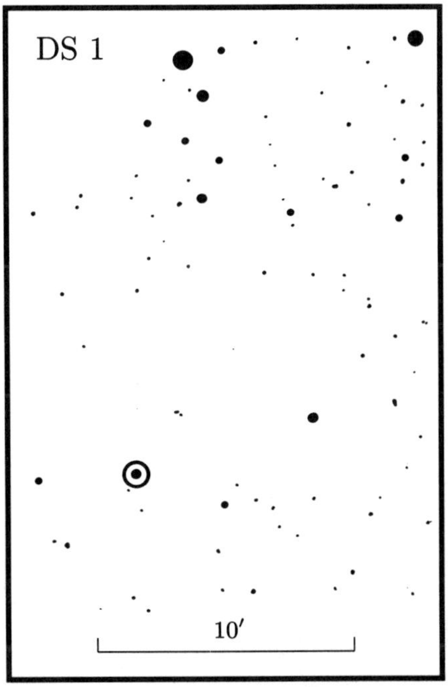
DS 1
10′

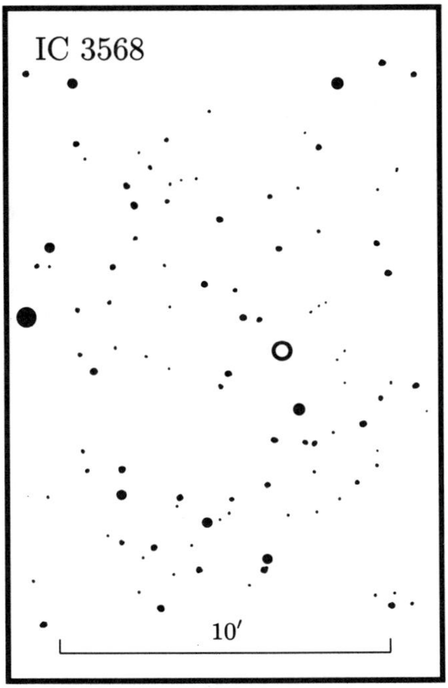
IC 3568
10′

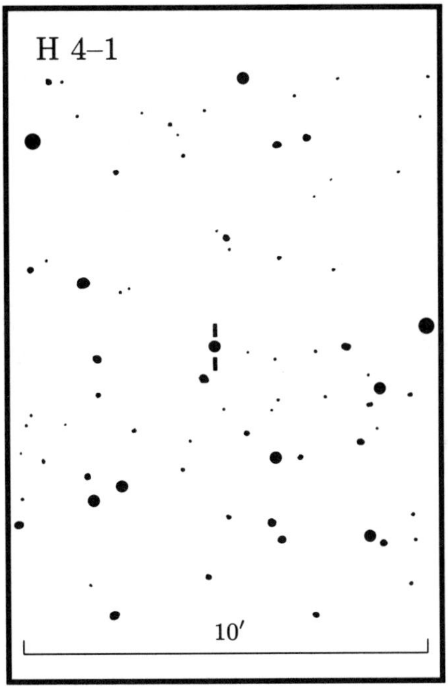
H 4–1
10′

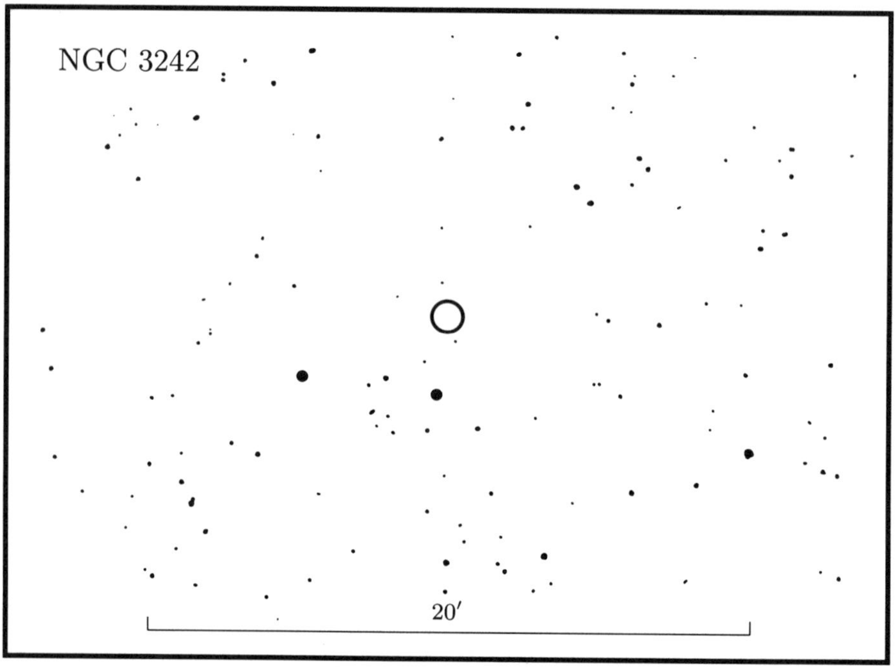
NGC 3242
20′

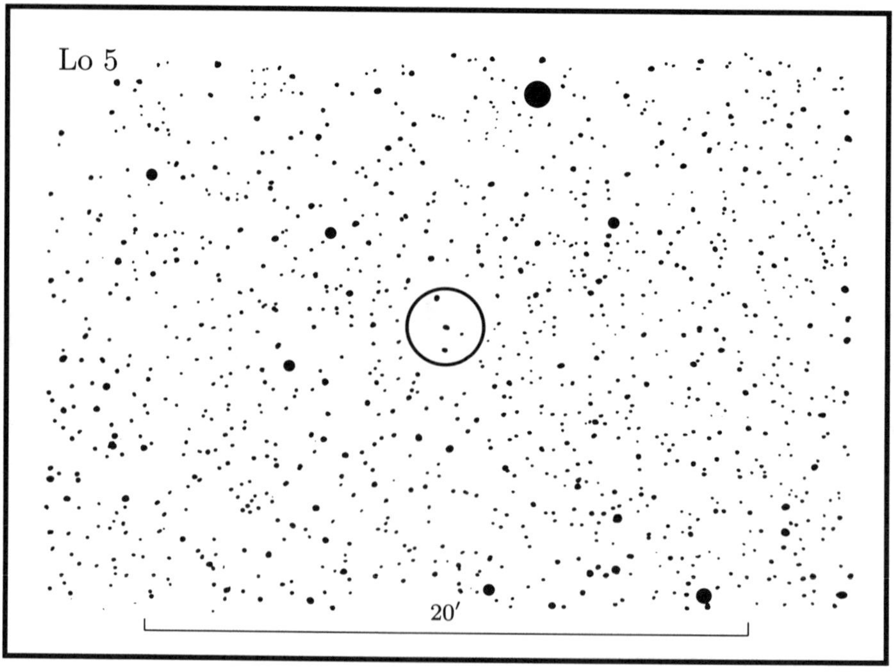
Lo 5
20′

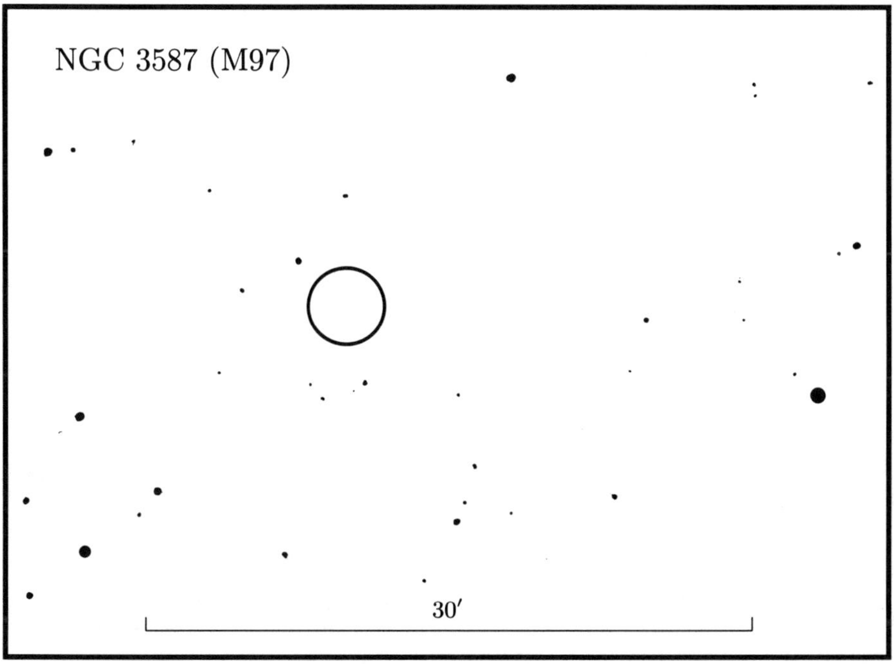
NGC 3587 (M97)
30′

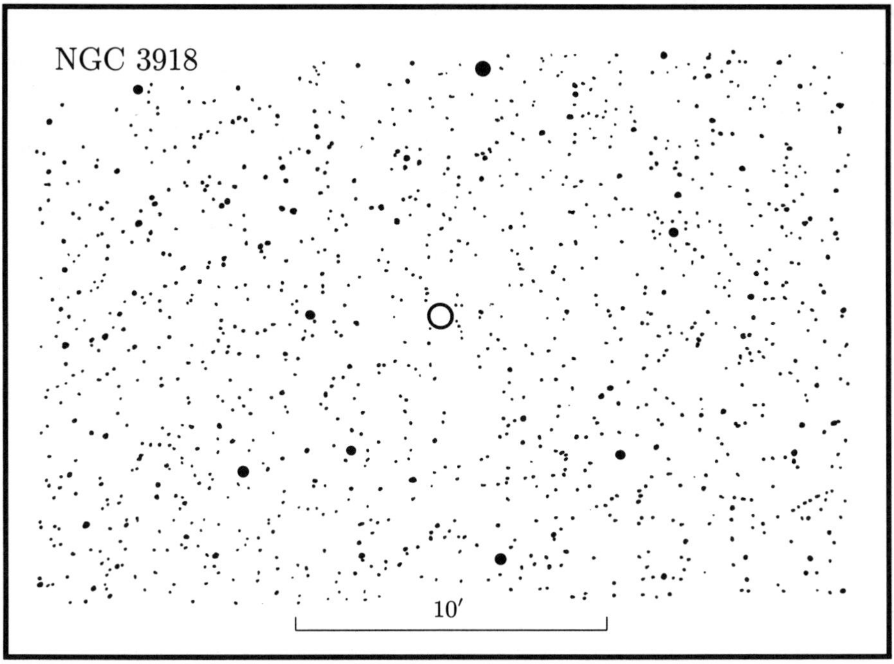
NGC 3918
10′

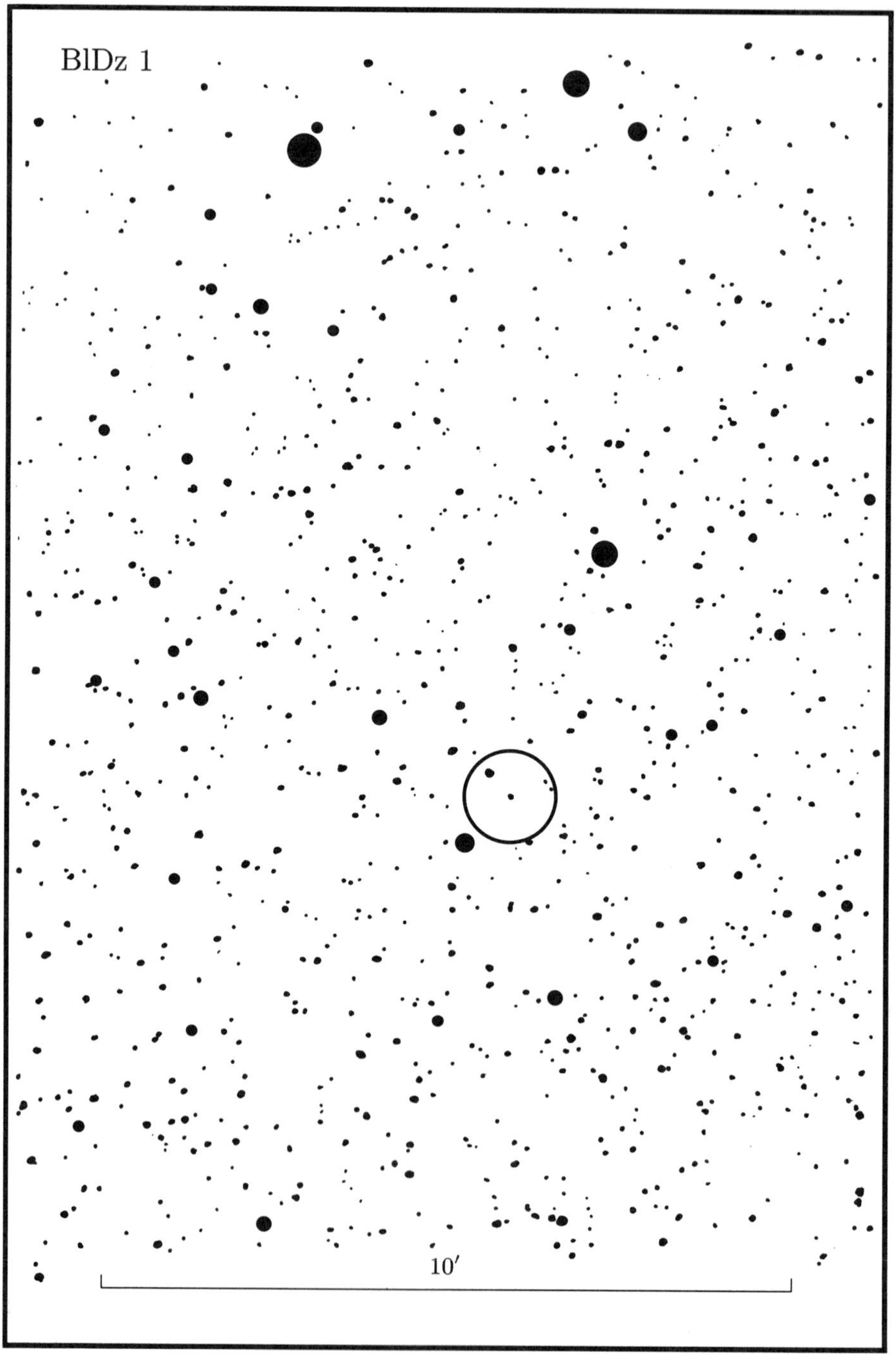
BlDz 1
10′

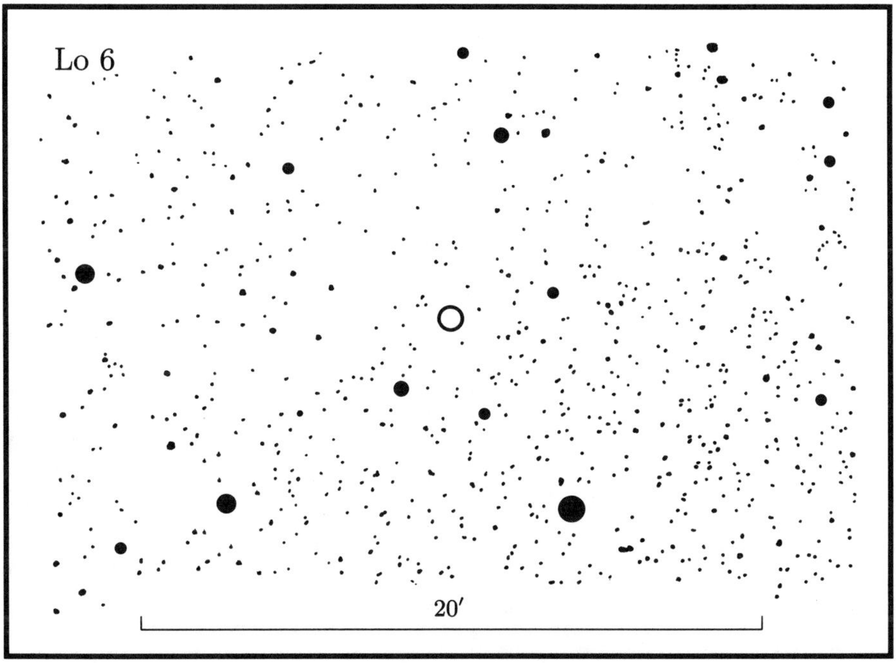
Lo 6
20′

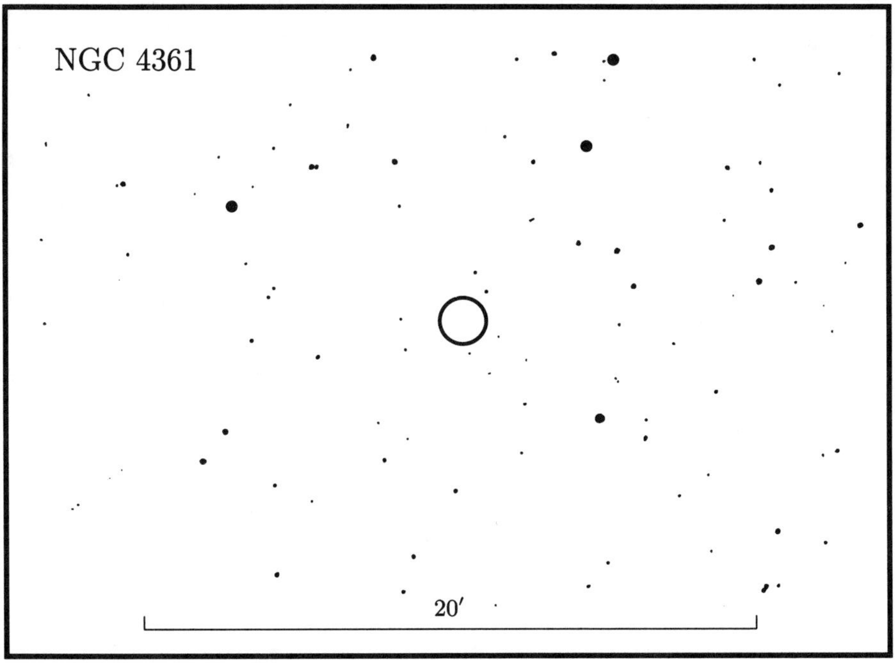
NGC 4361
20′

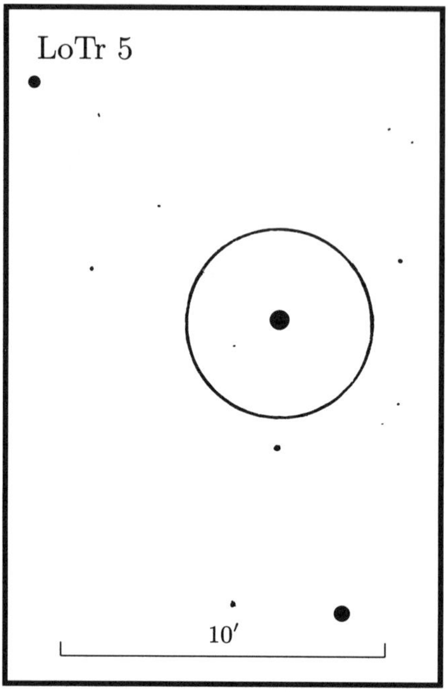
LoTr 5
10′

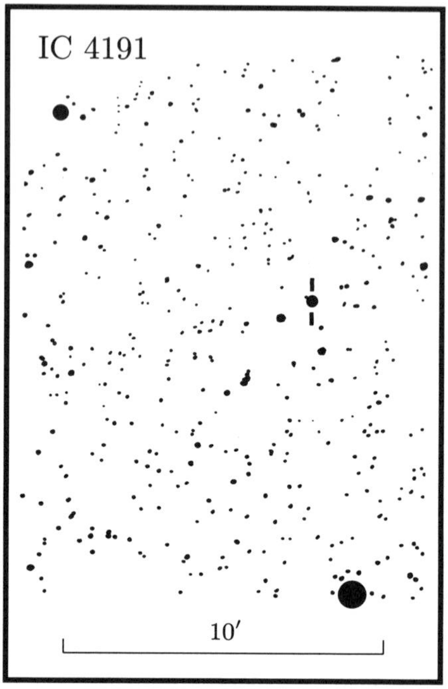
IC 4191
10′

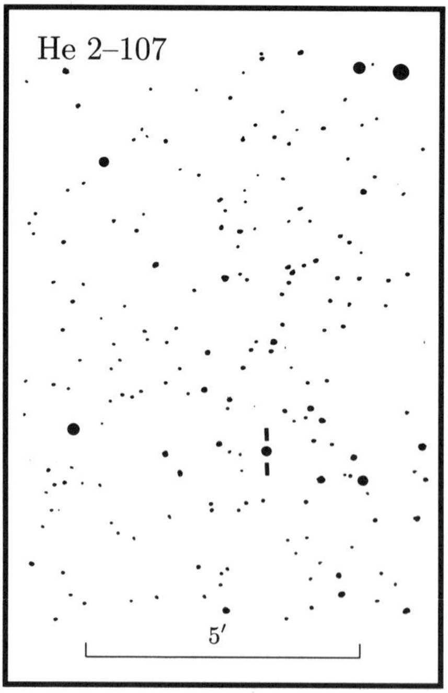
He 2–107
5′

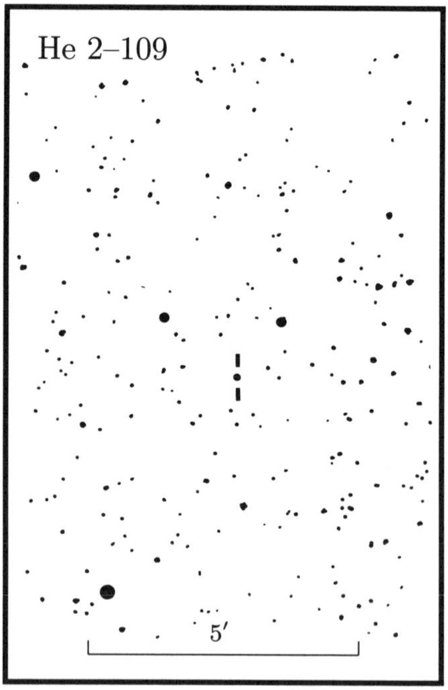
He 2–109
5′

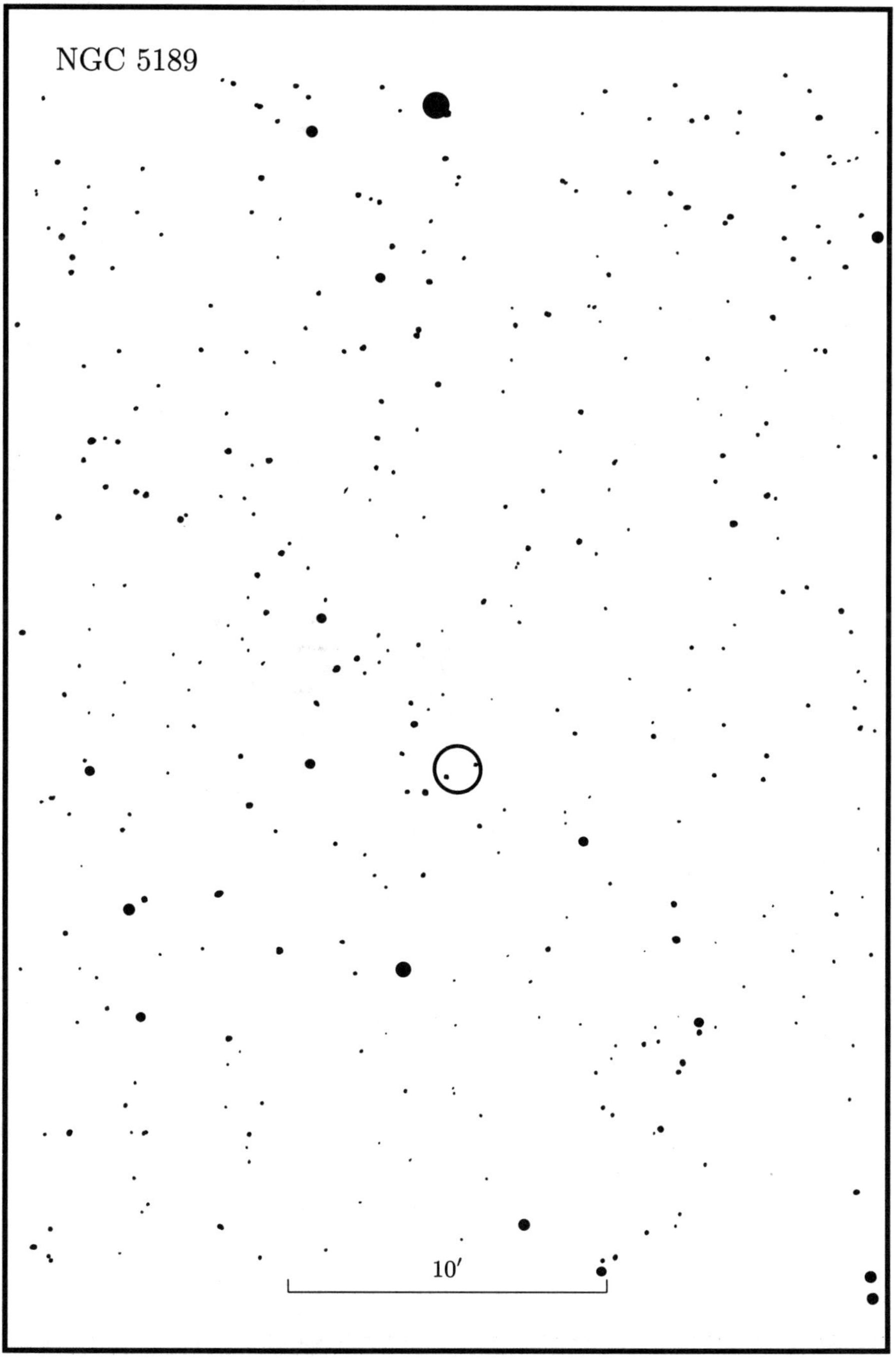
NGC 5189
10′

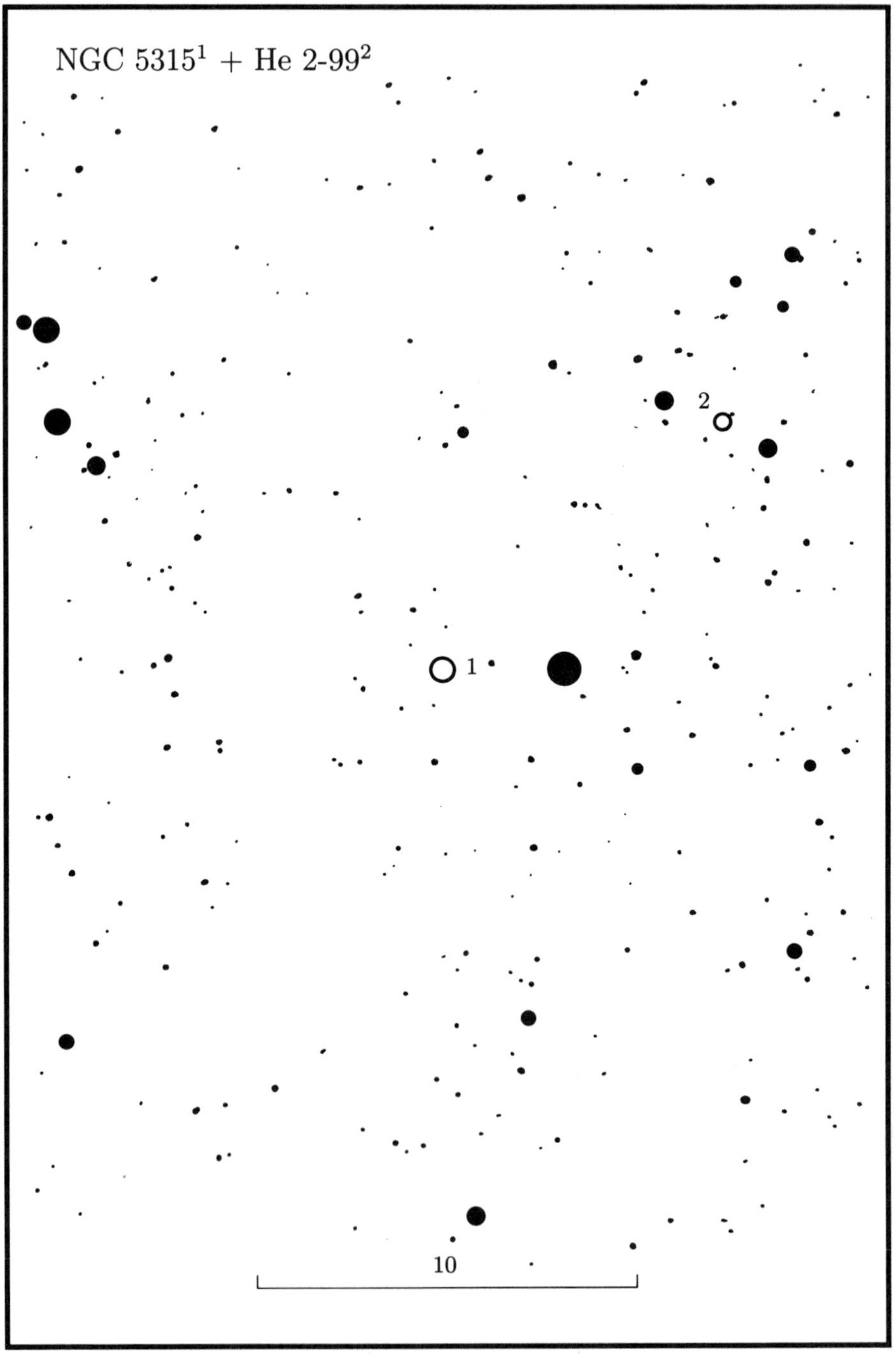
NGC 5315[1] + He 2-99[2]
2
1
10

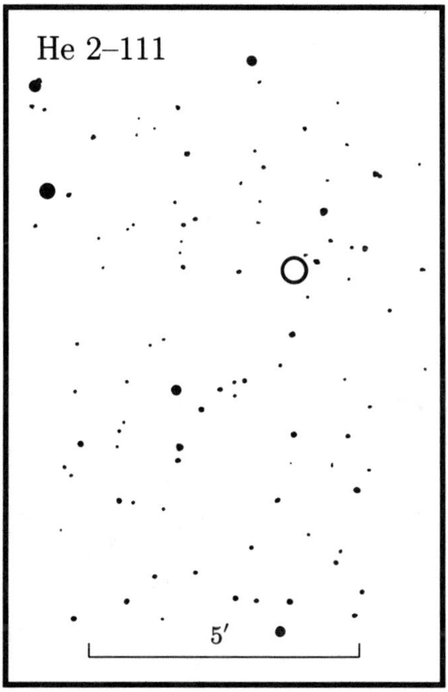
He 2–111
5′

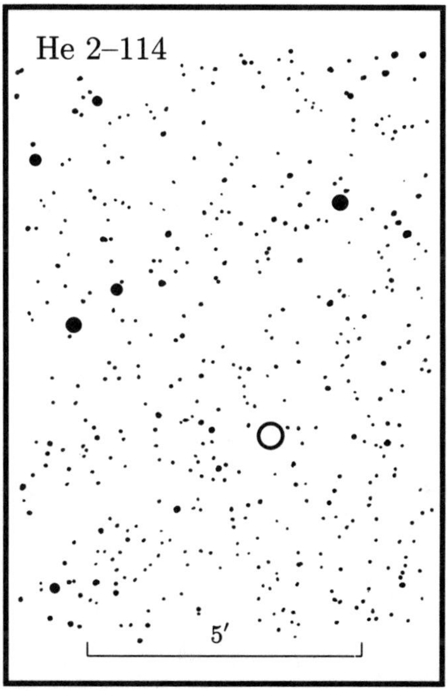
He 2–114
5′

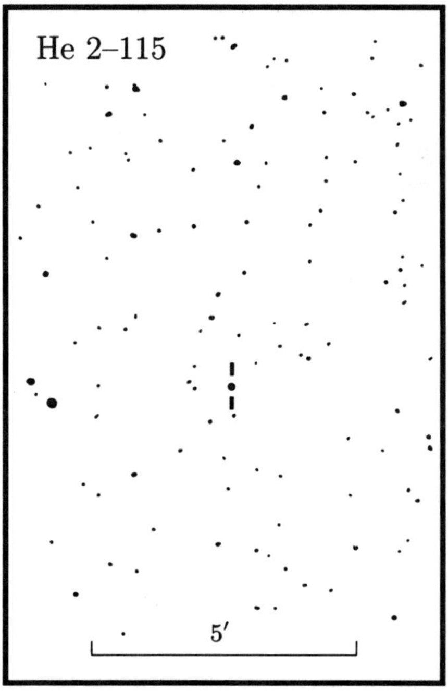
He 2–115
5′

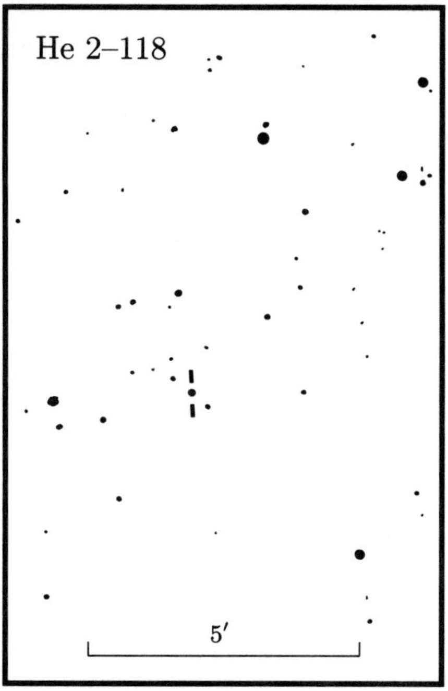
He 2–118
5′

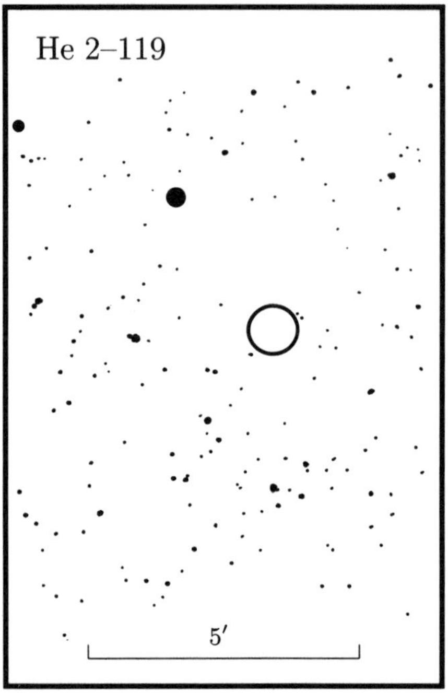
He 2–119
5′

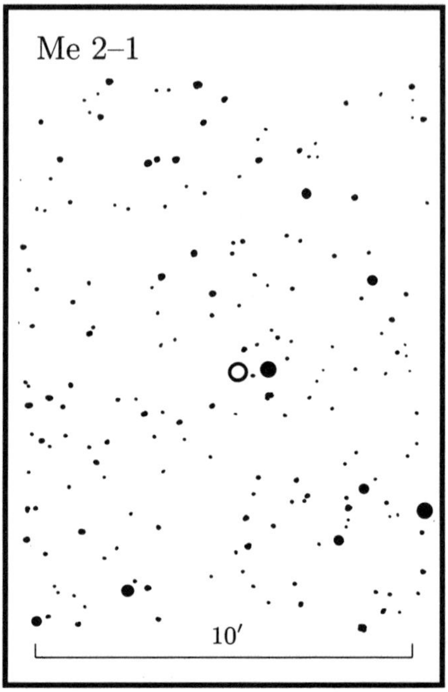
Me 2–1
10′

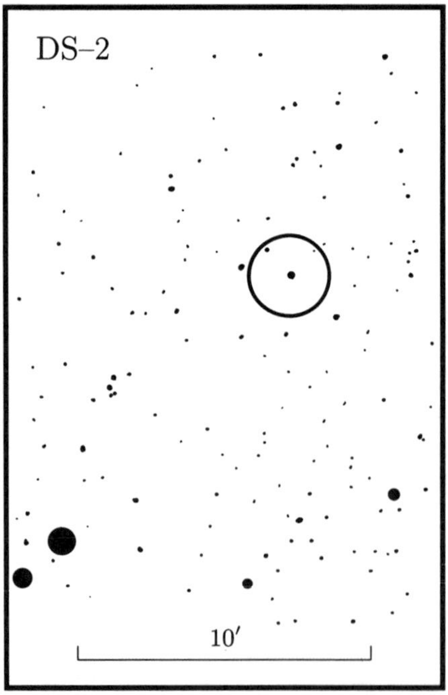
DS–2
10′

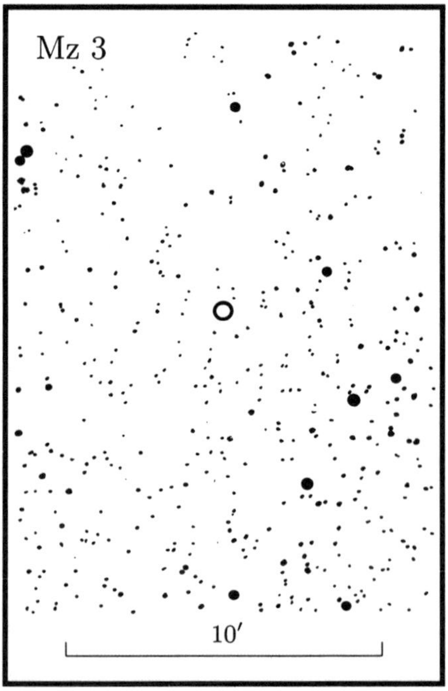
Mz 3
10′

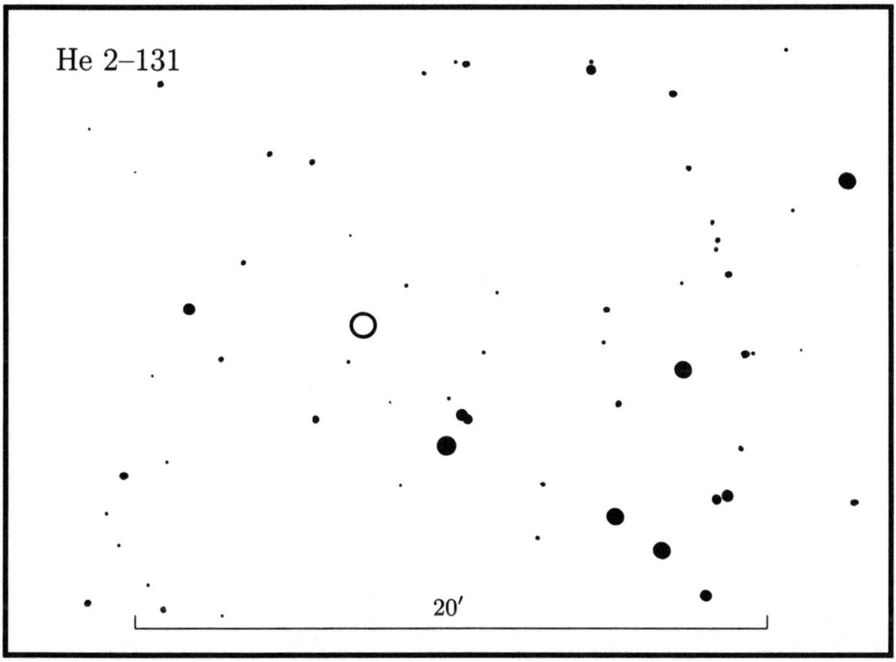
He 2–131
20′

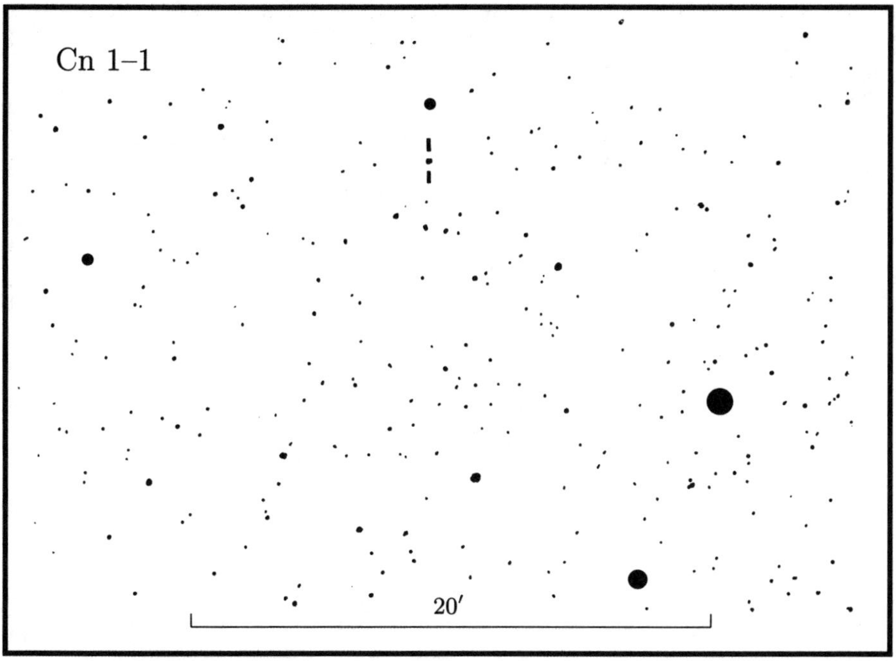
Cn 1–1
20′

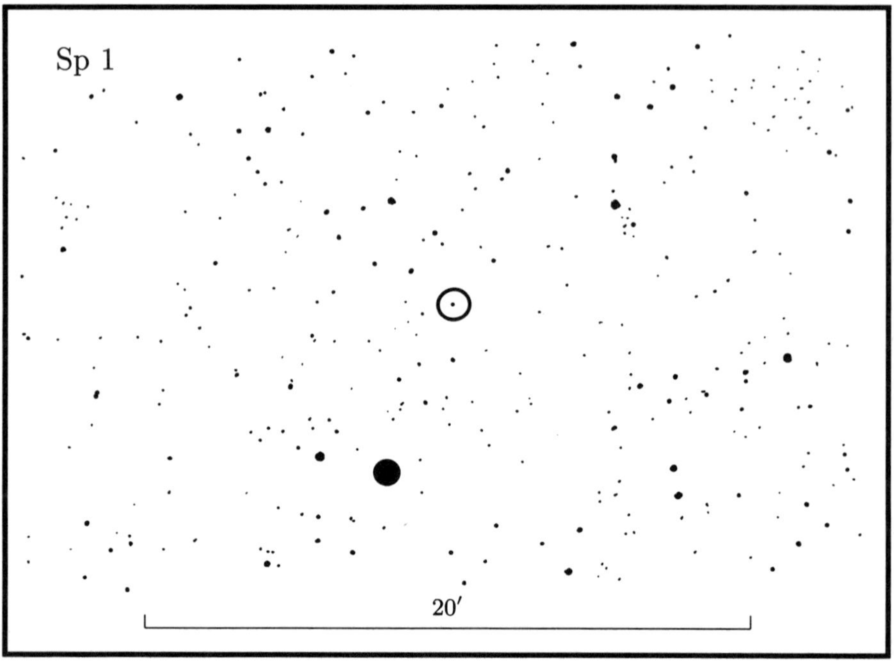
Sp 1
20′

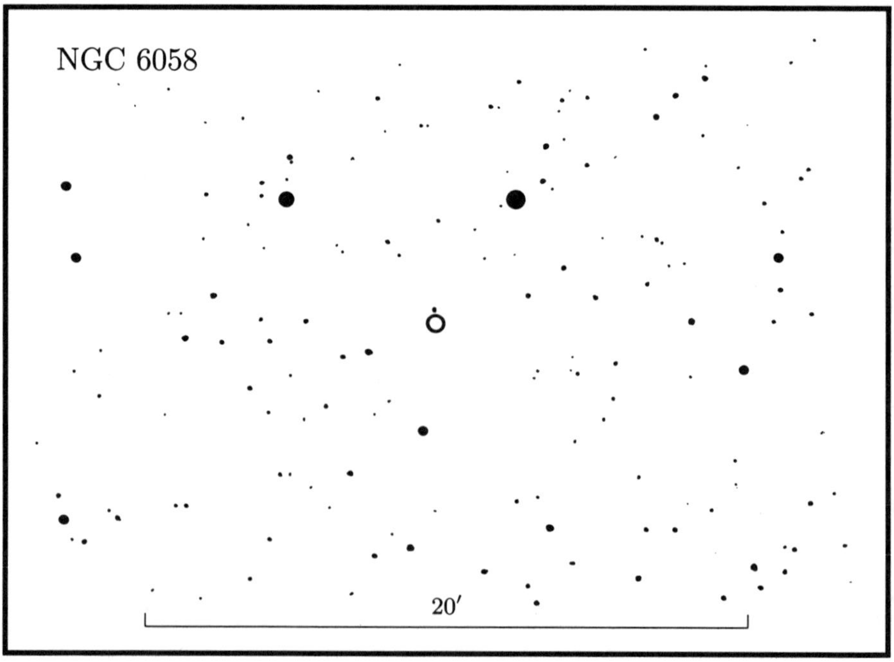
NGC 6058
20′

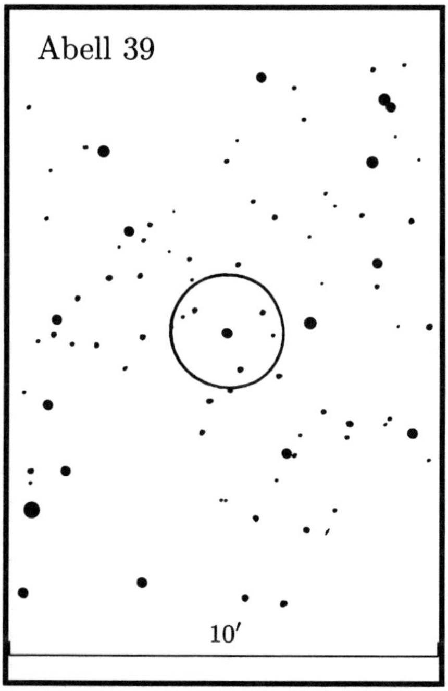
Abell 39
10′

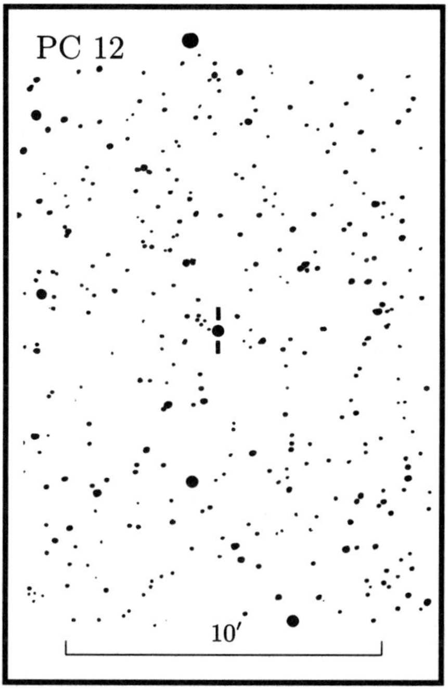
PC 12
10′

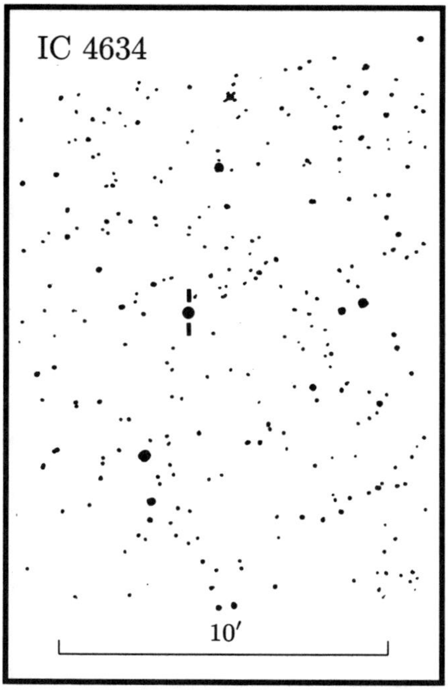
IC 4634
10′

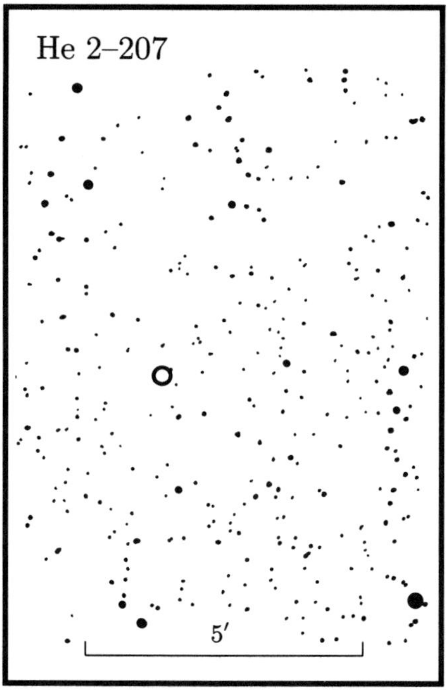
He 2–207
5′

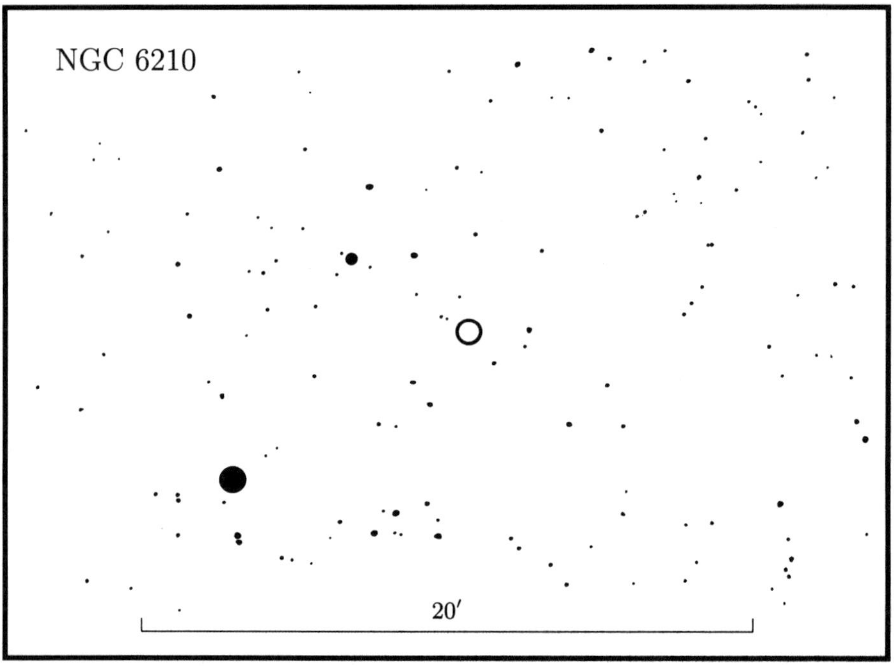
NGC 6210
20′

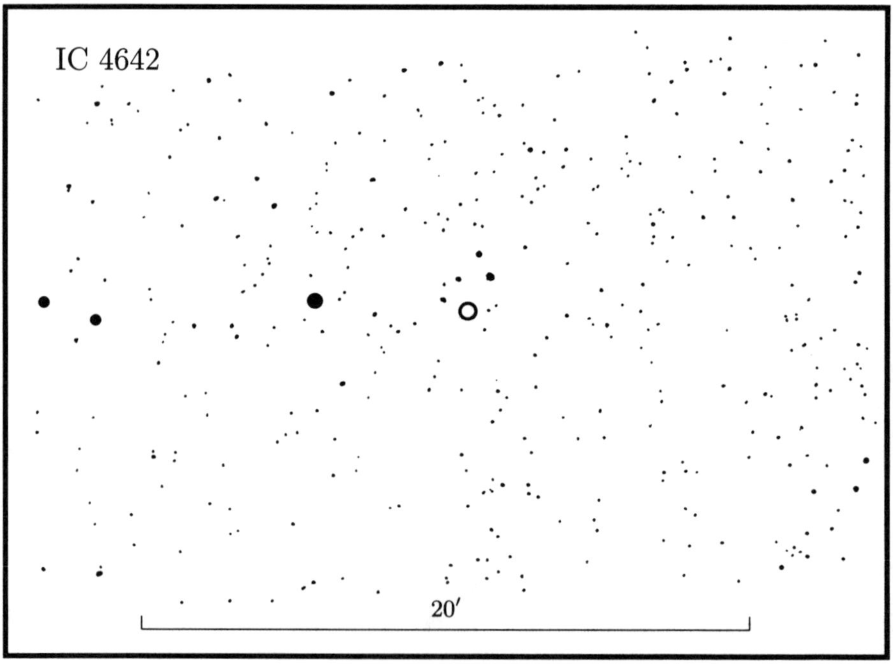
IC 4642
20′

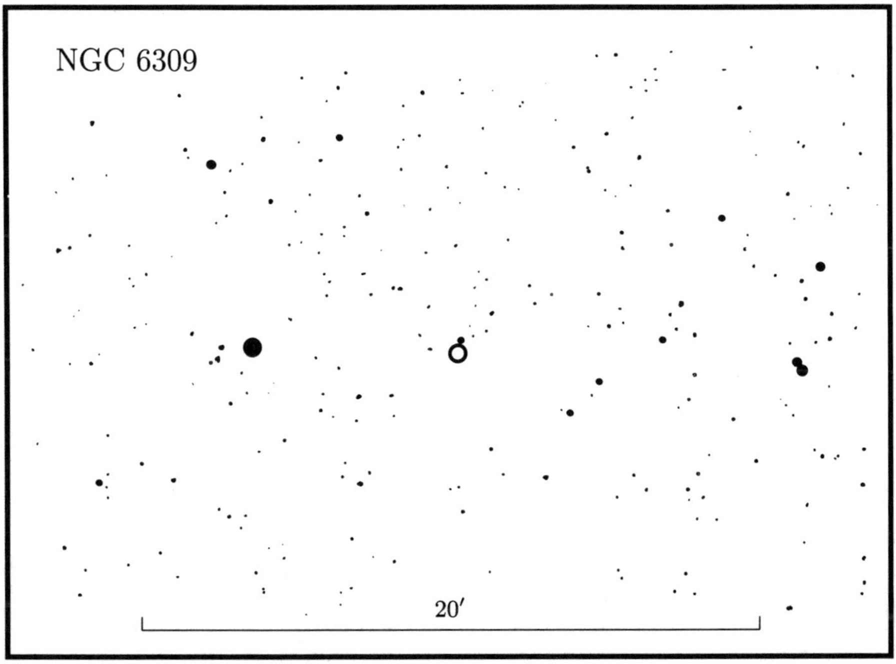
NGC 6309
20′

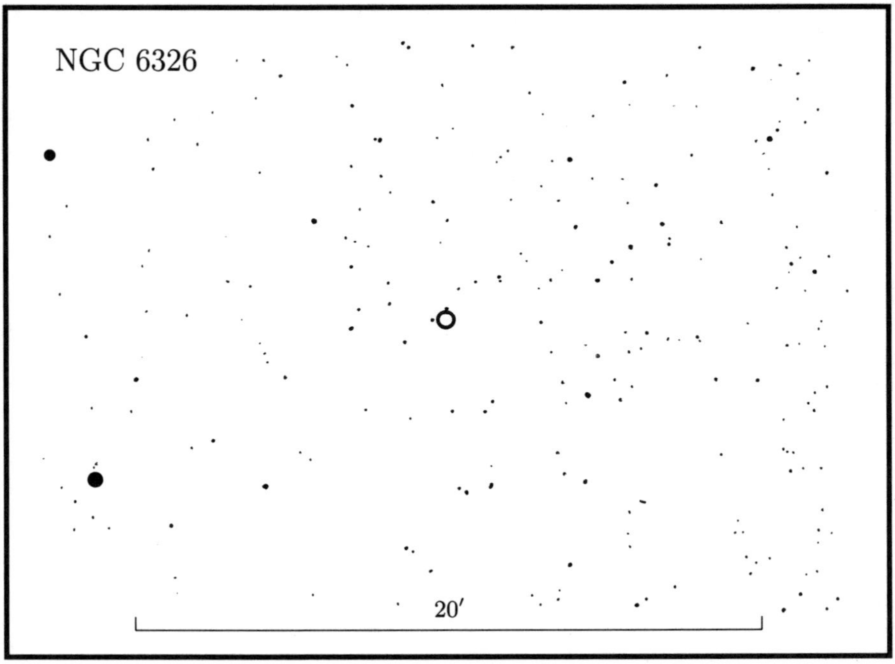
NGC 6326
20′

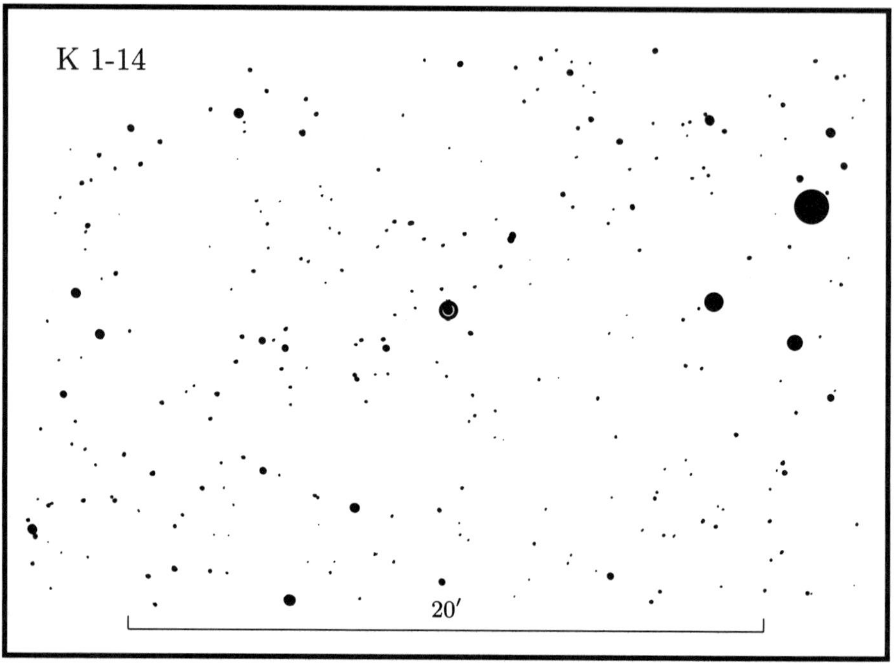
K 1-14
20′

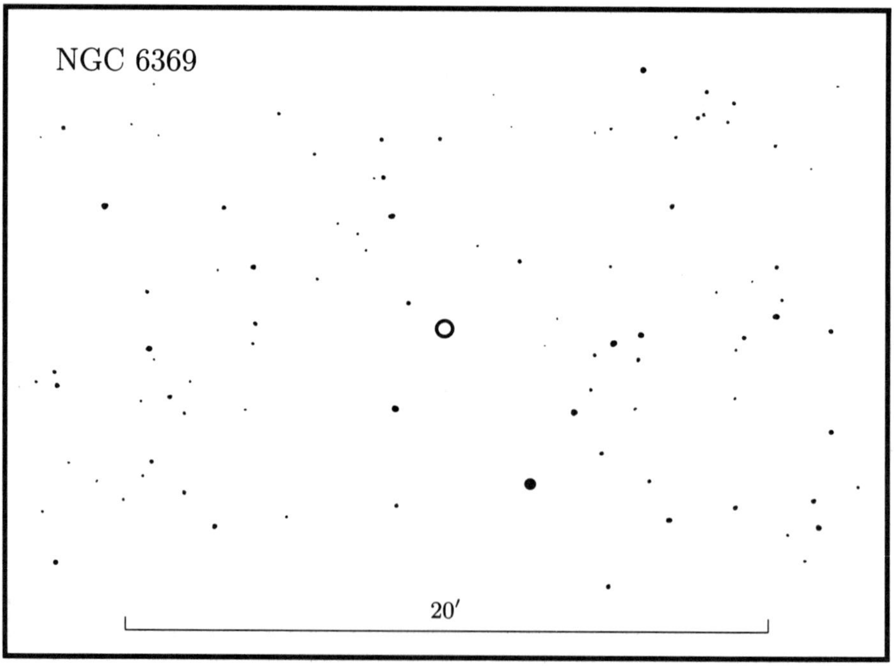
NGC 6369
20′

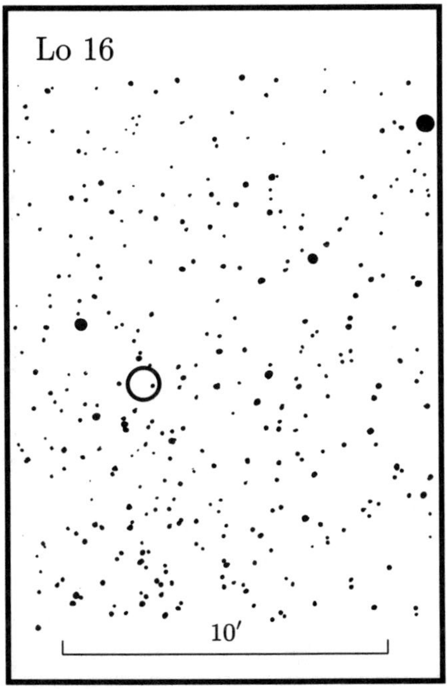
Lo 16
10′

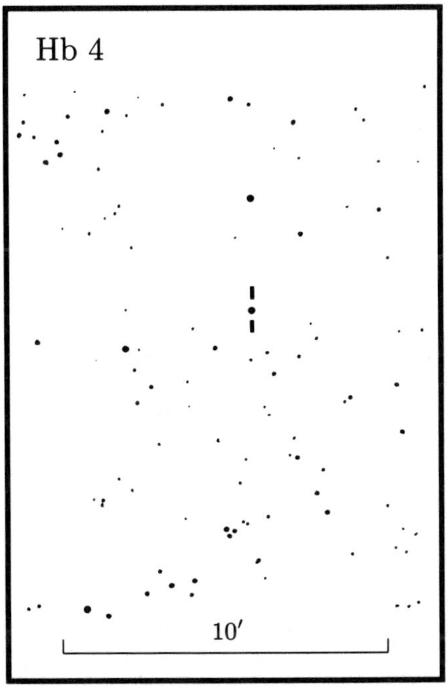
Hb 4
10′

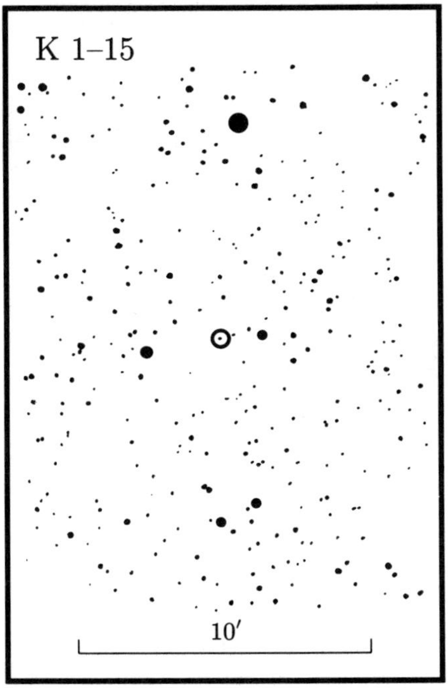
K 1–15
10′

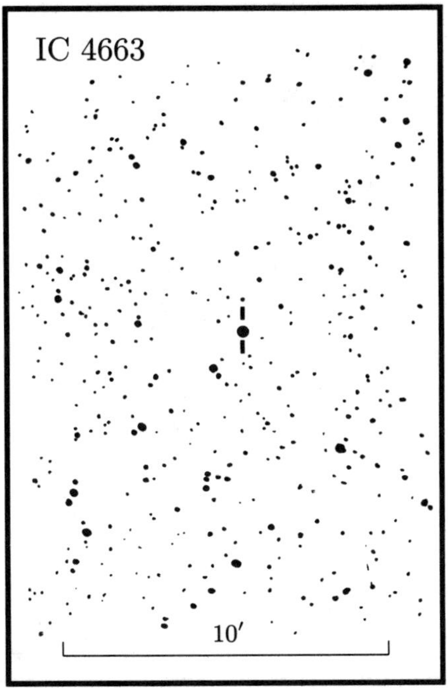
IC 4663
10′

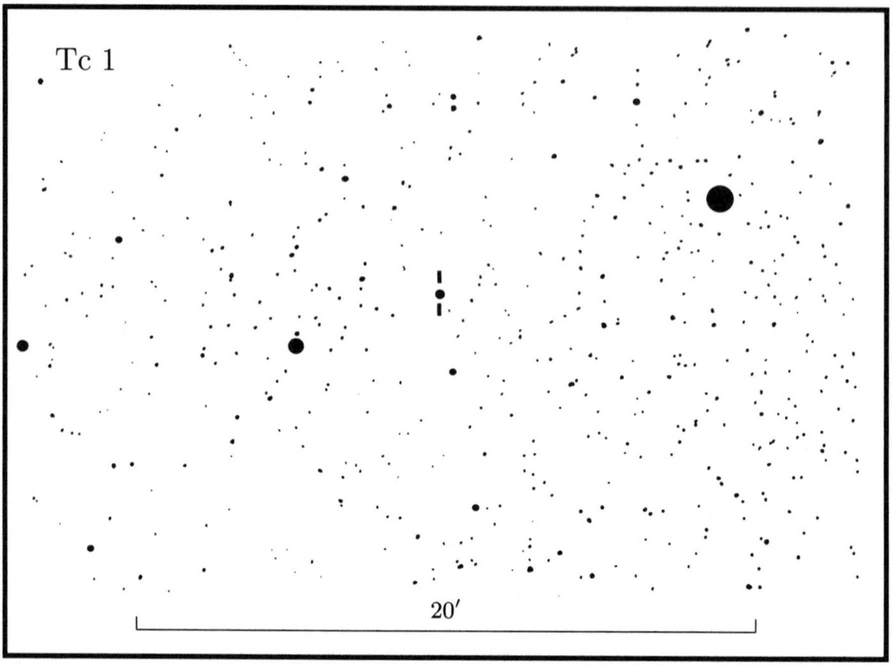
Tc 1
20′

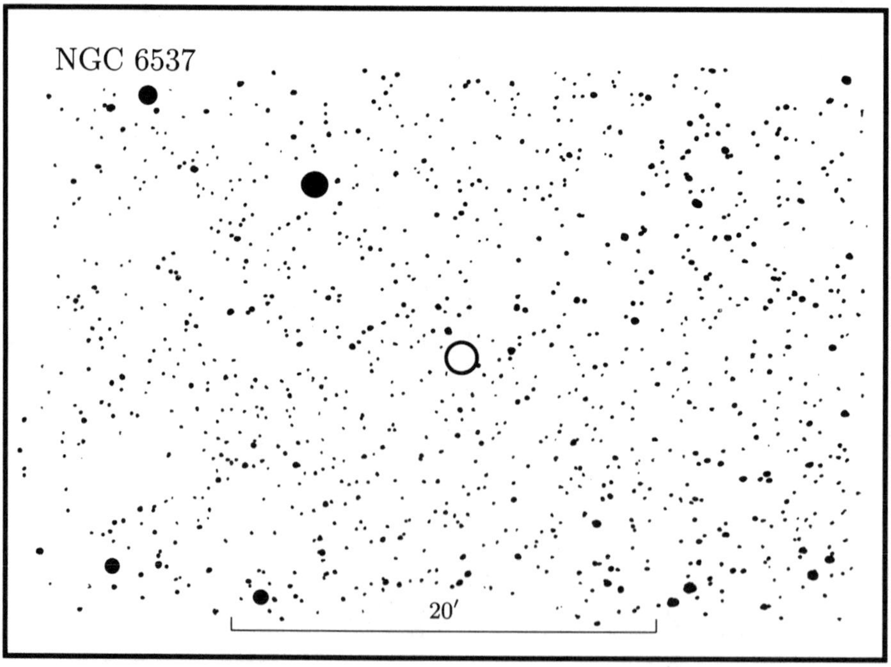
NGC 6537
20′

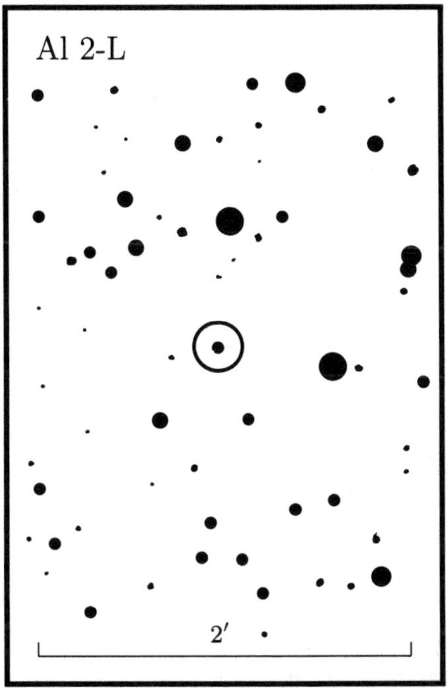
Al 2-L
2′

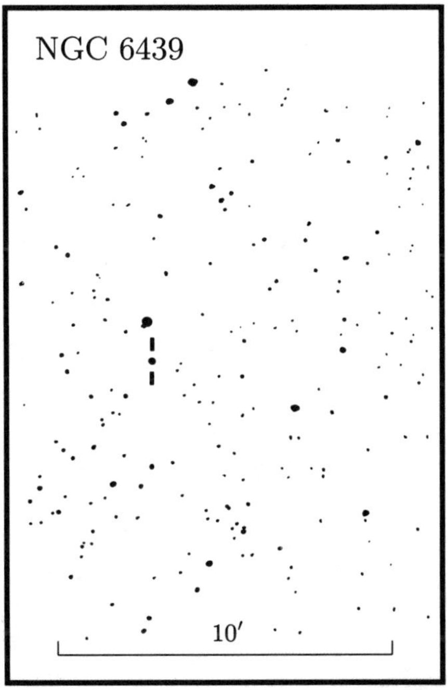
NGC 6439
10′

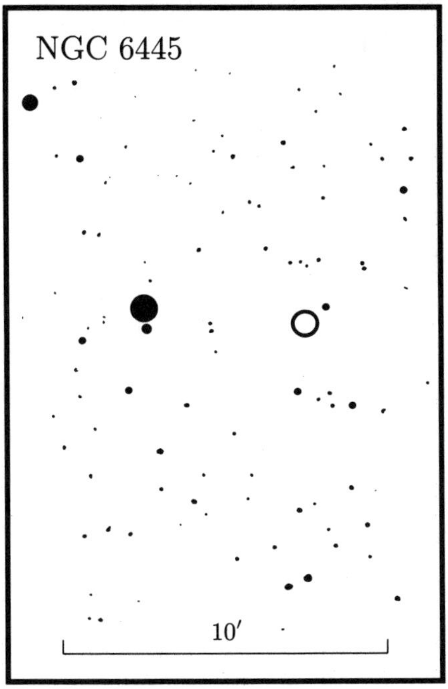
NGC 6445
10′

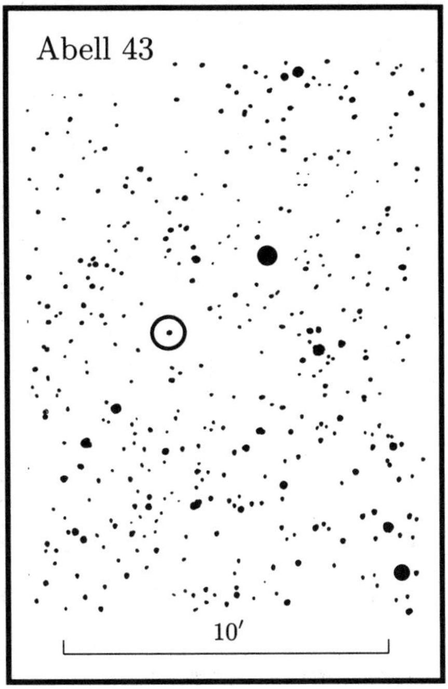
Abell 43
10′

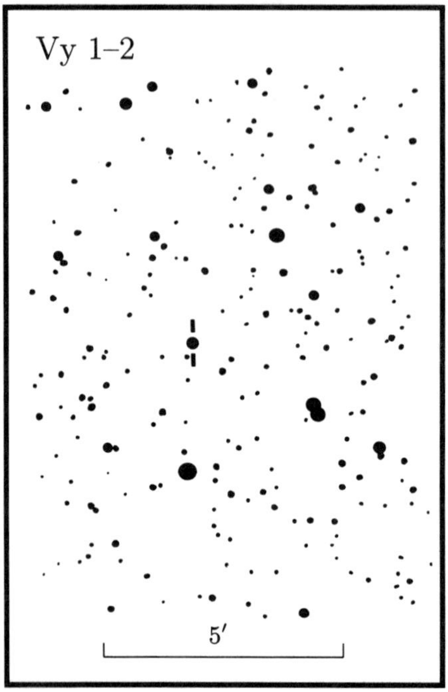
Vy 1–2
5′

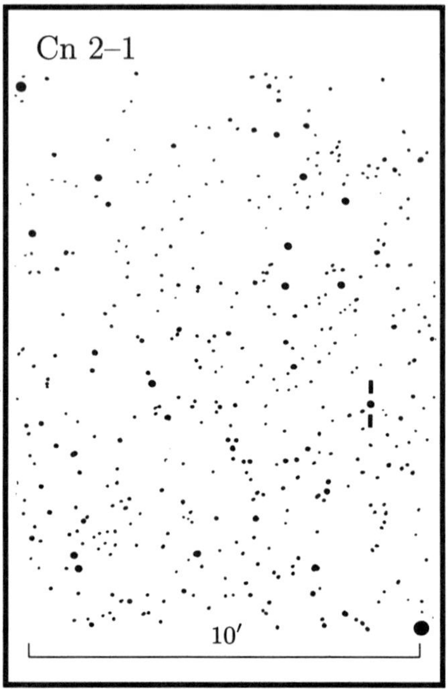
Cn 2–1
10′

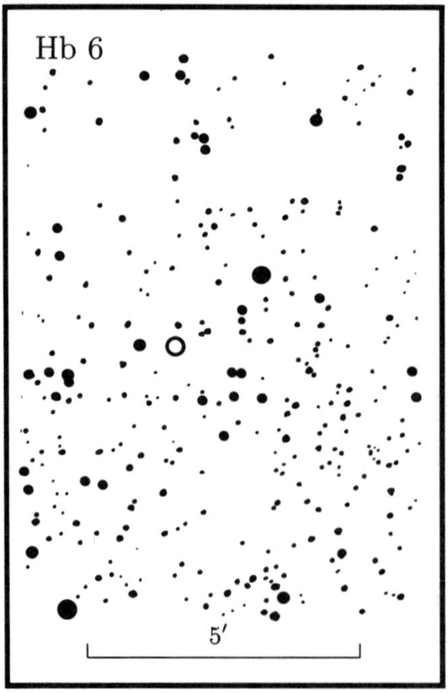
Hb 6
5′

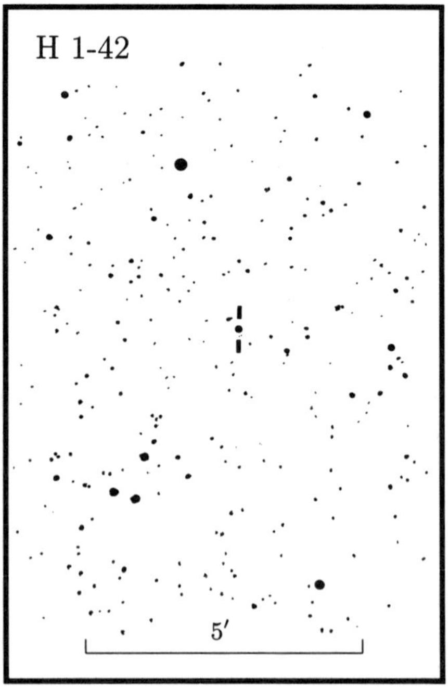
H 1-42
5′

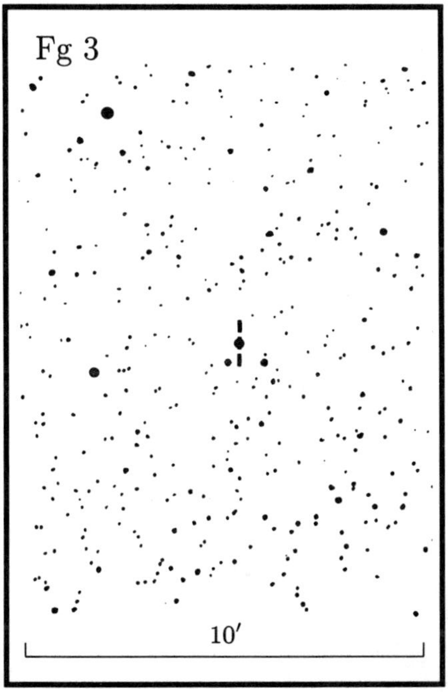
Fg 3
10′

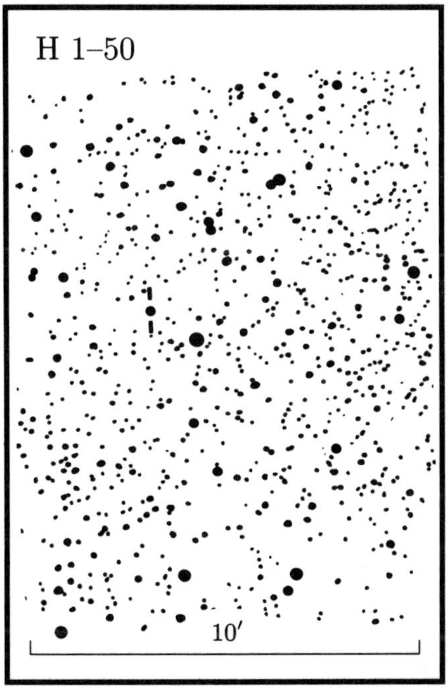
H 1–50
10′

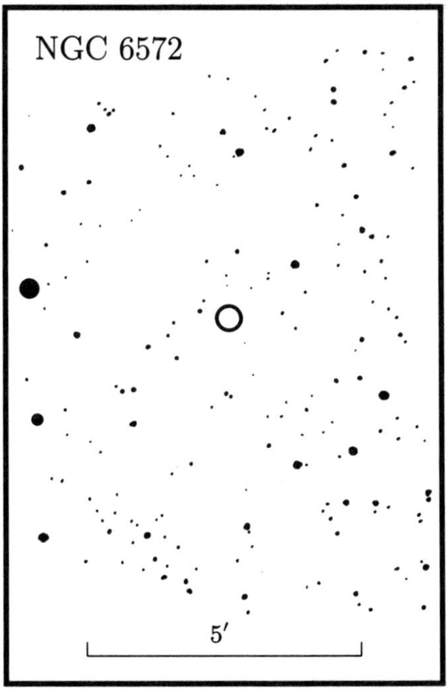
NGC 6572
5′

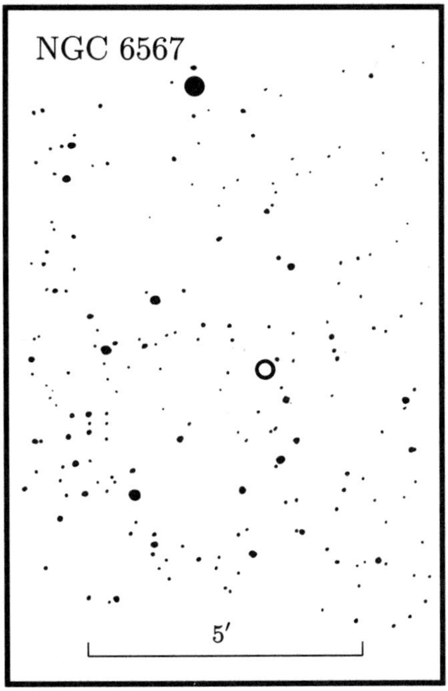
NGC 6567
5′

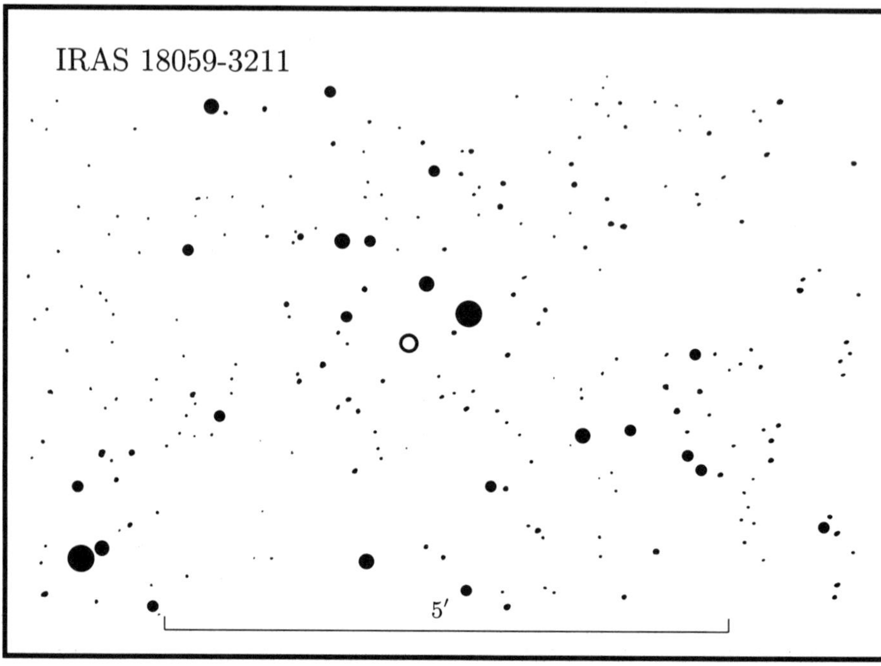
IRAS 18059-3211
5′

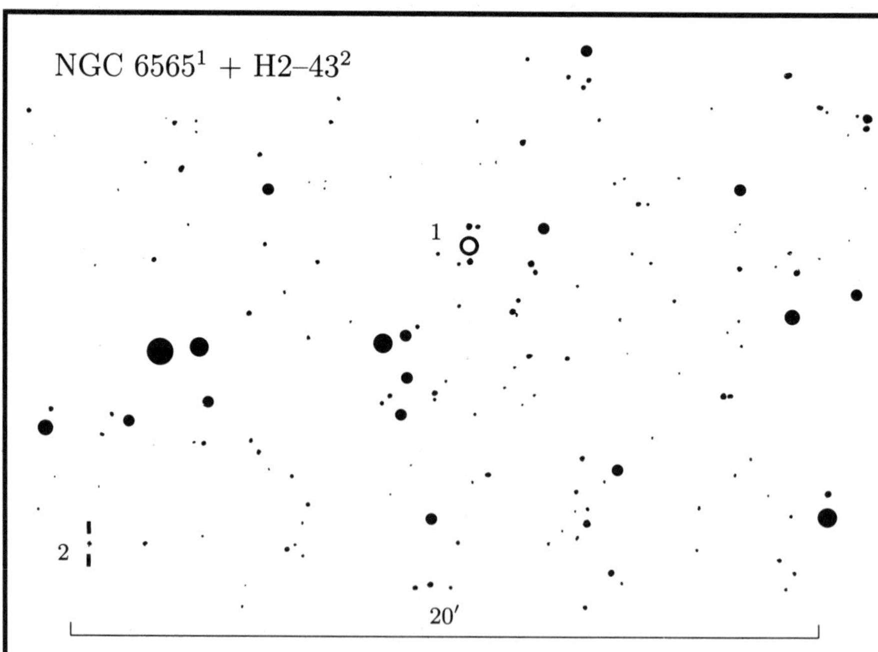
NGC 6565¹ + H2–43²
1
2
20′

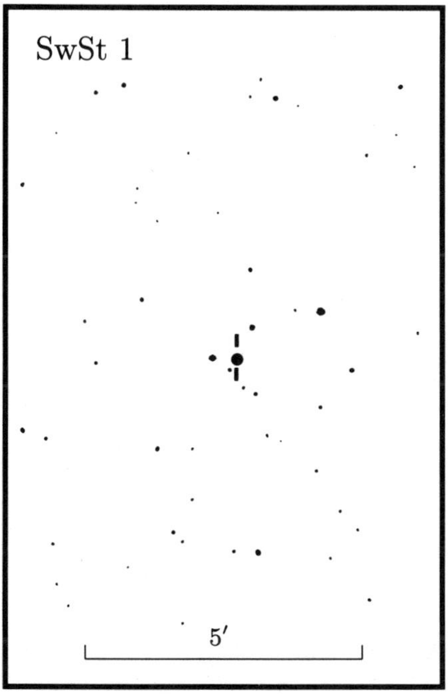
SwSt 1
5′

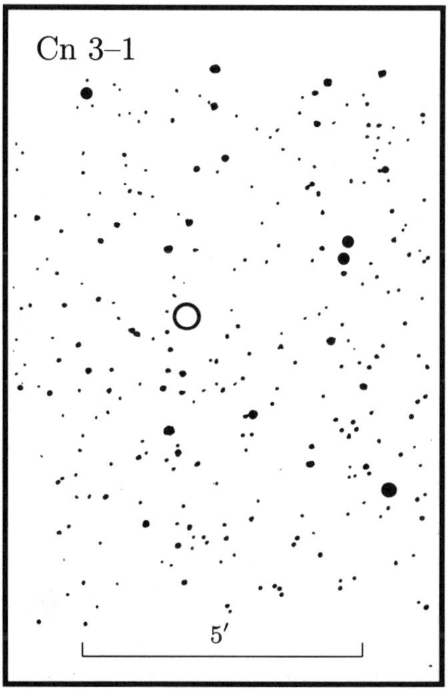
Cn 3–1
5′

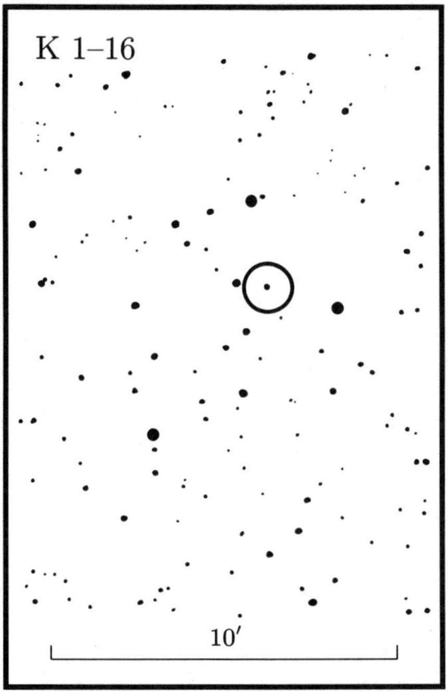
K 1–16
10′

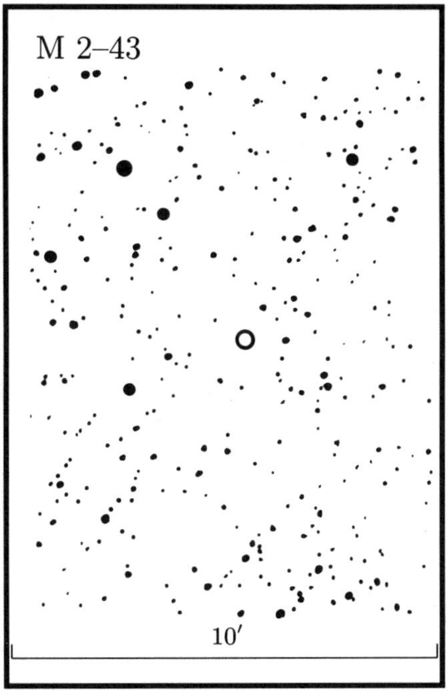
M 2–43
10′

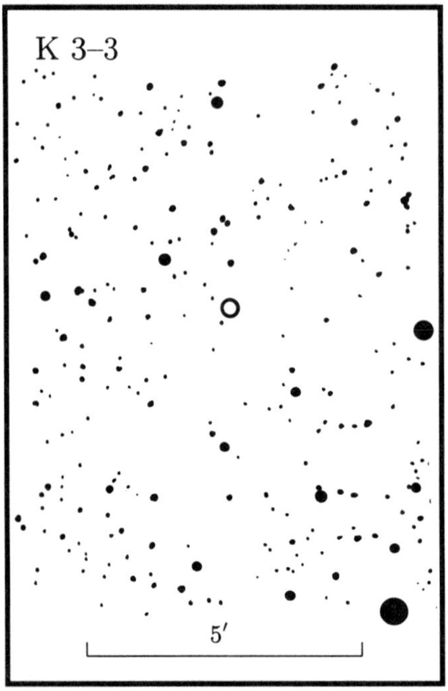
K 3–3
5′

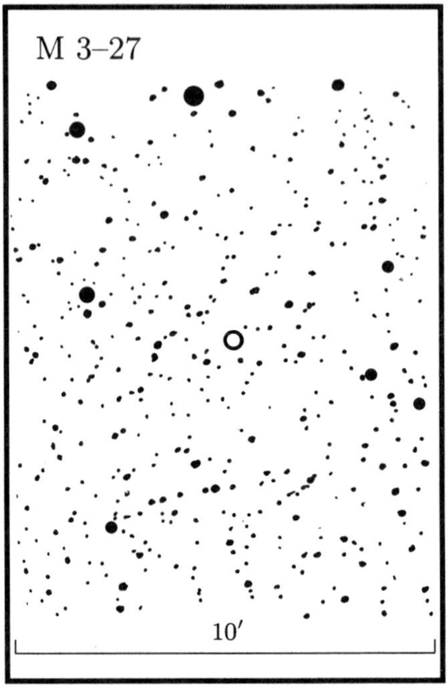
M 3–27
10′

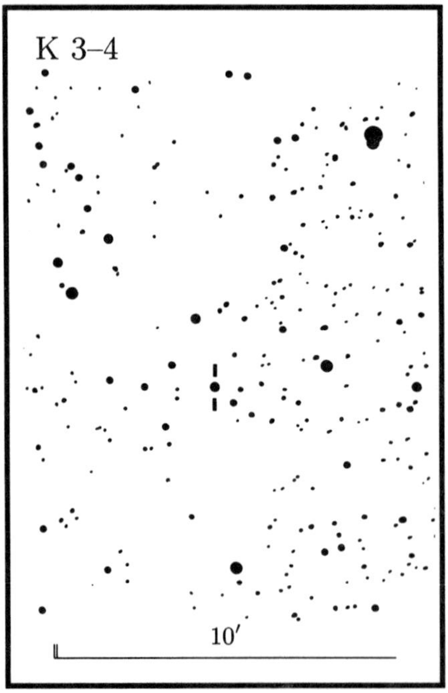
K 3–4
10′

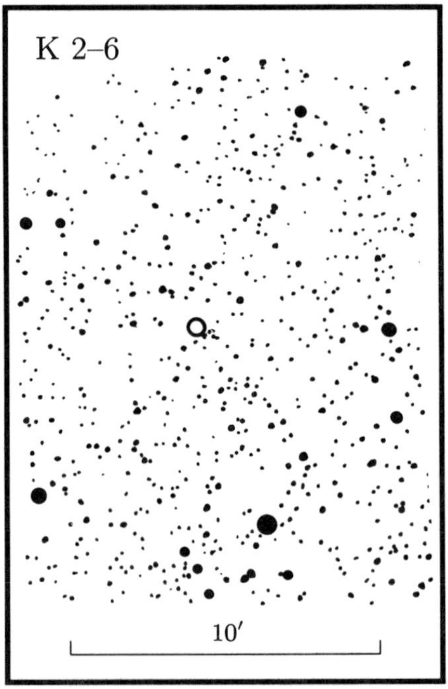
K 2–6
10′

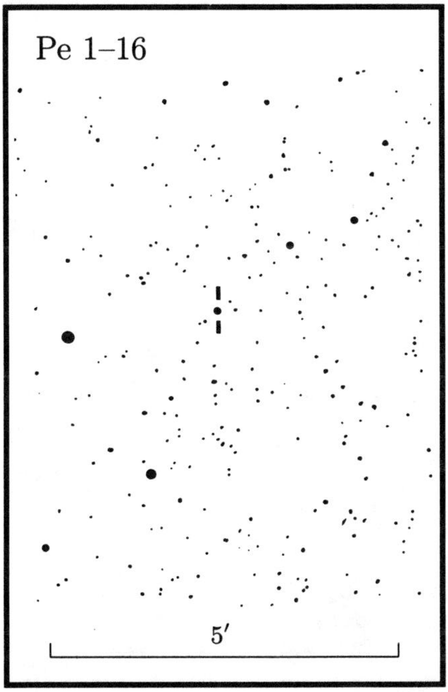
Pe 1–16
5′

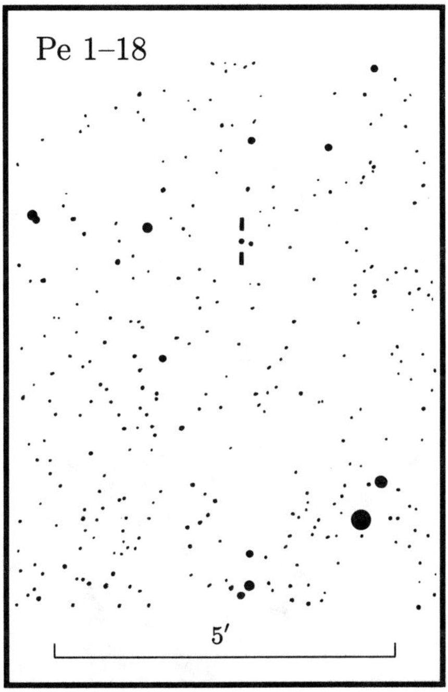
Pe 1–18
5′

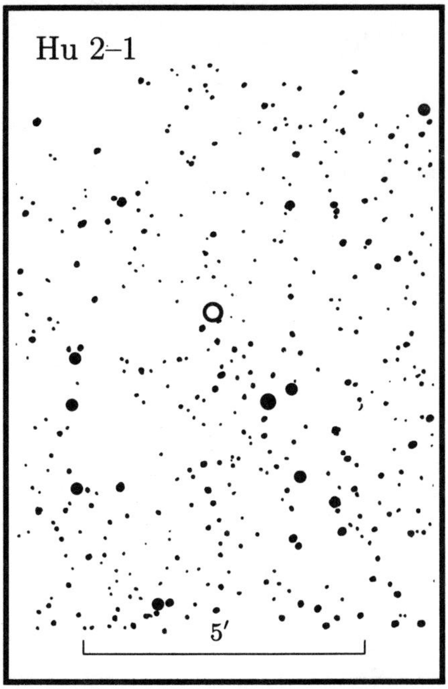
Hu 2–1
5′

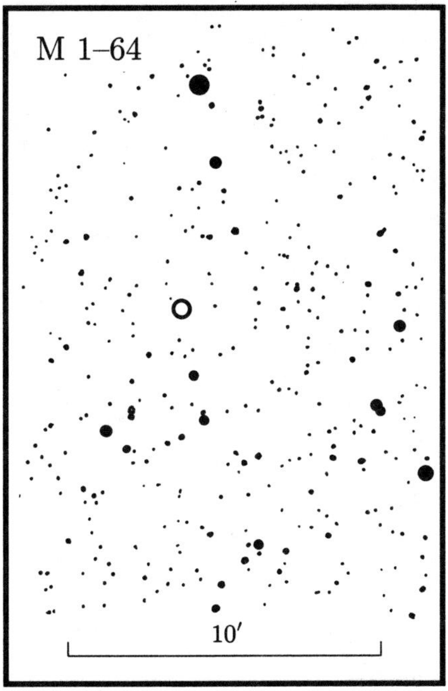
M 1–64
10′

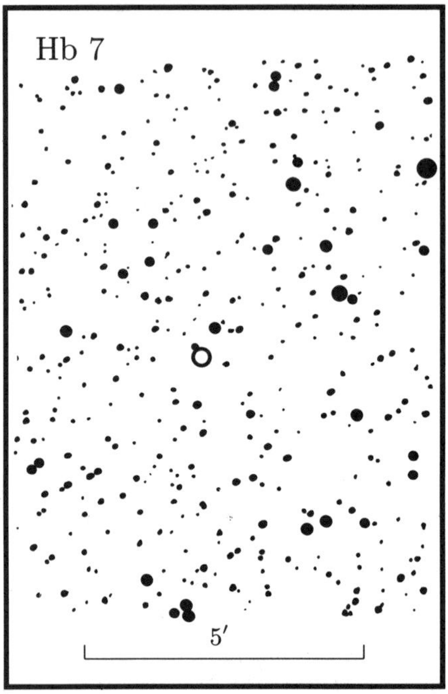

Hb 7
5′

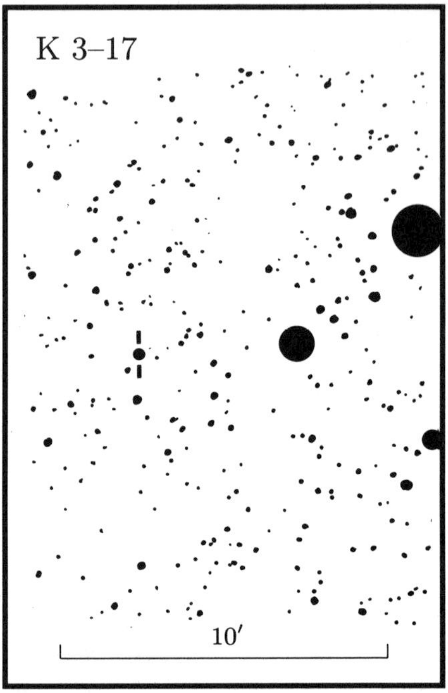

K 3–17
10′

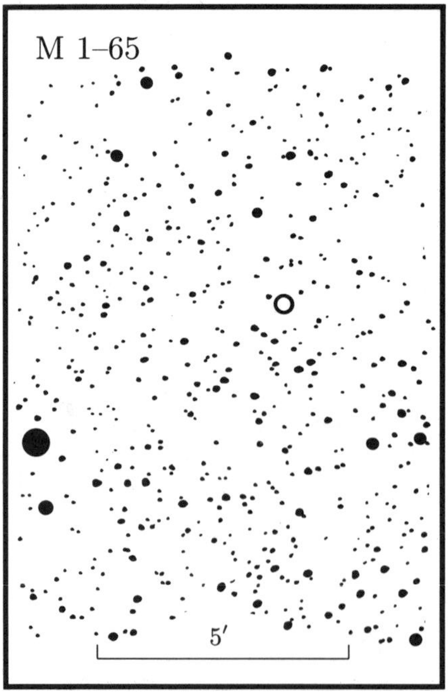

M 1–65
5′

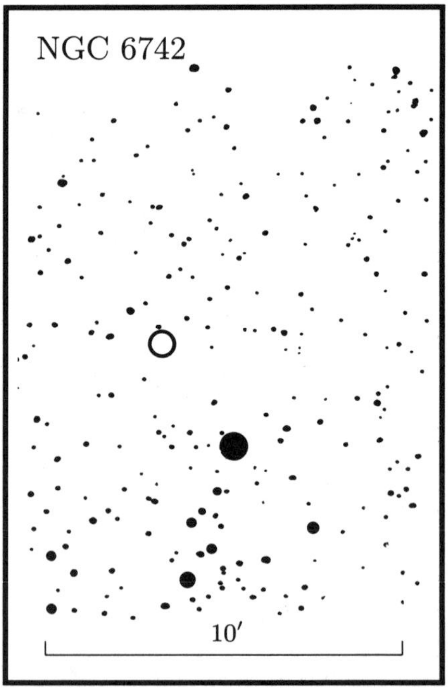

NGC 6742
10′

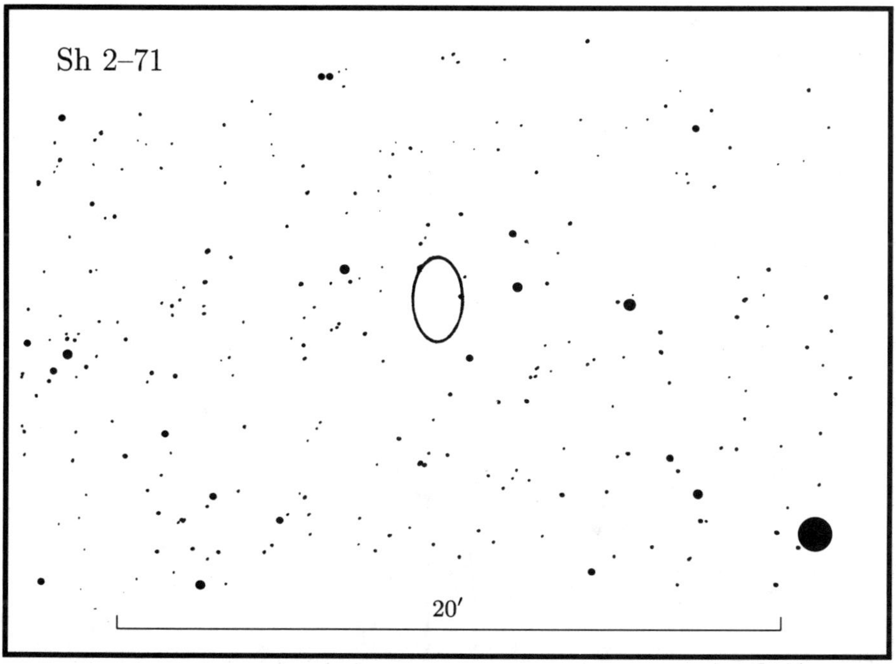
Sh 2–71
20′

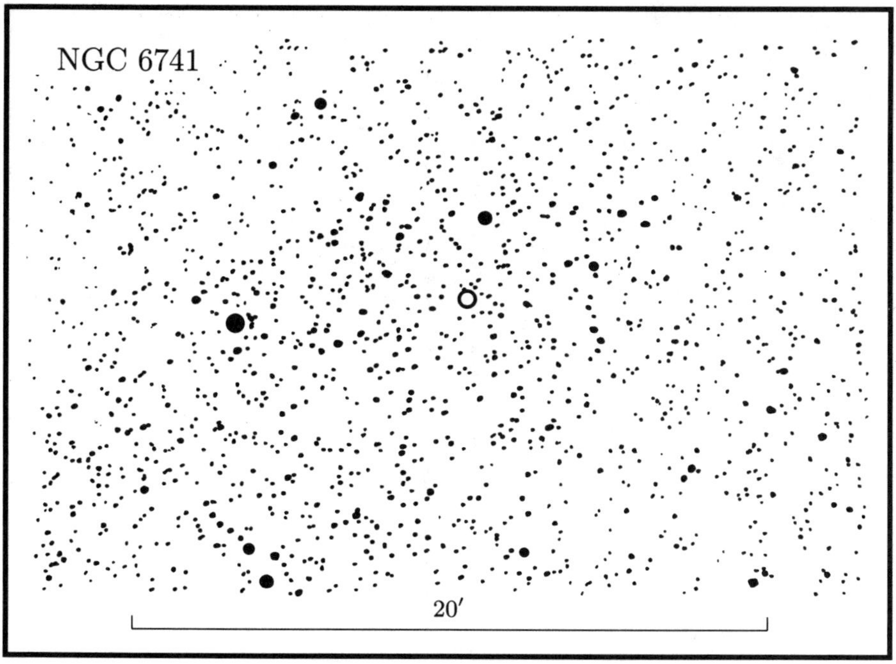
NGC 6741
20′

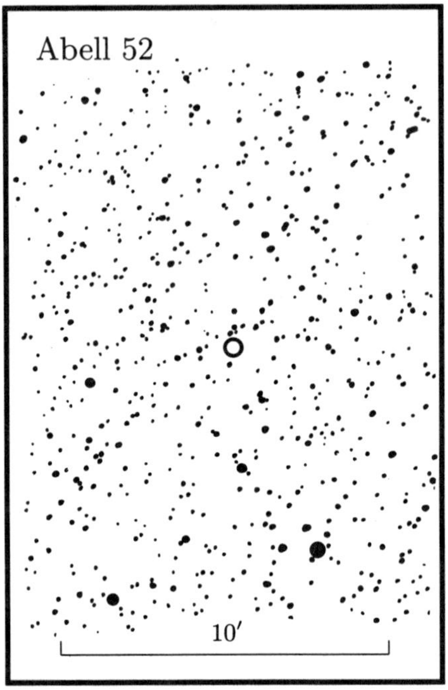
Abell 52
10′

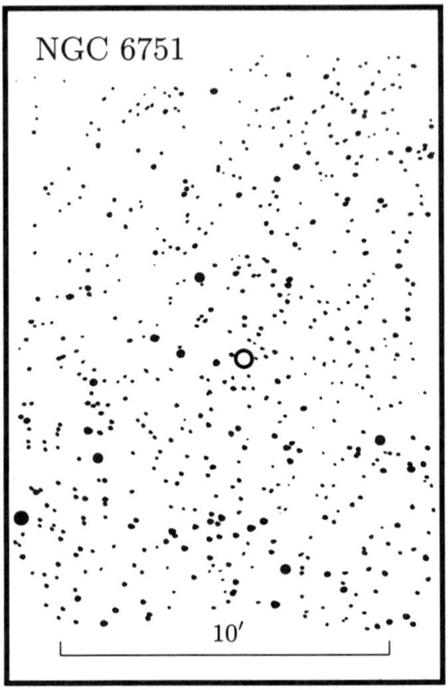
NGC 6751
10′

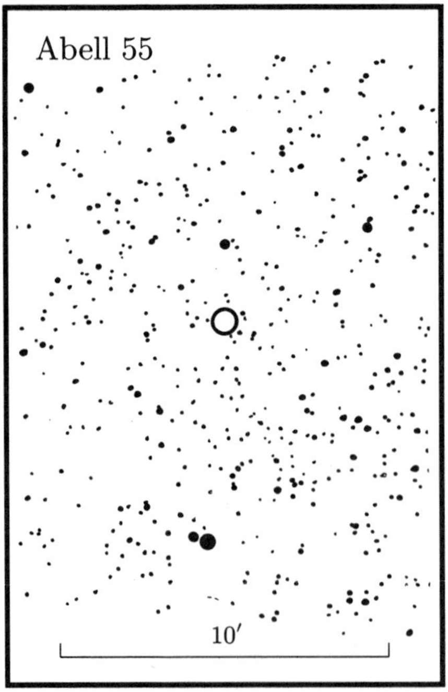
Abell 55
10′

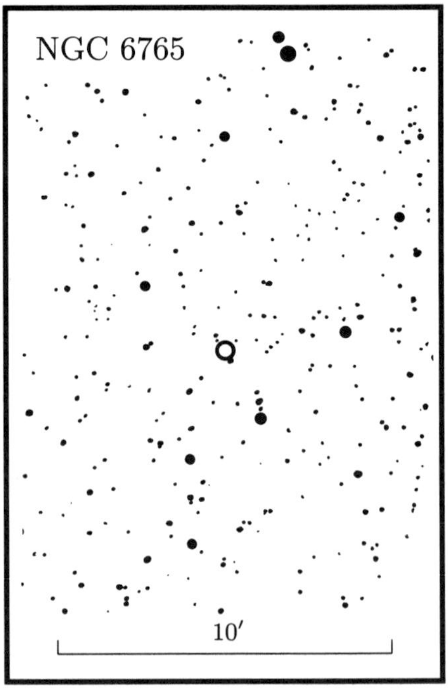
NGC 6765
10′

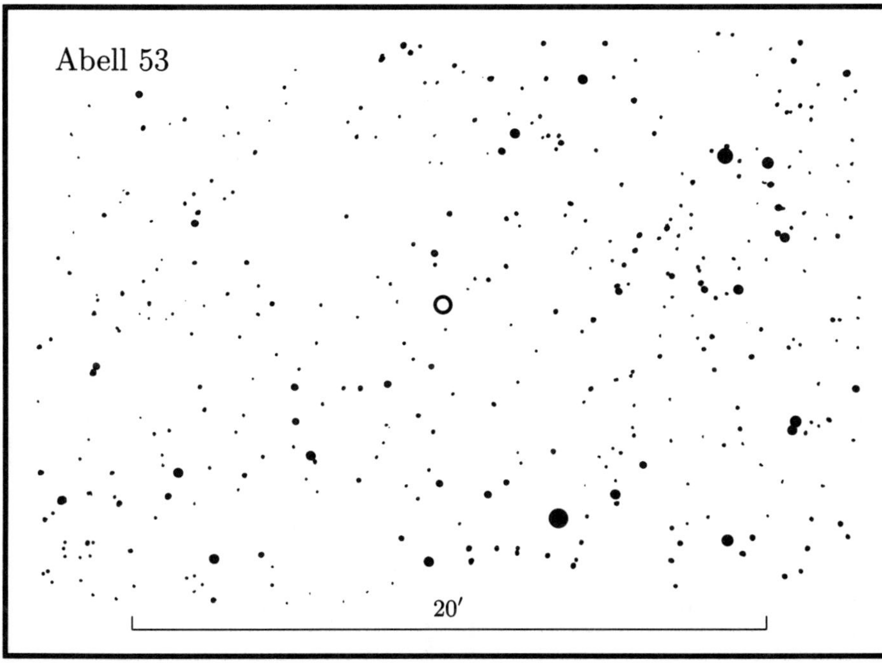
Abell 53
20′

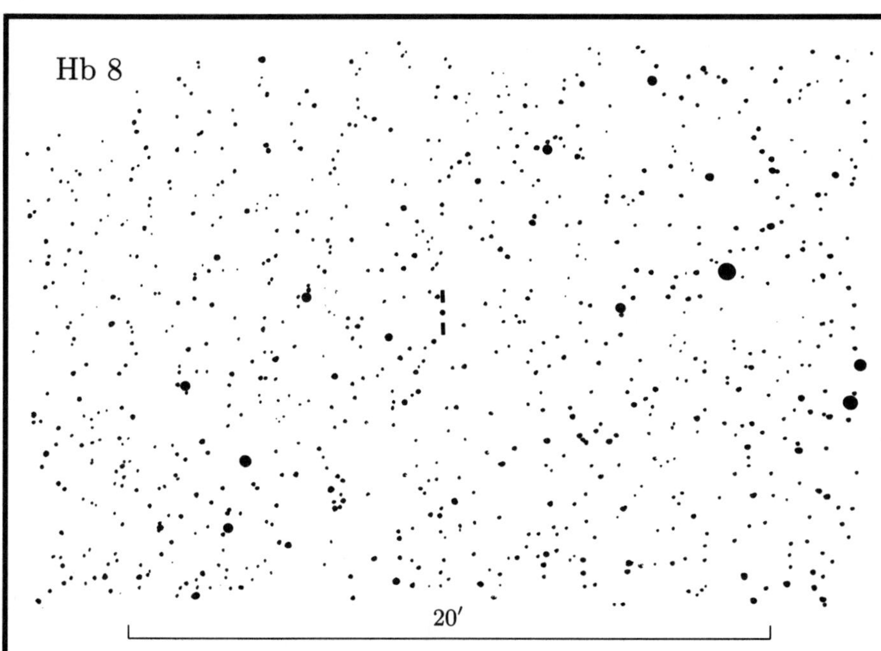
Hb 8
20′

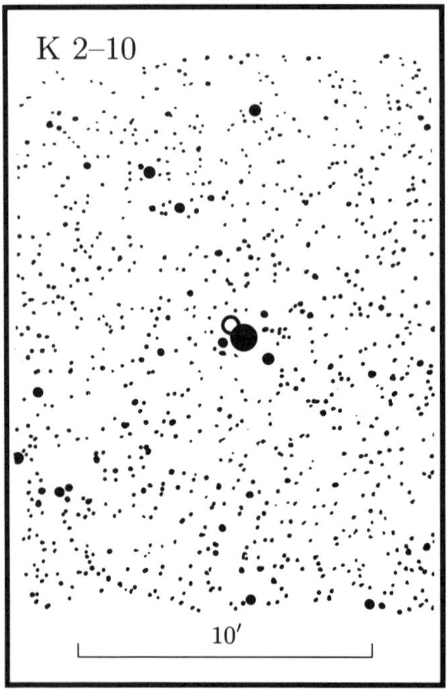
K 2–10
10′

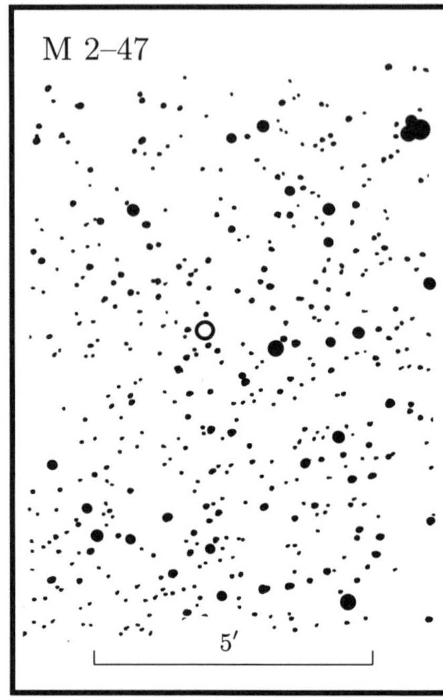
M 2–47
5′

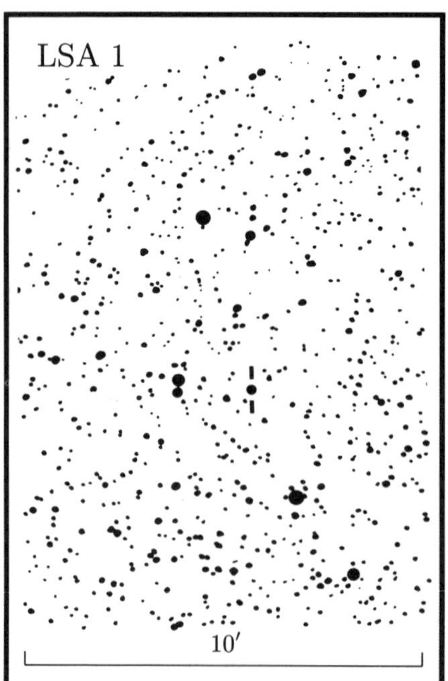
LSA 1
10′

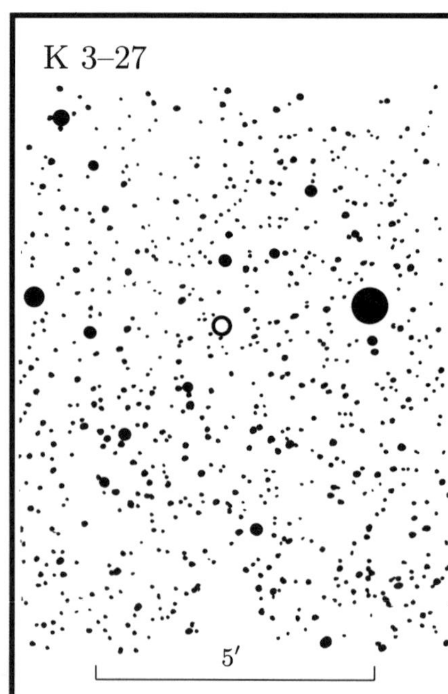
K 3–27
5′

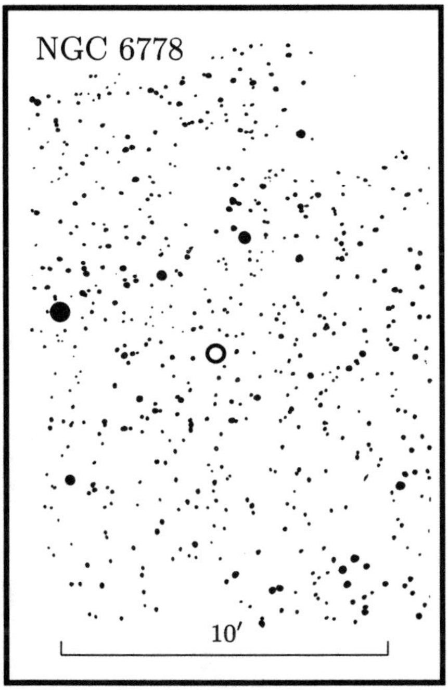
NGC 6778
10′

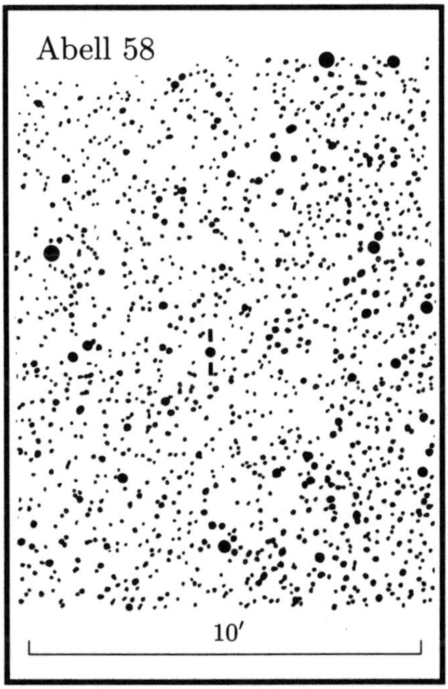
Abell 58
10′

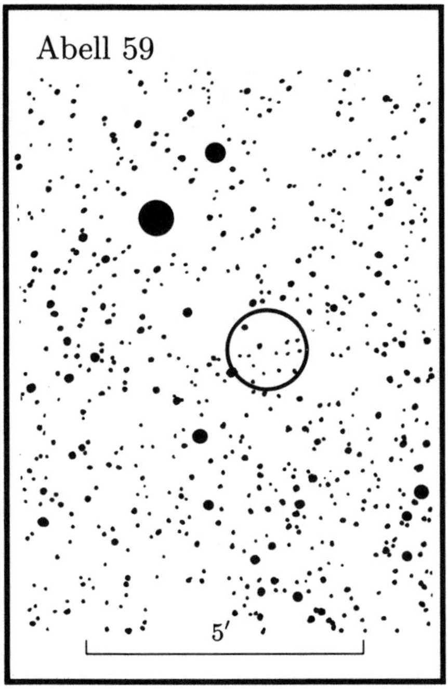
Abell 59
5′

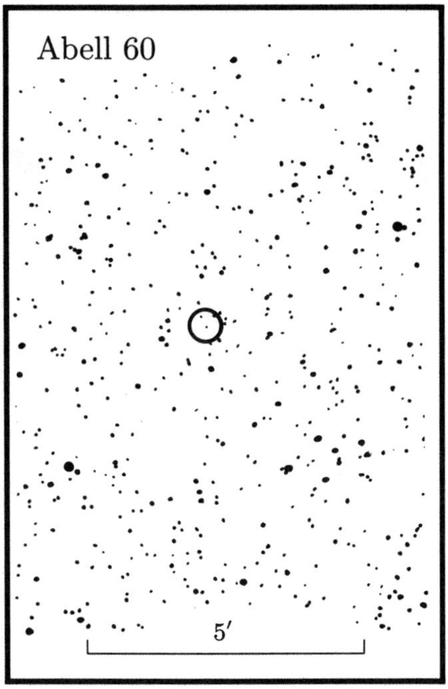
Abell 60
5′

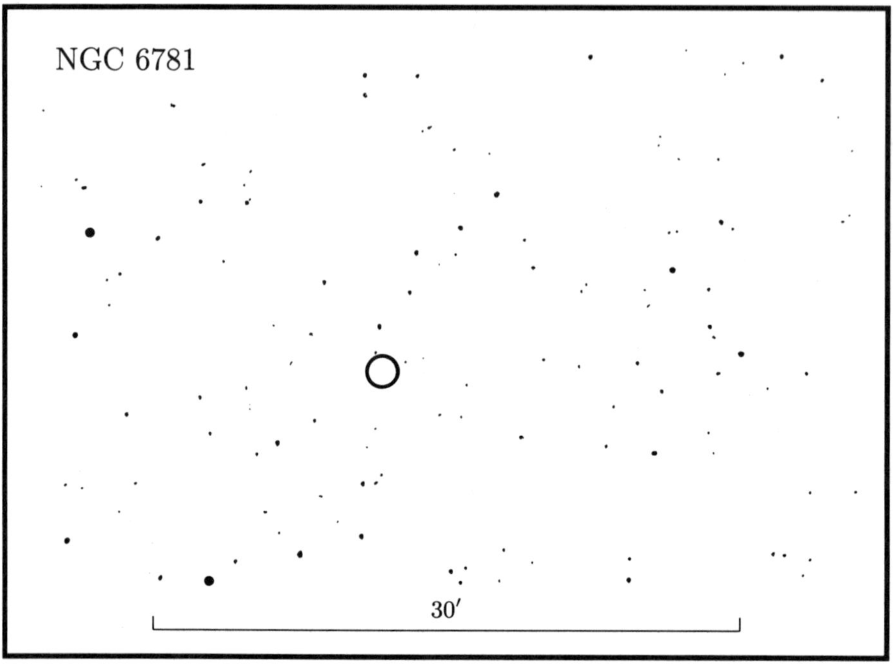
NGC 6781
30′

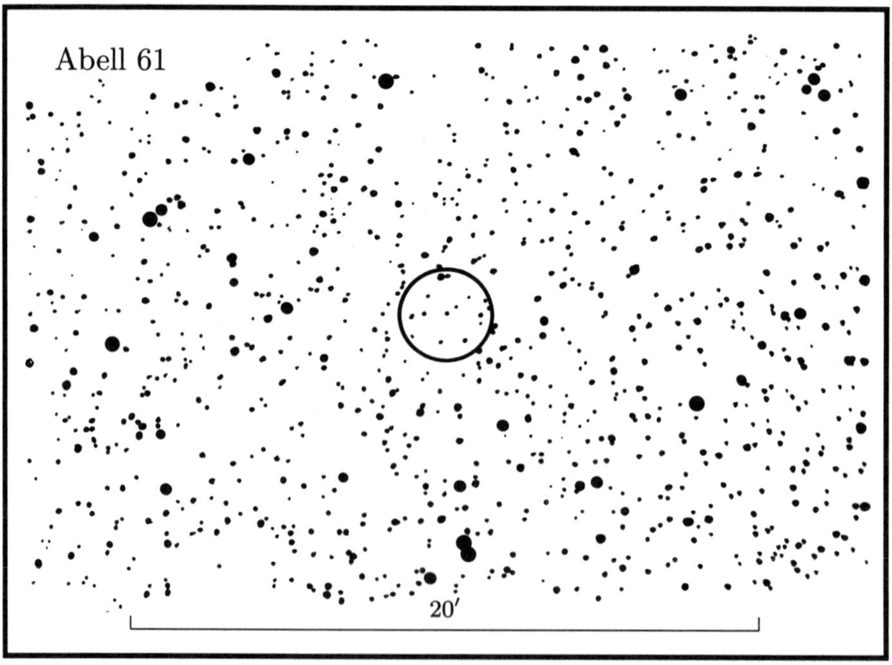
Abell 61
20′

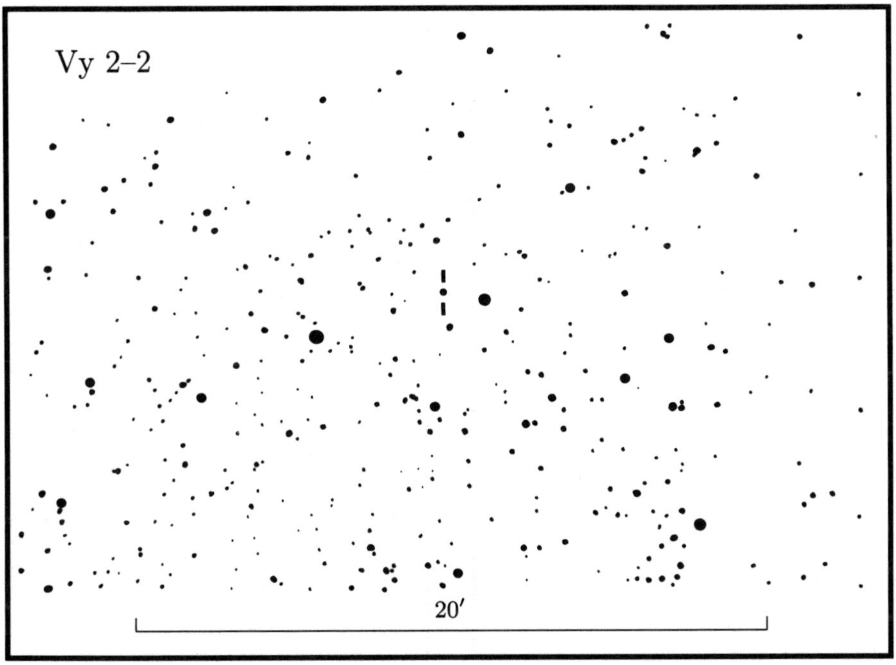
Vy 2–2
20′

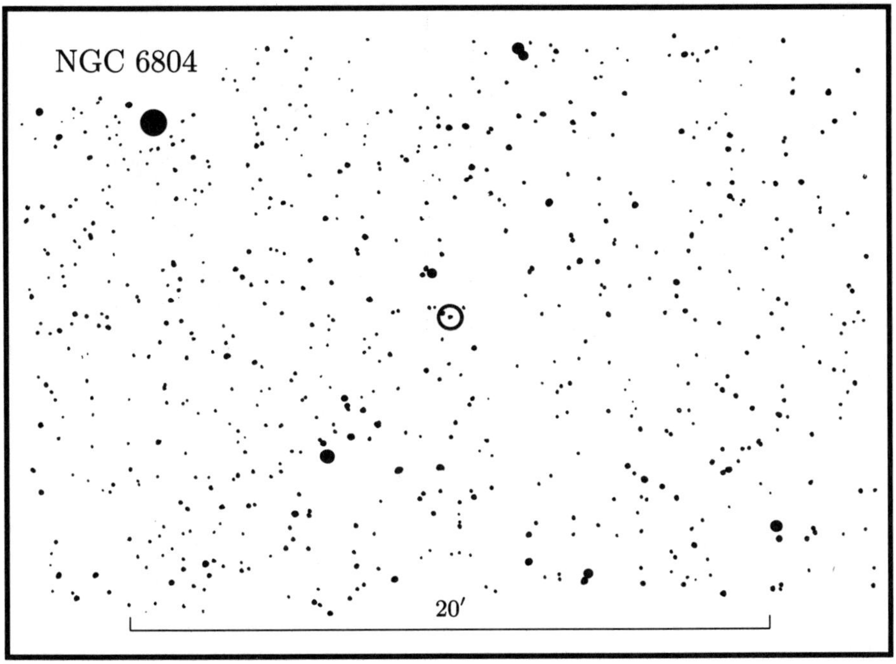
NGC 6804
20′

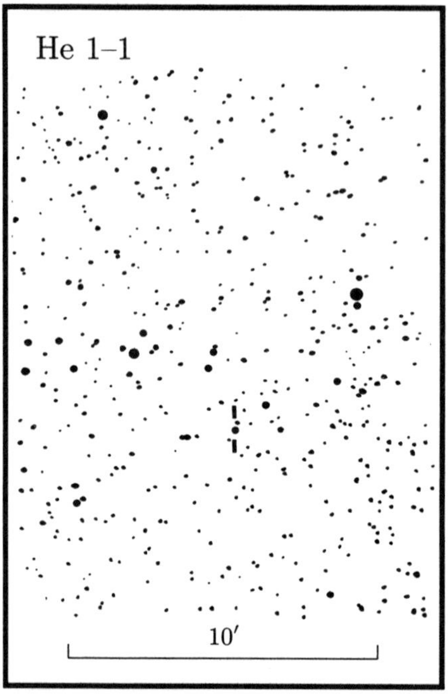
He 1–1
10′

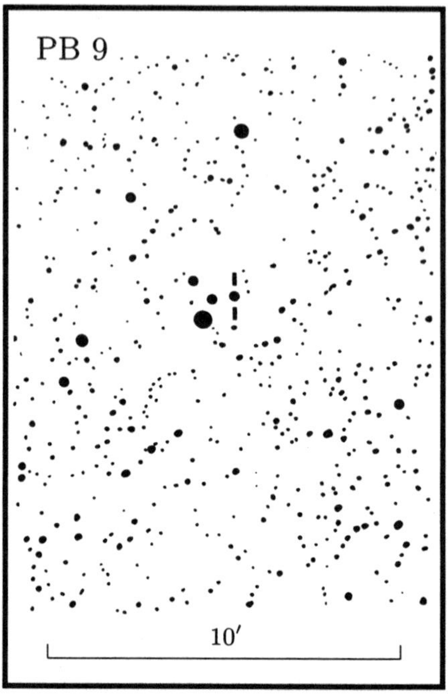
PB 9
10′

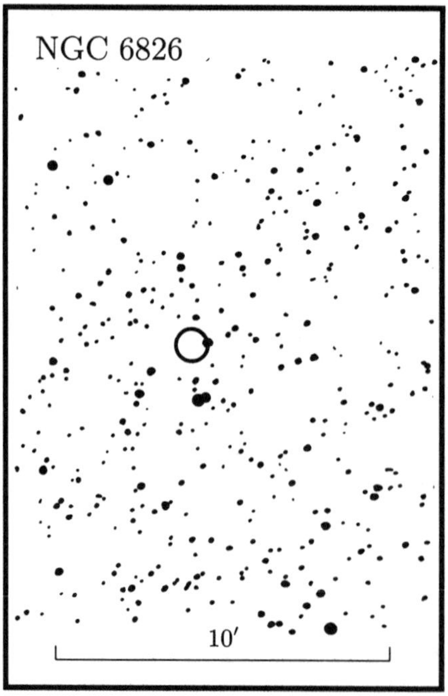
NGC 6826
10′

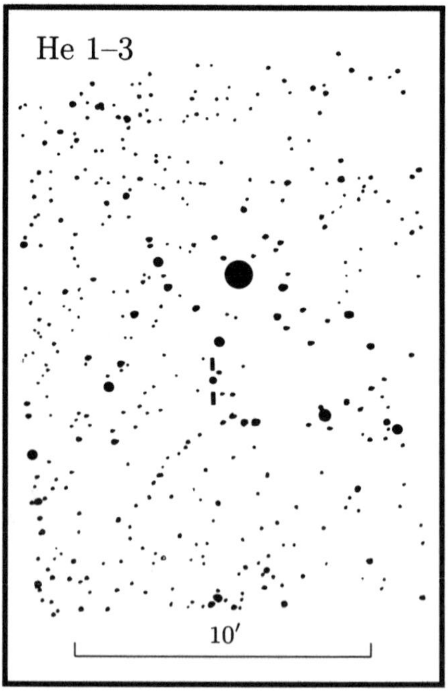
He 1–3
10′

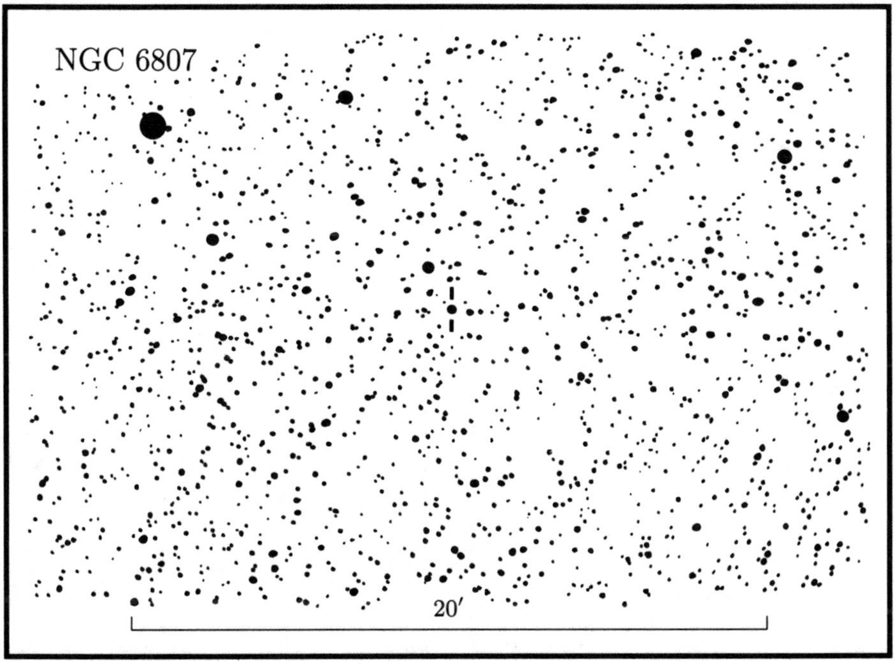
NGC 6807
20′

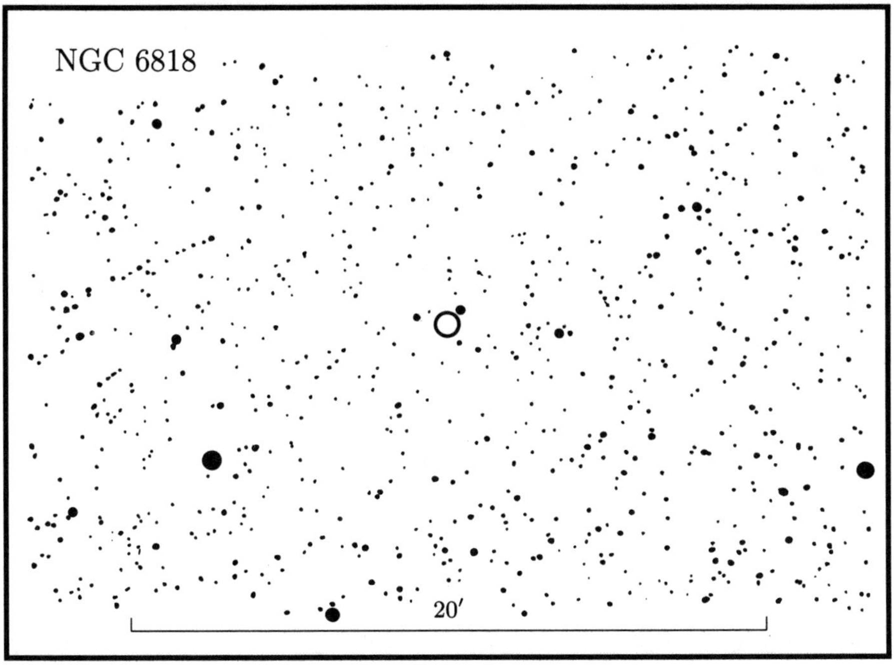
NGC 6818
20′

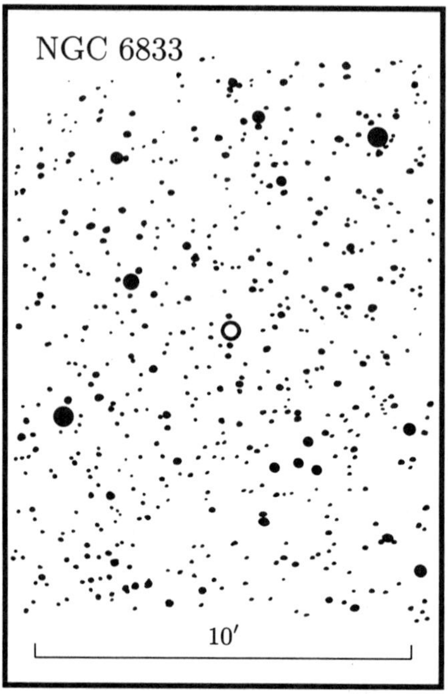
NGC 6833
10′

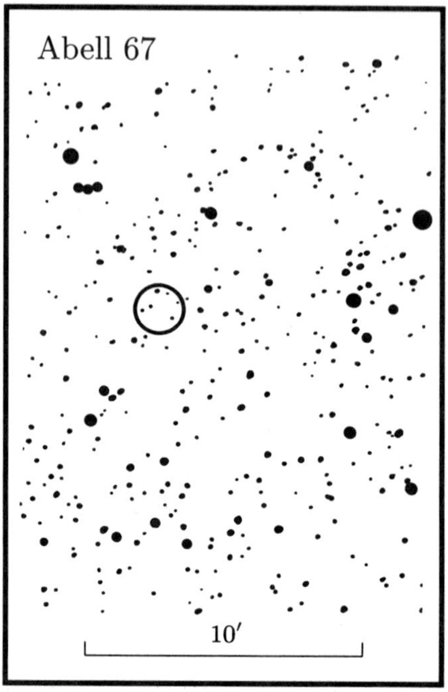
Abell 67
10′

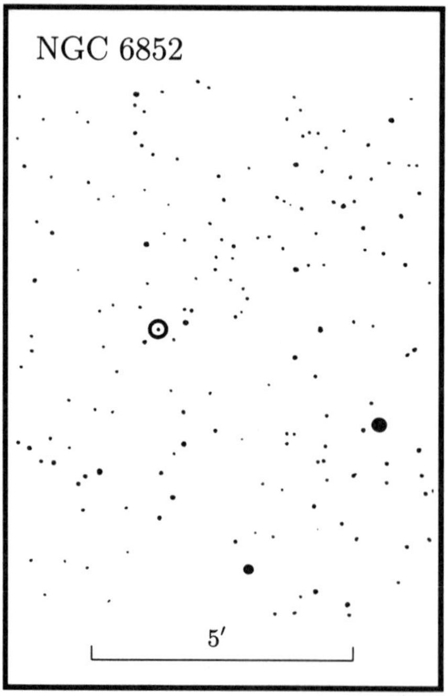
NGC 6852
5′

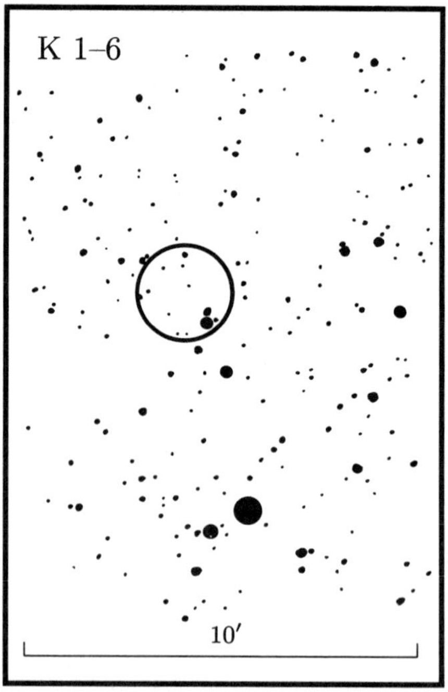
K 1–6
10′

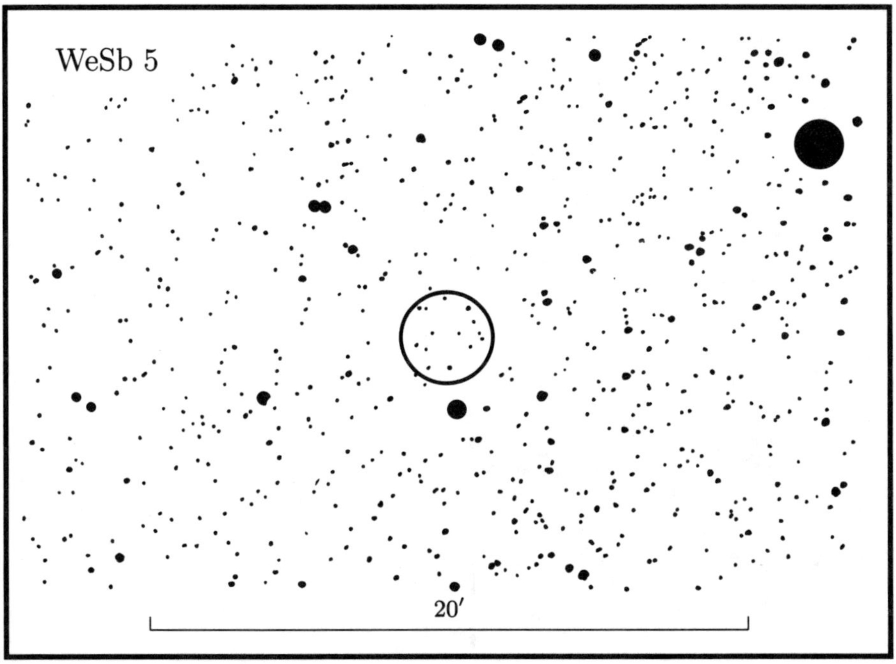
WeSb 5
20′

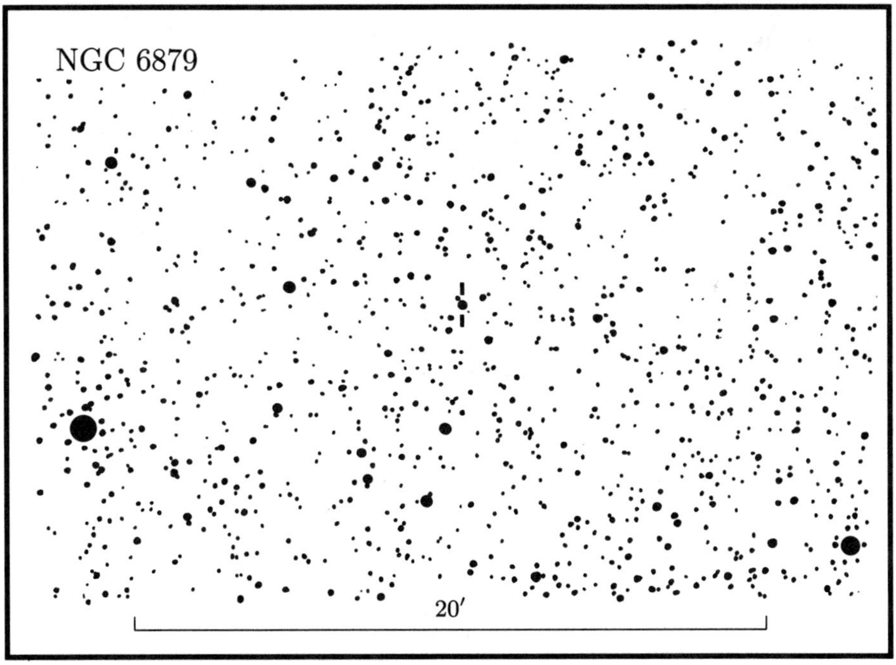
NGC 6879
20′

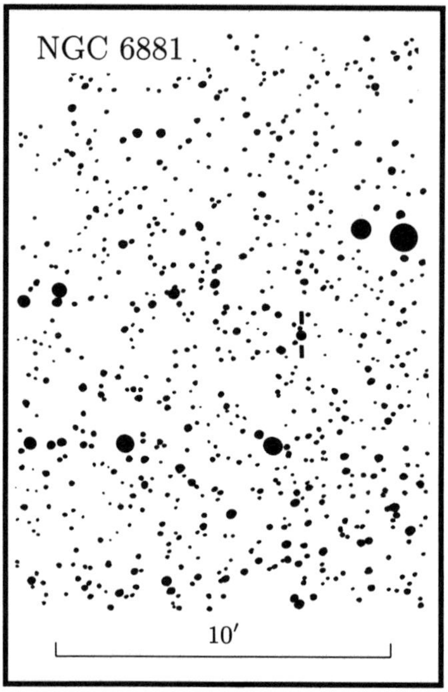
NGC 6881
10′

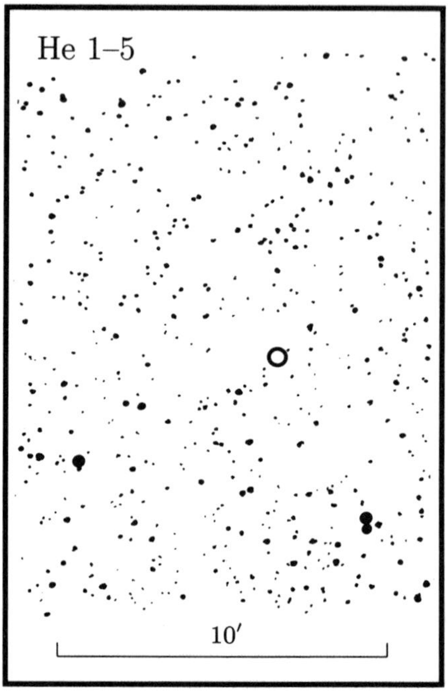
He 1–5
10′

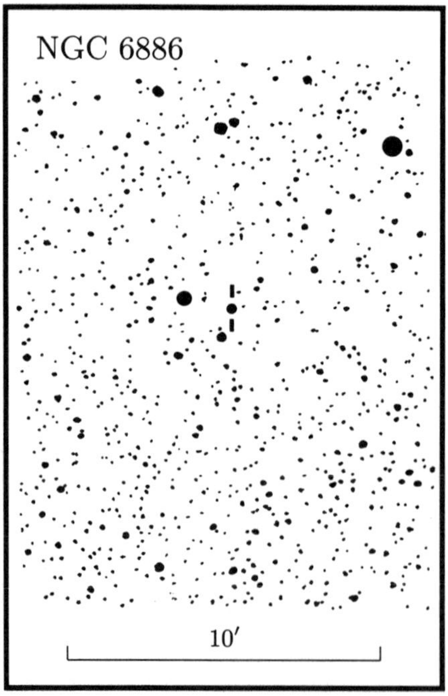
NGC 6886
10′

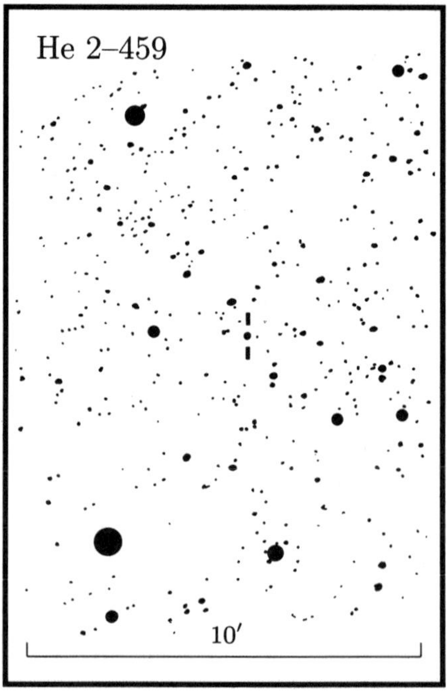
He 2–459
10′

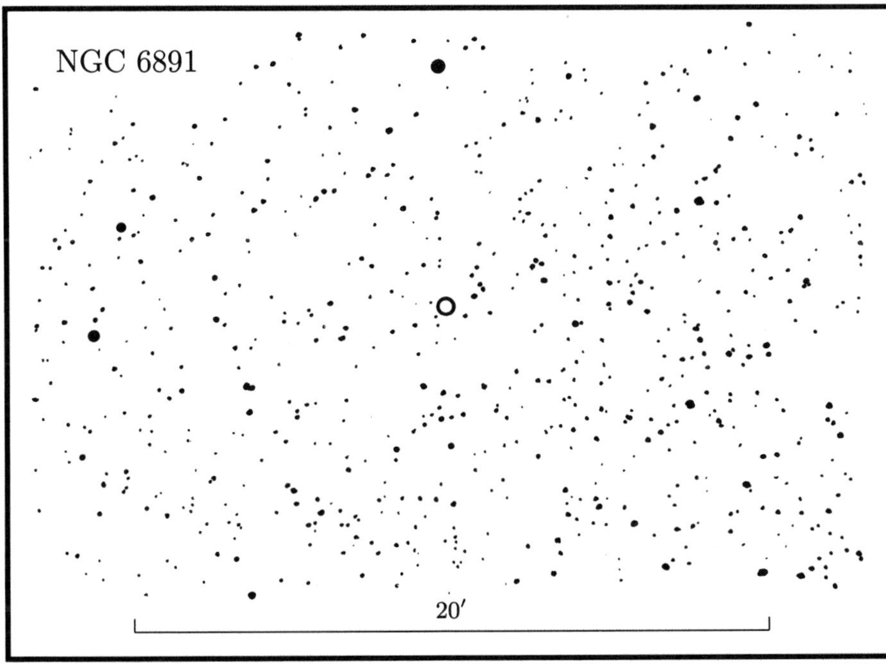
NGC 6891
20′

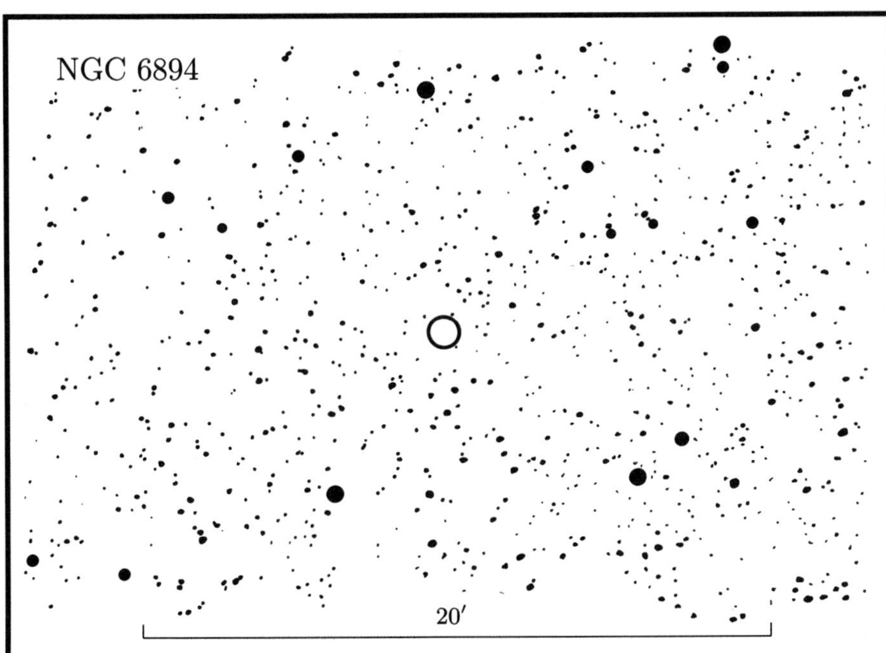
NGC 6894
20′

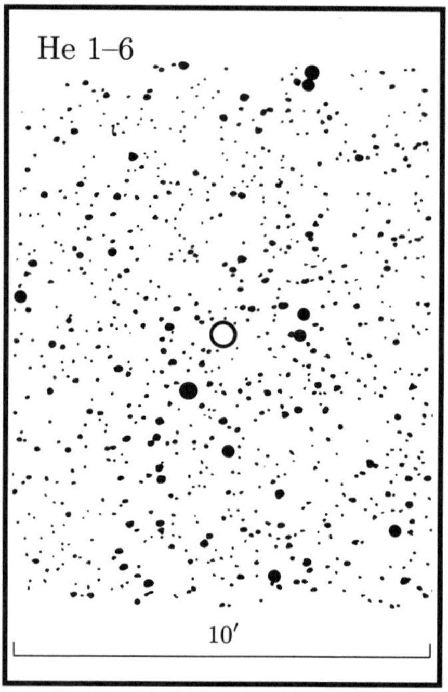
He 1–6
10′

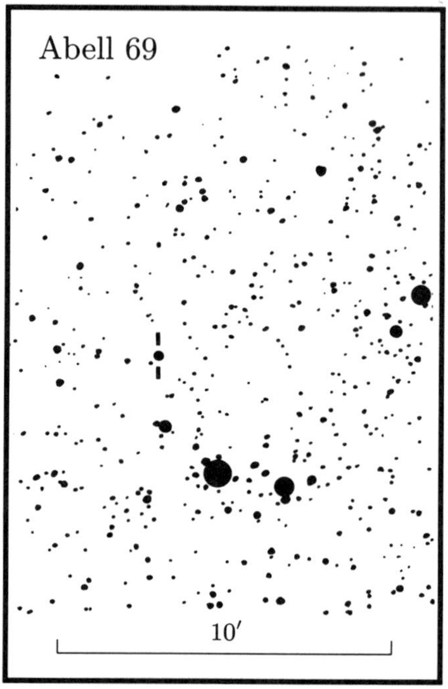
Abell 69
10′

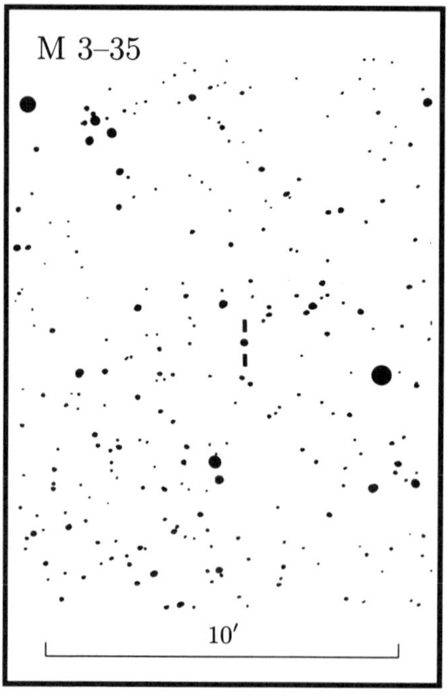
M 3–35
10′

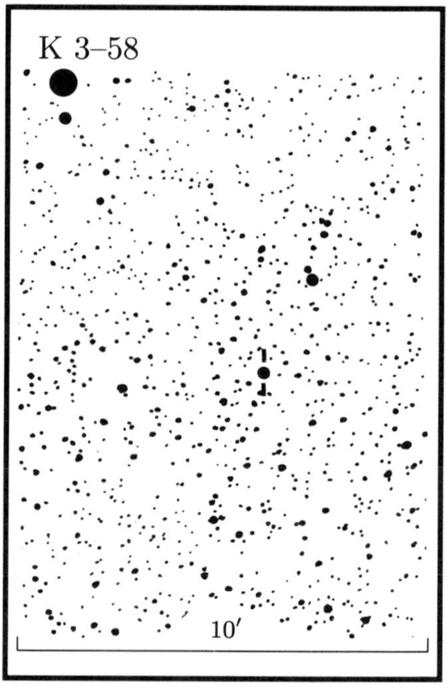
K 3–58
10′

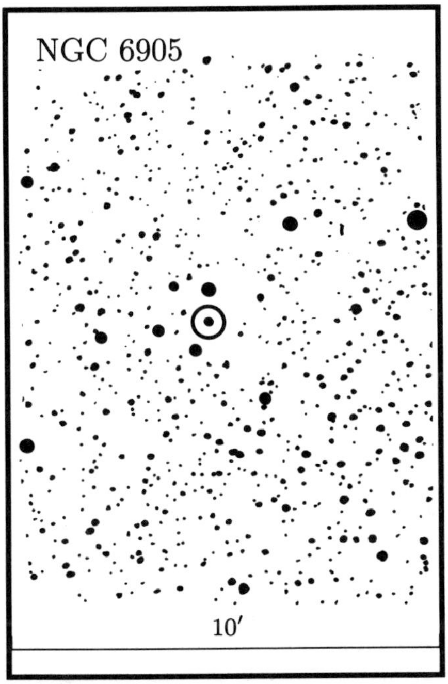
NGC 6905
10′

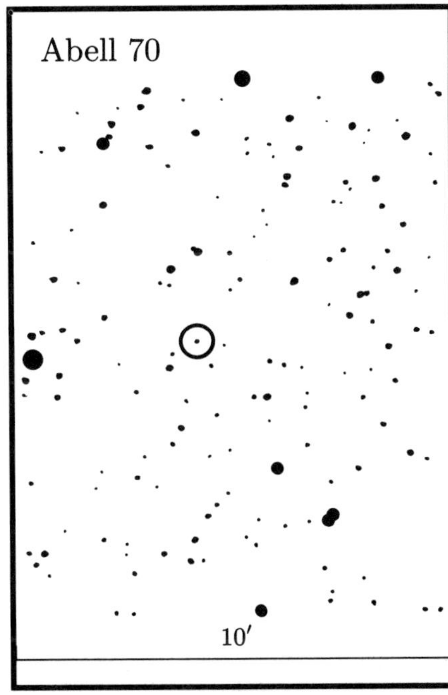
Abell 70
10′

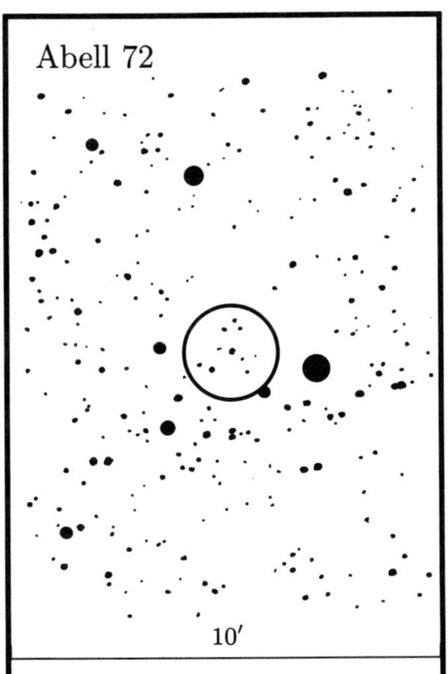
Abell 72
10′

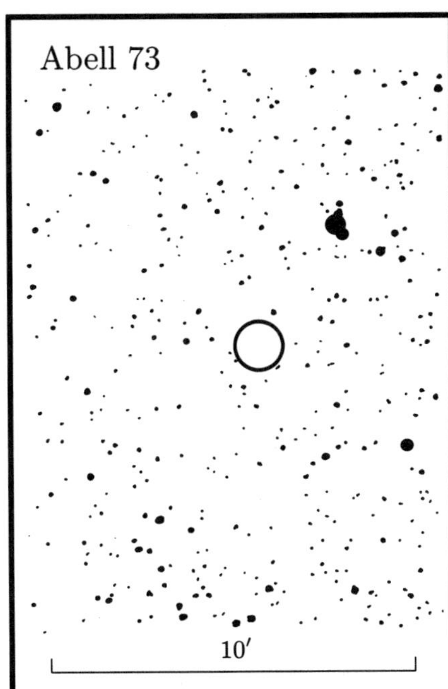
Abell 73
10′

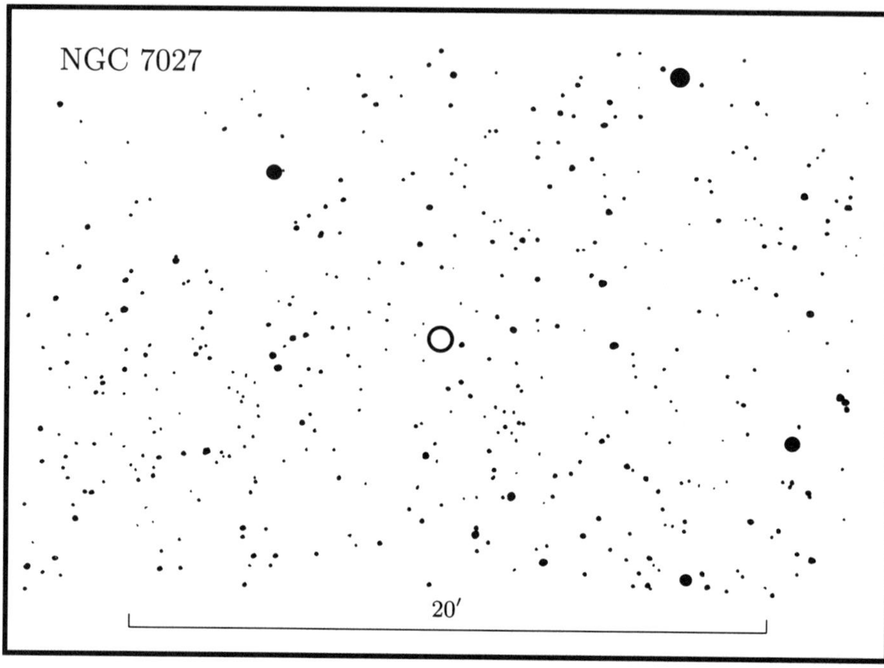
NGC 7027
20′

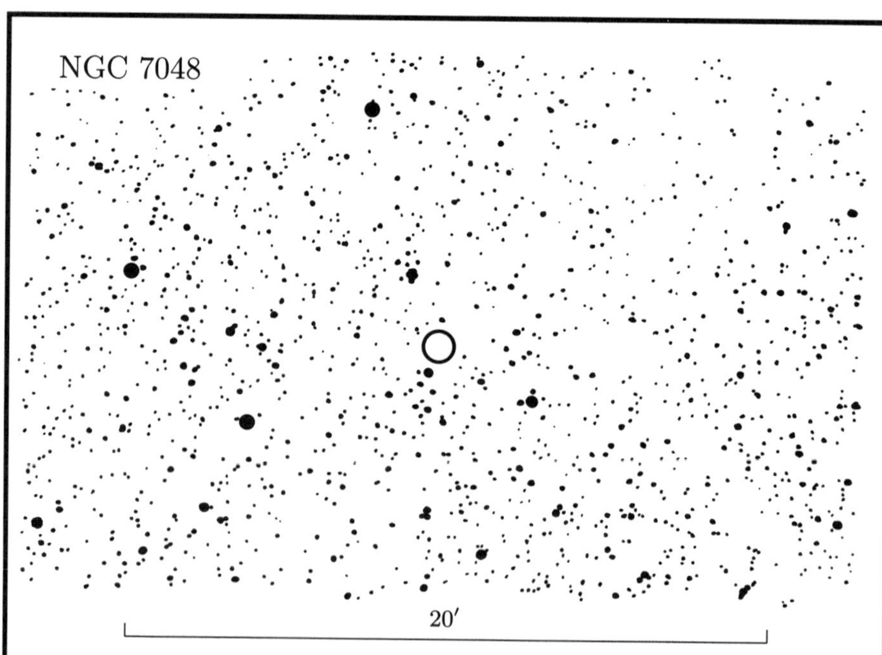
NGC 7048
20′

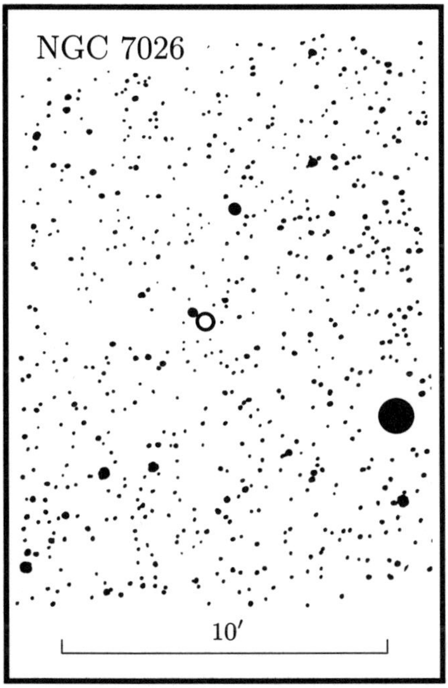
NGC 7026
10′

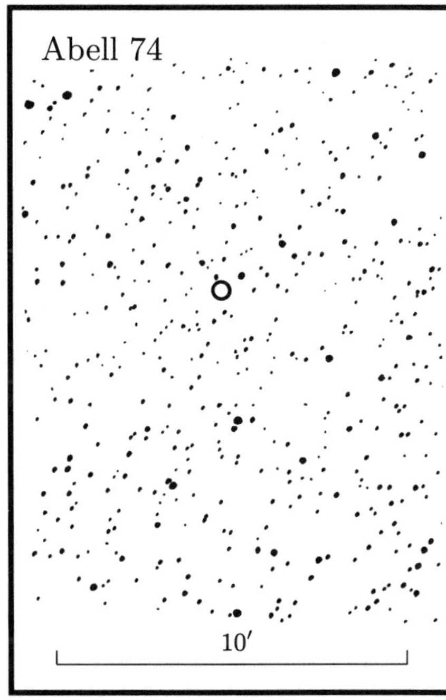
Abell 74
10′

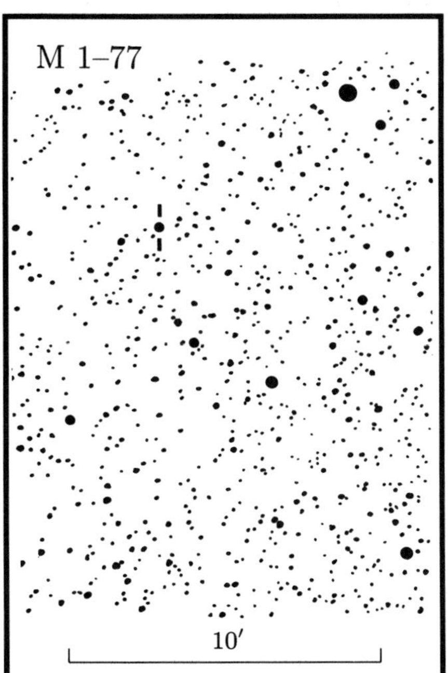
M 1–77
10′

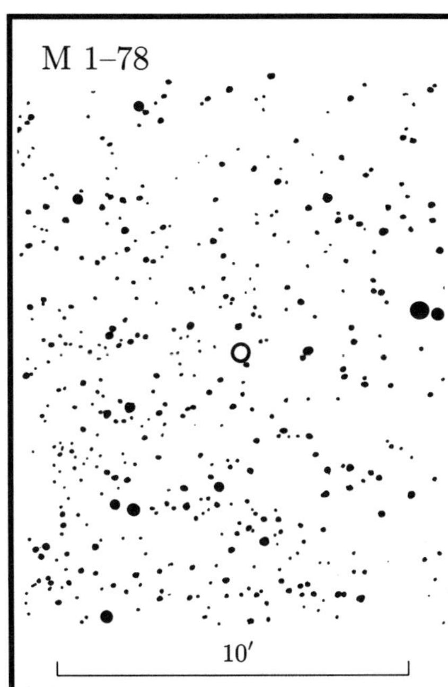
M 1–78
10′

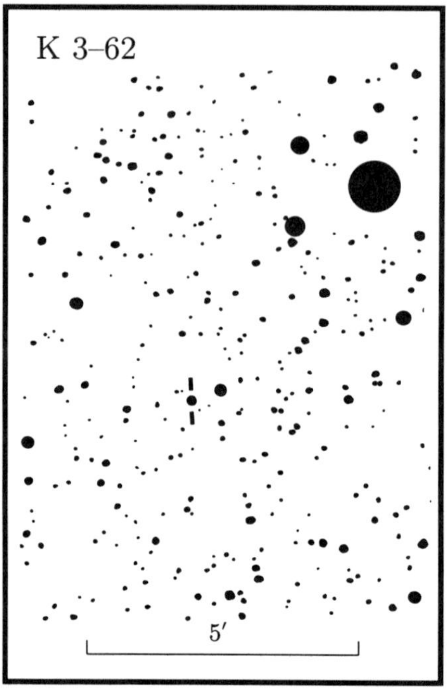
K 3–62
5′

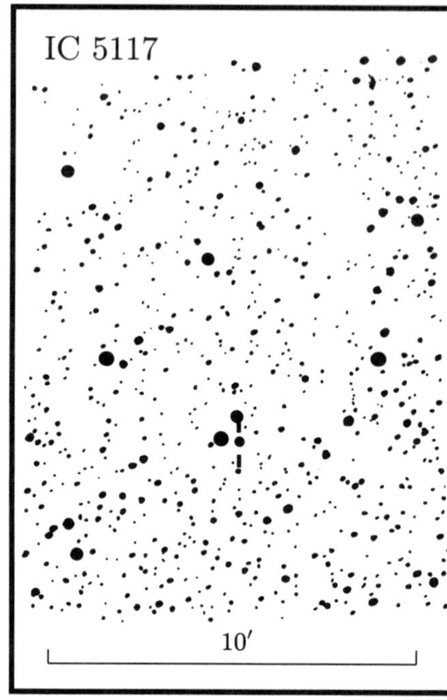
IC 5117
10′

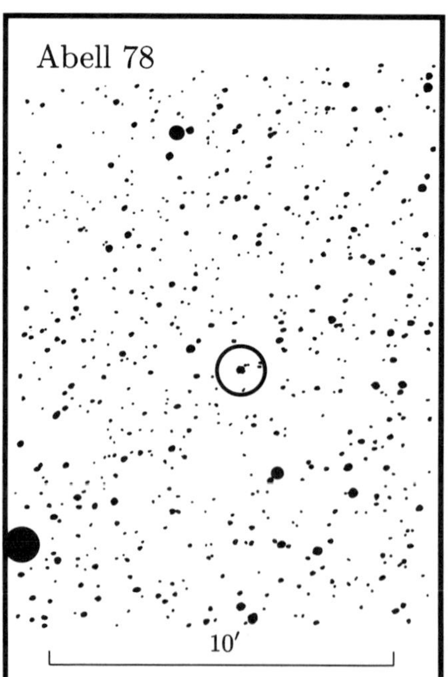
Abell 78
10′

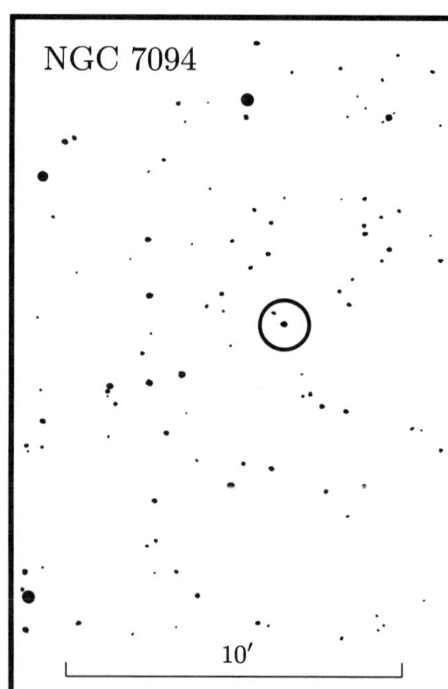
NGC 7094
10′

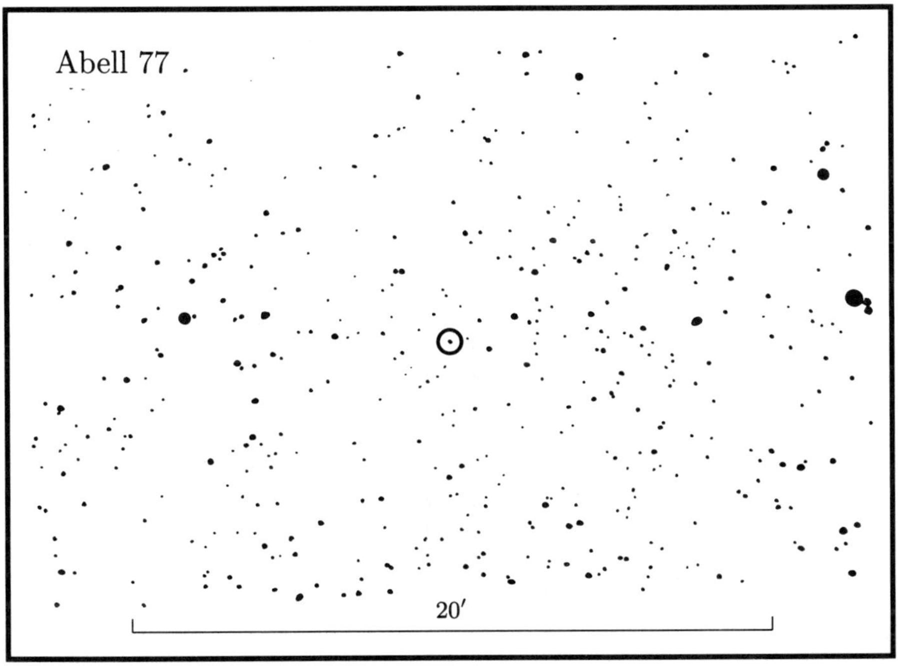
Abell 77
20′

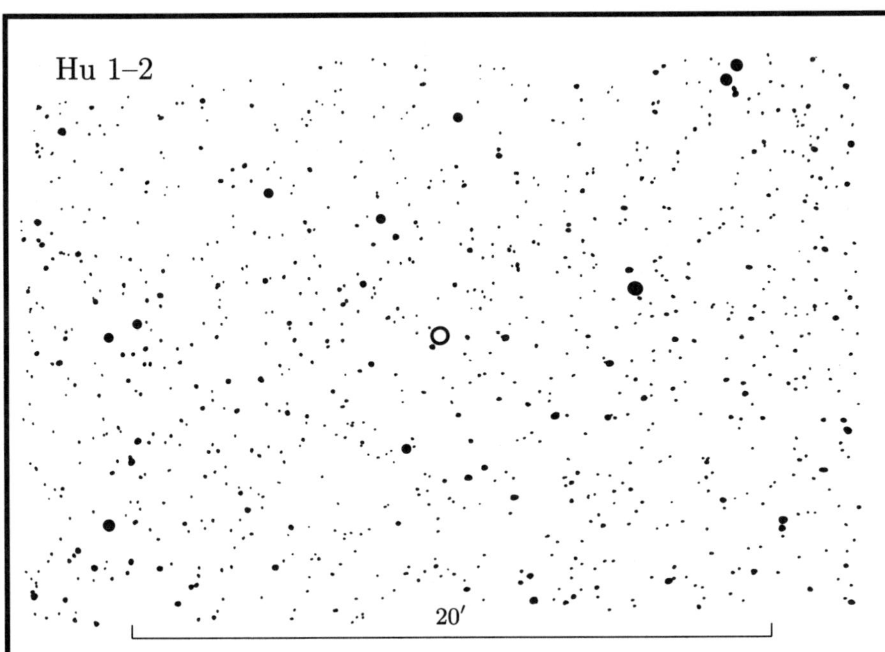
Hu 1–2
20′

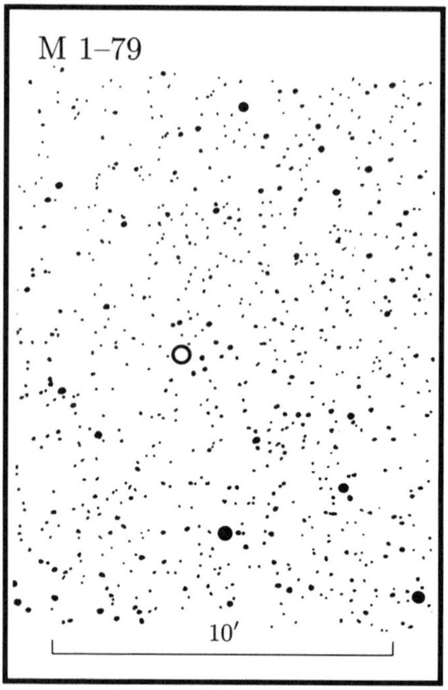
M 1–79
10′

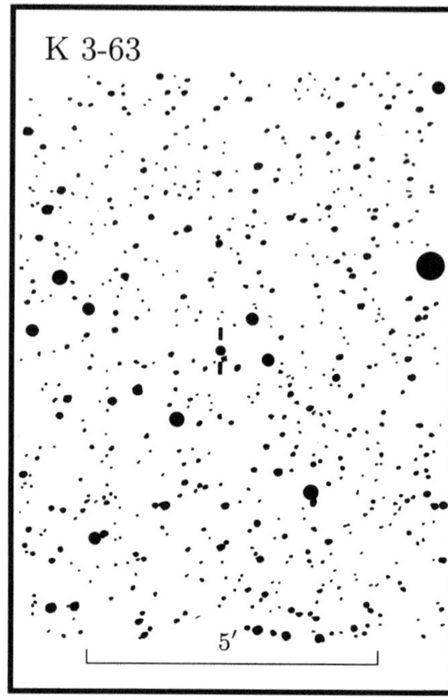
K 3-63
5′

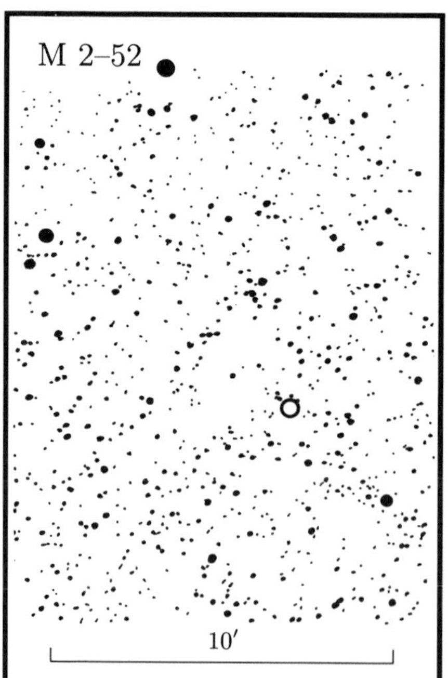
M 2–52
10′

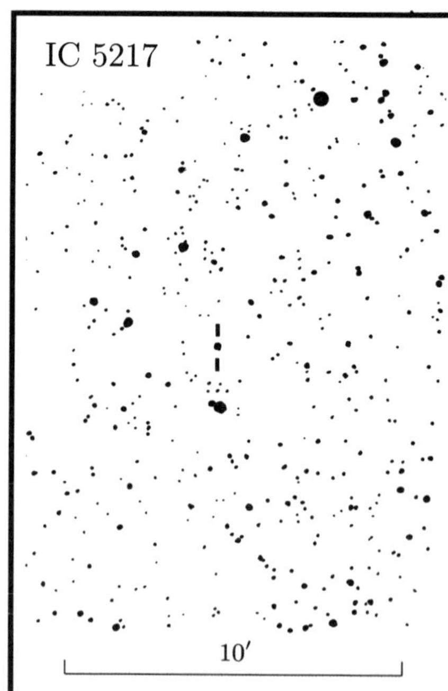
IC 5217
10′

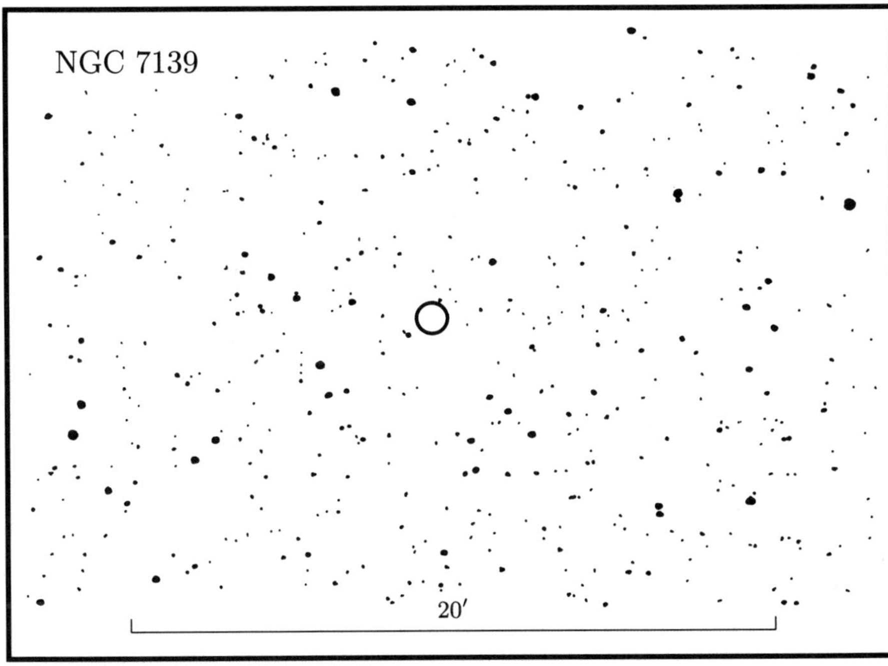
NGC 7139
20′

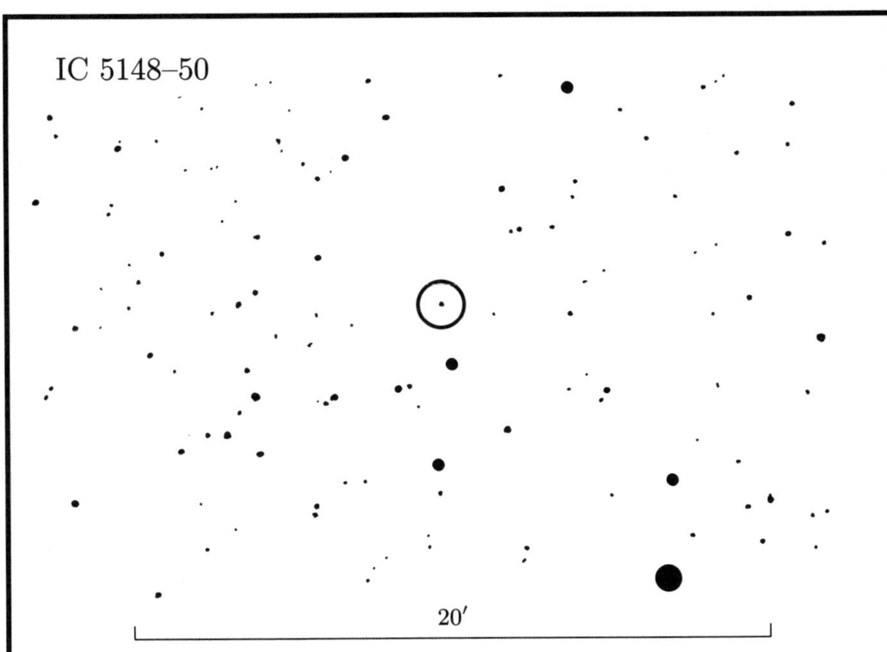
IC 5148–50
20′

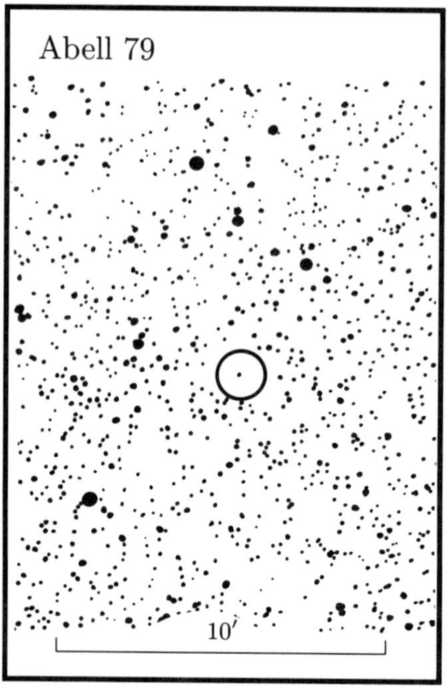
Abell 79
10′

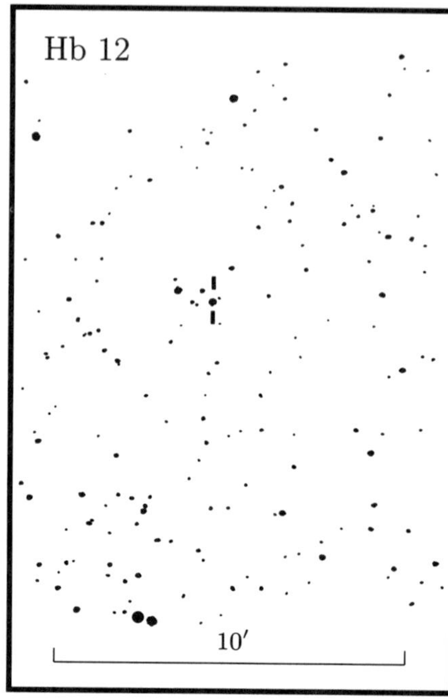
Hb 12
10′

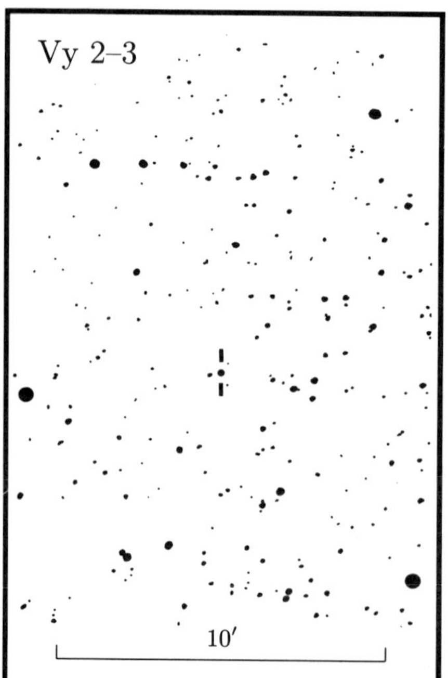
Vy 2–3
10′

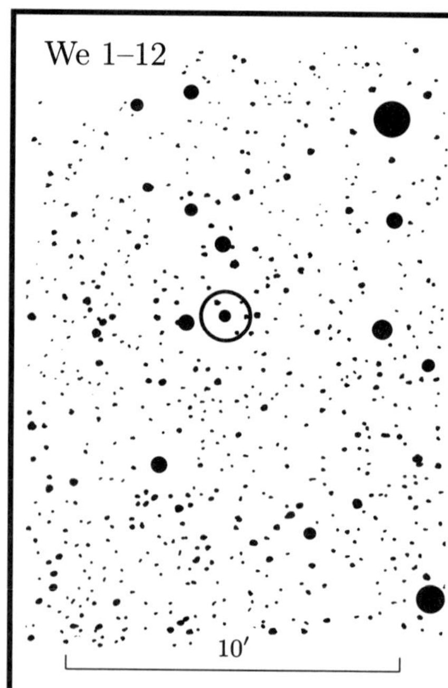
We 1–12
10′

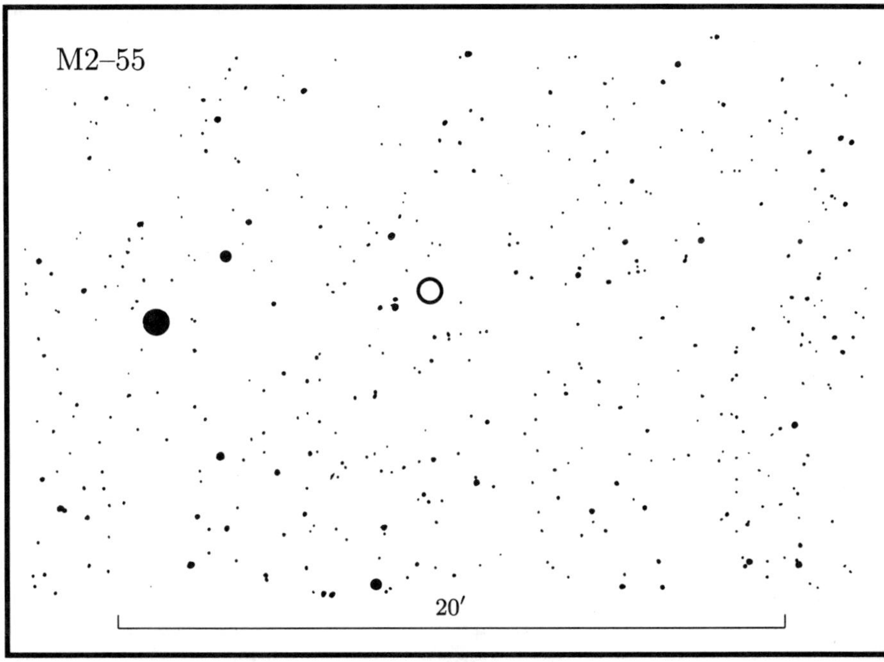
M2–55
20′

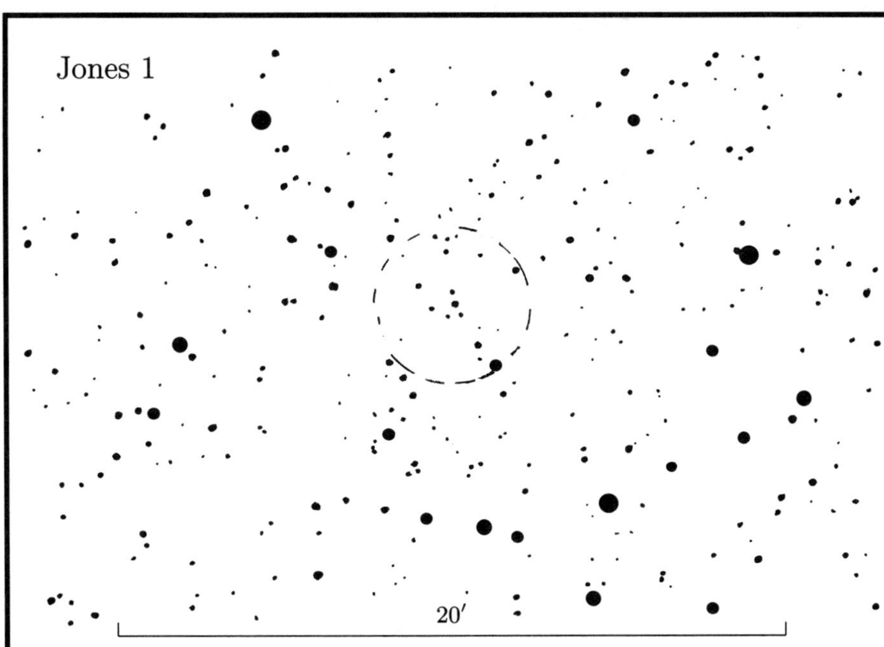
Jones 1
20′

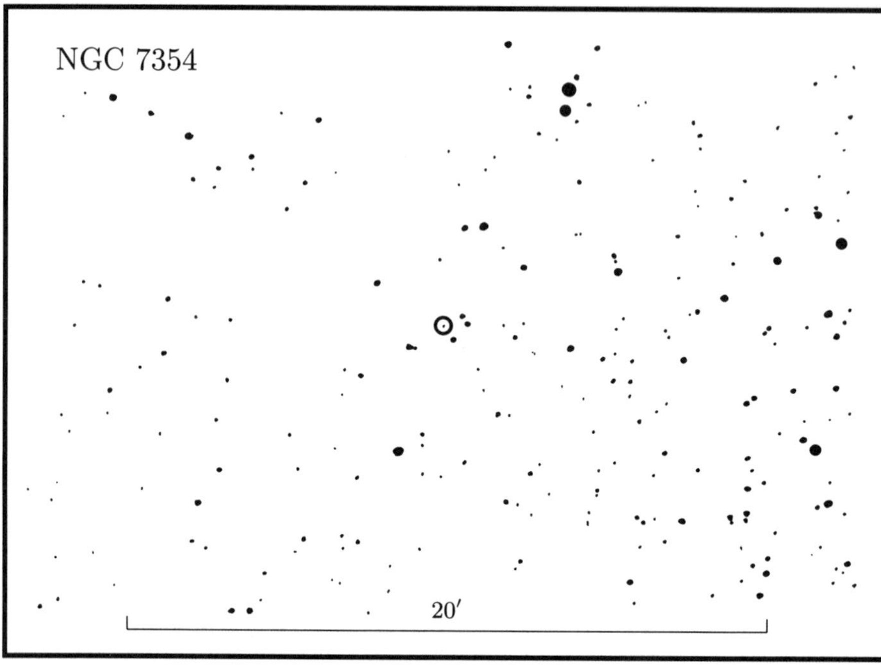
NGC 7354
20′

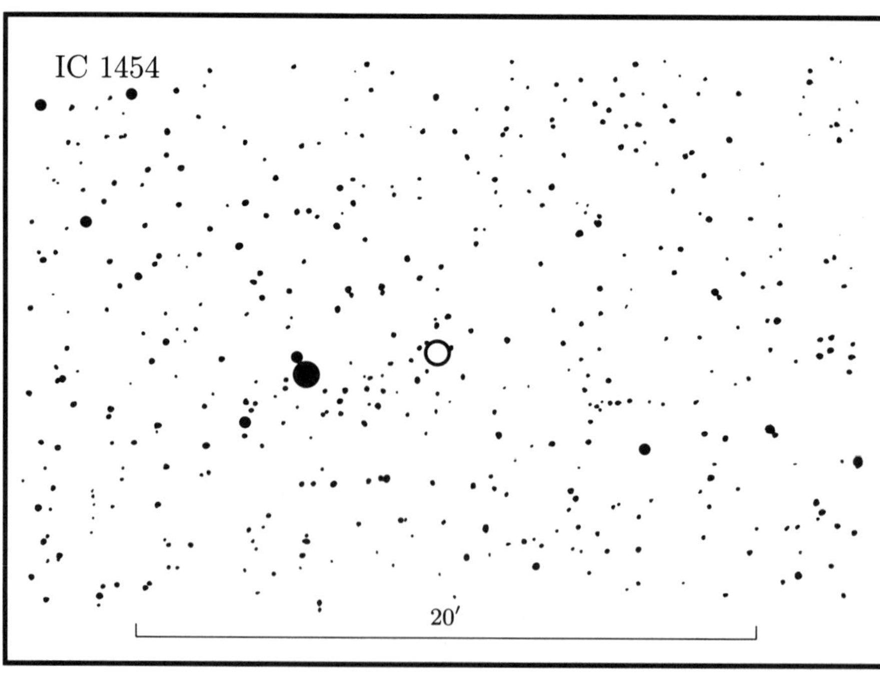
IC 1454
20′

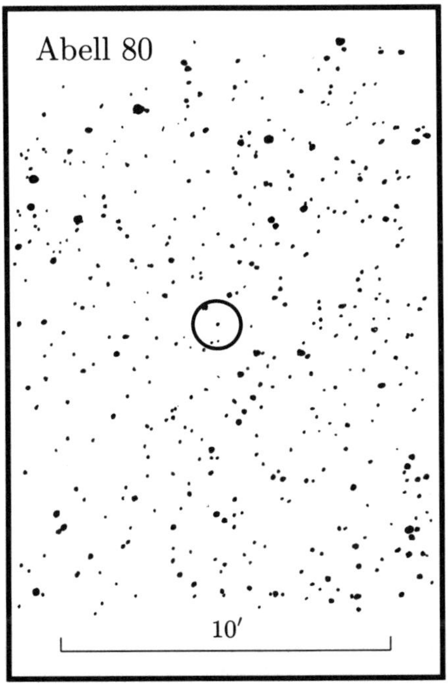
Abell 80
10′

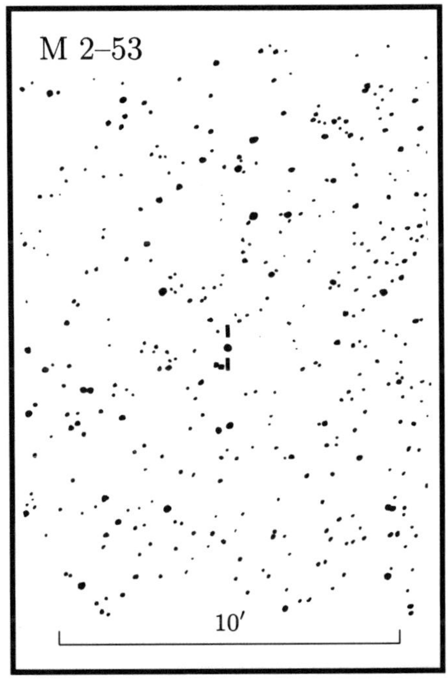
M 2–53
10′

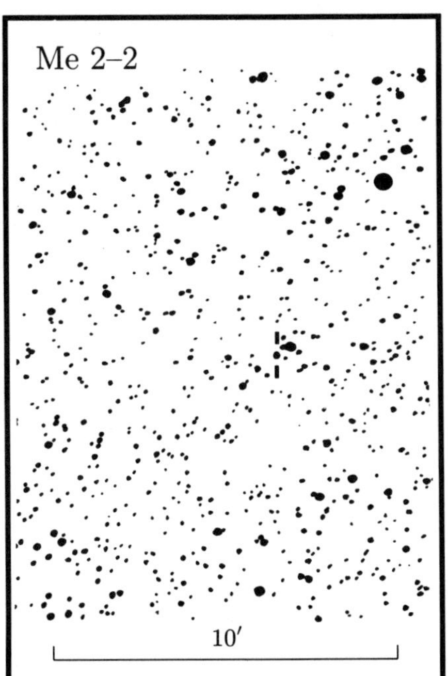
Me 2–2
10′

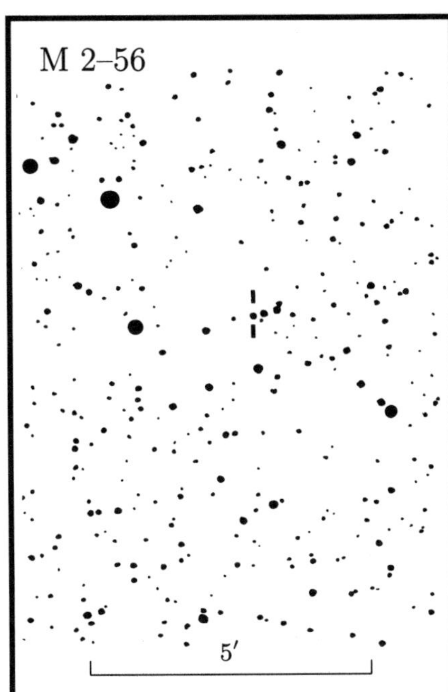
M 2–56
5′

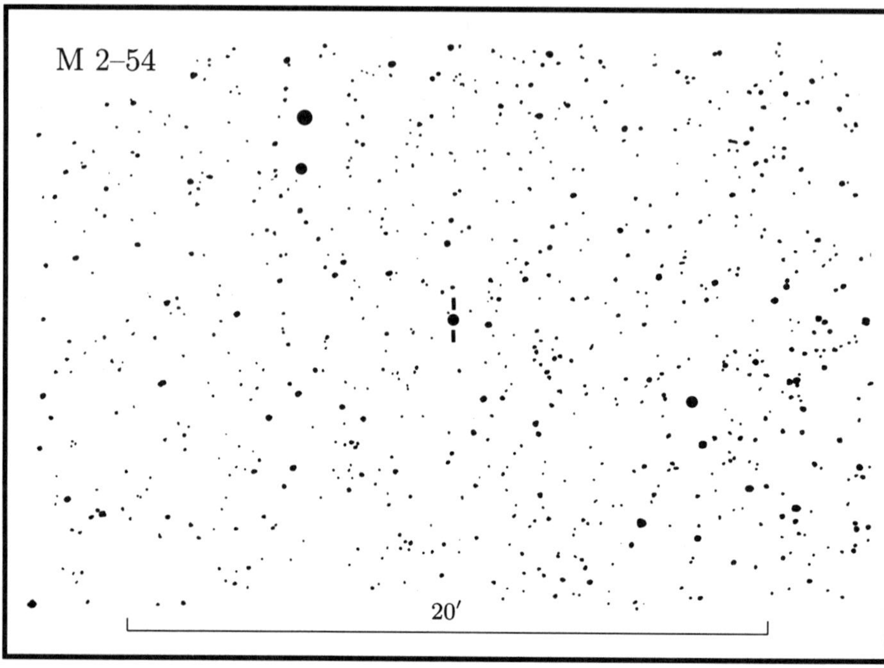
M 2–54
20′

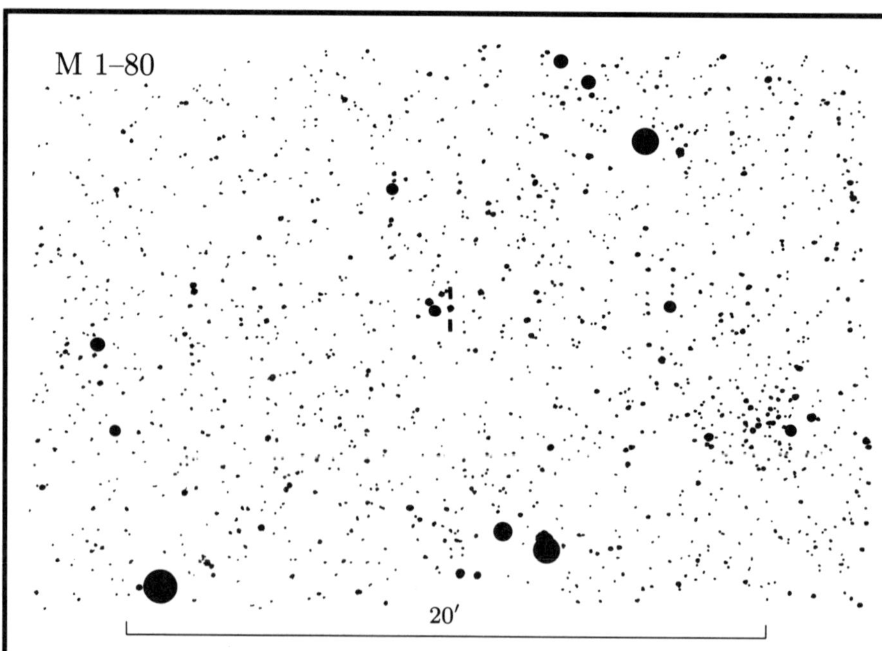
M 1–80
20′

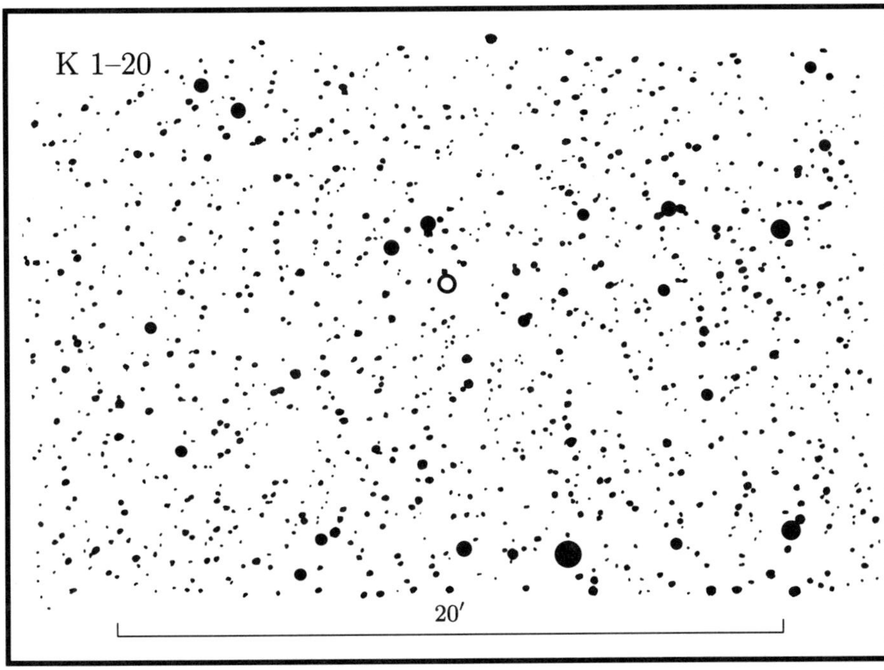
K 1–20
20′

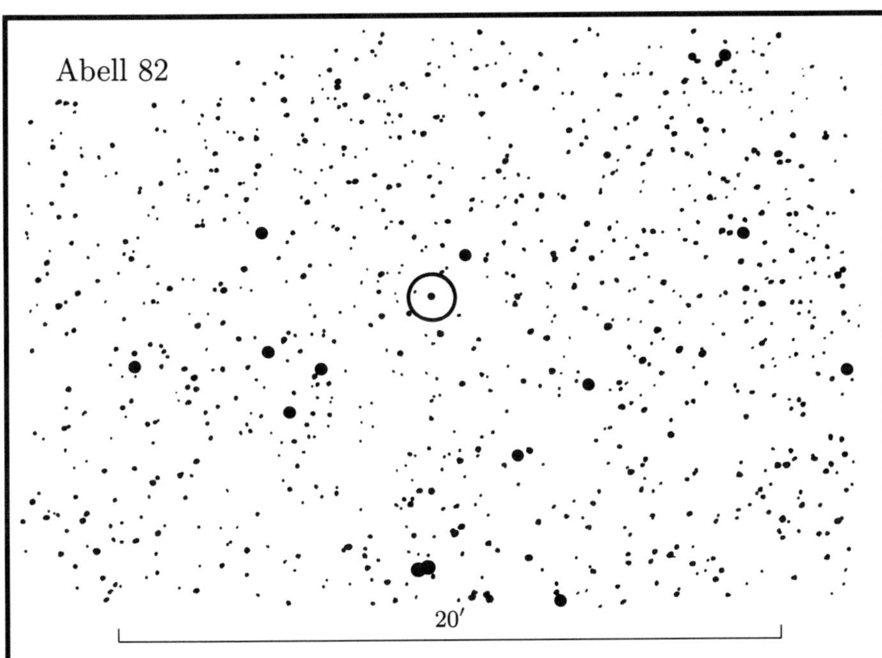
Abell 82
20′

Biblography

Abetti, G. & Hack, M.; *Nebulae and Galaxies*, Faber, 1964.

Acker, A. (et al.); 'Index and Cross-Identification of Planetary Nebulae,' *Astron. Astrophys. Supp. Ser.*, 54, 315, 1983.

Acker, A. (et al.); 'Strasbourg Catalog of Galactic Planetary Nebulae,' *Astron. Astrophys. Supp. Ser.*, **43**, 265, 1981.

Allen, D.A. & Barker, E.S.; *Webb Society Deep-Sky Observer's Handbook: Volume 2—Planetary & Gaseous Nebulae*, Enslow Publishers, 1979.

Aller, L.H.; 'The Planetary Nebulae: Parts I–XIV,' *Sky & Telescope*, May 1969 through July 1970 (except Feb. 1970).

Aller, L.H.; *Atoms, Stars and Nebulae*, Harvard Univ. Press, 1971.

Becvar, A.; *Atlas of the Heavens – II: Catalogue 1950.0*, Sky Publishing Corporation, 1964.

Flower, D.R. (ed.); *Planetary Nebulae: IAU Symposium 103*, D. Reidel Publ. Co., 1983.

Glyn Jones, K.; *The Search for the Nebulae*, Alpha Academic Press, 1975.

Gore, J.E.; *The Astronomical Observations and Theories of Sir William Herschel* (2nd Edition), P.M.E. Erwood, 1981.

Hirshfeld, A. & Sinnott, R.W. (ed); *Sky Catalogue 2000.0: Volume 2*, Cambridge University Press, 1985.

Kaler, J.B.; *Planetary Nebulae and their Central Stars*, Ann. Rev. Astron. Astrophys. (p. 89 - 117), 1985.

Kaler, J.B.; *Stars and their Spectra*, Cambridge University Press, 1989.

Kitchin, C.R.; *Stars, Nebulae and the Interstellar Medium*, Adam Hilger, IOP Publishing Ltd., 1987.

........; *Lick Publications Vol. XIII*, 1918.

Miller, J.S.;*Planetary Nebulae*, Ann. Rev. Astron. Astrophys. (p. 331 -358), 1974.

Osterbrock, D.E. & O'Dell, C.R. (ed); *Planetary Nebulae: IAU Symposium 34*, D. Reidel Publ. Co., 1968.

Osterbrock, D.E.; *Astrophysics of Gaseous Nebulae*, W.H. Freeman & Co., 1974.

Perek, L. & Kohoutek, L.; *Catalogue of Galactic Planetary Nebulae*, Academia, Prague, 1967.

Pottasch, S.R.; *Planetary Nebulae*, D. Reidel Publ. Co., 1984.

Sidgwick, J.B.; *Amateur Astronomer's Handbook*, Pelham Books, 1979.

Terzian, Y. (ed); *Planetary Nebulae. IAU Symposium 76*, D. Reidel Publ. Co., 1978.

Tirion, W.; *Sky Atlas 2000.0*, Sky Publishing Corporation, 1981.

Tirion, W., Rappaport, H. & Lovi, G.; *Uranometria 2000.0: Volume 1*, Willmann-Bell Inc., 1987. *Uranometria 2000.0: Volume 2*, Willmann-Bell Inc., 1988.

Torres-Peimbest, S, (ed.); *Planetary Nebulae. IAU Symposium No. 131*. Kluwer Academic Publ., 1989

Underhill, A. & Doazan, V.; *B Stars: With and Without Emission Lines*, NASA SP-456, 1982.

Whitney, C.A.; *The Discovery of Our Galaxy*, Angus & Robertson (U.K.) Ltd., 1971.

Appendix A

References to Catalogues and Lists of Planetary Nebulae

Code	Source
	Abell, G.O.; *P.A.S.P.* **67**, 258, 1955.
A	Abell, G.O.; *Ap.J.* **144**, 259, 1966.
Al 1	Allen, D.A.; *Observatory*, **93**, 85, 1973.
Al 2	Allen, D.A.; *Observatory*, **99**, 83, 1979.
Ap 1	Apriamasvili, S.P.; *Astron. Zh.* **39**, 256, 1962.
Ap 2	Apriamasvili, S.P.; *A.C.* **231**, 25, 1962.
Ap 3	Apriamasvili, S.P.; *A.C.* **232**, 3, 1962.
Ap 4	Apriamasvili, S.P.; *A.C.* **279**, 1, 1964
ARO	Algonquin Radio Observatory, Higgs, L.A.; *P.A.B.*, Vol. 1, No. 1, Domin. Obs., 1971.
Ba	Baade, W.; *P.A.S.P.* **47**, 99, 1935.
Bl	Blanco, V.M.; *Contr. Bosscha Obs.* **13**, 1961.
Bl 2	Blanco, V.M.; Private communication to P&K, 1964.
Bl 3	Blanco, V.M.; Private communication to P&K, 1964.
BlDz	Blaauw, A. *et al*; *Astron. Astrophys.* **44**, 469, 1975.
BoBn	Boeshaar, G.O. & Bond, H.E.; *Ap.J* **213**, 421, 1977.
BV	Bohm-Vitense, E.; *P.A.S.P* **68**, 430, 1956. (Table 5)
Cn 1	Cannon, A.J.; *Harvard Circ.* 224, 1921.
Cn 2	Cannon, A.J.; *Harvard Bull.* 784, 1923.
Cn 3	Cannon, A.J.; *Harvard Bull.* 837, 1926.
CnMy	Cannon, A.J. & Mayall, M.W.; *Harvard Bull.* 908, 1938.

Code	Source
	Cohen, M. & Jones, H.F.; *Ap.J* **321**, L151, 1987.
CTS 2	Turatto, M. *et al*; *Astron. J.* **99**, 1170, 1990
CTS 1	Cappellaro, E. *et al*; in *IAU Symp. 131: Planetary Nebulae*, Reidel, 1989. (p. 61)
CTIO	Cerro Tololo Interamerican Observatory. Smith, M.G. *et al*; *Ap.J* Supp. **32**, 217, 1976.
CTSS	Cappellaro, E. *et al*; *Astron. Astrophys. Supp. Ser.* **86** 503, 1990.
DeHt	Dengl, J. *et al*; *Astron. Astrophys.* **85**, 356, 1980.
Dd	Dolidze, M.W.; *Astron. Tsirk.* **629**, 6, 1971.
DdDm	Dolidze, M.W. & Dzhimsheleishvili, G.N.; *Astron. Tsirk.* **385**, 7, 1966.
DS	Drilling, J.S.; *Ap.J* **270**, L13, 1983.
EGB	Ellis, G.L. *et al*; *P.A.S.P* **96**, 283, 1984
ESO	European Southern Observatory, Holmberg, E., Lauberts, A., Schuster, H. & West, R. *Astron. Astrophys. Supp. Ser.* **18**, 463, 1974. *Astron. Astrophys. Supp. Ser.* **22**, 327, 1975. *Astron. Astrophys. Supp. Ser.* **27**, 295, 1977. *Astron. Astrophys. Supp. Ser.* **31**, 15, 1978. *Astron. Astrophys. Supp. Ser.* **34**, 285, 1978. *Astron. Astrophys. Supp. Ser.* **39**, 173, 1980. *Astron. Astrophys. Supp. Ser.* **43**, 307, 1981. *Astron. Astrophys. Supp. Ser.* **46**, 311, 1981.
	Fesen, R.A. *et al*; *P.A.S.P* **96**, 283, 1984.
Fg	Fleming, M.; *Harvard Circ.* 158, 1910.
	Gillett, F.C. *et at* *Ap.J* **338**, 862, 1989.
Fg	Fleming, M.; *Harvard Circ.* 167, 1911.
Gum	Gum, C.S.; *Mem. R.A.S* **67**, 155, 1955.
H 1	Haro, G.; *Bol. Obs. Ton. y Tac.*, **1**, 93, 1952. (Table 1)
H 2	(Table 2)
H 3	Haro, G. *et al*; *Bol. Obs. Ton. y Tac.*, **1**, No. 8, 3, 1953.
H 4	Haro, G.; *P.A.S.P* **63**, 144, 1951.
HtTr	Hartl., H. & Tritton, S.B.; *Astron. Astrophys.* **145**,41, 1985.
HtWe	Hartl., H. & Weinberger, R. *Astron. Astrophys. Supp. Ser.* **69**, 519, 1987
	Heber, U. & Drilling, J.S.; *Mitt. Astron. Ges.* **62**, 252, 1984.
HFG	Heckathorn, J.N. *et al*; *Astron. Astrophys.* **114**, 414, 1982.
He 1	Henize, K.G.; *P.A.S.P* **73**, 159, 1961.
He 2	Henize, K.G.; *Ap.J Supp.* **14**, 125, 1967.
HEN	Henize, K.G.; *Ap.J Supp.* **30**, 491, 1976.

Code	Source
Hf	Hoffleit, D., *Harvard Ann.* **119**, 37, 1953.
Hb	Hubble, E.P.; *P.A.S.P* **33**, 174, 1921.
Hu 1	Humason, M.L.; *P.A.S.P* **33**, 175, 1921.
Hu 2	Humason, M.L.; *P.A.S.P* **34,** 296, 1922.
IC	Index Catalog; Dreyer, J.L.E.; *Mem. R.A.S.*, 1895 & 1908.
IsWe	Ishida, K. & Weinberger, R.; *Astron. Astrophys.* **178**, 227, 1987.
IRAS	Joint IRAS Science Working Group, Washington, 1985
J	Jonckheere, R.; *Observatory* **39**, 134, 1916.
Kj	Kazarian, M.A.; *Byurakan Obs.* **12**, 385, 1976.
KjPn	Kazarian, M.A. & Parsamyan, E.; *Astron. Tsirk.* **602**, 6, 1971.
KO	Kazarian, M.A.; & Oganeyan, E.; *Astron. Tsirk.* **753**, 3, 1973.
KFL	Kinman, T.D. *et al*; *Astron. J.* **95**, 804, 1988.
KtRe	Koester, D. & Reimers, D.; *Astron. Astrophys.* **223**, 326, 1989
K 1	Kohoutek, L.; *Bull. Astr. Inst. Csl.* **13**, 120, 1962.
K 1	Kohoutek, L.; *Bull. Astr. Inst. Csl.* **14**, 70, 1963.
K 1	Kohoutek, L.; *Astron. Astrophys.* **13**, 493, 1971.
K 1	Kohoutek, L.; *Astron. Astrophys.* **59**, 137, 1977.
K 2	Kohoutek, L., *Bull. Astr. Inst. Csl.* **14**, 70, 1963.
K 2	Kohoutek, L., *Bull. Astr. Inst. Csl.* **15**, 162, 1964.
K 2	Kohoutek, L.; *Astron. Astrophys.* **13**, 493, 1971.
K 2	Kohoutek, L.; *Astron. Astrophys.* **59**, 137, 1977.
K 3	Kohoutek, L.; Private communication to P&K, 1965.
K 3	Kohoutek, L.; *Bull. Astr. Inst. Csl.* **20**, 307, 1969.
K 3	Kohoutek, L.; *Astron. Astrophys.* **16**, 291, 1972.
K 4	Kohoutek, L.; Private communication to P&K, 1965.
K 4	Kohoutek, L.; *Bull. Astr. Inst. Csl.* **20**, 307, 1969.
K 4	Kohoutek, L.; *Astron. Astrophys.* **16**, 291, 1972.
Kr	Krasnogorskaya, A.A.; *A.C.* **230**, 11, 1962.
Ku	Kustner, F.; *Veroff. Univ. Sternw.* Bonn 15, 1921.
Lo	Longmore, A.J.; *M.N.R.A.S.* **178**, 251, 1977.
LoTr	Longmore, A.J. & Tritton, S.H.; *M.N.R.A.S.* **193**, 521, 1980.
LSA	Lundstrom, I. *et al*; *Astron. Astrophys.* **196**, 233, 1988.
M	Messier, C. & Mechain, P.; *Conn. des Temps*, 1784.
Mac 1	MacConnell, D.J.; *Astron. Astrophys. Supp. Ser.* **33**, 219, 1978.
Mac 2	MacConnell, D.J.; *Astron. Astrophys. Supp. Ser.* **48**, 355, 1982. (Table III)
Em	MacCuskey, S.W.. *P.A.S.P* **73**, 264, 1961.
Ma	Maehara, H.; *Contr. Bosscha Obs.* **71**, 1, 1982.
	Manchado, A. *et al*; *Astron. Astrophys.* **218**, 267, 1989

Code	**Source**
My	Mayall, M.W.; *Harvard Bull.* **920**, 32, 1951.
MyCn	Mayall, M.W. & Cannon, A.J.; *Harvard Bull.* **913**, 7, 1940.
	Meaburn, J. & Rovithis, P.; *Astrophys. Sp. Sci.*, **46**, L7, 1977.
MrWe	Melmer, D. & Weinberger, R.; *MNRAS* **243**, 236, 1990
Mz	Menzel, D.N.; *Harvard Bull.* 777, 1922.
Me 1	Merrill, P.W.; *P.A.S.P* **53**, 245, 1941.
Me 2	Merrill, P.W.; *P.A.S.P* **54**, 107, 1942.
MWC	Merrill, P.W. & Burwell, C.G.; *Ap.J* **78**, 87, 1933.
MWC	Merrill, P.W. & Burwell, C.G.; *Ap.J* **98**, 153, 1943.
MWC AS	Merrill, P.W. & Burwell, C.G.; *Ap.J* **112**, 72, 1950.
Jn	Miller, F.D. & van Dien, E.; *Ap.J* **109**, 537, 1949.
Jn	Miller, F.D. & van Dien, E.; *Ap.J* **110**, 104, 1949.
M 1	Minkowski, R.; *P.A.S.P* **58**, 305, 1946.
M 2	Minkowski, R.; *P.A.S.P* **59**, 257, 1947.
M 3	Minkowski, R.; *P.A.S.P* **60**, 386, 1948.
M 4	Minkowski, R., *P.A.S.P* **76**, 197, 1964.
Na	Nassau, J. *et al*; *Ap.J* **139**, 864, 1964. (Table V)
NGC	*New General Catalogue* Dreyer, J.L.E.; Mem. R.A.S., 1888.
Ns	Nordstrom, H., *Astron. Astrophys. Supp. Ser.* **21**, 193, 1975.
PB	Peimbert, M. & Batiz, G.; *Bol. Obs. Ton. y Tac.* **2**,No. 19, 12, 1960.
PC	Peimbert, M. & Costerro, R.; *Bol. Obs. Ton. y Tac.* **3**, No. 1, 33, 1961.
Pe 1	Perek, L.; *Bull. Astr. Inst. Csl.* **11**, 256, 1960.
Pe 2	Perek, L.; *Bull. Astr. Inst. Csl.* **14**, 201, 1963.
Ps	Pease, F.G.; *P.A.S.P* **40**, 342, 1928.
A 06–09	Pena, M.; *Rev. Mex. Astron. Astrof.* **17**, 25, 1989
PRTM-1	Pena, M.; *Astron. Astrophys.* **237**, 454, 1990
Pt 1	Peterson, A.W.; *P.A.S.P.* **89**, 129, 1977
	Pollacco, D.L.; *M.N.R.A.S.* **245**, 204, 1990
	Pottasch, S.R. *et al*; *Astron. Astrophys.* **205**, 248, 1988.
PM 1	Preite-Martinez, A.; *Astron. Astrophys. Supp.* Ser. **76**
RWT 152	Pritchet, C.; *Astron. Astrophys.* **139**, 230, 1984.
Pu 1	Purgathofer, A.; *Astron. Astrophys.* **70**, 589, 1978.
Pu 2	Purgathofer, A.; *Astron. Astrophys.* **88**, 275, 1980.
PuWe	Purgathofer,A. & Weinberger, R.; *Astron. Astrophys.*, **87**, L5, 1980.
RCW	Rodgers, A.W., Campbell, C.T. & Whiteoak, J.H.; *M.N.R.A.S.* **121**, 103, 1960.
Sa 1	Sanduleak, N.; *P.A.S.P* **86**, 215, 1974.

Code	Source
Sa 2	Sanduleak, N.; *Publ. Warner & Swasey Obs.* **2**, 1, 1975.
Sa 3	Sanduleak, N.; *Publ. Warner & Swasey Obs.* **2**, 57, 1976.
Sa 4	Sanduleak, N.; *P.A.S.P* **95**, 619, 1983.
SaSt 1	Sanduleak, N. & Stephenson, C.; *Ap.J* **178**, 183, 1972.
SaSt 2	Sanduleak, N. & Stephenson, C.; *P.A.S.P* **84**, 816, 1972. (Table 1)
SrWe	Saurer, W. & Weinberger, R.; *Astron. Astrophys. Supp. Ser.* **69**, 527, 1987
SMC	Savage, A. *et al*; *Observatory* **102**, 229, 1982.
SuWt 1	Schuster, H.E. & West, R.M.; *Astron. Astrophys.* **46**, 139, 1976.
SuWt 2	Schuster, H.E. & West, R.M.; *Astron. Astrophys.* **88**, 350, 1980.
Sn	Shane, C.D.; private communication to P&K (in list of radial velocities provided by N.U. Mayall), 1964.
Sp	Shapley, H.; *Harvard Bull.* 902, 26, 1936.
Sh 1	Sharpless, S.; *Ap.J* **118**, 362, 1953. (Table II)
Sh 2	Sharpless, S.; *Ap.J Supp.* **4**, 257, 1959. (Table I)
Sh Wi	Shaw, R.A. & Wirth, A.; *P.A.S.P* **97**, 1071, 1985
Sd	Sherwood, W.A.; *Observatory* **89**, 207, 1969.
Ste	Stenholm, H.; *Astron. Astrophys.* **39**, 307, 1975.
St 3	Stephenson, C.B.; *P.A.S.P* **90**, 396, 1978.
St 4	Stephenson, C.B.; *P.A.S.P* **97**, 930, 1985.
	Stock, J. & Wroblewski, H.;*Publ. Dep. Astron. Univ. Chili* **2**, 259, 1972.
StWr 1	(Table Ib)
StWr 2	(Table IIb)
StWr 3	(Table IIIb)
StWr 4	(Table IV)
SwSt	Swings, P. & Struve, O.; *Proc. Nat. Acad. Sci.* **26**, 454, 1940.
TrBr	Terzan, A. *et al*; *Comptes Rendus Acad. Sci.* **287**, Serie 8, 235, 1978.
TrJu	Terzan, A. & Ju, K.H.; *ESO Messenger No. 20,* 6, 1980
	Terzan, A. & Ounnas, C.; *Astron. Astrophys. Supp. Ser.* 76(2), 205, 1988
Tc	Thackeray, A.D.; *M.N.R.A.S.* **110**, 524, 1950.
Th 1	The, P.S.; *Contr. Bosscha Obs.* **14**, Table V, 1962.
Th 2	The, P.S.; *Contr. Bosscha Obs.* **17**, Table IV, 1962.
Th 3	The, P.S.; *Contr. Bosscha Obs.* **26**, Table I, 1964. (No's. above 36 from a prvt. comm. to P&K)
Th 4	The, P.S.; *Contr. Bosscha Obs.* **28**, Table I, 1964.
PP 40	Turner, K.C. & Terzian, Y.; *Astron. J.* **90**, 59, 1985
VBe 1	Van den Bergh, S.; *Ap.J Supp. Ser.* **38**, 119, 1978.

Code	**Source**
VBe 2	Van den Bergh, S.; *Ap.J* **227**, 497, 1979.
VBRC	Van den Bergh, S. *et al*; *Ap.J.* **179**, 863, 1973.
Vd	Vandervort, G.L.; *Contr. Bosscha Obs.* 30, 1964.
VeRa	Vega, E.I. *et al*; *Astron. J.* **85** 1207, 1980.
	Van der Veen, W.E.C.J. *et al*; *Astron. Astrophys.* **216**, L1, 1989.
Ve	Velghe, A.G.; *Ap.J.* **126**, 302, 1957 (Table I: 22, 26 & 27, Table III: 59 to 62)
V-V 1	Vorontsov-Velyaminov, B.A.; *Astron. Zhurn.* **38**, 375, 1961.
VV'	Vorontsov-Velyaminov, B.A.; *Mitt. Staatl. Astron. Sternberga Inst.*, Moscow, **118**, 3 1962.
V-V Anon	Vorontsov-Velyaminov, B.A. *et al*; *Sov. Astr.* **19**, 163, 1975.
Vy 1	Vyssotsky, A.N.; *P.A.S.P* **54**, 152, 1942.
Vy 2	Vyssotsky, A.N. *et al*; *P.A.S.P.* **57**, 314, 1945.
We 1	Weinberger, R.; *Astron. Astrophys. Supp. Ser.* **30**, 343, 1977
We 2	Weinberger, R.; *Astron. Astrophys. Supp. Ser.* **30**, 353, 1977
We 3	Weinberger, R.; *Observatory* **98**, 137, 1978.
We a-f	Weinberger, R.; prvt. comm. in *Catalogue of Central Stars of True and Possible Planetary Nebulae*, A. Acker *et al*, 1981
WeSb	Weinberger, R. & Sabbadin, F.; *Astron. Astrophys.* **100**, 66, 1981.
WSDH	Weinberger, R. *et al*; *Ap.J* **265**, 249, 1983.
19W32	Wouterlout, J.G.A. & Dekker, E.; *Astron. Astrophys. Supp. Ser.* **36**, 323, 1979.
Wra	Wray, J.D.; Thesis, Northwestern University, 1966.
Y-C 2	Yale-Columbia; Cesco, C. & Gibson, J.; *Astron. Astrophys. Supp. Ser.* 11, 335, 1973. (Table 2)
Y-C	Cesco, C. *et al*; *Bol. Asoc. Argent. Astron.* No. 28, 159, 1984.
YM	Yerkes & McDonald Observatories; Johnson, H.M.; *Ap.J* **121**, 604, 1955.

Notes

(1) The abbreviations employed follow those used by Acker *et al* (ref. 1) with minor modifications where clarity would be improved. For lists produced since then I have generally used the abbreviation given by the authors.

(2) Several of the catalogues listed are not specifically devoted to planetary nebulae; some are catalogues of miscellaneous objects which happen to include planetary nebulae (e.g. M, NGC, IC and ESO) and others are lists of other types of object in which planetary nebulae have been found (e.g. the MWC catalogues of Hα emission stars).

References

1. Acker, A. *et al.* *Astron. Astrophys. Supp. Ser.* **54**, 315, 1983.

Index

Subject Index

A

B

C

D

E

F

G

H

Object Index

Name Index

Planetary Nebulae Chart Index

B

C

D

F

H

I

P

S

T

V

W